CAIA Level I

CAIA Level I

An Introduction to Core Topics in Alternative Investments

Mark J. P. Anson
The CAIA Association

WILEY

John Wiley & Sons, Inc.

Published by John Wiley & Sons, Inc., Hoboken, New Jersey.
Published simultaneously in Canada.

For general information on our other products and services or for technical support, please contact our Customer Care Department within the United States at (800) 762-2974, outside the United States at (317) 572-3993 or fax (317) 572-4002.

Wiley also publishes its books in a variety of electronic formats. Some content that appears in print may not be available in electronic books. For more information about Wiley products, visit our web site at www.wiley.com.

Library of Congress Cataloging-in-Publication Data:

CAIA Association.
  CAIA level I : an introduction to core topics in alternative investments / the CAIA Association.
      p. cm. — (Wiley finance series)
  Includes index.
  ISBN 978-0-470-44702-4 (cloth)
    1. Investments.   2. Securities.   3. Portfolio management.   I. Title.   II. Title: CAIA level one.   III. Title: CAIA level I.
  HG4521.C24 2009
  332.63'2—dc22

                                                                                                      2009021621

Printed in the United States of America

10 9 8 7 6 5 4 3 2 1

Contents

Preface

Since its inception in 2002, the Chartered Alternative Investment Analyst (CAIA) Association has strived to incorporate state-of-the-art reading materials in its curriculum. This latest curriculum reading, part of the Chartered Alternative Investment Analyst Series, represents a milestone in our efforts to continuously improve and update our curriculum. To ensure that the material best reflects current practices in the area of alternative investments, the CAIA Association invited a group of leading industry professionals to contribute to the production of the series, covering core areas of alternative investments: hedge funds, managed futures, commodities, real estate, and private equity. Similar to other books published by the CAIA Association, this book is grounded in the *CAIA Program Core Knowledge Outline*SM. Mark Anson, CAIA, has been contributing to the development of the CAIA curriculum since the Association's beginnings. He brings more than 20 years of experience in alternative assets to writing this first book in our series. We are proud to make this book available to our candidates and alternative investment professionals. This first edition of the series is being launched in 2009 when more than 5,000 aspiring, as well as accomplished, alternative investment professionals will endeavor to master the material covered in this book, as well as other readings as outlined in the CAIA study guides, in order to earn the prestigious CAIA designation.

In publishing the books in this series, we are guided by the Association's mission to provide its members with a comprehensive knowledge of alternative investments, advocate high standards of professional conduct, and establish the Chartered Alternative Investment Analyst designation as the educational gold standard for the alternative investment industry.

FOUNDATION

The quality, rigor, and relevance of this series derive from the ideals upon which the CAIA Association was based. The CAIA program offered its first Level I examination in February of 2003. We now have over 3,000 members, but in its first full year only 43 candidates, who passed Level I and Level II exams and met the other requirements of membership, were invited to join the CAIA Association. Many of these founding members were instrumental in establishing the CAIA designation as the global mark of excellence in alternative investment education. Through their support and with the help of the founding co-sponsors, the Alternative Investment Management Association (AIMA) and the Center for the International Securities and Derivatives Markets (CISDM), the Association is now firmly established as the most comprehensive and credible designation in the rapidly growing sphere of alternative investments.

The AIMA is the hedge fund industry's global, not-for-profit trade association, with over 1,100 corporate members worldwide. Members include leading hedge fund managers, fund of hedge funds managers, prime brokers, legal and accounting services, and fund administrators. They all benefit from the AIMA's active influence in policy development; its leadership in industry initiatives, including education and sound practice manuals; and its excellent reputation with regulators.

The CISDM of the Isenberg School of Management of the University of Massachusetts seeks to enhance the understanding of the field of alternative investments through research, education, and networking opportunities for member donors, industry professionals, and academics.

I first attended one of the early annual CISDM Research meetings as a CISDM fellow and doctoral student over 10 years ago, and recall being most impressed by the level and depth of discussion among the Center's sponsors regarding the need for education and research in the area of alternative investments. It has been truly rewarding to witness the development and growth of the CAIA, starting from only an idea to meet a real need.

Led by Craig Asche, Executive Director of the Association; Dr. Thomas Schneeweis, Director of the CISDM; Florence Lombard, of AIMA; and a core group of faculty and industry experts who were associated with the University of Massachusetts and AIMA, the CAIA program took shape and was introduced to the investment community through the publication of its first set of CAIA study guides in 2002. From the beginning, the Association recognized that a meaningful portion of its curriculum must be devoted to codes of conduct and ethical behavior in the investment profession. To this end, with permission and cooperation of the CFA Institute, we have incorporated its Code of Ethics and the *CFA Standards of Practice Handbook* in our curriculum. Further, we leverage the experience and contributions of our membership and other distinguished alternative investment professionals on our board and committees to create and update the *CAIA Program Core Knowledge Outline*[SM].

The CAIA Association has experienced rapid growth in its membership during the past seven years—a growth that has followed the expansion of the alternative investment industry into the mainstream of the investment industry. We strive to stay nimble in our process so that curriculum developments remain relevant and keep pace with the constant changes in this dynamic industry. Yet we never lose sight of the fact that we complement the still larger traditional and established investment arena.

This series focuses on the core topics that comprise each of the basic areas of alternative investments, but our original philosophy to stay nimble will serve us especially well now. Given the recent turmoil in the markets, the ability to keep pace with the regulatory and economic changes is more important today than it has ever been in our history. This series, including the annually revised, most advanced material contained in our *CAIA Level II: Current and Integrated Topics*, reflects the current state of the industry.

BENEFITS

While the CAIA Association's origins are largely due to the efforts of professionals in the hedge fund and managed futures space, these founders correctly identified a void in the wider understanding of the alternative investments space as a whole. From the beginning, the CAIA curriculum has also covered private equity, commodities, and real estate equally and always with an eye toward shifts in the industry. Today, several hundred CAIA members identify their main area of expertise as real estate or private equity; several hundred more members are from family offices, pension funds, endowments, and sovereign wealth funds that allocate across multiple classes within the alternative space. To accomplish this comprehensively, we have fully developed curriculum subcommittees that represent each area of coverage within the curriculum. All of these alternative investment areas share many distinct features such as the relative freedom on the part of investment managers to act in the best interests of their investors, alignment of interests between investors and management, relative illiquidity of positions for some investment products, and deviations from some of the underpinning assumptions of modern portfolio theory. These characteristics necessitate conceptual and actual modifications to the standard investment performance analysis and decision making paradigms.

The reader will find the publications in our series to be beneficial whether from the standpoint of allocating to new asset classes and strategies in order to gain broader diversification or from the standpoint of a specialist needing to better understand the competing options available to sophisticated investors globally. In either case, the reader will be better equipped to serve his or her clients' needs. The series has been designed to make studying more efficient relative to our past curriculum. Importantly, it is more relevant, having been written under the direction of the CAIA Association with the input and efforts of many practicing and eminent alternative investment professionals, as reflected in each publication's acknowledgments section.

THE CAIA PROGRAMS AND CAIA ALTERNATIVE INVESTMENT ANALYST SERIES

The CAIA Prerequisite Program is an assessment tool to determine a candidate's readiness to enter the CAIA program. These prerequisite materials cover the quantitative analytics commonly associated with traditional assets, as well as a blend of practical and theoretical knowledge relating to both traditional and alternative investments.

The first book in our series, *CAIA Level I: An Introduction to Core Topics in Alternative Investments*, is a revised edition of Mark Anson's *Handbook of Alternative Assets*. This new CAIA edition includes completely updated sections on hedge funds, managed futures and commodities, private equity, and credit derivatives, as well as new chapters on active management and real estate. Thus, the CAIA Level I required readings are contained in this one text, supplemented only by the CFA Institute's *Standards of Practice Handbook*. The reader should be aware, however, that the prerequisite program has been expanded, and that Level I candidates are assumed to have mastered all of its content in advance of taking the Level I exam.

The second book in our series, *CAIA Level II: Advanced Core Topics in Alternative Investments*, also represents a significant improvement to the coverage of our curriculum. Specifically, each section was developed to incorporate the expert practitioner input that comprises the *CAIA Program Core Knowledge Outline*^{SM}. We believe this new model of curriculum development accurately reflects the skill set required of industry practitioners.

The third book in the series, *CAIA Level II: Integrated Topics and Applications*, is the result of the work of our Curriculum Task Force members. They reviewed the newly developed drafts of the first two new books in the series in light of the *CAIA Program Core Knowledge Outline*^{SM}, updated the *Outline*, prioritized and developed supplemental topics, and reviewed practice problems designed for the Level II examinations and included in this publication.

The fourth volume in this series is titled *CAIA Level II: Current and Integrated Topics*. It is updated annually and designed to address topics that cut across all areas of alternative investments, such as asset allocation and risk management techniques, as well as new developments in the alternative investment research space and in the industry itself.

Finally, we will continue to update the *CAIA Level I Study Guide* and the *CAIA Level II Study Guide* every six months (each exam cycle). These are freely available on our web site. These guides outline all of the readings and corresponding learning objectives (LOs) that candidates are responsible for meeting. They also contain important information for candidates regarding the use of LOs, testing policies, topic weightings, where to find and report errata, and much more. The entire exam process is outlined in the *CAIA Candidate Handboo*k and is available at www.caia.org/enroll/candidatehandbook/.

I believe you will find this series to be the most comprehensive, rigorous, and globally relevant source of educational material available within the field of alternative investments.

June 2009   Kathryn Wilkens-Christopher, PhD, CAIA
                                                                        Director of Curriculum
                                                                        CAIA Association

Acknowledgments

We would like to thank the many individuals who played important roles in producing this book. Mark Anson authored the material, while several others were instrumental in bringing this project to its completion. Kathryn Wilkens-Christopher, Hossein Kazemi, Nelson Lacey, Donald Chambers, Craig Asche, Urbi Garay, Kristaps Licis, Raj Gupta, and Edward Szado contributed greatly by assisting with the development of the initial section outlines, which are based on the CAIA Core Knowledge (CKO) Outline[SM], and reviewing several section drafts. Michael Carolan, Meg Inners, and Aileen Cummings were also very helpful in the review stage. Jeanne Miller kept the project on schedule, and we owe many thanks to Bill Falloon and Meg Freeborn at John Wiley & Sons.

About the Authors

The CAIA Association is an independent, not-for-profit global organization committed to education and professionalism in the field of alternative investments, established in 2002 by industry leaders under the guidance of the Alternative Investment Management Association (AIMA) and the Center for International Securities and Derivatives Markets (CISDM) with the belief that a strong foundation of knowledge is essential for all professionals. The CAIA Association offers two exams (Level I and Level II) to professional analysts in this growing field so that, upon successful completion, an individual is designated a Chartered Alternative Investment Analyst (CAIA). This certification has a great deal of prestige in the global community, with members from over 50 countries on five continents.

Mark Anson is the President and Executive Director of Investment Services at Nuveen Investments. Previously, he was the Chief Executive Officer of Hermes Pensions Management Ltd. In addition, he was the Chief Executive Officer of the British Telecom Pension Scheme, the largest pension fund in the United Kingdom at $80 billion of assets under management (AUM). Before joining Hermes, Mark was the Chief Investment Officer of the $245 billion California Employees' Retirement System (CalPERS)—the largest pension fund in the United States. Prior to CalPERS, he worked on Wall Street as a portfolio manager, where he received the Series 3, 7, 24, and 66 National Association of Securities Dealers (NASD) securities industry licenses. Mark is the author of four financial textbooks, including the *Handbook of Alternative Assets*, which for several years was one of the primary textbook for the Chartered Alternative Investment Analyst program. In addition, he has published over 80 research articles on topics ranging from alpha and beta separation to corporate governance, and he serves on the editorial boards of several financial journals.

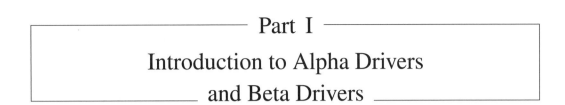

Part I

Introduction to Alpha Drivers
and Beta Drivers

What Is an Alternative Asset Class?

Part of the difficulty of working with alternative asset classes is defining them. Are they a separate asset class or a subset of an existing asset class? Do they hedge the investment opportunity set or expand it? Are they listed on an exchange or do they trade in the over-the-counter market?

In most cases, alternative assets are a subset of an existing asset class. This may run contrary to the popular view that alternative assets are separate asset classes.[1] However, we take the view that what many consider separate classes are really just different investment strategies within an existing asset class.

Additionally, in most cases, they expand the investment opportunity set, rather than hedge it. Last, alternative assets are generally purchased in the private markets, outside of any exchange. While hedge funds, private equity, and credit derivatives meet these criteria, we will see that commodity futures prove to be the exception to these general rules.

Alternative assets, then, are just alternative investments within an existing asset class. Specifically, most alternative assets derive their value from either the debt or the equity markets. For instance, most hedge fund strategies involve the purchase and sale of either equity or debt securities. In addition, hedge fund managers may invest in derivative instruments whose value is derived from the equity or debt markets.

In this book, we classify five types of alternative assets: real estate, hedge funds, commodity and managed futures, private equity, and credit derivatives. Investments in real estate may be made directly, or indirectly through a fund. Hedge funds and private equity are the best known of the alternative asset world. Typically, these investments are accomplished through the purchase of limited partner units in a private limited partnership. Commodity futures can be either passive investing tied to a commodity futures index or active investing through a commodity pool or advisory account. Private equity is the investment strategy of investing in companies before they issue their securities publicly, or taking a public company private. Credit derivatives can be purchased through limited partnership units, as a tranche of a special purpose vehicle, or directly through the purchase of distressed debt securities.

We will explore each of these alternative asset classes in detail, providing practical advice along with useful research. We begin this chapter with a review of super asset classes.

SUPER ASSET CLASSES

There are three super asset classes: capital assets, assets that are used as inputs to creating economic value, and assets that are a store of value.[2]

Capital assets

Capital assets are defined by their claim on the future cash flows of an enterprise. They provide a source of ongoing value. As a result, capital assets may be valued based on the net present value of their expected returns.

---

[1] See, for example, Chapter 8 in David Swensen, *Pioneering Portfolio Management* (New York: Free Press, 2000).

[2] See Robert Greer, "What Is an Asset Class Anyway?" *Journal of Portfolio Management* 23 (1997), 83–91.

Under the classic theory of Modigliani and Miller, a corporation cannot change its value (in the absence of tax benefits) by changing the method of its financing.[3] Modigliani and Miller demonstrated that the value of the firm is dependent on its cash flows. How those cash flows are divided up between shareholders and bondholders is irrelevant to firm value.

Capital assets, then, are distinguished not by their possession of physical assets, but rather by their claim on the cash flows of an underlying enterprise. Hedge funds, private equity funds, credit derivatives, and corporate governance funds all fall within the super asset class of capital assets because the values of their funds are all determined by the present value of expected future cash flows from the securities in which they invest.

As a result, we can conclude that it is not the types of securities in which they invest that distinguish hedge funds, private equity funds, credit derivatives, or corporate governance funds from traditional asset classes. Rather, it is the alternative investment strategies they pursue that distinguish them from traditional stock and bond investments.

Assets that can be used as economic inputs

Certain assets can be consumed as part of the production cycle. Consumable or transformable assets can be converted into another asset. Generally, this class of assets consists of the physical commodities: grains, metals, energy products, and livestock. These assets are used as economic inputs into the production cycle to produce other assets, such as automobiles, skyscrapers, new homes, and appliances.

These assets generally cannot be valued using a net present value analysis. For example, a pound of copper, by itself, does not yield an economic stream of revenues. Nor does it have much value for capital appreciation. However, the copper can be transformed into copper piping that is used in an office building or as part of the circuitry of an electronic appliance.

While consumable assets cannot produce a stream of cash flows, we will demonstrate in our section on commodities that this asset class has excellent diversification properties for an investment portfolio. In fact, the lack of dependency on future cash flows to generate value is one of the reasons why commodities have important diversification potential vis-à-vis capital assets.

Assets that store value

Art is considered the classic asset that stores value. It is not a capital asset because there are no cash flows associated with owning a painting or a sculpture. Consequently, art cannot be valued in a discounted cash flow analysis. It is also not an asset that is used as an economic input because it is a finished product.

Art requires ownership and possession. Its value can be realized only through its sale and transfer of possession. In the meantime, the owner retains the artwork with the expectation that it will yield a price that in real terms (i.e. adjusted by inflation) is at least equal to what the owner paid for it.

There is no rational way to gauge whether the price of art will increase or decrease because its value is derived purely from the subjective (and private) visual enjoyment that the right of ownership conveys. Therefore, to an owner, art is a store of value. It neither conveys economic benefits nor is used as an economic input, but retains the value paid for it.

Gold and precious metals are another example of a store of value asset. In the emerging parts of the world, gold and silver are a significant means of maintaining wealth. Residents of these countries

---

[3] Franco Modigliani and Merton Miller, "The Cost of Capital, Corporation Finance, and the Theory of Investment," *American Economic Review* (June 1958), 433–443.

often do not have access to the same range of financial products that are available to residents of more developed nations. Consequently, they accumulate their wealth through a tangible asset as opposed to a capital asset.

However, the lines between the three super classes of assets can become blurred. For example, gold can be leased to jewelry and other metal manufacturers. Jewelry makers lease gold during periods of seasonal demand, expecting to purchase the gold on the open market and return it to the lessor before the lease term ends. The gold lease provides a stream of cash flows that can be valued using net present value analysis.

Precious metals can also be used as transformable or consumable assets because they have the highest levels of thermal and electrical conductivity among the metals. Silver, for example, is used in the circuitry of most telephones and light switches. Gold is used in the circuitry of TVs, cars, airplanes, computers, and rocket ships.

REAL ESTATE

We include real estate in our discussion of alternative assets even though real estate was an asset class long before stocks and bonds became the investment of choice. In fact, in times past, land was the single most important asset class. Kings, queens, lords, and nobles measured their wealth by the amount of property that they owned. "Land barons" were aptly named. Ownership of land was reserved for only the wealthiest of society.

However, over the past 200 years, our economic society changed from one based on the ownership of property to one based on the ownership of legal entities. This transformation occurred as society moved from the agricultural age to the industrial age. Production of goods and services became the new source of wealth and power.

Stocks and bonds were originated to support the financing needs of new enterprises that manufactured material goods and services. In fact, stocks and bonds became the alternatives to real estate instead of vice versa. With the advent of stock and bond exchanges and the general acceptance of owning equity or debt stakes in companies, it is sometimes forgotten that real estate was the original and primary asset class of society.

In fact, it was only 28 years ago in the United States that real estate was the major asset class of most individual investors. This exposure was the result of owning a primary residence. It was not until the long bull market started in 1983 that investors began to diversify their wealth into the "alternative" assets of stocks and bonds.

Given the long-term presence of real estate as an asset class, several treatises have been written concerning its valuation.[4] Still, we believe a discussion of real estate is relevant within the framework of alternative assets. The reason is that other than a primary residence, real estate is often excluded from a diversified portfolio. Perhaps another way to look at real estate is as a fundamental asset class that should be included within every diversified portfolio. Therefore, it is an alternative asset class meant to diversify the stock and bond holdings within a portfolio context.

---

[4] See, for example, Howard Gelbtuch, David Mackmin, and Michael Milgrim, eds., *Real Estate Valuation in Global Markets* (Chicago: Appraisal Institute, 1997); James Boykin and Alfred Ring, *The Valuation of Real Estate*, 4th ed. (Englewood Cliffs, NJ: Prentice Hall, 1993); Austin Jaffe and C. F. Sirmans, *Fundamentals of Real Estate Investment*, 3rd ed. (Englewood Cliffs, NJ: Prentice Hall, 1994); and Jack Cummings, *Real Estate Finance & Investment Manual* (Englewood Cliffs, NJ: Prentice Hall, 1997).

ASSET ALLOCATION

Asset allocation is generally defined as the allocation of an investor's portfolio across a number of asset classes.[5] Asset allocation, by its very nature, shifts the emphasis from the security level to the portfolio level. It is an investment profile that provides a framework for constructing a portfolio based on measures of risk and return. In this sense, asset allocation can trace its roots to modern portfolio theory and the work of Harry Markowitz.[6]

Asset classes and asset allocation

Initially, asset allocation involved four asset classes: equity, fixed income, cash, and real estate. Within each class, the assets could be further divided into subclasses. For example, stocks can be divided into large-capitalization stocks, small-capitalization stocks, and foreign stocks. Similarly, fixed income can be broken down into U.S. Treasury notes and bonds, investment-grade bonds, high-yield bonds, and sovereign bonds.

The expansion of newly defined alternative assets may cause investors to become confused about the diversification properties of alternative assets and how they fit into an overall diversified portfolio. Investors need to understand the background of asset allocation as a concept for improving return while reducing risk.

For example, in the 1980s, the biggest private equity game was taking public companies private. Does the fact that a corporation that once had publicly traded stock but now has privately traded stock mean that it has jumped into a new asset class? We maintain that it does not. Furthermore, public offerings are the primary exit strategy for private equity; public ownership begins where private equity ends.[7]

Considered within this context, a separate asset class does not need to be created for private equity. Rather, this type of investment can be considered as just another point within the equity investment universe. Rather than hedging the equity class as altogether separate, private equity expands the equity asset class.

Similarly, credit derivatives expand the fixed income asset class, rather than hedging it. Hedge funds also invest in the stock and bond markets but pursue trading strategies that are very different from a traditional buy-and-hold strategy. Commodities fall into a different class of assets than equity, fixed income, or cash, and are treated separately in this book.

Strategic versus tactical allocations

Some alternative assets should be used in a tactical rather than strategic allocation. Strategic allocation of resources is applied to fundamental asset classes such as equity, fixed income, cash, and real estate. These are the basic asset classes that must be held within a diversified portfolio.

Strategic asset allocation is concerned with the long-term asset mix. The strategic mix of assets is designed to accomplish a long-term goal such as funding pension benefits or matching long-term liabilities. Risk aversion is considered when deciding the strategic asset allocation but current market conditions are not. In general, policy targets are set for strategic asset classes with allowable ranges

---

[5] See William Sharpe, "Asset Allocation: Management Style and Performance Measurement," *Journal of Portfolio Management* 18, no. 2 (1992), 7–19.

[6] See Harry Markowitz, *Portfolio Selection*, Cowles Foundation Monograph 16 (New Haven, CT: Yale University Press, 1959).

[7] See Jeffrey Horvitz, "Asset Classes and Asset Allocation: Problems of Classification," *Journal of Private Portfolio Management* 2, no. 4 (2000), 27–32.

around those targets. Allowable ranges are established to allow flexibility in the management of the investment portfolio.

Tactical asset allocation is short-term in nature. This strategy is used to take advantage of current market conditions that may be more favorable to one asset class over another. The goal of funding long-term liabilities has been satisfied by the target ranges established by the strategic asset allocation. The goal of tactical asset allocation is to maximize return.

Tactical allocation of resources depends on the ability to diversify within an asset class. This is where alternative assets have the greatest ability to add value. Their purpose is not to hedge the fundamental asset classes, but rather to expand them. Consequently, alternative assets should be considered as part of a broader asset class.

As already noted, private equity is simply one part of the spectrum of equity investments. Granted, a different set of skills is required to manage a private equity portfolio compared to public equity securities. However, private equity investments simply expand the equity investment universe. Consequently, private equity is an alternative investment strategy within the equity universe as opposed to a new fundamental asset class.

Another example is credit derivatives. These are investments that expand the frontier of credit risk investing. The fixed income world can be classified simply as a choice between U.S. Treasury securities that are considered to be default-free and spread products that contain an element of default risk. Spread products include any fixed income investment that does not have a credit rating on a par with the U.S. government. Consequently, spread products trade at a credit spread relative to U.S. Treasury securities that reflects their risk of default.

Credit derivatives are a way to diversify and expand the universe for investing in spread products. Traditionally, fixed income managers attempted to establish their ideal credit risk and return profile by buying and selling traditional bonds. However, the bond market can be inefficient and it may be difficult to pinpoint the exact credit profile to match the risk profile of the investor. Credit derivatives can help to plug the gaps in a fixed income portfolio and expand the fixed income universe by accessing credit exposure in more efficient formats.

Efficient versus inefficient asset classes

Another way to distinguish alternative asset classes is based on the efficiency of the marketplace. The U.S. public stock and bond markets are generally considered the most efficient marketplaces in the world. These markets are often referred to as semistrong efficient. This means that all publicly available information regarding a publicly traded corporation, both past information and present, is fully digested in the price of that company's traded securities.

Yet, inefficiencies exist in all markets, both public and private. If there were no informational inefficiencies in the public equity market, there would be no case for active investment management. Nonetheless, whatever inefficiencies do exist, they are small and fleeting. The reason is that information is easy to acquire and disseminate in the publicly traded securities markets. Top-quartile active managers in the public equity market earn excess returns (over their benchmarks) of approximately 1% a year.

In contrast, with respect to alternative assets, information is very difficult to acquire. Most alternative assets (with the exception of commodities) are privately traded. This includes private equity, hedge funds, real estate, and credit derivatives. The difference between top-quartile and bottom-quartile performance in private equity can be as much as 25%.

Consider venture capital, one subset of the private equity market. Investments in start-up companies require intense research into the product niche the company intends to fill, the background of the management of the company, projections about future cash flows, exit strategies, potential competition, beta testing schedules, and so forth. This information is not readily available to the investing public. It is time-consuming and expensive to accumulate. Further, most investors do not have the time or the talent to acquire and filter through the rough data regarding a private company. One reason why alternative asset managers charge large management and incentive fees is to recoup the cost of information collection.

This leads to another distinguishing factor between alternative investments and the traditional asset classes: the investment intermediary. Continuing with our venture capital example, most investments in venture capital are made through limited partnerships, limited liability companies, or special purpose vehicles. It is estimated that 80% of all private equity investments in the United States are funneled through a financial intermediary.

Last, investments in alternative assets are less liquid than their public markets counterparts. Investments are closely held and liquidity is minimal. Further, without a publicly traded security, the value of private securities cannot be determined by market trading. The value of the private securities must be estimated by book value, arrived at by appraisal, or determined by a cash flow model.

Constrained versus unconstrained investing

During the great bull market of 1983 to 2000, the asset management industry only had to invest in the stock market to enjoy consistent double-digit returns. During this heyday, investment management shops and institutional investors divided their assets between the traditional asset classes of stocks and bonds. As the markets turned sour at the beginning of the new millennium, asset management firms and institutional investors found themselves boxed in by these traditional asset class distinctions. They found that their investment teams were organized along traditional asset class lines and their investment portfolios were constrained by efficient benchmarks that reflected this "asset box" approach.

Consequently, traditional asset management shops have been slow to reorganize their investment structures. This has allowed hedge funds and other alternative investment vehicles to flourish because they are not bound by traditional asset class lines—they can invest outside the benchmark. These alternative assets are free to exploit the investment opportunities that fall in between the traditional benchmark boxes. The lack of constraints allows alternative asset managers a degree of freedom that is not allowed the traditional asset class shops. Further, traditional asset management shops remain caught up in an organizational structure that is bounded by traditional asset class lines. This provides another constraint because it inhibits the flow of information and investment ideas across the organization.

Asset location versus trading strategy

One of the first and best papers on hedge funds, by William Fung and David Hsieh,[8] shows a distinct difference between how mutual funds and hedge funds operate. They show that the economic exposure associated with mutual funds is defined primarily by *where* the mutual fund invests. In other words, mutual funds gain their primary economic and risk exposures by the locations of the asset classes in which they invest. Thus, we get large-cap active equity funds, small-cap growth funds, Treasury bond funds, and the like.

Conversely, Fung and Hsieh show that hedge funds' economic exposures are defined more by *how* they trade. That is, a hedge fund's risk and return exposure is defined more by a trading strategy

---

[8] William Fung and David Hsieh, "Empirical Characteristics of Dynamic Trading Strategies: The Case of Hedge Funds," *Review of Financial Studies* 10, no. 2, 1997, 275–302.

within an asset class than it is defined by the location of the asset class. As a result, hedge fund managers tend to have much greater turnover in their portfolios than mutual funds have.

Asset class risk premiums versus trading strategy risk premiums

Related to the idea of trading strategy versus investment location is the notion of risk premiums. You cannot earn a return without incurring risk. Traditional investment managers earn risk premiums for investing in the large-cap value equity market, small-cap growth equity market, and high-yield bond market, in other words, based on the location of the asset markets in which they invest.

Conversely, alternative asset managers also earn returns for taking risk, but the risk is defined more by a trading strategy than it is by an economic exposure associated with the systematic risk contained within broad financial classes. For example, hedge fund strategies such as convertible arbitrage, statistical arbitrage, and equity market neutral can earn a so-called complexity risk premium.[9]

These strategies buy and sell similar securities, expecting the securities to converge in value over time. The complexity of implementing these strategies results in inefficient pricing in the market. In addition, many investors are constrained by the long-only restriction—their inability to short securities. This perpetuates inefficient pricing in the marketplace, which enables hedge funds to earn a return.

OVERVIEW OF THIS BOOK

This book is organized into six parts plus four appendices. The first part provides a framework to consider alternative assets within a broader portfolio context. Specifically, in Chapter 2 we expand on the concept of strategic versus tactical asset allocation and the use of beta drivers versus alpha drivers to achieve these goals. Chapter 3 discusses in detail the concept of beta. Just as the market for alternative assets has become more sophisticated over the years, the market for beta has advanced as well. The traditional capital asset pricing model (CAPM) beta is not sufficient to describe the many ways of systematic risk capture that exist in the financial markets today. Further, a discussion of beta will help ground us in the reality and examination of alpha. Chapter 4 examines the separation of alpha and beta in the asset management industry. As investors have become more advanced in their portfolio construction, asset management companies have had to respond by developing a clearer understanding and pricing of beta and alpha. Chapter 5 explains the calculus of active management, which provides a discussion of the Fundamental Law of Active Management.

The second part of the book turns to real estate. Real estate has long been a significant holding of both retail (homeowners) and institutional (commercial, retail, multifamily, industrial) investors. We start in Chapter 6 with a review of real estate investment trusts (REITs). Chapter 7 discusses the formation of the National Council of Real Estate Investment Fiduciaries (NCREIF) and the construction of its National Property Index, the most widely used benchmark in the real estate industry. Chapter 8 takes a step back to discuss the five reasons why real estate is a necessary part of any diversified portfolio. Chapter 9 provides a discussion on the differences between core, value-added, and opportunistic real estate, exploring their different risk profiles and return expectations.

The third part of the book reviews hedge funds. Chapter 10 begins with a brief history on the birth of hedge funds and an introduction to the types of hedge fund investment strategies. Chapter 11 provides some practical guidance as to how to build a hedge fund investment program. Chapter 12 is devoted to conducting due diligence, including both a qualitative and a quantitative

---

[9] See Lars Jaeger, *Managing Risk in Alternative Investment Strategies* (Upper Saddle River, NJ: Prentice Hall/Financial Times, 2002).

review. In Chapter 13, we analyze the return distributions of hedge funds and begin to consider some risk management issues. In Chapter 14, we expand the discussion of hedge fund risks and highlight some specific examples of hedge fund underperformance. Chapter 15 provides an introduction to hedge fund benchmarks and discusses how these benchmarks impact the asset allocation decision with regard to hedge funds. In Chapter 16, we consider the fees charged by hedge fund managers, a key point of contention between hedge fund managers and their clients. Chapter 17 reviews some recent hedge fund explosions and implosions. We thought it worthwhile to look at recent exits of five hedge fund managers to determine what went wrong, to consider what might have been done to prevent their demise, and to see whether there are any other lessons learned. In the concluding Chapter 18, we have a bit of fun at the expense of the hedge fund industry and add a humorous note as we go through a top-ten list of hedge fund quotes (from actual hedge fund managers) and accompanying anecdotes.

Part IV is devoted to commodity and managed futures. We begin with a brief review in Chapter 19 of the economic value inherent in commodity futures contracts. Chapter 20 describes how an individual or institution may invest in commodity futures, including an introduction to commodity futures benchmarks. Chapter 21 considers commodity futures within a portfolio framework, while Chapter 22 examines the managed futures industry.

Part V covers the spectrum of private equity. In Chapter 23, we introduce venture capital, while Chapter 24 is devoted to leveraged buyouts. In Chapters 25 and 26, we show how two different forms of debt may be components of the private equity marketplace. In Chapter 27, we introduce alternative investment strategies within the private equity marketplace, and in Chapter 28, we review the economics associated with private equity investments.

Part VI is devoted to credit derivatives. In Chapter 29, we review the importance of credit risk and provide examples of how credit derivatives are used in portfolio management. In Chapter 30, we review the collateralized debt obligation market. Specifically, we review the design, structure, and economics of collateralized bond obligations and collateralized loan obligations. In Chapter 31, we discuss new developments.

Throughout this book, we attempt to provide descriptive material as well as empirical examples. In each chapter, you will find charts, tables, graphs, and calculations that serve to highlight specific points. Our goal is to both educate the reader with respect to these alternative investment strategies as well as provide a reference book for data and research. Along the way, we also try to provide a few anecdotes about alternative investing that, while providing some humor, also demonstrate some of the pitfalls of the alternative asset universe.

Appendices

The first three appendices cover essential material provided as a reference: Appendix A begins to apply some basic principles of return, compounding, expected return, and internal rate of return. Appendix B turns to measures of risk such as the variance, volatility, skewness, and kurtosis. These are risk measures that we use throughout the book with respect to each alternative investment class. Appendix C provides basic examples of correlation analysis and linear regression analysis. These deal with quantitative methods in finance. As the market has moved toward the separation of beta and alpha, more sophisticated mathematical concepts have been applied to accurately measure and manage alpha and beta. Last, Appendix D explores 130/30 funds, which are all the rage among both institutional and retail investors. Some consider 130/30 funds to be a poor man's hedge fund, but, in fact, these funds can play a vital part in portfolio construction.

2

Why Alternative Assets Are Important

Beta Drivers and Alpha Drivers

The 1980s and 1990s experienced an unprecedented equity market expansion that provided an average annual total return to the S&P 500 of over 18% per year. It was hard to ignore the premium that the equity market delivered over U.S. Treasury bonds during this time. Over the same period, the average yield to maturity for the 10-year U.S. Treasury bond was 8.63%, a historic high.

The long-term implied **equity risk premium** (ERP) (over 10-year U.S. Treasury bonds) has been estimated at 3.8%.[1] This is the risk premium implied by stock market valuations and forecasts of earnings in relation to current market value. It is the expected risk premium that long-term investors must earn to entice them to hold equities rather than government bonds. However, throughout the 1980s and 1990s, the realized risk premium frequently exceeded that implied by investors' expectations.

Exhibit 2.1 plots the realized equity risk premium compared to the long-term ERP. It also graphs the cumulative ERP earned over this period. Generally, over the 1980–1999 time period, the realized ERP was inconsistent, sometimes greater than the expected long-term risk premium, sometimes less. However, from the late 1980s through the end of the 1990s, the realized risk premium for holding equities exceeded the expected premium more often than not. As a result, investors were continually rewarded with equity market returns that exceeded their expectations.

This led large institutional investors to rely exclusively on asset allocation models where asset classes were defined by strict lines or so-called benchmark boxes.[2] For 20 years, this type of investing worked for large institutional investors. However, the global bear equity market of 2000 to 2002 demonstrated that mean reversion is a powerful force in finance.

Throughout the 19-year period 1981 to 2000, investors needed only to consider return, a traditional approach to asset allocation earned strong returns for many years.[3] In addition, consultants encouraged such an approach because it made for convenient asset allocation, benchmarking of performance, and style classification. However, looking forward, traditional asset class definitions may not be sufficient to deliver the kind of portfolio performance that investors have come to expect and demand.

---

[1] See Henry Dickson and Charles Reinhard, "Weekly Earnings Comment," Lehman Brothers Research, July 21, 2004. The long-term equity risk premium is measured for U.S. stocks and is remarkably consistent across international borders. Of interest, there were two time periods when the equity risk premium approached zero. The first was in the autumn of 1987 before the stock market undertook a massive correction in October of that year. At that time, portfolio insurance was all the rage. Of course, this turned out to be a fallacy, but at the time, the ERP was driven close to zero because investors believed that they could insure against losses so investing in the stock market was associated with a zero risk premium. The second time was at the height of the tech bubble. Then, investors so overvalued stocks based on the technology hype that the equity risk premium also approached zero.

[2] See Mark Anson, "Thinking Outside the Benchmark," *Journal of Portfolio Management*, 30th Anniversary Issue, 2004, 8–22.

[3] The same can be said for the 2003 to 2007 period. However, this bull market was much shorter and by then alternative investments had already become an important part of many portfolios.

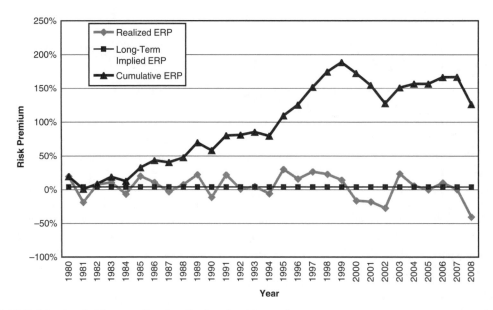

Exhibit 2.1   Implied (expected) and realized equity risk premium

This leads to the focus of this book. Alternative investments have the ability to generate greater yield, reduce risk, and provide return streams that are less than perfectly correlated with the traditional stock and bond market. Throughout this chapter, we refer to **beta drivers** and **alpha drivers**. Beta drivers capture financial market risk premiums in an efficient manner, while alpha drivers seek pockets of excess return often without regard to benchmarks. Most alternative assets fall squarely into the category of alpha drivers. Alpha drivers seek excess return or added value. They tend to seek sources of return less correlated with traditional asset classes, which reduces risk in the entire portfolio in the process. However, understanding alternative assets in institutional portfolios means we first must review the asset allocation process of large institutional investors.

STRATEGIC VERSUS TACTICAL ASSET ALLOCATION

Generally, the board of trustees of a pension fund, endowment, or foundation establishes the strategic allocation among the major asset classes. **Strategic asset allocation** (SAA) is the translation of an institutional investor's investment policy. This process identifies strategic benchmarks tied to broad asset classes that establish the policy risk for the fund, known as the beta or market risk for the fund.

SAA is not designed to beat the market. Rather, it is designed to meet the long-term funding goals of the organization. This includes paying retirement benefits, supplementing a university budget, or providing for philanthropic donations. It is the process by which long-term assets are matched against long-term pension fund liabilities, university budgets, foundation donation schedules, or high-net-worth wealth generation.

In contrast, **tactical asset allocation** (TAA) facilitates an institutional investor's long-term funding goals by seeking extra return. It does this by taking advantage of opportunities in the financial markets when those markets appear to be out of line with fundamental economic valuations. As a result, TAA

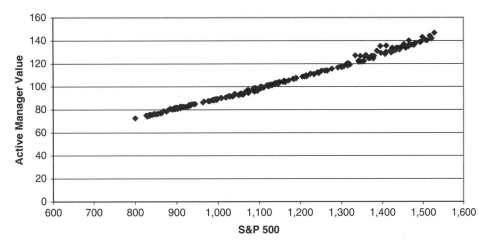

Exhibit 2.2   A large-cap active equity manager

Note: Beta 1.00; R-squared 0.994

Source: Morningstar.

requires more frequent trading than SAA. This process uses actively managed investment products as alternatives to passive benchmark risk.

Boards of trustees engage in SAA, which provides pension funds with target allocations among the major asset classes. Typically, percentage targets or ranges are set up to allocate a fund's investment capital across asset classes such as stocks, bonds, cash, and real estate. This type of allocation establishes the beta for the fund (i.e. the fund's exposure to broad asset classes). After the broad allocations are made, active returns, or alpha, is sought within each asset class.

Beta drivers are linear in their performance

Under the traditional paradigm of asset management, active management or alpha is pursued within an asset class. The beta of the asset class and the alpha are not separated or pursued independently. This is most apparent in the search for alpha by traditional long-only active equity managers.

Exhibit 2.2 plots the weekly returns of a large-cap active equity manager to those of the S&P 500. The result is a basically straight line. With a beta of 1.0 and a correlation coefficient of 0.99, this large-cap active equity manager essentially replicates the S&P 500.

Exhibit 2.2 demonstrates that the returns generated by this active equity manager are perfectly consistent with the up-and-down movement of the S&P 500. Beta drivers are linear in their performance compared to a financial index. Despite this manager's claim of "active" status, the fund is a beta driver, not an alpha driver—its returns are derived exclusively from the broad stock market.[4]

For comparison, we provide Exhibit 2.3, which shows the performance of a passive S&P 500 index manager. Again, we see a straight line where the performance of this investment manager is in precise lockstep with the up-and-down movement of the S&P 500. The only differences between this manager and the one in Exhibit 2.2 are the claim to active status by the manager in Exhibit 2.2

---

[4] In fact, over the five-year period studied, 2000 to 2004, this large-cap active equity manager underperformed the S&P 500 by 276 basis points.

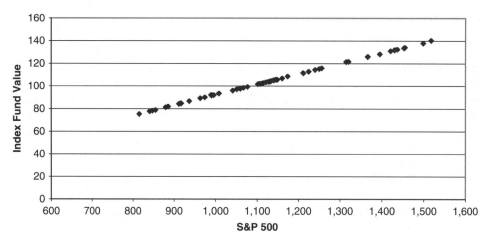

Exhibit 2.3   A passive index manager benchmarked to the S&P 500

Note: Beta 1.00; R-squared 1.00

Source: Morningstar.

and the level of fees charged. The manager in Exhibit 2.2 charges 65 basis points a year to deliver the S&P 500, whereas the manager in Exhibit 2.3 charges only four basis points.

SEPARATING ALPHA FROM BETA

Investors need to rethink asset management and break out of the traditional asset allocation model of trying to extract alpha from beta. A simple way to manage a total portfolio is to divide it into two classes of economic drivers: beta drivers and alpha drivers.

Beta drivers are designed to provide efficient economic exposure to establish the policy or market risk for an investor. This book does not seek to discredit beta drivers; they are an essential building block in institutional portfolios. They help to accomplish the primary funding and spending obligations of the investor.

In the traditional model, institutional portfolios find alpha but only when it is attached to beta. Institutional investors first make the allocation to strategic benchmarks to establish the policy risk of the institutional portfolio. Next, the investment staff tries to squeeze alpha out of these policy benchmarks but is often hampered by investing in the traditional asset classes of stocks and bonds to seek excess return. Consequently, alpha budgets are often misspent on the most efficient markets, those represented by the strategic benchmarks.

In the new investment model, alpha is sought independently of beta. Beta drivers remain important to implement the SAA established by the investor. However, the professional investment staff can seek alpha from investment products that are outside the benchmark.[5] This is where alternative assets are most useful.

More to the point, alpha risk budgets should not be spent on strategic benchmarks. Strategic benchmarks are designed to offer efficient beta exposure, the last place to look for extra value. Alpha risk budgets should be spent in less efficient markets, those described in this book: hedge funds, managed futures, commodities, private equity, and credit derivatives.

---

[5] See Anson, "Thinking Outside the Benchmark."

Broad categories of alpha drivers

Alpha drivers are expected to outperform the market. They fall into six general categories:

1. **Long/short investing.** These are strategies that go both long and short in the same asset class such as equity long/short hedge funds. These strategies may be market neutral (i.e. no beta exposure to market risk), but they typically retain some beta exposure. For example, many equity long/short hedge funds retain a net beta exposure to the stock market. Their goal is to optimize their total alpha from both positive and negative bets, generally without worrying about whether they retain some systematic (beta) risk exposure to the financial markets.
2. **Absolute return strategies.** These strategies are closely related to long/short investing. The key difference is that the hedge fund manager is unchained from a stock and bond index to pursue value-added strategies regardless of size, market direction, or benchmark restrictions. Many hedge fund managers simultaneously pursue long and short investment strategies to extract the greatest value associated with their financial market insights. A diversified portfolio of such strategies would be expected to have a low correlation with broad financial market indices, especially when measured over a full market cycle.
3. **Market segmentation.** Often investors deselect themselves from certain markets. Consider the collateralized debt market. Many investors avoid this market because of the default risk associated with the lower-rated tranches of securities in this market. In fact, some institutional investors are prohibited from investing in below-investment-grade bonds, while others eschew this market because it is less liquid than investment-grade securities. In fact, given the credit and liquidity crisis from the subprime mess in 2007 to 2009, we might expect to see more market segmentation along these lines. Commodities are another example of market segmentation. Commodities are less well understood than even hedge funds, and many investors avoid what they do not have the time to understand.
4. **Concentrated portfolios.** Most traditional active managers tend to hug their benchmark and maintain well-diversified portfolios (see Exhibit 2.2). Diversification is a way to minimize the risk of underperformance, but it also minimizes the probability of outperformance. In contrast, concentrated portfolios frequently have significant tracking errors to an established benchmark, but offer a greater opportunity for excess return. Corporate governance funds and private equity funds fall into this category because they typically have only a few very concentrated positions in their portfolios.
5. **Nonlinear return processes.** Nonlinear return functions exhibit option-like payoffs with a kinked distribution. These alternative investments may be explicitly linked to an option-like convertible bonds or may replicate an option payoff structure by virtue of their trading strategy. Examples of the latter include merger arbitrage, event-driven fixed income arbitrage, and managed futures. This type of return distribution may be particularly useful when combined with a linear beta driver.
6. **Alternative/cheap beta.** Another form of alternative investing is gaining access to a new source of systematic risk premium. Alternative beta is generally classified as anything that is outside the normal stock/bond portfolio. So commodities might be considered alternative beta as might real estate. The key point is that this bucket of alternatives provides an ability to diversify an investment portfolio beyond traditional asset classes.

The alternative assets discussed in the following chapters of this book all fall into one of these six broad categories of alternative investments. For example, many investors do not include real estate as an asset class in their diversified portfolios. This is another example of market segmentation. The categories discussed are not defined by asset class; they are defined by economic exposure or trading strategy.

The separation of alpha and beta

Exhibit 2.4 provides a graphical depiction of the separation of alpha and beta. This graph defines products by their contribution to active risk and active return. Active risk is the type of risk that an actively managed portfolio sustains as it endeavors to beat the returns of a benchmark. Active return is the return earned on an active investment relative to a benchmark. At the zero axis we find index products. These are the ultimate beta drivers, products that take no active risk, extract no added value, and are devoid of information (in fact, they toss any information aside). They passively capture the risk premium associated with a risky asset class.

Included in this group are exchange-traded funds (ETFs) and other replication products designed to efficiently capture systematic risk premiums. Slightly above the index products, we find enhanced index products, which are designed to take small amounts of risk within tightly controlled parameters and offer a little extra return, usually on a large pool of capital. Small, consistent alpha is their game.

Next, just slightly above the enhanced indices, we find the traditional long-only active manager. A word of caution: as Exhibit 2.2 demonstrates, these products are often beta drivers dressed up in alpha driver clothing.

Last along the beta spectrum, we find 130/30 portfolios. These have become very popular in recent years, and we devote a full chapter to them as a result. These products often retain a beta exposure to the stock or bond market close to 1.0 while adding long and short active bets around this systematic risk profile.

Collectively, these four products form the strategic core for the institutional portfolio to achieve the cost-effective implementation of the policy risk for the portfolio (although sometimes a traditional active manager will charge large fees for delivering a product that has considerable beta risk and only a smidgen of alpha risk).

Exhibit 2.4 then has a large gap between the beta drivers at the lower end of the active risk/return scale and the alpha drivers presented at the higher end of the risk/return scale. Note that this gap does not necessarily need to be as large as depicted in Exhibit 2.4. Well-designed alpha drivers may be delevered to match their tracking error along the active risk spectrum. We draw Exhibit 2.4 with a gap to highlight the difference between alpha and beta drivers in their natural state of active risk taking.

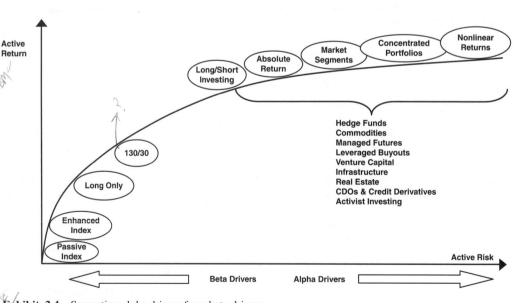

Exhibit 2.4   Separating alpha drivers from beta drivers

Alpha is not static. Over time, alpha can migrate and become beta. A number of recent articles provide examples of investment strategies that had once been considered manager skill (i.e. alpha), but are now regarded as a systematic capturing of existing risk premiums (i.e. beta).[6] In addition, alpha strategies go through cycles of profitability, sometimes in favor, sometimes out of favor. This is most appealing to those who pursue a tactical asset allocation among alpha drivers.

RETHINKING ASSET ALLOCATION

Asset allocation must allow for alpha drivers and beta drivers. Beta drivers will still play an important role in the construction of the pension portfolio, but the strict allocation lines to fixed income, real estate, public equity, and private equity will break down. Investors are migrating to sub-asset classes with inefficient markets and trading strategies that have high alpha content. Japanese pension funds have already moved in this direction. A 13-year bear market combined with near-zero interest rates have forced Japan to turn to alpha drivers. As of 2008, Japanese pension funds have allocated 9.3% of their assets to hedge funds, compared to 7.5% for U.S. institutional investors and 7.4% for European institutional investors.[7]

Rather than draw bright lines across asset classes, the strategic allocation should allow for broad ranges or tilts in the portfolio.[8] Tilts recognize that asset class lines may become blurred. An investor should commit assets to beta drivers within an asset class when the investor believes the class has the least amount of talent or insight to extract alpha. This approach has two implications.

First, investors should reduce their reliance on beta drivers for excess return generation and rely more on alternative assets that have the highest alpha content. Second, an institutional investor should commit the investment staff resources toward those alternative assets and trading strategies believed to add value. One of the greatest sources of alpha is derived from investments that fall between the cracks of traditional asset allocation. This means building teams of investment staff that bridge asset classes.

Exhibit 2.5 demonstrates a new way to allocate assets for an institutional portfolio. Four broad asset classes are identified: equity, fixed income, real estate, and inflation protection.[9] Within each asset class, there will be a blend of beta drivers that provide efficient asset class exposure and alpha drivers that are designed to extract greater value. For example, the strategic allocation to equity could be broken into the following subclasses, as displayed in Exhibit 2.6:

- Beta drivers—60%:
  - Passive equity
  - 130/30
  - Enhanced index equity
- Alpha drivers—40%:
  - Private equity.
  - Distressed debt.

---

[6] See Clifford Asness, "An Alternative Future," *Journal of Portfolio Management*, 30th Anniversary Issue, 2004, 94–103; Lars Jaeger, *Managing Risk in Alternative Investment Strategies* (Upper Saddle River, NJ: Prentice Hall/Financial Times, 2002); Greg Jensen and Jason Rotenberg, "Hedge Funds Selling Beta as Alpha," *Bridgewater Daily Observations*, June 17, 2004.

[7] See Russell Investment Group, "The 2007–2008 Russell Survey on Alternative Investing," Russell Investments, 2008.

[8] Joanne Hill and Meric Koksal, "The New Pension Paradigm: Implications for Investment Strategy, Managers and Markets," Goldman Sachs & Co., January 30, 2004.

[9] Hill and Koksal ("New Pension Paradigm") identify six portfolio tilts: equity-tilt, debt-tilt, alpha-only strategies, low-liquidity strategies, cross-market and overlay, and flexible absolute return. We provide a more simplified approach that retains some of the traditional asset allocation themes of most pension funds.

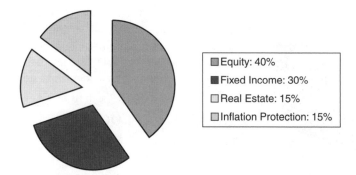

Exhibit 2.5   A different strategic asset allocation

- Equity-based hedge fund strategies: merger arbitrage, equity long/short, short-selling hedge funds.
- Convertible bonds.

Notice that two fixed income instruments are classified as equity alpha drivers: convertible bonds and distressed debt. This highlights the fact that alpha drivers are not necessarily defined by neat benchmark boxes or placed into clear asset classes. Convertible bonds, by the very nature of their hybrid structure, may be included in either the equity or the fixed income bucket. Alpha drivers need to be sought out wherever they can be found. Similarly, the fixed income portfolio may be broken down into alpha and beta drivers as displayed in Exhibit 2.7:

- Beta drivers—60%:
  - U.S. Treasury bonds.
  - Investment-grade corporate bonds.
  - Agency mortgage-backed securities.
- Alpha drivers—40%:
  - Convertible bonds, high-yield bonds, and mezzanine debt.
  - Collateralized debt obligations (CDOs) and collateralized loan obligations (CLOs).
  - Fixed income–based hedge fund strategies: fixed income arbitrage, relative value, distressed debt.
  - Emerging market debt.

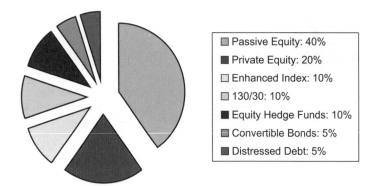

Exhibit 2.6   Equity beta and alpha drivers

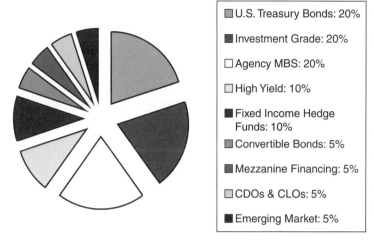

- U.S. Treasury Bonds: 20%
- Investment Grade: 20%
- Agency MBS: 20%
- High Yield: 10%
- Fixed Income Hedge Funds: 10%
- Convertible Bonds: 5%
- Mezzanine Financing: 5%
- CDOs & CLOs: 5%
- Emerging Market: 5%

Exhibit 2.7   Fixed income beta and alpha drivers

Convertible bonds may be included in either the fixed income portfolio or the equity portfolio. This sub-asset class contains both equity and debt components and highlights the point that pension plans should not adhere to strict asset allocation lines. Pension plans should acknowledge that certain sub-asset classes blur the distinction across traditional asset class lines.

To round out our asset allocation, Exhibits 2.8 and 2.9 show the allocation for our inflation hedging and real estate buckets. Notice that for the inflation hedging category, we include (1) Treasury Inflation-Protected Securities (TIPS), which might otherwise fall into our fixed income bucket; (2) infrastructure that could be classified as private equity within our equity bucket; and (3) public stocks that are geared to inflation (like health care stocks), which might otherwise fall into our equity bucket. This highlights the fact that asset allocation should not be held along strict asset class lines. Risk and return objectives are becoming more important, and these objectives cut across asset class lines.

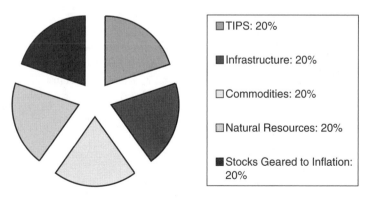

- TIPS: 20%
- Infrastructure: 20%
- Commodities: 20%
- Natural Resources: 20%
- Stocks Geared to Inflation: 20%

Exhibit 2.8   Inflation hedging bucket

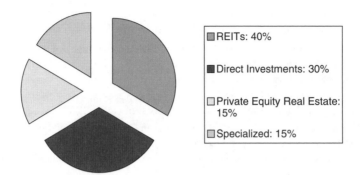

Exhibit 2.9   Real estate allocation

SUMMARY

Think outside the benchmark. Institutional investors need to remove the artificial restrictions associated with strategic asset allocation models. Traditional asset allocation models partition the financial markets into neat benchmark boxes. While this is useful for planning purposes, it can inhibit alpha extraction.

For example, active mandates should be sought throughout the equity spectrum and not be tied to an investor's equity benchmark. Active equity management may be extended to long/short investing, convertible bonds, distressed debt, and other equity-based alpha drivers. The equity asset class must be considered on a global basis rather than being segmented into benchmark boxes. This leads back to the concept of portfolio tilts.[10] Tilts recognize that asset class boundaries are not etched in stone but are flexible, even dynamic.

A cautionary note: Thinking outside the benchmark is a useful alpha-generating exercise but may meet resistance. In the asset management industry, consultants and institutional investors have long classified money managers into convenient style categories. The reasons are simple: categories make external manager searches easier (e.g. targeting a large-cap value manager search); provide consistent style analysis (e.g. large cap vs. small; growth vs. value); and allow for simpler recommendations (this manager outperforms its peer group of other large-cap managers). In addition, putting money managers into neat benchmark boxes makes the hiring and firing decisions easier.

 Recognize that alpha need not be captive to beta. Investors should worry less about the style of a manager and more about whether the manager has sufficient skill to generate consistent alpha. Find skill first, and then worry about the systematic risk that may be attached to that alpha.

Recognize that alpha may be generated across asset class boundaries. A good example is convertible arbitrage. Because convertible bonds contain both equity and fixed income characteristics, they fall outside the traditional boundaries of asset allocation. As a result, this strategy can capture a risk premium simply because the traditional marketplace is segmented into benchmark boxes. In later chapters, we show how convertible arbitrage managers pry apart convertible bonds into their different risk components to hedge what is expensive and keep what is cheap. Market segmentation is an inherent inefficiency that may be exploited if the investor can look across asset class boundaries. Alpha drivers should be sought out wherever they lie, and market partitioning is great place to find them. Examples include convertible arbitrage, distressed debt, mezzanine debt, and credit derivatives, to name a few.

---

[10] Hill and Koksal ("New Pension Paradigm") extend their analysis to consider both risk and return drivers within asset class tilts.

In a similar vein, institutional investors should deemphasize their organizational structure along traditional asset class lines. Most pension funds build their investment teams by partitions: public equity, fixed income, real estate, and private equity. This is the standard way to structure an institutional investor. Yet, strict adherence to asset class divisions inhibits the ability of the investment team to seek alpha-driven returns across asset boundaries.

Consider the risk of failing to outperform a peer group. There is safety in numbers and running with the pack. Institutional investors that hug their benchmarks will closely resemble their peer group. This is a conservative investment strategy designed to minimize the underperformance of the investor when compared to a group of similar investors. Beta drivers reduce the risk of peer group underperformance. This behavioral phenomenon is most often observed among pension funds.

This will leave alternative investments to other investors in the marketplace: traditionally, endowments and foundations. For example, endowments have an average allocation to hedge funds of almost 15% compared to 7% for corporate pension plans and 6% for public pension plans.[11] To effectively access alpha drivers, investors must be willing to accept the risk that their fund performance will differ significantly from their peer group's performance. Strict asset allocation reduces the risk of underperformance but increases the risk that the institutional investor will not generate superior performance.

Pursue alternative assets where you have the greatest informational advantage. It may not be possible to pursue every alternative asset discussed in this book. Every investor should figure out where he or she may apply his or her organizational resources to develop an informational advantage. For example, most institutional investors would not judge corporate governance to be an alpha driver. However, consider the California Public Employees' Retirement System (CalPERS), which has actively pursued shareowner rights for the past 20 years.[12] It has developed a competitive edge over other institutional investors through its corporate governance expertise applied to its investment portfolio. The insights gained from its program give CalPERS an informational advantage over other investors, which it has translated into significant added value. Conversely, it is not easy for an institutional investor to admit that it has no informational advantage in a particular market. As markets become more efficient, investors will recognize that they lack a competitive edge to translate into added value. When an institutional investor realizes no advantage in active management (or in selecting active managers), cost control becomes the most important value-added tool. Without an informational edge, institutional investors should exit the alternative asset arena and focus on reducing costs through indexation.

In summary, an investor should spend his alpha budget where it has the greatest ability to translate its competitive edge into added value. An informational advantage may be developed in external manager selection, superior risk control, extensive knowledge about an alternative asset class, better manager monitoring, or enhanced flexibility to practice tactical asset allocation.

[11] See Russell Investment Group, "2007–2008 Russell Survey on Alternative Investing." Part of this difference is also related to the size of pension funds compared to endowment and foundation funds.

[12] CalPERS calls itself a "shareowner" instead of a "shareholder" to emphasize its rights and obligations as an owner of a public corporation.

3

The Beta Continuum

Classic Beta, Bespoke Beta, Alternative Beta, Fundamental Beta, Cheap Beta, Active Beta, and Bulk Beta

INTRODUCTION

In the prior chapter, we introduced the concepts of alpha and beta. **Alpha** is the nomenclature associated with active portfolio management. Alpha is oftentimes an elusive concept, but much of the asset management industry is dedicated to active management—the quest to find and capture excess return. Since alpha can be expensive to acquire, it normally commands a fee premium by active managers. Hedge fund and private equity managers are renowned for the large fee structures they charge their investors in the generation of active returns.

Conversely, **beta** is defined as the efficient capture of risk exposures tied to broad asset classes. Beta represents the systematic risk exposure associated with the equity markets, bond duration, exposure to commodities, credit exposure, and even systematic returns that are associated with volatility embedded within stock options. Beta should be acquired cheaply since active management is not necessary to capture the systematic risk premium associated with an asset class.

For the most part, alpha and beta are considered as two points of an economic compass: as diametrically opposed as east and west. Generally, beta is defined as the art of passive portfolio management and alpha as active portfolio management. Both lie upon a continuum, from classic beta at one end to pure alpha at the other. Different forms of beta along the continuum recognize the efficiency of risk premium capture and acknowledge that one size of beta doesn't fit every investor.

In this chapter, we define the beta continuum.[1] Beta is not a point estimate. Rather there is a range of risk premiums that can be described as beta. Note that what is sometimes labeled as alpha is really more beta and belongs along the beta continuum. We begin by describing classic beta, then move to the beta continuum as we get closer to active management.

CLASSIC BETA

Classic beta is the beta we all grew up with, this is your father's beta. It is the market beta, the broad-based beta, the beta of the capital asset pricing model (CAPM) as defined by William Sharpe. Classic beta is typically defined with reference to a broad stock market index such as the S&P 500, Russell 1000, MSCI-EAFE, FTSE 100, or Nikkei 225. These widely based indexes are designed to passively track the systematic risk associated with investing in the equity markets.

A simple demonstration will help. Exhibit 3.1 shows the performance of Vanguard 500 Index Fund, the largest a U.S. mutual fund that tracks the S&P 500 index. This is an example of classic beta, tracking a well-known stock market index. This product produces a smooth, straight line that leads to one of the key conclusions about beta drivers: they are linear in their performance relative

---

[1] This chapter was reviewed by the Three Wise Men: Larry Pohlman, director of research at Wellington Asset Management; Eric Sorenson, CEO of Panagora Asset Management; and Andy Weisman, managing director and chief portfolio manager for the Merrill Lynch Hedge Fund Development and Management Group. Their comments saved me again from some embarrassing mistakes while contributing additional keen insights to make this chapter a success.

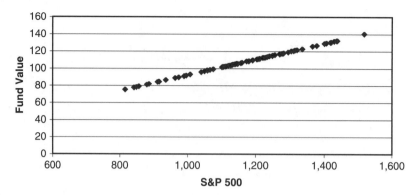

Exhibit 3.1   Vanguard 500 index fund and S&P 500 index

Note: Beta 1.00; R-squared 0.999; Tracking error 0.11%

to a traditional benchmark. This linear performance is a function of a high-rate (in fact, perfect) correlation between the investment product and the index that it tracks.

As we discussed in the preceding chapter, linearity is a common element of all beta drivers. The reason is that beta drivers are not designed to provide excess return, or alpha. Their goal is the efficient capture of systematic risk premiums in the market. The more efficient capture means lower costs of the beta driver and straighter lines respecting the risk premium being captured. Lining up all of the data points of this index fund with the S&P 500 leads to a straight line that connects the dots. Simply, the returns generated by this index fund exactly match the up-and-down movement of the S&P 500.

Interestingly, nonlinear return patterns can sometimes be induced by imposing an incentive fee. Effectively, when active managers' return patterns are grossed up to include their previously deducted performance fees, a much more linear pattern of returns can appear.[2]

BESPOKE BETA

Bespoke beta describes the method in which asset managers capture local risk premiums. The term comes from Saville Row in London where this adjective is used as a reference to custom-tailored clothing.[3] Therefore, bespoke beta is custom beta, designed to match a tailored risk exposure.

Exchange-traded funds (ETFs) are the best example of bespoke beta. These funds divide up the broader financial markets into submarkets, sectors, industries, and other localized risk exposures. ETF managers slice and dice the equity, bond, currency, and commodities markets to bring investors wedges of market risk for targeted economic exposures. Through ETFs, investors can make size, style, sector, subsector, country, and region bets in their portfolio. Think of ETFs as producing "local beta," the systematic risk associated with a smaller, local part of the financial market.

For example, Exhibit 3.2 shows the tracking of the iShares Russell 2000 Value ETF. This ETF tracks so-called value stocks in the small-capitalization range of the U.S. equity markets. We compare this product to the Russell 2000 Value Stock Index, a stock index of smaller-capitalized companies

---

[2] This is a neat point contributed by Andy Weisman.

[3] In days gone by, when lords would visit their tailors on Savile Row to look at clothing swatches, they would buy the complete bolt of cloth associated with a particular swatch so that no other person could use the same fabric for their garments. When a bolt of cloth was claimed in this manner, it was said to "be spoken for." From this phrase, we get the word *bespoke*.

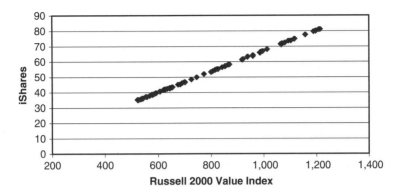

Exhibit 3.2 iShares Russell 2000 value ETF and Russell 2000 value index

Note: Beta 1.02; R-squared 0.98; Tracking error 0.27%

that exhibit value characteristics such as a larger book-to-market value and higher earnings payout ratios. From Exhibit 3.2, we can see that the iShares product tracks the benchmark extremely well, offering investors cheap and direct exposure to small-cap value stocks.

The first ETF was the Standard & Poor's Depositary Receipts (SPDRs or Spiders), first introduced in 1993. Since then ETFs have exploded, as represented by Exhibit 3.3. At the end of 2008 more than 200 ETF products traded globally with more than $700 billion of assets. ETFs have grown at a 38% cumulative average growth rate (CAGR) over the past 12 years.

Investors seek bespoke beta for several reasons. First, bespoke beta is a cheap and efficient way to make sector, style, size, country, and other bets. Even if an investor has no knowledge regarding individual securities, he may have some insight into macroeconomic fundamentals that may impact certain sectors differently. For example, a rise in interest rates usually has an adverse economic impact on heavily leveraged industries like the auto industry. However, such a rise would benefit the income statements of banks and other financial lenders. ETFs allow an investor to short the auto industry and overweight the financial sector.

In fact, it is the ability to short that makes ETFs so popular. As their name indicates, ETFs trade like stocks and other securities. Therefore, they can be purchased on margin, can be traded throughout the day, and may even be borrowed from a prime broker and shorted. These benefits make ETFs efficient tools for adjusting the tilts within a portfolio. In fact, the advent of ETFs makes for a more

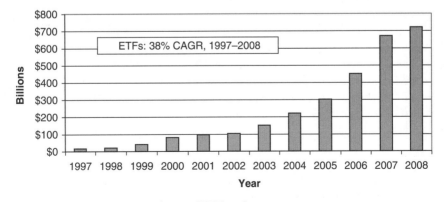

Exhibit 3.3 Cumulative average growth rate of ETF products

efficient construction of portfolios. The ability to add a macroeconomic, top-down overlay onto a stock or bond portfolio allows an active manager to extract the most from the information set. Even though ETFs are passive products themselves, they can be used in an active fashion to maximize the value of a portfolio manager's information coefficient.

ALTERNATIVE BETA

The growth of the ETF market has also given rise to another development: **alternative beta**. There are other systematic risk exposures that have been previously closed to investors because of the difficulty of accessing these risk exposures. However, with the advent of ETFs and the slicing and dicing they can produce, new betas, alternative betas, have been identified and accessed.

Consider the currency markets. Currency exposure has generally been considered a by-product of international economic exposure. For the most part, currency risk has been considered a necessary evil of globally diversified portfolios. Currency risk is often hedged out of institutional portfolios to provide a return that is consistent with the returns earned from assets in the investor's home currency.

However, new ETFs now allow investors to access this systematic risk and to include it as a return generator in a diversified portfolio. Consider Exhibit 3.4. This is a currency ETF linked to the price of the euro denominated in dollars. If the euro appreciates in value against the U.S. dollar, the net asset value of the ETF will increase. If the euro depreciates relative to the dollar, the net asset value of the ETF will decline as well. For investors who have watched the U.S. dollar decline in value relative to other currencies, this is a targeted manner to capture the systematic risk exposure associated with the variation of the U.S. dollar vis-à-vis other currencies.

The euro ETF is supported by a grantor trust, the common vehicle of most ETF structures, that backs the individual shares issued by the ETF with euro deposits in London. Previously, if investors wanted to gain exposure to the currency markets, they would have to buy futures or forward contracts. However, futures and forward contracts expire by the specific tenor of the instrument. Investors have to continually reinitiate or roll the futures or forward contracts to maintain their exposure. The euro ETF alleviates the burden of managing the economic exposure and allows the investor to access the systematic risk of the euro currency market in a consistent and efficient manner.

Exhibit 3.4 shows the euro ETF compared with the euro/U.S. dollar spot rate. We see a nice smooth line, another linear beta driver. With a beta of 0.99, a correlation of 1.00, and a tracking

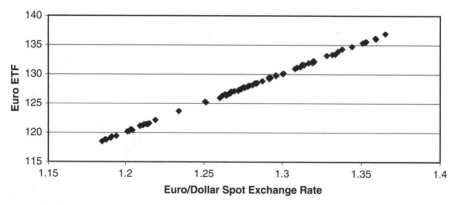

Exhibit 3.4   Euro ETF versus euro/dollar exchange rate
Note: Beta 0.99; Correlation 1.00; Tracking error 0.10%

error of 10 basis points, this product offers a new form of systematic risk for investor portfolios, the systematic exposure to the fluctuation of the U.S. dollar versus the euro.

FUNDAMENTAL BETA

A new form of beta, **fundamental beta**, has sprung up in the past few years, spurred on by the research of Arnott, Hsu, and Moore (2005) called *fundamental indexation*. The thesis is that capitalization-weighted stock indexes have an inherent inefficiency because they force index providers to purchase more stocks that have a higher weighting in the index (which may be overvalued) and to buy less and less of stocks that have a lower weighting in the index (which may be undervalued). This can produce a systematic bias of "buying high and selling low" in the returns associated with the cap-weighted index. Cap-weighted indexes also produce a large-cap bias by the very nature of the index construction. Therefore, Arnott devised a new stock index based on five fundamental factors associated with public companies: book value, dividend payout, sales revenue, operating income, and employees.

Other fundamental indexes have sprung up sponsored by Morningstar, Wisdom Tree, and Dow Jones based on similar economic fundamentals. The goal of these indexes is to capture a systematic risk premium tied to a fundamental economic driver of corporate performance instead of a company's market capitalization weight. The genesis of these products dates back to the Fama-French (1992, 1993) three-factor model for describing equity market risk premiums.

Consider Exhibit 3.5. This is the Dow Jones Dividend Index compared to the S&P 500, with monthly returns over the period 2003–2007. The Dow Jones Dividend Index weights stocks in the index by their dividend payout ratios instead of market capitalizations. In Exhibit 3.5, we observe that the beta associated with this index compared to the S&P 500 stock index is lower (0.76), with a correlation coefficient with the S&P 500 of 0.82. This is not surprising given that high-dividend-paying stocks tend to be so-called value stocks representing companies that are more mature in their growth cycles, generate more cash, are less risky than growth stocks, and produce higher dividend payout ratios.

Exhibit 3.5 also presents the average excess return, tracking error, and information ratio (IR) for the Dow Jones Dividend Index compared to the S&P 500. This index generated an impressive monthly excess return (ER) of 0.37% compared to the S&P 500 with an equally impressive IR of 0.35. We call this form of excess return **endogenous alpha** to recognize that the source of the alpha extraction comes from the index construction itself (see Schoenfeld 2006). This is in contrast to

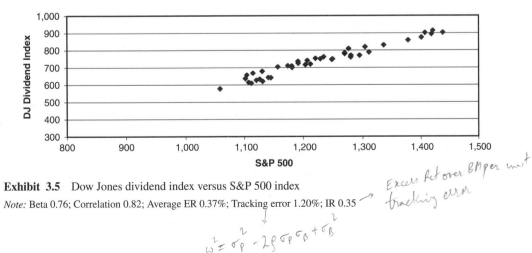

Exhibit 3.5   Dow Jones dividend index versus S&P 500 index
Note: Beta 0.76; Correlation 0.82; Average ER 0.37%; Tracking error 1.20%; IR 0.35

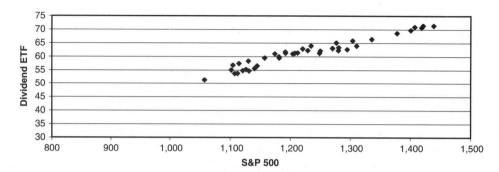

Exhibit 3.6   iShares Dow Jones Select Dividend ETF versus S&P 500 index

Note: Beta 0.78; Correlation 0.80; Average ER 0.09%; Tracking error 1.31%; IR 0.07

exogenous alpha, where the source of the excess return comes from actively managing a portfolio of stocks through underweights and overweights relative to a capitalization-weighted benchmark.

Nonetheless, fundamental beta products reflect an attempt to outperform a capitalization-weighted index. It is a form of active management based on the efficient capture of fundamental factors that drive corporate value. However, the capture of these fundamental values does lead to the erosion of the excess return.

Exhibit 3.6 plots the iShares Dow Jones Select Dividend ETF compared to the S&P 500. This ETF has been in operation since 2003 and its goal is to offer passive exposure to the Dow Jones Select Dividend Index. We note that this dividend ETF provides very similar values for beta, correlation, and tracking error as the Dow Jones Dividend Index when compared to the S&P 500. However, the monthly excess return for the dividend ETF compared to the S&P 500, while still positive at 0.09%, is much less than that demonstrated by the Dow Jones Dividend Index. Therefore, while fundamental beta products can produce excess return compared to capitalization-weighted indexes, the capture of these fundamental economic drivers does lead to an erosion of the alpha embedded within the fundamental index construction.

Note that fundamental beta is different from active beta, described later. Fundamental beta comes from the design of the index itself, while active beta is a way to outperform an existing index.

CHEAP BETA

Beta is not always accessed by traditional methods of risk premium capture such as index funds or ETFs. Instead, beta can be embedded as a complex basket of risk exposures contained within one security. Consider convertible debt. Convertible bonds are a mix of debt and equity, a hybrid mixture that makes their intrinsic risk exposures less transparent. We consider this issue by examining the returns to convertible arbitrage hedge fund managers. To determine whether alpha is generated by convertible arbitrage hedge fund managers, we need to apply some economics to determine what potential risk factors, betas, might affect the value of convertible bonds. When we look at a convertible bond, there are five potential systematic risk factors that can influence its value:

1. Interest rate risk: it is a bond.
2. Stock market risk: it is convertible into stock.
3. Credit risk: convertible bonds are usually issued by below-investment-grade companies.
4. Volatility risk: there is an embedded call option in the bond.
5. Autocorrelation risk: convertible bonds are illiquid, and current prices may be influenced by past prices (the absence of a random walk). Essentially, autocorrelation risk is a proxy for lack of

liquidity. Some of the biggest losses in the convertible arbitrage industry have come because of a mismatch between investors' ability to redeem their interests in a convertible arbitrage hedge fund and the ability of the hedge fund manager to unwind the arbitrage positions. Weisman (2002) provides a nice discussion of some of the pitfalls of hedge fund strategies.

To measure the alpha and the beta, we resort to a standard factor model based on the five risk factors identified earlier:

$$\text{Return to Alpha Manager}(t) = \alpha + \sum_i \beta_i \times \text{Factor}_{i,t} + \varepsilon_{i,t} \qquad (3.1)$$

where

$\alpha =$ a measure of active manager skill to select undervalued securities

$\varepsilon =$ a measure of random noise

$\beta =$ a factor loading measures how sensitive the active manager's returns are to the beta factor

Factor = a source of systematic risk premium that exists in the market and constitutes a component of the active manager's return[4]

Equation 3.1 is used to measure the alpha of an active manager by subtracting out all of the beta factors. What is left over is either alpha (α) or epsilon (ε), where alpha represents genuine skill that has statistical significance and epsilon represents random noise.

We use Equation 3.1 and regress the Hedge Fund Research Inc. (HFR) Hedge Fund Convertible Bond Arbitrage Index on the five beta factors identified earlier. We use the Russell 1000 to reflect stock market risk, 10-year Treasury bonds to reflect interest rate risk, the Lehman High Yield Index to represent credit risk, the change in the Chicago Board Options Exchange (CBOE) Volatility Index (VIX) to represent volatility risk, and ConvArb(–1) to represent the prior month's value of convertible arbitrage (autocorrelation risk).[5]

Exhibit 3.7 presents our results.[6] We start with summary return, risk, and Sharpe ratio statistics for convertible arbitrage hedge fund managers. The Sharpe ratio is positive, indicating a positive risk-return trade-off. That is, convertible arbitrage managers offer investors a positive, risk-adjusted rate of return, a clear demonstration of value added.

Next we look at the intercept in our factor analysis, a value that represents the alpha offered by convertible arbitrage hedge fund managers. We note that once we account for the five systematic beta factors associated with convertible bonds, the alpha associated with convertible bond arbitrage hedge fund managers is statistically significant and negative at –1% per month.[7] Therefore, what we define as alpha, finding undervalued securities, does not add value in convertible arbitrage returns.

---

[4] Fung and Hsieh (1997) were the first to apply factor modeling to hedge funds.

[5] We also included lagged variables for stock market risk, interest rate risk, volatility risk, and credit risk. We found only that credit risk had some lagged impact on the returns to convertible bond arbitrage hedge fund managers but that the explanatory power of the factor model increased only slightly.

[6] We use monthly data over the eight-year time period of 1999 to 2006. We chose to start in 1999 because of a fundamental shift in the way convertible arbitrage managers managed their portfolios after the liquidity crisis of late summer and early autumn 1998. In August 1998 the Russian government defaulted on outstanding bonds (spreads on Russian bonds increased to 5,000 basis points) followed by the near collapse of Long-Term Capital Management and the subsequent bailout of LTCM by large money center banks. Virtually all hedge fund arbitrage strategies suffered extreme losses during this time period, which led them to change the way they subsequently managed their portfolios. See Anson (2006).

[7] We can conclude that this is (negative) alpha and not epsilon because of the statistical significance of the intercept term—this is not random noise.

Exhibit 3.7   Factor analysis of HFR convertible arbitrage index (based on monthly data, 1999–2006)

Summary Statistics

Average Return	0.72%
Standard Deviation	0.95%
Sharpe Ratio	0.50

Factor Analysis

Factor	Intercept	Russell 1000	10-Year U.S. T-bond	High-Yield	VIX	ConvArb(-1)
Value	-1.02%	0.002	0.26	0.21	0.03	0.54
t-Statistic	-2.13	0.075	2.58	5.42	0.91	6.89

It is important to note that this estimate of alpha is an approximation because not all the variables on the right-hand side of the regression are investible products or are available at zero cost. For example, the lagged return on the convertible arbitrage index is not an investible product; that is, one cannot invest in a product today that would provide last month's return. Further, VIX itself is not an investible asset. It can be accessed through VIX futures contracts, but the return on the contract is likely to be different from the rate of change in the VIX itself. Finally, even though the high-yield index represents an investible product, it cannot be accessed at zero cost; that is, even a total return swap on the index is likely to cost several basis points.

Keep in mind as you read this book the following important point: To properly estimate the alpha of an active manager (see Equation 3.2):

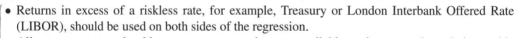

- Returns in excess of a riskless rate, for example, Treasury or London Interbank Offered Rate (LIBOR), should be used on both sides of the regression.
- All excess returns should represent returns that are available to investors through investable contracts on a timely basis at zero or very low costs.

If either of these two conditions are not satisfied, then the estimates of alpha may not be accurate and, at best, they should be viewed as approximates.

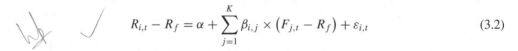

$$R_{i,t} - R_f = \alpha + \sum_{j=1}^{K} \beta_{i,j} \times \left(F_{j,t} - R_f \right) + \varepsilon_{i,t} \qquad (3.2)$$

where

$R_{i,t} =$ the rate of return on active manager i
$R_f =$ the riskless rate
$\beta_{i,j} =$ the exposure of manager i to investible factor or benchmark j
$F_{j,t} =$ the return on investible factor or benchmark j
$\varepsilon_{i,t} =$ the return on the active manager that is left unexplained by the factors

Bearing in mind the words of caution just offered, let's examine the active manager's risk exposure more closely. So how do convertible arbitrage hedge fund managers generate a positive Sharpe ratio? First, we can see that the beta associated with stock market risk is virtually zero (0.002) with no statistical significance. In addition, the beta for volatility risk associated with the equity call option is also virtually zero at 0.03. It is clear that convertible arbitrage hedge fund managers hedge out the equity and volatility components embedded within convertible bonds.

What's left? Credit risk, interest rate risk, and autocorrelation risk. Not surprisingly, after the liquidity and credit crisis of 1998, credit spreads rose dramatically. After peaking in 1998, the period of 1999 to 2006 was generally a time of credit spread compression, making it economically desirable to load up on credit risk exposure. Interest rates also peaked at the height of the tech bubble and declined as the Federal Reserve Bank in the United States cut interest rates dramatically. This was a good time to load up on interest rate exposure as interest rates fell and bond prices soared. Both of these variables have large positive betas, which are statistically significant at the 1% level.[8]

Based on the negative intercept term, the source of the good convertible arbitrage positive risk-adjusted returns is not manager skill (alpha) at selecting undervalued securities. Instead, convertible arbitrage hedge fund managers search for undervalued beta. They hedge out the expensive beta risk components of the convertible bond and keep embedded in the convertible bond those systematic risk premiums that are cheap. We call this undervalued beta **cheap beta**.

Convertible arbitrage managers carve up a convertible bond into its systematic risk components; they keep those beta pieces that are priced cheaply and hedge out (sell) those beta components that are overpriced. Some might call this skill and a form of active management. Value is clearly added, but it comes from managing beta exposure, not from insights into undervalued securities. Of course, a skilled convertible arbitrage manager may be able to identify undervalued convertibles and therefore generate alpha for investors. Another point that should be kept in mind is that the aforementioned analysis was performed using a broad index of convertible arbitrage managers. This index is calculated by equally weighting all managers who report to the HFR database and classify themselves as convertible arbitrage managers. Clearly, within this universe of hedge fund managers there are some who had significant positive alpha and some who had significant negative alpha. The due diligence process is supposed to help identify those managers who are likely to produce positive alpha.

ACTIVE BETA

Active beta constitutes the world of products that use quantitative tools and models to capture so-called systematic irregularities (an economic oxymoron) in the equity markets. The most popular of these products are known as 130/30 funds (we devote a full chapter to these types of products later in this book). These are equity-based products that can short individual stocks or the broader stock market up to 30% of the net assets of the fund while simultaneously leveraging the long portion of the portfolio up to 130% of the net asset value. Either the cash generated from the short positions is used to leverage the long positions or the fund borrows cash from a prime broker to leverage the long side of the portfolio.

These 130/30 funds can increase the active risk versus active return trade-off of an asset manager along two dimensions. First, a manager can increase the number of active bets in her portfolio if she can use both long and short positions in the portfolio. Second, relaxing the long-only constraint allows the asset manager a greater opportunity to act on her bets through larger overweights and underweights; again, this increases the IR.

But there is no magic to 130/30; it could be 120/20, 150/50, 200/100, and so on. A more appropriate name for these types of products is beta one products; there is a continuum from 100/0 to 200/100.

---

[8] We also note that autocorrelation risk has a significant and positive beta. This is a reflection of two factors. First, the convertible bond marketplace is an illiquid market—these are privately issued bonds that do not trade on an exchange and the pricing of the underlying convertible bond may be dependent on the prior month's price. Second, hedge fund managers have significant control over the pricing of their portfolios. Undoubtedly, there is some price smoothing embedded in the returns to convertible bond arbitrage managers.

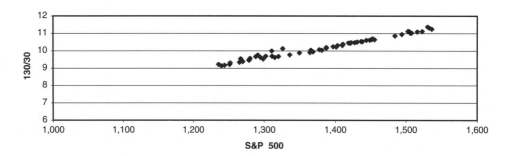

Exhibit 3.8   A 130/30 equity long/short product versus S&P 500 index

Note: Beta 1.05; Correlation 0.96; Excess return –0.06%; Tracking error 0.46%; IR –0.13

There is no special limit to 130/30 as some clients might want more octane in their accounts and others less. It really depends on the risk tolerance of the client. The key point is that asset managers can go both long and short in a client's portfolio while synchronizing the overall risk of the portfolio to the beta of a chosen benchmark. Hence, the term beta one, as the systematic risk of the resulting portfolio can be finely tuned to equal the systematic risk of a benchmark, but with greater active security selection around the selected benchmark.

Another name for these products is active beta. The goal is to maintain a closed systematic risk profile to the equity benchmark while adding excess return through long and short positions. Typically, the long and short positions tend to be small to medium size so as to manage the tracking error of the 130/30 fund. In other words, the long and short positions are monitored within a tight tracking error range to ensure that the active beta portion of the fund does not stray too far from the benchmark. Some users and purveyors might also call this type of fund an enhanced index fund.

Despite the high demand for active beta products, the track record of these products is short. Exhibit 3.8 presents the weekly track record of the ING 130/30 Fundamental Research Fund, an open-end mutual fund in the United States, compared to the S&P 500 index. This fund has been in operation since 2006 and has a large-cap focus. We can see that the beta of this fund closely tracks the S&P 500 with a value of 1.05 and with a correlation coefficient of 0.96. While this fund has a small negative IR of –0.13 to date, we note that its track record is brief. The key point is that this is an equity long/short product that maintains a beta very similar to that of a large-cap stock benchmark.

Another form of active beta is tactical asset allocation (TAA). TAA is the process by which systematic risk premiums are overweighted or underweighted depending on macroeconomic conditions. For example, Anson (2007) provides a mapping of the equity risk premium for the U.S. equity markets and demonstrates points in time when the equity markets were overvalued and undervalued relative to the U.S. Treasury bond market. TAA takes advantage of these risk premiums when they are distorted from historical norms by overweighting or underweighting equities accordingly. In fact, TAA could be considered another method of buying cheap beta and selling expensive beta, as discussed in the prior section.

BULK BETA

Last, we come to the heart of the active management industry. Traditional long-only equity management has long been the mainstay of the active management industry. Traditional active products are

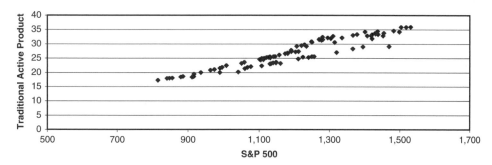

Exhibit 3.9   Active traditional long-only equity versus S&P 500 index
Note: Beta 1.02; Correlation 0.83; Excess return 0.24%; Tracking error 2.69%; IR 0.09

judged relative to a benchmark. This means that these products combine a blend of beta (systematic market risks) with alpha (excess returns). The question is: How much of the product returns are beta, and how much is alpha?

Exhibit 3.9 answers this question. This is a large-cap active equity product benchmarked to the S&P 500. Exhibit 3.9 does not provide the nice straight line of a pure beta driver such as the one presented in Exhibit 3.1. There is quite a bit of variation between the returns to this product and those of the S&P 500. This is demonstrated by a relatively large monthly tracking error of 2.69%. This active product does take active risk, and there is a trade-off for the active risk taking: a positive (monthly) information ratio of 0.09 and an average monthly alpha of 0.24%.

Although this active product is not a closet beta driver, by the very nature of being tied to a large-cap equity benchmark a considerable amount of systematic risk remains in the return stream associated with the product. The correlation coefficient for this product, while less than 1.00, is still quite high at 0.84. This demonstrates that a considerable amount of the variation of returns associated with this active product is influenced by the returns to the S&P 500 index. We call these products **bulk beta** to recognize that there is a considerable amount of systematic risk contained within their returns, but the trade-off is that there is large capacity for assets under management. Indeed, the product in Exhibit 3.9 has close to $50 billion under management.

We also note that bulk beta products produce a linear relationship with their stated benchmark. However, the linearity that we demonstrated in Exhibit 3.1 is not nearly as pronounced as in Exhibit 3.9. This is because bulk beta products are less than perfectly correlated with the index that they are designed to outperform. Still, you can see that there remains a linear relationship between the actively managed product in Exhibit 3.9 and its S&P 500 benchmark.

SUMMARY: THE BETA CONTINUUM

Beta does not come in a single flavor. There are many forms of beta and it is becoming more exotic with each passing day. Exhibit 3.10 summarizes the beta continuum. As you move left along the horizontal axis, toward the zero axis, an investor is driven to collect systematic market risk premiums (beta) as cheaply as possible, while farther out on the horizontal axis represents the attempt to collect active returns. Along the vertical axis, higher points on the axis represent a greater amount of active risk taking.

We classify classic beta, bespoke beta, and alternative beta as devoid of active risk taking. The purpose of these products is to capture systematic risk premiums that exist in the financial,

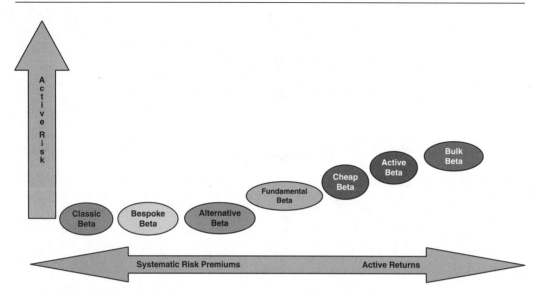

Exhibit 3.10   The beta continuum

commodity, and currency markets. Classic beta is designed to capture broad asset class risk premiums, while bespoke beta captures more local risk premiums (e.g. small-cap value premiums) and alternative beta captures systematic risk premiums that typically reside outside the standard asset classes of stocks and bonds.

We note that alternative beta can also be classified in the "alternatives" bucket for two reasons. First, alternative beta can provide another source of risk and return that is different from (in fact, an alternative to) the traditional sources of return found in stocks and bonds. Second, alternative beta is often designed to have a very low correlation with stocks and bonds. For example, a commodities ETF can provide easy and efficient access to the commodities markets for those investors that do not have this asset class exposure in their portfolios. Real estate ETFs would be another source of alternative beta as well.

Moving along to the right of the horizontal access, we find beta products that begin to take incremental amounts of active risk. Fundamental beta is a form of endogenous alpha, alpha embedded within the index construction itself to outperform traditional capitalization-weighted benchmarks. Cheap beta is the search for undervalued risk premiums embedded within complex securities such as convertible bonds. Active beta describes quant active, 130/30, and enhanced index products, where tight risk control maintains a beta exposure close to 1.0 with the benchmark while adding some form of enhanced return. Finally, traditional active management, what we call bulk beta, incorporates the most amount of active risk taking along the beta continuum, but still retains more beta exposure than alpha exposure. Bulk beta defines the end of the beta continuum.

The next phase of the developing asset management industry is to determine where the beta continuum ends and the alpha continuum begins. The remainder of this book is designed to explore the alpha continuum.

4

Alpha versus Beta

Separation in the Asset Management Industry

INTRODUCTION

A significant number of newspaper articles have been written about the changing nature of the asset management business. As asset owners have learned to separate beta from alpha in their investment portfolios, so too have asset managers learned to offer investment products that serve these investment needs. This means that the business models for asset management companies must change themselves. If not, they may find themselves trapped in the middle, stuck with balanced mandates that serve neither the beta-driven approach of core portfolios nor the alpha approach of satellite products.

The quest to serve alpha and beta mandates is driving asset management companies into what is called the tails of the distribution for product development. We will talk more about the tails of the distribution when we examine the return patterns for hedge funds and other alternative assets. For the moment, the best way to explain the tails of the distribution is that these are the more distant or extreme results along the asset management spectrum. At the one extreme, we find the large-scale index trackers that provide passive management at excruciatingly low margins. At the other extreme, we find successful alpha drivers that seek excess return while charging high fees. This paper provides an analysis of the increasing polarization of the asset management business.

ANOTHER DEMONSTRATION OF BETA VERSUS ALPHA DRIVERS

Before constructing a portfolio, every investor must recognize a liability stream. Take a pension fund, for example. Its liability stream is measured with actuarial precision to respect future benefit payments promised to its pensioners. Other investors have liability streams as well. For a foundation, consider the research and philanthropic donation schedule; for an endowment, the capital expenditure budget; and for a high-net-worth individual, the wealth transfer to the next generation.

As the demands for intelligent solutions to fund liability streams have grown, alpha and beta drivers have been invented. Beta drivers are low-cost investment products (as low as one basis point) designed to efficiently capture the risk premium associated with an asset class such as equity, fixed income, commodities, or real estate. Beta drivers are informationless; they do not attempt to outperform well-defined benchmarks. Their purpose is not to generate excess return but to provide a rate of return consistent with a fundamental risk premium. They help reduce the risk of the portfolio through diversification. Conversely, alpha drivers exploit an informational advantage in the financial markets. Their purpose is to generate excess return. Since they tend not to be highly correlated with traditional asset classes, they provide diversification benefits as well.

Unfortunately, the asset management industry is not so black and white. In between pure beta drivers and pure alpha drivers are a wide range of products, as our beta continuum chapter demonstrated. For example, some hedge fund managers provide portfolio diversification benefits while others focus on return enhancement. The key is that diversification benefits and earning risk premiums are generally gained at a relatively low cost while return enhancement is hard to find and expensive.

The separation of alpha and beta is at the heart of the dynamic change under way in the asset management industry. Anson (2004a and 2004b) describes how institutional investors apply alpha and beta drivers to implement tactical versus strategic asset allocation. While beta drivers passively capture the long-term risk premiums associated with strategic asset allocation, alpha drivers seek excess return as part of tactical asset allocation. Together, alpha and beta drivers[1] allow for a more cost-efficient portfolio.

PRODUCT INNOVATORS, PROCESS DRIVERS, AND BESPOKE BETA

The separation of alpha and beta by asset owners means that asset managers must build products to meet these demands. This has started a movement by the asset management industry into the tails of the distribution. At one end of the scale, the active management part of the investment industry is gravitating toward 130/30 products, hedge funds, tactical asset allocation, alternative betas, and other high-alpha-content active strategies. These are the **product innovators**.

At the other end of the scale, asset gatherers are striving to deliver beta as cheaply and efficiently as possible. These are the large-scale index trackers who produce passive products tied to well-recognized financial market benchmarks. They build value through scale and processing efficiency. These asset managers are the **process drivers**.

Process drivers increasingly provide finely tuned beta separation. As an example, these index trackers have introduced exchange-traded funds (ETFs) by the bucketful. ETFs are another form of beta, only it is bespoke beta, tailored for a particular market capitalization range, industry, asset class, or geographic market. The process drivers efficiently carve up financial assets into as many systematic risk factors as they can find. Exhibit 4.1 demonstrates the growth of the ETF market. The demand for tailored beta drivers is growing rapidly and it now exceeds $700 billion.

Similarly, the demand for alpha drivers has grown dramatically, demonstrated by the large increase of assets under management by hedge funds. Hedge funds are generally considered the least constrained of any asset manager. Therefore, they have the greatest ability to seek alpha. The growth of hedge fund assets, also plotted in Exhibit 4.1, closely tracks the ETF market. Exhibit 4.1 demonstrates the increased demand for the two extremes in the asset management industry. Of course, the extreme market turmoil of 2008 slowed the growth of both beta drivers and alpha drivers.

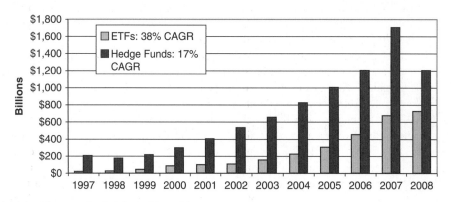

Exhibit 4.1   The growth of alpha and beta drivers

---

[1] Mark Anson, "Strategic vs. Tactical Asset Allocation: Beta Drivers vs. Alpha Drivers," *Journal of Portfolio Management* (Winter 2004): 8–22; Mark Anson, "Thinking Outside the Benchmark," 30th Anniversary Issue, *Journal of Portfolio Management* (2004): 104–112.

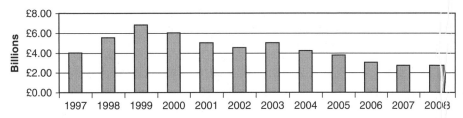

Exhibit 4.2   The rise and fall of a UK balanced mandate product

From 1997 to 2007, the cumulative average growth rate (CAGR) of ETFs was 51% and it was 26% for hedge funds. But when the year 2008 is added, the CAGRs fall to 38% for ETFs and 17% for hedge funds.

Unfortunately, asset managers with traditional balanced mandates are caught between product innovators and process drivers. Balanced mandates are declining because they use a peer group as their target return. Balanced mandate managers focus on what other balanced managers are doing; they concentrate on a performance benchmark consisting of peer groups and not on financial markets. This leads to what is known as herding. Managers of balanced mandates are unlikely to take more (or less) risk than their peer groups and invest in asset classes or active management approaches that are not included in the peer group. Exhibit 4.2 shows the decline of assets under management for a balanced mandate product in the United Kingdom.

Balanced funds are sometimes called consensus funds because they track the return given by the average balanced fund in the market as a whole. This means that investment decisions in a consensus fund are based on the average asset distribution of all balanced funds in the market. For instance, the consensus fund presented in Exhibit 4.2 states that its goals are to:

- Track the asset split and performance of all balanced mandate funds in the industry.
- Achieve the average return among these funds in the market.

Balanced mandates are no longer popular with pension funds for two reasons. First, balanced mandates reflect the average asset allocation in the marketplace, which places the focus exclusively on the asset side of the pension fund balance sheet and ignores the liability side. Each pension fund has a unique set of liabilities that may not be served best by investing in a balanced product that mimics the average asset allocation across all pension funds.

Second, with the new accounting regulations that require a mark-to-market or fair value accounting for liabilities, duration mismatches have been revealed between the asset side and liability side of a pension fund's balance. This means that maturing pension funds with maturing liabilities must shift the focus away from asset allocation to duration matching.

Traditional asset managers with balanced mandates and long-only products are moving away from the center of the investment product distribution into the tails. The highest growth will come from the pure beta drivers and those active managers with the fewest constraints. Leibowitz (2005) distinguishes between these managers by naming them "beta grazers" or "alpha hunters."[2] While beta drivers offer efficient capturing of risk premiums at razor-thin margins, hedge funds and other active alpha hunters capture very high profit margins for producing excess returns. Thus, to the degree that the market for alpha drivers is a seller's market, one would expect alpha drivers to expropriate as much of the alpha as possible in terms of fees. That is, after adjusting for various

---

[2] Marty Liebowitz, "Alpha Hunters and Beta Grazers," *Financial Analysts Journal* 61, no. 5 (September/October 2005).

risks, including manager risk and illiquidity risk, the alpha earned by investors could be close to zero if there is no competition among alpha drivers to attract capital.

SHERLOCK HOLMES AND THE CASE OF ALPHA GENERATION

One of the most challenging parts of the asset management industry is that at the outset of every investment, alpha is unobservable. You only judge alpha ex-post, not ex-ante. To paraphrase Sherlock Holmes:

"Once you eliminate the beta, whatever remains, however improbable, must be the alpha."[3]

Alpha is typically identified through the use of factor models. Everyone is familiar with at least one factor model: the capital asset pricing model (CAPM). It was the first pricing model that identified a systematic risk factor, the beta, associated with an asset class. A portfolio with a beta of 1.0 represents the systematic risk of the market portfolio, often represented by a broad-based benchmark such as the S&P 500, Russell 1000, or MSCI EAFE. The CAPM model is a single-factor model and has since been expanded by Fama and French (1992, 1993, and 1996), where they identified additional betas: a systematic risk premium associated with value stocks (high book value stocks minus low book value stocks) and another systematic risk factor associated with small-cap stocks (small-cap stock returns minus large-cap stock returns).[4] Since the Fama and French studies, other factors such as momentum have been identified.

Therefore, alpha is identified by regressing the excess return of an active manager on the excess returns on the factors that are sources of systematic risk premiums to determine how much of the manager's return is beta driven (i.e., driven by the up-and-down movement of the stock market and other systematic factors). After eliminating the beta, whatever remains is the alpha. Generally, these models follow the equation:

$$R_{i,t} - R_f = \alpha_i + \sum_{j=1}^{K} \beta_{i,j} \times \left(F_{j,t} - R_f \right) + \varepsilon_{i,t} \tag{4.1}$$

where

$R_{i,t} =$ the rate of return on active manager i

$R_f =$ the riskless rate

$\beta_{i,j} =$ the exposure of manager i to investible factor or benchmark j

$F_{j,t} =$ the return on investible factor or benchmark j

$\varepsilon_{i,t} =$ the return on the active manager that is left unexplained by the factors

Factor is a systematic risk premium that exists in the market and constitutes a component of the active manager's return.[5]

---

[3] As a former resident in London, I could not resist calling upon the help of that great detective, Sherlock Holmes, to help solve the mystery of alpha. This is, of course, a paraphrase of one of Holmes's greatest quotes: "Once you eliminate the impossible, whatever remains, however improbable, must be the truth." From *The Sign of the Four* (1890) and *The Adventures of Sherlock Holmes* (1892) by Sir Arthur Conan Doyle.

[4] E. Fama and K. French, "The Cross-Section of Expected Stock Returns," *Journal of Finance* 47, no. 2 (1992): 427–465; "Common Risk Factors in the Returns to Stocks and Bonds," *Journal of Financial Economics* 33, no. 1 (1993): 3–56; "Multifactor Explanations of Asset Pricing Anomalies," *Journal of Finance* 51, no. 2 (1996).

[5] Fung and Hsieh were the first to apply factor modeling to hedge funds, which they expanded in a subsequent paper. See W. Fung and D. Hsieh, "Empirical Characteristics of Dynamic Trading Strategies: The Case of Hedge Funds," *Review of Financial Studies* 10, no. 2 (1997): 275–302; "Asset-Based Style Factors for Hedge Funds," *Financial Analysts Journal* 58, no. 5 (September/October 2002).

Equation 4.1 is used to measure the alpha of an active manager by subtracting out all of the beta factors. Either alpha or epsilon is left over: Alpha represents genuine skill and epsilon represents random noise. How do we know which is which? Through statistical analysis. If the remaining term is statistically significant, it is alpha; otherwise it is just random noise represented by epsilon.

Let's take a simple example. From the prior chapter, in Exhibit 3.9, we looked at an investment product that we called bulk beta. This was an actively managed, long-only, large-cap U.S. equity manager, benchmarked to the S&P 500. Its only form of systematic risk is large-cap, U.S. stock market risk with a beta measured against the S&P 500 of 1.02. With this factor (large-cap U.S. stock market risk), we can measure the alpha of the product as:

$$\alpha_i = R_{i,t} - R_f - \sum_{j=1}^{K} \beta_{i,j} \times \left(F_{j,t} - R_f \right) + \varepsilon_{i,t}$$

Plugging in values from 2007, we get the alpha return:

$$\alpha = 6.1\% - 2\% - 1.02 \times (5.5\% - 2\%) = +0.53\%$$

The problem with determining the alpha component in this manner is that it depends on the systematic risk factors that we include in our analysis to determine the beta component. If we forget to include a relevant beta factor, then the alpha component could be artificially high. This leads to two implications for asset managers.

1. Asset managers must be rigorous and intellectually honest about what is beta and what is alpha. They must scour their performance returns to determine what the beta components are. In fact, some of these systematic risk factors are labeled alternative betas because they have a systematic impact on the returns in a portfolio even though most investors would not include these beta components in their portfolios. These alternative betas refer to exposures to systematic risk premiums that are not easily obtained through traditional asset classes. They may not require special skills and may not be expensive to obtain, but they are not available through long-only positions in stocks and bonds. Examples of these alternative betas are volatility risks, illiquidity risks, some currency risks, some commodity risks, and some credit risks.

2. An information asymmetry exists between asset managers and asset owners. Since alpha is not directly observable, asset managers have greater information about their true alpha-producing ability than the asset owners who hire them. Brown and de Figueiredo (2007) call this "hidden information."[6] The implication is that it is incumbent upon asset managers to make their investment process as transparent as possible to the asset owners. Eliminating this asymmetry of information leads to more efficient pricing of investment products. Furthermore, this asymmetry is exacerbated because the investment process or risk taking by the asset manager is not perfectly observable by the asset owners.

The natural question that arises is: "What incentives do managers have that reveal their true beta exposures?" Certain fee structures may lead active managers to take too much beta exposure in the hope of collecting short-term fees. If there is no clawback provision to recoup previous fees, the manager may have the incentive to expose the fund to certain hidden risks (e.g. writing deep-out-of-the-money put options).

In the absence of proper due diligence, certain incentives may encourage a certain class of risk hiding and deferred blowup. For example, take two active money managers. The first one has a true

---

[6] N. Brown and R. de Figueiredo, "Hedge Funds and the Active Management Industry," *Citigroup Alternative Investments Journal* (Winter 2007): 2–11.

alpha and no hidden exposure. She produces 2% true excess return per year, with no hidden risk. The second has the same set of skills but also assumes a significant amount of hidden beta exposure through the sale of deep-out-of-the-money put options, and apparently generates 5% excess return (the true excess return is 2%). The second is bound to have a significant large loss at some point in time (e.g. the deep-out-of-the-money put options expire in-the-money). Therefore, while the first asset manager might end up accumulating a relatively small amount of capital, the second one will do a lot better for himself by providing higher returns, but with hidden risk. He can earn steady amounts of fees for several years before the fund's true risk is revealed.

Several factors may help reduce the negative impact of this asymmetry in information. First, the manager may have his own capital at risk. It is common for hedge fund managers to have a significant portion of their own net worth invested in the fund along with investors. Second, the manager's human capital and reputation are negatively affected by a significant adverse outcome. This will serve as an incentive to reduce those hidden risks. Third, due diligence may reveal some of these hidden risks negatively affecting the reputation of the fund.

We gave one demonstration of alpha detecting in Chapter 3. In that demonstration, we applied our factor model to bring some transparency to the alpha generation of hedge fund managers who were engaged in convertible bond arbitrage. Convertible bonds are a mix of debt and equity. This hybrid mixture makes their value less transparent. If you recall our analysis from Chapter 3, we first used our understanding of convertible bonds and convertible arbitrage strategy to determine what betas to apply in our factor model. As a recap, the five economic factors that can influence the value of a convertible bond are:

1. Interest rate risk—It is a bond.
2. Stock market risk—It is convertible into stock.
3. Credit risk—Convertible bonds are usually issued by below-investment-grade companies.
4. Volatility risk—There is an embedded call option in the bond.
5. Autocorrelation risk—Convertible bonds are illiquid, and current prices may be influenced by past prices (the absence of a random walk).

As our factor analysis in Chapter 3 demonstrated, once you removed all of the betas from convertible bond arbitrage returns, the remaining component was a negative alpha. We concluded that convertible bond arbitrage is all about finding so-called cheap beta. In our example, convertible bond arbitrage managers are not searching for undervalued bonds; they are searching for undervalued beta. They hedge out the expensive components of the convertible bond and keep those systematic risk premiums embedded in the convertible bond that are cheap.

MARKETS ARE NEVER FULLY EFFICIENT

We should not despair in our search for alpha based on our results for convertible arbitrage. Opportunities to generate alpha exist all the time. The U.S. stock market is generally considered the most efficient stock market in the world. Yet, if this is the case, how do we explain the technology bubble of the late 1990s when dot-com stocks were going to take over the world? Or the portfolio insurance fallacy of the 1980s when investors collectively believed that the risk of holding equities could be eliminated?

Exhibit 4.3 presents a graph of the equity risk premium (ERP) in the United States over the period 1982–2008. The ERP is that return premium that investors must earn in order to entice them to hold stocks over bonds. Stocks are fundamentally more risky than bonds. Stockholders are the residual claimants on a public company. They are paid only after all other creditors and bondholders are paid first. As a result, the risk to a stockholder is greater than that of a bondholder. The ERP

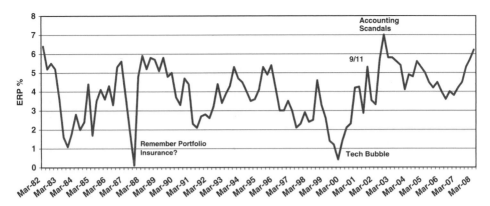

Exhibit 4.3   Estimate of S&P 500 risk premium, 1982–2008

is the additional compensation that investors demand to bear the extra risk of holding stocks over bonds.

Unfortunately, the ERP is not directly observable; it must be backed out of the current values in the financial markets. The five steps are:

1. Start with the current value of the stock market.
2. Forecast the future earnings and aggregate dividend payout ratio associated with the stock market.
3. Use a present value calculation: Determine the discount rate necessary to equate: Discounted future dividends = Current stock market value.
4. From the discount rate determined in step 3, subtract out a Treasury bond rate.
5. The remainder is the ERP, the additional return necessary to entice investors to hold stocks over bonds.

A few quick observations about Exhibit 4.3. First, the data is over a 28-year period, and during this period the average ERP is 3.9%; that is, on average, stocks have yielded 3.9% more than Treasury bonds to entice investors to purchase stocks over bonds.

Second, Exhibit 4.3 demonstrates two instances when the ERP approached zero, when stocks were perceived to be no more risky than bonds. The first instance was the portfolio insurance fallacy of 1987 that led to a significant crash of stock prices on the major U.S. stock exchanges (a 750-point decline over two days in the Dow Jones Industrial Average). This resulted in the development of so-called circuit breakers on the New York Stock Exchange to prevent future panic attacks by investors.

The second instance is the tech bubble of 1999 when Internet stocks were poised to take over the world. In both cases, the ERP approached zero. This cannot be. As stated earlier, stocks are fundamentally more risky than Treasury bonds, and there must be some premium earned by investors to hold this asset class instead of bonds. When the ERP declines toward zero, there is a fundamental disconnection with respect to the value of these two asset classes. A correction is sure to follow, as it did dramatically in October 1987 with a significant market crash and in the bursting of the tech bubble in 2000.

It is also interesting to note the highest level of the ERP came in 2002 at the height of the corporate accounting scandals in the United States. At that time, corporate governance significantly collapsed, leading to numerous corporate debacles like WorldCom, Enron, Adelphia, Tyco, and MCI. This so eroded the confidence of the U.S. stock market that the ERP rose to 7%. It is an excellent demonstration of how poor corporate governance can significantly increase the cost of capital to public corporations while simultaneously eroding their stock market value.

Let's use Exhibit 4.3 to demonstrate a numerical example.

The long-term average for the ERP is 3.9%.
The reading of the ERP as of the first quarter of 2008 was 6.2%.
The difference is: 6.2% – 3.9% = 2.3%.

The difference of 2.3% represents the excess discount rate applied to U.S. stocks over Treasury bonds given the credit and liquidity turmoil that existed in the U.S. economy during the first quarter of 2008. In fact, by the end of 2008, the implied ERP had risen to 7.2%.

Another way to say this is that to value U.S. stocks accurately, the discount rate applied to their future cash flows should be reduced by 2.3% to get a fair long-term value. It is important to note that the estimates of cash flows are just that, estimates. As subsequent events in 2008 demonstrated, the projected earnings held at the beginning of 2008 were too optimistic, and ex-post, the actual risk premium turned out to be negative.

In summary, modern portfolio theory assumes that investors are rational utility maximizers. Yet humans are not always rational; they are guided by emotions and behavioral patterns. These can introduce inefficiencies into the market, systematic irregularities, such as momentum, overconfidence, herding, emotional attachment to portfolio positions, and fixation on portfolio benchmarks. The point is that there will always be human biases embedded in the financial markets and this will provide opportunities for alpha generation. Finally, we have had several examples of irrational exuberance in stock or credit markets in the 1980s, 1990s, and 2000s, so what will the 2010s bring?

IS ALPHA A ZERO-SUM GAME?

This is a question that is debated almost endlessly. The answer is "Yes," but only if:

- Investors have the same investment horizon.
- Investors have the same level of risk tolerance.
- Investors are allowed the same access to all asset classes (there is no market segmentation).
- Investors have the same expectations about return and asset class risk premiums (homogeneous expectations, the key assumption of the CAPM).
- Investors pay the same tax rate, or equivalently, there is no tax.

Clearly, this is not the case; investors do indeed have different investment horizons (a pension fund versus a hedge fund, for example), risk tolerances (an endowment fund versus a high-net-worth investor), access to asset classes (many pension funds do not/are not allowed to invest in commodities or hedge funds), application of different tax rates (a high-net-worth investor compared to a tax-exempt pension fund), and certainly different expectations about return and risk (speculators versus hedgers). For example, Hill (2006) provides a great demonstration of how multiple investment horizons with different market access costs can distort the zero-sum alpha pie.[7]

The fact that there are so many varied investment horizons, market segments, risk tolerances, and expectations allows alpha to be generated across time, asset classes, and risk tolerances. For example, a bank that wishes to hedge its credit exposure to a certain industry (let us say automobiles) will be willing to trade some of the upside on its loan portfolio to satisfy its lower risk tolerance to this industry. Conversely, a high-yield investor may have an underexposure to autos and will be keen

---

[7] Joanne Hill, "Alpha as a Net Zero Sum Game," *Journal of Portfolio Management* 32, no. 4 (Summer 2006).

to buy those loans off of the bank's balance sheet; this is the whole basis for the collateralized debt obligation (CDO) market.

Therefore, the bank gives up some of the alpha associated with its auto loan exposure to be more in line with its risk tolerances while the high-yield manager loads up on an industry where it is willing to take more risk. However, both parties are better off: alpha is generated on both sides of the trade because of different risk tolerances to the auto sector.

GOVERNANCE MODEL FOR ALPHA AND BETA SEPARATION

The asset management industry, like any industry, is subject to good and bad corporate governance. However, the movement toward alpha/beta separation can improve the governance of the asset management industry. Unfortunately, the traditional model of long-only active managers is still the predominant form of investing for pension funds and other asset owners.

The existing paradigm of most of the asset management industry is still benchmark driven. While benchmarks are a useful tool for performance transparency, they are also a significant constraint that reduces the information ratios of active managers. To achieve consistent alpha, investors must think outside the benchmark in the construction of their portfolios.[8]

Consider a manager that is benchmarked to the S&P 500. This manager is allowed an active risk budget of 5% (tracking error volatility of 5%). This means that the remaining 95% of the risk of the portfolio is geared to nothing more than matching the volatility of the benchmark. Why pay active management fees for the 95% that does nothing more than track the S&P 500? Again, this gets back to poor governance in the asset management industry.

This constraint, in turn, reduces the value that an active manager can add to a client's portfolio. This is why hedge funds have become so popular: investors have turned away from traditional active managers, who packaged a big chunk of benchmark beta with small bits of alpha, toward hedge funds, which offered more alpha bang for the buck.

Fortunately, the financial markets and financial products have matured to the point where beta and alpha can be efficiently separated. The sophistication of the financial markets therefore leads to better corporate governance in the delivery of asset management services. Alpha no longer needs to be bundled up with beta.

The separation of beta from alpha provides for more efficient and transparent choices for asset owners. Transparency is a key element of every good governance regime, mitigating three risks associated with the asymmetric relationship between asset owners and asset managers:

1. *Asymmetry of information.* This asymmetry of information takes three forms:
    1. Asset managers have better information regarding their true level of skill, their information coefficient, in the nomenclature of Grinold and Kahn (1999).[9] As we demonstrated earlier, alpha, the output of asset manager skill, is not observable ex-ante. It is only after the asset manager has produced a return stream and the beta components have been accounted for that alpha can be observed. There, ex-ante, asset managers have much better information about their alpha-producing skills than the asset owners have.
    2. Asset owners get only a snapshot of their portfolio at any point in time. The amount or risk that is embedded in the portfolio may not be transparent. Also, the investment process by which the portfolio was constructed may not be transparent.

---

[8] See Anson (2004b).

[9] Richard Grinold and Ronald Kahn, *Active Portfolio Management*, 2nd rev. ed. (New York: McGraw-Hill, 1999).

3. Asset managers know how much beta they deliver with their alpha. In the traditional governance structure, asset owners receive a combination of alpha and beta from asset managers. In fact, because asset managers are fixated on benchmark-driven investing, there is much more beta than alpha in these products. This leads to the phenomenon of "closet beta drivers dressed up like alpha drivers" (see Anson, 2004a).[10]

2. *Asymmetry of incentives.* Alpha managers essentially have a so-called free option with respect to performance fees generated from their alpha-generative products. Profit-sharing fees of 20% to 25% are the norm for hedge funds, private equity, commodity trading advisers, and the like. This is the nature of a call option: to enjoy the upside but to bear no risk on the downside. In fact, given that hedge fund managers and the like are paid a management fee in addition to a profit-sharing fee, alpha managers are actually paid to take the free option. Conversely, traditional long-only asset managers also have an asymmetry of incentives. They provide much more beta than alpha and yet are paid an active management fee. Traditional managers, therefore, have the incentive to keep the amount of beta/alpha proportion in their portfolios as opaque as possible.

3. *Asymmetry of risk taking.* This asymmetry risk follows from the asymmetry of incentives. Asset managers who share in the gains from their performance but not the losses have an incentive to take excessive risk. Because asset managers do not bear the cost of losses from their investment strategies, this can lead them to take more risk than the asset owner is willing to bear. As noted earlier, incentive fees are like a call option. Call option values increase the more risk is taken. Therefore, hedge fund and other active managers who receive performance fees have an incentive to increase the volatility of the underlying portfolio to maximize the value of their incentive fee call option.

Governance in the asset management industry must address these asymmetries of information. Some clear conclusions are:

- *Beta is a commodity and should be priced cheaply.* To the extent there is skill associated with beta capturing, it is not in accessing the economic exposure to a systematic risk premium, but in delivering beta as cost-effectively as possible. Through the use of ETFs, swaps, futures, options, and computer tools to optimize or replicate benchmarks, beta capture is a relatively easy task. The cost is small and beta capture should be priced accordingly.

- *Unbundling drives price transparency.* The unbundling of alpha from beta allows asset managers to price their products more accurately and with greater transparency. No longer do asset owners have to pay an active management fee for a product that delivers much more beta than alpha.

- *Asset managers must demonstrate a clear and transparent investment process.* Because of the asymmetry of information, asset managers have a much better idea of whether they have an informational advantage that produces sustainable outperformance. In addition, asset managers have a better idea of whether future economic conditions will allow them to exploit their informational advantage as fully as their past performance might indicate.

- *Investors must accept a balance between transparency and alpha generation.* The ability to generate alpha will decline if information about the asset manager's competitive advantage is made public. Asset owners must have sufficient information to assure themselves that an alpha manager's performance is sustainable while recognizing that it is in the asset owner's best interest not to demand a public accounting of the asset manager's informational advantage.

- *Asset managers must be transparent in their risk taking.* Profit-sharing fees can lead to excessive risk taking by the asset manager. This problem is particularly acute for hedge fund managers.

---

[10] Mark Anson, "Thinking Outside the Benchmark," *Journal of Portfolio Management*, 30th Anniversary Edition, 2004.

Transparent monitoring of a hedge fund manager's risk taking will allow asset owners to assure themselves that the incentive fee structure has not created a risk profile that is inconsistent with their level of risk tolerance.

CONCLUSION: EVOLUTION IS A NECESSITY

Traditional active management is not dead, yet. However, sophisticated investors have become increasingly skeptical of the ability of traditional asset managers to extract alpha. Consequently, asset owners are increasingly shifting their assets away from traditional asset managers to the extremes of beta grazers and alpha hunters. Those asset management companies caught in the center are vulnerable to this disintermediation of fund flows. Without a plan, they will fall behind, may be acquired, or may even go under. There are four choices for those asset management companies stuck in the middle.

1. *Focus on beta-driven products.* Become efficient at processing trades rather than generating alpha. Spend significantly on order management systems, risk control, transition management, trade execution, and cost-efficient automation. Process drivers must attract and retain enough assets to cover their high fixed-cost base. In addition, a large scale of assets is needed to demonstrate that index tracking may be done efficiently no matter the size of assets under management. This is a commoditized business; attracting and retaining clients requires a high level of client marketing and constant advice provided to the client through as many channels as possible. This is a "high touch" business because clients can get the same product by crossing the street to another large index tracker.

    As a corollary, consider the development of bespoke beta products. These are the customized beta trackers that are tailored toward a more narrow definition of systematic risk such as small-cap stocks, commodity sectors, emerging markets, and international markets. Bespoke beta products are typically offered in the form of ETFs, which are more profitable than traditional index products. This is the growth market within the index tracking business. It is still small enough that there is sufficient opportunity for new entrants.

2. *Focus on alpha drivers.* These are investment products with a minimum of constraints, maximum flexibility, and considerable research to generate excess return. Hedge funds are the prime example, but so too are private equity, active commodities, tactical asset allocation, credit derivatives, real estate, and distressed debt investing. For these products, scale is not necessary; it can erode the alpha production. Instead, these managers must invest in highly paid staff, research, idea generation, innovative solutions to existing problems, sophisticated use of derivatives, and good trade execution. What these managers lack in scale they make up for with highly priced investment products, typically with a large performance fee of 20% to 30% for outperformance. We call these "high alpha content" products because of their ability to extract more value per unit of information than in the traditional active management space.

3. *Become an investment solutions provider.* This is the Citigroup model. Citigroup exited the traditional asset management business and sold its asset management company to Legg Mason. Instead, Citigroup chose to concentrate on client service, portfolio construction, manager selection, distribution of investment products, and risk management. This is a *solutions-based* business model. The key will be to focus on the distribution of its solutions model, demonstration of superior manager selection, construction of intelligent portfolio models, and better customer service. Access to high-performing funds will be important. While this model is also a "high touch" business, it builds revenues from value added to the portfolio construction process rather than collecting investment management fees.

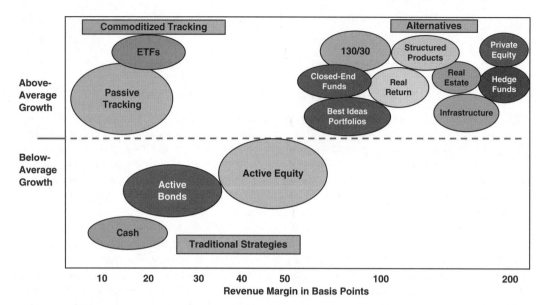

Exhibit 4.4   Polarization in the asset management industry

4. *Evolve into a multiboutique.* The multiboutique is a collection of specialized investment products
collected together under one brand identity. The multiboutique does not try to develop the huge
scale of large asset gatherers with commoditized products. Instead, the multiboutique focuses
on actively managed products across asset classes such as hedge funds, private equity, small-
cap stocks, emerging markets, credit investments, and commodities. A key advantage to the
multiboutique is its flexibility to develop additional capacity for active mandates. Scale is not
the driver of revenues and profits. The innovative nature of the investment products commands
higher fees. A smaller base of assets is found in the multiboutique but with investment products
that command premium pricing in the asset management industry. Many middle-of-the-road
asset management companies are moving to this model by developing 130/30 funds, hedge
funds, commodities funds, and special purpose vehicles such as collateralized debt obligations.
The multiboutique model alleviates the burden of raising a huge amount of assets. It relies on
performance fees (for outperformance) to generate its profits.

To summarize, there is a polarization under way in the asset management industry. As asset owners
have become more sophisticated about what is alpha and what is beta, asset managers have had to
revise their business models driving to alpha development at one end and beta providing at the other.
Exhibit 4.4 provides a demonstration of this change in the asset management industry. Above the
dotted line are the areas of growth in the asset management industry: beta drivers on the one hand
like enhanced index products, and alpha drivers on the other hand like closed-end funds (CEFs).
Below the dotted line lie the traditional components of the asset management industry: stock and
bond funds. The growth of traditional products is still positive; it is just that the growth rate is not as
high as for beta drivers or alpha drivers.

5

The Calculus of Active Management

INTRODUCTION

Alternative assets are all about active management. When we use the term **alternative** we should ask the question: Alternative to what? Alternative investments grew out of the benchmark-driven, style-denominated form of investing that plagues most of the long-only industry. Most asset managers still operate in the sphere of traditional stock and bond funds. These investments are constrained to remain close to their benchmarks or peer-group style boxes.

Alternatives were invented as a way to think outside the benchmark. They often operate with disdain to a benchmark, frequently eschewing a peer-group style of investing. These investments, in fact, are designed as an alternative to benchmark-driven or peer-group style boxes.

As a consequence, alternative assets focus on adding value to the portfolio through the use of active bets, both long and short, with and without concentrated portfolios. But how do we judge how effective an active manager is in her designated portfolio specialty? The answer lies with the Fundamental Law of Active Management.

FUNDAMENTAL LAW OF ACTIVE MANAGEMENT

We first begin with the **information ratio** (IR) of an active manager, a concept that was introduced in a previous chapter. The IR is measured as the active return, or alpha (α), produced by the manager divided by the tracking error (TE), or standard deviation of that alpha (σ_α):

$$IR = \frac{\alpha}{\sigma_\alpha} \qquad (5.1)$$

The information ratio is a measure of risk-adjusted return, much like the Sharpe ratio. Recall that the Sharpe ratio $[(R_i - R_f)/\sigma]$ is based on the excess return over the risk-free rate divided the standard deviation of the active manager's returns. The Sharpe ratio is a risk-adjusted return based on the total deviation of the active manager's returns because the benchmark that is used is the risk-free rate, which has no volatility. Further, the Sharpe ratio is based on the mean-variance approach of Markowitz. That is, it assumes the risk of the portfolio is entirely determined by the standard deviation of its return. Clearly, it is not appropriate to apply the Sharpe ratio to individual securities or even individual managers, because it ignores the fact that the manager's correlation with the rest of the portfolio is a major determinant of its risk-return profile. That is, the Sharpe ratio is appropriate only for comparing stand-alone investments. The decision to add a new manager (*mngr*) investment to a portfolio (*p*) must account for the correlation between the manager's returns and the portfolio returns ($\rho_{mngr,p}$) and should satisfy the following equation:

$$\frac{E(R_{mngr}) - R_f}{\sigma_{mngr}} > \left(\frac{E(R_p) - R_f}{\sigma_p}\right) \rho_{mngr,p} \qquad (5.2)$$

IR is a special form of a risk-adjusted rate of return where the performance is measured relative to a risky benchmark. Whereas the Sharpe ratio assumes a riskless benchmark (the risk-free rate), the information ratio incorporates a risky benchmark into the analysis. Therefore, it is not the total volatility that is measured, but rather the volatility of the active manager compared to its *volatile* benchmark. Similarly, the excess return is not compared to a risk-free benchmark, but instead is measured relative to a risky benchmark. The IR can be expressed as:

$$IR = \frac{\text{Return}_{\text{Active Manager}} - \text{Return}_{\text{Risky Benchmark}}}{\text{Tracking Error}_{\text{Active Manager}}} \tag{5.3}$$

where the tracking error of the active manager is the volatility of the difference between the active returns and the benchmark returns.

The information ratio is almost always reported on an ex-post basis. This means that the parameters of the model have to be estimated. Assuming that N observations are obtained, the IR is calculated using the following familiar expressions:

$$\alpha_t = (R_t - R_{Bt})$$

$$\alpha = \frac{1}{N} \sum_{t=1}^{N} \alpha_t$$

$$\sigma_\alpha = \sqrt{\frac{1}{N-1} \sum_{t=1}^{N} (\alpha_t - \alpha)^2}$$

$$IR = \frac{\alpha}{\sigma_\alpha} \tag{5.4}$$

where R_{Bt} is the per period return on the benchmark and R_t is the per period return on the active manager.

Since the parameters have to be estimated, the resulting IR is subject to estimation risk. This means the true value of IR may or may not be different from its estimated value. Under some assumptions, one can use a t-statistic to test whether the estimated value of α is significantly different from zero. In fact there is a simple approximate relationship between IR and the t-statistic.[1]

$$t\text{-Statistic} \approx IR \times \sqrt{T} \tag{5.5}$$

Since IR is typically reported on an annualized basis, T represents the length of manager's performance history measured in years. This relationship can be exploited to decide if a manager's IR is significantly greater than zero.

Example: Suppose a manager's alpha is 3% per year while its tracking error is 5% per year. The information ratio will be IR $= 3/5 = 0.6$. Also, suppose we have 10 years of data. Then the t-statistic will be 1.897. Is this significantly greater than zero? The critical value of this t-statistic at a 95% confidence level and 9 degrees of freedom is 1.833. Thus, the IR is barely significantly greater than zero. The same procedure can be used to test whether the IR exceeds a threshold. For instance, suppose we require the manager's IR to exceed 0.10. Then the t-statistic is given by:

$$t\text{-Statistic} = (IR - 0.10) \times \sqrt{T} \tag{5.6}$$

The IR can be expressed on an ex-ante basis as well. In this instance, the ratio is related to the manager's skill and the size of the portfolio.

Richard Grinold in his original thesis proposed that the Fundamental Law of Active Management is based on two key components of every actively managed investment strategy: breadth and skill.[2]

---

[1] The relationship is exact if we assume that the beta is known with certainty. Otherwise, σ_α is not the standard deviation of α and it has to be adjusted by the standard error of the estimated beta.

[2] Richard Grinold, "The Fundamental Law of Active Management," *Journal of Portfolio Management* 15, no. 3 (1989), 30–37.

The **breadth** of a strategy is the number of independent *active* bets placed into an active portfolio. I emphasize the term *active* because this will become important to understand in the analysis of portfolio construction. The second component is the *skill* of the manager as measured by the term **information coefficient** (IC).

Breadth is measured as the number of independent forecasts of excess return that a portfolio manager places into a portfolio. The information coefficient is a measure of skill as determined by the correlation between the active manager's forecasted return for every portfolio bet and the actual return earned from that active bet.

$$IC = \text{Correlation (Forecasted Returns, Actual Returns)} \qquad (5.7)$$

The **Fundamental Law of Active Management** connects breadth and skill to the information ratio in the following equation:

$$IR = IC \times \sqrt{\text{Breadth}} \qquad (5.8)$$

Suppose an active manager has an IR of 0.1. To increase the IR to 0.2 the active manager could double her skill (as measured by the IC) or increase the breadth by a factor of 4 (the square root of which is 2), or some combination of both.

This result can be obtained in the following manner. The alpha of each active position is denoted by α_i. If the net weight of each active position is denoted by w_i, then the manager is assumed to maximize the following function by choosing the optimal values of w_i:

$$U = \sum_{i=1}^{N} w_i \alpha_i - \lambda \sum_{i=1}^{N} w_i^2 \sigma_i^2 \qquad (5.9)$$

Here σ_i^2 is the variance of residual or idiosyncratic risk of active position i and λ is the risk aversion parameter of the manager. The higher the risk aversion parameter, the greater the weight assigned to reducing the total volatility of active positions. Note that this assumes that the manager is only concerned with mean and variance of active risk. The optimal weight of each active position can be shown to be:

$$w_i = \frac{\alpha_i}{\sigma_i} \frac{1}{2\lambda} \qquad (5.10)$$

Note that the higher the alpha of the position, the higher the weight. Also, the higher the risk of the active position or the risk aversion parameter, the lower the weight will be. The alpha of each active position is related to the absolute size of the correlation between the random return on each active position and the signal the manager uses to place the active position. Presumably, as the signal becomes more precise (i.e. absolute value of correlation increases), the alpha of each active position increases as well. As shown by Grinold, using this result, the IR of the portfolio can be expressed as in Equation 5.8.

There is a trade-off between breadth and the information coefficient. It is not generally possible for an active manager to increase breadth and the IC at the same time. Consider this example. Two managers actively invest in large-cap stocks with both portfolios benchmarked to the S&P 500. One manager does not have an industry specialty and makes active bets across all Global Industry Classification Standard (GICS) industry classifications in the S&P 500. Her breadth is great, but since she is not a specialist her IC will be low across each industry. Conversely, the second portfolio manager follows only the telecom and media industries. She does not have as many active bets to put into the portfolio, but by concentrating on only two industries she can extract more information

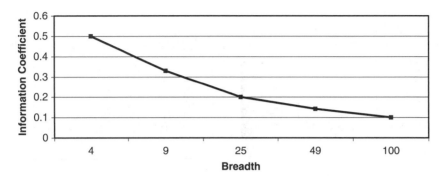

Exhibit 5.1   The trade-off between breadth and skill with IR fixed at 1.0

and value from a concentrated knowledge base. While the second portfolio manager will have a low breadth, she should have a higher IC.

Consider another definition of IC as information content (instead of information coefficient). This definition highlights that much of a manager's skill comes from developing a deeper informational advantage by accessing greater content of data than other active managers. Content drives knowledge, which leads to a bigger informational advantage and a higher IC.

Some additional examples will help. Let's hold the information ratio constant at 1.0 and consider what would be the IC necessary to establish this IR when we change the breadth of the portfolio.

- One portfolio manager is a market timer who makes bets each quarter on the up-and-down movement of the stock market. Her breadth = 4. Therefore to maintain an IR of 1.0, we solve for the value of IC that must be equal to 0.5: $IR = IC \times \sqrt{4}$.
- Next we consider a commodities trader who makes nine forecasts a year on the movement of crude oil prices. Again, using Equation 5.8 and solving for IC when breadth = 9 and IR = 1.0, we find that IC = 0.33.
- For our next example, we consider a hedge fund manager who includes 25 independent long and short positions in her portfolio. Using the same analysis as in Equation 5.5, we find that the hedge fund manager only needs to generate an IC of 0.2 to maintain an IR of 1.0.
- Next, consider a long-only manager who runs a concentrated portfolio with 49 active bets. Here, the IC need only be 0.1428.
- Last, we consider a traditional long-only manager who has 100 active bets in her portfolio. Here IC need only be 0.1.

Exhibit 5.1 demonstrates this relationship between the IC and breadth. As the breadth increases, the manager can be less smart and operate with a lower IC in order to achieve a constant IR of 1.0. Stated another way, the smaller the number of active bets in the portfolio, the more value (read skill) the active manager must extract from those bets to maintain her IR.

Consider another example involving the gambling of dice. Craps is a popular game of chance played in army barracks, casinos, and back alleys around the globe.[3] Many variations of this dice game exist, but they all revolve around "Lucky 7." Why is the number 7 so lucky? Because this is the number that has the highest probability or turning up when two dice are rolled together.

---

[3] In their book, *Active Portfolio Management*, 2nd ed. (New York: McGraw-Hill, 1999), Richard Grinold and Ronald Kahn use an example of the roulette wheel, but I have always been partial to craps myself.

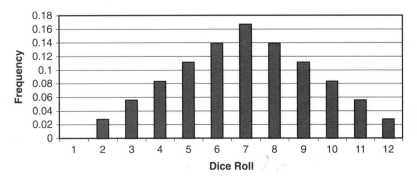

Exhibit 5.2 Frequency distribution for craps with two dice

Let's back up. Each die has six faces to it with dots on each face numbering from one dot to six. With two dice, the number of possible combinations is $6 \times 6 = 36$. Adding together the values of each die, the number 7 can come up in six different combinations: 6-1, 5-2, 4-3, 3-4, 2-5, 1-6. This means that a combination of the two dice producing the value of 7 has six chances in 36 total number combinations to occur, or a one-sixth probability of rolling a Lucky 7. Exhibit 5.2 demonstrates the frequency distribution associated with the game of craps.

Suppose we run a casino and the minimum bet for craps is $100. Let's take the simplest of craps games: The player wins if she rolls Lucky 7; otherwise we, the casino, win. If we pay out $500 whenever a player rolls Lucky 7, then our version of craps is a fair game where the expected value to both the player and to us, the casino owner, is 0:

$$\text{Player Wins: } (1/6 \times \$500) - \text{Casino Wins: } (5/6 \times \$100) = \$0$$

In effect, as the casino operator, we pledge $500 against every player's bet of $100, because if Lucky 7 turns up, we will have to pay out $500. What makes this a fair game is that the odds are in the favor of the casino, not the player. Now, being a capitalist casino operator, we decide to adjust the payout in our favor so that we can turn a profit. Note that we cannot adjust the odds associated with rolling two dice (unless the dice are loaded), so we have to adjust the amount we award the winner for rolling Lucky 7. Consequently, we decide to pay out to the player $400 if she rolls Lucky 7; otherwise we collect the minimum bet of $100.

The expected value to the casino is now:

$$(5/6 \times \$100) - (1/6 \times \$400) = \$16.67$$

Since we have to put up $100 to cover the player's bet, our return is $16.67/$500 = 3.33%. The standard deviation of this bet is 89.75%.[4] Therefore, if there is one bet of $100 each year at our casino, our excess return, or alpha, is 3.33%, and our standard deviation of the alpha is 89.75%, which leads to an IR of:

$$\frac{3.33\%}{89.75\%} = 0.0371$$

---

[4] The variance is measured as $5/6 \times (100\% - 100\%/6)^2 + 1/6 \times (-100\% - 100\%/6)^2 = 8,055\%$, and the standard deviation is the square root of this, or 89.75%. See Grinold and Kahn, *Active Portfolio Management*.

If 10,000 bets are placed on our craps tables in one year, our expected return per bet remains constant at 3.33%, but the standard deviation is reduced to a value of $89.75\%/\sqrt{10,000} = 0.8975\%$. Our new IR with more bets per year becomes:

$$\frac{3.33\%}{89.75\%} = 3.71$$

You can quickly see how casinos game the Fundamental Law of Active Management to their advantage.

SOME REAL-LIFE EXAMPLES

We now apply the Fundamental Law of Active Management to some real-life examples of mutual funds and hedge funds. We have chosen two well-known large-cap equity mutual funds operating in the United States as well as an index of equity long/short hedge fund managers to determine the information ratio of their portfolios compared to the S&P 500. The two mutual funds explicitly identify the S&P 500 as their benchmark to measure whether they can add value to an investor's portfolio.

For hedge funds, benchmark identification is not as easy. Most hedge funds claim that there is no appropriate benchmark by which to compare their performance. The topic of benchmarks for alternative assets is discussed later in this chapter. For the time being, let's use the S&P 500 index as the benchmark for an equity long/short manager with a long bias.

We start with Exhibit 5.3. We plot, compared to the total return for the S&P 500, the monthly net asset values (NAVs) for a large-cap active equity manager with over $50 billion in its mutual fund. Our time period is January 2000 through May 2008. This manager generates a small but positive monthly return on average of 0.01%. Its beta is less than 1.0, and this is not surprising given the size of this mutual fund. To maintain its capacity, it has to invest in the very largest-cap stocks, typically those of more mature companies and in more mature industries where the exposure to the systematic risk of the stock market is less than that for lower-capitalized companies.

You can see clearly from Exhibit 5.3 the linearity concept introduced in Chapter 2. The straight-line nature of this product compared to the S&P 500 indicates that it is more of a beta driver than an alpha driver. Its small monthly return and the negative Sharpe ratio confirm this. Not surprisingly, when its return is compared to the S&P 500, a negative alpha is produced; this mutual fund performs less well than the S&P 500. This leads to a negative information ratio. Simply, the active risk taking

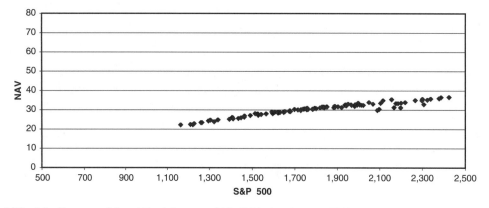

Exhibit 5.3   Return on Mutual Fund A versus S&P 500 index (January 2000–May 2008)
Note: Average return 0.01%; Sharpe ratio –0.029; Beta 0.76; Correlation 0.93; Alpha –0.15%; IR –0.092

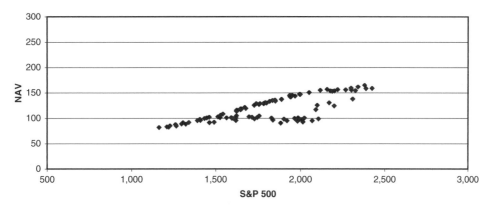

Exhibit 5.4   Return on Mutual Fund B versus S&P 500 index (January 2000–May 2008)
Note: Average return 0.30%; Sharpe ratio 0.046; Beta 0.74; Correlation 0.77; Alpha 0.13%; IR 0.05

of this manager is not worth it. Investors are not rewarded for the risk incurred by investing in this mutual fund.

Exhibit 5.4 shows us a different story. This is another long-only large-cap mutual fund operating in the United States. Fund B also has over $50 billion in assets under management. It, too, has a more conservative beta as it is forced to invest in larger-capitalized stocks with a lower beta exposure to the stock market. However, this fund generates both a positive Sharpe ratio and a positive information ratio.

Mutual Fund B is an alpha driver. It adds value for its clients through active risk taking compared to its benchmark. We can see visually that there is much more variation in this manager's returns compared to the S&P 500. True, there is still considerable beta risk in the portfolio, but this reflects the nature of all long-only equity mutual funds in the United States. However, this manager is not afraid to stray from its benchmark in the quest for added value. It's correlation with the S&P is much lower than that for Mutual Fund A.

Last, we consider Exhibit 5.5, where we plot the returns to equity long/short hedge fund managers to the S&P 500. We see more variation in the returns to equity long/short hedge fund managers compared to the S&P 500 than that for the mutual funds in Exhibits 5.3 and 5.4. True, some

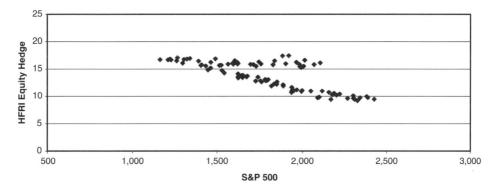

Exhibit 5.5   Long/short equity hedge fund versus S&P 500 index
Note: Average return 0.59%; Sharpe ratio 0.21; Beta 0.38; Correlation 0.66; Alpha 0.48%; IR 0.16

systematic risk exposure remains as measured by a beta value of 0.38, but the correlation of the hedge fund returns with the S&P 500 is much lower at 0.66. We also see a larger average monthly return and alpha compared to the S&P 500, leading to a larger Sharpe ratio and IR. To summarize, compared to traditional long-only mutual funds, equity long/short hedge funds offer more active risk taking, a larger excess return, and less exposure to the U.S. stock market than large-cap mutual funds. This result is not unexpected, but it is nice to confirm it using the Fundamental Law of Active Management.

BENCHMARKS FOR ALTERNATIVE ASSETS

Unlike traditional long-only stock and bond asset managers, alternative investment managers do not have a mandate to follow a benchmark. Therefore, the preceding results may not be applicable to many alternative investment managers.

To overcome this problem, investors may have to create custom-made benchmarks; the simplest method to do so is to use the Sharpe style analysis approach.[5] The goal is to create a portfolio of readily investable assets that best replicates the return on the active manager. The general expression for Sharpe style analysis is:

$$R_{i,t} - R_f = \alpha_i + \sum_{j=1}^{K} w_{i,j} \left(F_{j,t} - R_f \right) + \varepsilon_{i,t} \tag{5.11}$$

Here $R_{i,t}$ is the rate of return on active manager i, R_f is the riskless rate (e.g., LIBOR), $F_{j,t}$ is the rate of return on asset class j, $w_{i,j}$ is the estimate of the weight of asset class j in the portfolio that replicates active manager i, and $\varepsilon_{i,t}$ is the part of return that cannot be explained by these asset classes. Given the estimated values of $w_{i,j}$, then a portfolio is created where the weight of asset class j is given by $w_{i,j}$ and the weight of the riskless asset is given by $(1 - \sum_{j=1}^{K} w_{i,j})$.

When applied to traditional money managers, certain restrictions have to be imposed on the estimates of the weights (e.g., they may have to be positive), but no such restrictions need be considered when applied to most alternative investments.

Using the preceding Sharpe style analysis, one can immediately obtain the information ratio of the manager:

$$\begin{aligned} IR_i &= \frac{\alpha_i}{\sqrt{Variance(\varepsilon_{it})}} \\ &= \frac{\alpha_i}{\sqrt{(1 - R^2) \times Variance\left(R_{i,t} \right)}} \end{aligned} \tag{5.12}$$

Here R^2 is the r-squared of the preceding regression.

RISK MANAGEMENT

Many positions held in a portfolio by a traditional long-only manager are for "risk management purposes." This is another way of saying that the active manager holds portfolio positions designed to balance the portfolio back to its benchmark. These are not active bets in the sense that they are

---

[5] See W. Sharpe, "Asset Allocation: Management Style and Performance Measurement," *Journal of Portfolio Management* 18, no. 2 (Winter 1992): 7–19.

intended to add value to the portfolio, but rather they are added to keep the active manager from straying as little from the benchmark as possible.

Therefore, it is often difficult to determine exactly how many independent bets a portfolio manager puts into the portfolio. Consider the mutual fund displayed in Exhibit 5.4. This portfolio contains over 247 positions. As a result, this active manager has about one-half of the S&P benchmark in its portfolio. It is unlikely that all 247-plus portfolio positions are independent, active forecasts. Rather, only a small subset of these positions are active bets. Consequently, the true breadth for this portfolio is not 247 but a smaller number and the manager's IR is much larger than initially calculated.

Filtering through the holdings of this portfolio compared to its benchmark, suppose we come up with 61 stock holdings that differ significantly from their benchmark weights in the S&P 500. The remaining positions are used for risk management purposes. These are not active positions. They are not independent forecasts of the portfolio manager, but rather are used to tether the portfolio to its benchmark.

Recall from Exhibit 5.1 that there is a trade-off between breadth and IC (manager skill). As the breadth shrinks, the IC increases to achieve the same level of IR. If we use a value for breadth of 61, the manager's measure of skill, or information coefficient, increases to 0.006. We believe this to be a more accurate measure of the manager's skill.

THE TRANSFER COEFFICIENT

The long-only constraint on investing has been recognized as the most restrictive portfolio requirement in the asset management industry. The restriction on short sales has two important detrimental impacts on portfolio management. First, the inability to go short effectively removes from the portfolio the manager's "negative alpha bets." In the course of managing money, a portfolio manager typically comes across good buys and good sells. Buys can typically be effected by overweights without a specific limit on the overweight. However, with the long-only constraint, sells can be effected only to the extent of their weight in the benchmark index. This means that the portfolio manager cannot maximize the negative alpha bets in the portfolio.

Second, positive, active overweights require underweights elsewhere in the portfolio. To the extent that a portfolio manager is limited in her negative underweights (through the long-only constraint), positive overweights will also be limited. Grinold and Kahn refer to this as a "knock-on" effect. Simply, the long-only constraint also limits the size of long overweights in the active portfolio.

The nature of the long-only constraint has led to an expanded form of the Fundamental Law of Active Management:

$$IR = TC \times IC \times \sqrt{Breadth} \qquad (5.13)$$

where TC is the transfer coefficient and the other terms remain as defined before.

The transfer coefficient, defined precisely, is the cross-sectional correlation coefficient between risk-adjusted active weights and risk-adjusted forecasted residual returns in the portfolio.[6] More generally, the TC is a measure of the efficacy of translating active portfolio forecasts into real portfolio bets. It measures the degree to which active signals are transferred into active portfolio weights.

The transfer coefficient is always less than 1.0. In a perfect world, without portfolio constraints and transaction costs, the TC equals 1.0. However, even if the long-only constraint is eliminated, there are still trading costs, opportunity costs, liquidity constraints, and other market frictions that

[6] See Roger Clarke, Harindra de Silva, and Steven Thorley, "Portfolio Constraints and the Fundamental Law of Active Management," *Financial Analysts Journal* (September/October 2002).

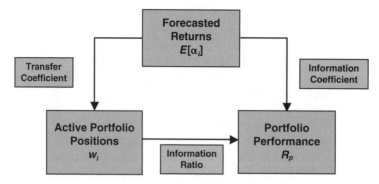

Exhibit 5.6   The generation of information ratios

erode the value of an active forecast as it is implemented into an active portfolio position. For example, Clarke, de Silva, and Thorley estimate that the long-only constraint can reduce the transfer coefficient by up to 42%.[7] This is a significant erosion of value.

Exhibit 5.6 shows the interplay of the information coefficient, information ratio, and transfer coefficient. The forecasted returns are a summary of all of the active alpha bets that the portfolio manager can add to the portfolio; we summarize this as $E[\alpha_i]$, which represents an $N \times 1$ vector of return forecasts. The manager tries to capture all of her active bets by adjusting the active weights of her security holdings in the portfolio; this is measured by a $1 \times N$ vector, w_i. The manager's ability to translate her active forecasts into active weights is limited by the transfer coefficient (e.g. a limitation as to the size of bets in the portfolio, or no shorting allowed). Last, we have the active return to the portfolio, measured by R_p, where $R_p = E[\alpha_i] \times w_i$. The correlation between the active manager's forecasted returns and the resulting portfolio returns is the measure of her skill, or information coefficient.

As Exhibit 5.6 shows, they are all intertwined in building value in an active portfolio. The identification of the transfer coefficient is perhaps the best argument for long/short investing. The ability to remove the long-only constraint adds tremendous value to an actively managed portfolio. This is the whole impetus for the hedge fund industry: unconstrained investing to add the greatest value.

130/30 EQUITY PORTFOLIOS

Within the past three years there has been a virtual explosion in the introduction of 130/30 funds by asset management companies, with some companies introducing several different versions of 130/30 products. **130/30 products** are similar to traditional long-only products in that their goal is to outperform an equity benchmark. These products start by allocating 100% of NAV to long positions in the equity markets. They differ from the traditional products to the extent that they can sell short equity securities, typically up to 30%. The proceeds from the short sales are then used to establish additional long positions (typically overweighted positions relative to a benchmark) up to 130% of the NAV.

These 130/30 products are a natural progression for both hedge fund managers and traditional asset managers. Generating excess returns, or alpha, is difficult. Alpha is a scarce and valuable commodity for which skillful active managers can charge large asset management fees. Hedge fund

---

[7] Ibid.

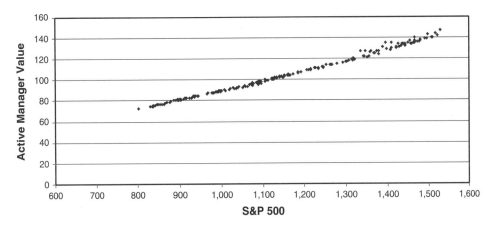

Exhibit 5.7   Large-cap active equity manager versus S&P 500 index

Note: Beta 1.0; R-squared 0.994

managers, for example, are typically constrained by capacity in their more turbocharged investment products. In seeking more capacity, they have gravitated to products that combine a small amount of shorting with a large amount of traditional stock picking.

Conversely, traditional long-only equity managers have observed the fees commanded by hedge fund managers who have the ability to short the market. Also, traditional asset managers have long been aware of the inefficiency of the long-only constraint in maximizing their equity market information set. Naturally, they have gravitated toward 130/30 products which lifts the long-only constraint by a reasonable amount and allows traditional asset managers to generate higher revenues.

For example, a typical institutional investor such as a pension fund will pay 30 to 70 basis points for an active, long-only investment product. However, for 130/30 products, an investor typically pays a management fee of around 1%. This is a significant boost up for a traditional asset manager. For a hedge fund manager, a 1% management fee is a long way from the "2 and 20" charged for a typical hedge fund, but with capacity for 130/30 programs running into the tens of billions of dollars, a 1% management fee applied to a large pool of investor capital can generate a significant amount of fees, and do so on a much more regular and stable basis than hedge fund fees.

One of the key reasons for the proliferation of 130/30 products can best be demonstrated by Exhibit 5.7. This is a traditional long-only equity product benchmarked to the S&P 500. This product, despite its active mandate, is really a closet index tracker. There is minimal variation from the S&P 500, limited risk taking and, unfortunately, limited performance. Simply, this active manager is not very active and the performance of the product demonstrates this. Investment performance like this has encouraged investors to turn to 130/30 products.

Background for 130/30 products

The largest constraint in active portfolio management is the long-only constraint. It is estimated that this constraint alone can reduce the transfer coefficient by one-third.[8] The limitation of the long-only constraint can best be demonstrated by Exhibit 5.8.

---

[8] Ibid.

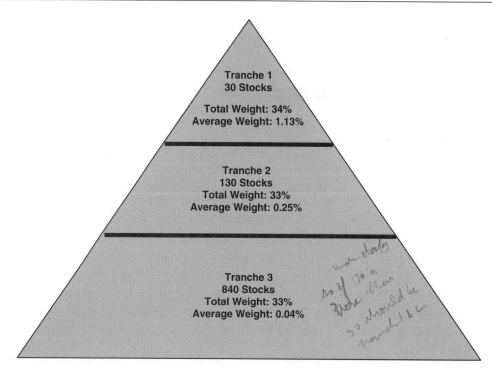

Exhibit 5.8   The capitalization of the Russell 1000 stock index

This exhibit shows a breakdown of the capitalization-weighted Russell 1000 stock index, a common equity benchmark. One-third of the capitalization of this index is represented by only 30 stocks with an average contribution to the capitalization of the index of 1.13%. The second tranche is made up of 130 stocks with an average cap weighting in the index of 0.25%. The last tranche of the index consists of 840 stocks with an average weighting of 0.04%. In fact, the median weight for a stock in the Russell 1000 stock index is 0.04%.

For active portfolio management, overweights in the portfolio must be funded with underweights. With the long-only constraint in place, the most a portfolio manager can underweight a stock in the portfolio is by its weight in the index. For 84% of the stocks in the Russell 1000, this underweight is only 0.04% or less, not much of an active bet. This forces an active manager to sell down more stocks from the first two terciles in order to fund the active overweights in the portfolio. Even more clearly, consider a portfolio manager whose strongest active overweight is with respect to a stock in the first tercile while her most negative bet is with respect to a stock in the third tercile. This means that her ability to fund her strongest overweight is constrained to only 0.04% from the most negative underweight.

This problem is by no means limited to the Russell 1000 index. The median weight of a stock in the S&P 500 is only 10 basis points. The smallest 250 companies in the S&P 500 have an index weight of less than 10 basis points.

Exhibit 5.9 demonstrates the advantage of relaxing the long-only constraint for 130/30 products. Additional funding is created for active overweights in the portfolio through the use of 30% short positions. The 30% short positions also increase the leverage of the portfolio. The total exposure to the market is 160%, the combination of both 30% short active positions and 130% long active positions.

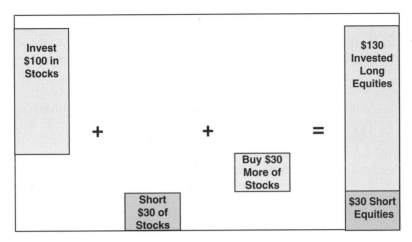

Exhibit 5.9   Breaking free of the long-only constraint

Further, the relaxation of the long-only constraint in 130/30 portfolios allows a manager to increase the information ratio along two dimensions. First, according to Exhibit 5.8, the active manager can increase the number of active bets in the portfolio, expanding the breadth. In addition, the manager can increase the size of her bets, in effect increasing the information coefficient.

The improvement in the information ratio of an investment manager follows from the concavity of the return versus risk trade-off common to all actively managed investment products. For both traditional, actively managed products and 130/30 products, an increase in tracking error (σ_a) leads to an increase in expected excess returns ($E[\alpha]$). With the long-only constraint, the relation between active risk taking and expected alpha is not proportional. This means that increases in risk lead to smaller and smaller increases in alpha. Relaxing the long-only constraint to allow up to 30% shorting leads to a better return for active risk-taking trade-off. Exhibit 5.10 demonstrates this trade-off.

In theory, a 130/30 strategy appeals to the intuition of the active asset management model. However, the mechanics of 130/30 products are not as simple as theory would like. Exhibit 5.11 presents the many moving parts associated with these strategies. The most important piece is the

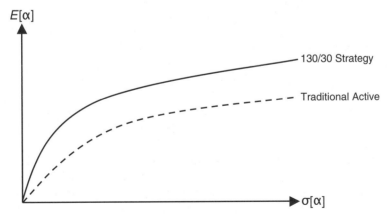

Exhibit 5.10   Expanding the active risk-taking frontier

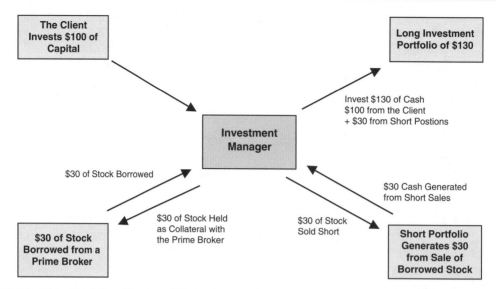

Exhibit 5.11   How a long/short portfolio is constructed

ability to borrow the stock from a prime broker from which to sell short. Stock can sometimes be hard to borrow, particularly those stocks that are in the lower capitalization range. Also, borrowed stock can be recalled by its owner, forcing the portfolio manager to cover the short position before maximizing the value of the position. Nonetheless, the relaxation of the long-only constraint, even if the constraint is not fully eliminated, provides the portfolio manager a better opportunity to increase the investment set.

A demonstration of 130/30

To demonstrate the power of 130/30 programs, assume the same, constant information coefficient for a long-only manager and a 130/30 manager. Each active manager has the same informational advantage but the long-only manager is limited in ability to overweight and underweight stocks based on the weight of a specific stock in the index. The 130/30 manager does not have the same constraint imposed and can introduce more negative bets into the portfolio.

With the IC held constant, there are two ways for the 130/30 manager to add value beyond the ability of a long-only manager. First, as previously discussed, the long-only constraint is the single greatest constraint on active portfolio management and can reduce the TC (and the IR) by over 40%. Although there are more costs associated with shorting stocks as demonstrated by Exhibit 5.11, these costs are small relative to relaxing the long-only constraint.[9]

Second, the breadth can be expanded by the 130/30 manager. In fact, the breadth can be expanded in two directions. On the long side, more active bets can be placed into the portfolio because the active manager now has the ability to short stocks to fund long positions that might otherwise not be implemented. On the short side, negative alpha bets that were previously impossible because of the long-only constraint may now be implemented.

---

[9] As Gastineau (2008) notes, 10% to 12% of the floating stock of every company in the S&P 500 is held in an index tracking fund, making the borrowing of these stocks cheap and easy.

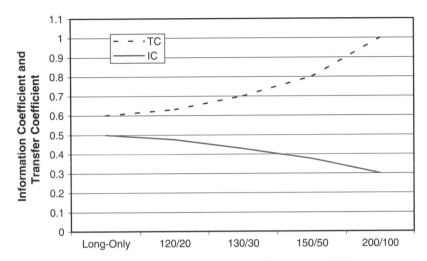

Exhibit 5.12 Decaying transfer coefficient and increasing information coefficient as one moves toward long-only

Note: IR 1.5; Breadth 25

The simple mathematics of Equation 5.13 demonstrate that if you can increase the transfer coefficient or the breadth of the portfolio while holding the information coefficient (manager skill) constant, the information ratio will increase. It really is not a fair fight between a long-only manager and a 130/30 manager.

To make this point explicit, we translate the math of Equation 5.13 into a simulation where we compare a 120/20 manager, a 130/30 manager, a 150/50 manager, and a 200/100 manager to a traditional long-only manager. The work by Clarke, de Silva, and Thorley demonstrates that the transfer coefficient is reduced by over 40% through the long-only constraint, or conversely, the full relaxation of the long-only constraint leads to an improvement in the TC of 40%.[10] We assume that the TC is at a maximum of 1.0 for 200/100; at this level of long and short investing the active manager has the full ability to implement both positive and negative alpha bets. However, the TC decays from 1.0 to 0.6 as we move from the 200/100 manager to the long-only manager. To simplify our demonstration we hold the IR constant at 1.5 and we assume that the breadth is also constant for each manager at a value of 25.

Exhibit 5.12 plots the decay of the transfer coefficient as we move from 200/100 to a long-only manager and also the increase in the information coefficient necessary to achieve an IR of 1.5. Remember that the IC is a measure of active manager skill. Effectively, Equation 5.13 and Exhibit 5.12 demonstrate that as the TC decays the IC must increase to maintain an IR of 1.5. In other words, the active manager must become more skillful to generate excess returns as the long-only constrain becomes more binding. Putting this statement in the converse, an active manager can be less skillful if the long-only constraint is removed and still maintain the same level of IR.

Exhibit 5.13 provides an additional demonstration of the power of removing the long-only constraint. Again, we keep the IR constant at 1.5. However, in this example, we now hold the transfer coefficient constant at 0.8 and we allow the breadth of the portfolio to increase as the active manager has a greater ability to add negative and positive alpha bets with the gradual removal of the long-only

---

[10] See Roger Clarke, Harindra de Silva, and Steven Thorley, "Portfolio Constraints and the Fundamental Law of Active Management," *Financial Analysts Journal* (September/October 2002).

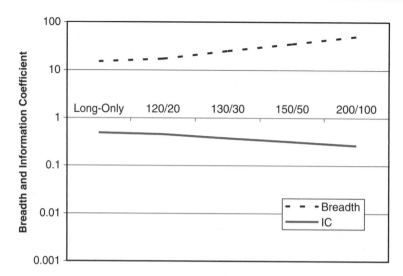

Exhibit 5.13   Decaying breadth and increasing information coefficient as one moves toward long-only
Note: IR 1.5; Transfer coefficient 0.8

constraint.[11] Exhibit 5.13 demonstrates that as the number of active bets in the portfolio increases (by relaxing the long-only constraint), the value of the information coefficient declines. This means that the skill level of the active manager can decline if the manager is allowed to put more active bets into the portfolio.

If we combine the demonstrations of Exhibits 5.12 and 5.13, we have a powerful story as to why 120/20, 130/30, 150/50, and 200/100 portfolios have become so popular. The ability to short securities in the portfolio not only increases the breadth of the portfolio, but it also increases the transfer coefficient. This one-two punch allows a manager with the same level of skill as a traditional long-only manager to generate a better risk versus return trade-off and a vastly superior information ratio.

CONCLUSION

The Fundamental Law of Active Management provides significant insights into the sources of alpha or value added by active managers. It states that a manager's added value is related to the manager's skills, as measured by the information coefficient, and the breath of skill in identifying profit opportunities in various segments of the market. As this law indicates, it is fundamental to every actively managed portfolio; none may escape this law.

Take the example of a 130/30 manager compared to a private equity manager. Most 130/30 portfolios are designated as quant active portfolios, meaning that they use quantitative computer programs to conduct massive research across a very large cross section of companies and a very large number of fundamental and behavioral factors. Simply, breadth is the name of this game. Quant active managers strive for as many independent active bets as they can come up with. They maximize their IR by increasing the number of their independent forecasts, but their information coefficient with respect to each forecast is low because they do top-down, macro analysis with many, many bets, instead of bottom-up micro analysis.

---

[11] We use a logarithmic scale in order to be able to graph the number of active bets in the portfolio versus the increase in the information coefficient.

Conversely, private equity managers apply the opposite technique. Each private equity fund has only 10 to 25 names in the portfolio. In fact, the portfolios are frequently as concentrated as only 10 to 15 independent bets. This means that private equity managers have very low breadth. However, they conduct tremendous research and due diligence on the individual companies that they put into their funds. Their advantage is a very high information coefficient associated with every bet they make.

Last, the transfer coefficient has implications for the whole alternatives space. Generally, alternative investing has been perceived to add value by being less constrained than traditional long-only products. This allows alternative managers to eschew the long-only constraint, build concentrated portfolios with very large active positions, or run market-neutral programs to eliminate market risk. However, the TC is a double-edged sword. It is not costless to borrow and short stocks, for example. Borrowing costs, covering of short positions, short rebates, and the like mean that there is still an erosion of the TC for alternative asset products. On the whole, there is a net improvement in the TC for alternative assets, but the construction of alternative products must still abide by the Fundamental Law of Active Management.

References

Anson, M. 2001. Hedge fund incentive fees and the free option. *Journal of Alternative Investments* (Fall).

Anson, M. 2004a. Strategic versus tactical asset allocation: Beta drivers vs. alpha drivers. *Journal of Portfolio Management* (Winter): 8–22.

Anson, M. 2004b. Thinking outside the benchmark. *Journal of Portfolio Management* (30th Anniversary Issue): 104–112.

Anson, M. 2006. *The handbook of alternative assets*. 2nd ed. Hoboken, NJ: John Wiley & Sons.

Anson, M. 2007. Business models in asset management part II. *Journal of Investing* (December).

Arnott, R., J. Hsu, and P. Moore. 2005. Fundamental indexation. *Financial Analysts Journal* 61, no. 2 (March/April): 83–99.

Black, F., and M. Scholes. 1973. The pricing of options and corporate liabilities. *Journal of Political Economy* 81 (May–June): 637–654.

Brown, N., and R. de Figueiredo. 2007. Hedge funds and the active management industry. *Citigroup Alternative Investments Journal* (Winter): 2–11.

Clarke, R., H. de Silva, and S. Thorley. 2002. Portfolio constraints and the fundamental law of active management. *Financial Analysts Journal* 58, no. 5 (September/October): 48–66.

Fama, E., and K. French. 1992. The cross-section of expected stock returns. *Journal of Finance* 47 (2): 427–465.

Fama, E., and K. French. 1993. Common risk factors in the returns on stocks and bonds. *Journal of Financial Economics* 33 (1): 3–56.

Fama, E., and K. French. 1996. Multifactor explanations of asset pricing anomalies. *Journal of Finance* 51.

Fung, W., and D. Hsieh. 1997. Empirical characteristics of dynamic trading strategies: The case of hedge funds. *Review of Financial Studies* 10, no. 2 (April): 275–302.

Fung, W., and D. Hsieh. 2002. Asset-based style factors for hedge funds. *Financial Analysts Journal* 58, no. 5 (September/October).

Fung, W., and D. Hsieh. 2003. The risk in hedge fund strategies: Alternative alphas and alternative betas. In *The New Generation of Risk Management for Hedge Funds and Private Equity Investment*, ed. Lars Jaeger. London: Euromoney Books.

Gastineau, L. 2008. The short side of 130/30 investing for the conservative portfolio manager. *Journal of Portfolio Management* 34, no. 2 (Summer): 39–52.

Grinold, R., and R. Kahn. 1999. *Active portfolio management*. 2nd rev. ed. New York: McGraw-Hill.

Hill, J. 2006. Alpha as a net zero sum game. *Journal of Portfolio Management* 32, no. 4 (Summer).

Jaeger, L. 2005. Factor modelling and benchmarking of hedge funds: Can passive investments in hedge fund strategies deliver? Working paper, Partners Group (November 7).

Leibowitz, M. 2005. Alpha hunters and beta grazers. *Financial Analysts Journal* 61, no. 5 (September/October).

Schoenfeld, S. 2006. Are alternatively weighted indexes worth their weight? White paper, Northern Trust (April).

Weisman, A. 2002. Informationless investing and hedge fund performance measurement bias. *Journal of Portfolio Management* (Summer).

Part II
Real Estate

6

Real Estate Investment Trusts

INTRODUCTION

As we discussed in Chapter 1, real estate was the original asset class. This was the primary way that wealth was accumulated, measured, and invested in days gone by. Noblemen and noblewomen such as kings, queens, dukes, and their relatives denominated their wealth in the land that they held. As the industrial revolution spread around the world, corporations, partnerships, and other commercial ventures became the new way to accumulate and measure wealth. Stocks and bonds became the alternatives to real estate, so much so that real estate is now considered an alternative to stocks and bonds.

More specifically, we include real estate in our discussion of alternative assets for three reasons:

1. First, real estate is an overlooked asset class. Many investors, even sophisticated investors, have only a small or no allocation at all to real estate.
2. Real estate provides a different systematic risk premium exposure from stocks and bonds. This means that it is a useful asset class for strategic asset allocation.
3. As a corollary to the preceding point, real estate is a tangible asset class (the "real" in real estate). As a result, it derives a return stream that is different from the cash flows generated by a corporation.

We begin our real estate discussion with real estate investment trusts (REITs). These are a simple and liquid way to bring real estate into an investor's portfolio.

REITs are stocks listed on major stock exchanges that represent an interest in an underlying pool of real estate properties. The first REIT was invented in the United States in 1961. REITs invest in the equity and/or mortgages of office, retail, industrial, apartment, housing, shopping center, hotel, and leisure properties. Effectively, REITs operate much in the same fashion as mutual funds. They pool investment capital from many small investors, and invest the larger collective pool in real estate properties that would not be available to the small investor.

The key advantage of REITs is that they provide access to an illiquid asset class for investors who would not otherwise invest in real property. For now, consider an investment in a REIT as providing a broad exposure to real estate properties that the investor would not otherwise be able to obtain.

ADVANTAGES OF REITs

The benefits of REITs are several. One of the biggest advantages is the pass-through tax status of a REIT. Subject to the several requirements discussed later, a REIT avoids double taxation that comes with paying taxes at both the corporate and individual levels and instead is able to avoid corporate income taxation by passing all of its income and capital gains to its shareholders (where the distributions may be subject to taxation at the individual level).

A second advantage is that investors in REITs can freely trade the shares of a REIT (e.g. in the United States they are traded on the New York, American, or NASDAQ stock markets), making REIT investing both convenient and liquid. Consequently, an investor can add to or trim her exposure to real estate quickly and easily through REITs. In fact, a REIT is a marginable security, which means that investors can typically borrow from their broker (up to 50%) to purchase shares in a REIT.

Another advantage of REITs is in facilitating asset allocation. This comes at two levels. First, an investor can use REITs as part of a strategic asset allocation to real estate as an asset class. Second, investors can use tactical asset allocation by tilting their real property exposure to certain parts of the real estate market. For example, an investor can choose different categories of REITs such as office building REITs, health care REITs, shopping center REITs, apartment REITs, and so on. Exhibit 6.1 demonstrates the size and diversity of the REIT market as represented by the NAREIT index. Exhibit 6.1 represents the market as of May 2009, which is a point of time when the REIT market had declined over 40% through 2008 and into 2009.

A fourth benefit of REITs is the professional asset management of real estate properties by the REIT executives. These are real estate professionals who know how to acquire, finance, develop, renovate, and negotiate lease agreements with respect to real estate properties to get the most return for their shareholders.

A fifth advantage is that REITs provide a consistent dividend yield for their shareholders. This is particularly important for retirees and others living on a fixed income. Having a dependable cash flow stream is a necessity to pay bills, medical expenses, and so on. Exhibit 6.2 shows the dividend yields for most categories of REITs. The cash flows from REITS can be quite generous. For example, the categories of Healthcare, Industrial, and Residential all had dividend yields over 7% as of May 2009.

Last, REITs are also overseen by an independent board of directors that is charged with seeing to the best interests of the REIT's shareholders. This provides a level of corporate governance protection similar to that employed for other public companies.

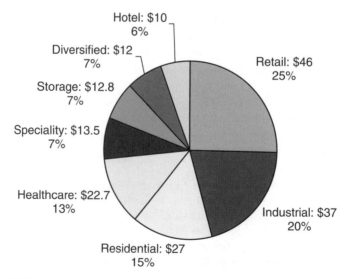

Exhibit 6.1 The NAREIT market (in $ billions), 2009

Source: FTSE Group and National Association of Real Estate Investment Trusts at www.reit.com, May 2009.

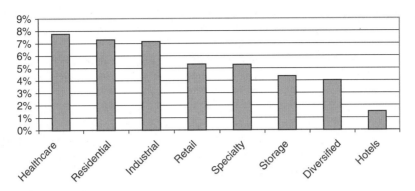

Exhibit 6.2   REIT annual yields as of 2008

Source: FTSE Group and National Association of Real Estate Investment Trusts at www.reit.com, May 2009.

DISADVANTAGES OF REITs

The single biggest disadvantage of REITs comes from being listed on a stock exchange or on NASDAQ. As a result, their prices pick up some of the systematic risk associated with the broader stock market. This reduces their diversification benefits, as an investor in a REIT obtains both real estate and stock market exposure. Therefore, REITs are less of a pure play in real estate. They are an imperfect substitute or proxy for direct real estate investing.

Most REITs fall into the capitalization range of $500 million to $5 billion—a range typically associated with small-cap stocks and the smaller half of mid-cap stocks. Therefore, they are more highly correlated with small-cap stocks than with large-cap stocks. This is demonstrated later in this chapter where REITs' correlation coefficient with small-cap stocks is 0.50, much higher than with large-cap stocks.

Using data from later in this chapter we can calculate the beta of REITs with the Russell 2000 small-cap stock index:

$$\text{Beta} = \text{Corr}_{(\text{REITs, RU2000})} \times \sigma_{\text{REITs}}/\sigma_{\text{RU2000}}$$
$$\text{Beta} = 0.68 \times 0.2354/0.2123 = 0.75$$

The size of the beta is relatively large, indicating that there is still a substantial amount of stock market risk embedded within REITs, which tends to reduce some of their diversification benefit.

Another disadvantage of REITs is that their dividend distributions are taxed at ordinary income rates. This is in contrast to dividends from most other public companies that are eligible for a 15% qualified dividend tax rate. The reason is that a REIT is a pass-through investment pool of underlying real estate properties. As a result the dividend tax advantages that apply to most public companies are not extended to REITs. Simply, REITs are less tax efficient for high-tax-bracket investors.

DIFFERENT TYPES OF REITs

REITs can differ by investment philosophy, type of structure, and the markets in which they invest.

Investment philosophy

There are three basic investment types of REITs: equity REITS, mortgage REITs, and hybrid REITs.

An **equity REIT** uses the pooled capital from investors to purchase property directly. The REIT is the equity owner of the properties underlying the REIT portfolio. An equity REIT will also manage, renovate, and develop real estate properties. An equity REIT produces revenue for its investors from the rental and lease payments it receives as the landlord of the properties it owns. An equity REIT also benefits from the appreciation in value of the properties that it owns as well as an increase in rents. In fact, one of the benefits of equity REITs is that their rental and lease receipts tend to increase along with inflation, making REITs a potential hedge against inflation.

A **mortgage REIT** derives its value from financing the purchase of real estate properties. A mortgage REIT invests in loans that are used to purchase real estate such as mortgages, mortgage-backed securities, subprime loans (we will have more to say about this later), or some other securitization of real property values. Mortgage REITs are lenders to owners, developers, and purchasers of real estate. Pure mortgage REITs, however, do not own any real estate property directly. They generate returns for their shareholders from the interest earned on the financing they provide.

Hybrid REITs invest in both the equity interests and the debt interests of real estate properties. They provide lending for the acquisition and development of real estate properties as well as purchase and develop real estate properties themselves. Some hybrid REITs are explicit as to the amount of equity ownership and mortgage financing they may provide (e.g. a 50–50 split). Other hybrid REITs are flexible as to the amount of ownership versus financing they may provide. As the name implies, hybrids can do an unlimited combination of real estate investing and mortgage financing.

REIT structures

There are many different ways a REIT can be structured, depending on the type of properties acquired or financed.

A **single-property REIT** accumulates capital to purchase a single large property. Rockefeller Center in New York City is a very large collection of office buildings, shopping promenades, and dining establishments grouped together in the center of Manhattan. The mortgage of the complex used to be owned by a single-property REIT.

A **finite life REIT** establishes a termination date by which the REIT will sell its underlying properties and wind up its affairs. The typical term is eight to 15 years. This provides sufficient time for the REIT manager, for example, to acquire the properties, renovate them, replace the existing tenants, increase the rents, and ultimately increase the value of the underlying properties upon their sale to new investors.

A **dedicated REIT** is typically established to invest in: (1) one type of property only (e.g. retail strip malls); (2) a single development (e.g. LaSalle Partners developed office buildings); or (3) a geographic region (e.g. Washington, D.C., office buildings). Another development in the dedicated REIT is the health care REIT. These are REITs that specialize in the purchase and sale/leaseback of health care facilities such as nursing homes, hospitals, and outpatient facilities. Dedicated REITs add value by providing a deep specialized knowledge of a small slice of the real estate market. However, they are often more risky because of the narrow focus of their investment universe.

An **umbrella partnership REIT** (an **UPREIT**) is a REIT where the REIT itself does not own any real estate properties directly but rather holds the properties in an operating partnership. The motivation for the UPREIT is to permit real estate investors to contribute properties in exchange for ownership in a manner such that they can defer built-in capital gains that would have to be recognized if the appreciated real estate properties were contributed directly in exchange for the REIT's stock. The UPREIT has been used since 1992. All of the properties are held through an operating partnership. Investment bankers like the UPREIT structure because it is a way for the REIT to reach a minimum level of capitalization before accessing the public capital markets. Exhibit 6.3 shows the structure of an UPREIT.

In contrast to an UPREIT is a **Down-REIT**. A Down-REIT is also driven by tax consequences. They were created as a way for property owners to contribute property to a REIT in exchange for stock as a nontaxable exchange of value. Down-REITs were created with the same technology that established UPREITs. These vehicles were created out of older REITs as a way to provide growth opportunities. In a Down-REIT, an older REIT forms a subsidiary partnership that holds the existing real estate assets. This subsidiary REIT then allows in new partners who contribute new properties for an equity stake in the more diversified REIT. Effectively, in a Down-REIT, the REIT downsteams its assets into a new partnership to which other partners can contribute real estate properties in exchange for stock in the Down-REIT. Exhibit 6.4 shows the structure for a Down-REIT.

Markets in which REITs invest

REITs also differ in terms of the markets in which they invest their capital. The primary distinction of markets is the property type (e.g. office, retail, industrial). REITs can also differ by property type subcategories such as by concentrating on upscale properties. The geographic region, or regions, of focus (if any) is another common distinction—along with other potential distinctions such as the typical sizes of portfolio investments.

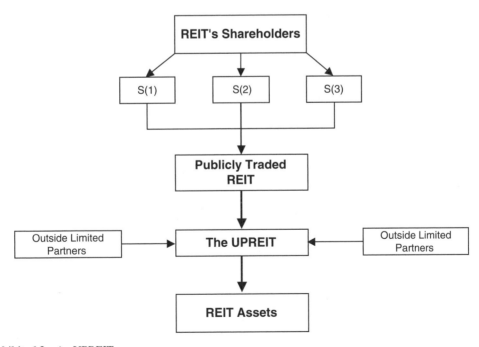

Exhibit 6.3 An UPREIT

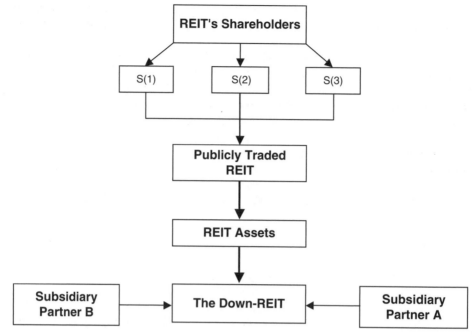

Exhibit 6.4   A down-REIT

REIT RULES

The main advantage of a REIT is its ability to pass on income and capital gains directly to its investors without suffering any tax at the corporate REIT level. However, there are many rules and regulations that must be obeyed for a REIT to obtain this tax-advantaged status.

Corporate structure

To be structured as a REIT, the following six rules apply:

1. It must be organized as a corporation, a trust, or an association.
2. It must be managed by one or more trustees or directors.
3. Its shares must be transferable, usually accomplished by listing the REIT shares publicly on an exchange.
4. It cannot be a financial institution or an insurance company.
5. It must be owned by 100 or more persons.
6. No more than 50% of the REIT's shares can be owned by five or fewer persons—this must be in the REIT organizational documents as a preventive measure against concentrated ownership.

Tax structure

To ensure the favorable tax status as a REIT, the following five rules apply:

1. At least 75% of the REIT's assets must be invested in (1) real estate assets, (2) cash and cash equivalents, (3) government securities, or (4) temporary investments (up to one year) while the REIT searches for new properties to purchase with its investment capital.

2. The remaining 25% of the REIT's assets may be held in the securities of other issuers, but they cannot exceed 5% of the total assets of the issuer or 10% of the total outstanding voting shares of the issuer.

3. At least 75% of the REIT's gross income must come from revenue related to real estate: (1) rents from real property, (2) interest from real estate and mortgage loans, (3) gains from the sale of real property, (4) dividends from ownership of other REIT shares, (5) gains from the sale of other REIT shares, (6) tax abatements from owning real property, (7) income from foreclosure of properties, and (8) commitment fees from investing in real property.

4. As a second income test, at least 95% of the REIT's income must come from: (1) sources that qualify for the 75% test, (2) dividends and interest, and (3) gains from the sale of stock or securities.

5. A REIT must distribute annually to its shareholders at least 95% of its taxable income (excluding capital gains). This test is required to prevent a REIT from being a vehicle for income accumulation.

If a REIT meets these tests, then it receives pass-through tax status where the REIT is not taxed on any gains and income passed through to its shareholders (but which are then potentially taxed at the shareholder level). Income not passed through to shareholders in the form of a distribution (i.e., retained by the REIT) is subject to tax at the corporate (REIT) level.

REIT distributions of income are generally taxed as dividends to the REIT shareholders. But portions of a REIT's distributions that are identified as long-term capital gains resulting from the sale of real estate properties are taxed as long-term capital gains to the REIT shareholders.

ECONOMICS OF REITs

This section discusses the economic benefits of REITs compared to other asset classes. Exhibit 6.5 shows the returns to the S&P REIT index for the past 12 years (since inception), including the disastrous years of 2007 and 2008. The S&P REIT index contains 100 publicly traded REIT stocks

Exhibit 6.5   Comparative financial performance for REITs

	SPREIT	RIY1000	RTY2000	SBHYCP	10-Year T-Bond	1-Year T-Bill	Inflation
2008	−37.95%	−37.60%	−33.80%	−24.68%	22.81%	2.30%	0.10%
2007	−16.21	5.78	−1.51	1.91	9.60	3.28	4.10
2006	35.03	15.38	18.34	11.72	2.04	5.00	2.50
2005	11.18	6.21	4.56	2.07	6.61	4.42	3.40
2004	30.98	11.25	18.28	10.51	7.78	2.79	3.30
2003	34.77	29.55	46.90	29.36	3.29	1.21	1.90
2002	4.12	−21.52	−20.34	−0.58	16.06	1.19	2.40
2001	13.82	−12.22	2.52	6.92	4.53	2.03	1.60
2000	27.97	−7.71	−2.87	−4.41	18.73	5.47	3.40
1999	−5.57	20.77	21.11	0.84	−8.98	6.14	2.70
1998	−19.41	26.56	−2.25	4.42	12.93	4.58	1.60
1997	13.41	32.28	22.06	13.10	14.45	5.62	1.70
Average	7.68%	5.73%	6.08%	4.27%	9.15%	3.67%	2.39%
Std. Dev.	23.54%	21.70%	21.23%	12.68%	8.59%	1.76%	1.09%
Sharpe	0.17	0.09	0.11	0.04	0.62		

Source: Bloomberg Finance, L.P.

higher the value
better it will

across all of the sectors of REITs listed in Exhibit 6.1. Consequently, it is a well-diversified portfolio of REITs, as well as a good snapshot into the performance of the real estate market generally.

Exhibit 6.5 also contains the average return, standard deviation, and Sharpe ratio for the S&P REIT index (SPREIT) as well as comparative returns for large-cap and small cap stocks (the Russell 1000 and Russell 2000 stock indexes), high yield bonds (the Salomon Smith Barney Cash Pay High Yield index, SBHYCP), 10-year U.S. Treasury bonds, 1-year Treasury bills (a measure of cash returns), and the annual inflation rate for the past 12 years. Keep in mind that 2008 was a brutal year for most asset classes. Every asset class that had some amount of risk attached to it lost value in 2008. The safest of the safe, U.S. Treasury bonds, soared in 2008 while other asset classes deteriorated.

Exhibit 6.5 indicates that the Sharpe ratio, a measure of risk-adjusted returns, is higher for REITs than for large-cap or small-cap stocks, and also is larger than for high-yield bonds. U.S. Treasury bonds have the highest Sharpe ratio, and this is due to their higher return and lower volatility. In fact, 10-year Treasury bonds were the best-performing asset class over this time period. Part of this is due to the flight to safety during the global market meltdown of 2008 when the total return soared to almost 23% as well as the safe haven they provided after the popping of the tech bubble and the recession years of 2001–2002. We do not calculate a Sharpe ratio for U.S. Treasury bills because this is the risk-free rate that we use as part of the Sharpe ratio calculation for the other asset classes.

During this time period, the average return to REITs was 200 basis points higher than for large-cap stocks, 160 basis points higher for small-cap stocks, almost 340 basis points higher than for high-yield bonds, and even 200 basis points higher than for U.S. Treasury bonds, despite the phenomenal year for Treasury bonds in 2008. Clearly, during the period 1997–2008, REITs delivered a favorable return premium over stocks and bonds. However, this extra return did come with extra risk, as the volatility for REITs was higher than for any other asset class. Still, the extra return from REITs offset this extra risk in that the Sharpe ratio is higher compared to stocks and high-yield bonds. In summary, REITs provided a good total return for investors but not without some additional risk.

However, the risk associated with real estate hit with a vengeance starting in May 2007. At that time, a meltdown in the subprime mortgage market sent a ripple effect—more closely resembling a tsunami—through the financial markets. In its wake, the subprime meltdown severely eroded real estate values across the United States. Exhibit 6.6 shows the recent declines in the S&P REIT index. At its nadir, this index was down 33 percent year over year before recovering slightly as 2008 wore on. However, the message is clear: real estate investing is subject to the risk of liquidity and credit events.[1] Interestingly, although the REIT declines originated from the problems in the subprime mortgage market, most of the REITs in the S&P REIT index had little or no direct involvement with the subprime market.

Another way to gauge the risk and return associated with investing in REITs is to use a histogram of returns. This concept is reviewed in Appendix B on risk and return measures where we produce a histogram for a sample of returns associated with equity long/short hedge fund managers. A histogram is a way of mapping returns with the frequency of their occurrence. It paints a picture of the return stream associated with an asset class. In fact, if we had many thousands of data points to plot, the histogram would, in fact, produce a smooth curve that we could label a probability distribution from which we could draw inferences about the probability of observing a return that is a designated number of standard deviations away from the mean (assuming that returns were and would continue to be generated by the same process).

---

[1] From its high point in February 2007 through its low point in March 2009, the S&P REIT index lost almost 77% of its value, a dramatic decline for any asset class.

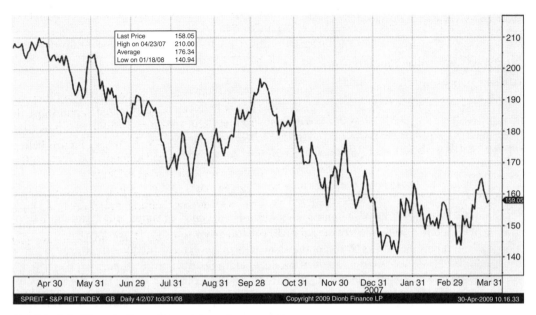

Exhibit 6.6 The subprime crisis and the real estate market

Source: Bloomberg Finance, L.P.

Exhibit 6.7 provides a histogram for the monthly returns to the S&P REIT index over the time period 1997 to May 2009. This 12½-year period provides us with enough data to draw some conclusions, but not enough observations to produce a full probability distribution. First, we can see that the mass of the distribution is centered around the return range of −2% to 4%. However, the average monthly return is much lower, only 0.25%, which reflects the fact that there is a wide dispersion of monthly returns. This is confirmed by our estimate of the standard deviation of 5.58% per month, resulting in a monthly Sharpe ratio of 0.02.

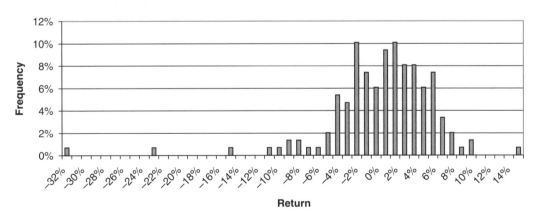

Exhibit 6.7 Frequency distribution for monthly return to REITs

Note: Average 0.25%; Std. dev. 5.58%; Sharpe ratio 0.02; Skew −1.91; Kurtosis 8.89

Source: Bloomberg Finance, L.P.

Exhibit 6.8   Correlation analysis: 1997–2008

	S&P REIT	RU1000	RU2000	SBHYCP	10-Year T-Bond	1-Year T-Bill	Inflation
S&P REIT	1.00						
RU1000	0.38	1.00					
RU2000	0.68	0.84	1.00				
SBHYCP	0.72	0.77	0.90	1.00			
10-Year T-bond	−0.32	−0.53	−0.68	−0.52	1.00		
1-Year T-bill	0.03	0.45	0.19	−0.07	−0.23	1.00	
Inflation	0.38	0.25	0.25	0.24	−0.30	0.26	1.00

Source: Bloomberg Finance, L.P.

Exhibit 6.7 also shows the skew and excess kurtosis[2] of the distribution (the third and fourth moment of the return distribution) for the S&P REIT index. These statistics are reviewed in Appendix B on risk and return measures. To recap, the skew tells us how the distribution of returns is tilted or leans in one direction. Asset classes that produce return distributions with positive skew are to be favored, as this indicates a bias to the upside. Kurtosis is a method to measure the fatness of the tails of the distribution. Return distributions that have large positive measures of kurtosis are called "leptokurtic" and have exposure to large outlier events that deviate greatly from the mean return.

Exhibit 6.7 shows a large negative skew of 1.91. This demonstrates a bias toward the downside—that there is a larger number of extreme negative returns than extreme positive returns. The value of kurtosis is a positive 8.89. This is the value measured compared to a normal distribution. This tells us that REITs have more exposure to outlier events than what would be predicted by a normal distribution. The combination of a large negative skew value and a large value of kurtosis demonstrates that REITs are exposed to large downside risks. This is a way of saying that REITs produce a return stream with a large or fat downside tail. The results in Exhibit 6.7 are skewed themselves because they are greatly influenced by the returns achieved by REITs in 2008, which were distinctly negative, and in many cases the negative monthly return was very large.

Last, Exhibit 6.8 reviews the portfolio diversification properties of REITs. As we discussed earlier, REITs provide both good access to real estate and diversification. We test the diversification abilities of REITs by running a correlation analysis compared to other major asset classes. The results are in Exhibit 6.8.

When two asset classes have a correlation less than 1.0 there is the ability to diversify the investor's portfolio by blending the two asset classes together in the portfolio. A correlation below zero indicates that the two asset classes tend to move in the opposite direction from one another—when the first asset class is up, the second is down and vice versa. This is an extreme example of diversification—return streams that do not track together but go their different ways to produce a portfolio that will tend to exhibit stability at all points of the business cycle.

Exhibit 6.8 indicates that REITs offer very good diversification properties to large-cap stocks, Treasury bonds, and T-bills. In fact, the correlation between REITs and Treasury bonds is negative, indicating excellent diversification potential. With respect to stocks, REITs have a much lower correlation to large-cap stocks than to small-cap stocks. This is not surprising since most REITs

---

[2] The normal distribution has a kurtosis value of 3. Excess kurtosis = kurtosis − 3; therefore, the normal distribution has an excess kurtosis value of zero. For simplicity, kurtosis is used throughout this chapter to mean excess kurtosis.

have a market capitalization range closer to small-cap stocks than large-cap stocks. It is rare for a REIT to have a large-cap market capitalization (more than $10 billion). More precisely, there are only 14 REITs in the S&P 500 index, which contains the stocks which are among the largest in the United States. These 14 REITs have an average market capitalization of only $13 billion. Also, REITs have the highest correlation with high-yield bonds. This reflects the credit risk that can creep into the REIT market that we discussed previously. During the credit and liquidity meltdown of 2008, REITs and high-yield bonds declined in value precipitously.

In summary, most REITs would be classified as small- to mid-cap rather than large-cap. Therefore, it is not surprising that the S&P REIT index would have moderately high correlation (0.68) to the small-cap Russell 2000 stock index and near zero correlation with the large-cap-dominated Russell 1000 stock index.

In the last row, we look at the correlation of REITs with the U.S. inflation rate. REITs are often considered to be a hedge against inflation. The reason is that as inflation rises, REIT managers can raise the lease rates to keep pace. Although there is a lag between inflation and higher lease rates, REITs would appear able to maintain some pace with inflation. However, Exhibit 6.8 shows a positive correlation coefficient of 0.38 with inflation. This demonstrates a good ability of REITs to hedge against inflation.

REITs tend to be a good hedge against inflation for two reasons. First, rental/lease payments are typically adjusted upward during times of inflation. Thus, properties with shorter term leases such as multifamily housing or even hotels can adjust their rental rates quickly in line with inflation. For multiyear commercial leases, there is often a clause to adjust the rent upward over the course of the lease for increases in inflation. Second, REIT values tend to increase during periods of inflation as investors shift their portfolios away from financial assets to real assets. However, there is a negative relationship between REIT dividend yields and inflation. The reason is that dividends often lag increases in lease rates and lease rates react to inflation. As a result, it may take one or two periods to adjust the dividends associated with a REIT after lease rates have already been adjusted. Exhibit 6.9 is a chart comparing dividend yields from REITs and the rate of inflation.[3]

Recent academic research continues to support the notion that REITs are good inflation-hedging assets. Simpson, Ramchander, and Webb reviewed prior studies that did not find a positive relationship between REITs and inflation and concluded that there is an asymmetric response of REIT returns to inflation.[4] Specifically, they proposed that the reason REITs may be potentially negatively correlated with inflation is that REIT returns increase in periods of both rising and declining inflation. They found that the negative correlation between REIT values and declining inflation leads to an overall negative correlation between REITs and inflation. Similarly, Chatrah and Liang found that while REIT returns may be negatively correlated with inflation over small periods of time, REITs provide a good inflation hedge over the long run.[5]

In summary, REITs have demonstrated very good diversification potential with stocks, bonds, and T-bills. In addition, REITs may be positively correlated with the inflation rate, especially in the long run, and therefore may possess some ability to retain real value as inflation creeps ahead. Combining these correlations with the favorable Sharpe ratio from Exhibit 6.5, it is clear why REITs are a popular investment choice for many investors.

---

[3] See www.reit.com, "REITs and the Mechanics of Inflation Hedging," 2008.

[4] See Marc Simpson, Sanjay Ramchander, and James Webb, "The Asymmetric Response of Equity REIT Returns to Inflation," *Journal of Real Estate Finance and Economics* 34, no. 4 (2007).

[5] See Arjun Chatrah and Youguo Liang, "REITs and Inflation: A Long Run Perspective," *Journal of Real Estate Research* (1999).

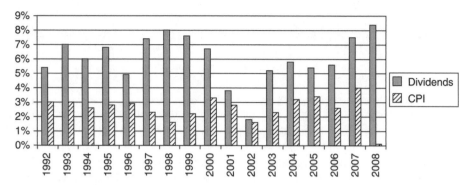

Exhibit 6.9   REIT dividends and CPI correlation = −0.13

Source: FTSE Group and National Association of Real Estate Investment Trusts at www.reit.com, May 2009.

CONCLUSION

This chapter has introduced the reader to REITs: the simplest way to access the real estate market. REITs are a convenient and liquid way to add real property exposure to a diversified portfolio. While REITs do contain some systematic risk, particularly associated with small-cap stocks, there is still plenty of diversification potential to make REITs a legitimate asset class choice. However, we end on a cautionary note. The recent financial crisis in general and the subprime mortgage market crisis in particular had a significant and severe impact on the value of REITs through the end of 2008. Into the beginning of 2009, REITs tended to experience typical declines of two-thirds or more from their highs of early 2007. These extreme returns are substantially affecting historical average returns, volatilities, and correlations—and making future REIT return behavior even more difficult to predict.

7

Introduction to NCREIF and the NCREIF Indexes

INTRODUCTION

This chapter serves as an introduction to the National Council of Real Estate Investment Fiduciaries (NCREIF) and its indexes. NCREIF is a not-for-profit industry association that was founded in 1982 to provide some guidance into the process of making direct real estate investments. Its members include pension funds, real estate investment professionals, appraisers, academics, and consultants.

The goals of NCREIF are straightforward:

- Collect and validate real estate performance data from its members.
- Calculate and publish performance indexes.
- Promote good standards in the real estate industry.
- Foster and support independent research on the real estate industry.
- Publish white papers and other educational materials for the real estate industry.

Perhaps the most important contribution of NCREIF is that it collects data regarding property values from its members and constructs an index of real estate values, the **NCREIF Property Index (NPI)**, based on the voluntary reporting of its members. We explore in this chapter the nature of the NPI, how it is constructed, and some of the challenges in using it as a performance indicator of real estate values.

THE NCREIF PROPERTY INDEX (NPI)

One of the key benefits of NCREIF is the development and publication of the NPI and a set of subindexes for direct real estate investing. Direct real estate equity investing involves direct property ownership as opposed to ownership of publicly traded claims to real estate. As the reader might imagine, it is very hard to gather pricing and other data for illiquid assets such as real properties that change hands infrequently. Consequently, one requirement for NCREIF membership is that members regularly share information on their real estate portfolios.

Every quarter, members of NCREIF submit their data about the real estate properties that they own to support the computation of the NPI. NCREIF aggregates this information from its members on an extremely confidential basis and builds indexes based on the member data. It then publishes these indexes for use by its members and the real estate industry.

The NPI is a proxy for the performance of direct investments in real property. More specifically, it provides the returns for an institutional-grade real estate portfolio held by large U.S. investors. Real estate properties are typically managed by investment fiduciaries on behalf of large institutional investors in the United States such as endowments, foundations, pension funds, and high-net-worth investors. As of the first quarter of 2009, the NPI had over 6,071 properties in the index worth more than $268 billion.

The NPI was created as a way to measure the performance of income-producing real properties. It is the primary benchmark used by institutional investors to assess the performance of their portfolios of real estate holdings. In addition, it can be used to compare the performance of real estate to other asset classes such as stocks, bonds, credit, and so on. As a result, the NPI is often used in asset allocation studies, diversification analysis, and portfolio construction.

Exhibit 7.1 shows the breakdown of the types of properties underlying the NPI. Not surprisingly, commercial office properties is the largest category, with the remainder of the index being almost equally split between apartments (sometimes called multifamily housing), retail, and industrial properties. These properties are best described as:

- *Offices:* Class A office buildings are the top-tier office buildings in major metropolitan centers around the United States where one would expect to find the headquarters and satellite offices of Fortune 1000 public companies in the United States as well as private companies in the asset management business, consulting, legal, accounting, engineering, and other professions. Class A office buildings are considered the least risky in the office market with prime locations, stable tenants, strong property management, and long leases.
- *Apartments:* Sometimes called multifamily housing, these are complexes of multiple-tenant properties. They can be located in urban areas or in the suburbs and cater to the working professionals who are earlier in their career and have not accumulated enough savings to purchase a first home. Rents and income tend to be high, but this is also a more volatile part of the real estate market.
- *Retail:* These are the commercial properties in major and regional shopping centers, strip malls, outlet malls, and so on.
- *Industrial:* These properties include warehouses, manufacturing facilities, office parks, and other productive facilities. They are a good addition to the front-office Class A buildings contained in the office sector.
- *Hotels:* These include luxury, budget, and midpriced hotels as well as other leisure properties. Hotels are a new addition to the NPI.

Collectively, these types of properties form the core of a real estate portfolio. We discuss the concept of core versus noncore properties in greater detail in the next chapter, but for the purposes of this chapter core refers to those property types that most institutional investors use as their basic real estate portfolios.

Exhibit 7.2 shows the returns, averages, standard deviations, and Sharpe ratios for the NPI composite and its four divisions of Apartments, Offices, Retail, and Industrial. We can see that the Apartments division of the NPI had the highest Sharpe ratio because it has the highest average or expected return and the lowest standard deviation.

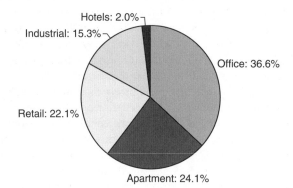

Exhibit 7.1   The components of the NPI (second quarter, 2009)
Source: NCREIF, www.ncreif.com.

Exhibit 7.2   NCREIF and its four divisions

	NCREIF Composite	NCREIF Apartments	NCREIF Office	NCREIF Retail	NCREIF Industrial
1990	2.29%	5.79%	−1.06%	5.96%	1.96%
1991	−5.59	−1.36	−11.44	−1.85	−3.86
1992	−4.26	1.72	−8.05	−2.25	−4.47
1993	1.38	8.72	−3.95	4.84	−0.77
1994	6.38	12.07	3.92	6.01	7.63
1995	7.53	11.66	7.18	3.98	12.30
1996	10.30	11.54	13.56	4.85	13.57
1997	13.90	12.90	17.87	8.53	15.94
1998	16.25	14.12	19.62	12.91	15.86
1999	11.36	11.73	12.22	9.55	11.65
2000	12.25	12.99	14.11	7.76	14.02
2001	7.28	9.37	6.20	6.74	9.30
2002	6.75	8.76	2.78	13.74	6.70
2003	9.00	8.90	5.67	17.15	8.23
2004	14.49	13.04	12.02	22.95	12.07
2005	20.06	21.15	19.46	19.98	20.31
2006	16.60	14.63	19.16	13.35	16.96
2007	15.85	11.36	20.51	13.51	14.95
2008	−14.70	−16.40	−16.30	−9.50	−14.10
Average	7.74%	9.09%	7.03%	8.33%	8.33%
Std. Dev.	8.79%	7.84%	11.14%	7.89%	8.88%
Sharpe Ratio	0.47	0.70	0.31	0.60	0.53

Source: NCREIF, www.ncreif.com.

Conversely, we can see that the Offices sector had the lowest average return and the highest volatility. Offices is the largest segment of the NPI, so its lower return influences the total return for the NPI. The lower return is due to two factors. First, the business tenants in the office sector tend to have more sophisticated negotiating clout in their lease negotiations, which can lead to lower property values. Second, the office sector is much more affected by the up-and-down movement of the economy. For example, in the recession of 1991 to 1992 as well as after the popping of the tech bubble in 2002, the Offices sector was impacted more negatively than any other sector. In addition, this higher exposure to the business cycle leads to greater volatility in the returns to the Offices sector, also contributing to a lower Sharpe ratio. Notice that in Exhibit 7.2, the NPI and each of its sectors showed positive returns in 2007 while the REIT returns we displayed in the prior chapter showed negative returns for 2007. This reflects the fact that real estate is an illiquid asset class and generally the returns to the real estate market will lag those of the current market environment. REITs, in contrast, because they are publicly listed and traded, react much more quickly to market events.

Exhibit 7.3 shows the allocation of real estate properties in the NPI classified by region. The higher weights to the West and the East demonstrate where the population centers are in the United States. The Midwest and the East have been shrinking over the past two decades as the South and the West grow not only in population, but also as centers of business development.

The NPI is calculated quarterly, which is a relatively infrequent interval compared to the daily calculations of most stock, bond, or even commodity indexes. The reason is the illiquid nature of real estate; properties simply do not turn over frequently enough to compute short-term returns using prices from transactions performed in an arm's-length manner. So how are values determined?

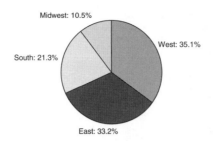

Exhibit 7.3   NPI by region (second quarter, 2009)
Source: NCREIF, www.ncreif.com.

The NPI is calculated every quarter on an "as if" basis: as if the property was purchased at the beginning of the quarter at its appraised value and sold at the end of the quarter at its end-of-quarter appraised value. The return on the index is then calculated as the change in appraised value of the real estate property plus the cash flow received for the quarter. Cash flow is calculated as the net operating income from the property less any capital expenditures. Capital expenditures include items such as new roofing, leasing commissions, tenant improvements, and new facades or lobbies that are capitalized as an asset on the balance sheet rather than expensed directly in the income statement.

The NPI is calculated on an unleveraged basis, as if the property being measured was purchased with 100% equity and no debt, so the returns are less volatile and there are no interest charges deducted. Obviously most equity positions in real estate are established with leverage, so this assumption of no leverage is unrealistic, as is discussed later. The returns to the NPI are calculated on a before-tax basis and therefore do not include income tax expense. Since the members of NCREIF are tax-exempt organizations (pension funds, endowments, and foundations), this assumption is more realistic. Finally, the returns are calculated for each individual property and then are value weighted in the index calculation.

The appraisal process

As noted earlier, because turnover of real estate properties is infrequent, the NPI is based on **appraised values**, rather than market transactions. The pension funds and other members of NCREIF report to NCREIF the value of their properties every quarter based on an estimate of their value know as an appraisal.

Appraisals are professional opinions and are a common way to estimate the market value of a real estate property. Appraisals are commonly used even in residential home purchases as part of the mortgage lending application process. For institutional investors, appraisals are performed typically once a year on real estate properties to assess the value of their real estate portfolios. These appraisals are then reported to NCREIF by its members.

Appraisals are generally based on two different methods. The first is the **comparable sales method**. In this approach, the real estate appraiser looks at sales of similar properties in the same geographic region (if not city) as the property being appraised. These actual sales prices give the appraiser an estimate of, for example, the cost (i.e. price) per square foot of similar real estate properties. The appraiser then adjusts this cost per square foot for similar property sales for the unique characteristics of the property being appraised: better parking or access, better location, newer lobby, longer-term tenants, and so on. This process has the advantage of being based on actual sales transactions. However, the accuracy of the process is lower when there is a lack of frequency of property sales, and since every property is unique it is hard to adjust a square-foot calculation value from one property to form the value of another.

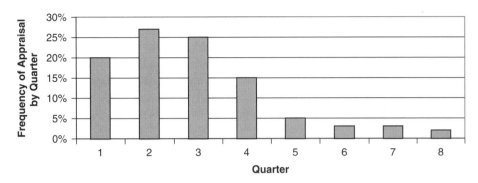

Exhibit 7.4   Frequency of appraisals in the NPI

Source: NCREIF, www.ncreif.com.

The second method is a discounted cash flow analysis. This has become the more accepted practice by real estate appraisers. In this valuation, the appraiser estimates the cash flows from a property and discounts them to form a present value to the property. In order to project cash flows, the appraiser examines the current lease agreements, looks at client turnover in the area, and considers the strength of the current property, positioning of the property, and likelihood for growth.[1] This approach has the advantage of valuing the unique characteristics of the property being appraised. However, it is subject to the usual forecasting errors of lease growth rates, holding period for the property, inflation estimates, and the like.

Problems with an appraisal-based index

A well-known criticism of the NPI is that the index tends to exhibit lower volatility than is believed to exist in the true underlying property values. This is attributed to the NPI being a smoothed index because it is based on appraisals, infrequent valuations, and other lagged information.

Although NPI is a quarterly index, NPI properties are not appraised every quarter. Most properties are valued once per year, but many are appraised only every two or even three years. The reason is that appraisals cost money and therefore there is a trade-off between the benefits of having frequent property valuations and the costs of those valuations as a drain on portfolio performance. Instead of conducting a full reevaluation of the property, property owners may simply adjust its value for any additional capital expenditures. In fact, many institutional real estate investors value their portfolio properties only when they believe that there is a significant change in value based on new leases, changing economic conditions, or the sale of a similar property close to the portfolio property.

Exhibit 7.4 demonstrates how frequently properties are appraised and reported to NCREIF. About 88% of properties in the NCREIF are valued at least once per year, while 12% are valued less frequently. Only 20% of the properties in the NCREIF are valued every quarter. In simple terms, the lack of regular frequency in property appraisals means that the NPI values lag the true market values for the properties contained in the index.

Another reason that the NPI is criticized as a smoothed index results from the nature of how appraisals are conducted. Specifically, both major appraisal types potentially contain aspects of being backward looking rather than purely forward looking.

For example, using the first method of appraising properties, the comparable sales method, the information on similar market transactions is obtained from previous sales. When it is time to do a

---

[1] Software packages such as Argus are explicitly designed for real estate appraisals based on cash flow analysis.

comparative analysis, the appraiser looks at transactions that happened over the past four quarters to estimate the current value of the real estate property being appraised. But these data are already stale and can be outdated by up to one year. Looking backward at prices does not reflect how the real estate market may have advanced (or declined) over the current quarter or year. This will cause appraised prices to lag the rise in true market value in rising real estate markets and lag the decline in true market value in declining real estate markets.

Using the second approach, the discounted cash flow method, also can lead to a lag in appraised values relative to true market values. The problem occurs when tenants in the building have negotiated their leases in prior years when market conditions were different and those revenues are used to forecast future revenues. In a rising market, the tenant lease payments may underestimate the true value of the cash flows that the property could now demand. Again, this will lead to a lag in valuations where in a rising market the property's true value will be underestimated, and in a declining market the property's true value will be overestimated.

Three impacts from smoothing

The practical effects of the smoothing process are threefold. First, the NCREIF index will lag the true values of the underlying real estate properties, both up and down. The NPI does not provide a true picture of current market value.

Second, the volatility of the index will be dampened. This issue is particularly important when using the NCREIF index for asset allocation purposes. The lower volatility will result in a more attractive risk-adjusted performance measure such as a higher Sharpe ratio. This, in turn, can undermine the portfolio construction and asset allocation process as an investor might be tempted to allocate more of the portfolio to real estate than would be allocated based on accurately measured Sharpe ratios.

Last, the slowness with which changes in market values are reflected in changes in the NPI means that the NPI does not react to changes in macroeconomic events as quickly as stock and bond indexes. This translates to lower correlation coefficients of real estate with stocks and bonds because, for example, the NPI does not react as quickly as the S&P 500 or the Salomon Brothers Broad Investment Grade Index. These underestimated correlation coefficients will exaggerate the diversification benefits to real estate and lead to an overallocation to real estate in the asset allocation process in a mistaken attempt to increase the diversification of the portfolio.

This does not mean that real estate cannot diversify a portfolio of stocks and bonds. Indeed, it can. It is just that the lagging/smoothing process of the NPI overstates the diversification value of real estate.

To demonstrate the smoothing effect, we compare the NPI with an index of REITs. As we learned in the preceding chapter, REITs are investment companies that collect investor capital and invest 75% or more of the REITs' assets in direct real estate. REITs are publicly traded, and therefore observed prices are able to react more quickly to market events than appraised values of illiquid individual properties.

Exhibit 7.5 plots the annual changes in values for REITs from the National Association of Real Estate Investment Trusts (NAREIT)[2] versus the NCREIF's NPI. We can see significant differences in the NAREIT index compared to the NPI. For example, the NAREIT index declines in 1998 and 1999 while the NPI increases.

---

[2] Information and data on the FTSE NAREIT indexes can be found at the National Association of Real Estate Investment Trusts (NAREIT) web site at www.reit.com.

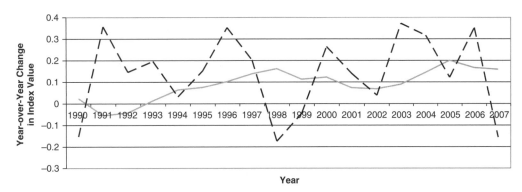

Exhibit 7.5 NPI-NCREIF (solid line, appraisal based) versus NAREIT (dashed line, REIT based)

Sources: NCREIF, www.ncreif.com; NAREIT, www.reit.com.

Could the differences observed between the indexes in Exhibit 7.5 be attributable to differences between the properties that REITs invest in versus those owned by institutional investors and reported to NCREIF? The answer is no. Real estate values took a tumble in 1998 into 1999 as a result of the Russian bond default in 1998 and the subsequent credit and liquidity crisis it spawned. The fact is that the embedded smoothing process associated with the appraisal process allowed properties contained in the NCREIF to react slowly to the declines in value. By delaying the appraisal of real estate values for up to a year (or even more), members of NCREIF could stave off reporting a significant decline in the value of their portfolios. As seen in Exhibit 7.5, the changes in values of the NPI between 1998 and 1999 are positive as opposed to the relatively large negative returns for the NAREIT index.

Unsmoothing the NPI

There are ways to correct for the smoothing process of the NPI. The simplest way to correct for the lagged effect is to use only those properties that have turned over (sold) during the most recent quarter. However, as Exhibit 7.4 indicates, only 20% of real estate properties are valued in the current quarter, mostly based on current transactions. While a transaction-based subindex of the NPI seems to be a good idea, there are simply not enough properties turning over each quarter to provide an accurate view of real estate values.

Another method based on transactions is called a **hedonic price index**.[3] In this method, a model simulates transaction prices for all untraded real estate properties based on sales of traded properties. The hedonic model examines price changes in properties that have traded and attributes those price changes to the characteristics of those properties. The results of the analysis are used to simulate prices for nontraded properties based on the characteristics of those properties. These factors include age, size, location, quality of the property, term of existing leases, region, and macroeconomic variables.

A third method to correct for the appraisal and lagging process is to use only those properties where there has been a significant effort to revalue the property. Appraisers tend to be creatures of habit. The same method is repeated over and over again until some event forces a significant revaluation of the property. This event could be a sale of a very similar property, a significant change

---

[3] See Jeremy Fisher, Dean Gatzlaff, David Geltner, and Donald Haurin, "Controlling for the Impact of Variable Liquidity in Commercial Real Estate Price Indices," *Real Estate Economics* 31, no. 2 (Summer 2003).

in macroeconomic conditions, a renovation of the property, or a significant new tenant (or loss of a tenant). These events often lead to a significant change in the value of the property, forcing an appraiser to break out of the prior process and take a fresh look at the property.

The drawback of this method is that it depends on a significant event happening that forces a wholly new appraisal of the property. Similar to the transaction-based index problem, there are simply too few events to force enough significantly new appraisals to facilitate construction of accurate indexes.

A method that is used most frequently is to unsmooth the index econometrically. Instead of being dependent on new transactions or other significant events, this method begins with the data in the NPI but transforms the prices using a model to explicitly recognize the embedded lag in the appraisal process. Another way to consider this method is that it reverse engineers the NPI to pull out the smoothing impact and reveal more of the volatility of real estate values that are hidden within the NPI. In this method, appraisal behavior is modeled as a moving average of current and prior comparable sales, a well-known method to smooth a time series of returns.

For example, one method of modeling a moving average of real estate prices is:

$$RE^*_t = \alpha RE_t + \alpha(1 - \alpha)RE_{t-1} + \alpha(1 - \alpha)^2 RE_{t-2} + \ldots \tag{7.1}$$

where

$$RE^*_t = \text{the optimal appraised value of the real estate property at time } t$$
$$RE_t, RE_{t-1}, \text{and } RE_{t-2} = \text{the real estate values at times } t, t-1, t-2, \text{ and so forth}$$
$$\alpha = \text{a parameter that captures the speed of the decay function. A decay function}$$
is simply a numeric construct that puts less weight on older valuations and more weight on more recent valuations.

Equation 7.1 expresses—in effect—a smoothed average (RE^*_t) as a function of true prices (RE_i from $i = 1$ to t). The goal is to turn the equation around so that the most recent true price (RE_t) can be expressed as a function of the smoothed averages. That way, we can estimate market values of real estate from smoothed series of prices such as appraisal indexes.

We next reduce Equation 7.1 to:

$$RE^*_t = \alpha RE_t + (1 - \alpha)RE^*_{t-1} \tag{7.2}$$

We can rearrange Equation 7.2 to get at the true value of RE_t displayed as:

$$RE_t = (1/\alpha) \times RE^*_t - [(1 - \alpha)/\alpha] \times RE^*_{t-1} \tag{7.3}$$

Equation 7.3 expresses the most recent true real estate prices as a simple equation involving the most recent smoothed index value and the previous smoothed index value.

Previous research estimates that the value of $\alpha = 0.40$.[4] Inserting $\alpha = 0.40$ into Equation 7.3 creates the following numerical equation:

$$RE_t = 2.5 \times RE^*_t - 1.5 \times RE^*_{t-1} \tag{7.4}$$

Using Equation 7.4, we can unsmooth the index. First, we have to convert the smoothed return sequence that we see in Exhibit 7.5 into an index of values instead of returns (or use the index values directly), use Equation 7.4 to unsmooth the values, and then convert the unsmoothed values back into a return index. Our results are presented in Exhibit 7.6.

The unsmoothed version of the index in Exhibit 7.6 demonstrates much more volatility than the smoothed NPI. Simply, there is much more variability in real estate values than is indicated by the

---

[4] See Jeffrey Fisher, "US Commercial Real Estate Indices: The NCREIF Property Index," BIS White Paper 21, 2003.

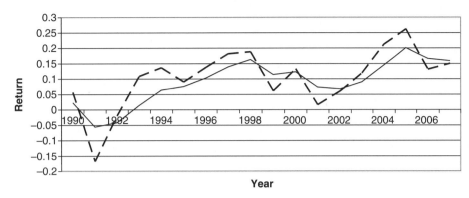

Exhibit 7.6   The unsmoothed return (dashed line) and smoothed return (solid line) NPI

Source: NCREIF, www.ncreif.com.

NPI. The appraisal process masks this volatility because of the lack of frequency with which real estate properties turn over.

Finally, in Exhibit 7.7 we present the time series returns for both the smoothed NPI index and the unsmoothed version of the index based on this unsmoothing process. We also examine expected returns, volatility, and Sharpe ratios. We can see that the average return, volatility, and Sharpe ratio are all higher with the unsmoothed index.

Exhibit 7.7   Smoothed and unsmoothed NPI

	NCREIF Composite Smoothed	NCREIF Unsmoothed
1990	2.29%	5.73%
1991	−5.59	−16.78
1992	−4.26	−1.95
1993	1.38	10.87
1994	6.38	13.62
1995	7.53	9.03
1996	10.30	13.79
1997	13.90	18.20
1998	16.25	18.86
1999	11.36	6.15
2000	12.25	13.29
2001	7.28	1.57
2002	6.75	6.07
2003	9.00	11.88
2004	14.49	21.21
2005	20.06	26.20
2006	16.60	13.14
2007	15.85	15.05
2008	−14.70	−16.10
Average	7.74%	8.94%
Volatility	8.79%	11.19%
Sharpe Ratio	0.41	0.63

Source: NCREIF, www.ncreif.com.

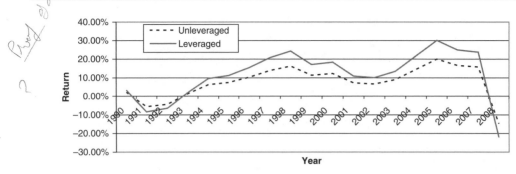

Exhibit 7.8   Leveraged and unleveraged returns

Source: NCREIF, www.ncreif.com.

Adding leverage to the NPI

Another issue with the NPI is that it is an unlevered index. As almost every homeowner knows, some amount of financing is usually necessary to purchase a new home. Leverage exists for small and tall investors alike. However, particularly in the real estate industry, leverage is a key component of most property purchases.

To demonstrate the returns that are actually earned from investing in direct real estate property, we recomputed the NPI adding 50% leverage as part of the property financing. Almost all institutional investors use leverage in the purchase of their real estate portfolios. The California Public Employees' Retirement System (CalPERS) uses up to 50% leverage in its real estate acquisitions.

Exhibit 7.8 demonstrates both the higher risks and the potentially higher returns of leverage. Markets on average are expected to move upward to compensate investors for bearing risk. The use of leverage increases risk. Accordingly, for the most part, leverage increases the expected and historic mean returns to a strategy such as that reflected in the NPI. However, leverage is a two-edged sword, as down years such as the beginning and end of the 1990s demonstrated. Thus, to get a better sense of the performance of an actual real estate portfolio, leverage must typically be included when analyzing unleveraged real estate indexes to understand the performance characteristics of the return on equity.

CONCLUSION

This chapter introduced the reader to investing in direct real estate properties. Unfortunately, given the illiquid and unique nature of property in the United States and abroad, the data collected for analyzing this asset class are fraught with errors. The errors in the data are not due to negligence; instead, they are due to the illiquidity of the asset class, the imperfections in the appraisal process, and the infrequent turnover of real estate properties. In our next chapter we turn more to the economics of real estate and explore the value of real estate in a diversified portfolio.

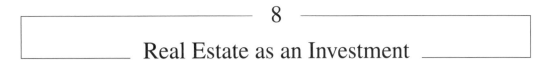

8

Real Estate as an Investment

INTRODUCTION

In the prior chapter we described how the NCREIF Property Index (NPI) works, including some of its disadvantages and caveats. In this chapter we use the NPI to explore real estate as an investment in a diversified portfolio. In this regard, the chapter focus is more on the economics of real estate and less on the difficulties in measuring its value.

We also explore other investment strategies beyond real estate investment trusts (REITs) and core real estate portfolios. Specifically, we review core, value-added, and opportunistic real estate investing, comparing and contrasting their styles and return expectations. We start with some basic comparative performance data, then consider the portfolio impacts of real estate, and conclude with a discussion of the extent to which the objectives of real estate investing are met.

THE BENEFITS OF REAL ESTATE INVESTING

Real estate has long been a staple of land barons everywhere. In ancient and medieval times, the way royalty denominated their wealth was by the amount and type of land they owned (although it should be noted that beachfront property back then did not have the cachet that it does today—there was little agricultural benefit to growing anything in sand).

However, starting in the 1700s and 1800s, a new way to hold wealth emerged: partnerships and corporations. Holding stock certificates or limited partnership interests began to take away some of the luster of real estate as these new forms of wealth denomination grew. Yet real estate remains a valuable part of any well-diversified portfolio. There are five goals for adding real estate to an investment portfolio.[1]

1. To achieve absolute returns above the risk-free rate.
2. To provide a hedge against inflation.
3. As a portfolio diversification tool that provides exposure to a different type of systematic risk and return than stocks and bonds.
4. To constitute an investment portfolio that resembles the global investment opportunity set.
5. To deliver strong cash flows to the portfolio through lease and rental payments.

As we go through our analysis in this chapter, we should keep in mind these five reasons and ask ourselves the extent to which real estate accomplishes these five goals.

REAL ESTATE PERFORMANCE

We begin our economic review of real estate by comparing the returns for this asset class to the returns for other asset classes. Our initial analysis is simply to see how real estate stacks up

---

[1] See Susan Hudson-Wilson, Jacques N. Gordon, Frank J. Fabozzi, Mark J.P. Anson, and S. Michael Gilberto, "Why Real Estate?" *Journal of Portfolio Management*, Special Real Estate Edition, 2005.

compared to other asset classes on a risk-adjusted basis. We include the following asset classes in Exhibit 8.1:

- Real estate: the NCREIF Property Index both smoothed and unsmoothed as well as the four (unsmoothed) divisions of the NPI.
- REITs as represented by the NAREIT index and a mutual fund that actively buys and sells REITs to add value (FRESX).
- Large-cap stocks represented by the Russell 1000 stock index.
- Small-cap stocks represented by the Russell 2000 stock index.
- Investment-grade bonds.
- High-yield bonds.
- Credit risk–free bonds represented by 10-year U.S. Treasury bonds.
- Cash equivalent, represented by one-year U.S. Treasury bills (which we use as the risk-free rate for our Sharpe ratio calculations).
- Inflation, not as an asset class but for historical perspective on real returns.

First, looking at risk-adjusted returns as measured by the Sharpe ratio, we can see that the NPI's performance compares very well to stocks, bonds, and credit. In fact, the highest Sharpe ratios are scored by the NCREIF Apartment index at 0.63, U.S. Treasury bonds at 0.54, and the NCREIF Retail index at 0.53. Over this time period, U.S. Treasury bonds provided a comparable yield and volatility compared to real estate.

So, looking at total returns, the NPI, both smoothed and unsmoothed, stacks up well against stocks, bonds, credit, and cash. Returns of 7.74% (smoothed) and 10.33% (unsmoothed) provide similar returns to large-cap stocks (7.21%) and small-cap stocks (7.97%). Further, using the unsmoothed NPI, with a volatility of 11.19% (about one-half of the annual volatility of small-cap stocks and about 40% of the volatility of large-cap stocks), provides for a very favorable risk versus return trade-off. This is demonstrated by the Sharpe ratios for the smoothed and unsmoothed NPI (0.41 and 0.63, respectively), which are twice those of large-cap and small-cap stocks—both, coincidently, with a Sharpe ratio of 0.33.

Also, we compare the NPI, smoothed and unsmoothed, to REIT returns. We use the NAREIT index as well as the mutual fund of actively managed returns. The NAREIT index provides a large total return of almost 11.2% but it has a much larger standard deviation, reflective of the fact that REITs are publicly traded and therefore pick up a significant amount of systematic risk from the stock market. This leads to a higher level of volatility than for direct real estate investing, and a lower Sharpe ratio. In fact, the NAREIT index has just about the same level of volatility as small-cap stocks (in fact, a little higher), not surprising since the market cap of most REITs is in the $500 million to $4 billion range, which is the market-capitalization range for small companies and the smaller segment of mid-cap companies.

Interestingly, when we turn to the actively managed REIT mutual fund, we find the lowest Sharpe ratio of all asset classes in Exhibit 8.1. The actively managed REIT product produces one of the lowest average returns (4.86%) with one of the largest measures of volatility (20.5%). The result is a lower Sharpe ratio. The conclusion is that while REITs provide a valuable way to access the real estate market, this actively managed REIT fund did not add value. Further, it is worth reminding the reader that each REIT is, in fact, an actively managed pool of real estate assets. Therefore, an actively managed REIT fund is simply an overlay of active management on top of active real estate management. The results do not bear out that a second layer of active management added value.

Finally, on an inflation-adjusted basis, real estate offers a significant return premium over inflation, leading to excellent real returns. The real returns (in excess of the inflation rate) for the NPI both smoothed and unsmoothed are 5.63% and 6.83%, respectively. In addition, the NAREIT index

Exhibit 8.1 Returns to real estate and other asset classes

REIT mutual fund ↓

	NCREIF (NPI) Composite	NCREIF Unsmoothed	NCREIF Apts.	NCREIF Offices	NCREIF Retail	NCREIF Industrial	NAREIT	FRESX	RU1000	RU2000	Inv.-Grade	High-Yield	10-Year T-Bond	1-Year T-Bill	Inflation
1990	2.29%	5.73%	5.79%	-1.06%	5.96%	1.96%	-15.35%	-13.87%	-7.50%	-21.45%	9.09%	-7.04%	6.58%	4.25%	5.70%
1991	-5.59	-16.78	-1.36	-11.44	-1.85	-3.86	35.70	32.45	28.83	43.68	15.98	34.22	17.29	4.37	-0.10
1992	-4.26	-1.95	1.72	-8.05	-2.25	-4.47	14.59	15.17	5.89	16.36	7.58	18.35	7.93	3.56	1.60
1993	1.38	10.87	8.72	-3.95	4.84	-0.77	19.65	7.70	7.33	17.00	9.92	17.37	16.22	3.59	0.20
1994	6.38	13.62	12.07	3.92	6.01	7.63	3.17	-2.73	-2.42	-3.18	-2.85	-0.82	-7.60	6.92	1.70
1995	7.53	9.03	11.66	7.18	3.98	12.30	15.27	5.15	34.44	26.21	18.53	19.23	27.30	5.22	2.30
1996	10.30	13.79	11.54	13.56	4.85	13.57	35.27	29.90	19.72	14.76	3.62	10.85	-0.49	5.62	2.80
1997	13.90	18.20	12.90	17.87	8.53	15.94	20.26	13.42	30.49	20.52	9.64	13.10	14.45	5.62	-1.20
1998	16.25	18.86	14.12	19.62	12.91	15.86	-17.50	-24.01	25.12	-3.45	8.71	4.43	12.93	4.58	0.00
1999	11.36	6.15	11.73	12.22	9.55	11.65	-4.62	-5.41	19.46	19.62	-0.83	0.84	-8.98	6.14	2.90
2000	12.25	13.29	12.99	14.11	7.76	14.02	26.37	25.85	-8.84	-4.20	11.59	-4.41	18.73	5.47	3.60
2001	7.28	1.57	9.37	6.20	6.74	9.30	13.93	0.11	-13.59	1.03	8.52	6.92	4.53	2.03	-1.60
2002	6.75	6.07	8.76	2.78	13.74	6.70	3.82	-0.70	-22.94	-21.58	10.09	-0.58	16.06	1.20	1.20
2003	9.00	11.88	8.90	5.67	17.15	8.23	37.13	28.93	27.54	45.37	4.20	29.36	3.29	1.21	4.00
2004	14.49	21.21	13.04	12.02	22.95	12.07	31.58	24.59	9.49	17.00	4.48	10.51	7.78	2.79	4.20
2005	20.06	26.20	21.15	19.46	19.98	20.31	12.16	5.48	4.37	3.32	2.57	2.07	6.61	4.42	5.40
2006	16.60	13.14	14.63	19.16	13.35	16.96	35.06	17.68	13.34	17.00	4.33	11.71	2.03	5.00	1.10
2007	15.85	15.05	11.36	20.51	13.51	14.95	-15.69	-29.15	3.86	-2.75	7.22	1.91	9.60	3.29	6.20
2008	-14.70	-16.10	-16.40	-16.30	-9.50	-14.10	-37.50	-38.21	-37.60	-33.80	-12.40	-24.68	22.81	2.30	0.10
Average	7.74%	8.94%	9.09%	7.03%	8.33%	8.33%	11.23%	4.86%	7.21%	7.97%	6.31%	7.55%	9.32%	4.08%	2.11%
Volatility	8.79%	11.19%	7.84%	11.14%	7.89%	8.88%	21.41%	20.50%	19.40%	20.73%	6.86%	13.44%	9.54%	1.64%	2.31%
Sharpe	0.41	0.63	0.63	0.26	0.53	0.47	0.33	0.03	0.16	0.18	0.31	0.25	0.54		

Sources: NCREIF, www.ncreif.com; NAREIT, www.reit.com; Bloomberg Finance, L.P.

provided a real return of 9.12%. Clearly, over this time period, real estate provided an excellent premium over the inflation rate. A better demonstration of the inflation hedging properties is provided later in this chapter.

REAL ESTATE RISK PROFILE

In this section we analyze histograms of real estate returns. A histogram is a convenient way to illustrate the return stream associated with an asset class, an investment product, or even an individual portfolio manager. The histogram provides a graphical description of a pattern of past returns. In fact, if we had many hundreds, if not thousands, of data points, the histogram would begin to resemble a probability distribution with a nice smooth curve reflecting the full range of potential values for real estate returns (assuming that past returns are indicative of future returns). As it is, the histogram still provides a revealing snapshot regarding the returns for real estate.

The histogram is an important way to observe the patterns of real estate returns. We can visualize whether the returns are skewed to the positive or negative, whether there are large outlier returns, how fat the tails are, and so forth. Exhibits 8.2 and 8.3 provide the histograms for the full NPI index for both smoothed and unsmoothed returns based on quarterly returns from 1980 through the first quarter of 2008. Exhibits 8.4 through 8.7 provide the histograms for the component parts of NPI index: Apartments, Offices, Retail, and Industrial. To be consistent in our analysis, we also unsmooth the returns to each of the four NCREIF sectors. Last, in Exhibit 8.8, we provide the histogram for the NAREIT index.

Starting with Exhibit 8.2, we see an average quarterly return of 2.2%, a standard deviation of 1.9%, and a very favorable Sharpe ratio of 0.61. Clearly, on a risk-adjusted basis, the returns to real estate provided a very favorable risk and return profile. However, Exhibit 8.2 exhibits a negative skew computed as −2.11. This indicates a bias to the downside—that there are more large negative returns than large positive returns. Also, we note a large value of kurtosis of 9.19, indicating fatter tails than a normal distribution or a greater exposure to outlier events. In general, we would like to see a positive skew with fat tails—indicating a bias toward large positive outlier returns. In this case, we see a return pattern that demonstrates a large negative downside tail. This means that there can

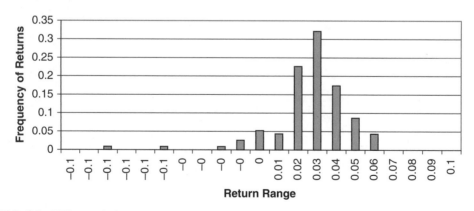

Exhibit 8.2   NPI smoothed quarterly returns, 1990–2008

Note: E(Return) 2.20%; Volatility 1.90%; Skew –2.11; Kurtosis 9.19; Sharpe 0.61

Source: NCREIF, www.ncreif.com.

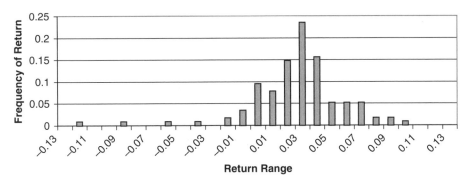

Exhibit 8.3   NPI unsmoothed quarterly returns, 1990–2008

Note: E(Return) 2.23%; Volatility 3.12%; Skew –1.36; Kurtosis 5.76; Sharpe 0.38

Source: NCREIF, www.ncreif.com.

be significant losses in real estate during short periods of time that can have a significantly negative impact on an investment portfolio.

Exhibit 8.3 is the histogram of quarterly returns for the unsmoothed NPI. These returns have a higher expected return of 2.23% but also a much larger value of volatility of 3.12%. This leads to a much lower Sharpe ratio of 0.38. Simply, once we unsmooth the NPI, the risk-adjusted returns decline, primarily as a result of higher volatility that is otherwise masked by the lagged effect of appraisal values in the NPI. We also see a negative skew of −1.36, similar to Exhibit 8.2, but a much larger value of kurtosis of 5.76. The negative skew of −1.36 combined with the large value of kurtosis of 5.76 indicates a large downside tail associated with the unsmoothed NPI. Consequently, once we unsmooth the NPI data, we find that the returns to real estate exhibit much more risk than otherwise thought as measured by a larger value of volatility and by a larger downside tail risk.

When we review the individual sectors of the NCREIF index, we find similar statistics. Quarterly returns are consistently positive in the 2% to 2.5% range with volatilities ranging from 1.73% (Apartments) to 2.53% (Offices). All Sharpe ratios are positive, with Apartments having the highest (0.86) and Offices having the lowest (0.37). Each of the subsectors also has a negative skew and a large value of kurtosis, indicating risk to the downside, or "fat tail" risk. These results are consistent

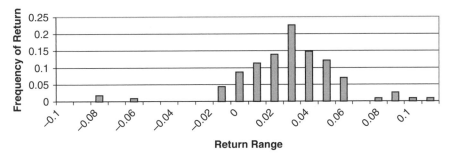

Exhibit 8.4   Quarterly returns for apartments, 1990–2008

Note: E(Return) 2.53%; Volatility 1.73%; Skew –2.20; Kurtosis 13.63; Sharpe 0.86

Source: NCREIF, www.ncreif.com.

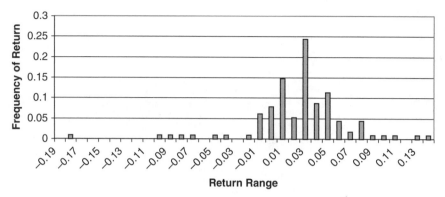

Exhibit 8.5   Quarterly returns for offices, 1990–2008

Note: E(Return) 1.98%; Volatility 2.53%; Skew –1.50; Kurtosis 5.29; Sharpe 0.37

Source: NCREIF, www.ncreif.com.

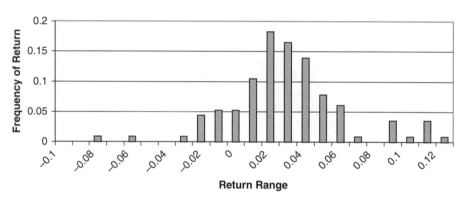

Exhibit 8.6   Quarterly returns for retail, 1990–2008

Note: E(Return) 2.40%; Volatility 1.88%; Skew –0.68; Kurtosis 4.47; Sharpe 0.73

Source: NCREIF, www.ncreif.com.

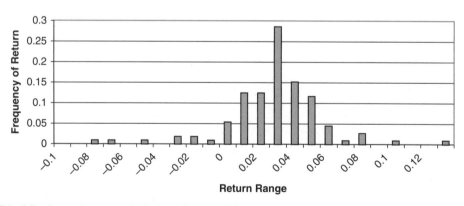

Exhibit 8.7   Quarterly returns for industrial, 1990–2008

Note: E(Return) 2.33%; Volatility 1.89%; Skew –1.85; Kurtosis 8.00; Sharpe 0.69

Source: NCREIF, www.ncreif.com.

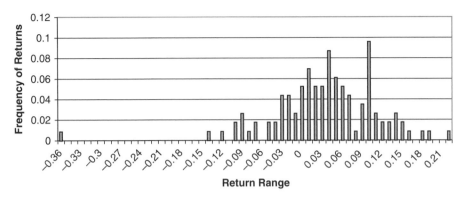

Exhibit 8.8   Quarterly returns for REITs, 1990–2008

Note: E(Return) 3.11%; Volatility 7.96%; Skew –0.99; Kurtosis 4.70; Sharpe 0.26

Source: Bloomberg Finance, L.P.

with the broader NCREIF index. We do note that the negative skew and large values of kurtosis are influenced by the brutal year for real estate of 2008.

Overall, if we could pick and choose our sectors, the Apartments component had the best risk versus return trade-off with a positive bias to upside returns, while the Offices component had the lowest risk versus return trade-off with the greatest exposure to downside fat tails. However, it should be noted that Apartments had the largest negative value of skew and the largest value of kurtosis, indicating the greatest amount of downside risk.

Last, in Exhibit 8.8, we include the histogram for REITs. Since REITs are publicly traded, their valuations are observed without the appraisal lag that infects the NPI. Consequently, there is no need to unsmooth the data. The distribution of returns for REITs demonstrates a smaller skew of −0.99 but still with a reasonably large value of kurtosis of 4.7. REITs are also exposed to downside fat tails; again, these statistics are influenced by the very difficult year of 2008. Average returns are much higher for REITs but so is volatility as the lack of smoothing reveals the riskiness of the real estate market. Last, the Sharpe ratio of 0.26 is lower compared to the NPI and its individual sectors, with the exception of the Office sector. Much of the lower Sharpe ratio can be explained by the much higher quarterly volatility for REITs of 7.96 compared to the appraisal-based NPI and its sectors.

REAL ESTATE AS PART OF A DIVERSIFIED PORTFOLIO

Correlation coefficients

When we think about real estate as part of a diversified portfolio, the first thing we need to consider is the correlation of returns for real estate with other asset classes. The lower the correlation coefficient, the greater the diversification benefits of combining real estate with stocks, bonds, and other asset classes.

Exhibit 8.9 displays the correlation coefficients for the NPI, its sectors, and REITs with other asset classes. We include both the smoothed and unsmoothed NPI numbers and use the unsmoothed numbers primarily for our discussion. First, we can see that the NPI is highly correlated with its sector components. The correlation coefficients of the NPI with its four sectors are all 0.81 or greater. This is what we would expect given that these four sectors should be driven by common factors that drive the returns of all four sectors of real estate that comprise the composite NPI.

Exhibit 8.9 Correlation coefficients for the NPI, NPI sectors, REITs with other asset classes

	NCREIF Composite	NCREIF Unsmoothed	NCREIF Apts.	NCREIF Offices	NCREIF Retail	NCREIF Industrial	NAREIT	FRESX	RU1000	RU2000	Inv.-Grade	High-Yield	10-Year T-Bond	1-Year T-Bill	Inflation
NCREIF Composite	1.00														
NCREIF Unsmoothed	0.90	1.00													
NCREIF Apts.	0.93	0.89	1.00												
NCREIF Offices	0.97	0.85	0.86	1.00											
NCREIF Retail	0.86	0.81	0.79	0.75	1.00										
NCREIF Industrial	0.98	0.85	0.93	0.97	0.77	1.00									
NAREIT	0.26	0.21	0.38	0.17	0.28	0.29	1.00								
FRSEX	0.16	0.13	0.29	0.07	0.19	0.19	0.97	1.00							
RU1000	0.39	0.31	0.44	0.37	0.24	0.43	0.51	0.47	1.00						
RU2000	0.16	0.07	0.25	0.10	0.16	0.19	0.76	0.72	0.84	1.00					
Inv.-Grade	0.19	0.09	0.33	0.13	0.11	0.24	0.43	0.40	0.47	0.40	1.00				
High-Yield	0.09	0.02	0.22	-0.01	0.13	0.10	0.76	0.71	0.77	0.92	0.60	1.00			
10-Year T-Bond	-0.34	-0.29	-0.37	-0.30	-0.32	-0.30	-0.11	-0.11	-0.10	-0.13	0.43	0.01	1.00		
1-Year T-Bill	0.27	0.26	0.36	0.33	-0.12	0.35	0.08	0.11	0.40	0.14	0.03	-0.03	-0.29	1.00	
Inflation	0.36	0.41	0.32	0.31	0.46	0.30	-0.06	-0.02	0.00	-0.07	-0.06	-0.15	-0.23	0.02	1.00

Sources: NCREIF, www.ncreif.com; NAREIT, www.reit.com; Bloomberg Finance, L.P.

Next we compare the unsmoothed NPI to the NAREIT index. Somewhat surprisingly, we find a very low correlation of 0.21. However, the answer lies with respect to how these two indices track with small-cap stocks. Recall from our prior chapter that REITs are publicly traded on an exchange, just like stocks. Further, most REITs are in the market capitalization range described as small-cap stocks. In fact, most REITs are contained in the Russell 2000, an index of 2,000 small-cap stocks traded in the United States. Therefore, it is not surprising to see that the NAREIT index, as a market-traded index, has a large positive correlation with the Russell 2000 of 0.76. Conversely, the NPI has almost a zero correlation with small-cap stocks of 0.07. This negative correlation may reflect the diversification benefits of direct investing in unique real estate properties compared to the stock market, or it may be caused by the use of appraisals.

Also, when we compare the unsmoothed NPI or smoothed NPI to large-cap stocks, represented by the Russell 1000, we find very low correlations of 0.31 and 0.39, respectively. We find very low correlation between the Russell 2000 and either the smoothed or unsmoothed NPI, demonstrating that direct real estate investing has very good diversification properties with small-cap stocks in addition to large-cap stocks. We also see that direct real estate investing is an excellent diversifier with respect to investment-grade, high-yield, and U.S. Treasury bonds. The correlation coefficients of the composite NCREIF index with these three bond classes are very consistent at 0.19, 0.09, and −0.34, respectively. Combined with the low or negative correlation coefficients observed between real estate and stocks, we would expect real estate to be an excellent diversifying asset class for a traditional stock and bond portfolio.

Last, we note that the unsmoothed NPI has a positive correlation with the inflation rate. This demonstrates that real estate is a good inflation hedge. The reason is that real estate properties can adjust their rental and lease rates to take into account higher inflationary costs. There is inevitably some lag in the ability to increase lease/rental rates with inflation, which is a reason why the NPI is not perfectly correlated with the inflation rate. We can also see that each of the four NPI sectors is also positively correlated with the inflation rate, with the Retail sector having the best inflation hedging properties. This simply demonstrates the ability of shopping centers and strip malls to adjust their lease rates more quickly in tune with higher inflation.

Turning to the other asset classes—small-cap stocks, investment-grade bonds, high-yield bonds, U.S. Treasury bonds, and even REITs—we can see that these asset classes have uniformly negative correlation coefficients with inflation (large-cap stocks have a zero correlation with the inflation rate). Simply, these asset classes form poor inflation hedges. For investment-grade bonds, high-yield bonds, and U.S. Treasury bonds, this is not surprising because higher inflation rates mean higher interest rates and lower bond prices. In sum, it is clear that direct real estate investing provides excellent diversification properties for a variety of asset classes. In addition, direct real estate investing also provides an excellent hedge against inflation. We next turn toward building a diversified portfolio.

Expanding the efficient frontier

We examine the power of adding real estate to a portfolio of stocks and bonds by examining the efficient frontier. The efficient frontier includes all potentially optimal combinations of assets in terms of their risk (standard deviation) and expected return. At every point along the efficient frontier, there is no transaction that can add expected return without adding risk, or that can lower risk without lowering expected return. This means that there is no combination of assets within the portfolio that can offer more return for a given level of risk, or less risk for a given level of return.

Exhibit 8.10 displays the efficient frontier for a combination of investment-grade bonds and large-capitalized stocks. Starting at the left-hand end of the frontier, our first data point is a portfolio consisting of 100% investment-grade bonds. Moving along toward the right-hand side of the efficient

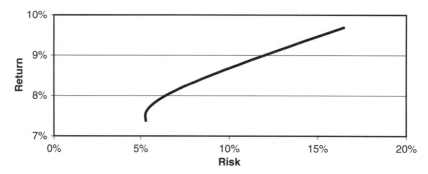

Exhibit 8.10   Efficient frontier with large-cap stocks and investment-grade bonds

frontier, we begin to add large-cap stocks to the portfolio in increments of 10%, so that the data points used to create the curve are 100% bonds, 90% bonds/10% stocks, 80% bonds/20% stocks, and so forth until we get to the end point at the right-hand side of the efficient frontier, which is 100% stocks in the portfolio.

Generally, we observe that the efficient frontier slopes upward. Given that a portfolio is diversified enough to lie on the efficient frontier, one can achieve more expected return only by taking on more risk. Said a different way, if an investor wishes to reduce the risk of her portfolio, she can do this only if she is willing to accept lower expected returns.

With our initial efficient frontier plotted, we can now observe how the efficient frontier that we have estimated reacts to the addition of real estate. We use the NPI unsmoothed index to determine the diversification benefits of direct real estate investing. Recall from our discussions in the chapters on asset allocation that the addition of major asset classes into an investment portfolio is all about diversification. Essentially, we are mixing in different risk exposures to provide more diversification and to expand the efficient frontier. This is the essence of strategic asset allocation. The goal is to blend asset classes to determine the best mix of risk premiums associated with those asset classes to provide the optimal investment portfolio.

Exhibit 8.11 demonstrates the power of adding real estate to a traditional investment portfolio. We use the same efficient frontier portfolio as in Exhibit 8.10 but instead we add an allocation of 10% real estate to each data point along the curve. So our first data point is 90% bonds/10% real estate, then 85% bonds/5% stocks/10% real estate, then 75% bonds/15% stocks/10% real estate, and so forth.

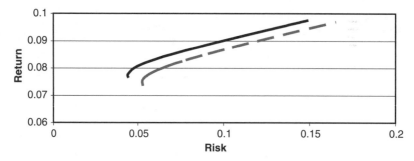

Exhibit 8.11   Expanding the efficient frontier with stocks, bonds, and direct real estate

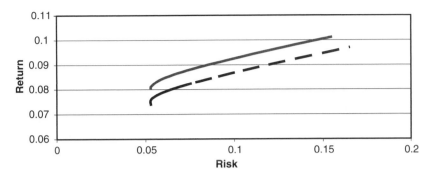

Exhibit 8.12 Expanding the efficient frontier with stocks, bonds, and REITs

In Exhibit 8.11, the dashed line represents the original efficient frontier from Exhibit 8.10, representing stocks and bonds, while the solid line represents the new efficient frontier combining stocks, bonds, and direct real estate. We observe a large movement of the new efficient frontier up and to the left of the original efficient frontier. This demonstrates a significant increase in efficiency. Simply, the addition of direct real estate investing into a portfolio of stocks and bonds increases the level of return for a given level of risk, or reduces the level of risk for a given level of return—a powerful combination.

The efficient frontier is also expanded when we use REITs as a diversifying asset class in a stock and bond portfolio. Exhibit 8.12 presents the efficient frontier when we add REITs. Again, the dashed line is the original efficient frontier from Exhibit 8.10, while the solid line is the new efficient frontier with stocks, bonds, and REITs. We add REITs to the stock and bond portfolio in exactly the same proportion that we added direct real estate to the investment portfolio in Exhibit 8.11. We observe that the efficient frontier is pushed upward, indicating a better risk versus return trade-off at every point along the efficient frontier.

Comparing Exhibits 8.11 and 8.12, we can see that direct real estate investing provides a slight edge to REIT investing. We note that in Exhibit 8.11, the new efficient frontier using direct real estate shifts not only upward but also to the left of the original frontier. This demonstrates that not only does direct real estate investment provide a higher return when combined with stocks and bonds, it actually reduces risk at the same time. As we noted earlier, this is a powerful combination. In contrast, Exhibit 8.12 demonstrates that the addition of REITs results in almost a linear shift upward of the efficient frontier. This is still a good thing—more return for a given level of risk or less risk for a given level of return. The distinction is that in Exhibit 8.11 we see not only more return *but with a lower level of risk* compared to the original efficient frontier. Both REITs and direct real estate investing provide excellent diversification to a stock and bond portfolio; it is just that direct real estate is a more efficient diversification tool.

CONCLUSION

In this chapter we explored the returns for real estate investing. We conclude by recapping the five objectives from the beginning of the chapter and discussing the extent to which real estate provides economic benefits as an asset class.

Absolute returns above the risk-free rate

Examining the first goal—high absolute returns above the risk-free rate and inflation—we found that both direct real estate investing and investing through REITs provide a very favorable risk-return trade-off compared to stocks and bonds. The Sharpe ratios for the NPI and its four sectors as well as the NAREIT index were significantly greater than those for large- or small-cap stocks, investment-grade bonds, and high-yield bonds. U.S. Treasury bonds had the second highest Sharpe ratio (after the NCREIF Apartment Index) based on their relatively high return and relatively low inflation. We also note that direct real estate investing and REITs provided a significant return premium above the inflation rate of over 6.83% and 9.12%, respectively. Clearly, access to either direct real estate or publicly traded REITs provided good long-term real rates of return.

We also note from Exhibit 8.1 that the average return to REITs offered a significant return premium to large- and small-cap stocks. The NAREIT index outperformed the Russell 1000 by 4.02% per year, while the return premium over small-cap stocks was 3.26% per year. REITs offered an enticing return premium over equity. We also note that the NAREIT index outperformed Treasury bonds by almost 2% per year.

A hedge against inflation

Considering our second goal of inflation hedging, we also found that direct real estate investing provided a hedge against inflation with a moderately positive correlation coefficient. Unfortunately, we did not observe the same hedging ability with REITs. The correlation coefficient between REITs and the inflation rate was negative, indicating that REITs have been adversely affected by inflation. Still, we note from Exhibit 8.1 that over the long term, REITs provided a return premium over the inflation rate.

We also note that the NCREIF Retail index provided the best hedge against inflation with a correlation coefficient with the inflation rate of 0.46. This is because current inflation increases the net operating income (NOI) of retail properties much faster than the expenses associated with retail properties. The reasons are that retail real estate properties charge percentage rents based on revenues (which adjust quickly to inflation) and retail leases have generous pass-through clauses that allocate escalating property costs to the lessees.

Conversely, we note that not all sectors of the NCREIF index provide the same level of inflation protection. Industrial properties have the lowest positive correlation with the inflation rate. The reason is that the revenues of these properties are often pegged to long-term leases that are difficult to adjust when inflation increases. Leases from these property types do not tend to reflect inflation for one to five years.

Portfolio diversification and reflection of investment universe

Goals 3 (diversification) and 4 (expand the investment opportunity set) were demonstrated by our correlation coefficient and efficient frontier analysis. Exhibit 8.9 showed that direct real estate and REITs are both excellent diversifying asset classes compared to stocks. The correlation coefficients between the different sectors of NCREIF and stocks, high-yield bonds, investment-grade bonds, and Treasury bonds demonstrate that real estate is an essential part of any diversified portfolio.

This analysis was confirmed in our efficient frontier analysis in Exhibits 8.10 through 8.12, where the addition of either direct real estate investments or REITs provided a significant positive expansion of the efficient frontier. Clearly, real estate should be considered a part of the global investment opportunity set.

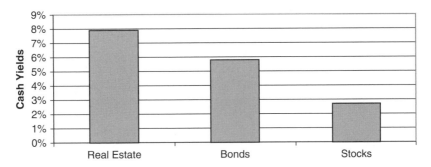

Exhibit 8.13   Annual cash yield, 2008

Source: NCREIF, www.ncreif.com; Bloomberg Finance, L.P.

In addition, real estate should be part of any well-diversified portfolio. The returns to real estate clearly contain different return drivers than stocks and bonds based on the low positive, or even negative, correlation coefficients in Exhibit 8.9. In fact, both the NPI and NAREIT indexes show a negative correlation with Treasury bonds. In addition, real estate has the nice benefit of capital preservation while producing a strong return stream. While real estate values can go up and down, their value is not as tied to the vicissitudes of the business cycle as stocks are, or as tied to the ravages of inflation as bonds are. While companies can go bankrupt, real estate will likely provide greater preservation of capital and value.

Furthermore, any diversified portfolio that does not include real estate is explicitly reducing the universe of investment opportunities. Real estate is an age-old but still relevant asset class. Including it in a diversified portfolio is an intelligent recognition of the investable universe.

However, we do strike one note of caution. Our risk analysis in Exhibits 8.2 through 8.8 did raise some concerns, as we did observe a significant negative skew combined with a large value of kurtosis for the unsmoothed NPI. This demonstrates a large negative downside exposure associated with direct real estate investment—a risk to be avoided if possible. When we examined the components of the NPI, we found a similar risk profile: large negative values of skew combined with large positive values of kurtosis. Combined, these statistics demonstrate a "fat" downside tail to the return distributions for real estate. A similar return pattern was observed for REITs.

Strong cash flows

Strong and consistent cash flows are a hallmark of real estate investing. Passing on inflation costs in the form of higher lease and rental payments indicates a strong ability to generate consistent cash flows. This is demonstrated in Exhibit 8.13, where we compare the average yields for real estate, bonds, and stocks in 2008. We can see that real estate provides a higher cash return than either stocks or bonds. This is one of real estate's key appeals: a combination of strong cash flows with some value appreciation.

9

Core, Value-Added, and Opportunistic Real Estate

INTRODUCTION

We complete our chapters on real estate investing with a description of core, value-added, and opportunistic real estate. Office, apartment, retail, and industrial properties are what most investors consider to be the core of any real estate portfolio. As large institutional investors have become more sophisticated they have expanded beyond the four sectors that make up the NPI. These opportunities, ranging from hotels to nursing homes, can provide a return boost beyond what core properties can offer.

This chapter explores other styles of real estate investing. Investment styles provide investors with a convenient way to categorize an investment such that return and risk expectations can be established. While **style boxes** have been used for many years in equity and fixed-income investing, real estate investment styles are relatively new. There are three main reasons for introducing styles into real estate portfolio analysis:

1. *Performance measurement.* Investors continually look for tools that can provide them with a better understanding of an investment sector's objectives. This includes identifying peer groups, return objectives, range of risk taking, return attribution, and peer performance.
2. *Monitoring style drift.* It is a fact of investment life that portfolio managers occasionally drift from their stated risk, return, or other objectives. Classifying different styles of real estate investments allows an investor to measure the overlap among investment products and to gain a better understanding of the risk level at any given point of time. Tracking style drift is another factor in monitoring and evaluating performance. The better the categorization of real estate, the better an investor can track the resulting risk and return of the portfolio relative to its stated style.
3. *Style diversification.* The ability to determine the risk and return profile of a manager relative to its style will allow for a better diversification of the portfolio since an investor can construct a portfolio that has a more robust risk and return profile if there is a better understanding of a real estate manager's style location.

Style boxes are essentially locators. Style investing is all about identifying the space in which the investment manager operates. Styles identify where and how an investment manager invests. Consequently, they identify dimensions in addition to simply risk and return.

THE NCREIF STYLE BOXES

In 2003, the National Council of Real Estate Investment Fiduciaries (NCREIF) took it upon itself to define style boxes within the real estate investment industry.[1] Specifically, NCREIF identified three styles that apply at the underlying asset level for direct real estate investing: core, value-added, and opportunistic. These styles may be thought of as a way to classify the individual real estate

---

[1] See John Baczewski, Kathleen Hands, and Charles R. Lathem, "Real Estate Investment Styles: Trends from the Catwalk," NCREIF white paper, October 2, 2003.

investment. In addition, NCREIF identified eight attributes to distinguish the three types of real estate asset styles:

1. Property type
2. Life cycle
3. Occupancy
4. Rollover concentration
5. Near-term rollover
6. Leverage
7. Market recognition
8. Investment structure/control

Exhibit 9.1 defines the three NCREIF real estate styles along with discussing the attributes that help to identify the type of property.

In addition to Exhibit 9.1, the following three subsections provide a summary to help distinguish core properties from value-added and opportunistic properties.

Core

Core properties are the most liquid, most developed, least leveraged, and most recognizable properties in a real estate portfolio. These properties have the greatest amount of liquidity but still are not sold quickly relative to traditional investments. Core properties tend to be held for a long period of time to take full advantage of the lease and rental cash flows that they provide. The majority of their returns come from the cash flows instead of value appreciation, and very little leverage is applied.

Value-added

These properties begin to get off the beaten path. This can include hotels, resorts, assisted care living, low-income housing, outlet malls, hospitals, and the like. These properties tend to require a subspecialty within the real estate market to manage well and can involve repositioning, renovation, and redevelopment of existing properties. Relative to core properties, these properties tend to produce less income and rely more on property appreciation to generate the total return.

These properties can also include new properties that might otherwise be core properties except that they are not fully leased, such as a new apartment complex or a new shopping center. A value-added property could also be an existing property that needs a new strategy like a facelift, new tenants, or a new marketing campaign. These properties tend to use more leverage and generate a total return from both capital appreciation and income.

For example, the Pennsylvania Public School Employees' Retirement System (PSERS) identifies value-added real estate as:

> Value-added real estate investing typically focuses on both income and growth appreciation potential, where opportunities created by dislocation and inefficiencies between and within segments of the real estate capital markets are capitalized upon to enhance returns. Investments can include high-yield equity and debt investments and undervalued or impaired properties in need of repositioning, redevelopment, or leasing. Modest leverage is generally applied in value added portfolios to facilitate the execution of a variety of value creation strategies.[2]

---

[2] See Pennsylvania Public School Employees' Retirement System, Investment Policy Statement, Objectives and Guidelines for Closed End Opportunistic and Value Added Real Estate Investments, Addendum U, June 22, 2007.

Exhibit 9.1   NCREIF style boxes for real estate assets

Core Definition	Value-Added Definition	Opportunistic Definition
Real estate assets that achieve a relatively high percentage of their return from income and are expected to have low volatility.	Real estate assets that exhibit one or more of the following attributes: (1) achieve a significant portion of their return from appreciation in value, (2) exhibit moderate volatility, and/or (3) are not considered to be core type properties.	A real estate asset that is expected to derive most of its return from property appreciation and that may exhibit significant volatility in returns. This may be due to a variety of characteristics such as exposure to development risk, significant leasing risk, or high leverage, but may also result from a combination of more moderate risk factors that in total create a more volatile risk profile.
Core Attributes	**Value-Added Attributes**	**Opportunistic Attributes**
1. The major property types only: Offices, Apartments, Retail, Industrial.	Major property types plus specialty retail, hospitality, senior/assisted care housing, storage, and low-income housing.	Nontraditional property types, including speculative development for sale or rent and undeveloped land.
2. Life cycle: fully operating.	Life cycle: operating and leasing.	Life cycle: development and newly constructed.
3. High occupancy.	Moderately to well leased and/or substantially preleased development.	Low economic occupancy.
4. Low rollover concentration; this means that core assets tend to be held for a long period of time—they form the central component of the real estate portfolio, which is geared toward generating income and not sales appreciation.	Moderate rollover concentration—a higher percentage of the assets are held for a short- to intermediate-term sale and rollover into new assets.	High rollover concentration risk—most of these assets are held for appreciation and resale.
5. Low total near-term rollover.	Moderate total near-term rollover.	High total near-term rollover.
6. Low leverage.	Moderate leverage.	High leverage.
7. Well-recognized institutional properties and locations.	Institutional and emerging real estate markets.	Secondary and tertiary markets and international real estate.
8. Investment structures with significant or direct control.	Investment structures with moderate control but with security or a preferred liquidation position.	Investment structures with minimal control; usually in a limited partnership vehicle and with unsecured positions.

Opportunistic

Opportunistic real estate moves away from a core/income approach to a capital appreciation approach. Often, opportunistic real estate is accessed through real estate opportunity funds, sometimes called **private equity real estate (PERE)**. PERE funds invest in real estate with a high risk and return profile, particularly those properties that require extensive development or are turnaround opportunities.[3]

Consistent with our description of opportunistic real estate in Exhibit 9.1, the majority of the return from these properties comes from value appreciation over a three- to five-year period of time. Rollover risk is high because total return is based on value appreciation. Compare this to core properties where sales of the underlying real estate are infrequent and core properties are held for a long period of time to harness their income-producing attributes. Due to their high focus on value appreciation, opportunistic real estate managers tend to resemble traders and value enhancers compared to core managers, who are operators of properties. Therefore, opportunistic managers tend to pursue some event that will result in the real estate being quickly and dramatically revalued. This can come from development of raw property, redevelopment of property that is in disrepair, or the purchase of property in an area that is undergoing significant urban renewal.

Using an example from PSERS again, its investment policy identifies opportunistic real estate as follows:

> Opportunistic real estate investing is the financing, acquisition, or investment in real estate assets, real estate companies, portfolios of real estate assets, private and public REITs that do not have access to traditional public equity or debt financing. Opportunistic real estate investing consists of strategies that seek to exploit market inefficiencies with an emphasis on total return. Opportunistic investments require specialized expertise and the flexibility to respond quickly to market imbalances or changing market conditions. Investments may include non-traditional property types and/or assets that involve development, redevelopment, or leasing risks. Leverage is typically incorporated into this strategy to further enhance total returns.

Last, opportunistic real estate investing is often the way institutional investors expand their property holdings outside their domestic country. Often, institutional investors access international property opportunities through a PERE limited partnership. For example, over the past five years, public companies in Germany have been selling their investment holdings of apartment housing to private investors, as these real estate properties represent investments outside the core expertise of the operating companies. The properties were held to house the workers of the operating companies. The workers still reside there but the properties are now in the hands of professional property managers.

In addition to defining style boxes for individual real estate assets, NCREIF also identified style boxes at the portfolio level. In other words, NCREIF defined the attributes of portfolios that could be described as core, value-added, or opportunistic. Thus, while each real estate property is unique, the combination of the unique attributes of each property form a portfolio that can resemble a core, value-added, or opportunistic style. Exhibit 9.2 provides these real estate style definitions at the portfolio level.

RETURN EXPECTATIONS

The unique nature of each real estate property and the general lack of liquidity make tracking real estate returns more difficult than tracking other asset classes. The most difficult part of the real estate

---

[3] See Thea C. Hahn, David Geltner, and Nori Gerardo-Lietz, "Real Estate Opportunity Funds," *Journal of Portfolio Management*, Special Real Estate Edition, 2005.

Exhibit 9.2   Real estate portfolio style definitions

Core Portfolio Definition	Value-Added Portfolio Definition	Opportunistic Portfolio Definition
A portfolio that includes a preponderance of core attributes. As a whole, the portfolio will have low lease exposure and low leverage. A low percentage of noncore assets is acceptable. Such portfolios should achieve relatively high income returns and exhibit relatively low volatility. The portfolio attributes should reflect the return versus risk profile of the NPI.	A portfolio that generally includes a mix of core real estate with other real estate investments that have a less reliable income stream. The portfolio as a whole is likely to have moderate lease exposure and moderate leverage. Such portfolios should achieve a significant portion of the return from the appreciation of real estate property values and should exhibit moderate volatility. A risk and return moderately greater than the NPI is expected.	A portfolio preponderantly of noncore investments that is expected to derive most of its return from the appreciation of real estate property values and that may exhibit significant volatility in total return. The increased volatility and appreciation risk may be due to a variety of factors such as exposure to development risk, significant leasing risk, high degree of leverage, or a combination of moderate risk factors. The risk and return profile is significantly greater than the NPI.

market is estimating returns for the value-added and opportunistic segments of the real estate investing market. A recent paper by the Center for International Securities and Derivatives Markets (CISDM) shows that there are reported data only for publicly traded REITs, exchange-traded funds that track REITs, and the NPI indices.[4] These issues are discussed in depth in Chapters 6 and 7. However, it is important in utilizing style boxes to have some range of risk and return expectations, in order to determine how a real estate property or investment manager should be monitored and evaluated.

Style box return objectives

Exhibit 9.3 provides a range of returns for the three style boxes. There is no exact specification for the returns and risks associated with real estate style boxes. Instead, general ranges are used. Some investors define their return expectations in absolute returns, citing an exact range of returns for each style box. Other investors define the risk and return ranges for value-added and opportunistic real estate in relation to the returns produced by the NPI.[5]

Exhibit 9.3 provides estimations of return expectations for real estate returns. It is really a matter of preferences based on objectives and circumstances as to whether an investor uses an absolute definition of real estate returns or a relative definition in relation to the NPI. The return expectations in Exhibit 9.3 have been dampened in light of the recent turmoil in this asset class over 2007 and 2008. Consequently, these return expectations have been reduced by 1% to 2% compared to estimates for these three styles during the real estate boom of 2000 to mid-2007.

Core returns

The easiest range of returns to define is the core portfolio. There are sufficient data from the NPI to set well-grounded expectations about core real estate assets. Using our data from Exhibit 8.1 in Chapter 8 we can see that the NPI had an average return of 7.74% with a volatility of a little more than 8.79% over the time period 1990 to 2008. Using unsmoothed NPI data, the average annual

---

[4] See CISDM Research Department, "The Benefits of Real Estate Investment: 2006 Update," May 2006.

[5] See Baczewski, Hands, and Lathem, "Real Estate Investment Styles."

Exhibit 9.3   Style box return objectives

Absolute Return Investor	Relative Return Investor
Core Returns: Target total returns of 9% to 10% per year. An expected real return of 5% to 7% per year. High percentage of total return from cash flows.	Core Returns: Stable current income and market-level returns commensurate with a low to moderate level of risk. Income is expected to make up the majority of returns, and total return performance is expected to mirror the composite NPI.
Value-Added: Target returns of 10% to 13% per year. Volatility expected to be in the same range.	Value-Added: Income is still a significant portion of total return, but value appreciation may be the source of the majority of the returns. Expected to outpace the NPI by 200 basis points.
Opportunistic: Target return of 13% or more. Higher level of volatility that may exceed 13%.	Opportunistic: Returns are primarily from property appreciation. Current income plays only a small role in total return. Returns are expected to exceed the NPI by 500 basis points.

return increases to almost 9% with a volatility of 11.19%. We maintain that this range of data is consistent with what investors can expect from their core portfolios. The period from 1990 to 2008 was filled with two recessions, two Gulf Wars, a technology boom and bust, the Asian contagion, the start of the subprime mortgage crisis, the Russian bond default, and the bailout of Long-Term Capital Management (LTCM), and a global financial meltdown not witnessed by this generation of investors. In short, this time period was diverse in its business cycle development, shocks to the financial markets, and global economic and political crises. Consequently, expected returns derived from this time period should be robust with respect to future economic and political events.

Value-added returns

While the range of returns for value-added and opportunistic properties given in Exhibit 9.3 come from NCREIF's definitions, actual institutional investors are a bit more conservative in their return expectations for the different style categories. However, PSERS defines value-added return expectations in total return terms. It cites an absolute return of 9% to 13% for value-added investments.[6] Compared to our return analysis for the NPI core properties in Exhibit 8.1, Chapter 8, we can see that PSERS's range of return expectations for value-added real estate is just above the historical return average for core real estate.

Opportunistic returns

PSERS also defines its opportunistic return target in absolute terms. It sets a hurdle rate for opportunistic real estate investing at 13% or greater, depending on the level of risk taken. A return below 13% falls into the value-added real estate style box. As another data point, the California Public Employees' Retirement System (CalPERS) also defines its opportunistic return target in absolute terms. It cites an expected return hurdle rate of 13% or greater.[7] The CalPERS investment policy goes further to note that investment staff may adjust this 13% hurdle rate depending on the characteristics

---

[6] See Pennsylvania Public School Employees' Retirement System, Investment Policy Statement, 2007.

[7] See California Public Employees' Retirement System, Statement of Investment Policy for Opportunistic Real Estate, February 14, 2006.

of the individual opportunistic real estate fund or changes in the marketplace, including changes to the inflation rate, capital market risk levels, or levels of available investment opportunities. The CalPERS investment policy for opportunistic real estate provides additional guidance:

> Opportunistic investments shall provide superior returns with acceptable risk levels when compared to direct equity US real estate investments. Additionally, rates of return will reflect the unique strategies associated with the investment opportunities and shall include, but are not limited to, such factors such as relative stages of development and/or redevelopment, targeted property types, entity or debt vehicles, relative control or liquidity or both that are associated with the investment, and other structuring techniques used to mitigate taxes and currency exposure, if any.

The last part of the CalPERS policy statement mentions taxes and currency exposure because many institutional investors look at real estate investing outside of their home country as being opportunistic in nature since it involves a different market where real estate is valued differently, where development issues such as planning and zoning can be much more difficult, and where property management must recognize the peculiar nature of the foreign market. So, for example, when a U.S. institution invests overseas, it loses its U.S. tax-exempt status and must also deal with the conversion of the total return back into U.S. dollars. This raises the currency and tax issues mentioned in the CalPERS investment policy. These are additional risk factors for which additional expected return must compensate.

One of the difficulties of assessing the return expectations for opportunistic real estate is that many of these investments take place through private limited partnerships (i.e. private equity real estate). Unfortunately, there is no voluntary reporting of data for PERE as there is for members of NCREIF. These private limited partnerships are just that: private. Consequently, data regarding opportunistic real estate investing is limited.

However, a recent study examined the returns to PERE funds over the time period 1991 to 2001.[8] Studying 68 opportunistic real estate funds over this time period, the researchers found that the arithmetic average of gross returns (e.g. no weighting for the amount of capital/size of the funds), before management and incentive fees, was 20.15%. However, after fees were deducted, net total returns were 14.24%. This is pretty much in line with the absolute hurdle rates of CalPERS and PSERS and just a little less than that cited by NCREIF.

Distribution of the NPI returns

In Chapter 8 we used a histogram to observe the pattern of real estate returns over time. That histogram utilized a time series of returns to the composite NPI and its four sectors to analyze the long-term performance of real estate as an asset class. However, we can also use a similar histogram to look at the dispersion of returns associated with individual real estate properties. This is a cross-sectional analysis. We want to observe the returns to all real estate properties at a point in time rather than examining the returns of a composite basket or real estate asset through time. The purpose of a cross-sectional analysis is to give us a sense of the dispersion of returns across real estate assets in a given year.

Exhibit 9.4 presents a cross-sectional histogram of returns. We draw breakpoints at the 5th percentile range, 25th percentile range, 50th percentile range, 75th percentile range, and 95th percentile range. We can see that the median return for the NPI (at the 50th percentile range) is 15.85%. Despite the beginning of the subprime mortgage crisis in 2007, it was a good year for core

---

[8] See Hahn, Geltner, and Gerardo-Lietz, "Real Estate Opportunity Funds."

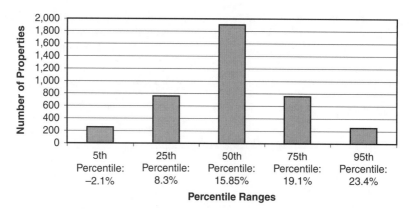

Exhibit 9.4   Cross-section distribution of NPI component property returns in 2007

Source: NCREIF, www.ncreif.com.

real estate returns. But we note that due to the lagged nature of the appraisal process for real estate assets, the returns in Exhibit 9.4 might not have yet fully incorporated the subprime meltdown that began in 2007. Conversely, if we were to plot the distribution of returns from 2008 we would not be plotting the returns from a normal year. The year 2008 was a year of epic upheaval in the financial markets and therefore is inappropriate as a benchmark for real estate return expectations. The year 2007 is a better measure of the expected return distribution for real estate investments.

We introduce a rule of thumb that uses the 5th, 25th, 75th, and 95th percentile ranges around the median as natural breakpoints for determining core, value-added, and opportunistic return expectations. For example, for a portfolio following a core approach in 2007, the rule of thumb suggests that we should expect to earn an average return of 15.85% but have a range of returns mostly ranging from the 25th to the 75th percentiles. Thus, a core portfolio could have a range of returns between 8.3% and 19.1% with an average of 15.85%. Core portfolios are not always within these ranges. They can occasionally fall into larger or smaller return ranges as occupancy and lease rates fluctuate, as some core properties are redeveloped or repositioned, or as new management changes its tenant strategies. The key point is that not all core portfolios in 2007 produced a return of 15.8%. This was simply the mean.

We use the ranges from core real estate returns in Exhibit 9.4 from the 5th percentile to the 25th percentile and from the 75th percentile to the 95th percentile to represent value-added portfolios. These are portfolios that deviate significantly from core portfolios in their risk and return profiles in that they fall outside the center mass of core portfolios more often. These properties can involve the gearing up of new leasing, pursuing a new leasing strategy, renovating and repositioning an existing core property, and occasionally redevelopment. Initially, we would expect that reported returns would fall into the 5th percentile to 25th percentile range as the new leasing strategy begins or as the repositioning of the property starts. Therefore, initially, these more risky properties earn a reported return in the −2.1% to 8.3% range. However, after successfully repositioning a property or initiating a new leasing program, we would expect returns to these types of properties to reflect their value appreciation and jump into the 75th to 95th percentile range with a range of returns from 19.1% to 23.4%.

Last, we look at the range of returns in the zero to 5th percentile and top 95th to 100th percentile to represent what we would expect for opportunistic real estate. As Exhibit 9.4 demonstrates, these properties are in the tails of the return distribution. Opportunistic real estate properties will

Opportunistic Real Estate Realized Returns		
23.40%		95th
Value-Added Real Estate Realized Returns		
19.10%		75th
Core Portfolio: Income Producing		
15.85%		50th
8.30%		25th
Value-Added Real Estate Initial Returns		
−2.10%	**Opportunistic Real Estate Initial Returns**	5th

Exhibit 9.5   Distribution of real estate returns for 2007

Source: NCREIF, www.ncreif.com.

often have negative reported returns early on as capital is deployed for the development, redevelopment, repositioning, restructuring, or ground-up building of the property. However, opportunistic properties would jump into the high end of the return distribution upon successful completion of the development, restructuring, and so on. Therefore, the initial returns can even be below the −2.1% average for the 5th percentile while the positive upside can be greater than the 23.4% average return for the top 95th percentile properties.

Exhibit 9.5 summarizes these return ranges and where core, value-added, and opportunistic properties should fall within these ranges. We can see visually that we would expect core assets to fall within the sweet spot of returns: limited downside, but also limited upside. For those investors willing to take on more risk, the rewards are apparent, but so are the downside risks, and core properties with such relatively extreme return characteristics may be more appropriately considered noncore properties.

Said differently, we can use Exhibits 9.4 and 9.5 to assess the style purity of a real estate manager. Keeping in mind that these returns are produced for the 2007 year only, a manager who professes to pursue a core style of real estate investing would expect to have a large portion of the properties under management generating a return between the 25th and 75th percentile ranges, 8.3% to 19.1%. If a significant number of these properties produce returns outside of this range, despite what the manager professes, the investor might wish to choose to categorize the real estate manager as a value-added or opportunistic real estate manager.

These ranges can also be used as a way to understand the risk profile of the real estate manager. A value-added manager, for example, would be expected to have a significant number of properties producing lower returns in the −2.1% to 8.3% range, as well as other properties producing very good returns in the 19.1% to 23.4% range. The fact that a value-added manager could have returns in the very low range, as well as the very high range is an indicator of the riskiness of the portfolio. The return range would be even more extreme for an opportunistic real estate manager, reflecting the greater risk of these strategies.

PRIVATE EQUITY REAL ESTATE

We provide a final section on PERE. This is a fast-growing part of the real estate market. These opportunistic real estate funds have grown rapidly from just a few billion dollars in 2000 to well over $119 billion in 2007; however, PERE investments in the second quarter of 2009 have dropped to 2004 levels. Exhibit 9.6 shows the growth of the PERE market over the past few years.

Leverage is typically used at a very high level in PERE. The capital structure of these investments is generally very complex. Compared to core properties, increased risks include leverage, development risk, zoning and public policy risk, environmental concerns, currency risk, tenant exposure, and property turnarounds. These investment strategies are hard to access, require considerable specialized expertise, and are hard to execute.

In recent years, many of these transactions have come from Europe, where government-owned real estate properties have become privatized. Also many corporations in Europe held significant real estate assets on their balance sheets that were not part of their core businesses. As in a previously discussed example, many public companies in Germany provided apartment housing for their workers. As these assets have moved off of corporate balance sheets and out of public control, they have provided excellent opportunities for redevelopment and repositioning, consistent with the specialized expertise required to manage opportunistic properties.

A significant problem of PERE investments is valuation. As the market is, by definition, private, transaction and carrying values do not have to be disclosed to anyone except the investors in the private limited partnership, and sometimes, depending on the governance of the private fund, not even to them. A valuation is placed on an asset at the time it is acquired, but often these properties are priced well below their potential. It is the redevelopment, repositioning, or restructuring that will add the value, and these are hard to value quantitatively. Appraisers try to assign interim values to opportunistic properties, but appraising redevelopment/repositioning/restructuring efforts is even more difficult than appraising core properties. Plus, there is a distinct lag in valuation just as discussed with the NPI in Chapter 7.

Valuations can also be subject to selection bias because opportunistic real estate investments change hands depending on the underlying market cycle. For example, in a cyclical downturn, prices may remain artificially high. The reason is that the buyers' bids may be below the sellers' asking prices. This leads to fewer transactions and means that the most recently reported price is the price

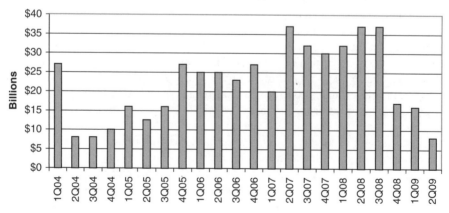

Exhibit 9.6   Private equity real estate

Source: Arleen Jacobius, "Real Estate Fundraising Near 5-Year Low," *Pensions & Investments*, July 7, 2009.

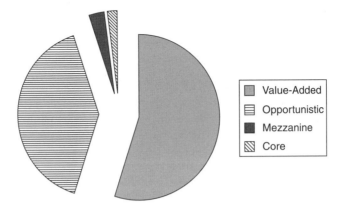

Exhibit 9.7   The PERE pie

Source: NCREIF, www.ncreif.com.

the seller originally paid for the property, which, in a market downturn, is often higher than what buyers are bidding.

Last, we note that PERE investments are not exclusive to opportunistic properties. PERE is being used more and more for value-added and even core properties.[9] Exhibit 9.7 shows a recent breakdown of PERE funds. Core properties are only a small portion of the overall PERE market, with value-added and opportunistic properties combining for the major part of the market. PERE structures are being used more and more for opportunistic as well as value-added and core properties.

CONCLUSION

Institutional investors have become more sophisticated in their real estate portfolio construction in the past eight years. With the advent of the NCREIF white paper on real estate investment styles (Baczewski et al.), institutional investors have been able to build diversified portfolios that stretch from core properties with consistent cash flows to developmental properties with no cash flows but significant value appreciation potential.

Also, the ability to classify real estate properties into different buckets has helped in performance measurement and in developing return expectations. The risks of the different property types have been made more transparent. While the real estate market does not divide the property universe into as many style boxes as the equity market or bond market, it is developing a more filtered view of the real estate investable universe. The result is better portfolio construction, clearer return benchmarks, enhanced performance evaluation, and clearer risk management.

The old adage of real estate was "location, location, location." The new adage is "core, value-added, opportunistic."

---

[9] See "Can Bumper Fundraising Be Sustained?" Preqin Real Estate Feature Article, *Real Estate Spotlight* 1, issue 2, July 2007.

Part III

Hedge Funds

10

Introduction to Hedge Funds

There is a joke in the hedge fund industry that goes like this. Question: "What is a hedge fund?" Answer: "Anything that charges you 2 and 20!"

The joke refers to the fact that hedge funds are not well defined as an investment vehicle and, in fact, are often defined by the fees they charge; "2 and 20" refers to a 2% management fee and a 20% incentive fee. An anecdote can help hammer home this point.

A new start-up hedge fund passed through the CalPERS investment office. I asked the managers of the fund, who were brand-new to the hedge fund game, what their fee structure was. They promptly responded: "We charge 2 and 20." When I inquired why they thought they should charge 2 and 20, given that they had never managed a hedge fund before, they replied: "If we don't charge 2 and 20, no one will think we are serious." Ah, yes.

Therefore, it must be understood that the phrase **hedge fund** is a term of art. In the United States, it is not defined in the Securities Act of 1933 or the Securities Exchange Act of 1934. In addition, hedge fund is not defined by the Investment Company Act of 1940, the Investment Advisers Act of 1940, the Commodity Exchange Act, or, finally, the Bank Holding Company Act. In fact, the Securities and Exchange Commission (SEC) has not attempted to define the term hedge fund and has stated that there is no regulatory or statutory definition of a hedge fund.[1]

So what is this investment vehicle that every investor seems to know but for which there is scant regulatory guidance? As a starting point, we turn to the American Heritage Dictionary (fourth edition), which defines a hedge fund as:

> An investment company that uses high-risk techniques, such as borrowing money and selling short, in an effort to make extraordinary capital gains.

Not a bad start, but we note that hedge funds are not investment companies, for in the United States they would be regulated by the SEC under the Investment Company Act of 1940.[2] Additionally, as we will see later, many hedge fund strategies produce consistent but conservative rates of return, and do not swing for the fences to earn extraordinary gains.

We define hedge funds as:

> A privately organized investment vehicle that manages a concentrated portfolio of public and private securities and derivative instruments on those securities, that can invest both long and short, and that can apply leverage.

Within this definition there are six key elements of hedge funds that distinguish them from their more traditional counterpart, the mutual fund.

First, hedge funds are private investment vehicles that pool the resources of sophisticated investors. One of the ways that hedge funds avoid the regulatory scrutiny of the SEC or the Commodity Futures

---

[1] See Securities and Exchange Commission, "Registration under the Advisers Act of Certain Hedge Fund Advisers," 17 CFR, parts 275 and 279, 69 Federal Register 72054, December 10, 2004.

[2] In fact, hedge funds take great pains to avoid being regulated by the SEC as an investment company. The National Securities Markets Improvement Act of 1996 greatly relieved hedge funds of any regulatory burden by increasing the number of "qualified purchasers" that hedge funds may have to 500. In 2004, the SEC disallowed managers to count each fund entity as a single client. However, the United States Court of Appeals for the District of Columbia overturned this regulation in 2006.

Trading Commission (CFTC) in the United States is that they are available only for high-net-worth investors. Under SEC rules, hedge funds cannot have more than 100 accredited investors in each fund. An **accredited investor** is defined as an individual who has a minimum net worth in excess of $1 million, or income in each of the past two years of $200,000 ($300,000 for a married couple) with an expectation of earning at least that amount in the current year. In addition, hedge funds may accept no more than 500 qualified purchasers in the fund. These are individuals or institutions that have a net worth in excess of $5 million.

There is a penalty, however, for the privacy of hedge funds. They cannot raise funds from investors via a public offering. Additionally, hedge funds may not advertise broadly or engage in a general solicitation for new funds. Instead, their marketing and fund-raising efforts must be targeted to a narrow niche of very wealthy individuals and institutions. As a result, the predominant investors in hedge funds are family offices, foundations, endowments, and, to a lesser extent, pension funds.

Second, hedge funds tend to have portfolios that are much more concentrated than their mutual fund brethren. Most hedge funds do not have broad securities benchmarks. One reason is that most hedge fund managers claim that their style of investing is skill-based and cannot be measured by a market return. Consequently, hedge fund managers are not forced to maintain security holdings relative to a benchmark; they do not need to worry about benchmark risk. This allows them to concentrate their portfolios only on those securities that they believe will add value to the portfolio.

Another reason for the concentrated portfolio is that hedge fund managers tend to have narrow investment strategies. These strategies tend to focus on only one sector of the economy or one segment of the market. They can tailor their portfolio to extract the most value from their smaller investment sector or segment. Further, the concentrated portfolios of hedge fund managers generally are not dependent on the direction of the financial markets, in contrast to long-only managers.

Third, hedge funds tend to use derivative strategies much more predominately than mutual funds. Indeed, in some strategies, such as convertible arbitrage, the ability to sell or buy options is a key component of executing the arbitrage. The use of derivative strategies may result in nonlinear cash flows that may require more sophisticated risk management techniques to control these risks.

Fourth, hedge funds may go both long and short securities. The ability to short public securities and derivative instruments is one of the key distinctions between hedge funds and traditional money managers. Hedge fund managers incorporate their ability to short securities explicitly into their investment strategies. For example, equity long/short hedge funds tend to buy and sell securities within the same industry to maximize their return but also to control their risk. This is very different from traditional money managers that are tied to a long-only securities benchmark.

Fifth, many hedge fund strategies invest in nonpublic securities (i.e. securities that have been issued to investors without the support of a prospectus and a public offering). In the United States, many bonds, both convertible and high-yield, are issued as what are known as **144A securities**. These are securities that are issued to institutional investors in a private transaction instead of a public offering. These securities may be offered with a private placement memorandum (PPM), but not a public prospectus. In addition, these securities are offered without the benefit of an SEC review as would be conducted for a public offering. Bottom line: with 144A securities it is buyer beware. The SEC allows this because, presumably, large institutional investors are more sophisticated than the average, small investor.

Finally, hedge funds use leverage, sometimes large amounts. In fact, a lesson in leverage is described later with respect to Long-Term Capital Management. Mutual funds, for example, are limited in the amount of leverage they can employ; they may borrow up to 33% of their net asset base. Hedge funds do not have this restriction. Consequently, it is not unusual to see some hedge fund strategies that employ leverage up to 10 times their net asset base.

We can see that hedge funds are different from traditional long-only investment managers. We next discuss the history of the hedge fund development.

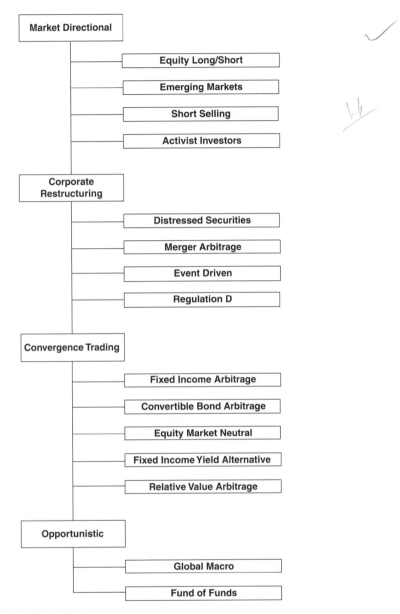

Exhibit 10.1 Categories of hedge funds

CATEGORIES OF HEDGE FUNDS

It seems like everyone has their own classification scheme for hedge funds.[3] This merely reflects the fact that hedge funds are a bit difficult to "box in." This is a topic we will address further when we examine a number of the hedge fund index providers. For purposes of this book, we try to break down hedge funds into broad categories as depicted in Exhibit 10.1.

---

[3] See, for example, Francois-Serge Lhabitant, *Hedge Funds: Quantitative Insights* (West Sussex, UK: John Wiley & Sons, 2004), and Joseph G. Nicholas, *Market Neutral Investing* (Princeton, NJ: Bloomberg Press, 2000).

We classify hedge funds into four broad buckets: market directional, corporate restructuring, convergence trading, and opportunistic. **Market directional** hedge funds are those that retain some amount of systematic risk exposure. For example, equity long/short (or, as it is sometime called, equity hedge) are hedge funds that typically contain some amount of net long market exposure. For example, they may leverage up the hedge fund to go 150% long on stocks that they like while simultaneously shorting 80% of the fund value with stocks that they think will decline in value. The remaining net long market exposure is 70%. Thus they retain some amount of systematic risk exposure that will be affected by the direction of the stock market.

Corporate restructuring hedge funds take advantage of significant corporate transactions like a merger, an acquisition, or a bankruptcy. These funds earn their living by concentrating their portfolios in a handful of companies where it is more important to understand the likelihood that the corporate transaction will be completed than it is to determine whether the corporation is under- or overvalued.

Convergence trading hedge funds are the hedge funds that practice the art of arbitrage. In fact, the specialized subcategories within this bucket typically contain the word *arbitrage* in their names, such as statistical arbitrage, fixed income arbitrage, or convertible arbitrage. In general these hedge funds make bets that two similar securities but with dissimilar prices will converge to the same value over the investment holding period.

Last, we have the **opportunistic category**. We include global macro hedge funds, as well as funds of funds (FOFs) in this category. These funds are designed to take advantage of whatever opportunities present themselves, hence the term *opportunistic*. For example, FOFs often practice tactical asset allocation among the hedge funds contained in the FOF based on the FOF manager's view as to which hedge fund strategies are currently poised to earn the best results. This shifting of the assets around is based on the FOF manager's assessment of the opportunity for each hedge fund contained in the FOF to earn a significant return.

A BRIEF HISTORY OF HEDGE FUNDS

The first hedge fund was established in 1949, the Jones Hedge Fund. Alfred Winslow Jones established a fund that invested in U.S. stocks, both long and short. The intent was to limit market risk while focusing on stock selection. Consequently, this fund was not tied to a securities benchmark and may be properly classified as an equity long/short fund.

Jones operated in relative obscurity until an article was published in *Fortune* magazine that spotlighted the Jones Hedge Fund.[4] The interest in Jones's product was large, and within two years a survey conducted by the SEC established that the number of hedge funds had grown from one to 140.

Unfortunately, many hedge funds were liquidated during the bear market of the early 1970s, and the industry did not regain any interest until the end of the 1980s. The appeal of hedge funds increased tremendously in the 1990s and in the early 2000s. By 2008, there were almost 10,000 hedge funds with close to $1.8 trillion in total assets. Compare this size to mutual funds, where the amount of total assets was $11.5 trillion in mid-2007.

Finally, according to some estimates reported in Anderson (2006), hedge funds account for around 50% of the trading on the New York and London exchanges.

Long-Term Capital Management

The hedge fund market hit another speed bump in 1998 when Long-Term Capital Management (LTCM) of Greenwich, Connecticut had to be rescued by a consortium of banks and brokerage firms. At the time, LTCM was considered one of the largest and best of the hedge fund managers.

---

[4] See Carol Loomis, "The Jones Nobody Keeps Up With," *Fortune*, April 1966, 237–247.

LTCM was founded in 1994 by several executives from Salomon Brothers Inc., as well as well-known academics in the field of finance. In addition, the fund had over 60,000 trades on its books. The gross notional amount of the fund's futures contracts totaled $500 billion, the notional amount of its swap positions totaled $750 billion, and its options and other over-the-counter derivative positions totaled $150 billion.[5] The leverage ratio implied by these derivative positions was a whopping 291.67 to 1.

The troubles for LTCM began in May and June of 1998 with losses in its mortgage-backed arbitrage portfolio. By August 1998, its balance sheet still showed $125 billion in assets but its capital base had shrunk to about $2.3 billion.[6] This was a leverage ratio of about 54 to 1. LTCM suffered further losses in August and September, losing approximately 42% and 83%, respectively. By the end of September, LTCM's capital base had declined to just $400 million.[7]

Unfortunately, LTCM's positions were directly impacted by the Russian bond default in the summer of 1998. In August 1998, the Russian government defaulted on the payment of its outstanding bonds. This caused a worldwide liquidity crisis with credit spreads expanding rapidly around the globe. The Federal Reserve Bank stepped in and acted quickly with three rate reductions within six months, but this action could not salvage LTCM.

The basis for most of LTCM's relative value trades was the expectation that the spread in prices between two similar securities would converge over time. LTCM would buy the cheaper security and short the more expensive security and wait for the spread between the two similar securities to narrow to lock in its profit. However, as a result of the Russian bond default, there was a sudden and drastic liquidity crisis, and spreads widened across a whole range of markets. The result was that instead of contracting as LTCM's pricing models had predicted, pricing spreads dramatically increased in most markets. LTCM quickly accumulated very large paper losses. The lost value of the paper positions led to a margin call from LTCM's prime broker. LTCM was forced to liquidate some of its positions in illiquid markets that were temporarily out of balance. This caused more losses, which led to more margin calls, and LTCM's financial positions began to spiral downward.

The situation for LTCM was bleak, and large financial institutions feared that if LTCM was forced to liquidate the majority of its portfolio there would be a negative impact in the financial markets. Finally, on September 23, at the neutral site of the Federal Reserve Bank of New York, 14 banks and brokerage firms met and agreed to provide a capital infusion of $3.6 billion to LTCM. In return the consortium of banks and brokerage firms received 90% ownership of LTCM.

While the cause of LTCM's demise was clear, the real question is: How did LTCM achieve such a huge amount of credit that it could leverage its cash positions at a 25 to 1 ratio, and its derivative positions at almost a 300 to 1 ratio? It was simple: LTCM did not reveal its full trading positions to any of its counterparties. Each counterparty was kept in the dark about the size of LTCM's total credit exposure with all other counterparties. As a result, LTCM was able to amass tremendous credit and nearly sent a shock wave of epic proportions through the financial markets.[8]

It should be noted that LTCM's spread trades would have worked if it had had more time to work its way out of the liquidity crisis that gripped the markets. It was not that LTCM had poor trade ideas. On the contrary, its valuation models were robust. Instead, it was a significant imbalance of liquidity brought on by the Russian bond default that caused a flight to quality. When this happened, LTCM's relative value positions diverged instead of converging, and this punished LTCM's capital

---

[5] The President's Working Group on Financial Markets, 17.

[6] See Philippe Jorion, "Risk Management Lessons from Long Term Capital Management," working paper, University of California at Irvine, January 2000.

[7] Ibid., 7.

[8] As it was, the near demise of LTCM had an impact on the hedge fund industry. We examine this point more closely in our chapters on risk management.

position. The liquidity crisis coupled with very large amounts of leverage only spelled trouble for LTCM. We explore other hedge fund disasters in Chapter 17.

Growth of the hedge fund industry

By any stretch of the imagination, the growth of the hedge fund industry has been explosive. Because the hedge fund industry is by and large a private industry based on private limited partnerships, the growth of the hedge fund industry cannot be precisely tracked. However, Exhibit 10.2 provides a reasonable estimate of the growth of hedge funds in the United States. As we mentioned before, by most estimates, the hedge fund industry now has almost 10,000 hedge funds with $1.8 trillion committed to it by 2008, a significant increase from just $500 billion in year 2000.

There are many reasons for the huge interest in hedge funds. First, the global three-year bear market of 2000–2002 fueled the interest of those investors who saw their traditional stock and bond portfolios decline in value. Second, many investors recognize the advantage that hedge funds have to go both long and short to maximize the value of their information about stocks, bonds, and other securities. Third, in the current economic environment of 2008, many investors are forecasting single-digit bond returns and low or even negative equity returns. This has encouraged investors all the more to seek the potential double-digit returns of the hedge fund industry. And this has taken place in spite of the fact that the hedge fund industry had its worst year on record in 2008, not only because the Bernie Madoff scandal exploded at the end of that year, but also because around 700 funds shut down in the first three quarters of 2008. Furthermore, according to Hedge Fund Research, hedge funds lost, on average, 18% of their value in 2008, their worst performance ever. The only other negative year on record was in 2002, when hedge funds lost an average of just 1.45%. Still, the performance of hedge funds in 2008 was not as dismal as that of stocks, considering that the Standard & Poor's 500 index fell 38%.

Last, there has been a consistent brain drain of investment talent drawn to the hedge fund industry. The ability to earn 2 and 20 fees is far greater than what a portfolio manager can earn running a mutual fund. The exodus of talent to the hedge fund industry continues to drive the growth of assets to this brand of investing, as well as set the stage for some amazing compensation.

The hedge fund industry continues to be a top wage producer for the asset management industry overall. The highest-paid hedge fund manager in 2007 was John Paulson at $3.7 billion, followed by George Soros at $2.9 billion, James Simons at $2.8 billion, and Phillip Falcone at $1.7 billion.[9]

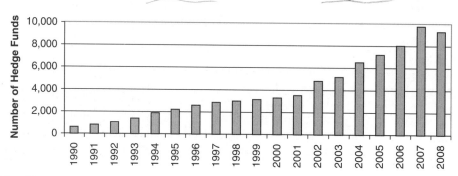

Exhibit 10.2   Growth of the hedge fund industry

Sources: CASAM CISDM Industry Report 2007, and Hedge Fund Research, Inc.

---

[9] See "Highest Paid Hedge Fund Managers 2007," Visualizing Economics, www.visualizingeconomics.com.

HEDGE FUND STRATEGIES

Hedge funds invest in the same equity and fixed-income securities as traditional long-only managers. Therefore, it is not the alternative assets in which hedge funds invest that differentiate them from long-only managers, but rather it is the alternative investment strategies that they pursue.

In this section we provide more detail on the types of strategies pursued by hedge fund managers. We also provide a performance history over the time period 1990 to 2008 for each hedge fund strategy compared to the U.S. stock market and the U.S. Treasury bond market.

Market directional hedge funds

The strategies in this bucket of hedge funds either retain some systematic market exposure associated with the stock market such as equity long/short or are specifically driven by the movements of the stock market such as short selling.

Equity long/short

Equity long/short managers build their portfolios by combining a core group of long stock positions with short sales of stock or stock index options and futures. Their net market exposure of long positions minus short positions tends to have a positive bias. That is, equity long/short managers tend to be long market exposure. The length of their exposure depends on current market conditions. For instance, during the bear market of 2000–2002, these managers decreased their market exposures as they sold more stock short or sold stock index options and futures, whereas during the bull stock market of 2003–2006 these managers tended to have much longer equity exposure.

For example, consider a hedge fund manager who at the beginning of 2008 went long by 150% of the portfolio value in the SPDR XME, an exchange-traded fund (ETF) that passively replicates exposure to the metals and mining sector of the S&P 500. Simultaneously, the hedge fund manager went short by 50% of the portfolio value in the SPDR XLF, an exchange-traded fund that passively replicates exposure to the financial sector in the S&P 500. The beta of the XME is 0.99 whereas the beta of the XLF is 0.98.

The weighted average beta of this equity long/short portfolio is:

$$(1.5 \times 0.99) - (0.5 \times 0.98) = 0.995$$

Therefore, this long/short equity portfolio is just about beta neutral to the S&P 500 benchmark.[10]

According to the capital asset pricing model (CAPM), the hedge fund manager has a portfolio that has just about the same systematic risk as the S&P 500. In 2008, the return on the market, represented by the S&P 500 was –13.64% through August 2008, while the risk-free rate was about 2.25%. Given the realized return on the market portfolio and beta of the hedge fund, the realized return on this portfolio, according to the model, should be:[11]

$$\text{Return} = 2.25\% + 0.995(-13.6\% - 2.25\%) = -13.52\%$$

---

[10] Beta is a well-known measure of market exposure (or systematic risk). A portfolio with a beta of 1.0 is beta neutral with respect to S&P 500 and therefore has the same stock market exposure or risk as a broad-based stock index such as the S&P 500.

[11] The capital asset pricing model is expressed as: E(Return on portfolio) = Risk-free rate + Beta × (Return on the market – Risk-free rate).

However, from January to August 2008, the return on the XLF was –33% while the return on the XME was +23%. This beta neutral portfolio would have earned the following return:

$$(1.5 \times 23\%) + (-0.5 \times -33\%) = 51\%$$

This is a much higher return than that predicted by the CAPM. This example serves to highlight two points. First, the ability to go both long and short in the market is a powerful tool for earning excess returns. The ability to fully implement a strategy not only about stocks and sectors that are expected to increase in value but also stocks and sectors that are expected to decrease in value allows the hedge fund manager to maximize the value of her market insights.

Second, the long/short nature of the portfolio can be misleading with respect to the risk exposure. This manager appears to be beta neutral to the S&P 500 and an investor might conclude that she should expect returns similar to those of the S&P 500. However, what the hedge fund manager has done is make two explicit bets: that financial stocks will decline in value and that metals and mining stocks will increase in value.

The CAPM assumes that investors hold well-diversified portfolios. That is not the case with this hedge fund manager. Most hedge fund managers build concentrated rather than broad portfolios. Consequently, traditional metrics such as the CAPM may not apply to hedge fund managers.

Equity long/short hedge funds essentially come in two flavors: fundamental or quantitative. **Fundamental** long/short hedge funds conduct traditional economic analysis on a company's business prospects compared to its competitors and the current economic environment. These shops will visit with management, talk with Wall Street analysts, contact customers and competitors, and essentially conduct bottom-up analysis. The difference between these hedge funds and long-only managers is that the former will short the stocks that they consider to be poor performers and buy those stocks that are expected to outperform the market. In addition, they may leverage their long and short positions.

Fundamental long/short equity hedge funds tend to invest in one economic sector or market segment. For instance, they may specialize in buying and selling Internet companies (sector focus) or buying and selling small market capitalization companies (segment focus).

In contrast, **quantitative** equity long/short hedge fund managers tend not to be sector or segment specialists. In fact, quite the reverse; quantitative hedge fund managers like to cast as broad a net as possible in their analysis. These managers are often referred to as statistical arbitrage because they base their trade selections on the use of quantitative statistics instead of fundamental stock selection.

In Exhibit 10.3, we provide a graph of a hypothetical investment of $1,000 in an equity long/short fund of funds compared to the S&P 500 index and 10-year U.S. Treasury bonds. The time period is 1990 through 2008. The dashed line represents the hedge fund strategy, the light gray line represents the S&P 500, and the dark line represents the U.S. Treasury bond return. As can be seen, the returns to this strategy were quite favorable compared to the stock market and the bond market. However, this strategy had its worst performance in 20 years in the midst of the financial crisis of 2008.

Included within the equity long/short category are so-called sector hedge funds. These are equity long/short managers that specialize in a specific sector such as biotechnology, health care, or natural resources. These are typically fundamental stock pickers that have considerable knowledge and experience in analyzing companies in a specialized sector of the economy. They go both long and short, using their fundamental information advantage to find both good and bad performing companies in that sector. Typically, they have a long beta exposure—sometimes a very long beta exposure with only a few short positions offsetting many long positions. Generally, these hedge funds are started by sector analysts or portfolio managers that wish to maximize the total value of

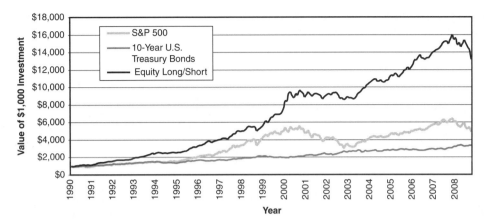

Exhibit 10.3   Equity long/short hedge funds

Source: Datastream and Hedge Fund Research, Inc., copyright 2009, www.hedgefundresearch.com.

their information set, as we described in our discussion in Chapter 5 on the Fundamental Law of Active Management.

Emerging markets

Emerging markets have become an increasingly important part of asset allocation for institutional investors. In addition, the maturity and sophistication of hedge fund investing is now extensive in the emerging markets.

Exhibit 10.4 shows the cumulative returns for emerging markets hedge funds. We can see that this category has performed significantly better than the S&P 500 and U.S. Treasury bonds, particularly during the current decade. This is partly due to a higher beta (systematic risk) associated with emerging compared to developed markets, and this was a period of good economic growth for emerging market economies. In addition, hedge funds became much more sophisticated investors in emerging markets during this time.

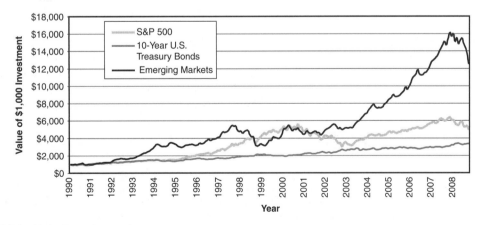

Exhibit 10.4   Emerging markets

Source: Datastream and Hedge Fund Research, Inc., copyright 2009, www.hedgefundresearch.com.

Note, however, that in the global bear market of 2008, the return for this strategy declined significantly. This reflects the long bias to stock market exposure that is retained in emerging market strategies. The MSCI Barra Emerging Markets index was down over 50% through October 2008, a more precipitous decline than the S&P 500.

Short selling

Short selling hedge funds have the opposite exposure of traditional long-only managers. In that sense, their return distribution should be the mirror image of long-only managers: they make money when the stock market is declining and lose money when the stock market is gaining.

These hedge fund managers may be distinguished from equity long/short managers in that they generally maintain a net short exposure to the stock market. However, short selling hedge funds tend to use some form of market timing. That is, they trim their short positions when the stock market is increasing and go fully short when the stock market is declining. When the stock market is gaining, short sellers maintain that portion of their investment capital not committed to short selling in short-term interest-rate-bearing accounts.

According to Stefanini (2006), the following are some of the necessary characteristics for a firm to be a short sale target: companies whose management lies to investors (e.g. use of accounting tricks), companies with insider trading, companies that are destroying value, companies with deteriorating fundamentals, and companies experiencing changes in their equity structure. Before setting up a short position, short selling hedge funds attempt to identify a catalytic event, an event that may have a negative impact on the company in the short-term.

Exhibit 10.5 demonstrates the return to short selling hedge funds compared to the S&P 500 and U.S. Treasury bonds. In general, short sellers do very well during a bear market. From Exhibit 10.5, short sellers provided strong positive performance during the bear market of 2000 to 2002 and the bear market of 2008, but otherwise the returns to this strategy are not generally favorable because there was a significant bull market from 1990 through 1999. Short selling strategies, therefore, provide good downside protection for bear markets, but otherwise do not add positive value to a portfolio. They should be included in a hedge fund of funds for their protective ability, but should not be the focal point for generating excess returns.

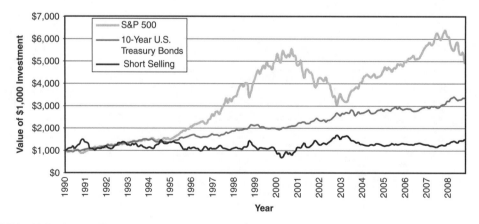

Exhibit 10.5   Short selling

Source: Datastream and Hedge Fund Research, Inc., copyright 2009, www.hedgefundresearch.com.

Activist investing

Corporate governance can be used as an alpha-driven investment strategy. Data from the California Public Employees' Retirement System (CalPERS) and well-identified market benchmarks demonstrate that corporate governance can generate returns in excess of the stock market while providing excellent return diversification.

The corporate governance style of investing has grown in importance. Essentially, this is the same type of corporate governance investing pursued by CalPERS, the California State Teachers Retirement System, Hermes Pensions Management, and other activist investors.

Essentially, it entails building a very concentrated portfolio of only 5 to 15 equity positions in publicly traded corporations. These positions are large, anywhere from 1% to 10% of the outstanding stock of the company. The activist investor then demands a meeting with the public company's board of directors and CEO. The purpose is to impose better governance techniques on the board of governors (e.g. to be less cozy with the CEO and to act in shareholders' interests). In addition, activist investors work with the CEO to implement a better business plan and even remove the CEO if he or she is ineffective. This manner of investing is also called corporate engagement, as the activist investor pursues a direct dialogue with the management and board of directors. The success of investors such as CalPERS and Hermes has encouraged many other investors to enter this form of equity investing to reap the rewards of better corporate governance. This strategy is included under market directional because these funds tend to take long-only positions. Even though their portfolios are very concentrated, there is still a considerable amount of stock market risk embedded in their portfolios.

Using a large hand-collected data set from 2001 to 2006, Brav, Jiang, Partnoy, and Thomas (2008) find that target firms in the United States experience increases in operating performance, payout, and higher CEO turnover after activism from hedge funds. Furthermore, they also calculate that the abnormal stock return upon announcement of activism is around 7%.

Exhibit 10.6 presents the results for **activist hedge funds**.[12] Not surprisingly, since 2002 these funds have tracked the broader U.S. stock market, but with a premium added for their skill. However,

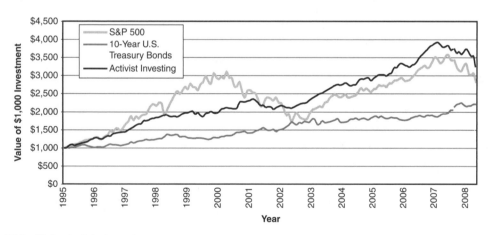

Exhibit 10.6   Activist investing

Source: Datastream and Hedge Fund Research, Inc., copyright 2009, www.hedgefundresearch.com.

---

[12] The data for this hedge fund strategy does not begin until 1995. Therefore, the value of a $1,000 investment will be different compared to those hedge fund strategies whose data history extends back to 1990.

we point out that these tend to be long-only funds with concentrated stock positions. Consequently, they are subject to up and down movements of the broader stock market. This is apparent from their poor performance during 2007 and 2008. Note that data tracking for activist investing does not begin until 1996. Consequently, the value of a $1,000 investment will be different compared to other hedge fund strategies where the data begins in 1990.

Corporate restructuring hedge funds

Many hedge fund articles call these strategies "event driven" or "risk arbitrage," but that does not really describe what is at the heart of each of these types of strategies. The focal point is some form of corporate restructuring such as a merger, acquisition, or bankruptcy. Companies that are undergoing a significant transformation generally provide an opportunity for trading around that event. These strategies are driven by the deal, not by the market.

Distressed securities

Distressed debt hedge funds invest in the securities of a corporation that is in bankruptcy, or is likely to fall into bankruptcy. Companies can become distressed for any number of reasons, such as too much leverage on their balance sheet, poor operating performance, accounting irregularities, or even competitive pressure. Some of these strategies can overlap with private equity strategies that we discuss in Part Five of this book. The key difference here is that hedge funds are less concerned with the fundamental value of a distressed corporation and, instead, concentrate on trading opportunities surrounding the company's outstanding stock and bond securities.

There are many different variations on how to play a distressed situation, but most fall into three categories. In its simplest form, the easiest way to profit from a distressed corporation is to sell its stock short. This requires the hedge fund manager to borrow stock from its prime broker and sell in the marketplace this stock that it does not own with the expectation that it will be able to purchase the stock back at a later date and at a cheaper price as the company continues to spiral downward in its distressed situation. This is nothing more than "sell high and buy low."

However, the short selling of a distressed company exposes the hedge fund manager to significant risk if the company's fortunes should suddenly turn around. Therefore, most hedge fund managers in this space typically use a hedging strategy within a company's capital structure.

A second form of distressed securities investing is called capital structure arbitrage. Consider Company A that has four levels of outstanding capital: senior secured debt, junior subordinated debt, preferred stock, and common stock. A standard distressed security investment strategy would be to:

- Buy the senior secured debt and short the junior subordinated debt.
- Buy the preferred stock and short the common stock.

In a bankruptcy situation, the senior secured debt stands in line in front of the junior subordinated debt for any bankruptcy-determined payouts. The same is true for the preferred stock compared to Company A's common stock. Both the senior secured debt and the preferred stock enjoy a higher standing in the bankruptcy process than either junior debt or common equity. Therefore, when the distressed situation occurs or progresses, senior secured debt should appreciate in value relative to the junior subordinated debt. In addition, there should be an increase in the spread of prices between preferred stock and common stock. When this happens, the hedge fund manager closes out its positions and locks in the profit that occurs from the increase in the spread.

Last, distressed securities hedge funds can become involved in the bankruptcy process in order to find significantly undervalued securities. This is where an overlap with private equity firms can occur. To the extent that a distressed securities hedge fund is willing to learn the arcane workings of the bankruptcy process and to sit on creditor committees, significant value can be accrued if a distressed company can restructure and regain its footing. In a similar fashion, hedge fund managers do purchase the securities of a distressed company shortly before it announces its reorganization plan to the bankruptcy court with the expectation that there will be a positive resolution with the company's creditors.

Exhibit 10.7 presents the value of distressed securities hedge funds compared to the U.S. stock and bond markets. It shows reasonably steady growth over the time 1990 through 2001, but significant growth from 2002 through 2006. This is indicative of distressed securities hedge funds capitalizing on the recovery of the U.S. credit markets and the U.S. economy after the three-year bear market of 2000 to 2002. It appears that many distressed securities hedge funds followed the third strategy during this time frame and enjoyed the benefits of successful reorganization of companies coming out of bankruptcy during a bull market. However, this strategy was not able to provide positive returns during the recession of 2008.

Merger arbitrage

Merger arbitrage is perhaps the best-known corporate restructuring investment among investors and hedge fund managers. Merger arbitrage generally entails buying the stock of the firm that is to be acquired and selling the stock of the firm that is the acquirer. Merger arbitrage managers seek to capture the price spread between the current market prices of the merger partners and the value of those companies upon the successful completion of the merger.

The stock of the target company will usually trade at a discount to the announced merger price. The discount reflects the risk inherent in the deal. Other market participants are unwilling to take on the full exposure of the transaction-based risk. Merger arbitrage is then subject to event risk. There is the risk that the two companies will fail to come to terms and call off the deal. There is the risk that another company will enter into the bidding contest, ruining the initial dynamics of the arbitrage. Last, there is regulatory risk. Various U.S. and foreign regulatory agencies may not allow the merger to take place for antitrust reasons. Merger arbitrageurs specialize in assessing event risk and building a diversified portfolio to spread out this risk.

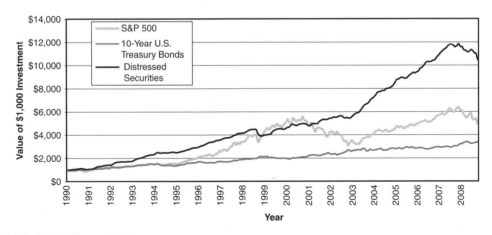

Exhibit 10.7   Distressed debt

Source: Datastream and Hedge Fund Research, Inc., copyright 2009, www.hedgefundresearch.com.

Merger arbitrageurs conduct significant research on the companies involved in the merger. They will review current and prior financial statements, SEC EDGAR filings, proxy statements, management structures, cost savings from redundant operations, strategic reasons for the merger, regulatory issues, press releases, and the competitive position of the combined company within the industry in which it competes. Merger arbitrageurs will calculate the rate of return that is implicit in the current spread and compare it to the event risk associated with the deal. If the spread is sufficient to compensate for the expected event risk, they will execute the arbitrage.

Hedge fund managers tend to use the term arbitrage somewhat loosely. As discussed earlier, there is plenty of event risk associated with a merger announcement. The profits earned from merger arbitrage are not riskless. Consider the saga of the purchase of MCI Corporation by Verizon Communications. Throughout 2005, Verizon was in a bidding war against Qwest Communications for the purchase of MCI. On February 3, 2005, Qwest announced a $6.3 billion merger offer for MCI. This bid was quickly countered by Verizon on February 10, which matched the $6.3 billion bid established by Qwest. The bidding war raged back and forth for several months before Verizon finally won the day in October 2005 with an ultimate purchase price of $8.44 billion.

To see the vicissitudes of merger arbitrage at work, we follow both the successful Verizon bid for MCI as well as the unsuccessful bid by Qwest.

Starting with Verizon: at the announcement of its bid for MCI, its stock was trading at $36, while MCI was trading at $20. Therefore the merger arbitrage trade was:

Sell 1,000 shares of Verizon at $36 (short proceeds of $36,000).
Buy 1,000 shares of MCI at $20 (cash outflow of $20,000).

For the Qwest bid, the trade was:

Sell 1,000 shares of Qwest at $4.20 (short proceeds of $4,200).
Buy 1,000 shares of MCI at $20 (cash outflow of $20,000).

Throughout the spring and summer of 2005, Qwest and Verizon battled it out for MCI, with Verizon ultimately winning in October 2005. At that time, MCI's stock had increased in value to $25.50, while Verizon's stock had lost value and was trading at $30. Qwest was trading unchanged at $4.20.

Total return for the MCI/Verizon merger arbitrage trade:

Gain on MCI long position	$1,000 \times (\$25.50 - \$20)$	= $5,500
Gain on Verizon short position	$1,000 \times (\$36 - \$30)$	= $6,000
Interest on short rebate	$4\% \times 1,000 \times \$36 \times 240/360$	= $960
Total		= $12,460

The return on invested capital is: $12,460 ÷ $20,000 = 62.3%

If the merger arbitrage manager had applied 50% leverage to this deal and borrowed half of the net outflow, the return would have been (ignoring financing costs): $12,460 ÷ $10,000 = 124.6% total return.

Turning to the MCI/Qwest merger arbitrage trade, the total return was:

Gain on MCI long position	$1,000 \times (\$25.50 - \$20)$	= $5,500
Gain on Qwest short position	$1,000 \times (\$4.20 - \$4.20)$	= $0
Gain on short rebate	$4\% \times 1,000 \times \$4.20 \times 240/360$	= $112
Total		= $5,612

The return on invested capital is: $5,612 ÷ $20,000 = 28.06%. With 50% leverage the return would be: $5,612 ÷ $10,000 = 56.12%.

While both merger arbitrage trades made money, clearly it made sense to bet on the Verizon/MCI merger rather than the Qwest/MCI merger. This is where merger arbitrage managers make their money: by assessing the likelihood of one bid over another. Also, in a situation where there are two bidders for a company, there is a very high probability that there will be a successful merger with one of the bidders. Consequently, many merger arbitrage hedge fund managers will play both bids. This is exactly what happened in the MCI deal, many merger arbitrage managers bet on both the MCI/Verizon deal and the MCI/Qwest deal, expecting that one of the two suitors would be successful in winning the hand of MCI.

Some merger arbitrage managers invest only in announced deals. However, other hedge fund managers will put on positions on the basis of rumor or speculation. The deal risk is much greater with the latter type of strategy, but so too is the merger spread (the premium that can be captured).

To control for risk, most merger arbitrage hedge fund managers have some risk of loss limit at which they will exit positions. Some hedge fund managers concentrate in only one or two industries, applying their specialized knowledge regarding an economic sector to their advantage. Other merger arbitrage managers maintain a diversified portfolio across several industries to spread out the event risk.

Merger arbitrage is deal driven rather than market driven. Merger arbitrage derives its return from the relative values of the stock prices of two companies as opposed to the status of the current market conditions. Consequently, merger arbitrage returns should not be highly correlated with the general stock market.

Exhibit 10.8 highlights this point. We see steady, consistent returns year after year. There are no years of extraordinary gains, and no years of extraordinary losses, not even in the bear market of 2008. Merger arbitrage is typically not driven by the systematic risk of the market; rather, it is mostly driven by the economics of the individual deals. However, during periods of market downturns, merger activities dry up and many announced mergers fall through, and as a result the merger arbitrage strategy performs poorly during such periods.

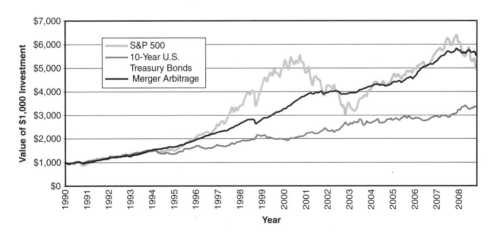

Exhibit 10.8 Merger arbitrage

Source: Datastream and Hedge Fund Research, Inc., copyright 2009, www.hedgefundresearch.com.

Event driven

Event driven hedge funds are very similar to distressed securities and merger arbitrage hedge funds in their approach to investing. The only difference is that their mandate is broader than the other two corporate restructuring strategies. Event driven transactions include mergers and acquisitions, spin-offs, tracking stocks, accounting write-offs, reorganizations, bankruptcies, share buybacks, special dividends, and any other significant market event. Event driven managers are nondiscriminatory in their transaction selection.

By their very nature, these special events are nonrecurring. Therefore, the financial markets typically do not digest the information associated with these transactions in a timely manner. The financial markets are simply less efficient when it comes to large, isolated transactions. This provides an opportunity for event driven managers to act quickly and capture a premium in the market. Additionally, most of these events may be subject to certain conditions such as shareholder or regulatory approval. Therefore, there is significant deal risk associated with this strategy for which a savvy hedge fund manager can earn a return premium. The profitability of this type of strategy depends on the successful completion of the corporate transaction within the expected time frame.

We would expect event driven strategies to be less influenced by the general stock market, since the returns are driven by company-specific events, not market driven events. However, in Exhibit 10.9, we do see that the value of event driven strategies does closely parallel that value of the S&P 500 from 1990 to 1999 and then significantly outperforms the stock market from 2000 to 2007. This may reflect the fact that event driven hedge fund managers participated in the many positive corporate mergers and acquisitions that occurred during the bull market, but then were also able to participate in the many corporate reorganizations that occurred during the bear market years of 2000 to 2002.

Regulation D hedge funds

This strategy is related to the regulatory environment of the United States. Regulation D (Reg D) hedge funds invest in privately issued securities of public companies. **Regulation D** is a regulation under the Securities Act of 1933 that allows public companies to issue stock or debt in an offering other than to the public. Under Reg D, the securities must be offered to only the most sophisticated

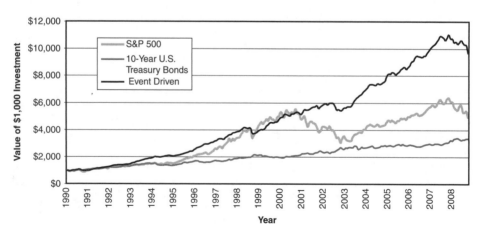

Exhibit 10.9 Event driven

Source: Datastream and Hedge Fund Research, Inc., copyright 2009, www.hedgefundresearch.com.

of investors and there cannot be any marketing materials. Corporations often raise capital by selling securities directly to sophisticated investors without the need for the lengthy public offering and registration process. The advantage is speed of completing the offering. The disadvantage is that the offering is made to a smaller pool of investors.

Hedge funds purchase Reg D offerings for two reasons. First, Reg D securities might be priced more cheaply than the similar, but publicly traded, securities of the issuer. This is just a value play where the hedge fund uses leverage to boost the returns of buying privately issued securities at a discount to their publicly traded counterparts. Second, Reg D hedge funds can perform a form of arbitrage where they buy the privately issued securities and short similar but publicly traded securities. It is a case of buying cheap and selling rich. This makes the Reg D strategy sound like more of an arbitrage strategy, but we include it within the corporate restructuring category because Reg D securities have an impact on the capital structure of a public company. Also, many Reg D offerings are made in debt form but are convertible to equity after a certain period of time. This allows a Reg D hedge fund manager to buy equity at a cheaper price than the publicly traded stock of the company. Alternatively, the hedge fund manager can buy the Reg D convertible debt of the issuer and short the publicly traded stock of the issuer to end up owning a cheap bond. However, if the hedge fund manager uses Reg D offerings, they have an impact on the capital structure of the issuing corporation.

Exhibit 10.10 shows the returns for Reg D hedge funds. Clearly, there is a return premium to purchasing Reg D securities cheaply. This strategy outperforms the U.S. stock market by a significant margin.

However, we note that the returns to this strategy plateaued in 2007 and began to decline in 2008. The reasons were several: There was a flight to security (mostly into U.S. Treasury bonds); the liquidity premium for less liquid securities soared, bringing down the prices of illiquid securities like Reg D securities; and credit risk was not rewarded.

Convergence trading hedge funds

As mentioned earlier, hedge fund managers tend to use the term arbitrage somewhat loosely. Arbitrage is defined simply as riskless profits. It is the purchase of a security for cash at one price

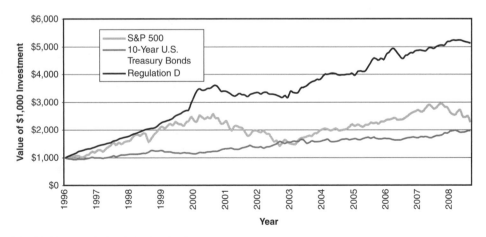

Exhibit 10.10   Regulation D hedge funds

Source: Datastream and Hedge Fund Research, Inc., copyright 2009, www.hedgefundresearch.com.

and the immediate resale for cash of the same security at a higher price. Alternatively, it may be defined as the simultaneous purchase of Security A for cash at one price and the selling of identical Security B for cash at a higher price. In both cases, the arbitrageur has no risk. There is no market risk because the holding of the securities is instantaneous. There is no basis risk because the securities are identical, and there is no credit risk because the transaction is conducted in cash.

Instead of riskless profits, in the hedge fund world arbitrage is generally used to mean low-risk investments. Instead of the purchase and sale of identical instruments, there is the purchase and sale of similar instruments. In addition, the securities may not be sold for cash, so there may be credit risk during the collection period. Last, the purchase and sale may not be instantaneous. The arbitrageur may need to hold on to the positions for a period of time, exposing him to market risk.

Fixed income arbitrage

Fixed income arbitrage involves purchasing one fixed income security and simultaneously selling a similar fixed income security with the expectation that over the investment holding period the two security prices will converge to a similar value. Hedge fund managers search continuously for these pricing inefficiencies across all fixed income markets. This is nothing more than buying low and selling high: waiting for the undervalued security to increase in value or the overvalued security to decline in value, or waiting for both to occur.

The sale of the second security is done to hedge the underlying market risk contained in the first security. Typically, the two securities are related either mathematically or economically such that they move similarly with respect to market developments. Generally, the difference in pricing between the two securities is small, and this is what the fixed income arbitrageur hopes to gain. By buying and selling two fixed income securities that are tied together, the hedge fund manager hopes to capture a pricing discrepancy that will cause the prices of the two securities to converge over time.

However, because the price discrepancies can be small, the way hedge fund managers add more value is to leverage their portfolios through direct borrowings from their prime brokers, or by creating leverage through swaps and other derivative securities. Bottom line: they find pricing anomalies, then crank up the volume through leverage.

Fixed income arbitrage does not need to use exotic securities. For example, it can be nothing more than buying and selling U.S. Treasury bonds. In the bond market, the most liquid securities are the on-the-run Treasury bonds. These are the most currently issued bonds issued by the U.S. Treasury Department. However, there are other U.S. Treasury bonds outstanding that have very similar characteristics to the on-the-run Treasury bonds. The difference is that off-the-run bonds were issued at earlier dates, and are now less liquid than the on-the-run bonds. As a result, price discrepancies occur. The difference in price may be no more than one-half or one-quarter of a point ($25) but can increase in times of uncertainty when investor money shifts to the most liquid U.S. Treasury bond. During the Russian bond default crisis, for example, on-the- run U.S. Treasuries were valued as much as $100 more than similar, off-the-run U.S. Treasury bonds of the same maturity.

Nonetheless, when held to maturity, the prices of these two bonds will converge to the same value. Any difference will be eliminated by the time they mature, and any price discrepancy may be captured by the hedge fund manager.

Fixed income arbitrage is not limited to the U.S. Treasury market. It can be used with corporate bonds, municipal bonds, sovereign debt, or mortgage-backed securities (MBSs).

Another form of fixed income arbitrage involves trading among fixed income securities that are close in maturity. This is a form of yield curve arbitrage. These types of trades are driven by temporary imbalances in the term structure of interest rates.

Exhibit 10.11 is a snapshot of the term structure in the U.S. Treasury bond market in August 2007. Instead of a smooth yield curve, there are kinks in the term structure between the three-month and five-year time horizons. Kinks in the yield curve can happen at any maturity and usually reflect an increase (or decrease) in liquidity demand around the focal point. These kinks provide an opportunity to profit by purchasing and selling Treasury securities that are similar in maturity.

Consider the kink that bottoms at the two-year maturity. The holder of the five-year Treasury bond profits by rolling down the yield curve toward the two-year rate. In other words, if interest rates remain static, the five-year Treasury note will age into a lower-yielding part of the yield curve. Moving down the yield curve will mean positive price appreciation. Conversely, Treasury bonds maturing in the two-year to three-month range will roll up the yield curve to higher yields. This means that their prices are expected to depreciate.

An arbitrage trade would be to purchase the five-year Treasury bond and short a two-year bond. As the two-year bond rolls up the yield curve, its value should decline, while the five-year Treasury bond should increase in value as it rolls down the yield curve. This arbitrage trade will work as long as the kinks remain in place.

However, this trade does have its risks. First, shifts in the yield curve up or down can affect the profitability of the trade because the two securities have different maturities and duration. To counter this problem, the hedge fund manager would need to purchase and sell securities in proper proportion to neutralize the differences in duration. Also, liquidity preferences of investors could change and the kink could reverse itself or flatten out. In either case, the hedge fund manager would lose money. Conversely, should liquidity preferences increase, the trade will become even more profitable.

Still another subset of fixed income arbitrage uses mortgage-backed securities (MBSs). An MBS represents an ownership interest in an underlying pool of individual mortgages lent by banks and other financial institutions. Therefore, an MBS is a fixed income security with underlying prepayment options. MBS hedge funds seek to capture pricing inefficiencies in the U.S. mortgage-backed market.

MBS arbitrage can be between fixed income markets, such as buying MBSs and selling U.S. Treasuries. This investment strategy is designed to capture credit spread inefficiencies between U.S. Treasuries and MBSs, which trade at a credit spread over U.S. Treasuries to reflect the uncertainty of

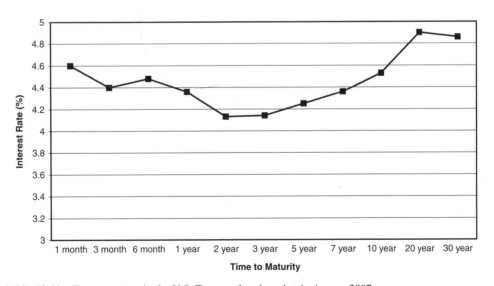

Exhibit 10.11   Term structure in the U.S. Treasury bond market in August 2007

cash flows associated with MBSs compared to the lack of credit risk associated with U.S. Treasury bonds.

As noted earlier, during a flight to quality, investors tend to seek out the most liquid markets such as the on-the-run U.S. Treasury market. This may cause credit spreads to temporarily increase beyond what is historically or economically justified. In this case the MBS market will be priced cheaply compared to U.S. Treasuries. The arbitrage strategy would be to buy MBSs and sell U.S. Treasury securities where the interest rate exposure of both instruments is sufficiently similar so as to eliminate most (if not all) of the market risk between the two securities. The expectation is that the credit spread between MBSs and U.S. Treasuries will decline and MBS bonds will increase in value relative to U.S. Treasuries.

MBS arbitrage can be quite sophisticated. MBS hedge fund managers use proprietary models to rank the value of MBSs by their option-adjusted spread (OAS). The hedge fund manager evaluates the present value of an MBS by explicitly incorporating assumptions about the probability of prepayment options being exercised. In effect, the hedge fund manager calculates the option-adjusted price of the MBS and compares it to its current market price. The OAS reflects the MBS's average spread over U.S. Treasury bonds of a similar maturity, taking into account the fact that the MBS may be liquidated early from the exercise of the prepayment option by the underlying mortgagors.

The MBSs that have the best OAS compared to U.S. Treasuries are purchased, and then their interest rate exposure is hedged to zero. Interest rate exposure is neutralized using Treasury bonds, options, swaps, futures, and caps. MBS hedge fund managers seek to maintain a duration of zero. This allows them to concentrate on selecting the MBSs that yield the highest OAS.

There are many risks associated with MBS arbitrage. Chief among them are duration, convexity, yield curve rotation, prepayment risk, credit risk, and liquidity risk. Hedging these risks may require the purchase or sale of other MBS products such as interest-only strips and principal-only strips, U.S. Treasuries, interest rate futures, swaps, and options.

What should be noted about fixed income arbitrage strategies is that they do not depend on the direction of the general financial markets. Arbitrageurs seek out pricing inefficiencies between two securities instead of making bets on market direction.

This is clear from Exhibit 10.12. Fixed income arbitrage earns a steady consistent rate year after year, regardless of the movement of the stock market. The exceptions have been 1998 and the dual

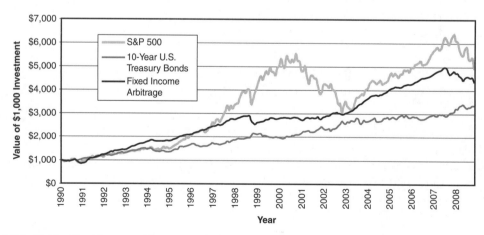

Exhibit 10.12   Fixed income arbitrage

Source: Datastream and Hedge Fund Research, Inc., copyright 2009, www.hedgefundresearch.com.

crisis of the Russian bond default and the LTCM bailout, and the subprime mortgage crisis that began in the summer of 2007. Otherwise, the hypothetical value of $1,000 invested in fixed income arbitrage is almost a straight line, matching that of the 10-year U.S. Treasury bond.

Convertible bond arbitrage

Convertible bonds combine elements of both stocks and bonds in one package. A convertible bond is a bond that contains an embedded option to convert the bond into the underlying company's stock.

Convertible arbitrage funds build long positions of convertible bonds and then hedge the equity component of the bonds by selling the underlying stock or options on that stock. Equity risk can be hedged by selling the appropriate ratio of stock underlying the convertible option. This hedge ratio is known as the **delta** and is designed to measure the sensitivity of the convertible bond value to movements in the underlying stock.

Convertible bonds that trade at a low premium to their conversion value tend to be more correlated with the movement of the underlying stock. These convertibles then trade more like stock than like a bond. Consequently, a high hedge ratio, or delta, is required to hedge the equity risk contained in the convertible bond. Convertible bonds that trade at a premium to their conversion value are highly valued for their bondlike protection. Therefore, a lower delta hedge ratio is necessary.

However, convertible bonds that trade at a high conversion premium act more like fixed income securities and therefore have more interest rate exposure than those with more equity exposure. This risk must be managed by selling interest rate futures, interest rate swaps, or other bonds. Furthermore, it should be noted that the hedging ratios for equity and interest rate risk are not static; they change as the value of the underlying equity changes and as interest rates change. Therefore, the hedge fund manager must continually adjust his hedge ratios to ensure that the arbitrage remains intact.

If this all sounds complicated, it is, but that is how hedge fund managers make money. They use sophisticated option pricing models and interest rate models to keep track of all the moving parts associated with convertible bonds. Hedge fund managers make arbitrage profits by identifying pricing discrepancies between the convertible bond and its component parts and then continually monitoring these component parts for any change in their relationship.

Consider the following example. A hedge fund manager purchases 10 convertible bonds with a par value of $1,000, a coupon of 7.5%, and a market price of $900. The **conversion ratio** for the bonds is 20. The conversion ratio is based on the current price of the underlying stock, $45, and the current price of the convertible bond (i.e. $900/$45). The delta, or hedge ratio, for the bonds is 0.5. Therefore, to hedge the equity exposure in the convertible bond, the hedge fund manager must short the following shares of the underlying stock:

$$\text{Number of bonds} \times \text{Conversion ratio} \times \text{Hedge ratio} = \text{Number of shares}$$
$$10 \text{ bonds} \times 20 \text{ conversion ratio} \times 0.5 \text{ hedge ratio} = 100 \text{ shares of stock}$$

To establish the arbitrage, the hedge fund manager purchases 10 convertible bonds and sells 100 shares of stock. With the equity exposure hedged, the convertible bond is transformed into a traditional fixed income instrument with a 7.5% coupon.

In addition, the hedge fund manager earns interest on the cash proceeds received from the short sale of stock. This is known as the **short rebate**. The cash proceeds remain with the hedge fund manager's prime broker, but the hedge fund manager is entitled to the interest earned on the cash balance from the short sale (a rebate).[13]

---

[13] The short rebate is negotiated between the hedge fund manager and the prime broker. Typically, large, well-established hedge fund managers receive a larger short rebate.

We assume that the hedge fund manager receives a short rebate of 4.5%. Therefore, if the hedge fund manager holds the convertible arbitrage position for one year, he expects to earn interest not only from his long bond position, but also from his short stock position.

The catch to this arbitrage is that the price of the underlying stock may change as well as the price of the bond. Assume the price of the stock increases to $47 and the price of the convertible bond increases to $920. If the hedge fund manager does not adjust the hedge ratio during the holding period, the total return for this arbitrage will be:

Appreciation of bond price	$10 \times (\$920 - \$900)$	$= \$200$
Appreciation of stock price	$100 \times (\$45 - \$47)$	$= -\$200$
Interest on bonds	$10 \times \$1,000 \times 7.5\%$	$= \$750$
Short rebate	$100 \times \$45 \times 4.5\%$	$= \$202.50$
Total		$= \$952.50$

If the hedge fund manager paid for the 10 bonds without using any leverage, the holding period return is: $\$952.50 \div \$9,000 = 10.58\%$.

Suppose the underlying stock price declined from $45 to $43, and the convertible bonds declined in value from $900 to $880. The hedge fund manager would then earn:

Depreciation of bond price	$10 \times (\$880 - \$900)$	$= -\$200$
Depreciation of stock price	$100 \times (\$45 - \$43)$	$= \$200$
Interest on bonds	$10 \times \$1,000 \times 7.5\%$	$= \$750$
Short rebate	$100 \times \$45 \times 4.5\%$	$= \$202.50$
Total		$= \$952.50$

What this example demonstrates is that with the proper delta or hedge ratio in place, the convertible arbitrage manager should be insulated from movements in the underlying stock price so that the expected return should be the same regardless of whether the stock price goes up or goes down.

However, suppose that the hedge fund manager purchased the convertible bonds with $4,500 of initial capital and $4,500 of borrowed money. We further assume that the hedge fund manager borrows the additional investment capital from his prime broker at a prime rate of 6%.

Our analysis of the total return is then:

Appreciation of bond price	$10 \times (\$920 - \$900)$	$= \$200$
Appreciation of stock price	$100 \times (\$47 - \$45)$	$= -\$200$
Interest on bonds	$10 \times \$1,000 \times 7.5\%$	$= \$750$
Short rebate	$100 \times \$45 \times 4.5\%$	$= \$202.50$
Interest on borrowing	$6\% \times \$4,500$	$= -\$270$
Total		$= \$682.5$

And the total return on capital is: $\$682.5 \div \$4,500 = 15.17\%$.

The amount of leverage used in convertible arbitrage will vary with the size of the long positions and the objectives of the portfolio. Yet, in this example, we can see how using a conservative leverage ratio of 2:1 in the purchase of the convertible bonds added almost 500 basis points of return to the strategy and earned a total return equal to twice that of the convertible bond coupon rate.

It is easy to see why hedge fund managers are tempted to use leverage. Hedge fund managers earn incentive fees on every additional basis point of return they earn. Further, even though leverage is a two-edged sword, it can magnify losses as well as gains. Hedge fund managers bear no loss if the

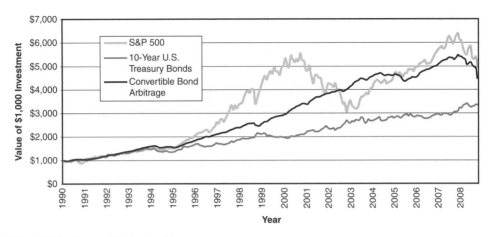

Exhibit 10.13   Convertible bond arbitrage

Source: Datastream and Hedge Fund Research, Inc., copyright 2009, www.hedgefundresearch.com.

use of leverage turns against them. In other words, hedge fund managers have everything to gain by applying leverage, but nothing to lose.

Additionally, leverage is inherent in the shorting strategy because the underlying short equity position must be borrowed. Convertible arbitrage leverage can range from two to six times the amount of invested capital. This may seem significant, but it is lower than other forms of arbitrage.

Convertible bonds earn returns for taking on exposure to a number of risks, such as liquidity (convertible bonds are typically issued as private securities), credit risk (convertible bonds are usually issued by below-investment-grade companies), event risk (the company may be downgraded or declare bankruptcy), interest rate risk (as a bond it is exposed to interest rate risk), negative convexity (most convertible bonds are callable), and model risk (it is complex to model all of the moving parts associated with a convertible bond). These events are only magnified when leverage is applied.

Since convertible bond managers hedge away the equity risk through delta neutral hedging, we should see little impact from the U.S. stock market. In addition, for undertaking all of the risks just listed, convertible bond arbitrage managers should earn a return premium to U.S. Treasury bonds. Exhibit 10.13 confirms these expectations, except for the bear market of 2008.

Market neutral

Market neutral hedge funds also go long and short the market. The difference is that they maintain integrated portfolios that are designed to neutralize market risk. This means being neutral to the general stock market, as well as having neutral risk exposures across industries. Security selection is all that matters.

Market neutral hedge fund managers generally apply the **rule of one alpha**.[14] This means that they build an integrated portfolio designed to produce only one source of alpha. This is distinct from equity long/short managers that build two separate portfolios, one long and one short, with two sources of alpha. The idea of integrated portfolio construction is to neutralize market and industry risk and concentrate purely on stock selection. In other words, there is no beta risk in the portfolio,

---

[14] See Bruce Jacobs and Kenneth Levy, "The Law of One Alpha," *Journal of Portfolio Management* (Summer 1995).

either with respect to the broad stock market or with respect to any industry. Only stock selection, or alpha, should remain.

Market neutral hedge fund managers generally hold equal positions of long and short stock positions. Therefore, the manager is dollar neutral; there is no net exposure to the market either on the long side or on the short side. Since returns to net positions tend to be small, some equity market neutral managers may use leverage to enhance their returns.

Generally, market neutral managers follow a three-step procedure in their strategy. The first step is to build an initial screen of investable stocks. These are stocks traded on the manager's local exchange, with sufficient liquidity so as to be able to enter and exit positions quickly, and with sufficient float so that the stock may be borrowed from the hedge fund manager's prime broker for short positions. Additionally, the hedge fund manager may limit his universe to a capitalization segment of the equity universe such as the mid-cap range.

Second, the hedge fund manager typically builds factor models. These models are often known as *alpha engines*. Their purpose is to find those financial variables that influence stock prices. These are bottom-up models that concentrate solely on corporate financial information as opposed to macroeconomic data. This is the source of the manager's skill, his stock selection ability.

The last step is portfolio construction. The hedge fund manager will use a computer program to construct a portfolio in such a way that it is neutral to the market, as well as across industries. The hedge fund manager may use a commercial optimizer, computer software designed to measure exposure to the market and produce a trade list for execution based on a manager's desired exposure to the market, or may use the manager's own computer algorithms to measure and neutralize risk.

Most market neutral managers use optimizers to neutralize market and industry exposure. However, more sophisticated optimizers attempt to keep the portfolio neutral to several risk factors. These include size, price-earnings ratio, and the ratio of market price to book value. The idea is to have no intended or unintended risk exposures that might compromise the portfolio's neutrality.

We will have more to say about transparency in our chapters regarding the selection of hedge fund managers (Chapter 12) and whether the hedge fund industry should be institutionalized (Chapter 11). For now it is sufficient to point out that black boxes tend to be problematic for investors.

We would expect market neutral managers to produce returns independent of the general market (they are neutral to the market). Exhibit 10.14 confirms this expectation. We see a steady linear progression of market neutral values compared to the S&P 500.

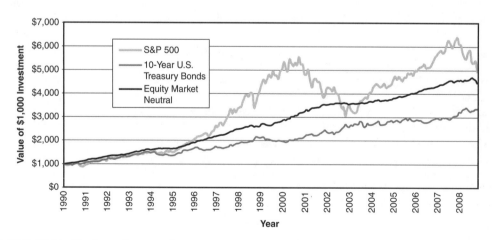

Exhibit 10.14   Equity market neutral

Source: Datastream and Hedge Fund Research, Inc., copyright 2009, www.hedgefundresearch.com.

Fixed income yield alternatives

The **fixed income yield alternatives** category includes many of the strategies discussed earlier with respect to fixed income arbitrage but also includes other strategies that are tied to fundamental value selection, both long and short. This exposes yield alternatives to the same problems of convergence as traditional fixed income arbitrage.

As a result, in Exhibit 10.15[15] we can see a steady increase in value with low volatility through 2006. However, starting in 2007 into 2008, these strategies declined significantly as the credit and liquidity markets dried up and virtually every security other than U.S. Treasury bonds was penalized. Also, yield alternatives work well in a low-volatility, normal market environment, not that of the financial markets in 2007 and 2008. As a result, we see a rapid decline in value from these strategies as the financial crisis unfolded.

Relative value arbitrage

Relative value arbitrage might be better named the smorgasbord of arbitrage. This is because relative value hedge fund managers are catholic in their investment strategies; they invest across the universe of arbitrage strategies. The best known of these managers was Long-Term Capital Management. Once the story of LTCM unfolded, it was clear that its trading strategies involved merger arbitrage, fixed income arbitrage, volatility arbitrage, stub trading, and convertible arbitrage.

In general, the strategy of relative value managers is to invest in spread trades: the simultaneous purchase of one security and the sale of another when the economic relationship between the two securities (the spread) has become mispriced. The mispricing may be based on historical averages or mathematical equations. In either case, the relative arbitrage manager purchases the security that is cheap and sells the security that is rich. It is called relative value arbitrage because the cheapness or richness of a security is determined relative to a second security. Consequently, relative value managers do not take directional bets on the financial markets. Instead, they take focused bets on the pricing relationship between two securities.

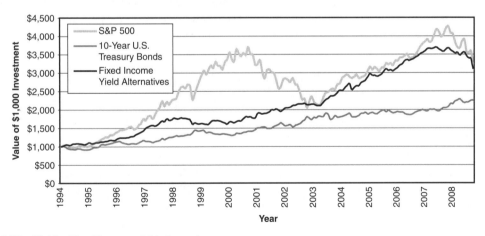

Exhibit 10.15   Fixed income yield alternatives

Source: Datastream and Hedge Fund Research, Inc., copyright 2009, www.hedgefundresearch.com.

---

[15] The data history for fixed income yield alternatives does not begin until 1994. Therefore, the value of a $1,000 investment will be different from those hedge fund strategies whose history extends back to 1990.

Relative value managers attempt to remove the influence of the financial markets from their investment strategies. This is made easy by the fact that they simultaneously buy and sell similar securities. Therefore, the market risk embedded in each security should cancel out. Any residual risk can be neutralized through the use of options or futures. What is left is pure security selection: the purchase of those securities that are relatively cheap and the sale of those securities that are relatively rich. Relative value managers earn a profit when the spread between the two securities returns to normal. They then unwind their positions and collect their profit.

We have already discussed merger arbitrage, fixed income arbitrage, and convertible bond arbitrage. Two other popular forms of relative value arbitrage are stub trading and volatility arbitrage.

Stub trading is an equity-based strategy. Frequently, companies acquire a majority stake in another company, but their stock price does not fully reflect their interest in the acquired company. As an example, consider Company A, whose stock is trading at $50. Company A owns a majority stake in Company B, whose remaining outstanding stock, or stub, is trading at $40. The value of Company A should be the combination of its own operations, estimated at $45 a share, plus its majority stake in Company B's operations, estimated at $8 a share. Therefore, Company A's share price is undervalued relative to the value that Company B should contribute to Company A's share price. The share price of Company A should be about $53, but instead, it is trading at $50. The investment strategy would be to purchase Company A's stock and sell the appropriate ratio of Company B's stock.

Let's assume that Company A's ownership in Company B contributes 20% of Company A's consolidated operating income. Therefore, the operations of Company B should contribute one-fifth to Company A's share price. A proper hedging ratio would be four shares of Company A's stock to one share of Company B's stock.

The arbitrage strategy is:

Buy four shares of Company A stock at $4 \times \$50 = \$200$.
Sell one share of Company B stock at $1 \times \$40 = \$40$.

The relative value manager is now long Company A stock and hedged against the fluctuation of Company B's stock. Let's assume that over three months, the share price of Company B increases to $42 a share and the value of Company A's operations remains constant at $45, but now the shares of Company A correctly reflect the contribution of Company B's operations. The value of the position will be:

Value of Company A's operations	$4 \times \$45$	$= \$180$
Value of Company B's operations	$4 \times \$42 \times 20\%$	$= \$33.60$
Loss on short of Company B stock	$1 \times (\$40 - \$42)$	$= -\$2$
Short rebate on Company B stock	$1 \times \$40 \times 4.5\% \times 3/12$	$= \$0.45$
Total		$= \$212.05$

The initial invested capital was $200 for a gain of $12.05 or 6.02% over three months. Suppose the stock of Company B had declined to $30, but Company B's operations were properly valued in Company A's share price. The position value would be:

Value of Company A's operations	$4 \times \$45$	$= \$180$
Value of Company B's operations	$4 \times \$30 \times 20\%$	$= \$24$
Gain on short of Company B's stock	$1 \times (\$40 - \$30)$	$= \$10$
Short rebate on Company B's stock	$1 \times \$40 \times 4.5\% \times 3/12$	$= \$0.45$
Total:		$= \$214.45$

The initial invested capital was $200 for a gain of $14.45 or 7.22% over three months. Stub trading is not arbitrage. Although the value of Company B's stock has been hedged, the hedge fund manager must still hold the position in Company A's stock until the market recognizes its proper value.

Volatility arbitrage involves options and warrant trading. Option prices contain an implied number for volatility. That is, it is possible to observe the market price of an option and back out the value of volatility implied in the current price using various option pricing models. The arbitrageur can then compare options on the same underlying stock to determine if the volatility values implied by their prices are the same.

The implied volatility derived from option pricing models should represent the expected volatility of the underlying stock that will be realized over the life of the option. Therefore, two options on the same underlying stock should have the same implied volatility. If they do not, an arbitrage opportunity may be available. In addition, if the implied volatility is significantly different from the historical volatility of the underlying stock, then relative value arbitrageurs expect that the implied volatility will revert back to its historical average.

Volatility arbitrage generally is applied in one of two models. The first is a mean reversion model. This model compares the implied volatility from current option prices to the historical volatility of the underlying security with the expectation that the volatility reflected in the current option price will revert to its historical average and the option price will adjust accordingly.

A second volatility arbitrage model applies a statistical technique called generalized autoregressive conditional heteroskedasticity (GARCH). GARCH models use prior data points of realized volatility to forecast future volatility. The GARCH forecast is then compared to the volatility implied in current option prices.

Both models are designed to allow hedge fund managers to determine which options have cheap versus rich prices. Once again, relative value managers sell those options that are rich based on the implied volatility relative to the historical volatility and buy those options with cheap volatility relative to the historical volatility.

Exhibit 10.16 presents the value of relative arbitrage compared to the S&P 500 and U.S. Treasury bonds. Once again, we see steady returns, without much influence from the direction of the stock or bond market.

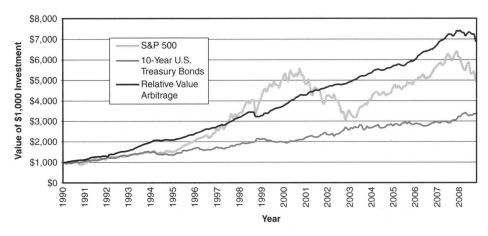

Exhibit 10.16   Relative value arbitrage

Source: Datastream and Hedge Fund Research, Inc., copyright 2009, www.hedgefundresearch.com.

Opportunistic hedge fund strategies

Along the lines of the smorgasbord comment for relative value hedge funds, these strategies have the broadest mandate across the financial, commodity, and futures markets. These all-encompassing mandates can lead to specific bets on currencies or stocks as well as a well-diversified portfolio.

Global macro

As their name implies, **global macro** hedge funds take a macroeconomic approach on a global basis in their investment strategy. These are top-down managers who invest opportunistically across financial markets, currencies, national borders, and commodities. They take large positions depending on the hedge fund manager's forecast of changes in interest rates, currency movements, monetary policies, and macroeconomic indicators.

Global macro managers have the broadest investment universe. They are not limited by market segment or industry sector, nor by geographic region, financial market, or currency. In addition, global macro hedge funds may invest in commodities. In fact, a fund of global macro funds offers the greatest diversification of investment strategies.

Global macro funds tend to have large amounts of investor capital. This is necessary to execute their macroeconomic strategies. In addition, they may apply leverage to increase the size of their macro bets. As a result, global macro hedge funds tend to receive the greatest attention and publicity in the financial markets.

The best known of these hedge funds was the Quantum Fund managed by George Soros. It is well documented that this fund made significant gains in 1992 by betting that the British pound would devalue (which it did). This fund was also accused of contributing to the Asian contagion in the fall of 1997 when the government of Thailand devalued its currency, the baht, triggering a domino effect in currency movements throughout Southeast Asia.

In recent times, however, global macro funds have fallen on hard times.[16] One reason is that many global macro funds were hurt by the Russian bond default in August 1998 and the bursting of the technology bubble in March 2000. These two events caused large losses for the global macro funds.

A second reason, as indicated earlier, is that global macro hedge funds had the broadest investment mandate of any hedge fund strategy. The ability to invest widely across currencies, commodities, financial markets, geographic borders, and time zones is a two-edged sword. On the one hand, this mandate allows global macro funds the widest universe in which to implement their strategies. On the other hand, it lacks focus. As more institutional investors have moved into the hedge fund marketplace, they have demanded greater investment focus as opposed to free investment rein.

Exhibit 10.17 compares global macro hedge funds to the S&P 500 and Treasury bonds over the period 1990 to 2008. During this time, global macro hedge funds earned steady, favorable returns. Also, global macro hedge funds significantly outperformed the U.S. stock market without the fluctuations that affected the stock market.

Fund of funds

Hedge funds of funds (FOFs) or funds of hedge funds are hedge fund managers that invest their capital in other hedge funds. These managers practice tactical asset allocation—reallocating capital across hedge fund strategies when they believe that certain hedge fund strategies will do better than others. For example, during the bear market of 2000 to 2002, short selling strategies performed the

---

[16] See "The Hedge Fund Industry Creates a Dinosaur: The Macro Manager," *New York Times*, May 6, 2000.

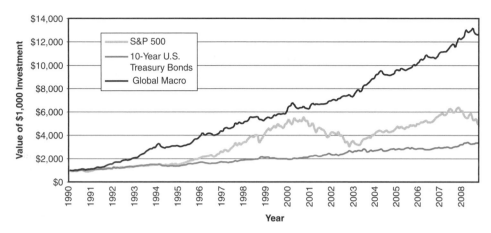

Exhibit 10.17   Global Macro

Source: Datastream and Hedge Fund Research, Inc., copyright 2009, www.hedgefundresearch.com.

best of all hedge fund categories. Not surprisingly, fund of funds managers allocated significant portions of their portfolios to short sellers during the recent bear market. Other strategies that are popular in funds of funds are global macro, fixed income arbitrage, convertible arbitrage, statistical arbitrage, equity long/short, and event driven.

One drawback on hedge funds of funds is the double layer of fees. Investors in FOFs typically pay management plus profit-sharing fees to the hedge fund of funds managers in addition to the management and incentive fees that must be absorbed from the underlying hedge fund managers. This double layer of fees makes it difficult for fund of funds managers to outperform some of the more aggressive individual hedge fund strategies. Brown, Goetzmann, and Liang (2004) document that individual hedge funds outperform funds of funds on an after-tax return or Sharpe ratio basis and argue that the nature of the FOF's fee arrangement (the fees on fees) is partly responsible for this result. However, the trade-off of investing in funds of funds is better risk control from a diversified portfolio. In this regard, Fung and Hsieh (2006) contend that FOF returns are a better reflection of the actual investment experience in hedge funds, as these returns are netting out the cost of due diligence, portfolio construction, and so on.

The comparison of a FOF versus a direct hedge fund investment is different for every investor, though. Thus, while a very wealthy and sophisticated investor might be inclined to invest directly in hedge funds, an investor without the knowledge of hedge funds may well choose to invest through funds of funds instead. However, the process of selecting hedge funds, which starts with the performance of a due diligence process on each potential hedge fund to be included in an investor's portfolio, can be very costly, complicated, and time consuming. Ang, Rhodes-Kropft, and Zhao (2008) present a model and find that, from a portfolio perspective, FOFs are the preferred investment vehicles for individuals with very high risk-aversion levels. Finally, Ineichen (2002) argues that investors should relate the double fee arrangement to the value-added of the fund of funds manager, although to a minority of institutional investors the total amount of fees charged will be unacceptable, whatever the net value-added.

Exhibit 10.18 shows the returns for hedge funds of funds. Not surprisingly, hedge funds of funds did not earn as good a return as the U.S. equity market over the period 1990 to 2008 but, at the same time, did not demonstrate the excessive volatility associated with the stock market.

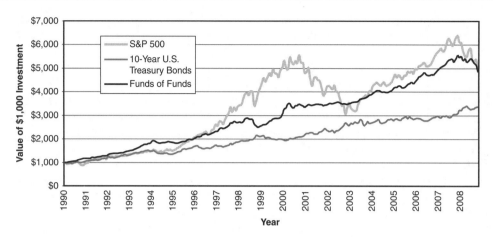

Exhibit 10.18 Hedge funds of funds

Source: Datastream and Hedge Fund Research, Inc., copyright 2009, www.hedgefundresearch.com.

Multistrategy hedge funds

Agarwal and Kale (2007) document the recent rapid growth in both FOFs and **multistrategy** (MS) **hedge funds**. An MS hedge fund has the ability to invest in different strategies, shifting capital among them according to their profitability, thus potentially benefiting from greater investment flexibility and from the ability to invest in less liquid investments because of longer lockup periods. However, Reddy, Brady, and Patel (2007) suggest that most multistrategy managers generally concentrate on two to four strategies and typically do not make significant shifts in investment allocation in the short run. According to Agarwal and Kale (2007), FOFs and MS hedge funds should yield similar risk-adjusted performances, as they represent similar forms of investments. However, they find that multistrategy funds outperform funds of funds by 2.6% to 4.8% per annum in gross of fees alphas and by 3.0% to 3.6% on a net of fees basis, thus suggesting that the higher fees charged by funds of funds cannot explain the differences in performance. They propose that the explanation for this result lies in that rational investors anticipate the additional agency risk that arises from investing in MS funds relative to FOFs and demand a higher return from them. This greater agency risk is the result of MS funds' investments being more opaque and their managers being strained to invest in strategies in which they do not have sufficient skill.

Reddy, Brady, and Patel (2007) make the case for investing in FOFs when compared to MS funds. First, they argue, similar to Ineichen (2002), that manager selection is a source of likely advantage for FOFs because these funds can choose managers from a large pool of hedge funds, whereas an MS fund manager is restricted by its capability to recruit skillful teams within each strategy in which it invests. Second, these authors also contend that FOFs generally provide greater diversification than MS funds and point to the case of the implosion of the large MS manager Amaranth Advisors, where institutions that invested directly in Amaranth experienced, by being undiversified, much higher losses than FOFs that invested in that same fund among others, which had an average investment of around 6% and recognized losses of close to 4%. Third, the potential effect of manager selection is greater than strategy allocation, something that tends to benefit FOFs above MS funds. Fourth, while investors in MS funds must bear the business and operational risks of the MS fund manager, an FOF diversifies these risks as it invests in different managers, each having its own risk management policy. Finally, FOFs offer an additional level of monitoring and due diligence. In spite of all this, Reddy,

Brady, and Patel (2007) caution that FOFs and MS funds are simply manifestations of different investment approaches, and that institutions may choose to invest in both investment vehicles.

CONCLUSION

This chapter was intended to provide an overview of the hedge fund market; it was not intended to draw any conclusions about the value of hedge funds as an investment vehicle. The issues associated with hedge fund investing will be addressed in the following chapters. In the meantime, there are three key points that the reader should take from this chapter.

First, the hedge fund industry has grown dramatically over the past decade. Although invested capital is approximately 20% of the size of the mutual fund industry (which is about $11.5 trillion), in terms of investment assets, its growth potential is much higher. New managers enter the hedge fund industry on a daily basis drawn by the tremendous fees that can be earned, and new capital, particularly from pension funds, is being drawn to the industry.

Second, the hedge fund strategies discussed in the chapter invest in the same securities as traditional long-only managers. This is a point that we made in Chapter 1, but it bears repeating. However, the distinguishing feature of hedge fund managers is the strategies they employ in investing in those securities. Therefore, hedge fund managers do not employ alternative assets, but rather alternative strategies.

Last, there are many different hedge fund strategies. Which is best for the investor? That will really depend on the strategic approach that the investor wishes to take. Some investors may be more focused on equity-based strategies. For them, equity long/short funds might be appropriate. For an investor with a fixed income bias, convertible arbitrage, fixed income arbitrage, or relative value arbitrage may be appropriate. Suffice it to say that there is sufficient variety in the hedge fund marketplace to suit most investors.

11

Establishing a Hedge Fund Investment Program

Before investors enter the hedge fund world they should have a plan of action to ensure the greatest opportunity for success. This chapter addresses the opportunities associated with hedge funds. We will discuss the hazards in later chapters. We begin with a review of the research on hedge funds where we address questions regarding the benefits of hedge funds within an investment portfolio, whether their performance is persistent, and whether hedge funds undermine the financial markets. We then consider the investment strategies that may be applicable to hedge funds.

SHOULD HEDGE FUNDS BE PART OF AN INVESTMENT PROGRAM?

Before considering hedged funds as part of a strategic investment program, we must first ask the question: Are they worth it? Initially, we must consider the return potential of hedge funds. Second, we must determine whether hedge funds have a place within a diversified portfolio that includes stocks and bonds.

The case for hedge funds is well established now. We cite several articles in a brief summary, but the first question, "Are hedge funds worth the investment?" has been answered several times. So we put the first question to bed quickly in this chapter and then focus on how to place hedge funds within a diversified portfolio.

Goldman, Sachs & Co. and Financial Risk Management Ltd. in two reports study the returns to hedge funds over two time periods, 1993 to 1997 and 1994 to 1998.[1] The returns to hedge funds during these two time periods were comparable to those of the U.S. stock market with less volatility. Furthermore, during the first time period, a portfolio of 60% S&P 500, 30% Lehman Aggregate Bond Index, and 10% absolute return hedge fund index outperformed the Pension Plan Index of 60/40 stocks/bonds by 78 basis points per year with a reduction in portfolio standard deviation of 31 basis points.

Over the second time period, a portfolio of 60% S&P 500, 30% Lehman Aggregate Bond Index, and 10% hedge funds increased the total return by 48 basis points per year over the 60/40 Pension Plan Index, but portfolio volatility also increased by 14 basis points.

Schneeweis and Spurgin document a range of hedge fund average annual returns of 7.8% for short selling funds to 27.9% for global macro funds.[2] Average annual standard deviation calculations ranged from 3.1% for market neutral funds to 18.4% for emerging market hedge funds. Correlation coefficients of the Hedge Fund Research hedge fund indices with the S&P 500 ranged from 0.60 for short selling hedge funds to 0.74 to hedge funds focusing on growth sectors.

[1] See Goldman, Sachs & Co. and Financial Risk Management Ltd., "The Hedge Fund 'Industry' and Absolute Return Funds," *Journal of Alternative Investments* (Spring 1999), 11–27; and "Hedge Funds Revisited," *Pension and Endowment Forum* (January 2000).

[2] See Thomas Schneeweis and Richard Spurgin, "Multifactor Analysis of Hedge Fund, Managed Futures, and Mutual Fund Return and Risk Characteristics," *Journal of Alternative Investments* (Fall 1998), 1–24.

Separately, Schneeweis finds that a portfolio consisting of 80% U.S. stocks and U.S. bonds (equally weighted) and 20% hedge funds outperforms the stand-alone stock and bond portfolio in terms or expected return, standard deviation, Sharpe ratio, and drawdown.[3]

Peskin, Urias, Anjilvel, and Boudreau find that over the time period of January 1990 through June 2000, the average annual return for all hedge funds in their sample was 18.9%, with a volatility of 5.5% and a Sharpe ratio of 2.5.[4] This compares quite favorably to the return for the S&P 500 of 17.2%, volatility of 13.7%, and a Sharpe ratio of 0.9. Edwards and Liew[5] study an unconstrained optimization including stocks, bonds, and funds of funds, and select an allocation of 83% to an equally weighted fund of hedge funds, 7% to the S&P 500, and 10% to long-term corporate bonds. Brown, Goetzmann, and Ibbotson[6] find that an equally weighted portfolio of offshore hedge funds earned an average return of 13.26%.

Ackermann, McEnally, and Ravenscraft review hedge funds within a portfolio context.[7] They find that over the period 1988–1995, the addition of hedge funds to either a stock, bond, or balanced portfolio results in an improved Sharpe ratio.

Fung and Hsieh[8] conduct a hedge fund performance attribution analysis similar to that performed by Sharpe for mutual funds.[9] They find low r-squareds between the returns to hedge funds and those of traditional asset classes. Almost half (48%) of the hedge fund regression equations had an r-squared below 25%. Further, they found that 25% of the hedge funds were negatively correlated with the standard asset classes.

In a subsequent study, Fung and Hsieh regress the HFRI Composite Index and the CSFB/Tremont Hedge Fund Index on nine financial market indices, including stocks, bonds, and currencies. They find the R-squared measure of overall regression fit to be 0.76 for the HFRI index and 0.55 for the CSFB/Tremont index.[10] This further demonstrates that hedge fund returns cannot be fully explained by market factors.

The body of research on hedge funds demonstrates two key qualifications for hedge funds. First, over the time period of 1989 to 2000, the returns to hedge funds were positive. The highest returns were achieved by global macro hedge funds, and the lowest returns were achieved by short selling hedge funds. Not all categories of hedge funds beat the S&P 500. However, in many cases, the volatility associated with hedge fund returns was lower than that of the S&P 500.[11]

In a more recent article, Ibbotson and Chen (2005) analyzed the performance of 3,538 hedge funds between January 1999 and March 2004 and found compounded average returns of 12.8% before

---

[3] See Thomas Schneeweis, "The Benefits of Hedge Funds," Center for International Securities and Derivatives Markets, University of Massachusetts (2006), 9–12.

[4] See Michael Peskin, Michael Urias, Satish Anjilvel, and Bryan Boudreau, "Why Hedge Funds Make Sense," *Morgan Stanley Dean Witter Quantitative Strategies* (November 2000).

[5] See Franklin Edwards and Jimmy Liew, "Hedge Funds versus Managed Futures as Asset Classes," *Journal of Derivatives* (Summer 1999), 45–64.

[6] See Stephen J. Brown, William N. Goetzmann, and Roger G. Ibbotson, "Offshore Hedge Funds: Survival and Performance, 1989–1995," *Journal of Business* 72, no. 1 (1999), 91–117.

[7] See Carl Ackermann, Richard McEnally, and David Ravenscraft, "The Performance of Hedge Funds: Risk, Return, and Incentives," *Journal of Finance* (June 1999), 833–874.

[8] See William Fung and David Hsieh, "Empirical Characteristics of Dynamic Trading Strategies: The Case of Hedge Funds," *Review of Financial Studies* 10 (Summer 1997), 275–302.

[9] William Sharpe, "Asset Allocation: Management Style and Performance Measurement," *Journal of Portfolio Management* (Winter 1992), 7–19.

[10] See William Fung and David Hsieh, "Hedge-Fund Benchmarks: Information Content and Biases," *Financial Analysts Journal* (January/February 2002), 22–24.

[11] See Goldman Sachs and Financial Risk Management, "Hedge Fund 'Industry'" and "Hedge Funds Revisited."

Exhibit 11.1 Realized return, standard deviations, and Sharpe ratios, 1990 to September 2008, using annual returns

Asset Class	Expected Return	Standard Deviation	Sharpe Ratio
S&P 500	9.92%	13.98%	0.43
10-Year U.S. Treasury	6.93	6.82	0.45
NASDAQ	11.74	23.96	0.33
EAFE	4.00	16.17	0.01
HFRI Composite	12.83 ⎫	6.85 ⎫	1.30 ⎫
HFRI FOF	8.97 ⎭	5.78 ⎭	0.88 ⎭
Cash	3.90	0.47	n/a

Note: "S&P 500" is a total return (capital appreciation and dividends) measure of large-capitalization U.S. stock returns calculated using the Standard & Poor's 500 index; "10-year U.S. Treasury" is a measure of U.S. bond returns using the Lehman Bond Index; "NASDAQ" is a total return (capital appreciation and dividends) measure of small-capitalization U.S. stock returns calculated using the NASDAQ Composite index; "EAFE" is a total return (capital appreciation and dividends) measure of large-capitalization international stock returns calculated using Morgan Stanley Capital International's Europe, Australasia, and Far East (EAFE) index; "HFRI Composite" represents the returns, net of fees, of an equally weighted composite of constituent hedge funds, as reported by the hedge fund managers listed within the Hedge Fund Research, Inc. Database; "HFRI FOF" is an equally weighted composite of constituent fund of hedge funds returns, net of fees, as reported by the fund of hedge funds managers listed within the Hedge Fund Research, Inc. Database; "Cash" is a measure of short-term interest rates, estimated using LIBOR.
Source: Datastream and Hedge Fund Research, Inc., copyright 2009, www.hedgefundresearch.com.

fees and 9.1% after fees. Out of this 9.1% return, 5.4% is attributable to exposure to market indices, while the remaining 3.7% is the average alpha of the hedge funds. Schneeweis, Martin, Kazemi, and Karavas (2005) studied the effect of leverage on hedge fund risk-adjusted performance and document that each hedge fund strategy uses a different amount of leverage. They also find that, interestingly, within a particular hedge fund strategy, there is no evidence of a significant disparity between the risk-adjusted performance of hedge funds with above-median and below-median leverage.

In Exhibit 11.1 we update the prior research by examining the returns to hedge funds over the period 1990 to September 2008 for the HFRI Hedge Fund Composite Index as well as the HFRI FOF index (both of these indices report returns to hedge fund investors net of fees) compared to large-capitalization stocks (measured by the returns of the S&P 500 index); small-capitalization stocks (measured using the NASDAQ Composite index returns, an index that is highly correlated to the returns on small stocks); U.S. Treasury bond returns; EAFE (a measure of returns on international stocks); and cash. As can be seen in the exhibit, the returns for the HFRI Composite index compare favorably with large-cap stocks but with much less volatility. The FOF index earns less than large-cap and small-cap stocks but significantly more than EAFE, and has significantly less volatility than any of the stock categories. Both the HFRI Composite and FOF indices earn premiums significantly in excess of a cash rate. Also, the HFRI FOF index has a volatility that is even lower than that of U.S. Treasury bonds. These findings are consistent with the prior research cited earlier.

Another benefit of hedge funds is that they provide good diversification benefits. In other words, hedge funds do, in fact, hedge other financial assets. Correlation coefficients with the S&P 500 range from −0.7 for short selling hedge funds to 0.83 for opportunistic hedge funds investing in the U.S. markets.[12] The less than perfect positive correlation with financial assets indicates that hedge funds can expand the efficient frontier for asset managers.

---

[12] See Brown, Goetzmann, and Ibbotson, "Offshore Hedge Funds," and Schneeweis and Spurgin, "Multifactor Analysis."

Exhibit 11.4, which will be analyzed later, presents the correlation of the HFRI Composite Index and HFRI Fund of Funds Index with large-cap stocks, Treasury bonds, small-cap stocks, and international stocks over the time period from 1990 to September 2008. The relatively low correlation coefficients of funds of hedge funds that can be observed in the exhibit reinforce the conclusion that funds of hedge funds provide good diversification benefits. In the case of the HFRI Composite Index, the correlations with stocks are somewhat higher, but the benefits of diversification are still present. In a section on funds of hedge funds that will be presented later in this chapter, we will come back to this point and illustrate, using a numerical example, the potential benefits of diversification that can be provided by funds of hedge funds.

In summary, the recent research on hedge funds indicates consistent, positive performance with low correlation with traditional asset classes. The conclusion is that hedge funds can expand the investment opportunity set for institutions, offering return enhancement as well as diversification benefits.

Nonetheless, there are several caveats to keep in mind with respect to the documented results for hedge funds. First, research provides clear evidence that shocks to one segment of the hedge fund industry can be felt across many different hedge fund strategies.[13] We will analyze this issue in more detail in a later chapter.

Second, most of the research to date on hedge funds has still not factored in the tremendous growth of this industry over the past 10 years. The impact on returns of this explosive growth has yet to be fully documented.

Third, some form of bias (survivorship bias, self-selection bias, or catastrophe bias) exists in the empirical studies. All of the cited studies make use of a hedge fund database. The building of these databases results in certain biases becoming embedded in the data. These biases, if not corrected, can unintentionally inflate the documented returns to hedge funds. It has been estimated that these three biases can add from 100 to 400 basis points to the estimated total return of hedge funds. We will address this issue in greater detail in the chapters that cover risk management.

IS HEDGE FUND PERFORMANCE PERSISTENT?

This is the age-old question with respect to all asset managers, not just hedge funds: Can the manager repeat her good performance? This issue, though, is particularly acute for the hedge fund marketplace because hedge fund managers often claim that the source of their returns is skill-based rather than dependent on general financial market conditions. Unfortunately, the existing evidence is mixed, and there is no clear conclusion.

Brown, Goetzmann, and Ibbotson present a year-by-year cross-sectional regression (parametric analysis) of past hedge fund returns on current hedge fund returns.[14] Over the six years studied, they find that three of the years have positive slopes (indicating persistent positive performance) and three years have negative slopes (indicating no persistence). In other words, it is only a 50–50 chance that good performance in one year will be followed by good performance in the following year. They conclude that there is no evidence of performance persistence in their hedge fund sample.

Park and Staum measure skill by the ratio of excess return as measured by the capital asset pricing model divided by the standard deviation of the hedge fund manager's returns.[15] They use this skill

---

[13] See Goldman Sachs and Financial Risk Management, "Hedge Fund 'Industry'" and "Hedge Funds Revisited"; and Mark Anson, "Financial Market Dislocations and Hedge Fund Returns," *Journal of Alternative Assets* (Winter 2002).

[14] See Brown, Goetzmann, and Ibbotson, "Offshore Hedge Funds."

[15] See James Park and Jeremy Staum, "Performance Persistence in the Alternative Investment Industry," working paper, 1999.

statistic to rank hedge fund managers on a year-by-year basis and then compare this ranking to the following year's skill ranking. Using a nonparametric test, they find strong evidence that hedge fund manager skill persists from year to year.

Agarwal and Naik use both a parametric (regression) test and a nonparametric (ranking) test to measure the persistence of hedge fund performance.[16] They find that under both tests a considerable amount of performance persistence exists at the quarterly horizon. However, the persistence is reduced as one moves to yearly returns, indicating that performance persistence among hedge fund managers is primarily short-term in nature.

Peskin, Urias, Anjilvel, and Boudreau's results are similar to those of Agarwal and Naik.[17] They find that performance among hedge fund managers persists on a monthly basis, but it is much less persistent on an annual basis.

A different approach to performance persistence looks at the persistence of volatility in hedge fund returns. Specifically, other researchers have noted that the volatility of returns is more persistent over time than the size or direction of the return itself. Schneeweis[18] and Park and Staum[19] demonstrate that the best forecast of future returns is one that is consistent with prior volatility, instead of a forecast that is based on prior returns.

The debate about hedge fund persistence continues. For example, using multifactor models, Amenc, el Bied, and Martellini in another study of hedge funds find strong evidence of predictability in hedge fund returns.[20] So do Edwards and Caglayan, who test for performance persistence using a nonparametric cross-product ratio of winners versus losers. They find significant performance persistence.[21] Compare these results with those of Harry Kat, who used a similar technique to measure hedge fund serial correlation over the time period 1994 to 2001 and found no performance persistence among hedge fund strategies.[22]

In a more recent article, Aggarwal, Georgiev, and Pinato (2007) find that a portfolio of equity-based hedge funds during a 31-month window period indicate its alphas are significantly more predictive than returns for short in-sample periods of six to nine months. Finally, Ammann and Moerth (2008) analyze the performance of funds of hedge funds between 1994 and 2005 and determine that results do not point to the existence of any statistically significant performance persistence in funds of hedge funds.

Another way to look at the performance persistence of hedge funds is to measure the serial correlation among the returns to hedge funds. Serial correlation measures the correlation of the return in the current year to the return performance of the previous year. If **performance persistence** is present, we should expect to see positive serial correlation, that is, good years followed by more good years. Exhibit 11.2 shows the serial correlation for large-cap stocks, small-cap stocks, EAFE, U.S. Treasury bonds, the cash return, and various hedge fund strategies.

---

[16] See Vikas Agarwal and Narayan Naik, "Multi-Period Performance Persistence Analysis of Hedge Funds," *Journal of Financial and Quantitative Analysis* (September 2000), 327–342.

[17] See Peskin, Urias, Anjilvel, and Boudreau, "Why Hedge Funds Make Sense."

[18] See Thomas Schneeweis, "Evidence of Superior Performance Persistence in Hedge Funds: An Empirical Comment," *Journal of Alternative Investments* (Fall 1998), 76–80.

[19] See Park and Staum, "Performance Persistence."

[20] See Noel Amenc, Sina el Bied, and Lionel Martellini, "Predictability in Hedge Fund Returns," *Financial Analysts Journal* (September/October 2003).

[21] See Franklin Edwards and Mustafa Onur Caglayan, "Hedge Fund Performance and Manager Skill," *Journal of Futures Markets* (2001).

[22] See Harry Kat, "10 Things That Investors Should Know about Hedge Funds," *Journal of Wealth Management* (Spring 2003).

Exhibit 11.2   Serial correlation of hedge fund returns, 1990 to September 2008

Asset Class	Serial Correlation
S&P 500	0.19
10-Year U.S. Treasury	(0.60)
NASDAQ	(0.10)
EAFE	(0.05)
Cash	0.33
HFRI Composite	(0.07)
Market Directional	
Equity Long/Short	0.13
Emerging Markets	(0.50)
Short Selling	(0.28)
Activist Investors	0.32
Corporate Restructuring	
Distressed Securities	0.06
Merger Arbitrage	0.11
Event Driven	(0.05)
Regulation D	0.56
Convergence Trading	
Fixed Income Arbitrage	(0.03)
Convertible Bond Arbitrage	0.11
Equity Market Neutral	0.32
Yield Alternatives	0.19
Relative Value Arbitrage	(0.03)
Opportunistic	
Global Macro	(0.64)
Fund of Funds	(0.30)

Source: For definitions of the first six asset classes included in this exhibit, see Exhibit 11.1. The serial correlations on hedge fund strategies were calculated from the respective HFR hedge fund index benchmarks. The source of this hedge fund strategies data is Hedge Fund Research, Inc., copyright 2009, www.hedgefundresearch.com.

As can be seen, the FOF index has negative serial correlation. This means that a good year tended to be followed by a year with lower returns, and a lower-returning year tended to be followed by a year with better returns. In other words, past performance was no indication of future results. In the case of HFRI, the serial correlation was only slightly negative. The two asset classes that had positive serial correlation were large-cap stocks and cash. Here good years tended to be followed by even better years and past performance was a reasonable indication of future performance.

Examining the performance of the different categories of hedge funds, we can see that the convergence trading strategies generated positive serial correlation, with the exception of fixed income arbitrage and relative value hedge fund managers. That is, these managers demonstrated the greatest affinity for performance persistence. In the case of market directional strategies, whereas equity long/short and activist investors showed positive serial correlations, emerging markets and short selling exhibited negative serial correlations. In the case of corporate restructuring, whereas distressed securities and merger arbitrage showed small but positive serial correlations, regulation

D strategies exhibited a higher level of serial correlation, and event driven had a slightly negative serial correlation. Finally, in the case of opportunistic strategies, both global macro funds and funds of funds showed negative serial correlations.

It is difficult to reconcile the varying conclusions regarding hedge fund performance persistence. The different conclusions could be due to different databases used or different time periods tested. This emphasizes all the more the need to conduct individual due diligence on each hedge fund manager.

DO HEDGE FUNDS UNDERMINE THE FINANCIAL MARKETS?

Hedge funds have often been made scapegoats for whatever ails the financial markets. This can be traced back to George Soros's currency attack on the British pound sterling and the Italian lira. In 1992, George Soros bet heavily and correctly that the British government would not be able to support the pound and that the pound would devalue. His similar bet on the Italian lira also paid off handsomely, for a combined total profit of close to $3 billion on both bets.

In 1997, Soros was once again blamed for a currency crisis by the Malaysian prime minister, Mahathir bin Mohammad. The prime minister attributed the crash in the Malaysian ringgit to speculation in the currency markets by hedge fund managers, including George Soros.

Brown, Goetzmann, and Park test specifically whether hedge funds caused the crash of the Malaysian ringgit.[23] They regress the monthly percentage change in the exchange rate on the currency exposure maintained by hedge funds. Reviewing the currency exposures of 11 large global macro hedge funds, they conclude that there is no evidence that the Malaysian ringgit was affected by hedge fund manager currency exposures. Additionally, they test the hypothesis that global hedge funds precipitated the slide of a basket of Asian currencies (the Asian contagion) in 1997. They find no evidence that hedge funds contributed to the decline of the several Asian currencies in the fall of 1997.

Fung and Hsieh measure the market impact of hedge fund positions on several financial market events from the October 1987 stock market crash to the Asian contagion of 1997.[24] They find that there were certain instances where hedge funds did have an impact on the market, most notably with the devaluation of the pound sterling in 1992. However, in no case was there evidence that hedge funds were able to manipulate the financial markets away from their natural paths driven by economic fundamentals. For instance, the sterling came under pressure in 1992 due to large capital outflows from the United Kingdom. The conclusion is that, for instance, George Soros bet correctly against the sterling and exacerbated its decline, but he did not trigger the devaluation.

Khandani and Lo (2007) analyze the extraordinary stock market return patterns observed in August 2007, when losses to quantitative hedge funds in the second week of that month were presumably started by a short-term price impact that was the result of a rapid unwinding of large quantitative equity market neutral hedge funds. These authors argue that the return patterns of that week were a sign of a liquidity trade that can be explained as the consequence of a major strategy liquidation. Khandani and Lo also contend that unlike banks, hedge funds can withdraw liquidity at any time, and that a synchronized liquidity withdrawal among a large group of funds could have devastating effects (i.e. systemic risk) on the basic functioning of the financial system. In spite of this potential shortcoming brought about by hedge funds, Khandani and Lo argue that the hedge fund industry has

---

[23] See Stephen Brown, William Goetzmann, and James Park, "Hedge Funds and the Asian Currency Crisis," *Journal of Portfolio Management* (Summer 2000), 95–101.

[24] See William Fung and David Hsieh, "Measuring the Market Impact of Hedge Funds," *Journal of Empirical Finance* 7 (2000).

facilitated economic growth and generated social benefits by providing liquidity, engaging in price discovery, discerning new sources of returns, and facilitating the transfer of risk.

HEDGE FUND INVESTMENT STRATEGIES WITHIN AN INVESTMENT PROGRAM

The preceding discussion demonstrates that hedge funds can expand the investment opportunity set for investors. The question now becomes: What is to be accomplished by the hedge fund investment program? The strategy may be simply a search for an additional source of return. Conversely, it may be for risk management purposes. Whatever its purpose, an investment plan for hedge funds may consider one of four strategies.

Hedge funds may be selected on an opportunistic basis, as a hedge fund of funds, as part of a joint venture, or as an absolute return strategy.

Opportunistic hedge fund investing

The term *hedge fund* can be misleading. Hedge funds do not necessarily have to hedge an investment portfolio. Rather, they can be used to expand the investment opportunity set. This is the opportunistic nature of hedge funds, they can provide an investor with new investment opportunities that cannot otherwise be obtained through traditional long-only investments.

There are several ways hedge funds can be opportunistic. First, many hedge fund managers can add value to an existing investment portfolio through specialization in a sector or in a market strategy. These managers do not contribute portable alpha. Instead, they contribute above-market returns through the application of superior skill or knowledge of a narrow market or strategy. In fact, this style of hedge fund investing describes most of the sector hedge funds in existence.

Consider a portfolio manager whose particular expertise is the biotechnology industry. She has followed this industry for years and has developed a superior information set to identify winners and losers. On the long only side, the manager purchases those stocks that she believes will increase in value, and avoids those biotech stocks she believes will decline in value. However, this strategy does not utilize her superior information set to its fullest advantage. The ability to go both long and short biotech stocks in a hedge fund is the only way to maximize the value of the manager's information set. Therefore, a biotech hedge fund provides a new opportunity: the ability to extract value on both the long side and the short side of the biotech market. This is nothing more than the Fundamental Law of Active Management, described in our earlier chapters, at work. As we noted, the long-only constraint is the most expensive constraint (in terms of lost alpha generation) that can be applied to active portfolio management.

Sector hedge funds tend to have well-defined benchmarks. Take the example of the biotech long/short hedge fund. An appropriate benchmark would be the AMEX Biotech Index that contains 17 biotechnology companies. The point is that opportunistic hedge funds are not absolute return vehicles (discussed later). Their performance can be measured relative to a benchmark.

All traditional long-only managers are benchmarked to some passive index. The nature of benchmarking is such that it forces the manager to focus on his benchmark and his tracking error associated with that benchmark. This focus on benchmarking leads traditional active managers to commit a large portion of their portfolios to tracking their benchmark. Oftentimes, the long-only manager will identify these positions as being utilized for risk management purposes. The necessity to consider the impact of every trade on the portfolio's tracking error relative to its assigned benchmark reduces the flexibility of the investment manager.

In addition, long-only active managers are constrained in their ability to short securities. They may short a security only up to its weight in the benchmark index. If the security is only a small part of the index, the manager's efforts to short the stock will be further constrained. For example, the median weight in the Russell 1000 stock index is only 0.04%. The inability to short a security beyond its benchmark weight deprives an active manager of the opportunity to take full advantage of the mispricing in the marketplace. Furthermore, not only are long-only managers unable to take advantage of overpriced securities, but they also cannot fully take advantage of underpriced securities because they cannot generate the necessary short positions to balance the overweights with respect to underpriced securities. The long-only constraint is a well-known limitation on the ability of traditional active management to earn excess returns.[25]

In summary, opportunistic (sector) hedge fund investing does not have to hedge the portfolio. Instead, it can lead to more efficient investing, a broader investment universe, and the freedom to allow managers to trade on an expanded information set. More to the point, opportunistic hedge fund managers can build a long/short market neutral portfolio based on biotech stocks if that is where they have the expertise to add value.

As another example, most institutional investors have a broad equity portfolio. This portfolio may include an index fund, external value and growth managers, and possibly private equity investments. However, along the spectrum of this equity portfolio there may be gaps in its investment lineup. For instance, many hedge funds combine late stage private investments with public securities. These hybrid funds are a natural extension of an institution's investment portfolio because they bridge the gap between private equity and index funds. Therefore a new opportunity is identified: the ability to blend private equity and public securities within one investment strategy.

Again, we come back to one of our main themes: that alternative assets are often alternative investment strategies within an existing asset class that are used to expand the investment opportunity set rather than hedge it. In summary, hedge funds may be selected not necessarily to reduce the risk of an existing investment portfolio, but instead to complement its risk versus return profile. Opportunistic investing is designed to select hedge fund managers that can enhance certain portions of a broader portfolio.

Another way to consider opportunistic hedge fund investments is that they are finished products because their investment strategy or market segment complements an institutional investor's existing asset allocation. No further work is necessary on the part of the institution because the investment opportunity set has been expanded by the addition of the hybrid product. These gaps may be in domestic equity, fixed income, or international investments. Additionally, because opportunistic hedge funds are finished products, this makes it easier to establish performance benchmarks.

Constructing an opportunistic portfolio of hedge funds will depend on the constraints under which such a program operates. For example, if an investor's hedge fund program is not limited in scope or style, then diversification across a broad range of hedge fund styles would be appropriate. If, however, the hedge fund program is limited in scope to, for instance, expanding the equity investment opportunity set, the choices will be less diversified across strategies. Exhibit 11.3 demonstrates these two choices.

Funds of funds

A hedge fund of funds (FOF) is an investment in a group of hedge funds, from 10 to more than 20. FOFs were already introduced in the previous chapter and discussed earlier in this chapter.

---

[25] See Richard Grinold and Ronald Kahn, *Active Portfolio Management* (New York: McGraw-Hill, 2000).

Exhibit 11.3   Designing a hedge fund investment program

Diversified Hedge Fund Portfolio	Equity-Based Hedge Fund Portfolio
Equity long/short	Equity long/short
Short selling	Emerging markets
Market neutral	Distressed securities
Merger arbitrage	Event driven
Distressed securities	Convertible arbitrage
Convertible arbitrage	Activist investing
Fixed income arbitrage	
Relative value arbitrage	
Global macro	

The purpose of these investment vehicles is to reduce the idiosyncratic risk of any one hedge fund manager. In other words, there is safety in numbers.

This is simply modern portfolio theory (MPT) applied to the hedge fund marketplace. Diversification is one of the founding principles of MPT and it is as applicable to hedge funds as it is to stocks and bonds. The success to any fund of hedge funds relies on manager selection. Typically, this is a winnowing process from the large universe of existing hedge funds down to a manageable pool that forms the FOF. Exhibit 11.4 demonstrates how the selection process works.

Typically, a FOF starts with the total universe of hedge funds, which was estimated at close to 10,000 at the end of 2007. However, databases such as that of Hedge Fund Research, Inc. and others cover only about 5,000 managers. From there, the list gets narrowed down further by quantitative screens and hedge fund styles to a list of 500 to 1,000 hedge funds that an FOF manager may do further analysis on (returns, risk profile, style bias, capacity limits, and other limiting criteria). The list gets further narrowed down to approximately 100 to 200 managers that are considered prospective and for which the FOF manager will conduct due diligence through actual on-site visits, interviews, reference checks, checking of trading programs and service providers, and so on. Finally,

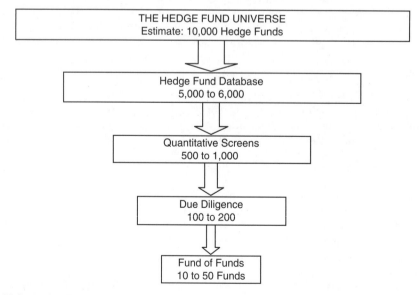

Exhibit 11.4   Hedge Fund Selection Process

from this list the FOF manager selects 10 to 50 individual hedge funds for the pool. Henker reviews the diversification benefits for three styles of hedge funds: equity long/short, event driven, and relative value.[26] Using random sampling within each hedge fund style, he finds that a portfolio of about five funds captures most of the diversification benefits that can be achieved within each style. The reduction of risk is achieved because of the heterogeneous return characteristics of hedge funds comprising the fund of funds portfolio. The fact that hedge funds within the same style have different return patterns is consistent with the findings of Fung and Hsieh.[27] They find no evidence of herding among hedge funds that pursued currency investment strategies.

Park and Staum consider the optimal diversification for a random pool of hedge funds selected from a database of 1,230 hedge funds of all different styles.[28] Consistent with Henker, they demonstrate that a fund of funds portfolio of five hedge funds can eliminate approximately 80% of the idiosyncratic risk of the individual hedge fund managers. After five hedge funds, the diversification benefits decline significantly. They find that a fund of funds portfolio of 20 hedge funds can diversify away about 95% of the idiosyncratic risk.

What, then, is left in terms of return with a hedge fund of funds? Along with the diversification of risk, funds of funds also provide diversification of return. That is, the return on a fund of funds product is generally below that of an individual hedge fund style. Generally, the return is cash-plus, with cash defined as LIBOR or Treasury bills and the plus equal to 200 to 600 basis points. Looking back at Exhibit 11.1, we can see that the HFRI FOF earns around 500 basis points over cash.

This low-volatility, cash-plus product may be applied in one of three ways: risk budgeting, portable alpha, or a bond substitute.

Risk budgeting

It seems odd to think of hedge funds as a risk budgeting tool. However, the empirical studies cited earlier demonstrate that funds of funds have low standard deviations and low correlations with traditional asset classes. Therefore, they are excellent candidates for risk budgeting.

We digress for a moment to discuss risk budgeting. **Risk budgeting** is a subset of the risk management process. It is the process of measuring the risk that an investor is actually taking, assessing the investor's appetite for risk, quantifying how much risk the investor is willing to take, and then deciding how to allocate that risk across a diversified portfolio. The process of allocating risk across a portfolio is what is known as risk budgeting. Risk budgeting allows a manager to set risk target levels throughout her portfolio.

Consider Exhibit 11.1, which was shown earlier. In this exhibit, we present the monthly expected return, standard deviation, and Sharpe ratios for the S&P 500, the 10-year U.S. Treasury bond, the NASDAQ index, Morgan Stanley Capital International's Europe, Australasia, and Far East (EAFE) index, two hedge fund indices, and one-year cash investment for the period 1990 to September 2008.

From Exhibit 11.1, we can see that hedge fund indices have much higher Sharpe ratios than stocks and bonds have. But hedge funds should not be considered in isolation. To assess their true value to a diversified portfolio, we need to see how hedge fund returns are correlated with the returns to stocks and bonds.

Suppose an investor has an annual risk budget of 15% for her overall portfolio and she wishes to invest in small-capitalized stocks. From Exhibit 11.1 we can see that small-cap stocks have a high

---

[26] See Thomas Henker, "Naive Diversification for Hedge Funds," *Journal of Alternative Assets* (Winter 1998), 33–38.

[27] See Fung and Hsieh, "Measuring the Market Impact of Hedge Funds."

[28] See James Park and Jeremy Staum, "Fund of Funds Diversification: How Much Is Enough?" *Journal of Alternative Investments* (Winter 1998), 39–42.

expected return. Unfortunately, the monthly expected volatility for the NASDAQ, which we use as a proxy measure of returns on small-cap stocks, is almost 24%, which exceeds her risk budget.

The investor can solve her problem by combining a hedge fund of funds investment with small-cap stocks to meet her risk budget of 15%. The returns received from hedge funds are less than perfectly correlated with stocks and bonds. For example, the correlation of the returns to the HFR FOF index with the returns to small-cap stocks (NASDAQ) is 0.54. Using the information in Exhibit 11.1, we can determine the optimal allocation to funds of hedge funds and small-cap stocks (which we assume are highly correlated to the returns on the NASDAQ Composite index) such that the investor can stay within her risk budget. The calculation, which is obtained from modern portfolio theory (Markowitz 1952), is:

$$\text{Risk budget} = \text{Square root of} [(w_h)^2 \times \sigma_h^2 + (1 - w_h)^2 \times \sigma_{\text{NASDAQ}}^2 + 2 \times (w_h)$$
$$\times (1 - w_h) \times \sigma_h \times \sigma_{\text{NASDAQ}} \times \rho_{h,\text{NASDAQ}}]$$

where

w_h = the weight in the portfolio allocated to a fund of hedge funds
$1 - w_h$ = the weight in the portfolio allocated to small-cap stocks
σ_h = the volatility (standard deviation) of fund of hedge fund returns
σ_{NASDAQ} = the volatility (standard deviation) of small-cap returns
$\rho_{h,\text{NASDAQ}}$ = the correlation between the returns to a fund of hedge funds and small-cap stocks

$$0.15 = \text{Square root of} [(w_h)^2 \times 0.0578^2 + (1 - w_h)^2 \times 0.2396^2 + 2 \times (w_h)$$
$$\times (1 - w_h) \times 0.0578 \times 0.2396 \times 0.54]$$

Solving the equation for w(FOF) yields a value of about 0.44. That is, the investor should invest around 44% of her portfolio in a fund of hedge funds and close to 56% in small-cap stocks to remain within her risk budget of 15% annual volatility.

Consider the power of a fund of hedge funds in this example. Without hedge funds, the investor could not allocate any of her portfolio to small-cap stocks because the annual standard deviation of small-cap stocks is 23.96%, exceeding her risk budget of 15%. However, when small-cap stocks are combined with a fund of funds product, the investor can allocate up to 56% of her portfolio to small-cap stocks.

Simply put, the investor uses hedge funds to buy units of risk that can then be allocated to other portions of her portfolio. This may run counter to intuition because hedge funds are perceived to be risky investments; yet in Exhibit 11.1 we can see that the risk associated with a portfolio of hedge funds, as measured by the annual standard deviation, is lower than for large-cap stocks, small-cap stocks, and foreign stocks. Additionally, hedge fund returns have less than perfect correlation with stock returns. This less than perfect correlation only enhances the risk budgeting power of hedge funds.

Risk budgeting can change portfolio asset allocations by highlighting the less than perfect correlation between two investment strategies. In the risk budgeting world, different asset classes or investment strategies are assigned different hurdle rates. These **hurdle rates** quantify an asset's correlation with the overall portfolio.

For example, most portfolios have a significant exposure to large-cap stocks. But from Exhibit 11.4, we can see that funds of hedge funds have a low correlation with large-cap stocks. As a result, the hurdle rate for funds of hedge funds would be lower than other asset classes or strategies.

Elton, Gruber, and Rentzler provide the calculation for determining the hurdle rate for funds of hedge funds vis-à-vis large-cap stocks.[29] In a study of commodity pools (i.e. funds that collect

---

[29] See Edwin Elton, Martin Gruber, and Joel Rentzler, "Professionally Managed, Publicly Traded Commodity Funds," *Journal of Business* (1987), 175–199.

investor contributions for use in commodity options and futures trading) within a portfolio context, they show that a commodity pool should be added to an existing portfolio if the following equation is satisfied:

$$\frac{R_c - R_f}{\sigma_c} > \frac{R_p - R_f}{\sigma_p} \times \rho_{c,p} \qquad (11.1)$$

where

R_c = the expected return to the commodity pool
R_p = the expected return to the portfolio
R_f = the risk-free rate
$\rho_{c,p}$ = the correlation between the returns to the commodity pool and the portfolio
σ_c = the volatility of returns to the commodity pool
σ_p = the volatility of returns to the portfolio

We can take Equation 11.1 and transform it into a hurdle rate calculation for funds of hedge funds, where funds of hedge funds (h) replace the previous commodity pool investment (c) from Equation 11.1:

$$R_h = R_f + (R_p - R_f) \times \frac{\sigma_h}{\sigma_p} \times \rho_{h,p} \qquad (11.2)$$

Defining the S&P 500 as the portfolio and using the data in Exhibit 11.1 and a correlation statistic of 0.47, the hurdle rate for funds of hedge funds is:

Hurdle rate = .0390 + (.0992 − .0390) × (.0578/0.1398) × 0.47

In other words, funds of hedge funds must earn a rate of at least 5.07% per year to be a valuable addition for risk budgeting purposes. Given that the expected return for a hedge fund of funds is 8.97% per year, the hurdle rate is met, and a fund of hedge funds is a valuable risk budgeting tool.

Compare this result to that obtained for international stocks. Using the EAFE stock index, we perform the same risk budgeting calculation for international stocks vis-à-vis large-cap stocks, given that the correlation of their returns is 0.67. The question is whether international stocks are appropriate risk budgeting tools versus large-cap stocks. Plugging the values from Exhibit 11.1 into Equation 11.2 we get the hurdle rate for international stocks

Hurdle rate = .0390 + (.0992 − .0390) × (.1617/0.1398) × 0.67

The hurdle rate for international stocks is 8.57% per year. From Exhibit 11.1, we can see that the expected return is only 4.00% per year. Therefore, international stocks are not suitable risk budgeting tools with respect to large-cap U.S. stocks.

Portable alpha

Portable alpha can be obtained from a diversified pool of hybrid managers with low correlation to traditional asset classes. This is a combination strategy of investing with multiple managers to achieve a portable alpha.

The idea is to invest with several hedge fund managers to achieve a distribution of returns that are uncorrelated with either stocks or bonds. Generally, this product yields a return equal to a cash rate of return plus a premium. The premium is the portable alpha. It represents the extra return that can be achieved with a fund of hedge funds above that which can be earned from investing in short-term cash instruments such as Treasury bills or high-grade commercial paper. The portable alpha is then applied to the equity or fixed income portion of the portfolio with futures contracts.

For example, Exhibit 11.4 demonstrates that the HFR fund of funds index has a less than perfectly positive correlation with the returns to the S&P 500. Furthermore, Exhibit 11.1 shows that hedge funds of funds earn an annual return of 8.97%, which is more than 2% greater than that for U.S. Treasury bonds. This extra return may be considered the alpha. It is the return earned above that of a fixed income rate of return while providing an alternative investment that has a very low correlation with large-cap U.S. stocks.

Consider an investor who has $1 billion to invest in large-cap U.S. stocks. The expected return for large-cap stocks is 9.92% per year. Instead of investing the full $1 billion in the S&P 500, she invests $500 million in the S&P 500 and $500 million in a hedge fund of funds. In addition, the investor purchases S&P 500 equity futures contracts such that the combination of hedge fund of funds plus equity futures contracts will be equivalent to an economic exposure of $500 million invested in the S&P 500. This process is known as **equitization**, and the investor does it to equitize her fund of hedge funds investment.

We digress for a moment to discuss the embedded financing cost associated with a portable alpha strategy. To prevent arbitrage in the financial markets, the S&P 500 futures contract reflects a short-term risk-free rate of financing. That is, the difference in the futures price and the current spot price of the S&P 500 reflects the relevant risk-free rate. This is because speculators who buy or sell the S&P 500 futures contracts must hedge their positions by selling or buying the underlying stocks. The cost of short-term financing to purchase or borrow the underlying stocks is reflected in the pricing of the S&P 500 futures contract.[30] Therefore, any portable alpha strategy must earn at least the cost of short-term financing embedded within the futures contract. Otherwise, the alpha will be negative, not positive.

For our example, we use the return of the cash rate from Exhibit 11.1 as the financing rate reflected in the S&P 500 futures contracts. Over the period 1990 through September 2008, this rate was 3.90% per year. Next we need to determine whether the FOF index provides an alpha.

In building the portable alpha strategy, we note that the systematic, or market, risk of hedge funds of funds is not zero. Therefore, we will need to take into account that our portable alpha strategy already contains a component of systematic or market risk. From Exhibits 11.1 and 11.4 we can calculate the beta of the funds of hedge funds, using the S&P 500 as the proxy for the market:[31]

$$\text{Beta} = (0.47 \times 0.1398 \times 0.0578)/(0.1398 \times 0.1398) = 0.19$$

The low beta value of the funds of hedge funds strategy demonstrates that it has minimal market risk. The question is whether the FOF has any alpha. To determine this we use the following relationship:

$$\alpha = (R_h - R_f) - \beta_{h,p} \times (R_p - R_f)$$
$$\alpha = (8.97\% - 3.90\%) - 0.19 \times (9.92\% - 3.9\%) = 3.93\%$$

---

[30] For instance, suppose this were not the case. Suppose that the futures contract was priced rich compared to the underlying S&P 500 stocks. Then the arbitrage would be to borrow cash to finance the purchase of the S&P 500 stocks and sell the futures contract to lock in an arbitrage profit. To prevent a risk-free arbitrage, therefore, futures contracts must reflect the cost of financing.

[31] The beta of an asset relative to the market portfolio is defined as:

$$\text{Beta} = \rho(a, m) \times \sigma(a) \times \sigma(m)/\sigma(m)^2$$

where $\rho(a, m)$ is the correlation coefficient between the asset return and the market return, $\sigma(a)$ is the standard deviation of the asset's returns, and $\sigma(m)$ is the standard deviation of the market's returns.

So the FOF has a positive alpha. Our goal is to add equity futures contracts to our $500 million investment in the hedge fund of funds until the combination of futures contracts and our hedge fund of funds investment matches the systematic risk of $500 million invested in the S&P 500. We then determine how much extra return we receive from this portable alpha strategy compared to what we could earn by purchasing large-cap stocks.

By definition, we establish the S&P 500 as the market portfolio. Therefore, its beta, or measure of systematic risk, is 1.0. We know that the beta of the funds of hedge funds strategy is 0.19. We need to add sufficient S&P 500 futures contracts so that the combination of hedge fund of funds and equity futures contracts matches the systematic risk of $500 million invested in the S&P 500. So we need to find the amount that should be invested in futures contracts to give us a portfolio that has the same beta as the S&P 500 index. Suppose instead of using futures contracts we were to borrow the funds needed to invest in the S&P 500 in the cash market. Then the beta of the portfolio would be:

$$\beta_{Portfolio} = 100\% \times \beta_h + w_{S\&P\ 500} \times \beta_{S\&P\ 500} - w_{S\&P\ 500} \times \beta_f$$
$$1 = 100\% \times 0.19 + w_{S\&P\ 500} \times 1 - w_{S\&P\ 500} \times 0$$
$$w_{S\&P\ 500} = 81\%$$

This means the position in the S&P 500 or the S&P 500 futures should be equal to 81% of the size of the portfolio. The equity futures contracts must contribute $1 - 0.19 = 0.81$, or 81%, of the systematic risk of the portable alpha strategy.

Since our goal is to match the systematic, or beta, risk of an investment of $500 million in the S&P 500, we must purchase equity futures contracts such that they contribute 81% of the beta risk of the portable alpha strategy. This amount is:

$$81\% \times \$500\ \text{million} = \$405\ \text{million of equity futures contracts}$$

In August 2008, the value of the S&P 500 was about 1,300, so this would translate into:

$$\$405,000,000 \times (\$250 \times 1,300) = 1,246\ \text{S\&P 500 futures contracts}^{32}$$

Finally, we now come to the amount of portable alpha we achieve with this strategy. The $500 million invested in the funds of hedge funds earns an expected annual return of 8.97%. Plus we have an investment in S&P 500 futures contracts that provides a return that is equivalent to 81% of that earned by an investment of $500 million in the S&P 500. In total, this portable alpha strategy is expected to earn a return of:

$$8.97\% + 0.81 \times (9.92\% - 3.90\%) = 13.85\%$$

Note that the return on the S&P 500 is reduced by the cash return to represent the approximate return to the S&P 500 futures contract. So how much alpha has been ported to this portfolio? Since this portfolio has the same beta as the S&P 500 index, the amount of alpha ported is given by:

$$13.85\% - 9.92\% = 3.93\%$$

This is the alpha of the FOF. Note that we have ignored the opportunity cost of the margin that has to be deposited for taking a position in the futures contract. In a sense, we have assumed that the entire investment in the S&P 500 can be financed by borrowing funds at 3.90%. If the cost of borrowing is higher or if the opportunity cost of margin requirements is accounted for, the alpha would be slightly smaller.

---

[32]Every point of the S&P 500 index is worth $250 under the S&P 500 futures contract. Therefore, one S&P 500 contract represents $250 × 1,300 = $325,000 of economic exposure to the S&P 500.

To summarize, the portable alpha strategy requires a cash investment in the fund of hedge funds of $500 million. Equity futures contracts are added so that the combination of the fund of hedge funds and the equity futures contracts matches the systematic, or beta, risk of an investment of $500 million in the S&P 500. The portable alpha strategy earns the combination return from the fund of hedge funds and the equity futures contracts.

This portable alpha strategy demonstrates part of the allure of hedge funds. The ability to use low-market-risk strategies to build portable alpha strategies that can outperform traditional investment strategies can add significant value to an investment portfolio.

Portable alpha strategies are beta driven because the purpose is to add an excess return component while maintaining systematic risk similar to that of the overall asset class. Equity futures or fixed income futures are added to equitize or "fixed income-ize" the generated alpha, matching the beta or market risk of the asset class, but at the same time adding the portable alpha. The investor receives the market return plus the alpha.

Bond substitute

Exhibit 11.1 demonstrates that hedge funds of funds have significantly lower risk than large-cap, small-cap, or foreign stocks. In fact, the HFRI FOF index generates a lower risk profile than even U.S. Treasury bonds while generating greater return.

This has led some researchers to consider whether hedge funds can replace bonds in an efficient portfolio. Lamm studies the issue of hedge funds as a **cash substitute**.[33] He combines hedge funds with stocks and bonds in an efficient frontier analysis, and finds that hedge funds enter efficient frontiers across all risk levels because of their superior risk-adjusted returns. More important, Lamm finds that hedge funds enter efficient portfolios largely at the expense of bonds. That is, hedge funds primarily displace cash and bonds in efficient portfolios. This suggests that hedge funds may be used as a cash substitute.

We note that in Exhibit 11.1 the FOF index has a superior Sharpe ratio compared to U.S. Treasury bonds. In addition, the correlation coefficients between FOFs and the different categories of stocks are positive, and relatively low. This also contributes to the ability of hedge funds to be a bond substitute. However, we do note that the correlation of U.S. Treasury bonds with small-cap, large-cap, and international stocks is either close to zero or negative, so that FOFs are a close but not perfect substitute for Treasury bonds.

Absolute return

Hedge funds are often described as **absolute return** products. This term comes from the skill-based nature of the industry. Hedge fund managers generally claim that their investment returns are derived from their skill at security selection rather than selection of broad asset classes. This is due to the fact that most hedge fund managers build concentrated portfolios of relatively few investment positions and do not attempt to track a stock or bond index. The work of Fung and Hsieh, discussed earlier, shows that hedge funds generate a return distribution that is very different from mutual funds.[34]

Further, given the generally unregulated waters in which hedge fund managers operate, they have greater flexibility in their trading style and execution than traditional long-only managers.

---

[33] See R. McFall Lamm Jr., "Portfolios of Alternative Assets: Why Not 100% Hedge Funds?" *Journal of Investing* (Winter 1999).

[34] See Fung and Hsieh, "Empirical Characteristics."

This flexibility provides a greater probability that hedge fund managers will reach their return targets. As a result, hedge funds have often been described as absolute return vehicles that target a specific annual return regardless of what performance might be found among market indices. In other words, hedge fund managers target an absolute return rather than determine their performance relative to an index.

The flexibility of hedge fund managers allows them to go both long and short without benchmark constraints. This allows them to set a target rate of return or an absolute return.

Specific parameters must be set for an absolute return program. These parameters will direct how the hedge fund program is constructed and operated and should include risk and return targets as well as the type of hedge fund strategies that may be selected. Absolute return parameters should operate at two levels: that of the individual hedge fund manager and for the overall hedge fund program. The investor sets target return ranges for each hedge fund manager but sets a specific target return level for the absolute return program. The parameters for the individual managers may be different than that for the program. For example, acceptable levels of volatility for individual hedge fund managers may be greater than what is acceptable for the program.

The program parameters for the hedge fund managers may be based on such factors as volatility, expected return, types of instruments traded, leverage, and historical drawdown. Other qualitative factors may be included, such as length of track record, periodic liquidity, minimum investment, and assets under management. Liquidity is particularly important because an investor needs to know with certainty her time frame for cashing out of an absolute return program if hedge fund returns turn sour.

Exhibit 11.5 demonstrates an example of absolute return program strategy. Notice that the return for the portfolio has a specific target rate of 10%, while for the individual hedge funds, the return range is 8% to 15%. Also, the absolute return portfolio has a target level for risk and drawdowns, while for the individual hedge funds a range is acceptable.

However, certain parameters are synchronized. Liquidity, for instance, must be the same for both the absolute return portfolio and that of the individual hedge fund managers. The reason is that a range of liquidity is not acceptable if the investor wishes to liquidate her portfolio. She must be able to cash out of each hedge fund within the same time frame as that established for the portfolio.

Exhibit 11.6 shows the breakdown with respect to hedge fund strategies for a large public pension plan in the United States. Although there is an overweight to equity long/short, the program is well diversified with respect to several hedge fund strategies. Again, portfolio diversification works. In this case, it is used to drive down the beta or systematic risk exposures to the traditional financial markets.

Exhibit 11.5 Absolute return portfolio of hedge funds

Absolute Return Portfolio	Individual Hedge Fund Strategies
Target return: 10%	Target returns: 8% to 15%
Target volatility: 7%	Target volatility: 10% to 15%
Largest acceptable drawdown: 10%	Largest acceptable drawdown: 15%
Liquidity: semiannual	Liquidity: semiannual
Correlation to U.S. stocks: 0	Maximum correlation to stocks: 0.5
Correlation to U.S. bonds: 0	Maximum correlation to bonds: 0.5
Hedge fund style: diversified	Hedge fund styles: convergence trading, corporate restructuring, and market directional

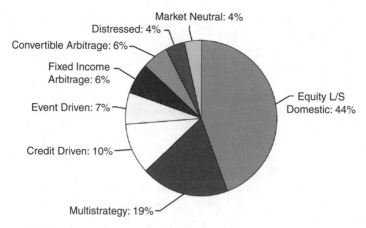

Exhibit 11.6 An absolute return strategies program

Source: Mark Anson, *Handbook of Alternative Assets*, 2nd ed. (Hoboken, NJ: John Wiley & Sons, 2006). Reprinted with permission by John Wiley & Sons, Inc.

CONCLUSION

Research indicates that hedge fund investments can expand the investment opportunity set for investors. The returns to hedge funds generally are positive, have lower volatility than the S&P 500, and have less than perfect correlation with traditional asset classes. Consequently, hedged funds provide a good opportunity to diversify a portfolio and are an excellent risk budgeting tool.

The issue of performance persistence will continue to dog hedge fund managers. Our simple study of the serial correlation associated with the returns to hedge funds found mixed results, as some strategies exhibited positive serial correlations (a positive or negative return in one year is followed by the same type of return in the following year), while others had negative serial correlations (a positive or negative return in one year is followed by the opposite type of return in the following year).

An investor must decide what the best strategy is for investing in hedge funds. Hedge funds may be invested in as part of an opportunistic strategy, a fund of funds strategy, a private equity investment strategy, or an absolute return strategy. In each case, hedge funds can add value to an existing portfolio.

Opportunistic hedge fund investing runs counter to the name hedge funds. This strategy uses hedge funds to expand the investment opportunity set, not hedge it. Typically, opportunistic hedge funds will have a benchmark associated with their performance.

Hedge fund of funds strategies may have one of three purposes: Fund of funds products may be used for risk budgeting, portable alpha, or as a fixed income substitute. In each case, the fixed-income-like volatility associated with a fund of funds product makes it an excellent portfolio diversifier.

Finally, absolute return strategies target a specific risk and return profile. The goal is to produce a consistent return no matter which part of the economic cycle the investor may find herself in.

Due Diligence for Hedge Fund Managers

In our prior chapters we addressed the questions of what (what are hedge funds?), why (why should hedge funds be included in an investment portfolio?), and how (how should a hedge fund program be constructed?). We now turn to the question of who: who should be selected as your hedge fund manager? The answer will depend on due diligence.

At the outset, we realize that this is one of the longest chapters in the book. This reflects the time it takes to perform proper due diligence on a hedge fund manager. Unfortunately, there is no substitute for detailed diligence on a hedge fund manager. This takes time and effort.

Due diligence starts the initial process of building a relationship with a hedge fund manager. It is an unavoidable task that investors must follow in order to choose a manager. Due diligence is the process of identifying the best and the brightest of the hedge fund managers. This is where the investor must roll up her sleeves and get into the devilish details that can prove to be so elusive with hedge fund managers.

Due diligence in the hedge fund world is of utmost importance. For example, Feffer and Kundro (2003) studied more than 100 fund liquidations over a 20-year period and attributed half of all hedge fund failures to operational risk alone. (The International Association of Financial Engineers [2001] defines operational risk as "losses caused by problems with people, processes, technology, or external events.") Feffer and Kundro also argue that structural problems with funds contributed to significant investor losses and that these problems could have been prevented by a comprehensive due diligence process.

Due diligence consists of seven parts: structure, strategy, performance, risk, administrative, legal, and references. This chapter reviews each part of the due diligence procedure. In the appendix to the chapter, we provide a due diligence checklist.

We start this chapter with three fundamental questions that every investor should ask a hedge fund manager. Although these questions seem simplistic, they should be part of the initial meeting with the hedge fund manager and should be addressed before an investor decides to put the hedge fund manager through a full-blown due diligence review.

THREE FUNDAMENTAL QUESTIONS

Although the first hedge fund was introduced more than 50 years ago,[1] the hedge fund industry is still relatively new because it has attracted attention only within the past couple of decades. In fact, most of the academic research on hedge funds was conducted during the 1990s. Further, the attrition rate among hedge funds is fairly high, and therefore it is difficult to find a large sample of hedge funds with each manager having a long track record. In fact, Park, Brown, and Goetzmann find that the attrition rate in the hedge fund industry is about 15% per year and that the half-life for hedge funds is about 2.5 years. Liang documents an attrition rate of 8.54% per year for hedge funds. Weisman and Abernathy indicate that relying on a hedge fund manager's past performance history can lead to

---

[1] Alfred W. Jones introduced the first hedge fund in 1949. See David Purcell and Paul Crowley, "The Reality of Hedge Funds," *Journal of Investing* (Fall 1999), 26–44.

disappointing investment results.[2] Consequently, performance history, while useful, cannot be relied upon solely in selecting a hedge fund manager.

Beyond performance numbers, there are three fundamental questions that every hedge fund manager should answer during the initial screening process. The answers to these three questions are critical to understanding the nature of the hedge fund manager's investment program. The three questions are:

1. What is the investment objective of the hedge fund?
2. What is the investment process of the hedge fund manager?
3. What makes the hedge fund manager so smart?

A hedge fund manager should have a clear and concise statement of the fund's investment objective. Second, the hedge fund manager should identify its investment process. For instance, is it quantitatively or qualitatively based? Last, the hedge fund manager must demonstrate that he or she is smarter than other money managers.

The questions presented in this chapter are threshold issues. These questions are screening tools designed to reduce an initial universe of hedge fund managers down to a select pool of potential investments. They are not, however, a substitute for a thorough due diligence review. Instead, these questions can identify potential hedge fund candidates for which due diligence is appropriate.

It must be noted that hedge fund due diligence is expensive, in terms of both money and time spent. Anson (2006) mentions that effective due diligence requires a work of 75 to 100 hours reviewing a fund manager. And, according to Brown, Fraser, and Liang (2008), the cost of due diligence depends on a series of factors, which include the time spent, the level of thoroughness, and whether accounting firms, law firms, third-party service providers and consulting firms are used. These authors also state, "Assuming a conservative cost of due diligence of $50,000 to $100,000 per hedge fund, the cost of performing initial due diligence on 10 hedge funds for a fund of funds portfolio would be $500,000 to $1 million. Obviously, the cost of performing due diligence on hedge funds in which a fund of funds does not invest would be additional" (pp. 10–11). In spite of these costs, Brown, Fraser, and Liang argue that effective due diligence of hedge funds generates alpha.

Investment objective

The question of a hedge fund manager's investment objective can be broken down into three additional questions:

1. In which markets does the hedge fund manager invest?
2. What is the hedge fund manager's general investment strategy?
3. What is the hedge fund manager's benchmark, if any?

Although these questions may seem straightforward, they are often surprisingly difficult to answer. Consider the following language from a hedge fund disclosure document:

> The principal objective of the Fund is capital appreciation, primarily through the purchase and sale of securities, commodities, and other financial instruments, including without limitation, stocks, bonds, notes, debentures, and bills issued by corporations, municipalities, sovereign nations, or other entities; options, rights, warrants, convertible securities, exchangeable securities, synthetic and/or structured

---

[2] See James Park, Stephen J. Brown, and William N. Goetzmann, "Performance Benchmarks and Survivorship Bias for Hedge Funds and Commodity Trading Advisors," *Hedge Fund News* (August 1999); Bing Liang, "Hedge Fund Performance: 1990–1999," *Financial Analysts Journal* (January/February 2001), 11–18; and Andrew Weisman and Jerome Abernathy, "The Dangers of Historical Hedge Fund Data," working paper, 2000.

convertible or exchangeable products, participation interests, investment contracts, mortgages, mortgage- and asset-backed securities, real estate, and interests therein; currencies, other futures, commodity options, forward contracts, money market instruments, bank notes, bank guarantees, letters of credit, and other forms of bank obligations; other swaps and other derivative instruments; limited partnership interests and other limited partnership securities or instruments; and contracts relating to the foregoing; in each case whether now existing or created in the future.

Let's analyze this statement in light of our three investment objective questions.

Question 1: In which markets does the hedge fund manager invest?
Answer: In every market known to exist.

By listing every possible financial, commodity, or investment contract currently in existence (or to exist in the future), the hedge fund manager has covered all of the bases but has left the investor uninformed. Unfortunately, the unlimited nature of the hedge fund manager's potential investment universe does not help to narrow the scope of the manager's investment objective.

Question 2: What is the hedge fund manager's general investment strategy?
Answer: Capital appreciation.

This answer, too, is uninformative. Rarely does any investor invest in a hedge fund for capital depreciation. Generally, hedge funds are not used as tax shelters. Furthermore, many institutional investors are tax-exempt so taxes are not a consideration. Capital appreciation is assumed to be the goal for most investments, including hedge funds. The language is far too general to be informative.

Question 3: What is the hedge fund manager's benchmark, if any?
Answer: There is no effective benchmark. The manager's investment universe is so widespread as to make any benchmark useless.

Unfortunately, the disclosure language, while very detailed, discloses very little. It does cover all of the manager's legal bases but it does not inform the investor.

By contrast, consider the following language from a second hedge fund disclosure document.

> The Fund's investment objective is to make investments in public securities that generate a long-term return in excess of that generated by the overall U.S. public equity market while reducing the market risk of the portfolio through selective short positions.

This one sentence answers all three investment objective questions. First, the manager identifies that it invests in the U.S. public equity market. Second, the manager discloses that it uses a long/short investment strategy. Last, the manager states that its objective is to outperform the overall U.S. equity market; therefore, a suitable benchmark might be the S&P 500, the Russell 1000, or a sector index.

In summary, long-winded disclosure statements are not necessary. A well-thought-out investment strategy can be summarized in one sentence.

Investment process

Most investors prefer a well-defined investment process that describes how an investment manager makes investments. The articulation and documentation of the process can be just as important as the investment results generated by the process. Consider the following language from another hedge fund disclosure document:

> The manager makes extensive use of computer technology in both the formulation and execution of many investment decisions. Buy and sell decisions will, in many cases, be made and executed algorith- mically according to quantitative trading strategies embodied in analytical computer software running the manager's computer facilities or on other computers used to support the Fund's trading activities.

This is a so-called black box. A black box is the algorithmic extension of the hedge fund manager's brainpower. Computer algorithms are developed to quantify the manager's skill or investment insight.

For black box managers, the black box itself is the investment process. It is not that the black boxes are bad investments. In fact, the hedge fund research indicates that proprietary quantitative trading strategies can be quite successful.[3] Rather, the issue is whether good performance results justify the lack of a clear investment process.

Black box programs tend to be used in arbitrage or relative value hedge fund programs. Hedge fund managers use quantitative computer algorithms to seek out pricing discrepancies between similar securities or investment contracts. They then sell the investment that appears to be expensive and buy the investment that appears to be cheap. The very nature of arbitrage programs is to minimize market risk. Leverage is then applied to extract the most value from the small net exposure to market risk.

A black box is just one example of process versus investment results. The hedge fund industry considers itself to be skill-based. However, it is very difficult to translate manager skill into a process. This is particularly true when the performance of the hedge fund is dependent upon the skill of a specific individual.

Let's consider another, well-publicized skill-based investment process. In the spring of 2000, the hedge funds headed by George Soros stumbled, leading to the departure of Stanley Druckenmiller, the chief investment strategist for Soros Fund Management. The *Wall Street Journal* documented the concentrated skill-based investment style of this hedge fund group:

> For years, [Soros Fund Management] fostered an entrepreneurial culture, with a cadre of employees battling wits to persuade Mr. Druckenmiller to invest.
>
> "[Mr. Druckenmiller] didn't scream, but he could be very tough. It could be three days or three weeks of battling it out until he's convinced, or you're defeated."[4]

This statement does not describe an investment process. It is a description of an individual. The hedge fund manager's investment analysis and decision making are concentrated in one person. This is a pure example of skill-based investing. There is no discernible process. Instead, all information is filtered through the brain of one individual. In essence, the institutional investor must trust the judgment of one person.

Mr. Druckenmiller compiled an exceptional track record as the manager of Soros's Quantum Fund. However, the concentration of decision-making authority is not an economic risk; it is a process risk.

Investors are generally unwilling to bear risks that are not fundamental to their tactical and strategic asset allocations. Process risk is not a fundamental risk. It is an idiosyncratic risk of the hedge fund manager's structure and operations.

Generally, process risk is not a risk that investors wish to bear. Nor is it a risk for which they expect to be compensated. Furthermore, how would an investor go about pricing the process risk of a hedge fund manager? It can't be quantified and it can't be calibrated. Therefore, there is no way to tell whether an institutional investor is being properly compensated for this risk.[5]

---

[3] See CrossBorder Capital, "Choosing Investment Styles to Reduce Risk," *Hedge Fund Research* (October 1999); Goldman, Sachs & Co. and Financial Risk Management Ltd., "The Hedge Fund 'Industry' and Absolute Return Funds," *Journal of Alternative Investments* (Spring 1999), and "Hedge Funds Revisited," *Pension and Endowment Forum* (January 2000).

[4] "Shake-Up Continues at Soros's Hedge-Fund Empire," *Wall Street Journal*, May 1, 2000, C1.

[5] See James Park and Jeremy Staum, "Fund of Funds Diversification: How Much Is Enough?" *Journal of Alternative Investments* (Winter 1998), 39–42. They demonstrate that idiosyncratic process risks can largely be eliminated through a diversified fund of funds program. They indicate that a portfolio of 15 to 20 hedge funds can eliminate much of the idiosyncratic risk associated with hedge fund investments.

Process risk also raises the ancillary issue of lack of transparency. Skill-based investing usually is opaque. Are the decisions of the key individual quantitatively based? Qualitatively based? There is no way to really tell. This is similar to the problems discussed earlier with respect to black boxes.

To summarize, process risk cannot be quantified, and it is not a risk that investors are willing to bear. Process risk also raises issues of transparency. Investors want clarity and definition, not opaqueness and amorphousness.

What makes the hedge fund manager so smart?

Before investing money with a hedge fund manager, an investor must determine that the manager is smarter and/or has better information than the next manager. One way to be smarter than another hedge fund manager is to have superior skill in filtering information. That is, the hedge fund manager must be able to look at the same information set as another manager but be able to glean more investment insight from that data set.

Alternatively, if the hedge fund manager is not smarter than the next manager, he must demonstrate that he has a better information set. His competitive advantage is not filtering information, but gathering it. To be successful, a hedge fund manager must demonstrate one or both of these competitive advantages.

Generally speaking, quantitative, computer-driven managers satisfy the first criterion. That is, hedge fund managers that run computer models access the same information set as everyone else, but have better (smarter) algorithms to extract more value per information unit than the next manager. These managers tend to be relative value managers.

Relative value managers extract value by simultaneously comparing the prices of two securities and buying and selling accordingly. This information is available to all investors in the marketplace. However, it is the relative value managers that are able to process the information quickly enough to capture mispricings in the market.

Alternatively, hedge fund managers that confine themselves to a particular market segment or sector generally satisfy the second criterion. They have a larger information set that allows them to gain a competitive edge in their chosen market. Their advantage is a proprietary information set accumulated over time rather than a proprietary data-filtering system.

Consider the following statement from a hedge fund disclosure document:

> The Adviser hopes to achieve consistently high returns by focusing on small and mid-cap companies in the biotechnology market.

The competitive advantage of this type of manager is his knowledge not only about a particular economic sector (biotechnology), but also about a particular market segment of that sector (small and mid-cap). This type of manger tends to take more market risk exposure than credit risk exposure and generally applies equity long/short programs.

Identifying the competitive advantage of the hedge fund manager is the key to determining whether the hedge fund manager can sustain performance results, although we note that the issue of performance persistence is undecided. Therefore, an investor cannot rely on historical hedge fund performance data as a means of selecting good managers over bad managers. Furthermore, every hedge fund disclosure document contains some variation of the following language:

> Past performance is no indication of future results.

Essentially, this statement directs the investor to ignore the hedge fund manager's performance history.

To assess the likelihood of performance persistence, the investor must then determine whether the hedge fund manager is an information gatherer or an information filterer. Consider the following language from a hedge fund disclosure document:

> The General Partner will utilize its industry expertise, contacts, and databases developed over the past 11 years to identify company investment ideas outside traditional sources and will analyze these investment opportunities using, among other techniques, many aspects of its proven methodology in determining value.

This hedge fund manager has a superior information set that has been developed over 11 years. It is an information gatherer. This manager applies an equity long/short program within a specific market sector.

Finally, consider the following disclosure language from a merger arbitrage hedge fund manager:

> [The] research group [is] staffed by experienced M&A lawyers with detailed knowledge of deal life cycle, with extensive experience with corporate law of multiple U.S. states, U.S. and foreign securities laws regarding proxy contests, and antitrust laws (of both the United States and the European Union), and who have made relevant filings before regulators and have closed a wide variety of M&A transactions.

This hedge fund manager is an information filterer. The hedge fund manager's expertise is sifting through the outstanding legal and regulatory issues associated with a merger or acquisition and determining the likelihood that the deal will be completed.

To summarize, a good lesson is that successful hedge fund managers know the exact nature of their competitive advantage and how to exploit it.

STRUCTURAL REVIEW

The structural review defines the organization of the hedge fund manager. We start with the basics: How is the fund organized? It is important to remember that the hedge fund manager and the hedge fund are separate legal entities with different legal structures and identities. We then consider the structure of the hedge fund manager, any regulatory registrations, and key personnel.

Fund organization

The hedge fund manager may invest the hedge fund's assets through an offshore master trust account or fund. An offshore **master trust** account is often used to take into account the various tax domiciles of the hedge fund's investors. Often, a hedge fund manager will set up two hedge funds, one onshore (U.S.-based) and one offshore. Master trusts are typically established in tax-neutral sites such as Bermuda or the Cayman Islands.

The purpose of the master trust is to invest the assets of both the onshore hedge fund and the offshore hedge fund in a consistent (if not identical) manner so that both hedge funds share the benefit of the hedge fund manager's insights. Investors in either fund are not disadvantaged by this structure. Instead, it allows the tax consequences to flow down to the tax code of each investor's domicile country.

Master trusts/funds are often viewed suspiciously as tax evasion vehicles. This is not their purpose. Their purpose is tax neutrality, not evasion. In Bermuda, for example, master trust funds do not pay any corporate income tax. They pay only a corporate licensing fee. Therefore, there are no adverse tax consequences to the hedge fund investors at the master trust level.

Instead, the tax consequences for the investors will depend on their domiciles. Investors in the onshore U.S.-based hedge fund are subject to the U.S. Internal Revenue Code. Investors in the

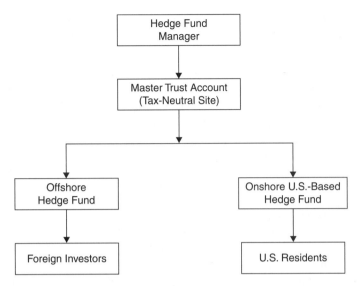

Exhibit 12.1 Master trust account

Source: Mark Anson, *Handbook of Alternative Assets,* 2nd ed. (Hoboken, NJ: John Wiley & Sons, 2006). Reprinted with permission by John Wiley & Sons, Inc.

offshore fund are subject to the tax codes of their respective domiciles. Therefore, master trust vehicles are used to accommodate the different tax domiciles of foreign and domestic investors.

Consider a hedge fund manager who has two investors: one based in the United States and one in France. Where should she locate her hedge fund? If she locates the hedge fund in the United States, the U.S. investor will be happy, but the French investor may have to pay double the income taxes: both in the United States and in France. The best way to resolve this problem is to set up two hedge funds, one onshore and one offshore. In addition, a master trust account is established in a tax-neutral site. The hedge fund manager can then invest the assets of both hedge funds through the master trust account and each investor will be liable only for the taxes imposed by the revenue codes of their respective countries.[6] Exhibit 12.1 demonstrates the master trust structure.

Hedge fund structures do not have to be as complicated as that presented in Exhibit 12.1. The majority of hedge fund managers in the United States operate only within the United States, have only an onshore hedge fund, and accept only U.S. investors. Nonetheless, the popularity of hedge fund investing has resulted in operating structures that are sometimes as creative as the hedge fund strategies themselves.

In addition to a master feeder structure, the hedge fund manager may also have **separate accounts**. These are single-client asset management accounts. An investor in a hedge fund should ascertain whether these separate accounts are managed in the same strategy as the hedge fund. If so, fee economics should be similar. In addition, these separate accounts must also be allocated trade ideas by the hedge fund manager. The investor should determine that there is a fair and equitable allocation of the hedge fund manager's trade ideas to the hedge fund as well as the separate accounts. This is a critical piece of the due diligence process because it is unlikely that the hedge fund manager's prime brokers or custodians will monitor whether the trade allocation was done in a fair and impartial manner.

---

[6] In reality, the United States and France have a tax treaty, so the threat of double taxation is minimal. However, there are many countries that do not have tax treaties, and the potential for double taxation is a reality.

Hedge fund manager organization

First, the basics: Where is the hedge fund manager located? Are there any satellite offices? Where is the nearest office to the investor? These questions can be very important if the hedge fund manager operates overseas and there are significant time differences between the manager's business hours and those of the investor.

Second, an organization chart is mandatory. Who are the chief executive officer, the chief investment officer, and chief operating officer? A warning: It is not a good business plan if they are all the same person. Hedge fund managers should do what they do best: invest money, and leave the operating details to someone else.

Of special importance is the chief financial officer (CFO). The CFO will be the investor's most important link with the hedge fund manager after an investment is made because the CFO will be responsible for reporting the hedge fund manager's performance numbers. Consequently, the investor should make certain that the CFO has a strong background in accounting, preferably a certified public accountant, a chartered accountant, or another professional accounting designation. Last, the investor must determine who are the senior managers in charge of trading, information systems, marketing, and research and development.

The educational and professional background of all principals should be documented. It should be determined whether they have graduate degrees, whether there are any professional certificates such as Chartered Alternative Investment Analysts, and what their prior investment experience was before starting a hedge fund.

Another warning: Many equity long/short hedge fund managers were former long-only managers. Yet shorting stocks is very different from going long stocks. The ability to locate and borrow stock, limit losses in a bull market, and short on the uptick rule are special talents that cannot be developed overnight.

Before investing money with a long/short hedge fund manager, an investor should find out where the hedge fund manager learned to short stocks. If it is a hedge fund manager that previously managed a long-only portfolio, chances are that she might not have much experience with respect to shorting stocks, and therefore will be learning to short stocks with your money.

Ownership

Ownership of the hedge fund manager must be documented. It is imperative to know who owns the company that advises the hedge fund. This is important for "key person" provisions of the contractual documentation.

Additionally, ownership is essential for ensuring that there is a proper alignment of interests with the hedge fund manager's employees as well as retention of employment. By sharing the ownership of the hedge fund management company with key employees, the hedge fund manager can ensure proper alignment of interests, as well as retention of key personnel.

Registrations

The investor should document the **regulatory registrations** of the hedge fund manager. The hedge fund manager might be registered with the Securities and Exchange Commission (SEC) as an investment adviser under the Investment Advisers Act of 1940. If so, the hedge fund manager must file annually with the SEC Form ADV which contains important financial and structural information regarding the hedge fund manager.

Alternatively, the hedge fund manager might be registered with the National Futures Association (NFA) and the Commodity Futures Trading Commission (CFTC) as either a Commodity Trading

Advisor (CTA) or a Commodity Pool Operator (CPO). The NFA is the self-regulatory organization for the managed futures industry. It is approved by the CFTC to handle all registrations for CTAs and CPOs. Also, the hedge fund manager might be registered with the NFA as an introducing broker or futures commission merchant. If the hedge fund manager is registered as either a CTA, a CPO, an introducing broker, or a futures commission merchant, it must obey the rules and regulations of the NFA and the CFTC.

If the hedge fund manager is registered with either the SEC or the CFTC, the investor should ascertain the date of the original registration and whether there are any civil, criminal, or administrative actions outstanding against the hedge fund manager. This information must be filed with either the NFA (for the managed futures industry) or the SEC (for investment advisers).

Outside service providers

The investor must document who is the hedge fund manager's outside auditors, prime broker, and legal counsel. Each of these service providers must be contacted.

First, the investor should receive the hedge fund manager's latest annual audited financial statement as well as the most current statement. Any questions regarding the financial statements should be directed to the CFO and the outside auditors. Any opinion from the auditors other than an unqualified opinion must be explained by the outside auditors. Additionally, outside auditors are a good source of information regarding the hedge fund manager's accounting system and operations.

The investor should speak with the hedge fund manager's outside counsel. This is important for two reasons. First, outside counsel is typically responsible for keeping current all regulatory registrations of the hedge fund manager. Second, outside counsel can inform the investor of any criminal, civil, or administrative actions that might be pending against the hedge fund manager. Outside counsel is also responsible for preparing the hedge fund manager's offering document. This is with whom the investor will negotiate should an investment be made with the hedge fund manager.

There was an incident on Presidents' Day in 1997 when a prime broker contacted one of its hedge fund manager clients with a margin call demanding that the hedge fund manager post more cash or collateral to cover either her short positions or her borrowing from the manager.

Margin calls can happen for several reasons. First and foremost, a short position can move against a hedge fund manager creating a large negative balance with the hedge fund manager's prime broker. To protect itself from the credit exposure to the hedge fund manager, the prime broker will make a margin call, in effect demanding that the hedge fund manager either put up cash or more securities as collateral to cover the prime broker's credit exposure to the hedge fund manager.

On this particular Presidents' Day, a prime broker made a margin call on a hedge fund manager that invested in the mortgage-backed securities market. The essence of the margin call was that the prime broker was skeptical of the market value of positions that the hedge fund manager claimed. The prime broker demanded that the hedge fund manager either confirm the market value of her positions by soliciting bids in the mortgage-backed securities market to buy some of the hedge fund manager's portfolio or post more collateral.

Unfortunately, Presidents' Day is a national holiday in the United States when banks and insurance companies, two key investors in the mortgage-backed securities market, are closed. As a result the market for mortgage-backed securities was very thin that day and the hedge fund manager had no choice but to be a price taker. Additionally, the hedge fund manager's marking-to-market values proved to be optimistic. The resulting fire sale had a significant impact on the hedge fund manager's performance.

This unfortunate example demonstrates the important relationship between the prime broker community and the hedge fund community. Every hedge fund manager has at least one prime broker, and these prime brokers monitor the hedge fund manager's portfolio.

Prime broker

Without a doubt the most important service provider is a hedge fund's prime broker. The lessons of Long Term Capital Management (LTCM) have taught us that it is best for a hedge fund manager to work with a designated prime broker even though the hedge fund manager may have relationships with many broker-dealers.

The prime broker is responsible for providing the leverage to the hedge fund manager for his trading program. This leverage can come in the form of a short-term floating-rate loan, overdraft privileges, margin on security purchases, and other forms of short-term financing. In addition, the prime broker provides execution and clearing services for the hedge fund manager, finds securities for lending and shorting, and even acts as matchmaker to hook up the hedge fund manager with potential investors. This last bit is known as the "hedge fund dating services" and is provided by most Wall Street banks and brokerage firms.

With so many services provided by the prime broker, it is essential that a potential hedge fund investor contact the prime broker to assess the strength of the relationship, any problems that may have arisen in the past, frequency of turnover of the portfolio, financing and leverage amounts, and the amount of exposure the hedge fund manager has to the prime broker.

The biggest stick (and it is a huge one) that prime brokers have with respect to their hedge fund clients is the ability to make margin calls. The prime broker has the absolute right to demand that the hedge fund manager deposit more cash into its prime brokerage account to support its leveraged trading. In addition, the prime broker can demand that the hedge fund manager liquidate outstanding portfolio positions to raise cash to deposit with the prime broker. Last, and the ultimate threat, the prime broker can, in fact, seize collateral from the hedge manager and liquidate the collateral itself to raise cash. In the past, this last step (seizure of collateral) was used rarely by prime brokers. However, in the midst of the credit and liquidity crisis that gripped most of the world from the summer of 2007 through 2008, prime brokers exercised this last power with much greater frequency.

STRATEGIC REVIEW

The second phase of due diligence is a review of the hedge fund manager's investment strategy. This should include a clear statement of the hedge fund manager's style, the markets and securities in which she invests, what competitive advantage the hedge fund manager brings to the table, the source of her investment ideas, the current portfolio position, and what benchmark, if any, is appropriate for the hedge fund.

Investment style

In Chapter 10, we listed several styles of hedge fund managers. While these are the major hedge fund styles, they are by no means exhaustive. The creativity of hedge fund managers is such that there are as many styles as there are colors of the rainbow.

For instance, convergence trading is a hedge fund style frequently seen. Recall that convergence trading compares two similar securities and buys the security that is cheap relative to the other security while selling the security that is relatively rich. Convergence trading can be subdivided into economic arbitrage and statistical arbitrage (stat arb). Economic arbitrage compares the pricing fundamentals of two similar securities to determine if the prices set by the market are inconsistent with the fundamentals. If an inconsistency is identified, the cheap security is purchased and the rich security is sold. The hedge fund manager will hold on to these positions until the market corrects itself and the two security prices are in proper balance. This holding period may be a day, a week, or several months. In some cases, it may be necessary to hold the two securities to maturity (in the case of bonds).

Conversely, statistical arbitrage (or "stat arb") is another form of convergence trading where the trading is based not on economic fundamentals, but rather on statistical anomalies that temporarily occur in the market. Typically, these anomalies occur only for a moment or for a day at most. Consequently, statistical arbitrage is a very short-term relative value trading program with positions entered and exited within the same trading day.

Additionally, economic relative value or statistical arbitrage can occur in the fixed income, equity, or convertible bond markets. Exhibit 12.2 diagrams how an investment strategy should be documented.

Investment markets

Next, the investor should document in which markets the hedge fund manager invests. Recall that this was one of our basic questions previously discussed. We provided an example of a well-defined equity long/short manager.

For other hedge fund managers, however, the answer is not so obvious. For instance, global macro managers typically have the broadest investment mandate possible. They can invest in equity, bond, commodity, and currency markets across the world. Pinning down a global macro manager may be akin to picking up mercury. Nonetheless, the investor should document as best she can in what markets the hedge fund manager invests. If the hedge fund manager is a global macro manager, the investor may have to accept that the manager can and will invest in whatever market he deems fit.

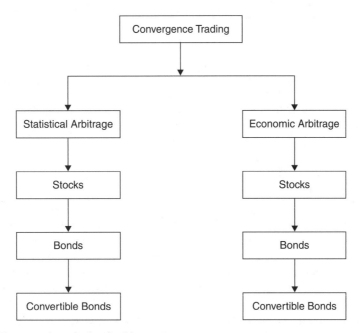

Exhibit 12.2 Documenting a hedge fund investment strategy

Source: Mark Anson, *Handbook of Alternative Assets*, 2nd ed. (Hoboken, NJ: John Wiley & Sons, 2006). Reprinted with permission by John Wiley & Sons, Inc.

The investor should also determine the extent to which the hedge fund manager invests in derivative securities. Derivatives are a two-edged sword. On the one hand, they can hedge an investment portfolio and reduce risk. On the other hand, they can increase the leverage of the hedge fund and magnify the risks taken by the hedge fund manager.

Investment securities

Closely related to the investment markets are the types of securities in which the hedge fund manager invests. For some strategies, this will be straightforward. For instance, the sample language provided earlier indicates that the hedge fund manager will invest in the stock of U.S. companies.

However, other strategies will not be so clear. Recall the language from the first example in this chapter where one hedge fund manager listed every security, futures contract, option, and derivative contract "in each case whether now existing or created in the future." This manager needs to be pinned down, and the due diligence checklist is the place to do it.

Oftentimes, hedge fund disclosure documents are drafted in very broad and expansive terms. The reason is that the hedge fund manager does not want to be legally painted into an investment corner. The purpose of due diligence is not to legally bind the hedge fund manager but to document the types of securities necessary to effect her investment strategy.

It is very important that the investor determine the hedge fund manager's strategy for using derivatives, the types of derivatives used, and in which markets derivatives will be purchased. Of particular concern is the extent to which hedge fund manager may "short volatility."

 Shorting volatility is a strategy where a hedge fund manager sells out-of-the-money call or put options against the investment portfolio. If the options expire unexercised, the hedge fund manager receives the option premiums and this increases the return for the hedge fund. However, if the options are exercised against the hedge fund manager, significant negative results may occur. In Chapters 13 and 14 on risk management, we demonstrate the dangers of shorting volatility.

Benchmark

Establishing a benchmark for hedge fund managers is one of the thorniest issues facing the industry. One reason is the skill-based nature of their investment styles. Manager skill cannot be captured by a passive securities benchmark. Skill, in fact, is orthogonal to passive investing.

Second, most hedge fund managers apply investment strategies that cannot be captured by a passive securities index. For instance, it can be argued that a long-only passive equity index is not an appropriate benchmark for an equity long/short hedge fund. In addition, hedge fund managers also use derivative instruments, such as options, that have nonlinear payout functions. Passive securities indices do not reflect nonlinear payout strategies.

Last, hedge fund managers tend to maintain concentrated portfolios. The nature of this concentration makes the investment strategy of the hedge fund manager distinct from a broad-based securities index.

Nonetheless, some performance measure must be established for the hedge fund manager. For instance, if the hedge fund manager runs a long/short equity fund concentrating on the semiconductor sector of the technology industry, a good benchmark would be the SOX semiconductor index maintained by the Philadelphia Stock Exchange.

If the hedge fund manager does not believe that any index is appropriate for his strategy, then a hurdle rate must be established. Hurdle rates are most appropriate for absolute return hedge fund managers whose rate of return does not depend on the general economic prospects of a sector or a broad-based market index.

Competitive advantage

Recall the three fundamental questions at the beginning of this chapter. One of the key factors that must be uncovered during the due diligence process is the competitive advantage of the hedge fund manager (what makes the manager smarter than others). What does this manager do that is special compared to other hedge fund managers? What is her insight? Is it better fundamental analysis, good risk control, better quantitative models? Further, how does she exploit this in the financial markets? This advantage must be documented as part of the due diligence process.

Another way to ask this question is: What makes the hedge fund manager different from the other managers? For instance, there are many merger arbitrage managers. However, some invest only in announced deals while some speculate on potential deals. Some merger arbitrage funds invest in cross-border deals while others stay strictly within the boundaries of their domicile. Some participate in deals of only a certain market capitalization range while others are across the board. And finally, some merger arbitrage funds use options and convertible securities to capture the merger premium while others invest only in the underlying equity.

As we demonstrated earlier, another competitive advantage consists in that some merger arbitrage experts develop large in-house legal staffs to review the regulatory (antitrust) implications of the announced deals. These managers rely on their expert legal analysis to determine whether the existing merger premium is rich or cheap. They exploit the legal issues associated with the merger instead of the economic issues.

Current portfolio position

This part of the due diligence is meant to provide a current snapshot of the hedge fund. First, the investor should ascertain the fund's current long versus short exposure. Additionally, the investor should determine the amount of cash that the hedge fund manager is keeping and why. Too much cash indicates an investment strategy that may be stuck in neutral.

The investor should also ascertain how many investments the hedge fund manager currently maintains in the fund. As we have previously discussed, hedge fund managers typically run concentrated exposure. Therefore, the investor is exposed to more stock-specific risk than market risk. Again, this is the essence of hedge fund management: Hedge fund managers do not take market risk; they take security-specific risk. This stock- or security-specific risk is the source of the hedge fund manager's returns.

Last, the investor should ask the hedge fund manager how she has positioned the hedge fund portfolio in light of current market conditions. This should provide insight as to not only how the hedge fund manager views the current financial markets, but also her investment strategy going forward.

Source of investment ideas

What is the source of the hedge fund manager's investment ideas? Does she wait until it just hits her? Wait until to you get to Chapter 18, "Top Ten Hedge Fund Quotes." Indeed, one manager readily admitted, "Basically I look at screens all day and go with my gut." Conversely, is there a rigorous process for sourcing investment ideas? Idea generation is what hedge fund investing is all about. This is the source of the manager's skill.

The source of investment ideas is closely tied in with the nature of competitive advantage. The hedge fund manager's competitive advantage could be her research department that generates investment ideas better or faster than other hedge fund managers. Conversely, some hedge fund managers, such as merger arbitrage managers, wait for deals to be announced in the market.

In addition, the investor should determine in which type of market the hedge fund manager's ideas work best. Do they work best in bear markets, bull markets, flat markets, volatile markets, or no one type of market more than others? For instance, an absolute return hedge fund manager (a manager with a hurdle rate for a benchmark) should be agnostic with respect to the direction of the market. Otherwise, an argument could be made that the hedge fund manager's performance should be compared to a market index.

Capacity

A frequent issue with hedge fund managers is the **capacity** of their investment strategy. Hedge fund managers have investment strategies that are more narrowly focused than traditional long-only managers. As a consequence, their investment strategies frequently have limited capacity. This is more the case for hedge fund managers that target small sectors of the economy or segments of the financial markets.

For instance, the convertible bond market is much smaller than the U.S. equity market. Consequently, a convertible bond hedge fund manager may have more limited capacity than an equity long/short manager. Global macro hedge fund managers, with their global investment mandate, have the largest capacity. This large capacity is derived from their unlimited ability to invest across financial instruments, currencies, borders, and commodities.

Capacity is an important issue for the investor because the hedge fund manager might dilute her skill by allowing a greater number of investors into the hedge fund than is optimal from an investment standpoint. This may result in too much money chasing too few deals.

PERFORMANCE REVIEW

Although every hedge fund disclosure document will state that past performance is no indication of future results, the performance review forms the heart of most due diligence reports. Even though past performance cannot guarantee future results, it provides some guidance of the likelihood of the hedge fund manager's success.

List of funds and assets under management

First, the investor should document how many hedge funds the hedge fund manager advises and the assets under management for each fund. The investor should know the size of the hedge fund manager's empire. This is important not only for the collection of performance data, but also to give the investor some sense of the hedge fund manager's investment capacity.

Verifying the assets of the hedge fund manager may not be as easy as it sounds. First, the hedge fund manager may have onshore and offshore accounts or hedge funds. Second, the hedge fund manager may use multiple prime brokers and custodians to keep and trade its assets. The investor should ask how many custodians and prime brokers the hedge fund manager uses and get the latest monthly statement of each. Then the investor can piece together the total size of the hedge fund manager's empire.

There are three important questions to ask:

1. How long has the hedge fund manager been actively managing a hedge fund?
2. Have the manager's performance results been consistent over time?
3. Are the investment strategies the same or different for each hedge fund?

Previously, we noted that the attrition rate in the hedge fund is very high, up to 15% a year according to one study. Successful hedge fund managers have a long-term track record with consistent results. However, *long-term* in the hedge fund industry is a relative term. For hedge funds, five years is generally sufficient to qualify as long-term.

If a hedge fund manager manages more than one hedge fund, the investment strategy and style should be documented for both. If the hedge funds follow the same style, then the issue of trade allocation must be resolved. The investor should determine how the hedge fund manager decides which trades go into which hedge fund.

Drawdowns

Drawdowns are a common phenomenon in the hedge fund industry. Simply defined, a **drawdown** is a decline in the net asset value of the hedge fund. Drawdowns are not unique to the hedge fund industry; they also occur in the mutual fund industry. However, in the long-only world of mutual funds, drawdowns are often motivated by declines in market indices. This reflects the market risk associated with mutual funds.

The difference with hedge funds is that they eschew market risk in favor of security-specific risk. The amount of security-specific risk in the hedge fund is reflective of the hedge fund manager's skill level of finding overpriced and underpriced securities regardless of the condition of the general financial markets. Therefore, drawdowns in the hedge fund world indicate a lapse of hedge fund manager skill.

Hedge fund managers often claim that their industry is skill-based. This claim is a two-edged sword. On the one hand, it protects hedge fund managers from being compared to a passive long-only index as a benchmark. On the other hand, it also means that when the hedge fund declines in value, the blame rests solely with the hedge fund manager and not with the condition of the financial markets.

Therefore, it is important to measure how much a lapse of hedge fund manager skill cost the fund, and how long it took for the hedge fund manager to regain her skill and recoup the losses. Last, the hedge fund manager should explain her temporary loss of skill.

Statistical data

This section covers the basic summary information that is expected of all active managers: the average return over the life of the fund as well as the standard deviation (volatility) or returns and the Sharpe ratio.

As an aside, Sharpe ratios can be misleading statistics when measuring hedge fund performance because of the nonlinear strategies that hedge fund managers can pursue. We provide an example of this danger in our two chapters on risk management.

Additionally, if a benchmark can be identified for the hedge fund, then the systematic risk of the hedge fund with that benchmark should be measured. This statistic is known as the beta of the hedge fund, and it measures the extent by which the hedge fund returns move in tandem with the benchmark.

Also, if a benchmark is identified, then an information ratio (IR) statistic can be calculated. As was explained in Chapter 5, the IR is the excess return of the hedge fund (the returns to the hedge fund minus the returns to the benchmark) divided by the standard deviation of the excess returns. The IR measures the amount of active return that is earned for each unit of active risk exposure. As a rule of thumb, successful long-only managers generally earn an IR between 0.25 to 0.5. With respect to hedge funds, an investor should expect to receive an IR greater than 1.0.

Withdrawals

Withdrawals can be detrimental to fund performance. If a hedge fund manager is fully invested at the time of a redemption request, fund performance will suffer. First, the hedge fund manager must sell securities to fund the withdrawal. This means transaction costs that would not otherwise be incurred will be charged to the fund and will be borne by all investors. Additionally, to the extent that a hedge fund manager cannot liquidate a portion of her investment strategy on a pro rata basis to fund the withdrawal, there may be a loss to the hedge fund from forgone investment opportunities.

Finally, the less liquid the securities in which the hedge fund manager invests, the greater these costs will be. Equity long/short hedge funds usually have the lowest cost associated with a withdrawal because the equity markets are typically the most liquid markets in which to transact. More arcane investment strategies and securities such as mortgage-backed arbitrage can have significant costs associated with a withdrawal.

Recall the incident discussed earlier with respect to a prime broker executing a margin call on Presidents' Day to a mortgage-backed hedge fund manager. The timing of the margin call had severe implications for fund performance. A withdrawal request is similar to a margin call in that a hedge fund investor demands that the hedge fund manager liquidate some of her positions to fund the redemption request. The results, if unexpected, can have a negative impact of fund performance.

Pricing

One of the biggest issues with hedge fund performance is how the hedge fund manager values the securities in her portfolio in order to create performance records. This issue is particularly acute for hedge fund managers that invest in esoteric and illiquid securities such as collateralized debt obligations, distressed debt, or convertible bonds. One of the reasons that hedge fund managers can earn significant excess returns is because the lack of liquidity in these markets provides the hedge fund manager with two sources of return: (1) a liquidity premium for simply buying and holding securities that trade infrequently, and (2) the ability to earn excess returns in a less efficient market.

For publicly traded securities such as stocks and bonds, the issue is less acute, but still has the potential for unscrupulous behavior. For example, every publicly traded stock has both a bid and an offer price. For a stock like IBM where the bid is $101.86 and the offer is $101.87, the issue is nonexistent, because the difference between the bid and the offer price is only one penny.

However, consider the stock of Sohu.com Inc., a NASDAQ-listed Internet company that provides news, entertainment, and communication services in China. Sohu.com had a market capitalization of less than $2 billion in mid-April of 2009. Its bid price was $47.50 while its offer was $47.54, a spread of four cents. Depending on whether the hedge fund manager is long or short this stock, marking her positions to the bid or offer can create an instant four-cent swing in the value of her position.

The best hedge fund managers take a conservative approach to pricing their positions. For example, for a long position in Sohu.com, the hedge fund manager could mark to the bid price of $47.50, whereas a hedge fund manager that is short could mark her position to the offer of $47.54. A common practice in the hedge fund industry is to take the midmarket price between the bid and offer prices, or $47.52, and use this for both short and long positions with respect to Sohu.com. Also, many hedge fund managers (or their administrators) use outside pricing services for their portfolio positions.

For stocks and bonds that are not publicly traded, the solution to marking the portfolio becomes especially problematic. Many hedge fund managers "mark to model." That is, they use their own internal valuation models to determine the price of illiquid securities. However, this pricing is neither independent nor objective. Further, as the lessons of Long-Term Capital Management show us, even if the pricing models are theoretically correct, there can be periods of illiquidity where the prices of less liquid securities decline significantly.

The bottom line is that every investor must document how the hedge fund manager marks to market her portfolio. The issue of illiquid securities must be especially detailed. If the hedge fund manager uses a mark to model methodology for less liquid securities, then the investor should determine how the hedge fund manager's model works under periods of market stress. This is all the more important because investors tend to flee hedge funds during periods of market stress, and therefore this might be a scenario when the hedge fund manager will have to sell a significant portion of her portfolio.

Liang (2003) examined the accuracy of performance figures reported to hedge fund databases. He compared performance figures for the same funds' returns across different data sources, and found that audited hedge funds had smaller return discrepancies in the returns reported to different databases than nonaudited funds, thus suggesting that auditing makes an important difference in the quality of the data reported. He also found that defunct funds were less effectively audited than live funds, and that there was a higher probability for a large fund to be audited than a small fund. Finally, funds of funds, funds listed on exchanges, funds with both U.S. and non-U.S. investors, funds invested in a single sector, and funds open to the public all had better data quality than other types of hedge funds. It is important to note that most funds have audited returns regardless of whether they are indicated by a database. The finding that defunct funds were more likely not to have audited returns could be due to the fact that defunct funds do not check the database for accuracy of information it provides about them.

RISK REVIEW

Risk is the other side of the equation from return. Understanding the risks embedded in a hedge fund manager's portfolio is just as important as measuring the return earned from underwriting those risks.

Risk management

There are four important questions that must be answered to understand the risk profile of the hedge fund:

1. What is the level of risk involved in the hedge fund manager's strategy?
2. What risks are managed?
3. How is risk measured?
4. How is risk managed?

First, investors need to understand whether the hedge fund manager pursues a conservative or an aggressive strategy. For example, the hedge fund manager may pursue an equity long/short strategy. The investor should assess whether the manager attempts to hedge away unwanted market risk and just focuses on his stock calls. Additionally, does the hedge fund manager borrow to leverage up the long/short positions? Or does the hedge fund manager concentrate in small-cap stocks where liquidity is less available and the underlying stocks are more volatile? In sum, the investor should ensure that his level of risk tolerance/aversion is consistent with that of the hedge fund manager's investment strategy.

Second, it is important to determine what risks the hedge fund manager monitors. Does she have limits on the percentage of the portfolio that may be invested in any one company or security? Additionally, does the manager monitor her gross long exposure, gross short exposure, and net market exposure? To what extent can the manager be long and to what extent can she be short the market? What is the minimum or maximum market exposure that the hedge fund manager will take? Does the hedge fund manager hedge against currency risk, interest rate risk, credit risk, or market risk?

Third, risk can be monitored through measures of standard deviation, semivariance, Sortino measures, and value at risk, and by style analysis. The investor must document what type of risk measurement system the hedge fund manager applies.

Last, the investor must determine how the hedge fund manager manages the risk of her positions. As indicated earlier, one way to control risk is by setting limits on the size of any investment position. This is particularly important because of the concentrated nature of most hedge fund portfolios.

Another way to manage risk is to set an upper boundary on the standard deviation of the hedge fund's returns. Alternatively, the hedge fund manager could set a limit on the amount of active risk (the standard deviation of excess returns) in the hedge fund.

Two additional risks that must be discussed are short volatility risk and counterparty risk. As already mentioned, hedge fund managers can sell options as part of their investment strategy. When a hedge fund manager sells an option, she collects the option premium at the time of the sale. If the option expires unexercised, the hedge fund manager keeps the option premium and the hedge fund's returns will be increased by the amount of the option premium. However, if the option is exercised against the manager, this may have a negative impact on the hedge fund performance.

Additionally, hedge fund managers frequently trade in over-the-counter derivative instruments. These are essentially private contracts between two parties: the hedge fund manager and her counterparty. The counterparty to such trades is often a large Wall Street investment house or large money center bank. Nonetheless, when a hedge fund manager negotiates these custom derivative contracts with a counterparty, the hedge fund manager takes on the credit risk that her counterparty will fulfill its obligations under the derivative contract.

Exchange-traded derivative contracts such as listed futures and options contracts do not have this counterparty risk because the clearinghouse for the exchange will make good on any defaulted contract. However, in the over-the-counter world of derivatives, the hedge fund manager must rely on its counterparty's good faith and credit to perform its obligations under the derivative contract.

In sum, the investor must determine how the hedge fund manager looks at risk, what are the most important risk exposures in the portfolio, and how the hedge fund manager reacts to excess risk.

Leverage

Some hedge fund managers specifically limit the leverage they will employ. This limit is typically set in the limited partnership agreement so that the hedge fund manager is legally bound to stay within a leverage limit. Nonetheless, within the leverage limit, the hedge fund manager has considerable flexibility. Also, many hedge fund managers never set a limit on the amount of leverage that they may apply.

If leverage is applied, the investor should document the highest amount of leverage used by the hedge fund manager as well as the average leverage of the fund since inception. As we indicated in Chapter 3, one of the reasons for the demise of Long-Term Capital Management was the massive amount of leverage employed in its strategy. While leverage can be a successful tool if employed correctly, it will have a significantly detrimental impact on hedge fund performance during periods of minimal liquidity.

Risk officer

Last, and most important, who monitors risk? The chief investment officer and the chief risk officer should not be the same person. If so, there is a conflict in risk control because risk management should function separately from investment management. Without this independence, there can be no assurance that risk will be properly identified and managed.

Often the chief financial officer serves as the risk officer. This is a good solution as long as the CFO is not also the chief investment officer (rarely is this the case). In the smaller hedge fund shops, this is the usual procedure. However, larger hedge funds have established a chief risk officer who monitors the hedge fund manager's positions across all hedge funds and separate accounts.

If the amount of leverage is not contractually specified in the limited partnership agreement, then the risk manager must set the limit. Even if there is a limit on leverage, the risk manager must monitor the leverage in each hedge fund to ensure that it is consistent with that fund's investment strategy. Finally, the risk manager should establish the position limits for any one investment within a hedge fund portfolio.

ADMINISTRATIVE REVIEW

Another revealing part of the due diligence process is the review of the hedge fund manager's operations and administration. Simply, does the hedge fund manager run a tight ship, or is there a lot of employee turnover? Have there been prior investigations by regulatory authorities? Has the hedge fund manager ever been sued? All of these can be red flags to your investment in a hedge fund.

Civil, criminal, and regulatory actions

The hedge fund manager should fully disclose all civil, criminal, and regulatory actions against the hedge fund manager or any of its principals over the past five years. Normally a three-year history is asked for, but five years is also common.

The hedge fund manager may balk at listing civil or criminal actions previously or currently pending against its principals. However, in addition to the expected red flags that legal actions raise, this is necessary information for two more reasons.

First, a history of civil or criminal actions filed against one of the hedge fund manager's principals is a valuable insight into that principal's character. Given the litigious nature of current society, it would not be unusual for a principal to be involved in a civil lawsuit outside the operating business of the hedge fund. However, a pattern of such lawsuits might indicate trouble.

Second, lawsuits are distracting. They take a toll in terms of time, money, and emotions. Such a distraction could impede a principal's performance with respect to the hedge fund.

Employee turnover

Given the skill-based nature (or claim thereof) of the hedge fund industry, a hedge fund manager's personnel is its most valuable resource. This is where the skill resides.

A complete list of hired and departing employees is important for three reasons. First, as previously discussed, a good hedge fund manager knows her competitive advantage and how to exploit it. One type of competitive advantage is the people employed by the hedge fund manager. Preserving this workforce may be one of the keys to maintaining her advantage.

Second, similar to lawsuits, turnover is distracting. It takes time, money, and sometimes emotions to recruit new talent. In addition, new employees take time to climb the learning curve and comprehend all of the nuances of a hedge fund manager's investment strategy.

Last, high employee turnover may be indicative of a volatile chief executive officer. If the employees do not have faith enough in the CEO to remain with the hedge fund manager, why should the investor?

Account representative

This is very simple. A primary contact person should be designated. This representative will handle issues regarding performance, withdrawals, increased investment, distributions, and meetings. Ideally it should be someone other than the chief executive officer, whose job it is to keep the hedge fund manager on course rather than take client phone calls.

Disaster planning

Disaster planning has become commonplace in the aftermath of the terrorist attacks of 9/11. Hedge fund managers employ sophisticated trading models that require considerable computing power. This is especially true for those hedge fund managers that employ quantitative arbitrage models. The loss of trading time can severely hurt a hedge fund manager's performance.

The hedge fund manager should have a recovery plan if a natural or other disaster shuts down its trading and investment operations. This plan could be leasing space at a disaster recovery site owned by a computer service provider, a backup trading desk at another remote location, or the sharing of facilities with other trading desks.

Consider the case of Hurricanes Katrina and Rita in 2005 and the total evacuation of New Orleans. How would a hedge fund manager located in Louisiana monitor its investment positions and its risk exposures? How would it trade without the use of its analytical computer programs? How would the hedge fund manager maintain connectivity with its employees if they cannot get to the recovery site?

LEGAL REVIEW

The hedge fund industry is generally unregulated. Therefore, the legal documentation supporting an investment in a hedge fund (e.g. private placement memorandum, subscription agreement, side letter agreements, etc.) tend to be heavily negotiated between attorneys. Therefore, not only is the legal structure an important consideration, but so are the many legal documents that an investor must sign to access the hedge fund manager's skill set.

Type of investment

Most hedge fund investments are structured as limited partnerships. Limited partnership units are purchased by the investor where the number of units that the investor owns entitles her to a pro rata share of the returns earned by the hedge fund.

Some hedge fund managers offer separate accounts for their investors. These are individual investment accounts that are dedicated solely to one investor. There are pros and cons of both types of investments.

In a limited partnership structure, the hedge fund manager acts as the general partner, and invests a portion of her own capital in the hedge fund side by side with that of the limited partners. This ensures an alignment of interests between the hedge fund manager and her investors.

Also, a limited partnership provides a financial firewall for the investor. Limited partnership laws protect the limited partners so that they are at risk only to the extent of their capital committed. Therefore, the limited partner's maximum downside is known with certainty. Any excess risk is borne by the hedge fund manager as the general partner.

Separate accounts do not have the advantages of alignment of interests or financial firewalls. There is more risk associated with this type of investment. However, there are two advantages of a separate account.

First, the investor need only worry about her own motivations. In our section on performance review, we discussed how withdrawals of capital from a hedge fund can be detrimental to the fund's performance. Therefore, the withdrawal of capital by one limited partner could disadvantage the remaining investors in the hedge fund. With a separate account, this issue does not exist because there is only one investor per account.

Second, separate accounts facilitate reporting and risk management. In a limited partnership, the investor receives her pro rata share of the fund's return and owns a pro rata share of each individual investment. Reporting these pro rata shares, or aggregating them for risk management purposes, can be cumbersome. However, with a separate account, all gains, losses, and investments are owned 100% by the investor. This simplifies any reporting or risk management requirements.

Fees

The standard in the hedge fund industry is "2 and 20." This means a 2% management fee and a 20% profit sharing or incentive fee. However, this structure is by no means uniform. Some of the larger hedge funds charge up to a 3% management fee and a 30% incentive fee, while some newer hedge funds may charge less than the standard 2 and 20.

In addition to the fee structure, the investor should determine how frequently fees are collected. Typically, management fees are collected on a quarterly basis, but they may also be structured semiannually or annually. Incentive fees are usually collected on an annual basis.

The investor should also determine if there is a high-water mark or a clawback with respect to the incentive fees. A **high watermark** means that a hedge fund manager cannot collect any incentive fee until she exceeds the highest previous net asset value.

This is particularly important because of the nature of drawdowns. If a hedge fund manager suffers a drawdown, she should not collect any incentive fees while she recoups this lost value. Incentive fees should begin only after the manager has regained the lost fund value and produced new value for her investors. Most hedge funds have high-water marks.

Clawbacks are rare in the hedge fund world. They are much more common in the private equity marketplace. As its name implies, a clawback provision allows the investors in the fund to take back incentive fees previously received by the hedge fund manager. Clawback arrangements generally apply if, over the life of the fund, the hedge fund manager has failed to produce an agreed-upon hurdle rate.

Lockups and redemptions

While lockup periods are the standard in the private equity world, they are less common in hedge funds. However, more and more hedge funds are requiring lockup periods for their investors. A **lockup period** is just that: The investor's capital is locked up for a designated period. During this time, the investor cannot redeem any part of her investment.

Lockup periods provide two benefits. First, they give the hedge fund manager time to implement her investment strategy. Imagine how difficult it might be to implement a sophisticated investment strategy while at the same time one is worrying about how to fund redemption requests.

Second, ill-timed withdrawals of capital by one limited partner in a hedge fund can disadvantage the remaining investors. During the lockup period, this is not an issue. Nervous investors have no choice but to have their capital committed for a specified period of time. Investors can be assured that their investments will not be undermined by a fickle limited partner.

Third, should the SEC require hedge fund managers to register as investment advisers, longer lockup periods would be expected. In the past the SEC proposed an exemption from registration for investment funds that have lockup periods exceeding two years.

Last, the investor should determine whether there is a redemption fee. Hedge fund managers may charge a fee to redeem shares in the hedge fund. This redemption fee serves two purposes. First, it discourages investors from leaving the fund and maintains a larger pool of funds for the hedge fund manager; second, it allows the hedge fund manager to recoup some of the costs associated with liquidating a portion of the hedge fund portfolio to redeem shares (or to make up for the drag on performance from a cash balance that the hedge fund manager maintains to fund investor redemptions).

Withdrawals and redemptions are specified in the limited partnership agreement. Some hedge funds provide monthly liquidity, but the norm is quarterly or semiannual redemption rights. Also, limited partners typically must give notice to the hedge fund manager that they intend to redeem. This notice period can be from 30 to 90 days in advance of the redemption. The purpose of the notice is to give the hedge fund manager the ability to position the hedge fund's portfolio to finance the redemption request.

A last risk to consider is whether the liquidity provisions provided by the hedge fund manager match the liquidity of the underlying securities in which the hedge fund manager invests. For example, the distressed debt market is one of the least liquid securities markets. Liquidity is virtually nonexistent and typically comes only with the private negotiation between two parties. It can take several months to find a willing seller and buyer. Now, if the hedge fund manager was to allow monthly redemptions, there would be a liquidity mismatch that could cause a run on the hedge fund's assets when there is no ready market to buy the assets the hedge fund manager needs to sell to fund the redemptions of its investors.

Subscription amount

All hedge funds have a minimum subscription amount. Generally, this amount is quite high for two reasons. First, the hedge fund manager needs sufficient investment capital to implement his investment strategy. Second, higher capital commitments ensure that only sophisticated investors with a large net worth will subscribe in the hedge fund. Hedge fund investing is not for the average investor. Rather, hedge funds are designed for sophisticated investors who can appreciate and accept the risks associated with hedge funds.

Some hedge funds may also have a maximum subscription amount. This is done so that no single investor becomes too large relative to other investors in the fund. Also, the hedge fund manager may have capacity issues that require limits on an investor's capital contribution.

Advisory committee

Advisory committees serve as a source of objective input for the hedge fund manager. They are comprised of representatives from the hedge fund manager and investors in the hedge fund.

Advisory committees may provide advice on the valuation of certain investments, particularly illiquid investments. The committee may advise the hedge fund manager when it is time to mark down or mark up an illiquid security where objective market prices are not available.

The advisory committee may also advise the hedge fund manager as to whether she should open up the hedge fund for new investors, and how much more capacity the hedge fund manager should take. Before allowing new investors into the fund, the hedge fund manager may wish to seek the counsel of the advisory committee to see if the existing investors have concerns about capacity or the types of additional investors that may be allowed to invest.

While advisory committees are a useful device for control by the hedge fund limited partners, they are more common in the private equity world than with hedge funds.

REFERENCE CHECKS

You would not hire a new employee without reference checks, so why would you give money to an unregulated hedge fund manager without checking his references? Just think of Bernie Madoff! Enough said.

Service providers

We indicated previously in the structural review section the importance of speaking with a hedge fund manager's primary service providers. For instance, with respect to the outside auditors, the investor should ask when the last audit was conducted and whether the auditors issued an unqualified opinion. Additionally, the investor should inquire about any issues that outside auditors have raised with the hedge fund manager over the course of their engagement.

With respect to the prime broker, the investor should inquire how frequently margin calls have been made, the size of the calls, and whether any calls have not been met. Remember that the prime broker is in the best position to evaluate the market value of the hedge fund manager's investments. A discussion with the prime broker should give the investor a reality check as to whether the hedge fund manager is recognizing the proper value of the hedge fund's portfolio.

Legal counsel is important to check on the veracity of any civil, criminal, or regulatory actions against the hedge fund manager or its principals. This conversation should confirm those actions listed by the hedge fund manager under the administrative review. Last, the legal counsel can confirm the status of any regulatory registrations under which the hedge fund manager operates.

Existing clients

Talking to existing clients is a necessary step to check the veracity of the hedge fund manager's statements and to measure his client responsiveness.

Typical questions to ask are: Have the financial reports been timely? Have the reports been easy to understand? Has the hedge fund manager responded positively to questions about financial performance? Has the hedge fund manager done what she said she would do (maintain her investment strategy)? What concerns does the current investor have regarding the hedge fund manager or the hedge fund's performance? Would the existing client invest more money with the hedge fund manager?

In sum, this is a chance for a prospective investor to ask current investors for their candid opinion of the hedge fund manager. If the prospective investor has any doubts regarding the hedge fund manager, these doubts should be either confirmed or dispelled.

MEASURING OPERATIONAL RISK

Christory, Daul, and Giraud (2006) offer a model for operational default for hedge funds. They also attempt to quantify the risk of default of hedge funds and reach the following three conclusions. First, a diversified portfolio consisting of at least 40 hedge funds would allow an investor to naively diversify away operational risk. Second, they highlight the importance of conducting an informed operational hedge fund due diligence that takes into consideration the relative importance of the main risk factors affecting hedge funds in general. Finally, they conclude that the risk-adjusted profile of a portfolio can be improved when the operational risk of hedge funds is properly assessed.

In a more recent paper, Brown, Goetzmann, Liang, and Schwarz (2008) propose a quantitative approach to measure operational risk for hedge funds, the "w-score." This measure is a function of a fund's age, size, past performance, volatility, and fee structure; the score was designed to use the information provided in the SEC filing information (Form ADV), and variables from the Lipper-Tass database. The authors were able to devise their measure of operational risk using the information provided by hedge funds in February 2006, when funds were required by the SEC to register as investor advisers. Some of the questions that hedge fund managers had to answer were designed to uncover past legal or regulatory issues that the manager has had to deal with. Hedge funds based in the United States possessing assets of at least $25 million, requiring a lockup period less than two years, and having at least 14 clients, as well as any internationally based hedge fund having at least 14 U.S.-based investors, were required by the SEC to file Form ADV.

Brown et al. find that the "w-score" can predict the future disappearance of funds from the sample. They also conclude that "operational risk is of course not the only factor explaining fund failure. We find that there is a significant positive interaction with financial risk, which suggests that funds with high degrees of operational risk are more subject to failure from excessive financial risk. This is consistent with rogue trading anecdotes that suggest that fund failure associated with excessive risk taking occurs when operational controls and oversight are weak." (p. 19)

CONCLUSION

In this chapter we addressed the question of who should be selected as a hedge fund manager. We provided a comprehensive discussion on due diligence. This process is not a simple exercise. A thorough investor should expect to spend 75 to 100 hours of their time reviewing a hedge fund manager.[7]

In the appendix, we provide an easy-to-follow due diligence checklist. In developing this checklist, we attempted to err on the side of being overly inclusive. An investor may choose to use all of this checklist, expand it, or edit it to suit his or her purposes. We believe, however, that the attached checklist is a good starting point for the best practices with respect to hedge fund due diligence.

---

[7] We know of at least one hedge fund of funds manager who spends between 75 and 100 hours of due diligence with each hedge fund manager.

APPENDIX: DUE DILIGENCE EXECUTIVE SUMMARY

Name of Hedge Fund _____

Hedge Fund Manager _____

Address _____

Phone Number _____

Fax Number _____

Chief Executive Officer _____

Key Contact Person _____

Hedge Fund Style _____

Assets under Management _____

Years of Operation _____

DUE DILIGENCE CHECKLIST

I. STRUCTURAL REVIEW

Type of Investment

    Hedge Fund (name) _____

    Separate Account _____

    Other (specify) _____

    Onshore Account or Fund?   _____ Yes _____ No

    Master Trust Account?   _____ Yes _____ No

Hedge Fund Manager

    Main Business Office _____

    Nearest Satellite Office _____

    Telephone Number _____

    Fax Number _____

    Type of Legal Entity _____

    Ownership Structure _____

Key Personnel

    Chief Executive Officer _____

    Chief Operating Officer _____

    Chief Investment Officer _____

    Chief Risk Officer _____

Chief Financial Officer _____

Head of Trading _____

Attach biographies of key principals: include education, work experience, and professional degrees (this may be taken from the offering memorandum).

Regulatory Registrations (please check)

Commodity Pool Operator _____

Commodity Trading Advisor _____

Investment Adviser _____

Investment Company _____

Broker-Dealer _____

Futures Commission Merchant _____

Introducing Broker _____

Other _____

If any of the above were checked, please indicate the regulatory authority with whom the hedge fund manager is registered, and the date of the registration.

Outside Service Providers

Independent Auditor _____

Legal Counsel _____

Prime Broker _____

Banker _____

II. STRATEGIC REVIEW

Hedge Fund Style (e.g. Market Neutral, Global Macro, etc.)

_____

_____

Description of investment strategy

_____

_____

_____

Description of instruments used to implement strategy

_____

_____

_____

What is your benchmark or hurdle rate?

_____

_____

What is your competitive advantage? What makes your strategy different from other hedge fund managers?

_____

_____

_____

How many investments are in your current portfolio?

_____

_____

_____

What is your current long/short/cash position?

_____

_____

_____

What is your current strategy given the current market conditions?

_____

_____

_____

What is the source of your investment ideas?

_____

_____

In which markets do your strategies perform best?

_____

_____

What is the maximum capacity of your strategy?

_____

_____

Identify key members of your investment team.

_____

_____

III. PERFORMANCE DATA

List all funds managed, assets under management for each fund, and date of performance inception.

_____

_____

_____

List the maximum drawdown for each fund, including: percent of drawdown, recovery period, and reason for drawdown.

_____

_____

Provide the average return, standard deviation, Sharpe ratio, and number of positive versus negative months of performance for each fund since inception. Also please attach a track record for each fund.

_____

_____

_____

List the largest withdrawal from each fund, including the date, percentage of equity, and reason for the withdrawal.

_____

_____

_____

If there is a benchmark for each fund, provide each fund's beta relative to the benchmark and information ratio.

_____

_____

_____

What pricing services does the hedge fund manager use for its portfolio?

_____

_____

_____

How does the hedge fund manager mark long positions and short positions?

_____

_____

_____

Does the hedge fund manager use midmarket quotes for publicly traded securities?

_____

_____

_____

How does the hedge fund manager mark to market illiquid securities?

_____

_____

_____

If the hedge fund manager uses a "mark to model" methodology for its illiquid securities, has this model been tested for periods of market stress?

_____

_____

_____

IV. RISK

Risk Management

What risks are measured?

_____

_____

How is risk measured?

_____

_____

How is risk managed?

What level of risk is associated with the hedge fund manager's investment program?

Are position limits used?

What is your gross long exposure, your gross short exposure, and your net market exposure?

What types of derivatives do you use in your investment strategy, and how do you monitor the risks associated with these instruments?

How do you monitor counterparty credit risk?

Do you hedge market, interest rate, credit, or currency risk?

How do you decide which of these economic exposures to hedge or maintain?

Leverage

What is the current level of leverage?

_____

What is the maximum amount of leverage that may be employed in your strategy?

_____

Historically, what is the maximum amount of leverage that you have employed?

_____

Historically, what is the average leverage amount employed?

_____

Risk Officer

Who is responsible for monitoring risk?

_____

If the person responsible for risk is also the chief investment officer or another investment person, please explain how the risk function can remain independent.

_____

_____

_____

V. ADMINISTRATION

Have there been any civil, criminal, or regulatory actions against the hedge fund manager or any of its principals within the past three years?

_____

_____

_____

Has there been any significant turnover or personnel within the past three years?

_____

_____

_____

Who will be the primary account representative for our investment?

_____

_____

_____

What is your disaster recovery plan?

_____

_____

_____

VI. LEGAL REVIEW

What type of investment product is being offered?

_____

_____

_____

What is the management fee?

_____

What is the incentive fee?

_____

Is there any fee recapture or high-water mark?

_____

Is there a lockup period?

_____

How frequently can investors redeem their investments?

_____

Is there a redemption fee?

_____

What is the minimum and maximum subscription?

_____

Is there an advisory committee?

_____

VII. REFERENCES

Accounting firm contact

_____

_____

Prime broker contact

_____

_____

Legal counsel contact

_____

_____

Banker contact

_____

Existing investors (please provide at least two)

_____

_____

_____

13

Risk Management Part I: Hedge Fund Return Distributions

Most of the prior studies of hedge funds have generally examined hedge funds within a mean-variance efficient frontier. Generally, Sharpe ratios are used to compare hedge fund returns to those of stock and bond indices. However, hedge funds may pursue investment strategies that have nonlinear payoffs or are exposed to significant event risk, both of which may not be apparent from a Sharpe ratio analysis because Sharpe analysis assumes a symmetry of return patterns measured by the mean and the variance. For instance, Bernardo and Ledoit (2000) demonstrate that Sharpe ratios are misleading when the distribution of returns is not normal, and Spurgin (2001) shows that fund managers can enhance their Sharpe ratios by selling off the potential return distribution's upper end (e.g. by selling out-of-the-money calls against a long position). Consequently, the distributions associated with hedge funds may demonstrate properties that cannot be fully captured by the mean and variance.

The purpose of this chapter is to take some of the mystery out of hedge funds by examining their return distributions. Analyzing these return distributions will provide us with necessary insight to understand and manage the risks associated with hedge fund investing. Additionally, we should be able to determine whether there is, in fact, skill at work. Last, we attempt to provide a snapshot of hedge fund returns. Painting a picture of what hedge fund managers actually deliver is a valuable tool in risk management.

We start with a brief review of the hedge fund literature on mapping the distribution of returns to hedge funds. We then expand on our prior description of hedge funds versus traditional long-only investors. We use this graphical description to classify and examine the types of return distributions we might expect from hedge funds. Last, we discuss the risk management implications for hedge funds.

A REVIEW OF HEDGE FUND STUDIES

In previous chapters we reviewed a growing body of empirical research that demonstrates that hedge funds can be a valuable addition to a diversified portfolio of stocks and bonds. These portfolio optimization studies demonstrate that the low correlation between the returns to hedge funds and those of traditional asset classes makes hedge funds a valuable portfolio addition.

In summary, the prior research indicates that hedge funds are a valuable addition to a diversified portfolio within a mean-variance efficient frontier. Yet hedge fund returns may exhibit properties that cannot be described by the first two moments of a distribution.

The moments of a distribution are statistics that describe the shape of the distribution. When an investor invests capital in a security, a hedge fund, or some other asset, she receives a distribution of returns from that investment. This distribution of returns can be described by certain statistics called **moments**. Everyone is familiar with the first moment of a distribution; this is the mean, or average return, and it is denoted by $E(R)$, where R represents the returns. The second moment of the distribution is used to determine the variance and the standard deviation of the distribution.

The normal, or bell-shaped, distribution can be completely described by its first two moments—effectively, the mean and the variance. Note that there are many other distributions that are completely explained by only two parameters, but are not necessarily symmetrical. Lognormal, for example, is such a distribution that is described by two parameters but is not symmetrical. Further, unlike normal, it is not a stable distribution, which means that the sum of two lognormal variables is not lognormal, whereas the sum of two normal random variables is still normal.

Often in finance the returns to most securities are assumed to follow a normal distribution. However, several studies have demonstrated that hedge funds generate returns that differ significantly from those generated by traditional financial asset classes. As a result, additional statistics must be used to describe the return patterns generated by hedge fund managers. Specifically, the skewness and kurtosis of a hedge fund return distribution might be necessary to paint the full picture. Since many hedge fund managers follow dynamic trading strategies, the return distributions of their funds are not likely to have fixed properties. This means that even if the return distribution of a fund is normal at each point of time, its mean and standard deviation may change through time. As a result, the estimated empirical distribution is a random combination of a series of normal distributions. Such a return process may display a number of properties not shared by a typical normal distribution (e.g. it may have fatter tails).

Fung and Hsieh attempt to analyze the returns to hedge funds by applying the factor or **style analysis** conducted by William Sharpe with respect to mutual funds.[1] In his 1992 study, Sharpe compared the returns of mutual funds to the returns from financial asset class indices in order to determine the amount of variation in mutual fund returns explained by asset class returns. His results indicated that up to 90% of mutual fund returns are explained by asset class returns.

Fung and Hsieh find that the amount of variation of hedge fund returns that is explained by financial asset class returns is low; R-squared measures were less than 25% for almost half of the hedge funds studied. They then apply a principal components analysis based on a hedge fund's trading style. They find that five different trading styles (systems/opportunistic, global/macro, value, systems/trend following, and distressed) explain about 45% of the cross-sectional variation in hedge fund returns. In a second study of asset-based style factors, Fung and Hsieh find that mapping hedge fund returns onto traditional long-only indices results in R-squared measures from 0.17 (equity market neutral) to 0.82 (equity long/short). Again, the lack of uniformity of hedge fund styles when mapped onto traditional financial market indices demonstrates that traditional mean-variance analysis does not fully capture the return patterns of hedge funds.[2]

In a more recent paper, Fung and Hsieh (2006) propose an asset-based style (ABS) factor model consisting of seven risk factors attempting to capture the systematic risk that diversified portfolios of hedge funds are subject to. It is important to note that the term **asset-based** arises because these risk factors are all based on observable, tradable securities and their derivatives. The seven factors are:

1. The excess return of the S&P 500 (i.e. the return of the S&P 500 above the risk-free return).
2. Small-cap stocks minus large-cap stock returns, represented by S&P 500.
3. The return of the 10-year Treasury bond above the risk-free return.
4. The return of Baa bonds above the return of the 10-year Treasury bond.

---

[1] See William Fung and David Hsieh, "Empirical Characteristics of Dynamic Trading Strategies: The Case of Hedge Funds," *Review of Financial Studies* 10 (1997), 275–302; and William Sharpe, "Asset Allocation: Management Style and Performance Measure," *Journal of Portfolio Management* (Winter 1992), 7–19.

[2] See William Fung and David Hsieh, "Asset-Based Style Factors for Hedge Funds," *Financial Analysts Journal* (September/October 2002), 16–27.

5. A portfolio of call and put options on bonds.
6. A portfolio of call and put options on currencies.
7. A portfolio of call and put options on commodities.

The options portfolios mentioned refer to portfolios of calls and puts that are constructed to mimic the behavior of a series of look-back options.

We will have more to say on the results of this study later in this chapter.

Liang conducts a style analysis similar to Sharpe and finds R-squareds in the range of 20% for hedge funds that invest in foreign exchange to 77% for hedge funds that invest in emerging markets.[3] Schneeweis and Spurgin conduct a regression analysis of the returns of various hedge fund categories to the returns of stocks, bonds, commodities, and currencies.[4] They find R-squared measures that range from near zero for relative value hedge funds to 0.67 for hedge funds that pursue primarily a long equity investment strategy.

These studies indicate that hedge fund return patterns do not map as well onto financial assets as do mutual fund returns. It is possible that hedge funds generate return distributions that are very different from traditional financial assets. In this chapter, we consider some common characteristics shared between hedge fund returns and those of financial asset classes and their impact on the shape of hedge fund return distributions.

Recall that we define four broad categories of hedge funds: market directional, corporate restructuring, convergence trading, and opportunistic. These four categories present different exposures to the financial markets, as well as corporate events and macroeconomic trends.

Equity long/short, short selling, emerging market strategies, and activist hedge funds have exposure to stock market risk. Long/short equity hedge funds are exposed to the stock market, but this exposure varies depending on the ratio of long positions to short positions. Equity long/short managers have some amount of net long stock market exposure, so their predominant risk is that of the broader stock market. Short sellers also have market exposure. They take the opposite position to long-only managers. Emerging market hedge fund managers also go both long and short, retaining some amount of beta exposure to the emerging stock markets. Last, activist investors run concentrated portfolios of long-only investments and actively engage the company's board of directors and executive management to change the direction of the corporate strategy. As a result, they also have a good amount of stock market exposure embedded in their portfolios.

As we saw in a previous chapter, corporate restructuring involves investing in the securities of companies that are about to undergo a significant transaction such as a merger, an acquisition, a spin-off, or a bankruptcy. The key risk associated with these hedge fund strategies is the risk that the proposed transaction will fail to come to fruition. The transaction can fail because of lack of shareholder approval, lack of regulatory approval, squabbling parties, or a significant drop in the share price of the concerned company. These strategies bet on the completion of the corporate transaction, and underwrite the risk that the transaction will, in fact, proceed as planned.

In this sense, corporate restructuring hedge fund strategies provide financial market insurance against the completion of the transaction. If the corporate event is successful, the hedge fund manager reaps the rewards. However, if the corporate transaction fails, the hedge fund manager is on the hook for the losses—very similar to an insurance contract. In return for insuring against the

---

[3] Bing Liang, "On the Performance of Hedge Funds," *Financial Analysts Journal* (July/August 1999), 72–85.

[4] Thomas Schneeweis and Richard Spurgin, "Multifactor Analysis of Hedge Fund, Managed Futures, and Mutual Fund Return and Risk Characteristics," *Journal of Alternative Investments* (Fall 1998), 1–24.

loss from a failed corporate transaction, the hedge fund manager collects an "insurance premium" for being willing to bear the risk of loss should the corporate event fail to come to fruition.

It is important to understand this insurance analogy because insurance contracts are essentially the sale of a put option. For example, in a homeowner's policy, if a house burns down, the homeowner can put the losses back to the insurance company. If the house doesn't burn down, the insurance company that has collected the insurance premium (put option premium) records a profit.

The sale of put options is also known as a **short volatility exposure**. Short volatility trading strategies are exposed to event risk. Under normal market conditions, a short volatility exposure will make a profit through the collection of premiums, but in rare cases, it will incur a significant loss when the unexpected happens. Consequently, if a merger breaks down, or a company fails to exit bankruptcy proceedings, or the corporate spin-off fails to happen, corporate restructuring hedge fund managers are liable for the loss associated with the failure of the expected event.

Convergence trading strategies are also subject to the same type of event risk as corporate restructuring hedge fund strategies. As we saw in a previous chapter, convergence trading strategies bet that the prices of two similar securities will converge to the same price over the investment holding period. These strategies earn a return premium for holding the less liquid or lower-credit-quality security while going short the more liquid or creditworthy security. At maturity, the two securities are expected to converge in price and the hedge fund manager earns the spread, or premium, that once existed between the two securities.

This is similar to selling financial market insurance. Under normal market conditions, the two securities are expected to converge in price.

If so, the hedge fund manager earns an insurance premium for betting correctly that the spread between the two securities will decline by maturity of the holding period. However, if there is an unusual or unexpected event in the financial markets, then the two securities will likely diverge in price and the hedge fund manager will lose on the trade. Again, this is similar to the sale of an insurance contract. Convergence trading strategies are essentially short volatility strategies, much like corporate restructuring hedge fund strategies.

Last, opportunistic hedge fund strategies like global macro can place bets across a wide spectrum of financial, commodity, and currency markets. Their ability to seek profits across such a wide range of investment opportunities provides the ability for excellent diversification. As a consequence, we would expect that the distribution of returns of these strategies will be closer to a normal distribution.

Exhibit 13.1 provides a brief summary of the major risks affecting these four categories of hedge fund returns.

With respect to corporate restructuring and convergence trading hedge funds, these strategies bear similarities to investing in credit-risky securities such as high-yield bonds. Credit risk distributions are generally exposed to significant downside risk. This risk is embodied in the form of credit events such as downgrades, defaults, and bankruptcies.

Consequently, credit-risky investments are also similar to insurance contracts or the sale of put options. An investment in high-yield bonds is essentially the sale of an insurance contract that says that the investor will be on the hook for any credit events that may occur (downgrades, defaults, bankruptcies). Under normal market conditions, a credit event is not expected, and the investor collects the high coupons (insurance premiums) associated with the high-yield bond. But if an unexpected event occurs, such as a default, a downgrade of credit ranking, or a bankruptcy filing, the high-yield investor is on the hook for the losses.

We use the example of credit-risky securities because their return distributions should be similar to those of corporate restructuring hedge funds and convergence trading hedge funds. This is because both are exposed to event risk that can result in significant downside risk exposure if an unexpected event occurs.

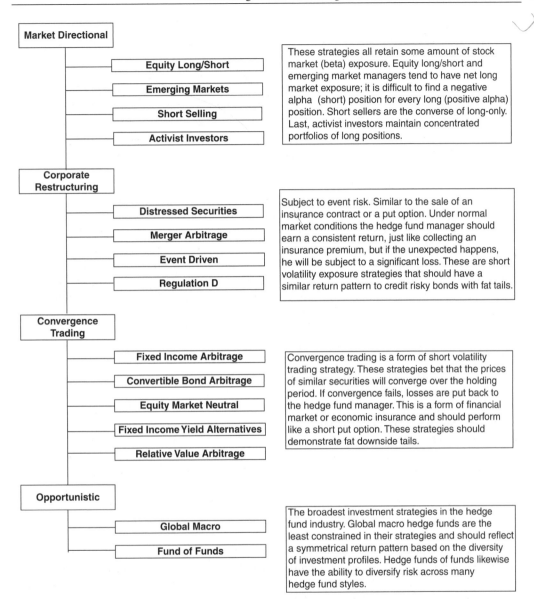

Exhibit 13.1 Major risks of hedge fund strategies

We began this chapter with a discussion of the first two moments of a distribution that describe the mean and the volatility of the distribution. We now provide a brief review of the terms kurtosis and skewness. **Kurtosis** is a term used to describe the general condition that the probability mass associated with the tails of a distribution, or outlier events, is different from that of a normal distribution. The condition of large tails in the distribution is known as **leptokurtosis**. This term describes a distribution of returns that has significant mass concentrated in outlier events. Therefore, to say a distribution of returns is leptokurtic is to mean that the distribution of returns has a greater exposure to outlier events.

+ive Skew (a) Mean 7 Median
(b) Less than 50% of positive side
So, fewer and larger gain
(c) More sort of negative more frequent loss.
208   CAIA Level I

The converse of leptokurtosis is **platykurtosis**, the condition where the tails of a distribution are thinner than would be expected by a normal distribution.[5] A platykurtic distribution has less probability mass concentrated in outlier events. Generally, platykurtic distributions are less risky than leptokurtic distributions because they have less exposure to extreme events.

The **skewness** (or skew) of a distribution is again measured relative to a normal (i.e. bell-shaped) distribution. A normal distribution has no skew; it is perfectly symmetrical. Distributions with a negative skew indicate downside exposure, while a positive skew indicates an upward bias. More specifically, in a positively skewed distribution, the mean value of the distribution is greater than the median value. With a median value less than the mean, this indicates that more than half of the observations in the return distribution are less than the mean value and less than half of the deviations from the mean are positive. In order for all of these deviations from the mean to balance out, the average magnitude of the positive deviations above the mean must be larger than the average magnitude of the negative deviations below the mean. There will be fewer but larger outliers above the mean, in effect, pulling the distribution forward toward the right with a positive skew.

Credit-risky investments experience leptokurtosis because they are exposed to event risk: the risk of downgrades, defaults, and bankruptcies. These events cause more of the probability mass to be concentrated in the left-hand tail of the return distribution. In fact, credit risk is a general way to describe the several types of event risk affecting the return distribution of credit-risky investments. In addition, credit-risky investments also tend to have a negative skew. The combination of leptokurtosis and negative skew results in large downside tails associated with the return distribution. This translates into considerable downside risk. This downside risk is sometimes referred to as "fat tail" risk because it reflects that credit-risky investments have a large probability mass built up in the downside tail of their return distributions. We will demonstrate this fat tail effect in just a moment.

We expect that convergence trading and corporate restructuring hedge funds should demonstrate distributions similar to those of credit-risky securities, that is, fat downside tails with a distribution skewed to the left. The fat downside tails and the skewed distribution reflect the event risk inherent in arbitrage investment strategies.

Conversely, those hedge funds that have more market exposure should exhibit symmetrical distributions. This should be consistent with the findings of Fama[6] and Blume,[7] who found that the returns to stocks have no skew. However, they also observed that equity market returns exhibit the condition of leptokurtosis, or fat tails in the distribution. Consequently, we expect hedge funds with market exposure to also exhibit leptokurtosis.

Finally, there are the hedge funds that minimize credit risk and market risk. These would be the market neutral and market timing hedge funds. We would expect these hedge funds to have a small skew or none at all and exhibit low values of leptokurtosis, or even platykurtosis, where the tails of the distribution are thinner than a normal distribution.

HEDGE FUND RETURN DISTRIBUTIONS

We use data from Hedge Fund Research, Inc. in examining the monthly returns to hedge fund strategies over the time period of January 1990 through September 2008, although for a few strategies

---

[5] My wife Mary calls this "scrunching the bell curve."

[6] See Eugene Fama, *Foundations of Finance* (New York: Basic Books, 1976).

[7] Marshall Blume, "Portfolio Theory: A Step toward Its Practical Application," *Journal of Business* (April 1970).

Exhibit 13.2   Summary statistics for hedge fund returns, the S&P 500, and high-yield bonds

	Expected Monthly Return	Monthly Standard Deviation	Skewness	Excess Kurtosis	Sharpe Ratio
S&P 500	0.79%	4.03%	−0.47	0.79	0.12
SB High Yield Index	0.77	1.66	−1.48	7.65	0.27
HFRI Composite Index	1.01	1.98	−0.63	2.54	0.35
Equity Long/Short	1.18	2.56	0.00	1.58	0.34
Emerging Markets	1.21	4.13	−0.84	3.83	0.22
Short Sellers	0.34	5.66	0.15	2.14	0.00
Activist Investors	0.73	2.20	−1.39	8.29	0.18
Distressed Securities	1.06	1.74	−0.65	5.00	0.43
Merger Arbitrage	0.77	1.24	−2.27	9.15	0.36
Event Driven	1.03	1.90	−1.24	4.12	0.37
Regulation D	1.10	2.00	0.78	2.05	0.39
Fixed Income Arbitrage	0.67	1.78	−0.78	6.23	0.20
Convertible Bond Arbitrage	0.66	1.39	−4.14	33.22	0.24
Equity Market Neutral	0.67	0.92	−0.13	1.25	0.38
Fixed Income Yield Alternatives	0.66	2.03	−0.89	4.16	0.17
Relative Value Arbitrage	0.87	1.11	−1.24	9.64	0.49
Global Macro	1.16	2.29	0.41	0.77	0.37
Fund of Funds	0.72	1.67	−0.49	3.67	0.24

Source: Datastream and Hedge Fund Research, Inc., copyright 2009, www.hedgefundresearch.com.

the initial date of the sample period is in the mid-1990s, as we will see.[8] We also include some standard asset classes such as large-cap stocks and high-yield bonds over this time period as a comparison to the hedge fund strategies.

Exhibit 13.2 presents the monthly realized returns, standard deviations, and Sharpe ratios for the asset classes and the different hedge fund styles. Except for short selling hedge funds, the Sharpe ratios of the hedge fund strategies are all higher than those for stocks. However, as alluded to earlier, Sharpe ratios may not fully capture the risks associated with hedge fund return distributions. For this reason we also include two additional distribution statistics, the skewness and the kurtosis. Finally, it is important to bear in mind that results presented in Exhibit 13.2 are based on historical data, so they are time-period specific. This implies that one should be cautious about any conclusions that one may reach based on the analysis of the statistics presented in this exhibit.

For comparison, we include two financial asset classes that can be interpreted as measuring market risk and credit risk. For market risk, we use large-capitalization stocks represented by the S&P 500 index. For credit risk, we use high-yield bonds represented by the Salomon Brothers High Yield Cash Pay Index. These two asset classes provide us with distribution benchmarks for analyzing hedge fund returns. We analyze the returns to these two financial asset classes over the same time period as for hedge funds. Risks and returns for stocks and bonds can also be used as a way to compare the risks and returns of hedge fund strategies to those of traditional investments.

We take the raw data contained in the HFRI Database and recalibrate it to plot a frequency distribution of the returns associated with each hedge fund investment style. Such a distribution provides a graphical depiction of the range and likelihood of returns associated with a hedge fund

---

[8] One significant caveat must be mentioned with respect to using hedge fund indices for economic analysis. Hedge funds are not as accessible to all investors as are stocks and bonds. Normally, the hedge fund managers impose minimum net worth or earning power requirements on investors in their funds. Additionally, there are issues of capacity when pursuing alternative investment as well as regulatory restrictions as to the number of investors in a hedge fund. Consequently, an index of hedge funds is not as investable as a stock or bond index is.

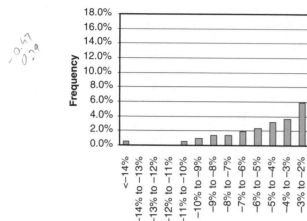

Monthly Return Range

Exhibit 13.3   Frequency distribution for the U.S. stock market, 1990 through 2008

Source: Datastream.

return. We calculate the mean, standard deviation, skewness, and kurtosis associated with the returns to each hedge fund strategy.

We begin by graphing the frequency distribution for large-cap stocks and high-yield grade bonds. In Exhibit 13.3 we can see that the S&P 500 has a distribution with a negative skew of −0.47 and a low but positive value of kurtosis of 0.79 (from Exhibit 13.2). We measure kurtosis relative to a normal distribution so that a positive value of kurtosis indicates more mass is built up in the tails of the return distribution than a normal distribution, whereas a negative value of kurtosis indicates thinner tails than a normal distribution.

The small value of kurtosis indicates that the return distribution of the S&P 500 has slightly greater probability mass in the tails of the distribution than would be expected for a normal distribution. This means that there are more outlier events associated with the distribution of returns to the S&P 500 than would be predicted by a normal distribution. A negative value for kurtosis would indicate the reverse—that there is less probability mass in the tails (fewer outlier events) than in a normal distribution. The excess value of kurtosis indicates that large-capitalization stocks had slightly larger tails than a normal distribution.

The negative skew found in the returns to stocks is contrary to the findings of both Fama and Blume discussed earlier. This could be due to the different time period examined in this study compared to earlier research rather than indicating a fundamental change in the distribution of equity returns. However, the negative skew is small and does not deviate greatly from the symmetry of a normal distribution.

A negative skew indicates that the mean of the distribution is to the left of (less than) the median of the distribution. A positive skew indicates the reverse of a negative skew—that the mean of the distribution is to the right of the median and that there are more frequent large positive returns than there are large negative returns. A positive skew demonstrates a bias to the upside.

For high-yield bonds, the return distribution is distinctly nonnormal. In Exhibit 13.4 we see a negative skew value of −1.48, as well as a large positive value of kurtosis of 7.65. This distribution demonstrates significant leptokurtosis. Specifically, the distribution of returns to high-yield bonds demonstrates a significant downside tail. This fat tail reflects the event risk of downgrades, defaults, and bankruptcies, which tend to occur in cycles, thus affecting the whole index in aggregate.

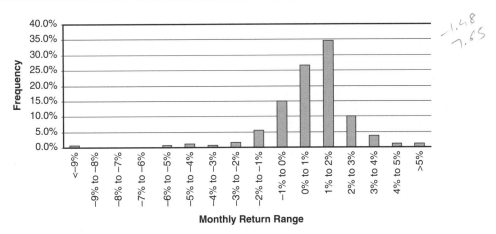

Exhibit 13.4   Frequency distribution for high-yield bonds, 1991 through 2008

Source: Datastream.

We note again that credit risk is simply another way to describe event risk. For example, the down-grade of General Motors debt to below investment grade (junk status) by Moody's Investors Service in 2005 caused a significant one-day decline in the value of GM debt from 87 to 78, an 11% decline.

We also include for comparison the HFRI Composite Index of all hedge fund styles as Exhibit 13.5. We can see from Exhibit 13.2 that this index has a higher Sharpe ratio than either stocks or high-yield bonds. However, it also has a negative skew, and a value of kurtosis between stocks and high-yield bonds.

Hedge funds that exhibit market risk

We begin with those hedge funds that are exposed to stock market risk: equity long/short, emerging market, and short sellers. These hedge funds invest primarily in equity securities and always retain some stock market exposure.

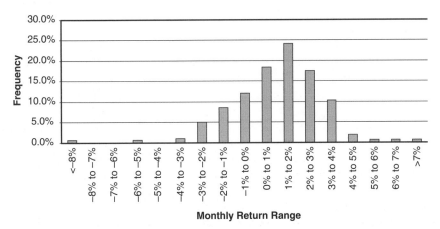

Exhibit 13.5   Frequency distribution for HFRI Composite Index, 1990 through 2008

Source: Hedge Fund Research, Inc., copyright 2009, www.hedgefundresearch.com.

Equity long/short hedge funds

This type of investing focuses on stock selection. This is the source of what many hedge fund mangers claim is skill-based investing. Rather than mimic an equity benchmark, these managers focus their skill on a particular market segment or industry sector to generate their returns.

Equity long/short strategies tend to have a **long bias**. That is, equity long/short managers tend to be more on the long side of the market than they are on the short side. This is partly because it is more difficult to borrow stocks to short, and it is partly because many long/short equity managers came from the traditional long-only investment world and thereby have a built-in long bias. Therefore, we would expect equity long/short hedge fund return distributions to also demonstrate the leptokurtic properties of the S&P 500.

Yet, the ability to short stocks at appropriate times should reduce some of the outlier events associated with the stock market. Therefore, while we still expect a positive value of kurtosis, we also expect it to be less than that of the broad stock market. Furthermore, the ability to go both long and short in the stock market should give equity long/short hedge fund managers an advantage over long-only passive investing. This added dimension to their strategy should reduce the negative skew associated with long-only investing.

Exhibit 13.6 presents the distribution for the HFRI Equity Long/Short Hedge Index. According to the statistics presented in Exhibit 13.2, this distribution has a skew of 0.0. This is particularly noteworthy given the negative skew observed with respect to the S&P 500 returns over the same time period.

The lack of a negative skewness to the equity long/short distribution is consistent with the hypothesis that hedge fund managers in this strategy have alpha. The ability to shift the distribution of stock returns to eliminate a negative skew is a concrete example of skill-based investing with which the hedge fund industry is so often associated. It must be pointed out that positive skewness is not always evidence of skill. For example, the put-protected long position would show positive skewness. Of course, in this case the positive skewness comes at the expense of lower return, which is caused by the cost of the put option.

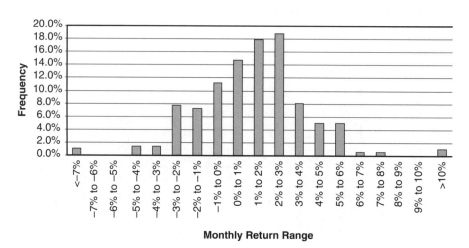

Exhibit 13.6   Frequency distribution of equity long/short, 1990 through 2008

Source: Hedge Fund Research, Inc., copyright 2009, www.hedgefundresearch.com.

Additionally, the distribution of returns for equity long/short investing has a positive kurtosis value of 1.58, consistent with that of the stock market. However, the value of kurtosis is slightly greater than that for the S&P 500, instead of less, which is what we had predicted. Last, we note that the Sharpe ratio for equity long/short managers is greater than that for large-cap stocks and on par with that for the broad HFRI Index.

One explanation for the higher value of kurtosis might be that these hedge fund managers attempt to generate a so-called double alpha strategy. That is, they attempt to add value by investing long in those companies that they expect to increase in value and short those companies that they expect to decrease in value. This is a **double alpha strategy** in that the short sales are not generated to reduce exposure to market risk, but instead to provide additional value through stock selection. The double alpha strategy would also be consistent with a positive skew if manager skill can indeed select both winners and losers. However, it is possible that the pursuit of a double alpha strategy increases the hedge fund's exposure to outlier events, resulting in a larger value of kurtosis for the distribution than would be predicted by observing the returns to the broad stock market.

Emerging markets hedge funds

Emerging markets hedge funds generally follow the same long/short investing as equity long/short hedge funds. However, they often follow a broader market than domestic equity long/short for two reasons. First, in developed countries, a greater information advantage can be achieved if an active manager focuses on only one or two sectors within the economy. Emerging markets, however, are still sufficiently inefficient that a broader perspective can be applied. Second, there is greater liquidity in developed countries such that an equity long/short strategy can be applied on a sector or industry basis. In contrast, liquidity is still an issue in many emerging market countries.

Exhibit 13.7 provides the histogram for emerging markets hedge fund managers. We can see from this chart a significant downside tail with negative returns reaching greater than −21% on a

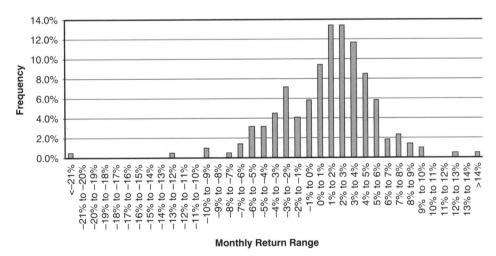

Exhibit 13.7 Frequency distribution of emerging markets hedge funds, 1996 through 2008

Source: Hedge Fund Research, Inc., copyright 2009, www.hedgefundresearch.com.

monthly basis. This leads to a negative value of skewness and a large value of kurtosis. Simply, emerging markets hedge fund strategies have a fatter downside tail than either the U.S. stock market or equity long/short strategies. We also note that emerging markets hedge fund strategies also have a lower Sharpe ratio than equity.

Short selling hedge funds

Short selling hedge funds perform well in down markets and poorly in up markets. Short selling hedge funds should be the mirror image of long-only investments. However, they may attempt to limit their short positions in up markets, thus timing their positions to limit their losses when the financial markets are improving. Consequently, we might expect a slight positive skew to their return distribution.

With respect to fat tails, we would expect to see a value of kurtosis similar to that for long-only stocks. This is because they have the reverse position from a traditional long-only manager. Short selling hedge funds are down when long-only managers are up and vice versa. Consequently, their returns should reflect the same type of kurtosis as that for a long-only equity benchmark.

Exhibit 13.8 presents the frequency distribution for the HFRI Short Selling Index. We can see that this distribution has a slightly positive skew of 0.15 and a kurtosis of 2.14 similar to that of the general stock market. We note that this distribution is centered slightly above zero. However, short selling hedge funds, on average, earn a low positive return of about 0.34% per month, leading to a Sharpe ratio of zero.

Also, short sellers have the largest standard deviation of any hedge fund style or of the traditional asset classes. This is the most volatile hedge fund strategy, which further contributes to its poor Sharpe ratio.

Given the positive returns associated with the stock market over the time period 1990–2000 and again from 2003 through 2007, the positive return of short selling hedge funds indicates a bias to market timing. This bias allowed them to produce a positive skew to their return distribution.

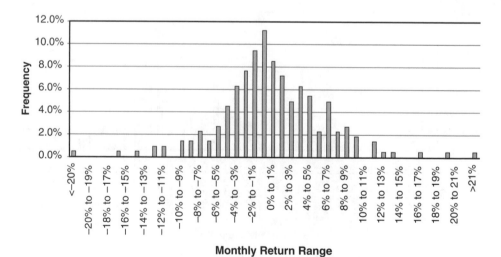

Exhibit 13.8 Frequency distribution for short selling, 1990 through 2008

Source: Hedge Fund Research, Inc., copyright 2009, www.hedgefundresearch.com.

Unfortunately, this positive bias was not sufficient to produce a favorable Sharpe ratio compared to stocks or high-yield bonds.

Activist hedge funds

Activist hedge funds tend to take large long-only positions in public companies and then challenge the executive management and the board of directors to change their governance structure in an attempt to favor the creation of shareholder wealth. This may include shaking up the board of directors, firing senior management, spinning off underperforming units, revising the business plan, or simply just getting back to the basics of the business instead of empire building. In any event, given the long-only nature of most activist investors, we would expect to see a return distribution that resembles the stock market somewhat.

Exhibit 13.9 presents our results. First, we note from Exhibit 13.2 that the skewness is negative at 1.39. This is not an improvement over the broader stock market. We also note that the kurtosis associated with the return pattern is almost the same as that of the general stock market: 8.29. Unfortunately, activist hedge fund managers are subject to significant event risk. This is the nature of their investment style. By directly engaging the board of directors and executive management, activist hedge fund managers intend to provide the spark or catalyst to generate superior performance. This strategy is at the mercy of event risk if the catalyst does not develop, leading to significant tail events, both positive and negative.

Corporate restructuring hedge funds

The investment strategies of these funds involve taking less market exposure and substantial company-specific risk. Note carefully that these strategies do not offer a diversified portfolio. Quite the reverse; their investment strategies may be concentrated in only a handful of significant corporate transactions. Consequently, these funds are exposed to event risk: the risk that the corporate transaction will fail to be completed. Their exposure to event risk should be demonstrated with a large, downside tail in their return distributions. In other words, they should exhibit distributions with a large value of kurtosis and a negative skew.

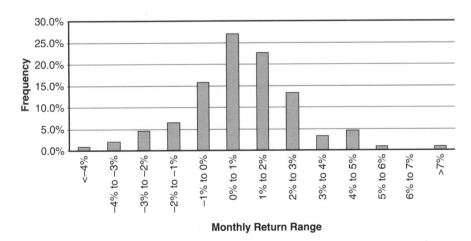

Exhibit 13.9   Frequency distribution for activist investors, 1995 through 2008

Source: Hedge Fund Research, Inc., copyright 2009, www.hedgefundresearch.com.

Distressed securities hedge funds

Distressed securities hedge fund managers can pursue a number of strategies regarding a company that is in financial distress, in bankruptcy, or about to enter bankruptcy. A company can become distressed because of liquidity problems, a credit downgrade, the need to reorganize, or simply to hold off its creditors until its cash flows improve.

Distressed securities hedge fund managers can short the securities of companies that they expect to experience financial stress, or can go long the securities of companies that are in financial distress with the expectation that the companies' fortunes will improve.

The key is that distressed hedge fund managers are exposed to significant event risk such as bankruptcy, liquidation, foreclosure, creditors seizing assets, and so on. In fact, distressed hedge fund managers invest in the lowest of the credit rating categories. They might be viewed as the ultimate in credit-risky investments. Consequently, we would expect their return distribution to resemble that for high-yield bonds.

Exhibit 13.10 confirms our expectations. Distressed hedge fund managers generate a negative skew of −0.65 with a value of kurtosis of 5.00. This demonstrates a fat downside tail similar to the return distribution for high-yield bonds. However, for taking on this additional risk, distressed hedge fund managers generate a larger average monthly return than high-yield bonds and a larger Sharpe ratio. Also, distressed hedge fund managers generate very consistent returns. Over 50% of the mass of the distribution is centered in the 0% to 2% range.

Merger arbitrage hedge funds

Merger arbitrage hedge funds seek to capture the spread between the market prices of two companies engaged in a merger and the value of those securities upon successful completion of the merger or takeover.

The spread in the market reflects the unwillingness of other market participants to take on the risk that the transaction might not be completed. Mergers collapse because the two firms may fail to come to complete agreement on terms, government agencies may intervene (e.g. review of possible monopolies), or because a third party may bid on the target firm.

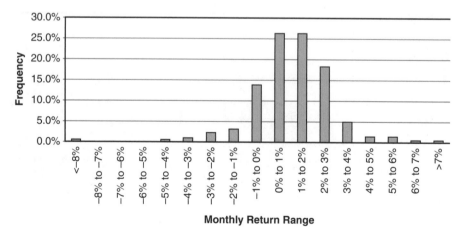

Exhibit 13.10   Frequency distribution for HFRI distressed debt, 1990 through 2008

Source: Hedge Fund Research, Inc., copyright 2009, www.hedgefundresearch.com.

Some hedge fund managers transact only in announced deals, while others take on more transaction risk based on speculation or rumors of mergers. In either case, the transaction risk is large. If a deal craters, merger arbitrage funds stand to lose a considerable portion of their investment. Merger arbitrageurs tend to be long deal risk because they are betting on the successful completion of a merger. According to Fung and Hsieh (2006, 26–27):

> Typically, mergers fail for idiosyncratic reasons and can be diversified away in a portfolio of such transactions. However, when the stock market has a severe decline, mergers tend to be called off for a variety of reasons—ranging from funding and pricing issues to concerns over the long-term prospects of the economy. This is one scenario where there is a convergence of deal-risk that cannot be easily diversified. Consequently, we expect the distribution of returns to demonstrate a large downside tail. This is similar to what we find with credit risk—the risk of bankruptcy has the ability to wipe out an investment in that company.

In addition to the event risk of a collapsed deal, merger arbitrage funds also apply leverage. Leverage exposes merger arbitrage funds to additional event risk that should magnify the tails of the distribution.

The upside potential for merger arbitrage is limited. Once the terms of a merger deal are announced, the amount of value to be gained is known with precision. There is no upside beyond what is offered in the spread between the price of the target company and the price of the acquiring company. The greater the transaction risk, the larger the spread, but the spread represents all that the merger arbitrage manager can expect to earn. Because the upside to a merger deal is limited and the downside can be considerable, we expect to see a distribution with a negative skew.

Fung and Hsieh (2006) argue that returns from merger arbitrage hedge funds are a form of insurance premium arising from selling a policy against the risk that a merger will not materialize. Merger arbitrage hedge funds tend to hold a portfolio of merger transactions as a way to mitigate the substantial idiosyncratic risk to which they are exposed.

Exhibit 13.11 presents our results for merger arbitrage. This distribution is consistent with our expectations. From Exhibit 13.2, a very large kurtosis value of 9.15 indicates a significant exposure to outlier events such as failed merger deals. In addition, we observe a negative skew of 2.27 to

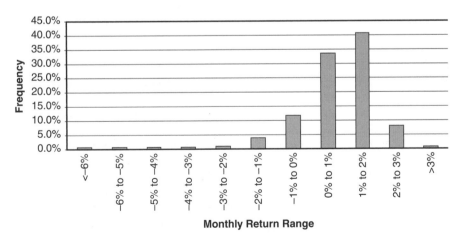

Exhibit 13.11   Frequency distribution for merger arbitrage, 1990 through 2008

Source: Hedge Fund Research, Inc., copyright 2009, www.hedgefundresearch.com.

the distribution that further reflects the transaction or deal risk associated with merger arbitrage. Together, these two statistics indicate a large negative fat tail, in fact, our largest fat tail yet.

Despite the large downside tail associated with merger arbitrage, Exhibit 13.11 also demonstrates very consistent positive returns. Notice how the probability mass of the distribution is concentrated in the 0% to 2% range. About 75% of the time merger arbitrage funds deliver 0% to 2% returns per month. This is consistent with our previous analysis with respect to the amount of premium that merger arbitrage managers can earn. The premium is known with precision at the time of the merger announcement. If all goes according to plan, the hedge fund manager knows exactly how much premium he will earn as the spread between the stock prices of the target company and the acquiring company. This produces very consistent returns with the occasional hiccup when the merger fails to come to fruition. Therefore, when merger deals go bad, merger arbitrage managers experience significant losses. The trade-off is that the overwhelming majority of the time, they generate positive monthly returns in the 0% to 2% range with a long-term expected return of 0.77% per month.

Event driven hedge funds

Event driven hedge funds follow the same pattern of investing as merger arbitrage managers, but their investment mandate is broader. In addition to mergers and acquisitions, these hedge fund managers can invest in spin-offs, liquidations, reorganizations, recapitalizations, share buybacks, and other events. The very nature of the investing exposes this type of hedge fund to event risk: the risk that the anticipated event will not come to fruition. Additionally, these hedge funds may apply leverage to amplify their investment bets. Consequently, we would expect to see large fat tails in the distribution and a negative skew to the distribution to reflect the event risk associated with this strategy. However, given their broader mandate than that of merger arbitrage hedge funds, we would expect to see more diversification compared to merger arbitrage hedge funds and a less obese downside tail to their return distribution. Exhibit 13.12 confirms this analysis. According to Exhibit 13.2, event driven hedge funds have a large negative skew value of 1.24 and a large positive kurtosis value of 4.12. This is consistent with the exposure to event risk but also is consistent with the expectation that

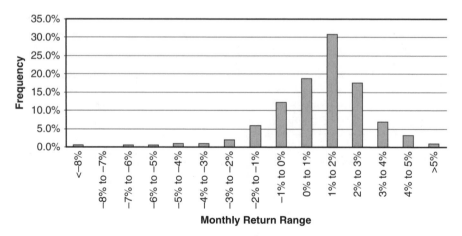

Exhibit 13.12   Frequency distribution for event driven, 1990 through 2008

Source: Hedge Fund Research, Inc., copyright 2009, www.hedgefundresearch.com.

event driven hedge fund managers should have a less fat tail to their return distribution than merger arbitrage managers because they participate in a broader opportunity set of corporate events than just mergers.

Also, notice that the probability mass for event driven hedge funds is less concentrated than it is for merger arbitrage managers. Only about 50% of the probability mass is concentrated in the 1% to 2% range. Therefore, there is a trade-off compared to merger arbitrage hedge funds: a smaller downside tail, but less consistency of returns.

Regulation D hedge funds

As we discussed earlier, Regulation D (or "Reg D") hedge fund managers purchase private securities issued by public corporations under a securities regulation (Regulation D) that allows public companies to sell their securities to large institutional investors without the need for a public offering or registration statement. This simplifies the capital raising for public companies, as large institutional investors are sophisticated investors that do not need the full protection of the securities laws.

Reg D securities are often offered at a discount to the publicly traded securities of the public company and are often issued in debt form but are convertible into equity. Reg D securities are also often issued as part of a capital restructuring for the public company.

Exhibit 13.13 displays our results for Reg D hedge funds. Contrary to the other forms of corporate restructuring hedge funds, Exhibit 13.2 shows a positive skew of 0.78. Visually, we can see in Exhibit 13.13 that the return pattern for Reg D hedge funds favors positive returns leading to its positive skew. In addition, we find a positive value of kurtosis of 2.05. This is a very favorable return pattern compared to the other forms of corporate restructuring. Possibly, Reg D hedge fund managers might not be best classified as part of corporate restructuring hedge funds. Also, the consistency of returns is much less for Reg D hedge fund managers than for the other forms of corporate restructuring. Returns in the 0% to 2% range occur about 40% of the time. Still, the Sharpe ratio for Reg D hedge fund managers is on a par with Sharpe ratios for the other corporate restructuring strategies.

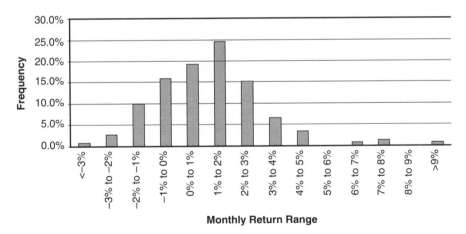

Exhibit 13.13   Frequency distribution for Regulation D, 1996 through 2008

Source: Hedge Fund Research, Inc., copyright 2009, www.hedgefundresearch.com.

Convergence trading hedge funds

Convergence trading strategies are often called arbitrage strategies. The reason is that hedge fund managers go long and short securities that reflect similar economic characteristics to arbitrage any pricing differential that may exist at the time of the purchase and sale. Over time, any price difference between two securities with similar economic characteristics should dissipate as the securities converge to the same price. When this happens, the hedge fund manager captures the spread between the two securities.

However, if the two securities do not converge in price, the hedge fund manager will lose money. As we described earlier, this is similar to selling financial market insurance. Convergence trading hedge fund managers underwrite the risk that two securities might not converge in price over time. Under normal market conditions convergence is expected and the hedge fund manager collects a premium. However, if an unusual market event occurs, then the hedge fund manager will bear the loss.

Fixed income arbitrage hedge funds

Fixed income arbitrage, as its name suggests, involves the buying and selling of similar types of fixed income securities to capitalize on mispricing opportunities. For example, fixed income arbitrage funds may combine an interest-only mortgage-backed strip and a principal-only mortgage-backed strip to form a traditional mortgage pass-through certificate and then sell a similar pass-through certificate to take advantage of any differences in price. Or the hedge fund manager may short the more liquid on-the-run U.S. Treasury bond and purchase an off-the-run U.S. Treasury bond with similar duration and convexity characteristics. The key to all of these trades is that the hedge fund manager expects the two securities to converge in value over the investment holding period. Leverage is applied to extract the most value from any difference in price.

Fixed income arbitrage is dependent on the prices of the two similar securities converging. However, there are many events that might prevent this conversion. For instance, the Federal Reserve Bank may decide to cut interest rates, encouraging mortgage refinancing and thereby speeding up the rate by which mortgage holders prepay their mortgage debt. The change in prepayment rates is a considerable risk for a mortgage-backed fixed income hedge fund manager. This type of event risk should manifest itself in a large downside tail to the return distribution.

Exhibit 13.14 presents a distribution consistent with this conclusion: a large positive value of kurtosis of 6.23 and a negative skew of -0.78 (see also Exhibit 13.2). In sum, a large downside tail indicates significant exposure to event risk. However, like merger arbitrage, fixed income arbitrage produces consistent monthly returns. The probability mass of the return distribution is concentrated in the 0% to 2% range. 60% of the time, fixed income arbitrage produces a return in the range of 0% to 2% per month. This is much more consistent than either the stock market or the high-yield market, and reflects the consistent insurance premium that can be earned through convergence trading.

Convertible bond arbitrage hedge funds

Convertible bonds combine the holding of a bond with a call option on the issuing company's stock. Because the call option associated with the convertible bond does not trade separately, mispricing opportunities can occur. Convertible arbitrage funds seek to buy undervalued convertible bonds and then hedge out the systematic risk associated with them. For convertible bonds that trade more like equity, the hedge fund manager shorts an appropriate ratio of stock (the delta) to neutralize the equity position. For convertible bonds that trade more like fixed income instruments, the hedge fund

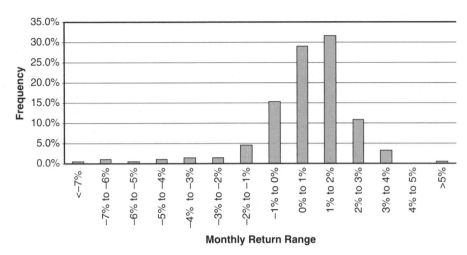

Exhibit 13.14   Frequency distribution for fixed income arbitrage, 1990 through 2008

Source: Hedge Fund Research, Inc., copyright 2009, www.hedgefundresearch.com.

manager may short interest rate futures to hedge the interest rate risk. In either case, the investor is betting that the option to exchange the bond for stock is mispriced by the market.

More specifically, convertible bond arbitrage is often the search for cheap volatility. That is, convertible arbitrage managers seek to buy convertible bonds where the embedded call option is not priced at its full value. This is known as buying cheap volatility because one of the most important inputs into the Black-Scholes option pricing model is the underlying volatility of the issuing company's stock price. A higher volatility translates into higher option prices. So an option that is undervalued usually has a lower volatility associated with its value than the market would predict. Hedge fund managers search for this cheap volatility in the embedded stock options contained within a convertible bond.

The upside potential of the trade is typically known with precision; it is usually based on an option pricing model. However, the downside cannot be determined with the same certainty. Convertible arbitrage can fail because of redemption risk, the risk that the company may redeem the convertible bonds and the option value will be lost. In addition, there is the credit risk associated with distressed security investing. If the company goes bankrupt, the bonds and any equity option attached to them may be worthless. In sum, convertible arbitrage is exposed to event risk.

In addition, convertible arbitrage funds employ leverage. This leverage is implicit in the margin account used to borrow stock or bonds for the short position. These funds may also borrow additional capital to boost their returns. For these reasons, we expect a large downside tail and a negative skew to the distribution.

Exhibit 13.15 confirms these expectations. From Exhibit 13.2, we observe the largest negative skew for any hedge fund strategy of −4.14 and a mind-blowing value for kurtosis of 33.22, which indicates significant tail risk. These observations are consistent with the redemption risk and event risk faced by convertible arbitrage managers. With the advent of the credit derivatives market, convertible arbitrage managers have more tools today to hedge credit event risk than they did in the past. Recall from prior discussions on convertible bonds that they contain considerable credit risk and liquidity risk. With the almost complete meltdown of the credit and liquidity markets in 2008, convertible arbitrage hedge fund managers were in for some nasty times and large negative

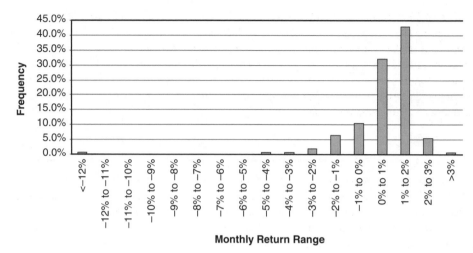

Exhibit 13.15 Frequency distribution of HFRI convertible arbitrage, 1990 through 2008
Source: Hedge Fund Research, Inc., copyright 2009, www.hedgefundresearch.com.

values. These large losses show themselves in the large negative value of skewness and huge value of kurtosis.

Despite the meltdown in the financial markets in 2008, we can see from Exhibit 13.15 that approximately 75% of the time an investor should expect to receive a return of 0% to 2% a month from convertible arbitrage. This consistency of returns is a good indication of manager skill and is much more consistent than what an investor might expect to earn from the stock market or high-yield bonds. Still, in a year like 2008, the risks embedded in convertible arbitrage can lead to an extreme meltdown, which happened in September 2008 when this category of hedge funds recorded a one-month decline of 12.2%.

Equity market neutral hedge funds

Market neutral hedge funds go long and short the market. These funds seek to maintain neutral exposure to the general stock market as well as have neutral risk exposures across industries, countries, currencies, market capitalization ranges, and style (value versus growth) ranges. The hedge fund manager builds an integrated portfolio so that market, industry, and other factor exposures cancel out. Security selection is all that matters. There is no beta, or market risk, in the portfolio either with respect to the broad stock market or with respect to any industry. Only the alpha associated with stock selection should remain.

With risk factors all balanced to zero, convergence trading might seem like a strange category in which to place these managers. However, the underlying fundamental strategy of these managers is that two similar securities are mispriced and will converge to a similar price over the investment holding period. Market neutral managers simply take this strategy one step further and ensure that all extraneous risk factors are neutralized (sounds sinister, doesn't it?).

All kidding aside, with minimal market and credit risk exposure, we would expect a distribution that does not have a negative skew (from either market or credit risk) or large tails. In fact, if a market neutral hedge fund manager is successful in removing credit risk and market risk from his portfolio, we would expect to see the statistical biases of skewness and leptokurtosis disappear.

Exhibit 13.16 confirms our expectations. The values for skewness and kurtosis are very low, with a −0.13 for the skew and the value of kurtosis is 1.25 (see Exhibit 13.2). This is as close to a normal distribution as we have seen with any hedge fund investment strategy. Further, equity market neutral managers produce consistent returns. 72% of the return distribution mass is concentrated in the range of 0% to 2% return per month.

In summary, market neutral hedge funds exhibit the properties of minimal credit and market risk, consistent with their intended strategy.

Fixed income yield alternatives hedge funds

We include this type of hedge fund strategy because it captures all of the trading strategies associated with fixed income, but not necessarily those that are strictly convergence trades. This could be a form of yield curve arbitrage, or a more directed bet on the flattening or steepening of the yield curve. In sum, while these hedge fund managers may pursue fixed income arbitrage as part of their bag of tricks, they have a more expanded repertoire to seek yield and return.

Exhibit 13.17 presents their histogram. We can see that the returns for this hedge fund strategy are much more spread out than those for fixed income arbitrage. While fixed income arbitrage has much of its mass concentrated around the 0% to 2% range, in Exhibit 13.17 we see that the mass of the distribution for fixed income yield alternatives is much more diffuse; there is not the same regularity of returns compared to fixed income arbitrage.

Also, while there is still a negative skew of −0.89, the value of kurtosis, while large, is not as large as that for fixed income arbitrage. Clearly, while this strategy is still exposed to outlier returns, the ability of fixed income yield alternatives hedge funds to diversify their strategies more broadly leads to less exposure to a downside fat tail.

Relative value arbitrage hedge funds

Relative value strategies are short volatility strategies. These funds seek out arbitrage pricing opportunities wherever they exist: merger arbitrage, convertible arbitrage, fixed income arbitrage,

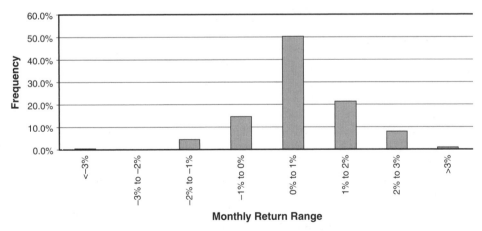

Exhibit 13.16   Frequency distribution for equity market neutral, 1990 through 2008

Source: Hedge Fund Research, Inc., copyright 2009, www.hedgefundresearch.com.

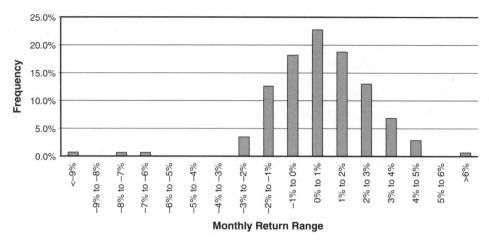

Exhibit 13.17   Frequency distribution for fixed income yield alternatives, 1994 through 2008

Source: Hedge Fund Research, Inc., copyright 2009, www.hedgefundresearch.com.

mortgage-backed securities arbitrage, and options arbitrage. As we stated earlier, relative value hedge fund managers are the smorgasbord of convergence trading. They do not limit the scope of their arbitrage opportunities. Often, they apply considerable leverage in their investment strategies. Long-Term Capital Management is the best example of a relative value hedge fund.

Exhibit 13.18 presents the results for the relative value hedge fund managers. Similar to the other arbitrage funds, we find a large (fat) downside tail and a large negative skew to the distribution. From Exhibit 13.2, relative value funds have a large positive value of kurtosis equal to 9.64, indicating large fat tails. Additionally, relative value hedge funds also have a large negative skew value of −1.24. This is consistent with the event risk expected of this investment strategy.

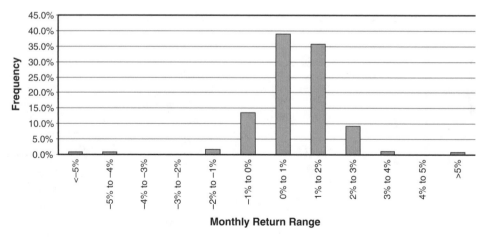

Exhibit 13.18   Frequency distribution for relative value arbitrage, 1990 through 2008

Source: Hedge Fund Research, Inc., copyright 2009, www.hedgefundresearch.com.

Relative arbitrage managers also produce consistent results. 74% of the distribution mass is concentrated in the 0% to 2% range, with a long-term average just under 1% per month. As previously noted, consistency of performance results is an indication of manager skill.

Opportunistic hedge funds

Opportunistic hedge fund managers have the greatest ability to diversify their portfolios. They are not constrained to any hedge fund strategy or market and have a mandate that allows them to be nimble and quick as they move across financial markets (global macro players) or hedge fund strategies (fund of funds managers).

Global macro hedge funds

Exhibit 13.19 presents the distribution for global macro hedge funds. This distribution more closely resembles a normal distribution than that demonstrated by large-cap stocks or high-yield bonds. From Exhibit 13.2, global macro funds exhibit a slightly positive skew of 0.41 with a low value of leptokurtosis of 0.77. This is consistent with our expectations for global macro hedge funds. Given their broad investment mandate across all financial markets, we are not surprised to find a return pattern that most closely resembles a normal distribution.

By definition, global macro hedge funds invest across the currency, stock, bond, and commodity markets. They are not limited either by geographic scope or by asset class. Their broad investment mandate allows them to achieve the most widely diversified portfolio where the idiosyncratic distribution properties of specific markets are diversified away. Indeed, global macro hedge funds invest across financial, commodity, and currency markets around the world. This breadth of investment strategies provides the best opportunity to achieve a diversified portfolio of returns, to minimize the impact of outlier events, and to approximate a normal distribution.

In any event, the ability to produce a positive skew to their return distribution while providing less exposure to outliers (a lower value of kurtosis) than the general stock market indicates that global macro hedge fund managers have provided a positive level of skill.

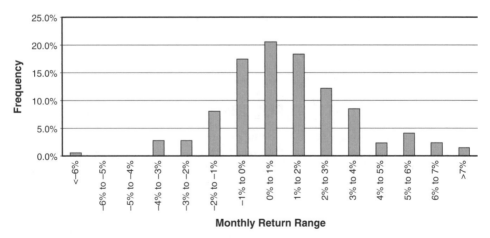

Exhibit 13.19   Frequency distribution for global macro, 1990 through 2008

Source: Hedge Fund Research, Inc., copyright 2009, www.hedgefundresearch.com.

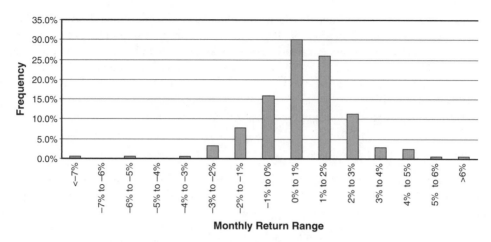

Exhibit 13.20   Frequency distribution for funds of funds, 1990 through 2008

Source: Hedge Fund Research, Inc., copyright 2009, www.hedgefundresearch.com.

Hedge funds of funds

Hedge funds of funds have the mandate to pick and choose hedge fund strategies depending on which strategies have the greatest current profitability expectation. This is the definition of opportunistic investing, allocating capital across strategies based on the FOF manager's expectation about which hedge fund strategies will produce the greatest return.

Similar to what we saw for global macro hedge funds, we would expect the diversification potential of this strategy to produce a return distribution consistent with a normal distribution of returns. Presumably, FOF managers have the ability to diversify the risks of the individual hedge funds in which they invest. However, Exhibit 13.20 does not confirm our expectations. We find (from Exhibit 13.2) a negative skew of −0.49 and a large value of kurtosis of 3.67, very similar to the results for credit risk investments and indicative of a large downside tail. These are very similar to the statistics found for the total HFRI Hedge Fund Index, a small but negative skew and a large value of kurtosis.

This is somewhat surprising since one of the skills a FOF manager is presumed to have is the ability to limit the exposure to large downside events. Yet Exhibit 13.20 demonstrates otherwise. However, returns are reasonably consistent, with 56% of the return mass concentrated in the 0% to 2% return range.

IMPLICATIONS FOR RISK MANAGEMENT

Before risk management of hedge funds can be applied, the risks of the several hedge fund strategies must be understood. Specifically, the distribution of returns of each hedge fund strategy must be analyzed to determine its shape and properties. In this chapter we found that many hedge fund return distributions exhibit properties that are distinctly nonnormal. The issue before us is how to apply this information when constructing a hedge fund program. We offer some practical observations and suggestions.

One observation is: do not construct a hedge fund program based on only one type of hedge fund strategy. As indicated in Exhibits 13.6 through 13.19, the different hedge fund styles exhibit different return distributions. Therefore, benefits can be obtained by diversifying across single hedge fund strategies. This is plain old portfolio theory: do not put all of your eggs into one hedge fund basket. An alternative to this would be to consider the average returns of investing in funds of hedge funds, because they directly reflect the actual investment experience of investors in hedge funds (Fung and Hsieh 2000b). Furthermore, the databases on FOFs have fewer biases than those on individual hedge funds, and, finally, the net performance of funds of hedge funds is net of the costs of due diligence (and also portfolio construction) of investing in hedge funds. These costs, which are borne by investors, are not reflected in the returns of individual hedge funds.

Hedge funds that exhibit market risk

The news here is mixed in that four types of market risk hedge funds, equity long/short, emerging markets, short sellers, and activist investors, exhibit risk profiles that have positive and negative skews. Ideally, we want return distributions that have a bias to the upside, a positive skew. Unfortunately, for our market risk hedge funds, we found two that exhibited a negative skew (activist investors and emerging markets), while the other two strategies were able to shift away from a negative market skew (equity long/short and short sellers).

Equity long/short hedge funds were able to generate a skew of zero, much better than having a distribution skewed to the left. Surprisingly, a positive shift in skew was not observed by emerging market or activist hedge funds. Presumably, one of the advantages of going long and short the equities market is to remove the negative skew from investing in the equity markets in the first place. Consequently, it is interesting to find that emerging market hedge fund managers still maintain a negative skew. So too do activist hedge fund managers. While they are subject to event risk, we would expect these managers to choose their concentrated bets very, very carefully so as to improve their distribution of returns to the upside with a positive skew. Apparently not, and this is an area that is deserving of more research, but we can only draw conclusions from what our analysis presents us with through 2008.

Short sellers also produce a positive skew with a value of kurtosis similar to that for equity long/short managers. However, the biggest detraction for short sellers is the volatility of returns. At a 5.66% volatility for monthly returns, short sellers were the most volatile of any hedge fund strategy, more volatile than even stocks or high-yield bonds. Further, short sellers have a negative Sharpe ratio, indicating a poor risk versus return trade-off, although they had an excellent year in the bear market of 2008.

The large downside tail exposures reflect the event risk inherent in arbitrage and event driven strategies.

Consider merger arbitrage. As Exhibit 13.11 demonstrates, about 74% of the time you should expect monthly returns in the 0% to 2% range. These results are very favorable compared to the S&P 500, where the frequency of returns is much more dispersed. Therefore, the consistency with which merger arbitrage funds deliver performance is less risky than the consistency of the S&P 500's performance. Further, the standard deviation of merger arbitrage returns is less than one-third that for the S&P 500.

However, merger arbitrage is exposed to significant event risk. Exhibits 13.2 and 13.11 show that merger arbitrage has the second largest negative skew and the third largest value of leptokurtosis. This means that when deals break down, significant losses will be incurred. The reason is that merger arbitrage is similar to selling a put option or selling insurance. In effect, merger arbitrage managers underwrite the risk of loss associated with a failed merger or acquisition.

With a short put option, the hedge fund manager sells the put and collects a cash premium from the sale. If the put expires unexercised (the merger is completed), the hedge fund manager keeps the premium and adds it to the total return. However, if the merger fails to be completed and the stock prices of the two companies diverge instead of converging, the put option will be exercised against the hedge fund manager. The manager must either purchase the underlying asset at the strike price (which is above the market price) or settle the option in cash. In both cases, the hedge fund manager incurs a loss.

The payoff for a short put option is presented in Exhibit 13.21. Notice that, as the value of the underlying asset declines, the short put option earns a consistent payout until the strike price is reached, and then declines in value. This is similar to the payout expected from merger arbitrage: a consistent payout, but a loss of value if the merger is not completed. Therefore, the distribution of returns associated with a short put option strategy will also be skewed to the left, because a short put option holder is exposed to downside risk.

Another way to consider this risk is that it is similar to the sale of an insurance contract. Insurers sell insurance policies and collect premiums. In return for collecting the insurance premium, they take on the risk that there will be no unfortunate economic events. Therefore, an insurance contract is like the sale of a put option. If nothing happens, the insurance company gets to keep the insurance/option premium. However, if there is an event, the insurance policy holder can put his policy back to the insurance company for a payout. The insurance company must then pay the face value (the strike price) of the insurance contract and accept a loss. Insurers make money by spreading these insurance contracts across many different types of policyholders, and thereby diversifying the risk of loss on any one economic event.

What is most important to note about this type of risk is that it is off-balance-sheet risk. If you were to look at the balance sheet of a merger arbitrage hedge fund manager, you would see offsetting long and short equity positions reflecting the purchase of the target company's stock and the sale of the acquiring company's stock. Looking at these offsetting long and short equity positions, an investor might conclude that the hedge fund manager has a hedged portfolio with long positions in stock balanced against short positions in stock.

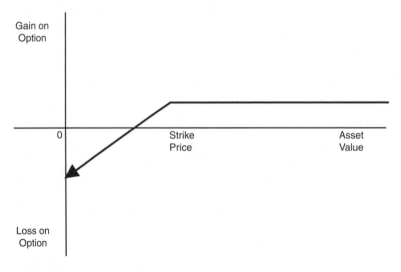

Exhibit 13.21   Payoff to a short put option

Yet the balance sheet positions mask what is really the true risk of merger arbitrage: financial market insurance against the possibility that the deal will break down. This short volatility strategy will not show up from just an observation of the hedge fund manager's investment statement. Therefore, it is vital that investors understand a hedge fund manager's risk exposure and not just its trading positions.

Merger arbitrage hedge funds can then be viewed as insurance agents. What they are insuring is the risk of loss should the deal collapse. By purchasing the stock of the target company and selling the stock of the acquiring company from investors who do not have as much confidence in the merger deal, merger arbitrage hedge funds accept/insure against the risk of the deal collapsing. If the merger fails, they are on the hook for the loss instead of the shareholders from whom or to whom they purchased or sold shares.

When viewed as insurance agents, three risk management suggestions can be made for merger arbitrage funds. First, apply the same principles as insurance companies: Diversify the risks. It is better to invest with two or three merger arbitrage funds than with one, because this will spread the insurance risk among three different funds, even though the costs of due diligence (applicable to two or three funds versus only one) will certainly be higher. In the insurance industry, this is called reinsurance. Second, do not invest in merger arbitrage funds that concentrate in the same industry or market capitalization range. This will concentrate and compound the insurance risk. Last, limit the amount of leverage that the merger arbitrage manager may apply. The more leverage, the larger the size of the short put option risk.

While we used merger arbitrage to highlight the downside risk exposure, this risk is similar for every arbitrage or event driven strategy. Each of these strategies has a similar short put option exposure. They are all at risk to outlier events.

For instance, recall our discussion of the demise of Long-Term Capital Management. LTCM was a relative value arbitrage hedge fund manager. Its strategy was simple: Securities with similar economic profiles should converge in price by maturity. This strategy worked well as long as a severe economic event did not occur. Year in and year out LTCM was able to collect option-like premiums in the financial markets for insuring that the prices of similar securities would converge.

However, a disastrous economic event eventually occurred: the default by the Russian government on its bonds in the summer of 1998. There was an instantaneous flight to quality in the financial markets as investors sought the safety of the most liquid and creditworthy instruments. Instead of converging as LTCM had bet they would, prices of similar securities diverged. LTCM's short put option profile worked against it, and it lost massive amounts of capital.[9] Those investors who had sold their positions to LTCM benefited, and just like an insurance company, LTCM was forced to accept the losses. In addition, the huge leverage LTCM employed only exacerbated its short put option exposure.

In summary, convergence trading and corporate restructuring hedge funds act like insurance companies: if there is a disastrous financial event, they bear the loss. This is consistent with the ideas of Fung and Hsieh.[10] This exposure is exacerbated to the extent arbitrage funds apply leverage. Therefore, a simple risk management tool is to invest with those hedge funds that employ limited leverage. A two-to-one ratio should be sufficient for these funds to effect their strategies.

---

[9] See Philippe Jorion, "Risk Management Lessons from Long-Term Capital Management," working paper, University of California at Irvine, January 2000.

[10] William Fung and David Hsieh, "A Primer on Hedge Funds," *Journal of Empirical Finance* 6, no. 3 (September 1999), 309–331.

Hedge funds that have low market and insurance risk

We found that two hedge fund strategies, equity market neutral and global macro, have the most conservative risk profiles. Equity market neutral hedge funds have a slight negative skew, while global macro hedge funds have a positive skew, indicating a bias to larger positive returns than negative returns. Also, each has a low value of kurtosis. In fact, global macro hedge fund managers exhibit a return pattern that is remarkably symmetrical, very close to that bell-curve distribution that is so elusive to asset managers.

For risk-averse investors, these would be the ideal investment. Also, both earn Sharpe ratios significantly greater than that of the stock market. However, these two strategies diverge with respect to the concentration of return mass. Market neutral managers have 71% of their distribution mass concentrated in the 0% to 2% range while for global macro this is only 38%. Global macro hedge funds have a much greater dispersion of returns than equity market neutral managers.

CONCLUSION

This chapter explored the different natures of hedge fund strategies by providing a frequency distribution of their returns. We found that the return patterns for hedge funds are differ greatly, reflecting different trading strategies, different levels of exposure to the financial markets, and different levels of off-balance-sheet risk. This emphasizes the point of diversifying across the hedge fund strategies to ensure the best complementary risk exposure. However, we note that the risk exposure of funds of funds was not much better than that for high-yield bonds; there was still considerable exposure to downside risk events. Consequently, it does not appear that FOF managers use diversification techniques to full advantage.

We found considerable evidence of hedge fund manager skill throughout the hedge fund manager strategies examined. This skill manifested itself in one of three ways: the ability to shift the distribution of returns from a negative skew to a positive skew; the ability to shrink the tails of the return distribution (reduce exposure to outlier events); and last, the ability to produce consistent returns with greater frequency than is observed in the stock and bond markets. Last, we note that we incorporated into our analysis of hedge fund return patterns the performance values through September 2008. The year 2008 was definitely a year of unusual financial events, challenged by as close to a financial market meltdown as I hope we will ever see. Undoubtedly, the credit and liquidity crisis that swept through global financial markets had an impact on hedge fund returns, potentially skewing those returns more toward the negative side and also expanding the tails of the distributions. However, when conducting risk management, one of the questions you should ask is: what is the worst that can happen to this strategy? In 2008 we saw it, and those returns are embedded in our analysis in this chapter.

14

Risk Management Part II: More Hedge Fund Risks

In the prior chapter we focused on drawing a picture of risk through frequency distributions of hedge fund returns. We showed that these distributions are often distinctly non-normal. In consequence, most of these distributions displayed return patterns very different from the traditional bell curve often assumed in the financial markets.

In this chapter we explore a number of additional risks that are peculiar to hedge funds, namely: process risk, mapping risk, transparency risk, risk management risk, data risk, performance measurement risk, event risk, beta expansion risk, and short volatility risk. Some of these risks are described qualitatively, while others can be documented in an empirical fashion. The purpose of this discussion is not to scare off the reader from hedge funds but rather to illuminate some of the less obvious issues associated with hedge fund investing.

In general, regulators, mainly the Securities and Exchange Commission (SEC) and the Commodity Futures Trading Commission (CFTC), maintain that hedge fund investors can fend for themselves. This is because hedge funds are accessible only to institutional investors and to sophisticated wealthy individuals. These are accredited investors having the knowledge and the sufficient wealth to bear the risk of experiencing significant investment losses.

PROCESS RISK

Most investors prefer a well-defined investment process that describes how an investment manager makes investments. Previously we highlighted the investment process as one of the three basic questions that must be documented as part of the due diligence process. Yet documenting a hedge fund manager's investment process is not always a straightforward task. Consider the following language from a hedge fund disclosure document:

> The General Partner makes extensive use of computer technology in both the formulation and execution of many investment decisions. Buy and sell decisions will, in many cases, be made and executed algorithmically according to quantitative trading strategies embodied in analytical computer software running the General Partner's computer facilities or on other computers used to support the Fund's trading activities.

We also used this example in our chapter on due diligence to demonstrate what is known as a "black box." Hedge fund managers that can be classified as information filterers rely on sophisticated computer programs to sift through current market data to find securities that appear to be mispriced. Yet, to describe a hedge fund manager's investment process as "computer software" is insufficient documentation. The problem is that for black box managers, the black box itself is the investment process.

The lack of transparency in the investment process is what we describe as **process risk**. There are two ways to manage this risk. The first is quite direct: don't invest in what you cannot document. This is a blunt risk management policy, but if an investor cannot understand the investment process, chances are he may not be able to comprehend the risks associated with the process. This is especially true for a hedge fund manager that will not let an investor examine its investment algorithms.

The second way to manage this risk is to "pop the hood" (or, as I have learned to say in the United Kingdom, "pop the bonnet") of the hedge fund manager's black box. It is not necessary to read the underlying computer code behind every computer algorithm. Instead, the investor must understand the structure of the algorithms.

First, the investor should determine that different computer algorithms are used to evaluate different financial instruments. As an example, mortgage-backed securities and convertible bonds are affected by different economic variables and pricing dynamics. One computer algorithm size does not fit all of the financial markets.

Second, the investor should determine that the computer algorithm includes all relevant variables. For instance, with respect to convertible bond arbitrage, appropriate economic inputs might be the underlying stock price, the historical volatility, the implied volatility, the current term structure of interest rates, the credit rating of the instrument, the duration of the bond, the convertible strike price, and any call provisions in the bond indenture.

Third, the investor should determine what the computer algorithms attempt to accomplish. Convertible arbitrage funds, for example, build long positions of convertible bonds and then hedge the equity component of the bond by selling the underlying stock or options on that stock. Equity risk can be hedged by selling the appropriate ratio, or delta, of stock underlying the convertible option. The delta is a measure of the sensitivity of the convertible bond value to movements in the underlying stock, and it changes as the price of the underlying stock changes. Therefore, convertible bond arbitrage algorithms must be designed to measure and track the delta hedge ratio and to provide a signal as to when an existing hedge ratio must be adjusted.

Black boxes are an example of a sophisticated process risk. However, process risk need not be embedded in a computer program; it can also exist with an individual.

Consider another example of the hedge funds run by George Soros. (We also used this example in Chapter 12 on due diligence.) Back in the 1990s, Mr. Soros had ceded much of the day-to-day investment management of his hedge funds to Stanley Druckenmiller. The *Wall Street Journal* documented the concentrated skill-based investment style of this hedge fund group:

> For years, [Soros Fund Management] fostered an entrepreneurial culture, with a cadre of employees battling wits to persuade Mr. Druckenmiller to invest.
>
> "[Mr. Druckenmiller] didn't scream, but he could be very tough. It could be three days or three weeks of battling it out until he's convinced, or you're defeated."[1]

This is another example of process risk. There is no documented investment process. Instead, there is one person who is the decision maker. An investor may be able to document the existence of a person, but not the thought process of that individual. Filtering all information through the brain of one individual raises two issues.

First, the investment process is dependent on a single person. Should that person leave the hedge fund, the investment process will leave with him. Hedge fund documents often contain a "key person" provision for this reason. If a key investment person leaves or dies, then the investors have the right to withdraw from the hedge fund.

Second, hedge fund investment strategies that are dependent on one person also lack transparency. Skill-based investing usually is opaque. There is no way to really tell whether the decisions of the key investment person are quantitatively or qualitatively based.

---

[1] "Shake-Up Continues at Soros's Hedge-Fund Empire," *Wall Street Journal*, May 1, 2000, C1.

Investors should accept the fundamental economic risks of the asset classes in which they invest. However, investors are generally unwilling to bear risks that are not fundamental to their tactical and strategic asset allocations.

Process risk is not a fundamental risk. It is an idiosyncratic risk of the hedge fund manager's structure and operations. Generally, it is not a risk that investors wish to bear. Unfortunately, process risk is peculiar to the hedge fund industry because of the industry's skill-based nature.

The solution to this problem is diversifying across hedge fund styles or investing in funds of hedge funds. Modern portfolio theory (MPT) teaches us that a diversified basket of stocks will eliminate most, if not all, of the idiosyncratic risk of the individual companies, leaving only market risk to be compensated. Similarly, MPT can be applied to hedge fund investing. Park and Staum[2] and Henker[3] indicate that a portfolio of 15 to 20 hedge fund managers can eliminate up to 95% of the idiosyncratic/process risk associated with hedge fund managers. However, investors need to be aware of the increasing due diligence costs that investing across an ever larger number of hedge funds implies.

MAPPING RISK

Another issue with hedge fund risk management is that there is no standard platform for measuring risk and no standard format for reporting risk. Different hedge funds map risk differently. For example, hedge fund managers may use different time periods and different confidence levels to measure the value at risk of their portfolios. Consequently, it is difficult to combine the risks of several hedge funds.

Fung and Hsieh (1997) apply Sharpe's style analysis to hedge funds. They find that the amount of variation of hedge fund returns that is explained by financial asset class returns is low; r-squared measures were less than 25% for almost half of the hedge funds studied. They then apply a principal components analysis based on a hedge fund's trading style, and find that five different trading styles (systems/opportunistic, global macro, value, systems/trend following, and distressed) explain about 45% of the cross-sectional variation in hedge fund returns.

A good example of the mapping problem is the work done by Fung and Hsieh[4] and Liang.[5] Both studies attempt to analyze the returns to hedge funds by applying the factor or style analysis conducted by William Sharpe with respect to mutual funds.[6] In his 1992 study, Sharpe compared the returns of mutual funds to the returns from financial asset class indices to determine the amount of variation in mutual fund returns explained by asset class returns. His results indicated that up to 90% of mutual fund returns are explained by asset class returns.

In a subsequent study, Fung and Hsieh (2004) regress the returns to the HFRI Composite Index and the CSFB/Tremont Hedge Fund Index on nine financial indices including large- and small-cap stocks, international stocks, bond indices, currencies, and commodities.[7] They find an R-squared measure for the HFRI Composite to be 70%, whereas for the CSFB/Tremont Index it was only 52%.

---

[2] James Park and Jeremy Staum, "Fund of Funds Diversification: How Much Is Enough?" *Journal of Alternative Investments* (Winter 1998), 39–42.

[3] Thomas Henker, "Naive Diversification for Hedge Funds," *Journal of Alternative Assets* (Winter 1998), 33–38.

[4] William Fung and David Hsieh, "Empirical Characteristics of Dynamic Trading Strategies: The Case of Hedge Funds," *Review of Financial Studies* 10 (1997), 275–302.

[5] Bing Liang, "On the Performance of Hedge Funds," *Financial Analysts Journal* (July/August 1999), 72–85.

[6] William Sharpe, "Asset Allocation: Management Style and Performance Measure, *Journal of Portfolio Management* (Winter 1992), 7–19.

[7] William Fung and David Hsieh, "Hedge Fund Benchmarks: A Risk-Based Approach," *Financial Analysts Journal* (September/October 2004), 65–80.

Liang conducts a style analysis similar to Sharpe and finds R-squareds in the range of 20% for hedge funds that invest in foreign exchange to 77% for hedge funds that invest in emerging markets.

The point of these studies is that hedge fund returns do not map as well onto standard asset classes as do mutual funds. One reason is the skill-based nature of the hedge fund industry. Hedge fund managers tend to hold concentrated portfolios that do not resemble passive indices. Another reason is that hedge funds often invest in derivative instruments that have nonlinear payoffs, and nonlinear derivative instruments map poorly onto linear (financial) asset classes.

To demonstrate the difficulty of mapping hedge fund returns onto financial asset returns, consider Exhibit 14.1. In this exhibit we map the returns to convertible bond arbitrage managers onto four fundamental variables.

One reason why convertible bonds are so difficult to value and are so popular with hedge fund managers is that a convertible bond is a basket of several systematic risk premiums. There are five fundamental factors that impact the value of a convertible bond:

1. It is a bond, so it has interest rate/duration risk.
2. It is convertible into stock, so it has stock market risk.
3. It is usually issued by companies with less than stellar credit ratings.
4. It has an embedded option that increases or decreases in value with the level of stock market volatility.
5. It trades infrequently, so there is a liquidity premium; convertible bond prices do not follow a random walk.

To capture these five economic drivers, we regress the returns to the HFRI Convertible Bond Arbitrage Index against the S&P 500 (stock market risk), U.S. Treasury bonds (duration risk), the Salomon Brothers High Yield Cash Pay Index (credit risk), the Chicago Board Options Exchange VIX Volatility Index (implied volatility for stock options on the S&P 500), and the prior month's value of convertible bonds (**liquidity risk**). We examine monthly data from the period 2000 to 2008.

Exhibit 14.1 provides our results. We can see that the betas for both stock market risk and volatility risk are almost zero. This indicates that hedge fund managers hedge out effectively, selling stock market risk and volatility risk. What remains are credit, interest rate, and liquidity exposures, all with significant betas.

However, note that the R-squared measure is still only 0.51. Despite breaking down convertible bonds into their five primary economic drivers, a considerable amount of the variation of hedge fund manager returns is left unexplained. This unexplained variation is embedded in the intercept or alpha for convertible arbitrage managers, which, disappointingly, is negative. Note that the alpha (intercept) term is a negative 1.02% with a t-statistic of -2.14, which is significant at the 5%

Exhibit 14.1 Regression results for convertible bond arbitrage

Variable	Alpha	RU1000	VIX	10-Year T-Bond	High-Yield	Convert(-1)	R-Squared
Coefficient value	-0.0102	0.002	0.027	0.26	0.21	0.54	0.51
t-statistic	-2.14^*	0.075	0.9	$2.58^\dagger$	$5.42^\dagger$	$6.89^\dagger$	

Note: The dependent variable is the monthly return on the HFRI Convertible Bond Arbitrage Index. Alpha is the intercept of the regression. The independent variables are: "RU1000" is the monthly index return of the Russell 1000, "VIX" is the volatility index, "10-Year T-Bond" is the monthly return on 10-year U.S. Treasury bonds, "High-Yield" is the monthly return on high-yield bonds, and "Convert(-1)" is the previous monthly return of the HFRI Convertible Bond Arbitrage Index.
*Significant at the 5% level.
†Significant at the 1% level.

level. Earlier we made the point that convertible bond arbitrage is not about finding undervalued convertible bonds, but rather about finding cheap beta. Despite a negative alpha associated with security selection, convertible bond arbitrage hedge fund managers generate a positive Sharpe ratio by hedging/selling expensive systematic risks embedded in the convertible bond and keeping the inexpensive systematic risks. During this time period, convertible arbitrage hedge fund managers hedged (sold) stock market and volatility risk and kept interest rate, credit, and liquidity risk, earning an excess return for these risk premiums.

Second, different hedge fund managers have different types of concentrated risk exposure that cannot simply be added to give a total exposure. For instance, equity long/short hedge funds have considerable market risk. Conversely, merger arbitrage hedge funds are exposed to significant event risk but little market risk. Even if they all measured risk in a consistent manner, their risk exposures are sufficiently different such that combining them into one risk statistic would be misleading.

Two solutions to the mapping problem are possible. First, institutions can act as global risk managers. It is the hedge fund manager's responsibility to generate the excess returns, and the investor's job to manage the risks that arise from that investment. This is a macro approach to risk management.

Under this solution, the investor loads each hedge fund manager's risk exposures into her risk management system and determines the risk of her overall portfolio. This solution has the advantage that the investor controls the mapping of the risk exposures rather than the individual hedge fund managers. The difficulty is getting sufficient performance data from the hedge fund managers to be able to measure the managers' exposures accurately.

As a second solution, the investor could ask for each hedge fund manager's investment positions. This is a micro approach.

Unfortunately, this is problematic for two reasons. First, hedge fund managers are reluctant to reveal their individual investment positions, because these tend to be the manager's proprietary data. The concern is that the distribution of such detailed information might erode the hedge fund manager's competitive edge should this information be inadvertently disclosed. However, this reluctance is changing. As more institutional investors have entered the hedge fund investment world, more hedge fund managers have become comfortable with providing full transparency.

Second, the detailed disclosure of the thousands of positions of all hedge fund managers in a hedge fund portfolio can choke a risk management system. For example, at the time of its demise, it was estimated that Long-Term Capital Management had over 100,000 individual risk positions in its portfolio.

One possibility is that the hedge fund managers could report this information to a central agent such as a prime broker or a hedge fund administrator, which could use its risk platform to prepare the risk analysis. In fact, more and more hedge fund administrators have begun to offer their position reporting and risk management services to investors. While hedge funds have long been their exclusive clientele, hedge fund administrators have realized that their services are equally valuable to investors in hedge funds.

TRANSPARENCY RISK

We alluded to transparency risk as an ancillary issue associated with process risk. Transparency is a continuing issue with hedge fund managers because of their mostly unregulated nature. In the past, the SEC has asked hedge fund managers to register by completing an annual Form ADV with the SEC. This form provides basic information regarding the hedge fund manager's place of business, products offered, key individuals, and so on, but does not require performance data. Hedge fund managers that operate outside the regulatory jurisdiction of the SEC or the CFTC typically do not provide as complete disclosure as their regulated counterparts. Even if hedge fund managers are required again to register with the SEC in the United States, the information provided because of this process will be insufficient to satisfy investors' transparency requirements.

Hedge funds generally provide an annual financial statement and performance review. However, hedge funds rarely disclose their existing portfolio positions. Without an accounting of their trading and portfolio positions, three issues arise for the investor.

The first is the authenticity of the hedge fund manager's performance. For instance, did an equity long/short manager really earn 10% in the current quarter from stock selection, or did she make market timing bets on the S&P 500 using SPX futures contracts? Without a position report, there is no way to establish the provenance of the hedge fund manager's performance results.

Second, without disclosure of trading and portfolio positions, an investor cannot appropriately monitor and measure the risks of the hedge fund manager. Again, using the example of an equity long/short manager, did the manager earn 10% in the quarter from long/short stock selections in the media sector of the economy as described in the manager's offering memorandum, or did she stray into other sectors?

Third, without transparency, investors cannot aggregate risks across their entire investment program to understand the implications at the portfolio level. It will be difficult for an investor to verify whether the hedge fund managers in her program are making stock selections in the same economic sector, and therefore compounding their collective risk positions instead of diversifying them.

Hedge fund managers are reluctant to disclose their trading and portfolio positions for several reasons. First, hedge fund managers contend that if they were to disclose their investment positions, other managers might be able to reverse engineer the hedge fund manager's investment strategy. In effect, a snapshot of the hedge fund manager's portfolio might reveal useful investment information to other market participants.

A second concern for hedge fund managers is that if they disclose to the financial markets their investment intentions, they will not be able to execute their trades as advantageously as possible. Essentially, this contention is that other market participants might line up in an attempt to pick off the hedge fund manager as she attempts to either establish or unwind her investment portfolio.

In an effort to resolve the competing needs and concerns of investors and hedge fund managers, the International Association of Financial Engineers and the Global Association of Risk Professionals jointly sponsored a Steering Committee on "Hedge Fund Risk Disclosure." This industry committee consists of hedge fund managers, investors, risk management professionals, and prime brokers. The purpose of the Steering Committee is to establish transparency guidelines that will satisfy hedge fund managers and investors alike.

The Steering Committee reached the conclusion that full, daily position reporting by hedge fund managers is not the solution. First, daily position reporting may compromise the hedge fund manager's investment strategy. Second, the vast quantity of position data generated by a hedge fund manager may overwhelm an investor's risk monitoring system.

The Steering Committee concluded that exposure reporting, combined with delayed position reporting is sufficient for risk monitoring and management purposes. Exposure reporting is the practice of reporting the risk exposures of the hedge fund manager instead of her individual trading positions. These exposures are known as **risk buckets**. It is much more practical to manage risk buckets than it is to manage individual trading positions. In fact, the practice of risk management is to measure and manage the aggregate risk exposures across a diversified portfolio. Risk buckets accomplish this task by identifying the factors that most impact the value of an investment portfolio.

For instance, exposure reporting might indicate the total dollar exposure to each industry or sector in which the hedge fund manager invests. It might also report the top 10 investment positions, as well as net market exposure, total long exposure, and total short exposure. Exposure reporting might also indicate the amount of leverage in the portfolio, as well as the duration and convexity (for a bond portfolio) or beta exposure (for a stock portfolio). Last, exposure reporting might indicate the extent to which the hedge fund manager is exposed to market events (short volatility).

Second, the Steering Committee concluded that position reporting could be reported with a sufficient lag to protect the hedge fund manager's investment strategy. Ninety days, for example, might be a sufficient delay between when a hedge fund manager executes a trade and when the manager reports its positions to investors. The investors can satisfy themselves that the hedge fund manager has not incurred any style drift (we will have more to say about style drift in the next chapter), while the hedge fund manager is secure in the secrecy of her positions.

RISK MANAGEMENT RISK

Value at risk (VaR) is a statistical method of quantifying a potential risk of loss. VaR can be defined as the maximum loss that can be expected under normal market conditions over a specified time horizon and at a specified level of confidence. For instance, a VaR calculation might determine that, with a 95% level of confidence, the worst loss that a hedge fund manager might incur over one month's trading horizon is $10 million.

The following expression shows how VaR is calculated:

$$VaR_a = [L : \Pr(P < L) = 1 - \alpha]$$

It states that VaR for a significance level of α (e.g. 99%) is given by L, such that probability that the value of the portfolio, P, will be less than L with the probability $(1 - \alpha)$. If the portfolio's return is assumed to be normally distributed (a very strong assumption), the VaR can be written as

$$VaR_\alpha = \mu_p + z_\alpha \times \sigma_p$$
$$\Pr(z < z_\alpha) = (1 - \alpha)$$

where

$z =$ a standard normal random variable
$\sigma_p =$ the standard deviation of the return on the portfolio
$\mu_p =$ the expected return on the portfolio

If the expected return and standard deviation measure daily performance of the portfolio, then the VaR would represent the daily VaR. By the same token, monthly or annual VaRs can be calculated as well. When daily VaR is calculated, it is customary to ignore the mean, for it is likely to be very small. In that case the daily VaR is given by

$$VaR_\alpha(Daily) = z_\alpha \times \sigma_p(Daily)$$
$$\Pr(z < z_\alpha) = (1 - \alpha)$$

Ignoring the mean and under very restrictive assumptions, one can use the daily VaR to obtain the T period VaR:

$$VaR_\alpha(T \; Day) = VaR_\alpha(Daily) \times \sqrt{T}$$

That is, VaR grows with the square root of the length of time period. So if the daily VaR at 99% confidence is 1%, then the 10-day VaR will be approximately $1\% \times \sqrt{10} = 3.16\%$.

As you can see, VaR calculations are based on several statistical inputs: the level of confidence, the time horizon, the volatility of the underlying asset, and the expected return of the underlying asset. The level of confidence is chosen by the hedge fund manager. For example, a 95% confidence level translates into a 1 in 20 chance of the loss exceeding $10 million. The manager also chooses the time horizon. This might be daily if the risk being monitored is a trading desk, monthly if the risk is a hedge fund's performance, or annually for long-only managers.

The volatility and expected return of the underlying asset are determined by historical data. Hedge fund managers might wish to look at only the most recent data, possibly the last 90 trading days, to ensure the most current information regarding the hedge fund manager's return distribution. Alternatively, a hedge fund manager might wish to look at a longer period of time such as a year or more to capture the long-term volatility and expected return associated with her performance.

This short discussion highlights the first risk in VaR. The hedge fund manager has control over three critical variables that underlie the VaR calculation: confidence level, time horizon, and time period over which to measure volatility and expected return. Hedge fund managers will have different time horizons, confidence levels, and measuring periods. VaR is not applied consistently across hedge fund managers, and therefore cannot be properly compared from hedge fund manager to manager.

A second issue is that VaR measures are not additive. As we saw, VaR is a statistic that measures the likelihood of a loss exceeding a certain threshold dollar amount over a specified period of time. It is a measure of probability that is dependent on a manager's time horizon, specified confidence level, and asset mix. Given that hedge fund managers may have different time horizons, confidence levels, and asset mixes, VaR measures will vary widely across hedge fund managers. Additionally, different types of hedge fund strategies will have different types of risk exposures.

Third, VaR is often based on the assumption that the returns to an underlying asset, such as a hedge fund investment, are normally distributed. Under this assumption, VaR considers only the mean and standard deviation of a distribution of returns. However, as we indicated in the prior chapter, the return distributions to hedge fund managers are distinctly nonnormal, exhibiting considerable skewness and excess kurtosis.

Fourth, VaR is based on normal market conditions (i.e. that market outliers occur infrequently). In fact, outlier events occur more frequently than predicted by a normal distribution of returns. Consequently, VaR calculations based on the normality assumption may lead to unfortunate surprises.

Exhibit 14.2 demonstrates the summary statistics and VaR analysis for the monthly return to the S&P 500 from 2000 through September 2008. The expected monthly return was 0.10% and the monthly standard deviation of S&P 500 returns was 4.04%. Under the assumption of normally distributed returns, VaR analysis would say that, with a 97.5% level of confidence, the monthly returns on the S&P 500 should not exceed 1.96 standard deviations from the expected return. Therefore, a VaR of 97.5% confidence interval would predict that the return to the S&P 500 in any given month should not exceed 8.01% or be less than −7.84%. In other words, there is a 1 in 40 chance that the monthly return to the S&P 500 will exceed 8.01% or be less than −7.84%.

Despite the 97.5% confidence level from the VaR analysis, consider the monthly returns to the S&P 500 over the period 2000 and 2001. Exhibit 14.3 demonstrates that in these two years, there were four months that exceeded the VaR confidence interval. Therefore the "1 in 40" event that should occur only once in every 40 months occurred four times within a space of 24 months. Or

Exhibit 14.2   VaR calculation for the S&P 500, monthly returns, 2000 to September 2008

Expected return	0.10%
Standard deviation	4.04%
$E(R) + 1.96 \times SD$	8.01%
$E(R) - 1.96 \times SD$	−7.84%

Source: Datastream and author's calculations.

Exhibit 14.3   Monthly returns to the S&P 500, 2000–2001

Jan-00	−5.05%	Jan-01	3.55%
Feb-00	−1.88	Feb-01	−9.12
Mar-00	9.77	Mar-01	−6.34
Apr-00	−3.00	Apr-01	7.77
May-00	−2.04	May-01	0.67
Jun-00	2.44	Jun-01	−2.43
Jul-00	−1.54	Jul-01	−0.98
Aug-00	6.21	Aug-01	−6.26
Sep-00	−5.28	Sep-01	−8.08
Oct-00	−0.45	Oct-01	1.91
Nov-00	−7.86	Nov-01	7.67
Dec-00	0.51	Dec-01	0.88

Source: Datastream.

we could consider the turbulent months of September and October of 2008. In fact, on Thursday, October 9, 2008, the S&P dropped almost 9% in a day! This example simply highlights that the financial markets are uncertain and descriptive statistics such as VaR can only describe; they cannot predict.

Therefore, if VaR is to be used in hedge fund risk management, it must be used with care. First, the VaR calculations of hedge fund managers must be synchronized. An investor should ask hedge fund managers to use consistent time horizons, confidence levels, and measuring periods.

Second, the VaR calculations of the hedge fund managers cannot be added together to achieve a total VaR for a hedge fund program. However, this is good news because the total VaR for a hedge fund program will be less than the sum of the individual VaR calculations for each hedge fund manager. The reason is that the returns to each hedge fund manager will be less than perfectly correlated with the returns to other hedge fund managers.[8]

Third, VaR may not capture the complete risk profile of a hedge fund manager. Additional information might be necessary. In particular, the extent to which a hedge fund manager is short volatility must be determined. In Chapter 13 we demonstrated how corporate restructuring hedge fund managers mimic a strategy of selling put options. This is a short volatility strategy, and the expected loss from this strategy should be calculated.

Last, the financial markets are anything but normal. Financial events have a way of occurring with greater frequency than expected. One way to compensate for this in a VaR calculation is to increase the confidence level. By specifying a 1 in 100 probability (99% level of confidence) in the VaR calculation, an investor can project a more realistic expectation of the worst loss that might occur. For instance, using our example of the S&P 500, if we had used a 99% confidence level for assessing VaR, only one month, February 2001, would have exceeded the confidence range.

Finally, Gupta and Liang (2005) apply the VaR approach to close to 500 hedge funds, finding that only 3.7% of active funds were undercapitalized (as of March 2003).[9] However, they also find that a higher 11% of the hedge funds that had stopped reporting to the database were undercapitalized, confirming that one of the reasons that hedge funds may die is because they do not have enough capital. The authors also determine that undercapitalized funds tend to be relatively small in size and represent only a small portion (only 1.2%) of the total fund assets in their sample. More important,

---

[8] In fact, the individual VaR calculations would be additive only if the returns to each hedge fund were perfectly correlated.

[9] Anurag Gupta and Bing Liang, "Do Hedge Funds Have Enough Capital? A Value-at-Risk Approach," *Journal of Financial Economics* 77, no. 1 (July 2005).

they also conclude that VaR is superior to standard deviation and leverage ratios in measuring hedge fund risk when returns are not assumed to be normally distributed.

DATA RISK

Much of the desire to invest in hedge funds stems from the academic research regarding the performance of this asset class. The empirical studies with respect to hedge funds demonstrate convincingly that hedge funds are a valuable addition to a diversified portfolio. In summary, these studies demonstrate that an allocation to hedge funds can increase the overall return to the portfolio while reducing its risk.[10] However, there are numerous data biases associated with these studies.

A reason to be skeptical of hedge fund performance data is the inherent biases found in hedge fund databases used in most of the research regarding hedge funds.[11] As a reminder, hedge funds are generally organized as private investment vehicles and do not generally disclose their investment activities to the public. Therefore, many hedge funds do not disclose their performance record to a reporting service in the same way that mutual funds do. A complete performance record of every hedge fund is simply unobtainable.

Within this imperfect framework there are three data biases that can affect the reported performance of hedge funds. The first is survivorship bias. **Survivorship bias** arises when a database of hedge funds includes only surviving hedge funds. Those hedge funds that have ceased operations may be excluded from the database. This leads to an upward bias in performance reporting because presumably those hedge funds that ceased operations performed poorly. In other words, only the good hedge funds survive, and their positive performance adds an upward bias to the reported financial returns.

In addition, the database may be biased downward in risk relative to the universe of all hedge funds because those hedge funds that ceased operations may have had more volatile returns (the cause for their demise). Survivorship bias is a natural result of the way the hedge fund industry (or any new financial industry) evolved. Databases were not developed until sufficient interest by the academic and institutional community rendered such a service necessary. By that time, many hedge funds that had started and failed were never recorded.

Survivorship bias has been documented in the mutual fund industry. One way to measure this bias is to obtain the population of all funds that operated during a certain period. The average return of all funds operating during that period is compared to the average return generated by the funds in existence at the end of the period. The difference is the amount of survivorship bias.[12]

The amount of survivorship bias in the hedge fund industry has been estimated at 2% to 3% per year.[13] This is the amount of upward bias reflected in the returns reported to a hedge fund database if not corrected for hedge funds that ceased operations. Fung and Hsieh (2006) determine that survivorship bias amounts to approximately 2.5% a year. They also contend that the importance of the survivorship bias will decline as the hedge fund industry matures. Clearly, this

---

[10] For a more detailed summary of these studies, see our discussion in Chapter 11.

[11] For a thorough discussion on the subject of data biases, see William Fung and David Hsieh, "Hedge-Fund Benchmarks: Information Content Biases," *Financial Analysts Journal* (January/February 2002), 22–34.

[12] See Burton Malkiel, "Returns from Investing in Equity Mutual Funds 1971 to 1991," *Journal of Finance* 50, no. 2 (1995), 549–572.

[13] See William Fung and David Hsieh, "Performance Characteristics of Hedge Funds and Commodity Funds: Natural versus Spurious Biases," *Journal of Financial and Quantitative Analysis* 25 (2000), 291–307; Stephen Brown, William Goetzmann, and Roger Ibbotson, "Offshore Hedge Funds: Survival and Performance, 1989–1995," *Journal of Business* 72, no. 1 (1999), 91–117; and Bing Liang, "Hedge Funds: The Living and the Dead," *Journal of Financial and Quantitative Analysis* 35, no. 3 (September 2000), 309–326.

is a very large bias that, if not corrected, can provide misleading conclusions about the investment benefits of hedge funds.

Survivorship bias is all the more important in the hedge fund industry compared to the mutual fund industry because of hedge funds' high turnover rate. It has been estimated that the average life of a hedge fund is about three years and that the yearly attrition rate is greater than 15%.[14] Consequently, hedge funds cease operations with great frequency, and this should be expected to exacerbate the survivorship problem.

Ackermann, McEnally, and Ravenscraft, however, find no systematic bias in their study of hedge funds.[15] Specifically, they find that there are competing forces in survivorship bias: termination bias and self-selection bias. Some funds stop reporting their information because they terminate their operations, while other funds stop reporting their performance because they have become so successful that it is no longer in their best interests to publicly report their performance.

A second bias affecting hedge fund performance results is **selection bias.** Generally, those hedge funds that are performing well have an incentive to report their results to a database in order to attract new investors into the fund. This would result in hedge funds included in the database having better performance than those that are excluded because of their (presumably) poor performance. Exhibit 14.4 shows a number of studies that have attempted to measure the survivorship bias. Most estimates are in the 3% to 5% per year range.

A process known as **backfilling** further magnifies this selection bias. When a database adds a hedge fund's historical performance to its pool of funds, it backfills the hedge fund's performance to the date it began operations. This is also called "backfill bias." This creates an instant history of hedge fund returns. Because hedge fund managers hold the option of when to reveal their historical performance, it is reasonable to expect that they will disclose their performance when their results look most favorable. This leads to an upward bias in performance results within the hedge fund database. To eliminate a backfill bias, it has been estimated that the first 12 to 24 months of reported data should be eliminated from a hedge fund manager's performance history. Barry finds that this instant history bias adds up to 40 basis points per year.[16] Ibbotson and Chen (2006) find this to be a much more serious problem. Their estimate of backfill bias is 5% per year.

There is a converse to the selection bias. It is also possible that those hedge funds that are very successful have no incentive to report their performance to a database because they have already attracted a sufficient number of investors to their fund. This would lead to a downward bias of hedge fund performance reported by the databases. Ackermann, McEnally, and Ravenscraft find that selection bias is offset with no impact on hedge fund reported performance, while Fung and Hsieh find that selection bias adds approximately 1.4% to reported hedge fund returns.[17]

Finally, a third bias is called **catastrophe** or **liquidation bias**. This bias arises from the fact that hedge funds that are performing poorly and likely to cease operations stop reporting their performance before they actually close shop. A hedge fund that is performing poorly and likely to go out of business has no incentive to continue to report its performance. Indeed, the hedge fund probably has greater issues to deal with than reporting its performance, such as liquidating positions

---

[14] See Franklin Edwards and Jimmy Liew, "Hedge Funds versus Managed Futures as Asset Classes," *Journal of Derivatives* (Summer 1999), 45–64; and James Park, Stephen Brown, and William Goetzmann, "Performance Benchmarks and Survivorship Bias for Hedge Funds and Commodity Trading Advisors," *Hedge Fund News* (August 1999).

[15] See Carl Ackermann, Richard McEnally, and David Ravenscraft, "The Performance of Hedge Funds: Risk, Return, and Incentives," *Journal of Finance* (June 1999), 833–874.

[16] See Ross Barry, "Hedge Funds: A Walk through the Graveyard," MFAC Research Paper 25, September 20, 2002.

[17] See Fung and Hsieh, "Performance Characteristics," and Ackermann, McEnally, and Ravenscraft, "Performance of Hedge Funds."

Exhibit 14.4   Biases associated with hedge fund data

Bias	Park, Brown, and Goetzmann, 1999	Brown, Goetzmann, and Ibbotson, 1999	Fung and Hsieh, 2000	Ackermann, McEnally, and Ravenscraft, 1999	Barry, 2003	Ibbotson and Chen, 2006
Survivorship	2.60%	3.00%	3.00%	0.01%	3.70%	5.68%
Selection	1.90%	Not estimated	Not estimated	No impact	Not estimated	Not estimated
Instant history	Not estimated	Not estimated	1.40%	No impact	0.40%	5.01%
Liquidation	Not estimated	Not estimated	Not estimated	0.70%	Not estimated	Not estimated
Total	4.50%	3.00%	4.40%	0.71%	4.10%	

Sources: James Park, Stephen Brown, and William Goetzmann, "Performance Benchmarks and Survivorship Bias for Hedge Funds and Commodity Trading Advisors," *Hedge Fund News* (August 1999); Stephen Brown, William Goetzmann, and Roger Ibbotson, "Offshore Hedge Funds: Survival and Performance, 1989–1995," *Journal of Business* 72, no. 1 (1999), 91–117; William Fung and David Hsieh, "Performance Characteristics of Hedge Funds and Commodity Funds: Natural versus Spurious Biases," *Journal of Financial and Quantitative Analysis* 25 (2000), 291–307; Carl Ackermann, Richard McEnally, and David Ravenscraft, "The Performance of Hedge Funds: Risk, Return, and Incentives," *Journal of Finance* (June 1999), 833–874; and Ross Barry, "Hedge Funds: A Walk through the Graveyard," MFAC Research Paper 25, September 20, 2002.

to fund customer redemptions. To illustrate the magnitude that this bias may have on reported returns in times when several hedge funds fail, Fung and Hsieh (2006) mention that during the Russian crisis of August 1998, several hedge funds (including Long Term Capital Management) lost all of their capital and went bankrupt and that, as a result of this, hedge fund managers stopped reporting their funds' returns in July of that year. Had they reported the corresponding −100% returns in August 1998, observed hedge fund returns would have been substantially lower during that month.

Catastrophe bias results in an upward bias in returns and a downward bias in risk because poor performance history is excluded from the data bias. Ackermann, McEnally, and Ravenscraft attempted to measure this bias by contacting hedge fund managers directly to determine their return performance subsequent to the termination of reporting. Their study measures the impact of liquidation bias to be approximately 70 basis points.

As Exhibit 14.4 demonstrates, the combination of survivorship and selection bias can add up to 450 basis points in hedge fund returns before the impact of catastrophe bias is considered. As a consequence, it is safe to say that studies of hedge funds, if not properly discounted for inherent data biases, will inflate the returns to hedge funds.

Every hedge fund disclosure document contains the language: "Past performance is no indication of future results." This is all the more apparent when considering the data biases associated with historical hedge fund performance.

PERFORMANCE MEASUREMENT RISK

The Sharpe ratio is the statistic most often used to compare the performance of two investment managers. As we have mentioned in a previous chapter, the Sharpe ratio is a measure of risk-adjusted returns that divides the performance of an investment manager in excess of the risk-free rate by the standard deviation of that manager's performance results. Its purpose is to provide a basis to compare the performance of different managers that may invest in different financial assets.

However, there are some practical difficulties with using a Sharpe ratio analysis to compare hedge fund returns. As previously indicated, many hedge funds use derivatives with nonlinear payoff structures as part of their investment plan. These nonlinear instruments can lead to misleading Sharpe ratio conclusions.

In the prior chapter, we demonstrated that many hedge fund managers have investment styles that contain a short option exposure. When a hedge fund manager shorts/sells an option, she collects the option premium. If the option expires worthless, the hedge fund manager pockets the option premium at no cost and can thereby increase her total return.

Selling options results in an asymmetric payoff profile. The upside potential is limited to the option premium collected, while the downside can be quite large, depending on the size of the market event. As we previously discussed, this type of strategy is similar to selling insurance contracts against a decline in the financial markets.

Short options exposure also helps to boost a manager's Sharpe ratio because the hedge fund manager collects the option premium and deposits it in a cash account with low volatility. The result is high total return with low (apparent) risk. Portfolio optimization techniques will tend to overallocate to these hedge fund managers because of their high total returns and Sharpe ratios and the fact that the risk inherent in short option positions did not manifest itself during the hedge fund manager's short operating history.

This overallocation process is sometimes referred to as a **short volatility bias,** and it is a dangerous trap for unaware investors.[18] Hedge fund managers using a short volatility strategy can pump up their returns with low risk in the short run by collecting option premiums. Selling options is just like selling insurance: Premiums continue to be collected and invested in short-term cash instruments until some catastrophe hits the financial markets and the options are exercised just like an insurance policy. This strategy will work until a hedge fund manager experiences a volatility event.

To the extent that risk-adjusted returns are inflated through the short selling of options, portfolio optimizers will tend to overallocate to those strategies. Yet, allocating to these hedge fund managers will increase portfolio risk rather than reduce it, because the portfolio has now increased its exposure to a financial market catastrophe event.

The trap is that hedge fund managers can boost their short-term risk-adjusted performance through a short volatility strategy, only to increase their exposure to a volatility event. Portfolio optimizers base their selections only on patent risk, the volatility of the hedge fund manager's returns to date. However, optimizers do not incorporate latent risk (i.e. the risk of a volatility event).

Consistent with what has just been mentioned, Goetzmann, Ingersoll, Spiegel, and Welch (2002) identify a class of strategies that maximize certain performance measures without requiring any manager skill. They demonstrate the rules under which a manager can increase the Sharpe ratio of his portfolio even if he does not have any skill. This takes place by taking positions in options. These authors state:

> Our analysis shows that the best static manipulated strategy has a truncated right tail and a fat left tail. The optimal strategy involves selling out-of-the-money calls and selling out-of-the-money puts in an uneven ratio that insures a regular return from writing options and a large exposure to extreme negative events. We also show that the best dynamic strategy for maximizing the Sharpe ratio involves leverage conditional upon underperformance. (p. 2)[19]

To highlight the risk measurement problem, consider the following example. A hedge fund manager accepts a $1 million investment from a pension fund and invests this money in six-month U.S. Treasury bills. In addition, at the beginning of every month, the hedge fund manager sells fairly priced out-of-the-money call options and out-of-the-money put options on the S&P 500 that will expire at the end of the month. (This type of option strategy is known as a strangle.) The strike

---

[18] See Andrew Weisman and Jerome Abernathy, "The Dangers of Historical Hedge Fund Data," working paper, 2000.

[19] William Goetzmann, Jonathan Ingersoll, Jr., Matthew Spiegel, and Ivo Welch, "Sharpening Sharpe Ratios," NBER Working Paper, No. W9116, August 2002.

prices are chosen to be 2.5 standard deviations away from the current market price. The hedge fund manager invests the option premiums received in U.S. Treasury bills. The hedge fund manager writes enough of these options to generate a return equal to 1.5 times that of the risk-free rate.

Since a 2.5 standard deviation event occurs only about 1% of the time, the manager has a 99% chance of outperforming the risk-free rate in any one month. In other words, it would take a 1 in 100 type of market event to trigger the exercise of the options in any given month. This means that a volatility event is expected once about every eight years (100 months divided by 12). A volatility event occurs when the S&P 500 trades outside the 2.5 standard deviation range of the put/call option strangle.

In the meantime, the manager collects the option premiums and produces impressive Sharpe ratios. In addition, a sufficient track record is established that can be fed into an optimizer, resulting in the selection of the hedge fund manager. This hedge fund house of cards will come tumbling down, however, when the market turns against this short volatility investment strategy. The large short option exposure will result in a large negative cumulative return for the hedge fund manager that will wipe out most of the prior gains.

Let's put some actual numbers on this. For simplicity, we will assume that the U.S. Treasury bill rate stays constant at 6% a year. Using monthly data from 1990 through September 2008, we find that the monthly standard deviation of the S&P 500 index is about 4%. Therefore, a 2.5 standard deviation move up or down means that the S&P 500 would have to increase or decrease by more than 10% for the put/call option strangle to be exercised against the hedge fund manager.

Option pricing simulation shows that a 10% out-of-the-money option strangle on the S&P 500 would cost about $7.50 per strangle. The goal of the hedge fund manager is to collect enough option premiums each month to generate a rate of return that is 150% greater than the Treasury bill rate. Therefore, each month the hedge fund manager must leverage her invested capital by selling enough strangles so that her return on invested capital is 9% or 1.5 times the Treasury bill rate of 6%.

As an example, assume that in the first month the hedge fund manager receives $1 million from her client, which she will invest for one month so that the yearly rate of return will be 9% (0.75% per month). This would generate an end-of-period total of $1,000,000 × 1.0075 = $1,007,500. The catch is that the manager invests the money in U.S. Treasury bills earning 6%. Therefore, the hedge fund manager must sell enough put/call strangles and take in enough option premiums so as to generate a total return equal to $1,007,500. The calculation is:

$$(\$1,000,000 + \text{Option premiums}) \times (1 + 0.06/12) = \$1,007,500$$

The amount of option premiums is $2,487. At an expected cost of $7.50, the hedge fund manager must sell 331 put/call strangles to generate a return of 9%.

This strategy will work until a volatility event occurs and the expected loss of capital results. At that point, if the S&P 500 moves by more than the 10% limit (2.5 standard deviations), the strangle will be exercised. Also, as the size of the investment increases, the hedge fund manager must sell more and more options to maintain the 9% return.

We performed a Monte Carlo simulation to determine how long it would take for a volatility event to occur. Running 5,000 simulations, our model estimated that it would take 80 months (almost seven years) for the options to be exercised against the hedge fund manager. This is a little less than what we predicted initially for our 1 in 100 event. Our simulation indicated that a volatility event could occur as early as the first month and take as long as 237 months. Additionally, we used a conservative estimate that the option is in-the-money by 10 S&P 500 points when exercised.

Exhibit 14.5 demonstrates what happens when the manager employs this strategy. It works fine for almost seven years. Then a volatility event occurs and the options are exercised against the

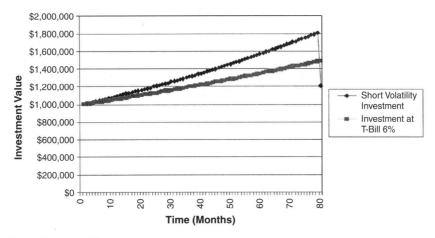

Exhibit 14.5   Short volatility investment strategy

Source: Mark Anson, *Handbook of Alternative Assets*, 2nd ed. (Hoboken, NJ: John Wiley & Sons, 2006). Reprinted with permission of John Wiley & Sons, Inc.

portfolio manager. The exercise of the options does not wipe out all of the manager's gains, but it does eliminate a good portion. In the end, the manager is left with an effective annual return of 2.85%, well below that of U.S. Treasury bills.

Exhibit 14.6 shows the returns and Sharpe ratios generated by the hedge fund manager before the volatility event and after the volatility event. As can be seen, the hedge fund manager looks like a star before the volatility event, but is unmasked once the event occurs. Unfortunately, before the volatility event is reached, the hedge fund manager can achieve a stellar track record. The low volatility associated with Treasury bill returns allows the hedge fund manager to achieve a large, positive Sharpe ratio before the volatility event occurs.

The volatility event, however, not only decreases the total return of the investment strategy; it also increases the volatility of the hedge fund manager's returns. In the month that the options are exercised against the hedge fund manager, the hedge fund earns a −33% return. This severe decline in one month causes the volatility of the hedge fund manager's returns to jump from 0.42% to 3.71%. Therefore, the volatility event reveals the latent risk associated with the hedge fund manager's strategy.

The preceding example may seem extreme, but at least one well-known hedge fund manager employed this strategy (and lost). Victor Niederhoffer was a well-known trader and author of a

Exhibit 14.6   Performance statistics for short volatility investment strategy

	Pre-Volatility Event	Post-Volatility Event
Average annual return	9.00%	2.85%
Excess return	3.00%	−3.15%
Standard deviation	0.42%	3.71%
Sharpe ratio	7.14	−0.85

Source: Mark Anson, *Handbook of Alternative Assets*, 2nd ed. (Hoboken, NJ: John Wiley & Sons, 2006). Reprinted with permission of John Wiley & Sons, Inc.

successful book: *The Education of a Speculator* (1998). Dr. Niederhoffer, generally considered to be an excellent investor and a savvy trader, earned a doctorate from the University of Chicago Graduate School of Business. He built trading programs based on statistical analysis. After analyzing stock market returns over many prior years, Dr. Niederhoffer believed that the stock market would never fall by more than 5% on any given day. He put this idea to work by selling out-of-the-money put options on stock index futures. His strategy worked successfully for several years. In fact, he was able to generate a 20% compound annual return.[20] However, his investment strategy eventually hit a volatility event.

On October 27, 1997, the S&P 500 declined by 7%. The put options that Victor Niederhoffer had sold increased in value dramatically, and he was faced with a margin call of $50 million from his prime brokers. Unable to meet the margin call, he was forced to close his hedge fund after his brokers liquidated his trading positions and wiped out his hedge fund portfolio.

Curiously, Mr. Niederhoffer's analysis did not include (or, even more curiously, chose to ignore) the history of the market crash on October 19, 1987. On that day, the S&P 500 declined by 20%.[21]

The preceding simulation and the history of Dr. Niederhoffer highlight the problems associated with the short selling of options. Short volatility positions can increase performance of the hedge fund manager but they expose the hedge fund to large downside risk should a volatility event occur.

Unfortunately, there is no simple solution for this problem; but there are some practical suggestions. First, hedge fund managers with short track records and high Sharpe ratios should be scrutinized carefully. They may not have experienced a volatility event sufficient to damage their performance history. It is possible that selecting managers based on their history of risk-adjusted returns may in fact be a negative selection process if their trading history is too short.

The second suggestion gets to the age-old issue with respect to the hedge fund industry: transparency. Just what is the hedge fund manager doing? How is she generating her excess performance? To what extent does she use options (particularly, short options) in her trading strategies? In Chapter 12 we included these questions as part of our due diligence process.

Last, new analytical tools are needed. Risk-adjusted ratios were developed for the linear investment world of traditional long-only investment managers and mutual funds. Additional analysis is needed to account for the nonlinear investment strategies employed by many hedge funds.

EVENT RISK

Hedge funds, by their very name, are supposed to hedge the risk and return profile of a diversified portfolio. Indeed many, if not most, hedge fund managers claim that their return distributions are skill-based; that is, returns are not readily identifiable with the returns for financial asset classes. This argument is the source for the additional claim that hedge funds are "total return" or "absolute return" investments, for which no benchmark is appropriate. The lack of an identifiable benchmark for a hedge fund would indicate that hedge fund returns are independent of financial market returns.

In addition, we would also expect the returns for hedge funds to be independent of each other. Again, this stems from the skill-based, absolute return claim of hedge fund managers. If hedge fund returns are truly skill-based, not only should they be independent of the returns in the financial markets, but their returns should also be uncorrelated with each other. Benchmarks would be inappropriate.

---

[20] See David Segal, "Market's Crash Destroys Trader: A Risky Bet Brings Down a Millionaire Money Manager," *Washington Post*, November 17, 1997, A1.

[21] The history of Victor Niederhoffer's trading strategy is documented in Philippe Jorion, "Risk Management Lessons from Long Term Capital Management," working paper, University of California at Irvine, January 2000.

Economists and other financial researchers often ask the question, What is the impact of an economic event on the value of a financial asset? Under the principle of efficient capital markets, the effect of the event should be reflected immediately in the asset value. Therefore, the economic impact of the event can be measured using asset prices over a short interval of time.

The objective of an event study is to measure the difference between the actual returns observed with respect to an investment and the returns that are expected to occur in the absence of the observed event. The difference between the actual returns observed and those expected is called the abnormal or excess return. The excess returns are observed around the event date, and conclusions are drawn as to whether the event had a significant impact on an asset class.[22]

We put these claims to the test by conducting an event analysis. The summer of 2007 saw the start of the subprime mortgage meltdown and subsequent credit and liquidity crisis (we will have much more to say about this in our chapters on credit derivatives). July and August of 2007 were the beginning of a long crisis of confidence in the financial markets that lasted for several months.

We use the data from the Hedge Fund Research Inc. Hedge Fund Indices. Using data from 1990 through September of 2008 we conducted an event analysis. We focus on the two-month event period of July and August 2007. These two months capture the beginning of the turmoil from the subprime mortgage meltdown crisis and were characterized by substantial volatility in financial markets. Exhibit 14.7 presents the results of our analysis.[23] For each hedge fund style, we present the excess returns for July and August 2007. We also present the t-statistics associated with these two event months. Student t-statistics greater than or equal to 1.68, 1.97, and 2.30 in absolute value are significant at the 10%, 5%, and 1% level of confidence, respectively. Last, we present the cumulative excess return for the two-month event period of July and August combined. For comparison, in Exhibit 14.7 we also present the excess returns associated with large-cap stocks, high-yield bonds, and U.S. Treasury bonds. As might be expected, high-yield bonds were significantly negatively impacted in July, but did recover somewhat in August. U.S. Treasury bonds performed well as many investors sought the safe haven of U.S. Treasury bonds during this period of uncertainty.

When we examine the two-month event period of September and October of 2008, we can reach some quick conclusions. For example, every hedge fund strategy, with the exception of short sellers, earned negative returns over this two-month time period. Further, all of these negative returns, with the exception of global macro hedge funds, were statistically significant.

Several lessons can be gleaned from this analysis. First, many of the mispricing (arbitrage) opportunities that hedge funds attempt to capture can require an investment horizon of several months or greater. In addition, arbitrage strategies generally make the assumption of normal liquidity. However, when that liquidity dried up, many of the mispricing relationships increased instead of decreasing, thus creating large temporary paper losses. This situation was further exacerbated by margin calls from prime brokers, which forced some hedge fund managers to liquidate their positions and turned paper losses into realized losses.

Second, many lending institutions that provided liquidity to hedge funds were themselves invested in the same markets and under pressure to manage their own risk exposures. These institutions were unable to provide liquidity to the market at the time hedge fund managers needed it the most. Third, many hedge fund strategies are premised on the convergence in pricing of similar securities. At times of market crisis, prices often diverge instead of converging. This temporary imbalance can lead to large short-term losses.

---

[22] For a review of event studies and their application to hedge funds, see Mark Anson, "Financial Market Dislocations and Hedge Fund Returns," *Journal of Alternative Investments* (Winter 2002), 78–88.

[23] For each hedge fund style we use the 102 months of data prior to August 2007 to estimate mean and standard deviation of the index.

In declining mkt, margin call increase and failing that increase the roles by exchange ie selling pressure is high. Also Failure of margin call

248   CAIA Level I   *increase bankruptcy & declining mkt price*

Exhibit 14.7   Hedge fund excess returns

Strategy	Sep-08	t-Stat	Oct-08	t-Stat	Sept-Oct	t-Stat
Equity Long/Short	−8.14%	−3.44	−9.46%	−3.93	−17.60%	−5.21
Market Timing	−10.38%	−2.69	−14.45%	−3.64	−24.83%	−5.53
Short Selling	5.12%	0.84	9.58%	1.62	14.70%	2.46
Activist	−5.91%	−5.48	−5.86%	5.44	−11.77%	−7.72
Regulation D	−1.50%	−1.21	−4.44%	−2.64	−5.94%	−2.72
Distressed Securities	−5.87%	−3.53	−7.93%	−4.59	−13.80%	−5.75
Merger Arbitrage	−2.90%	−2.96	−2.47%	−2.61	−5.37%	−3.95
Event Driven	−6.01%	−3.41	−8.19%	−4.48	−14.20%	−5.59
Fixed Income Arbitrage	−1.71%	−2.02	−1.62%	−1.87	−3.33%	−2.70
Convertible Arbitrage	−11.81%	−6.63	−16.01%	−8.86	−27.82%	−10.96
Market Neutral	−2.87%	−3.72	−0.50%	−1.20	−3.37%	3.48
Statistical Arbitrage	−7.66%	−3.83	−6.01%	−3.07	−13.67%	−4.88
Relative Value	−5.90%	−5.13	−8.03%	−6.76	−13.93%	−8.41
Global Macro	−1.21%	−1.04	1.63%	0.21	0.42%	−0.58
HFRI FOF	−6.54%	−4.13	−6.22%	−3.95	−12.76%	−5.73
HFRI Composite	−6.13%	−3.43	−6.84%	−3.77	−12.97%	−5.09
S&P 500	−9.78%	−2.41	−16.82%	−4.04	−26.60%	−4.60
High Yield	−8.07%	−3.37	−14.96%	−6.03	−23.03%	−6.70
10-Year U.S. Treasury	0.30%	−0.13	−0.90%	−0.70	−0.60%	−0.59

Source: Hedge Fund Research and Datastream.

Finally, hedge fund managers received redemption calls from their investors during this period. This forced hedge fund managers to liquidate positions to fund their customers' redemption requests. Hedge fund managers were faced with a liquidity mismatch between the investment horizons of their arbitrage strategies, the lending horizons of their prime brokers, and the investment horizons of their investors. This was, in fact, a "triple witching hour" of sorts for hedge fund managers. You could not engineer a worse scenario.

In conclusion, what this event analysis demonstrates is that hedge fund returns are influenced by the same financial market dislocations as traditional asset classes. An absence of liquidity in the financial markets can have the same impact on hedge fund managers as it does on long-only managers. A hedge fund manager may have all of its economic risks appropriately balanced or hedged, only to be caught in a liquidity crisis. This is all the more exacerbated to the extent that a hedge fund manager invests in less liquid financial markets or custom-tailored derivative transactions.

BETA EXPANSION RISK

Beta expansion risk is a phenomenon that can happen with respect to those hedge funds that short securities, which is virtually all hedge fund strategies except long-only. To short a security, a hedge fund manager must borrow the security from her prime broker. The prime broker lends the security to the hedge fund manager, who then sells the security in the market with the intention to purchase the security back at a later date once the security has declined in value.

The problem is that hedge fund managers often short the same security in the collective belief/ analysis that the value of that security will decline. This can lead to the condition known as "crowded shorts" (we will have more to say about crowded shorts in Chapter 18, "Top Ten Hedge Fund Quotes").

Exhibit 14.8   Beta expansion risk

Hedge Fund Strategy	Beta Up	R-Squared Up	Beta Down	R-Squared Down	Total Beta	R-Squared Total
HFRI Composite Index	0.18	0.11	0.41	0.36	0.33	0.49
HFRI Event Driven	0.09	0.03	0.43	0.37	0.30	0.42
HFRI Equity Long/Short	0.28	0.12	0.43	0.27	0.42	0.45

Source: Hedge Fund Research.

When a short position in a security becomes crowded, there is extra selling pressure on that security. This can lead to a greater sensitivity of that security to downward changes in the financial markets than to upward movements. In turn, this means that hedge fund managers' performance may have greater sensitivity to downward stock market movements instead of upward movements.

Exhibit 14.8 documents the phenomenon of beta expansion risk. We use the HFRI Composite Index as well as two strategies that specifically incorporate shorting stocks into their investment process: event-driven and equity long/short. We can see that the beta of the hedge fund managers' returns is significantly larger for down markets than for upward market movements, that is, the hedge fund manager's performance is more sensitive to downward stock market movements.

What is the pragmatic conclusion from this example? Simply that hedge fund managers are more sensitive to downward movements, and therefore provide less hedging in a down stock market. This is also confirmed by the R-squared measures in Exhibit 14.8, which demonstrate that a greater percentage of a hedge fund manager's performance is explained by negative stock market movements than by positive stock market movements.

SHORT VOLATILITY RISK

We discussed the situation in the prior chapter that certain hedge fund strategies replicate a short put option position. These are known as short volatility positions because the trading strategy resembles the sale of (shorting) put options. Specifically, we discussed how the corporate restructuring hedge fund strategies most resemble a short put option strategy.

The reason is that these strategies bet on the completion of the corporate event, whether that be a merger, spin-off, restructuring, or successful emergence from bankruptcy. These hedge fund managers underwrite the risk of a successful corporate transaction much the same way as typical insurance companies underwrite the risk of homeowner's insurance. If a home burns to the ground, the homeowner can put his losses back to the insurance company. Similarly, if a corporate event fails to reach fruition, financial market participants collectively put the losses back on the hedge fund manager. Under normal market conditions, no loss is expected, and the hedge fund manager collects a premium for underwriting the risk of the corporate transaction.

To demonstrate this exposure to short volatility, we regress three corporate restructuring strategies, merger arbitrage, distressed debt, and event driven, on the VIX volatility index. If these strategies have significant exposure to short volatility, we should expect to see a negative beta associated with stock market volatility. That is, these strategies should suffer when stock market volatility increases, because they are short volatility strategies.

Exhibit 14.9 confirms our expectations. Each of the corporate restructuring strategies does indeed have a negative beta associated with stock market volatility, indicating a significant relationship between increasing stock market volatility and negative hedge fund returns. The *t*-statistics for each

Exhibit 14.9   Corporate restructuring and short volatility

Hedge Fund Strategy	Beta	*t*-Statistic
Distressed Securities	−0.04	−6.06
Merger Arbitrage	−0.03	−6.28
Event Driven	−0.06	−8.91

strategy are significant at the 0.001% level. Clearly, there is a negative impact of volatility on these hedge fund strategies.

As we noted earlier, an important point with respect to this risk is that it is an off-balance-sheet risk. If you were to look at the balance sheet of a corporate restructuring hedge fund manager, you would see a series of long and short stock positions. From this you might conclude that the hedge fund manager maintains a low-risk portfolio because his stock market exposure is minimized by the offsetting long and short security positions. True enough; corporate restructuring hedge fund managers have limited exposure to the broad securities markets. However, they have considerable exposure to event risk or short volatility risk, and this risk cannot be observed by looking at the hedge fund manager's trading positions.

MULTIMOMENT OPTIMIZATION

The discussion of the prior sections with respect to short volatility strategies shows that hedge fund strategies are exposed to significant short volatility risk. This leads to return distributions that are distinctly nonnormal, with negative skews and long downside fat tails. Furthermore, short volatility risk is off the balance sheet of the hedge fund manager and is not apparent from reviewing the hedge fund manager's trading positions.

To capture the off-balance-sheet risk of a hedge fund manager, higher moments of the return distribution must be incorporated into the optimization procedure. Specifically, the skew and kurtosis of each hedge fund manager must be considered in addition to the mean and volatility of their returns. This requires an optimization process more advanced than the standard mean-variance models used by most investors.

The assumption of normality in hedge fund returns is a weak link in portfolio construction. Anson, Ho, and Silberstein explore this issue and fashion a solution that rejects the assumption of a normal distribution of returns for hedge fund managers.[24] Following the work of Davies, Kat, and Lu, they incorporate higher moments of the return distribution to select a live portfolio of hedge fund managers.[25] They build an optimal portfolio of hedge funds based on the mean return, variance, skewness, and kurtosis. This type of optimization is known as a multiple objective approach to portfolio selection.

To solve this problem, the solution may be expressed as a series of optimized equations. This is called polynomial goal programming. The following notation is used:

$$\text{Mean} = X' E[R]$$

---

[24] See Mark Anson, Ho Ho, and Kurt Silberstein, "Building a Hedge Fund Portfolio with Skewness and Kurtosis," *Journal of Alternative Investments* (2007).

[25] See Ryan Davies, Harry Kat, and Sa Lu, "Fund of Hedge Funds Portfolio Selection: A Multiple Objective Approach," working paper, ISMA Centre, Business School for Financial Markets, University of Reading, 2004.

where

$X = (x_1, x_2, x_3...)$ and $x(i)$ is the percentage of wealth invested with hedge fund (i)

$E[R] = (E[r_1], E[r_2], E[r_3] ...)$ and $E[r(i)]$ is the expected return associated with hedge fund (i)

$$\text{Variance} = X'VX$$

where

$V =$ the variance-covariance matrix of all of the returns (vector $E[R]$) associated with the hedge funds available for selection in the hedge fund portfolio

$$\text{Skewness} = E[X'(R - E[R])/(X'VX)^{1/2}]^3$$

where

$R = (r_1, r_2, r_3 ...)$ and $r(i)$ is the actual return associated with hedge fund (i)

$$\text{Excess kurtosis} = E[X'(R - E[R])/(X'VX)^{1/2}]^4 - [3(t - 1)^2/(t - 2)(t - 3)]$$

referred to henceforth as kurtosis.

With the four moments of the return distribution identified, the portfolio optimization problem may be expressed as:

$$\text{Maximize } X'E[R] \qquad \text{Max Mean} \qquad (14.1)$$

$$\text{Maximize } E[X'(R - E[R])/(X'VX)^{1/2}]^3 \qquad \text{Maxi Skewness.} \qquad (14.2)$$

$$\text{Minimize } E[X'(R - E[R])/(X'VX)^{1/2}]^4 - [3(t - 1)^2/(t - 2)(t - 3)] \quad \text{Mini Kurt} \quad (14.3)$$

Subject to

$$X'VX = 1 \qquad \text{Variance = 1} \qquad (14.4)$$

$$\sum x_i = 1$$

For all $x_i \geq 0$.

Our goal is to select an optimal amount of wealth to be allocated to each hedge fund in the portfolio, represented by the vector of weights $X = (x_1, x_2, x_3 ...)$. The vector of weights must sum to 1 (all money must be invested). Also, we constrain each investment (every x_i) to be positive; that is, the investor cannot go short a hedge fund manager. Last, since the purpose of this exercise is to select the relative percentage to be invested in any hedge fund, the vector of weights, X, can be rescaled so that the variance of the portfolio is restricted to the unit variance space: $X'VX = 1$.

It is unlikely that Equations 14.1 through 14.4 can be satisfied simultaneously. To solve this problem, the PGP solution is typically expressed as:

$$\text{Minimize } Z = (1 + d_1)^a + (1 + d_3)^b + (1 - d_4)^c \qquad (14.5)$$

Subject to

$$X'E[R] + d_1 = Z^* \tag{14.6}$$

$$[X'(R - E[R])/(X'VX)^{1/2}]^3 + d_3 = Z_3 \tag{14.7}$$

$$E[X'(R - E[R])/(X'VX)^{1/2}]^4 - [3(t - 1)^2/(t - 2)(t - 3)] + d_4 = Z_4 \tag{14.8}$$

$$\sum x_i = 1 \tag{14.9}$$

$$\text{For all } x_i \geq 0 \tag{14.10}$$

where

$d_1,\ d_3 \geq 0$
$\quad d_4 \leq 0$

Z_1^*, Z_3^*, and Z_4^* represent the optimal values for Equations 14.1, 14.2, and 14.3. The value d_1 represents the distance or deviation of the expected portfolio mean from the optimal value expressed in Equation 14.1. Similarly, d_3 is the distance or deviation from the expected portfolio skewness and the optimal value represented by Z_3, and d_4 represents the distance or deviation from the expected portfolio kurtosis and the optimal portfolio kurtosis represented by Z^*.

The goal of Equation 14.5 is to minimize the deviations associated with the mean return (d_1), skewness (d_3), and kurtosis (d_4) of the resulting portfolio from the optimal portfolio values of mean return, skewness, and kurtosis. The parameters a, b, and c represent an investor's preferences for the values of mean return, skewness, and kurtosis. In a traditional mean-variance optimization, the values of b and c are zero.

Exhibit 14.10 shows the distributional statistics for an existing portfolio of hedge fund managers. Note that all of these strategies have significant skewness and kurtosis and the assumption of normality is explicitly rejected. Exhibit 14.11 provides a demonstration of using multimoment optimization. The top line, marked by small triangles, is the performance of the hedge fund portfolio incorporating skewness and kurtosis into the optimization process. The bottom line, marked by squares, is the standard mean-variance (MV) optimization. Clearly, the multimoment optimization provides superior performance. (The mean-variance portfolio represents the existing portfolio returns, whereas the multimoment portfolio was constructed going back in time and building an optimal hedge fund portfolio as if skewness and kurtosis had been incorporated from the beginning.)

CONCLUSION

The hedge fund industry has received tremendous attention over the past decade as an alternative investment strategy to hedge traditional portfolio returns. However, as a relatively new investment strategy, there are new risks that bear consideration. This chapter does not purport to cover every risk associated with hedge fund managers. Indeed, such a full discussion would require a whole separate treatise of several hundred pages. Instead, in this chapter we selected the essential risk factors that every investor must confront when investing in hedge funds. While the discussion is not exhaustive, we believe an investor can structure a successful hedge fund program if she can successfully manage the risks outlined in this chapter.

We also need to be aware of another type of risk when investing in hedge funds, the systemic risk (Fung and Hsieh 2006). This is the risk that large losses from one or more hedge funds may affect their counterparties, thus creating a domino effect with regard to other institutions and investors.

Exhibit 14.10 Descriptive statistics and statistical tests (equally weighted hedge fund strategy portfolio)

	Data Range	Normality Test at 5%	Autocorrel. Test at 5%	Maximum	Minimum	Mean	Monthly Std. Dev.	Mean/Std. Dev.	Skewness	Kurtosis
Equity L/S	1/99–5/05	No	No	0.096	−0.029	0.012	0.021	0.572	1.093	5.916
Multistrategy	1/99–5/05	Yes	Yes	0.065	−0.049	0.011	0.020	0.549	−0.284	3.788
Statistical Arbitrage	1/99–5/05	No	Yes	0.188	−0.065	0.011	0.038	0.278	1.722	9.085
Convertible Arbitrage	1/99–5/05	Yes	Yes	0.073	−0.056	0.009	0.024	0.375	0.297	3.786
Global Macro	1/99–5/05	Yes	No	0.044	−0.034	0.008	0.018	0.425	−0.095	2.567
Credit L/S	1/99–5/05	No	No	0.066	−0.034	0.011	0.016	0.693	0.059	4.733
Fixed Income Arbitrage	1/99–5/05	No	Yes	0.110	−0.040	0.007	0.023	0.316	1.473	8.336

Source: Mark Anson, Ho Ho, and Kurt Silberstein, "Building a Hedge Fund Portfolio with Skewness and Kurtosis," *Journal of Alternative Investments* (2007).

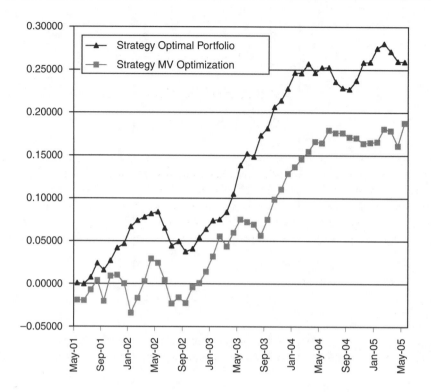

Exhibit 14.11   Multimoment Optimization

Source: Mark Anson, *Handbook of Alternative Assets*, 2nd ed. (Hoboken, NJ: John Wiley & Sons, 2006). Reprinted with permission of John Wiley & Sons, Inc.

Although regulators consider that systemic risk should be dealt with by existing regulation of other counterparties and banks, rather than by new laws, the events of 2008 have once again reignited this issue.

A number of regulators worry about the impact that a hedge fund failure may have on financial markets (e.g. the effects of the near bankruptcy of Long-Term Capital Management in 1998); others, however, contend that most hedge funds are still too small to be able to influence particular markets. In this regard, Fung and Hsieh (2006) argue that the impact that hedge funds may have on markets has changed from the failure of a mega hedge fund to that of a "convergence of leveraged opinions" among hedge funds that individually may function unnoticed. A convergence of leveraged opinions is an event in which the forecasts of a group of hedge funds converge onto the same set of bets, thus potentially threatening the normal functioning of financial markets and creating systemic risk.

15

Hedge Fund Benchmarks and
Asset Allocation

Initially, hedge funds were the domain of high-net-worth individuals. However, in the latter half of the 1990s, large institutional investors discovered the charms of these investments. Endowments and foundations were first, followed by corporate and public pension plans. As more and more institutional investors entered the hedge fund arena, they demanded many of the investment parameters that they had come to expect from their traditional long-only programs.

Generally, with respect to external investment managers, institutional investors demand three things:

1. A well-defined investment process.
2. Transparency.
3. Relative returns.

It is the last requirement, relative returns, that we explore in this chapter. Relative returns are one of the primary reasons for index construction. Index construction, in turn, has three benefits:

1. Transparency.
2. Performance measurement.
3. Asset allocation.

We begin by reviewing issues regarding the construction of hedge fund indices. Next we compare and contrast the hedge fund indices in existence. We then consider some issues regarding the selection of hedge fund indices. Last, we review several of the hedge fund indices to see how useful they might be in determining the appropriate amount of assets to be allocated to the hedge fund sector.

HEDGE FUNDS AS AN INVESTMENT

As Brown, Goetzmann, and Ibbotson note, the most interesting feature of the hedge fund industry is that an investment in a hedge fund is almost a pure bet on the skill of a specific manager.[1] Hedge fund managers tend to seek out arbitrage or mispricing opportunities in the financial markets using a variety of cash and derivative instruments. They take small amounts of market exposure to exploit mispricing opportunities, but employ large amounts of leverage to extract the greatest value. The key point is that hedge fund managers pursue investment strategies unfettered by conventional financial market benchmarks. Their investment styles are alpha-driven rather than beta-driven.

In prior chapters we have shown that hedge funds have favorable risk/return benefits compared to traditional stocks and bonds and that hedge funds have demonstrated ability to add value to a traditional portfolio of stocks and bonds.

---

[1] Stephen Brown, William Goetzmann, and Roger Ibbotson, "Offshore Hedge Funds: Survival and Performance, 1989–1995," *Journal of Business* 72, no. 1 (1999), 91–117.

However, capturing this pure skill can be problematic. Still, hedge fund indices serve two key purposes. First, they serve as a proxy for the hedge fund asset class. This is important for asset allocation studies. Second, hedge fund indices can serve as performance benchmarks to judge the success or failure of hedge fund managers. However, as we demonstrate later, there are many differences among the several hedge fund index products offered. We begin with a discussion on index construction.

ISSUES WITH HEDGE FUND INDEX CONSTRUCTION

In this chapter we review the information on 17 hedge fund indices. Each index is based on a different number of hedge funds, ranging from 38 to over 8,500. Most of these indices use simple averages, whereas others use capital-weighted indices. Also, some index providers collect the underlying data themselves, whereas others allow the hedge fund managers to enter the data. Some hedge fund indices include managed futures, whereas some do not. In sum, there are many different construction techniques of hedge fund indices. We discuss the challenges of implementing these methodologies in the following pages.

The size of the hedge fund universe

One of the problems with constructing a hedge fund index is that the size of the total universe of hedge funds is not known with certainty. It is currently estimated that there are some 9,200 hedge funds in existence with assets of about $1.5 trillion.[2] 2008 was an especially difficult year for hedge funds. Hedge Fund Research, Inc. measured 1,471 hedge fund liquidations in 2008, while only 328 new hedge funds came to the market, for a net decline of 1,143 hedge funds.

The uncertainty regarding the true size of the hedge fund industry stems from the fact that for most of its history it was an unregulated industry. For a short period of time, the Securities and Exchange Commission (SEC) required hedge funds to register as investment advisers under the Investment Advisers Act of 1940. Indeed, one of the reasons the SEC cited for pursuing this rule making was to provide census data on the number and size of hedge fund managers. These rules were applied for hedge fund managers beginning in 2006. Previously, hedge funds had no requirement to report their performance to an index provider. They enjoyed relative secrecy, in contrast to their mutual fund counterparts. Although the SEC rule has since been abandoned, most hedge funds have now registered as investment advisers; this is in keeping with the continued entrée of institutional investors into the hedge fund arena.

Mutual funds are regulated investment companies that are required to register with the SEC. In addition, investment advisers to mutual funds are also required to register with the SEC. In fact, mutual funds are considered public investment companies that issue public securities (mutual fund shares) on a continual basis. Therefore, they are required by law to report and publish their performance numbers to the SEC and to the public.

Although the hedge fund industry has become more transparent, a good example of the lack of knowledge about the exact size of the hedge fund universe was demonstrated by Liang.[3] He studied the composition of indices constructed by two well-known providers: TASS and Hedge

---

[2] See Hedge Fund Research, Inc., "Record Number of Hedge Funds Liquidate in 2008," March 18, 2009; and London Business School, BizResearch, "Hedge Funds 2009—Assets Under Management Fell by Nearly 30% in 2008," April 7, 2009.

[3] Bing Liang, "Hedge Funds: The Living and the Dead," *Journal of Financial and Quantitative Analysis* 35, no. 3 (September 2000), 309–326.

Fund Research Inc.[4] At the time of his study, there were 1,162 hedge funds in the HFR index and 1,627 hedge funds in the TASS index. He found that only 465 hedge funds were common to both hedge fund indices. Further, of these 465 common hedge funds, only 154 had data covering the same time period.

Another problem with measuring the size of the hedge fund universe is that the attrition rate for hedge funds is quite high. Park, Brown, and Goetzmann[5] and Brown, Goetzmann, and Ibbotson[6] find that the average life of a hedge fund manager is 2.5 to 3 years. The short half-life of the average hedge fund means that there will be considerable turnover on an annual basis with respect to hedge fund index construction. In conclusion, the hedge fund universe is not known with certainty, there is a large gap in the overlap between hedge fund index providers, and the high attrition rate for hedge funds results in constant turnover of the index construction.

Data biases

In Chapter 14 we talked about data risk when reviewing hedge fund performance. There are several data biases associated with hedge fund databases. The first is the well-known survivorship bias. **Survivorship bias**, which was introduced in the previous chapter, arises when constructing a hedge fund index today based on hedge fund managers that have survived the time period of study and are available for index construction. Those hedge fund managers that have not survived are excluded from the index construction. This creates an upward bias to the performance of a hedge fund index because, presumably, the remaining hedge funds survived as a result of their superior performance. The survivorship bias can be measured as the average return of surviving funds in excess of the average return of all funds, both surviving and defunct. Survivorship bias can amount from 2.6% to 5% a year. This bias is also common with mutual fund studies.

A common misperception is that available published hedge fund indices have significant survivorship bias. Survivorship is a problem that affects databases, but not necessarily hedge fund indices. The reason is that most published hedge fund indices use all available managers who report to the database to create the index. Subsequently, some of these managers may stop reporting to the database for a variety of reasons. Performance of these managers will not be reflected in the future values of the index. However, the historical performance of these managers will continue to be reflected in the past values of the index. In this sense, published indices are similar to public equity indices. For example, historical performance of Lehman Brothers or Enron will continue to be part of historical performance of the Russell 1000 index. Also, if one were to start a new index today based on the managers who report as of today, then historical performance of this index will suffer from survivorship bias because it does not include performance of all those managers who stopped reporting to the database during previous periods.

The lack of a regulatory environment for hedge funds creates the opportunity for other data biases that are unique to the hedge fund industry. In addition to survivorship bias, there are three other biases that may affect average performance figures estimated from databases. First, there is *selection* bias. Essentially, hedge fund managers have a free option to report their data. This bias is also present in published databases. Since hedge fund managers report to public databases on a voluntary basis, there is selection bias present in all databases. This bias affects past values of the

---

[4] The TASS database is now used by the joint venture of CSFB/Tremont Advisors.

[5] Brown, Goetzmann, and Ibbotson, "Offshore Hedge Funds."

[6] James Park, Stephen Brown, and William Goetzmann, "Performance Benchmarks and Survivorship Bias for Hedge Funds and Commodity Trading Advisors," *Hedge Fund News*, August 1999.

indices as well as their future values.[7] It is very difficult to quantify the magnitude of this important bias.

Closely related to selection bias is **instant history** or **backfill bias**. Instant history bias occurs because once a hedge fund manager begins to report his performance to a database provider, the provider backfills the hedge fund manager's historical performance into the database. Again, because it is more likely that a hedge fund manager will begin reporting his performance after a period of good performance, this bias pushes the historical performance of managers upward. Again, similar to survivorship bias, this bias does not affect historical performance of most published indices. The reason is that most index providers do not revise the history of an index once a new manager is added to the index. That is, only current and future performance of the manager affects the index. Users of hedge fund indices must check to determine the date that an index went public, because the performance figures of the index for periods prior to the launch date are subject to both survivorship and backfill biases.

Estimates for backfill bias are highly dependent on the database that is being used. In general, average value of backfilled performance can be as low as 1% to as high as 5% per year higher than the performance of the manager after being listed in a database.

A related concept is that of the **hazard rate**, which is defined as the proportion of hedge funds that drop out of a database at a given age. For example, Fung and Hsieh (2006) find that the highest dropout rate occurs when a hedge fund is 14 months old. The impact of this bias is that if an index is constructed that would require at least 24 months of performance history, a large number of funds may be excluded from this index, introducing a bias.

Last, there is **liquidation bias**. Frequently, hedge fund managers go out of business or shut down an unsuccessful hedge fund. When this happens, these managers stop reporting their performance in advance of the cessation of operations. In other words, several months of poor performance are lost because hedge fund managers are more concerned with winding down their operations than they are in reporting their performance to an index provider.[8] To the degree that managers do not report large negative returns to databases, these figures do not get reflected in published databases. Therefore, this bias increases the reported performance of published indices.

In Chapter 14 on risk management, we noted that these biases can add up to 3% to 10% of annual enhancement to an average performance of the managers who report to a database. It is important to take note of these biases because they cannot be diversified away by constructing a portfolio of indices since all indices suffer from these biases. We reprint the biases table from Chapter 14 here as Exhibit 15.1 to refresh the reader's memory on the size of these biases and their impact on hedge fund returns.

Strategy definition and style drift

Strategy definitions can be very difficult to establish for index providers. An index must have enough strategies to capture the broad market for hedge fund returns. Index providers determine their own hedge fund strategy classification system, and this varies from index to index.

Consider a hedge fund manager that goes long the stock of a target company subject to a merger bid and short the stock of the acquiring company. The strategy of this hedge fund manager may

---

[7] As we mentioned in the previous chapter, a contrary argument can be made for selection bias: that good hedge fund managers choose not to report their data to hedge fund index providers because they have no need to attract additional assets.

[8] The flip side to liquidation bias is participation bias. This bias may occur for a successful hedge fund manager who closes his fund and stops reporting his results because he no longer needs to attract new capital.

Exhibit 15.1   Biases associated with hedge fund data

Bias	Park, Brown, and Goetzmann, 1999	Brown, Goetzmann, and Ibbotson, 1999	Fung and Hsieh, 2000	Ackermann, McEnally, and Ravenscraft, 1999	Barry, 2003	Ibbotson and Chen, 2006
Survivorship	2.60%	3.00%	3.00%	0.01%	3.70%	5.68%
Selection	1.90%	Not estimated	Not estimated	No impact	Not estimated	Not estimated
Instant history	Not estimated	Not estimated	1.40%	No impact	0.40%	5.01%
Liquidation	Not estimated	Not estimated	Not estimated	0.70%	Not estimated	Not estimated
Total	4.50%	3.00%	4.40%	0.71%	4.10%	

Sources: James Park, Stephen Brown, and William Goetzmann, "Performance Benchmarks and Survivorship Bias for Hedge Funds and Commodity Trading Advisors," *Hedge Fund News,* August 1999; Stephen Brown, William Goetzmann, and Roger Ibbotson, "Offshore Hedge Funds: Survival and Performance, 1989–1995," *Journal of Business* 72, no. 1 (1999), 91–117; William Fung and David Hsieh, "Performance Characteristics of Hedge Funds and Commodity Funds: Natural versus Spurious Biases," *Journal of Financial and Quantitative Analysis* 25 (2000), 291–307; Carl Ackermann, Richard McEnally, and David Ravenscraft, "The Performance of Hedge Funds: Risk, Return, and Incentives," *Journal of Finance* (June 1999), 833–874; and Ross Barry, "Hedge Funds: A Walk through the Graveyard," MFAC Research Paper 25, September 20, 2002.

be classified alternatively as merger arbitrage by one index provider (e.g. HFR), relative value by another index provider (e.g. CASAM/CISDM), or event driven by still another index provider (e.g. CSFB/Tremont). In summary, there is no consistent definition of hedge fund styles among index providers. Indeed, the dynamic trading nature of hedge funds makes them difficult to classify, and this is part of the appeal of hedge fund managers.

Further complicating the strategy definition is that most hedge fund managers are classified according to the disclosure language in their offering documents. However, consider the following language from an actual hedge fund private placement memorandum:

> Consistent with the General Partner's opportunistic approach, there are no fixed limitations as to specific asset classes invested in by the Partnership. The Partnership is not limited with respect to the types of investment strategies it may employ or the markets or instruments in which it may invest.

Where to classify this manager? Relative value? Global macro? Market neutral? Unfortunately, with hedge funds, this type of strategy description is commonplace. The lack of specificity may lead to guesswork on the part of index providers with respect to the manager's strategy. Alternatively, some index providers may leave this manager out because of lack of clarity (e.g. Zurich Hedge Fund Indices), but this adds another bias to the index by purposely excluding certain types of hedge fund managers. In sum, there is no established format for classifying hedge funds. Each index provider develops its own scheme without concern for consistency with other hedge fund index providers, and this makes comparisons between hedge fund indices difficult.

Even if an index provider can successfully classify a hedge fund manager's investment strategy, there is the additional problem of strategy drift. Again, because of the mostly unregulated nature of hedge fund managers, there is no requirement for a hedge fund manager to notify an index provider when his investment style has changed.

Let's continue with our example of merger arbitrage managers. During the recession of 2001 and the financial crisis of 2008, the market for mergers and acquisitions declined significantly (except for investment banks, brokerage firms, and traditional banks!). There were simply too few deals to feed all of the merger arbitrage manager mouths. Consequently, many of these managers changed their investment style to invest in the rising tide of distressed debt deals, which are countercyclical from mergers and acquisitions. In addition, many merger arbitrage managers expanded their investment portfolios to consider other corporate transactions, such as spin-offs and recapitalizations. Typically, once a hedge fund manager has been classified as merger arbitrage it will remain in that category despite significant changes in its investment focus.

Finally, a growing recent trend in the industry has been for hedge funds to evolve from single-strategy specialists into multistrategy hedge funds. Furthermore, Fung and Hsieh (2006) comment on the growing research of so-called synthetic hedge funds, which are defined as the replication of hedge-fund-like returns using mathematical models; these funds are available at a lower cost to investors.[9]

Index investability

A key issue is whether a hedge fund index can be or should be investable. This is an issue for hedge funds that is distinct and different from their mutual fund counterparts. Mutual funds are public companies. They can and do continually offer their shares to the public. Capacity issues are virtually nonexistent. However, hedge funds generally do have capacity issues, as certain strategies work well only within certain limits of investment capital. This means that hedge fund managers often refuse further capital when they have achieved a maximum level of assets under management. Consequently, it is very difficult for hedge fund indices to remain investable when the underlying hedge funds close their doors to new investors.

A related issue is whether hedge fund indices should be investable. The argument is that an investable index will exclude hedge fund managers that are closed to new investors and therefore will exclude a large section of the hedge fund universe. Most index providers argue that to be a truly representative index that acts as a barometer for hedge fund performance, both open and closed funds should be included. The trade-off, therefore, is between having as broad a representation as possible of hedge fund performance versus having a smaller pool of hedge fund managers that represent the performance that may be accessed through investment.

In a recent working paper, Billio, Getmansky, and Pelizzon (2007) examine four different daily data sets of investable hedge fund return indices (MSCI, FTSE, Dow Jones, and HFRX), and three different monthly data sets of hedge fund return indices (CSFB, CASAM/CISDM, and HFR), which include both investable and noninvestable funds. The authors compare the characteristics of these databases and determine that investability is an important characteristic that affects the distributions of hedge funds' returns. The authors report that daily indices have different properties than monthly indices. The reason is that daily indices may suffer from access bias. To construct these daily indices, the index providers must have access to managers who are willing to provide daily performance figures. This means these managers may not be able to invest in illiquid assets. Further, these managers must have the capacity to accept new capital. The managers who report on a monthly basis to various databases are not subject to these restrictions. This is one of the reasons that investable indices have generally underperformed noninvestable indices.

HEDGE FUND INDICES

In this section we provide summary information on 17 hedge fund index providers. These indices vary as to the number of hedge fund managers, types of strategies employed, and investability. Exhibit 15.2 summarizes the key attributes of the hedge fund indices.

---

[9] William Fung and David Hsieh, "Hedge Funds: An Industry in its Adolescence," *Federal Reserve Bank of Atlanta Economic Review*, fourth quarter, 2006.

Exhibit 15.2 Summary of hedge fund indices

Index Provider	Provides a Single Index	Data History	Number of Subindices	Number of Funds	Includes CTAs	Equal or Asset Weighted	Investable or Noninvestable	Net of Fees	Web Site
Altvest Hedge Fund Indices	Yes	1993	13	8,000	Yes	Equal	No	Yes	www.altvest.com
Barclay Hedge Fund Indices	Yes	1980	27	3,000	Yes	Equal	Both	Yes	www.barclayhedge.com
Bloomberg Active Indices for Funds Indices	Yes	2005	18	475	Yes	Equal	No	Yes	www.bloomberg.com
CASAM/CISDM Indices	Yes	1972	15	6,000	Yes	Equal	No	Yes	www.casamhedge.com
Credit Suisse/Tremont TASS Hedge Fund Indices	Yes	1994	13	5,000	Yes	Asset	Both	Yes	www.hedgeindex.com
Dow Jones Hedge Fund Indices	Yes	2002	6	38	No	Equal	Yes	Yes	www.djhedgefundindices.com
EDHEC Alternative Indices*	No	1997	13	10	Yes	Other	No	Yes	www.edhec-risk.com
Eurekahedge	Yes	2000	10	7,000	Yes	Equal	No	Yes	www.eurekahedge.com
FTSE Hedge Indices	Yes	2002	12	43	Yes	Asset	Yes	Yes	www.ftse.com
Greenwich Alternative Investments Indices	Yes	1995	24	7,000	Yes	Equal	Both	Yes	www.greenwichai.com
Hedge Fund Net/Tuna Hedge Fund Indices	Yes	1990	37	8,500	Yes	Equal	No	Yes	www.hedgefund.net
Hedge Fund Intelligence Indices—InvestHedge	No	1998	61	2,600	Yes	Equal	No	Yes	www.hedgefundintelligence.com
Hennessee Hedge Fund Indices	Yes	1993	26	3,500	No	Equal	No	Yes	www.hennesseegroup.com
HFR Hedge Fund Indices	Yes	1990	28	2,800	No	Both	Both	Yes	www.hedgefundresearch.com
Morningstar Hedge Fund Indices	Yes	1993	17	8,500	Yes	Equal	No	Yes	www.morningstar.com
MSCI Hedge Fund Indices	Yes	2002	8	3,600	No	Both	Yes	Yes	www.mscibarra.com
RBC Hedge 250	Yes	2005	9	250	Yes	Equal	Yes	Yes	www.rbchedge250.com

*Index of indices.

At a glance, we see that these index providers have significant variation in the number of hedge funds they track, the number of subindices that they offer, whether they are capitalization weighted or equally weighted, the date they were launched, and so on. Beyond the information presented, the key takeaway from this table is the distinct lack of consistency in hedge fund index construction. Each index is unique, and very little overlap should be expected. We discuss some of their key differences next.

Management and incentive fees

Similar to the case of mutual funds, hedge funds charge a fixed management fee (calculated as a percentage of net assets under management). According to Fung and Hsieh (2006), more than 70% of live hedge funds (in TASS, HFR, and CASAM/CISDM databases) charge a management fee between 1% and 2%.[10] However, unlike mutual funds, hedge funds also charge an incentive or performance fee (a fee that is a portion of hedge fund remuneration that is tied to the hedge fund's performance). The same authors also determine that approximately 80% of live hedge funds in the aforementioned three databases charge a 20% incentive fee.

All of the hedge fund indices listed in Exhibit 15.2 calculate hedge fund performance net of fees. However, there are two issues related to fees that can result in different performance than portrayed by a hedge fund index. First, incentive fees are normally calculated on an annual basis. However, all of these indices provide month-by-month performance. Therefore, on a monthly basis, incentive fees must be estimated and subtracted from performance. The actual fees collected at year-end may be very different from the monthly estimates.

Second, hedge funds are a form of private investing. Indeed, virtually all hedge funds are structured as private limited partnerships. As a consequence, the terms of specific investments in hedge funds often may not be negotiated in a consistent manner among different investors or across different time periods. The lack of consistency means that the net-of-fees returns earned by one investor may not be what another investor can negotiate. In fact, the more successful the hedge fund manager, the greater the likelihood that he will increase his fee structure to take advantage of his success. The end result is that index returns may overstate what a new investor can obtain in the hedge fund marketplace. We call this the fee bias.

At least one index provider has offered an investment product tied to the performance of the index. Credit Suisse First Boston (CSFB) in conjunction with the Tremont Hedge Fund Index has offered an investable CSFB/Tremont product tied to the total return of the Tremont Hedge Fund Composite.

Turnover

Most of the turnover with respect to hedge fund indices tends to be one-sided. That is, the index composite grows as more hedge funds report their performance to the index provider. However, some hedge funds go out of business or close to new investors and cease reporting their returns. This can lead to several of the data biases presented in Exhibit 15.1. In sum, turnover tends to be low, with more hedge fund returns added to the composite over time.

Inclusion of managed futures

Managed futures, or Commodity Trading Advisors (CTAs), are sometimes considered a sub-set of the hedge fund universe. These are investment managers who invest in the commodity

---

[10] Ibid.

futures markets using either fundamental economic analysis or trend-following models. CTAs may invest in financial futures, energy futures, agriculture futures, metals futures, livestock futures, or currency futures. Because their trading style and the markets in which they invest are different from other hedge fund managers (mostly trend-following models), CTAs and managed futures accounts are sometimes segregated from the hedge fund universe. In fact, we discuss managed futures separately in Part IV, which follows our discussion of hedge funds. From Exhibit 15.2, we can see that most of the hedge fund index providers include managed futures in their databases.

Performance

Exhibit 15.3 demonstrates the historical performance of the 17 indices. The most striking observation is that the risk-return performance of the indices varies significantly. The highest return is associated with the Tuna funds, with an average annual return of almost 16%, and the lowest return is associated with HFRX (4.64%). Also, the standard deviation of annual returns ranges from 7.4% for the CSFB/Tremont TASS Hedge Fund Index to 3% for the Dow Jones Hedge Fund Index.

We also include as an additional reference the risk and return of the S&P 500, the Russell 1000 and 2000 stock indices, the Mount Lucas Trend-following Index (an index used to replicate CTA returns), and 10-year U.S. Treasury bonds. What is distinctly noticeable from Exhibit 15.3 is that all

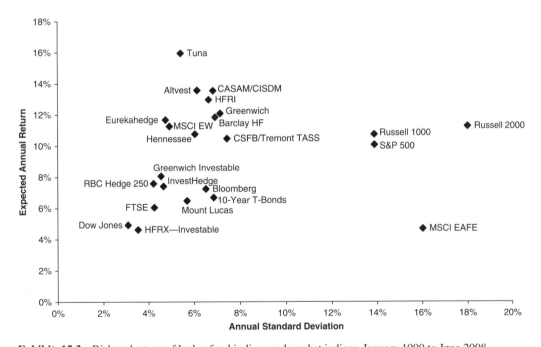

Exhibit 15.3   Risk and return of hedge fund indices and market indices, January 1990 to June 2008

Source: Own calculations based on Datastream and Altvest Hedge Fund Indices, Barclay Hedge Fund Indices, Bloomberg Active Indices for Funds Indices, CASAM/CISDM Indices, Credit Suisse/Tremont TASS Hedge Fund Indices, Dow Jones Hedge Fund Indices, EDHEC Alternative Indices, Eurekahedge FTSE Hedge Indices, Greenwich Alternative Investments Indices, Hedge Fund Net/Tuna Hedge Fund Indices, HedgeFund Intelligence Indices—InvestHedge, Hennessee Hedge Fund Indices, HFR Hedge Fund Indices, Morningstar Hedge Fund Indices, MSCI Hedge Fund Indices, and RBC Hedge 250.

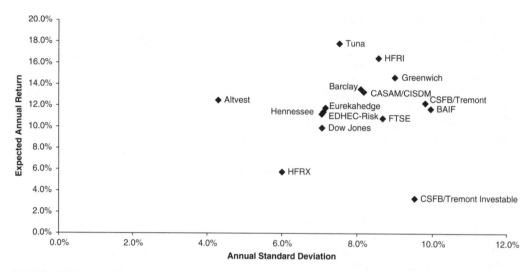

Exhibit 15.4   Long/short equity hedge fund subindices, January 1990 to June 2008

Source: Own calculations based on Datastream and Altvest Hedge Fund Indices, Barclay Hedge Fund Indices, Bloomberg Active Indices for Funds Indices, CASAM/CISDM Indices, Credit Suisse/Tremont TASS Hedge Fund Indices, Dow Jones Hedge Fund Indices, EDHEC Alternative Indices, Eurekahedge FTSE Hedge Indices, Greenwich Alternative Investments Indices, Hedge Fund Net/Tuna Hedge Fund Indices, HedgeFund Intelligence Indices—InvestHedge, Hennessee Hedge Fund Indices, HFR Hedge Fund Indices, Morningstar Hedge Fund Indices, MSCI Hedge Fund Indices, and RBC Hedge 250.

of the hedge fund indices have much lower volatility than the equity indices have. The stock market indices have volatility in the 14% to 18% range, double and even triple that for the hedge fund indices. In fact, most of the hedge fund indices demonstrate even less volatility than the 10-year U.S. Treasury bond, and many have higher returns than U.S. Treasury bonds. In an earlier chapter we discussed how hedge funds might be used as a fixed income substitute. Exhibit 15.3 demonstrates clearly this applicability.

Exhibit 15.3 underscores our earlier comments regarding the diversity of index construction and the fact that the size of the hedge fund universe is not known with certainty. Further, the wide range of historical risk-return performance carries over to the hedge fund subindices. In Exhibit 15.4, we present the historical risk-return profile for equity long/short indices.[11] There is just as much variability with an individual hedge fund style as there is with the composite indices.

All of this means that when choosing a hedge fund composite index or subindex, an investor must use care to ensure that the chosen index is representative of her hedge fund investment program. For example, the HFRI Equity Hedge Index and the FTSE Equity Hedge Index have almost the same volatility, 8.56% and 8.61%, respectively. However, their expected returns vary significantly, with 16.47% earned by the HFRI Equity Hedge Index and 10.81% for the FTSE Index. Consequently, a program that is constructed with hedge funds that resemble more the risk and return profile of the FTSE Index would lead to poor comparative performance metrics for an equity long/short program that resembles more the universe of equity long/short managers contained in the HFRI Subindex.

---

[11] Equity long/short hedge fund subindices are also referred to as equity hedge (HFR and EACM), or long/short hedged (Tuna).

Correlation across hedge fund indices and stock indices

Exhibit 15.5 presents a table of correlation measures between the hedge fund indices and the stock indices. We omit the S&P Hedge Fund Index and the MSCI Hedge Fund Index from this analysis because of their shorter, pro forma track records.

The variability of historical risk-return profiles is demonstrated in the correlation coefficients between the hedge fund indices. The coefficients range from a high of 0.99 between the Barclay Hedge Fund Index and the CASAM/CISDM Index to a low correlation coefficient of 0.00 between the Barclay BTOP Index and the Hennessee Hedge Fund Index. Most of the correlation coefficients are in the range of 0.7 to 0.9. Compared to correlation coefficients between the equity stock indices, the correlation coefficients between the hedge fund indices are similar.

It is worthwhile to note that the Barclay CTA Composite Index is negatively correlated with the stock indices and has a very low correlation with the hedge fund indices. With respect to hedge fund indices, a large component of these strategies comprises convergent (arbitrage) type managers. That is, many hedge fund managers engage in arbitrage trades where they expect the prices of two securities to converge over time. As we discussed in a previous chapter, these types of strategies are also known as short volatility. However, managed futures strategies tend to be long volatility trades, or divergent trading. They thrive on higher volatility. As a result, managed futures provide good diversification benefits for other hedge fund styles.

It is interesting to note that the hedge fund indices are much more highly correlated with small-cap stocks (represented by the Russell 2000) than with large-cap stocks (S&P 500) or mid-cap stocks (Russell 1000).[12] We offer two suggestions for this observation. First, the small-cap stock market is generally considered to be less efficient than large-cap or mid-cap stocks. To the extent that this market is driven by the similar pricing anomalies that drive hedge fund investment returns, a higher correlation of returns would be expected. Second, hedge fund managers may concentrate in small-cap stocks as a way to avoid the phenomenon of so-called crowded shorts. That is, hedge fund managers prefer to short stocks that do not already have a large short interest typically associated with larger-capitalized companies.

Last, we observe that most of the hedge fund index returns are negatively correlated with the returns to U.S. Treasury bonds. This provides another source of diversification with respect to fixed income investments. This is even more interesting because, as we noted earlier in this chapter, the long-term returns demonstrated by the hedge fund indices show returns that are more bondlike than equitylike. When we combine this observation with the results of Exhibit 15.5, we reach the conclusion that we can achieve bondlike returns with hedge funds and, at the same time, provide diversification benefits from bonds, a fascinating conclusion.

Asset-weighted versus equally weighted

An asset-weighted index is susceptible to disproportionate representation from large funds that have a very large gain or loss in any given time period. An asset-weighted index can also be distorted by errors in reporting by larger funds. Further, some of the largest funds choose not to report their data to public databases, and it may be difficult to interpret an asset-weighted index return that does not include some of the larger hedge funds.

Equal weighting has the advantage of not favoring large funds or hedge fund strategies that attract a lot of capital (like global macro or relative value). Investors may be prone to chasing either returns or the latest hedge fund flavor of the year. This can distort a market-capitalization index because

---

[12] I am indebted to Matt Moran of the Chicago Board Options Exchange for pointing this out to me.

Exhibit 15.5 Correlation coefficients between hedge fund indices and stock indices, January 2000 to June 2008

	10-Year T-Bond	Russell 1000	Russell 2000	MSCI EAFE	S&P 500	Barclay CTA	Barclay HF	Barclay BTOP	CASAM/ CISDM	FTSE	Hennessee	HFRI	Mount Lucas	MSCI AW	MSCI EW	TASS	Eurekahedge	Greenwich	InvestHedge	Tuna	Altvest
10-Year T-Bond	1.00																				
Russell 1000	−0.37	1.00																			
Russell 2000	−0.36	0.76	1.00																		
MSCI EAFE	−0.30	0.84	0.74	1.00																	
S&P 500	−0.37	1.00	0.72	0.84	1.00																
Barclay CTA	0.32	−0.19	−0.04	−0.03	−0.20	1.00															
Barclay HF	−0.24	0.70	0.83	0.76	0.66	0.09	1.00														
Barclay BTOP	0.30	−0.23	−0.08	−0.06	−0.23	0.94	0.03	1.00													
CASAM/CISDM	−0.23	0.70	0.84	0.75	0.65	0.07	0.94	0.00	1.00												
FTSE	−0.12	0.37	0.53	0.49	0.35	0.32	0.75	0.34	0.71	1.00											
Hennessee	−0.26	0.70	0.86	0.75	0.65	0.06	0.97	0.00	0.98	0.69	1.00										
HFRI	−0.24	0.73	0.86	0.78	0.69	0.10	0.98	0.03	0.99	0.70	0.98	1.00									
Mount Lucas	0.24	−0.20	−0.06	−0.13	−0.21	0.50	0.06	0.49	0.04	0.26	0.06	0.04	1.00								
MSCI AW	−0.15	0.48	0.68	0.62	0.44	0.34	0.91	0.31	0.90	0.83	0.91	0.90	0.25	1.00							
MSCI EW	−0.17	0.57	0.73	0.68	0.54	0.31	0.95	0.27	0.93	0.85	0.92	0.92	0.21	0.97	1.00						
TASS	−0.08	0.44	0.69	0.60	0.39	0.28	0.86	0.24	0.87	0.69	0.89	0.88	0.20	0.92	0.92	1.00					
Eurekahedge	−0.13	0.56	0.73	0.68	0.52	0.36	0.95	0.30	0.93	0.84	0.92	0.93	0.22	0.96	0.99	0.87	1.00				
Greenwich	−0.21	0.68	0.83	0.73	0.64	0.09	0.98	0.02	0.99	0.69	0.97	0.98	0.07	0.90	0.92	0.87	0.92	1.00			
InvestHedge	−0.14	0.42	0.57	0.58	0.38	0.28	0.87	0.25	0.84	0.83	0.85	0.83	0.23	0.96	0.94	0.87	0.92	0.83	1.00		
Tuna*	−0.08	0.58	0.78	0.66	0.54	0.36	0.95	0.28	0.93	0.83	0.92	0.93	0.23	0.95	0.99	0.85	0.99	0.93	0.90	1.00	
Altvest*	−0.14	0.60	0.80	0.66	0.56	0.20	0.97	0.11	0.97	0.74	0.95	0.97	0.11	0.92	0.94	0.88	0.94	0.97	0.86	0.95	1.00

Source: Own calculations based on Datastream and Altvest Hedge Fund Indices, Barclay Hedge Fund Indices, Bloomberg Active Indices for Funds Indices, CASAM/CISDM Indices, Credit Suisse/Tremont TASS Hedge Fund Indices, Dow Jones Hedge Fund Indices, EDHEC Alternative Indices, Eurekahedge FTSE Hedge Indices, Greenwich Alternative Investments Indices, Hedge Fund Net/Tuna Hedge Fund Indices, HedgeFund Intelligence Indices—InvestHedge, Hennessee Hedge Fund Indices, HFR Hedge Fund Indices, Morningstar Hedge Fund Indices, MSCI Hedge Fund Indices, and RBC Hedge 250.
*Correlations for Tuna and Altvest are for the period from January 2000 to September 2007.

the returns of a market-cap index will be influenced by the flows of capital. Most hedge fund index providers argue that a hedge fund index should be equally weighted to fully reflect all strategies.

Yet there are two worthwhile arguments for an asset-weighted hedge fund index. First, smaller hedge funds can transact with a smaller market impact. An asset-weighted index would more accurately reflect the full market impact from the hedge fund universe as it conducts its transactions. This is all the more important for hedge fund managers because of the nature of the high portfolio turnover associated with their frequent and opportunistic trading patterns.

Second, many other asset classes are benchmarked against capital-weighted indices. The S&P 500 and the Russell 1000, for example, are cap-weighted equity indices. This is important because large institutional investors use these cap-weighted indices in their asset allocation decision models. Therefore, to compare on an apples-to-apples basis, hedge fund indices should also be cap-weighted when used for asset allocation decisions. However, these arguments might really be moot. As an example, in Exhibit 15.5, we include the return streams for both the MSCI Equally Weighted (EW) Hedge Fund Index and the MSCI Asset Weighted (AW) Index. While there is some difference in the correlation coefficients with the other hedge fund indices and other asset classes, for the most part these differences are small. The biggest difference in correlation coefficients is with respect to the S&P 500 where the MSCI AW has a correlation coefficient of 0.44 compared to MSCI EW with a correlation coefficient of 0.54. Otherwise, the differences are small between the equally weighted index and the asset-weighted index when compared to the other hedge fund and asset indices in Exhibit 15.5.

Index diversification

The sizes of the 17 hedge fund indices vary from 38 funds to over 8,500. In addition, each index provider constructs several subindices so that the performance of specific hedge fund strategies can be tracked more closely.

But what is the right size of an index? For instance, do 38 funds offer sufficient diversification such that the idiosyncratic risks of individual managers are diversified away? Two studies have examined the issue of the proper diversification for hedge funds. Henker finds that the majority of idiosyncratic risk associated with equity long/short hedge funds can be diversified away with as few as 10 funds, while most of the risk is diversified away with about 20 funds.[13] Similarly, Park and Staum find that in the case of funds of funds, about 95% of hedge fund idiosyncratic risk can be diversified away with 20 hedge funds.[14] Therefore, each hedge fund index listed in Exhibit 15.2 should provide a well-diversified benchmark of hedge fund performance.

However, another question that should be asked is: how many hedge funds are necessary in an investment program to produce a correlation with a chosen hedge fund index that is sufficiently high? This is important since hedge fund indices may be used for asset allocation purposes, and the resulting hedge fund investment program should meet the expectations of the asset allocation study. Lhabitant and Learned examine several hedge fund strategies, and find that an investment program of 20 hedge funds captures 80% to 90% of the correlation with the chosen hedge fund index.[15]

---

[13] Thomas Henker, "Naive Diversification for Hedge Funds," *Journal of Alternative Investments* (Winter 1998), 33–38.

[14] James Park and Jeremy Staum, "Fund of Funds Diversification: How Much Is Enough?" *Journal of Alternative Assets* (Winter 1998), 39–42.

[15] Francois-Serge Lhabitant and Michelle Learned, "Hedge Fund Diversification: How Much Is Enough?" *Journal of Alternative Investments* (Winter 2002), 23–49.

ASSET ALLOCATION WITH HEDGE FUND INDICES

As we noted previously in this chapter, one of the benefits of a hedge fund index is that it can be used for asset allocation studies. Asset allocation studies are used to determine the target weights in a diversified portfolio to allocate across individual asset classes. In this example, we seek to find the allocation that might be made to hedge funds using different hedge fund indices. Asset allocation studies attempt to solve for the portfolio that provides the greatest utility to the investor.

When presented with various outcomes of portfolio return and volatility, an investor will choose the portfolio that provides the greatest expected utility. The issue we examine is whether the addition of hedge funds to a portfolio of stocks and bonds will increase an investor's expected utility beyond that obtained with only stocks and bonds.

The following expected utility maximization equation has been used by many researchers to determine the target allocation level to be made across individual asset classes:[16]

$$E(U_i) = E(R_p) - A_i \sigma^2(R_p)$$

where

$E(U_i) =$ the expected utility of the ith investor
$E(R_p) = \Sigma_i w_i E(R_i) =$ the expected return of the portfolio
$\sigma^2(R_p) = \Sigma_i \Sigma_j w_i w_j \sigma_i \sigma_j \rho_{ij} =$ the variance of the portfolio returns
$A_i =$ a measure of relative risk aversion for the ith investor
w_i and $w_j =$ the portfolio weights of the ith and jth asset classes
σ_i and $\sigma_j =$ the volatilities of the ith and jth asset classes
$\rho_{ij} =$ the correlation coefficient between the ith and jth asset classes

The expected utility in the equation may be viewed as the expected return on the investor's portfolio minus a risk penalty. The risk penalty is equal to the risk of the portfolio multiplied by the investor's relative risk aversion. This is another way to say that the equation is just a risk-adjusted expected rate of return for the portfolio, where the risk adjustment depends on the level of an investor's risk aversion.

It should be noted that the equation is based on the mean and variance and does not include the higher moments of the return distribution such as skewness and kurtosis that we have discussed in prior chapters. Three comments are necessary. First, incorporating higher moments into a utility function can lead to the counter economic results of investors exhibiting increasing marginal utility.[17] Second, the impact of skewness or kurtosis for an asset class should have a lesser impact within a diversified portfolio. Last, most investors apply a mean-variance analysis in their asset allocation models.

Whether we call the equation the expected utility or the risk-adjusted return, solving this function requires quadratic programming. This is because solving for $E(U)$ involves both squared terms (the individual asset variances) and multiplicative terms (the covariances of the various asset classes).

---

[16] See Philippe Jorion, "Risk Management Lessons from Long Term Capital Management," working paper, University of California at Irvine, January 2000; Richard Grinold and Ronald Kahn, *Active Portfolio Management* (New York: McGraw-Hill, 2000); William Sharpe, "Asset Allocation," in *Managing Investment Portfolios: A Dynamic Process*, ed. John Maginn and Donald Tuttle (New York: Warren, Gorham and Lamont, 1990); and Mark Anson, "Maximizing Expected Utility with Commodity Futures," *Journal of Portfolio Management* (Summer 1999), 86–94.

[17] See Pierre-Yves Moix, "The Measurement of Market Risk," PhD dissertation, University of St. Gallen, 2000. Increasing marginal utility would mean that the more an investor invests in hedge funds, the greater the utility. There is no point of saturation. This would lead to an even higher allocation to hedge funds than shown in the accompanying exhibit.

The important point to realize is that quadratic solutions recognize that the risk of the portfolio depends on the interactions among the asset classes.

There are two problems with determining the exact asset allocation for hedge funds. First, utility functions are hard to define in terms of all of the factors that affect investors' behavior. Second, even if a utility function could be specified for each investor, these functions would be as varied and as different as the investors they attempt to describe. Consequently, asset allocation and expected utility will be unique for each investor.

Instead of trying to describe the unique benefits of hedge funds for every investor, we develop a simple scale to measure risk aversion. An asset allocation study should consider how an investor's behavior is affected by his or her tolerance for risk. In this asset allocation example, we specifically incorporate investors' risk preferences into their investment decisions by maximizing expected utility as the objective function, with the level of risk aversion incorporated into the equation.

In this example, we consider three levels of investor risk aversion: low, moderate, and high. At low risk aversion, the investor is driven to maximize total return instead of reducing risk. At the moderate level of risk aversion, risk reduction becomes a more important factor. Last, at a high level of risk aversion, reducing risk becomes more important than maximizing total return. As the level of risk aversion increases, portfolio volatility becomes a greater concern in the investor's utility function, and the investor will seek greater diversification to manage her risk.

We use five hedge fund indices that have data back at least 14 years: HFRI, Barclay, CASAM/CISDM, CSFB/Tremont, and Tuna. We also include the Barclay CTA Index as another reference point. It is important to have as long a historical track record as possible when conducting asset allocation studies, because in any short time period (five years, for example) the relationships among asset classes can become distorted.[18] We include the S&P 500 to represent stock market exposure, 10-year Treasury bonds to represent bond market exposure, the High Yield Bonds to represent credit exposure, and one-year Treasury bills to represent cash. Our objective is to mix these asset classes together with hedge funds according to the equation, to see what is the optimal asset allocation to hedge funds.

A constrained optimization program is run to solve the equation at each level of risk aversion.[19] In Exhibit 15.6 we present the results for each hedge fund index.

At low levels of risk aversion, each of the utility programs allocates 100% of the asset allocation to the hedge fund index. Realistically, this would not happen. Most asset allocation programs have limits so that a single asset class does not dominate. Furthermore, it may not be possible to allocate all of an investor's assets to a single asset class. Still, this demonstrates the appeal of hedge funds—they offer a very favorable risk-return trade-off such that an objective utility function will allocate the full portfolio to hedge funds. However, as the investor's level of risk aversion increases, we see that the amount allocated to hedge funds declines. The reason is that these asset classes have less than perfect correlation with each other. By diversifying across a number of asset classes, the investor can reduce the volatility of her investment portfolio. This volatility dampening effect has greater utility as the level of risk aversion increases. In fact, at a high level of risk aversion, the allocation to hedge funds declines close to zero for many of the hedge fund indices.

Notice that there is a very large range of allocations to hedge funds, depending on the hedge fund index selected and the level of risk aversion of the investor. Allocation levels range from 4% to

---

[18] For an example of this, see Mark Anson, "Maximizing Utility with Private Equity," *Journal of Investing* (Summer 2001), 17–25.

[19] To solve the utility maximization equation, we program an optimization as follows:

$$\text{Maximize } E(U) = \Sigma_i w_i E(R_i) - A_i \Sigma_i \Sigma_j w_i w_j \sigma_i \sigma_j \rho_{ij}$$
$$\text{Subject to the constraints } \Sigma w_i = 1, \text{ and } 0 \leq w_i \leq 1.$$

Exhibit 15.6   Asset allocation with different hedge fund indices

HFRI Index

Risk Aversion	Hedge Fund	10-Year T-Bond	S&P 500	1-Year T-Bill	High-Yield	Expected Utility	Sharpe Ratio	Expected Return	Expected Variance
Low	1.00	0.00	0.00	0.00	0.00	0.138	1.40	13.77%	0.44%
Moderate	0.87	0.13	0.00	0.00	0.00	0.095	1.46	12.85%	0.33%
High	0.11	0.03	0.00	0.85	0.01	0.048	1.24	5.56%	0.01%

Barclay HF Index

Risk Aversion	Hedge Fund	10-Year T-Bond	S&P 500	1-Year T-Bill	High-Yield	Expected Utility	Sharpe Ratio	Expected Return	Expected Variance
Low	1.00	0.00	0.00	0.00	0.00	0.125	1.16	12.50%	0.48%
Moderate	0.74	0.26	0.00	0.00	0.00	0.085	1.31	11.04%	0.25%
High	0.08	0.04	0.00	0.85	0.03	0.046	1.04	5.32%	0.01%

CASAM/CISDM HF Index

Risk Aversion	Hedge Fund	10-Year T-Bond	S&P 500	1-Year T-Bill	High-Yield	Expected Utility	Sharpe Ratio	Expected Return	Expected Variance
Low	1.00	0.00	0.00	0.00	0.00	0.144	1.46	14.42%	0.47%
Moderate	0.88	0.12	0.00	0.00	0.00	0.099	1.51	13.51%	0.36%
High	0.11	0.03	0.00	0.85	0.01	0.048	1.29	5.63%	0.01%

CSFB/Tremont TASS

Risk Aversion	Hedge Fund	10-Year T-Bond	S&P 500	1-Year T-Bill	High-Yield	Expected Utility	Sharpe Ratio	Expected Return	Expected Variance
Low	1.00	0.00	0.00	0.00	0.00	0.110	0.88	10.99%	0.55%
Moderate	0.43	0.10	0.00	0.00	0.46	0.071	1.04	9.52%	0.24%
High	0.04	0.01	0.00	0.89	0.06	0.045	0.77	5.00%	0.01%

Tuna Hedge Fund Aggregate Average

Risk Aversion	Hedge Fund	10-Year T-Bond	S&P 500	1-Year T-Bill	High-Yield	Expected Utility	Sharpe Ratio	Expected Return	Expected Variance
Low	1.00	0.00	0.00	0.00	0.00	0.172	2.35	17.17%	0.29%
Moderate	1.00	0.00	0.00	0.00	0.00	0.142	2.35	17.17%	0.29%
High	0.22	0.01	0.00	0.77	0.00	0.056	2.17	7.24%	0.02%

Barclay Trader Index CTA

Risk Aversion	Hedge Fund	10-Year T-Bond	S&P 500	1-Year T-Bill	High-Yield	Expected Utility	Sharpe Ratio	Expected Return	Expected Variance
Low	0.00	0.00	1.00	0.00	0.00	0.105	0.44	10.55%	1.93%
Moderate	0.20	0.03	0.05	0.00	0.72	0.065	0.90	8.45%	0.20%
High	0.02	0.00	0.00	0.89	0.09	0.045	0.66	4.89%	0.00%

Source: Own calculations based on Datastream and Altvest Hedge Fund Indices, Barclay Hedge Fund Indices, Bloomberg Active Indices for Funds Indices, CASAM/CISDM Indices, Credit Suisse/Tremont TASS Hedge Fund Indices, Dow Jones Hedge Fund Indices, EDHEC Alternative Indices, Eurekahedge FTSE Hedge Indices, Greenwich Alternative Investments Indices, Hedge Fund Net/Tuna Hedge Fund Indices, HedgeFund Intelligence Indices—InvestHedge, Hennessee Hedge Fund Indices, HFR Hedge Fund Indices, Morningstar Hedge Fund Indices, MSCI Hedge Fund Indices, and RBC Hedge 250.

100%. Such a wide range of results would not be expected for a homogeneous asset class. This simply highlights our earlier point that the hedge fund universe is unknowable. Each index has its own methods of construction, which results in very little overlap with other available hedge fund indices.

One caveat to the conclusions reached here is that hedge fund returns are subject to massaging by managers; hence, some authors have argued that reported returns often offer a picture of the performance of a fund that exhibits a lower volatility and a higher persistence (serial correlation) than what was actually registered (Getmansky, Lo, and Makarov 2004). In any case, while it is still not clear whether this serial correlation of returns is the result of trading of illiquid securities by funds or manipulation by fund managers to smooth their funds' returns, this is an issue that should not be underestimated when analyzing data on hedge fund returns.

Therefore, should a hedge fund index be used for asset allocation purposes, the investor must take care to select an index that reflects the economic parameters of the hedge fund program that is expected to be implemented. Otherwise, unusual results may arise from an asset allocation study.

As a final note, as a practical matter, most large institutional investors would not normally allocate more than 25% of their investment portfolios to hedge funds, although some endowments and foundations do go as high as 50%. In fact, most public pension funds have a less than 5% allocation to hedge funds, and many place a specific asset allocation limit on hedge fund investing in the 1% to 10% range. Therefore, many of the allocation examples presented in Exhibit 15.6 might be beyond an explicit asset allocation constraint.

CONCLUSION

Benchmarks serve two useful purposes. First, they provide a yardstick for measuring performance of an asset class or an individual external manager. Second, they can be used in asset allocation studies to determine how much to allocate among broad asset classes. Benchmarks are tools for building and monitoring portfolios.

With respect to hedge funds, investors have a wide variety to choose from. Unfortunately, there is a lack of consistency in the construction of hedge fund indices. This lack of consistency was demonstrated in the wide range of risk and return measures in Exhibits 15.3 and 15.4 as well as the wide range of correlation coefficients in Exhibit 15.5.

This creates two distinct problems. First, given the large range of performance among the hedge fund indices, an investment manager who invests in hedge funds can significantly outperform or underperform her bogey by the choice of hedge fund index. Second, asset allocation studies that are driven by the risk-return trade-off of different asset classes may over- or underallocate to hedge fund investments based on the simple choice of hedge fund index. Some variability among hedge fund indices is good, but too much can result in misleading asset allocation decisions. Last, all of these indices suffer from several data biases that can boost returns by 3% to 4%.

In summary, the world of hedge fund performance measurement is still maturing. Currently, there are many indices to choose from, each with its own pros and cons. Also, the consistency among hedge fund indices is considerably less than that for equity indices. Perhaps the best way to choose a hedge fund index is to first state clearly the risk and return objectives of the hedge fund investment program. With this as a guide, the investor can then make an informed benchmark selection.

16

Hedge Fund Incentive Fees
and the Free Option

As we described in the previous chapter, hedge fund managers earn money from two sources of fees: management fees and incentive (or performance) fees. The management fee is a constant percentage applied to the amount of assets managed in the hedge fund, while the incentive fee is a form of profit sharing. Incentive fees are received only if the hedge fund manager earns a profitable return for its investors.

While management fees are widely accepted throughout the money management industry, it is the incentive fee that draws the most scrutiny and publicity. The fact is that incentive fees may be considered a so-called free option. In this chapter we review the nature of this incentive fee option, provide a way to value the option, and then consider some of the interesting ways this option can motivate hedge fund manager behavior.

HEDGE FUND INCENTIVE FEES

One attraction of the hedge fund marketplace for money managers is the ability to share in the profits earned for clients. Mutual fund managers, for example, are prohibited by law from accepting fees based on performance.[1] Mutual funds may only charge a management fee. In contrast, hedge fund managers may charge both a management fee and a profit-sharing fee.

Optimal contracting between investors and hedge fund managers must align the interests of both parties. In this regard, some authors (e.g. Fung and Hsieh, 2006) contend that the co-investing by the hedge fund manager and the investors improves this alignment of interests on the downside but can also cause "excessive conservatism" by the hedge fund's manager on the upside. The compensation contract design between the investors and the hedge fund manager will, in turn, determine the features of the business model to be adopted (e.g. the allocation of capital to factor-related bets, degree of leverage, etc.).

The general rule of thumb in the hedge fund market is "2 and 20." That is, a 2% management fee and a 20% incentive fee. However, hedge fund fees may range from 1% to 3% for management fees and up to 40% for incentive fees.

The management fee is collected whether or not the hedge fund manager earns a profit. The management fee may be collected on a quarterly, semiannual, or annual basis, while the incentive fee is collected annually. An incentive fee is collected by the hedge fund manager if the end-of-year net asset value (NAV) of the hedge fund is greater than the beginning-of-year NAV (assuming that the beginning-of-year NAV is above the high-water mark; see the following pages). This feature of hedge fund contracts led Agarwal, Daniel, and Naik (2006) to test the hypothesis that hedge funds have incentives to manage returns upward as the year is ending. Consistent with this hypothesis, they find that December returns for hedge funds are higher by 1.5% and that, after controlling for risk, residual returns continue to be 0.4% higher. They also determine that hedge funds that have greater incentives and greater investment opportunities show a larger December spike. The authors conclude

---

[1] See Section 205 of the Investment Advisers Act of 1940.

that the combination of these two results suggests that hedge funds may be managing (massaging) their reported returns. However, the paper could not explain why returns were unusually low between June and October of each year.

HEDGE FUND FEES AND OPTION THEORY

Hedge fund incentive fees can be considered a call option on a portion of the profits that the hedge fund manager earns for investors. If the manager earns a profit, she collects an incentive fee. If the hedge fund manager does not earn a profit, she collects no fee. This binary type of payoff is the same as the payout for a call option and may be described as:

$$\text{Payout on incentive fees} = \text{Max}[i(\text{ENAV} - \text{BNAV}),\ 0] \tag{16.1}$$

where

$i =$ the incentive fee rate (e.g. 20%)
ENAV $=$ the ending net asset value of the hedge fund
BNAV $=$ the strike price of the call option; it is equal to the beginning NAV of the hedge fund at the start of the period, assuming that BNAV is equal to the fund's high-water mark.

The high-water mark at a point in time is equal to the maximum value of the NAV observed up to that point. Typically, the manager must recoup previous losses before she can earn an incentive fee.

For the rest of this chapter we will focus on a one-period model of incentive fees, and we will assume that the fund's hurdle rate is zero. In a more realistic framework, not only will the manager be concerned with the value of the current period's incentive fees, but she will have to examine the effects of her decisions on the future value of incentive and asset management fees as well.

The option on incentive fees is free because the manager does not have to pay for it. If the option is out-of-the-money at maturity (the end of the year) the hedge fund manager is not out of pocket any option premium. Conversely, if the option is in-the-money at the end of the year, the hedge fund manager can be considered as exercising the option and collects her incentive fee.

The maturity of the incentive fee option is one year. That is, at the beginning of every year, the hedge fund manager receives a new call option from investors to share in the increase in hedge fund value at year-end. If the hedge fund does not increase in value over the course of the year, the incentive fee call option expires worthless. If the hedge fund increases in value over the course of the year, the hedge fund manager exercises the option at year-end and collects an incentive fee.

Equation 16.1 describes the payout at maturity for a call option. Using risk-neutral pricing, the current value of the **incentive fee option** may be expressed as:[2]

$$\text{Call(incentive fee)} = e^{-r(T-t)} \times \text{Max}[i(\text{ENAV} - \text{BNAV}),\ 0] \tag{16.2}$$

where

$r =$ the risk-free rate
$T - t =$ the time until maturity of the option contract
$e =$ the exponential operator

---

[2] One of the great insights of Black and Scholes is that an option's position can be combined with positions in the underlying stock to form a portfolio that is precisely hedged from market risk, thus creating a risk-free portfolio, because for every cent that a stock goes up in price the increase in the value of the stock in the portfolio is exactly offset by a decline in the value of the option's position (see Fischer Black and Myron Scholes, "The Pricing of Options and Corporate Liabilities," *Journal of Political Economy* 81 (1973), 637–654). With this insight, Black and Scholes demonstrate that an option can be priced using a risk-free discount rate.

If an investor could approximate the expected return for the hedge fund, $E(R)$, then Equation 16.2 can be expressed as:

$$\text{Call(incentive fee)} = e^{-r(T-t)} \times \text{Max}[i(e^{R(T-t)} \times \text{BNAV} - \text{BNAV}),\ 0] \tag{16.3}$$

where

$R =$ the expected return earned by the hedge fund manager

Equation 16.3 says that the current value of the call option is equal to the discounted value of the expected future incentive fees collected at the end of the reporting period. The expected future fees are dependent on the hedge fund manager earning a rate of return of $E(R)$ over time period $(T - t)$.

We measure the value of the hedge fund manager's call option on incentive fees using the Black-Scholes Option Pricing Model:

$$\text{Call(incentive fees)} = i \times [\text{NAV} \times N(d_1) - e^{-r(T-t)} \times \text{BNAV} \times N(d_2)] \tag{16.4}$$

where

$$\text{NAV} = \text{the monthly NAV for the hedge fund}$$
$$\text{BNAV} = \text{the beginning NAV}$$
$$N(d1) \text{ and } N(d2) = \text{the cumulative probability distribution function for a standard unit normal}$$
$$\text{variable}[3]$$

The other terms are defined as before.

The Black-Scholes Option Pricing Model is dependent on five inputs: the current value of the asset, the strike price, the time until maturity of the option, the risk-free rate, and the volatility of the underlying asset's returns. The call option on incentive fees is affected by these five variables, plus one more: the size of the profit-sharing percentage, i:

$$\text{Call(incentive fees)} = f(\text{NAV},\ \text{BNAV},\ T - t,\ r,\ \sigma,\ i) \tag{16.5}$$

There are some issues with applying the Black-Scholes formula to hedge fund incentive fees. First, the Black-Scholes Model assumes continuous trading and pricing. Unfortunately, hedge fund asset values are determined discretely, often at monthly intervals.[4] In addition, the Black-Scholes Model

---

Another way to infer the risk-neutral valuation property is to consider the Black-Scholes differential equation for pricing derivative securities:

$$\delta f/\delta t + rS\delta f/\delta S + (\sigma^2/2)S^2\delta^2 f/\delta S^2 = rf$$

where

$S =$ the underlying stochastic variable (e.g. stock prices)
$f =$ the price of the derivative security, a function of S and time, t
$r =$ the risk-free rate
$\sigma =$ the volatility of the underlying stochastic variable (e.g. the volatility of stock price)

The preceding equation does not involve any variable that is affected by the risk preferences of investors. Black and Scholes demonstrated that, given that risk preferences do not enter into the equation, they cannot affect its solution. Therefore, any set of risk preferences will satisfy the equation, including the simplifying assumption of risk-neutral preferences.

[3] $d_1 = [\ln(\text{NAV}/\text{BNAV}) + (r + \sigma^2/2) \times (T - t)]/[\sigma\sqrt{(T - t)}]$ and $d_2 = d_1 - \sigma\sqrt{(T - t)}$.

[4] One solution to this problem might be a discrete-time option pricing model such as a binomial tree. See John Cox, Stephen Ross, and Martin Rubinstein, "Options Pricing: A Simplified Approach," *Journal of Financial Economics* (September 1979), 229–263, and Richard Rendleman and Clifford Smith, "Two-State Option Pricing," *Journal of Finance* (December 1979), 1093–1110. Alternatively, Goetzmann, Ingersoll, and Ross provide a continuous-time diffusion process for hedge fund net asset values. See William Goetzmann, Jonathan Ingersoll Jr., and Stephen Ross, "High-Water Marks and Hedge Fund Management Contracts," working paper presented at the Berkeley Program in Finance, March 2001.

assumes that short selling of all securities is permitted. In the case of hedge fund limited partnership units, this assumption does not hold. Last, each security is assumed to be perfectly divisible. In the case of hedge funds, limited partnership units are not divisible and may be denominated in large values of $1,000 or more.

Conversely, there are some distinct advantages to applying the Black-Scholes Option Pricing Model with respect to valuing hedge fund incentive fees. First, the Black-Scholes Model was developed for European options—options that can be exercised only at maturity. This is consistent with the way hedge fund managers collect their incentive fees; they collect incentive fees only at year-end—at the expiration of the option. Second, the Black-Scholes Model assumes that no dividends are paid during the life of the option. This is also consistent with the fact that hedge funds rarely make intermediate distributions to their investors.

DATA AND RESULTS

In this section, we attempt, using market data, to assess the value that the incentive fee option has for the hedge fund manager. We use data from Hedge Fund Research, Inc. over the time period 1990 to June 2008. We examine the returns for three of the most popular types of hedge fund strategies: equity hedge (long/short), convertible arbitrage, and merger arbitrage. These strategies provide a spectrum of return distributions and resulting call option values. Exhibit 16.1 provides summary statistics for these three strategies.

Exhibit 16.1 demonstrates that equity hedge managers have the highest volatility associated with their strategy, which more than doubles those of convertible arbitrage and merger arbitrage strategies. The Black-Scholes Model teaches us that the higher the volatility, the more valuable the option, other factors held equal. Consequently, equity hedge managers benefit from the higher volatility created by their trading strategies.

At the beginning of each calendar year, the strike price for the call option on incentive fees is struck to the beginning-of-year net asset value, provided that the hedge fund manager earned a profit in the prior year. This is equivalent to setting the strike price for the incentive fee call option to be at-the-money each year.

However, should the hedge fund manager lose money in any calendar year, the strike price for the incentive fee call option is struck at the previous high-water mark for the hedge fund. The high-water

Exhibit 16.1   Summary performance statistics, 1990 to June 2008

Trading Strategy	Expected Return	Standard Deviation	Sharpe Ratio
Net of Fee Returns			
Equity Long/Short	16.27%	8.63%	1.40
Convertible Arbitrage	9.35%	3.70%	1.39
Merger Arbitrage	10.12%	4.19%	1.41
Gross Returns			
Equity Long/Short	22.53%	9.73%	1.88
Convertible Arbitrage	13.44%	4.04%	3.33
Merger Arbitrage	14.58%	4.57%	3.19
Gross of Incentive Fee Returns			
Equity Long/Short	20.14%	9.73%	1.64
Convertible Arbitrage	11.22%	4.04%	2.78
Merger Arbitrage	12.33%	4.57%	2.70

Source: Based on data from Hedge Fund Research, Inc.

mark is the previous highest net asset value achieved by the hedge fund manager. Typically, a hedge fund manager may not collect incentive fees until it has exceeded the previous high-water mark. The high-water mark becomes the new strike price for the incentive fee call option.

Consequently, if a hedge fund manager loses money in any calendar year and the strike price for the incentive fee call option is struck at the previous high-water mark, this is the same as setting the strike price to be out-of-the-money. Setting the strike price for the incentive fee call option out-of-the-money means that the strike price is set at a net asset value that is greater than the current net asset value of the hedge fund. This is done because if the hedge fund manager loses money in any calendar year, the current net asset value of the hedge fund will be below the high-water mark. Call options that have strike prices struck out-of-the-money are less valuable than call options struck at-the-money.

Most hedge fund managers collect the incentive fee annually. Therefore, we measure the value of the call option on incentive fees over the course of one year. From month to month, the value of the call option will increase or decrease depending on whether the net asset value is higher or lower than the beginning net asset value.

Exhibit 16.2 provides the month-by-month return earned by equity long/short managers and the month-by-month incentive fee call option value.[5] In each of Exhibits 16.2, 16.3 (convertible arbitrage), and 16.4 (merger arbitrage), we assume an incentive fee of 20% for the purpose of valuing the call option. Each month represents the value of the incentive fee call option to the hedge fund manager per $1 million of assets managed. Notice how the value of the incentive fee call option increases with positive monthly returns and decreases with negative monthly returns. Looking at Exhibit 16.2, we can see that in Panel A equity hedge managers earned negative returns in March and June of 2008. This, in turn, translated into reduced call option values in Panel B of Exhibit 16.2. Conversely, in months when returns were positive, the option value increased.

At maturity, the value of the incentive fee call option reduces to the formula in Equation 16.1. It is simply a percentage (20%) of the increase in the net asset value in the hedge fund.

Exhibit 16.2 presents the simple case where the incentive fee call option is struck at-the-money at the beginning of every calendar year, unless there was a negative return in the prior year. We can see that for equity hedge managers, there was only one negative year, 2002. Therefore, for year 2003, the hedge fund incentive fee for equity long/short managers was out-of-the-money, and the strike price for the option was set at the prior high-water mark. In all prior years where a positive return was earned, the incentive fee option was in-the-money where the ending net asset value of the prior year became the strike price for the incentive fee option in the following year. As long as the hedge fund manager earns a positive return, a new high-water mark will be established, and the incentive fee call option will be struck at-the-money in the following year.

Exhibits 16.3 and 16.4 demonstrate the same results for convertible arbitrage and merger arbitrage hedge fund managers. For example, convertible bond arbitrage hedge fund managers earned negative returns in 1994 and 2005. Consistent with these returns, there was no exercise of the incentive fee option in those years. It expired worthless. It is clear from these exhibits that the incentive fee option is quite valuable to hedge fund managers. We also note that equity hedge, convertible arbitrage, and merger arbitrage all earned negative returns in 2008, so the incentive fee call option was out-of-the-money as of the start of 2009. That is, high-water marks apply to these three categories of hedge fund managers in 2009. It will be interesting to see if hedge fund managers in these three categories can bring the incentive fee option back into the money in 2009.

---

[5] HFRI databases provide hedge fund returns net of incentive and management fees. Therefore, the returns have been adjusted to provide returns before management and incentive fees have been deducted.

Exhibit 16.2 HFRI equity hedge index monthly returns and incentive fee call option

Panel A: Monthly Net Returns (in Percent)

Year	Jan.	Feb.	March	April	May	June	July	August	Sep.	Oct.	Nov.	Dec.	YTD
2008	-4.49	1.27	-2.73	3.67	2.85	-2.52	0.17	-1.67	3.18	3.09	-2.84	0.50	-2.21
2007	1.16	0.63	1.01	1.86	2.24	0.89	-0.54	1.03	0.16	1.86	2.00	1.35	10.53
2006	3.95	0.02	2.55	1.76	-2.32	-0.54	2.95	0.74	2.25	-1.87	2.14	2.32	11.71
2005	-0.58	2.13	-1.05	-2.23	1.55	1.96	-1.88	-0.37	1.99	0.48	3.37	1.76	10.61
2004	1.95	1.11	0.36	-2.08	-0.19	1.07	-1.88	2.38	0.78	3.12	1.14	1.93	7.69
2003	-0.01	-0.78	-0.07	2.43	4.08	1.52	2.41	0.28	-1.96	0.56	2.67	-1.14	20.53
2002	0.22	-0.89	2.03	0.17	0.00	-2.63	-3.93	-1.22	-3.73	1.85	1.97	1.99	-4.71
2001	2.88	-2.56	-2.30	2.27	0.90	-0.32	-1.06	5.35	-1.08	-2.01	-4.30	3.16	0.40
2000	0.25	10.00	1.73	-4.19	-2.44	4.85	-1.58	0.04	0.35	2.33	6.76	10.88	9.09
1999	4.98	-2.41	4.05	5.25	1.22	3.80	0.61	-7.65	3.16	2.47	3.84	5.39	44.22
1998	-0.16	4.09	4.54	1.39	-1.27	0.50	-0.67	1.35	5.69	0.39	-0.93	1.42	15.98
1997	2.78	-0.24	-0.73	-0.27	5.04	1.97	5.05	2.63	2.18	1.56	1.66	0.83	23.41
1996	1.06	2.82	1.90	5.34	3.70	-0.73	-2.87	2.93	2.90	-1.44	3.43	2.56	21.75
1995	0.30	1.68	2.09	2.64	1.22	4.73	4.46	1.27	1.32	0.40	-1.48	0.74	31.04
1994	2.35	-0.40	-2.08	-0.37	0.41	-0.41	0.91	3.84	2.52	3.11	-1.93	3.59	2.61
1993	2.09	-0.57	3.26	1.30	2.72	3.01	2.12	-0.85	2.51	2.03	4.51	3.38	27.94
1992	2.49	2.90	-0.28	0.27	0.85	-0.92	2.76	2.17	4.30	1.16	-1.08	5.02	21.32
1991	4.90	5.20	7.22	0.47	3.20	0.59	1.41						40.15
1990	-3.34	2.85	5.67	-0.87	5.92	2.52	2.00	-1.88	1.65	0.77	-2.29	1.02	14.43

Panel B: Incentive Fee Call Option (per $1,000,000 of Net Assets)

Year	Jan.	Feb.	March	April	May	June	July	August	Sep.	Oct.	Nov.	Dec.
2008	$ 30,998.30	$ 30,484.43	$ 16,853.37	$ 25,633.22	$ 39,115.42	$ 23,341.74	$109,775.57	$ 91,168.23	$119,226.25	$147,055.62	$118,563.67	$120,021.73
2007	73,514.54	71,668.17	79,116.47	90,701.92	108,271.46	111,730.26	83,433.26	87,918.26	84,743.87	97,211.91	114,430.62	124,842.45
2006	89,425.58	84,769.62	108,443.78	122,044.26	100,087.59	91,194.00	73,792.23	78,284.32	98,702.78	79,303.04	99,474.91	121,159.27
2005	44,344.49	56,201.55	48,865.05	33,828.20	39,592.50	50,594.99	32,654.12	27,700.73	36,818.67	36,853.41	68,876.48	86,750.54
2004	54,409.23	60,287.65	61,385.90	45,793.34	42,414.19	46,610.31	45,886.10	60,507.83	64,604.10	90,405.13	99,806.88	116,141.97
2003	17,488.35	13,244.35	11,577.32	15,982.65	29,207.49	34,177.82	9,165.44	7,346.27	2,202.77	1,160.19	1,461.64	0.00
2002	47,307.12	38,912.40	48,128.52	46,342.51	43,732.22	26,212.05			5,976.62	6,670.50	7,818.92	9,528.27
2001	95,871.50	66,062.61	47,420.38	53,838.83	54,477.51	46,220.17	35,070.14	23,660.31			89,055.63	112,209.32
2000	67,450.80	149,242.19	165,534.76	125,900.71	101,966.59	136,114.62	118,743.09	167,612.97	154,334.87	132,965.52	276,080.33	356,976.76
1999	101,601.53	77,196.43	112,896.60	158,906.42	168,471.90	200,858.53	204,423.66	201,744.14	201,808.71	220,600.92	112,036.96	162,779.58
1998	64,582.89	90,928.24	132,625.79	140,847.55	126,648.64	125,642.88	116,473.64	46,440.01	65,422.87	82,206.53	215,837.96	225,583.72
1997	87,819.88	78,670.46	72,207.94	65,125.43	107,162.71	121,384.54	167,681.20	177,231.93	226,292.52	226,670.17	207,056.07	211,431.39
1996	74,759.74	91,485.03	105,948.46	152,226.02	185,331.83	175,267.71	147,903.49	166,042.33	183,391.56	194,993.00	259,626.31	278,370.33
1995	69,730.53	77,413.61	95,198.07	114,704.01	122,831.75	163,728.55	202,498.69	225,431.76	247,285.52	232,861.15	32,266.55	33,142.38
1994	70,446.55	63,386.40	49,236.67	44,373.84	44,517.13	38,313.15	40,170.85	44,069.18	50,999.67	50,399.51	229,133.24	259,035.68
1993	68,804.38	59,613.19	84,739.48	93,203.80	117,354.40	144,567.60	163,938.80	198,511.63	219,734.46	245,994.49	179,233.76	209,195.36
1992	78,225.18	97,346.93	93,650.85	91,122.35	95,853.43	83,514.54	107,181.60	96,051.32	118,338.77	137,036.85	296,031.44	333,273.85
1991	118,504.64	155,627.18	220,457.40	218,353.56	243,471.27	244,040.70	253,630.87	268,753.29	300,710.21	307,023.00	150,426.77	153,734.81
1990	$ 60,288.99	$ 68,831.04	$118,212.46	$103,630.07	$155,896.91	$173,533.40	$187,714.53	$165,943.69	$172,996.22	$175,415.62		

Source: Based on data from Hedge Fund Research, Inc.

Exhibit 16.3 HFRI convertible arbitrage index monthly returns and incentive fee call option

Panel A: Monthly Net Returns (in Percent)

Year	Jan.	Feb.	March	April	May	June	July	August	Sep.	Oct.	Nov.	Dec.	YTD
2008	-1.40	-0.92	-4.50	0.34	1.20	0.83							-4.47
2007	1.34	1.05	0.46	0.34	1.26	0.11	-0.48	-1.02	1.57	1.96	-1.03	-0.30	5.33
2006	2.40	1.17	1.04	0.64	0.79	0.10	0.73	1.11	0.91	0.34	1.11	1.22	12.17
2005	-0.90	-0.44	-1.48	-2.64	-1.17	1.03	1.08	0.58	1.27	-0.07	0.04	0.91	-1.86
2004	1.01	0.18	0.68	0.25	-1.19	-1.04	0.46	0.27	-0.25	-0.48	0.88	0.43	1.18
2003	2.50	1.29	0.73	1.36	1.14	-0.57	-0.70	-0.69	1.41	1.40	0.81	0.88	9.93
2002	1.38	0.19	0.46	0.87	0.53	0.22	-1.28	0.35	1.59	1.00	2.02	1.42	9.07
2001	2.73	1.70	1.68	1.57	0.71	0.13	0.76	1.26	0.64	0.93	0.62	-0.08	13.37
2000	1.91	2.21	1.75	1.78	1.34	1.66	0.68	1.42	1.21	0.42	-0.71	-0.01	14.50
1999	2.11	0.25	1.53	2.66	1.40	1.09	1.05	0.42	0.66	0.33	0.99	1.08	14.41
1998	1.91	1.52	1.58	1.35	0.40	0.22	0.49	-3.19	-1.07	-0.48	3.33	1.60	7.77
1997	1.01	1.11	0.59	0.68	1.40	1.71	1.61	1.14	1.11	1.19	0.09	0.41	12.72
1996	1.82	1.06	1.17	1.88	1.73	0.44	-0.37	1.40	1.23	1.27	1.40	0.66	14.56
1995	0.55	0.98	1.83	1.90	1.88	2.32	2.13	0.96	1.55	1.25	1.58	1.33	19.85
1994	0.66	0.24	-2.11	-2.79	0.03	0.15	1.55	0.80	0.12	-0.09	-0.79	-1.48	-3.73
1993	0.93	0.86	2.19	1.50	1.24	1.04	1.41	1.40	1.03	1.29	0.60	0.77	15.22
1992	2.12	0.94	0.99	0.80	1.70	0.71	1.85	1.65	1.46	1.24	0.70	1.09	16.35
1991	0.44	1.61	1.39	1.49	0.94	0.98	1.57	2.09	1.31	1.22	1.66	1.63	17.60
1990	-1.47	-0.92	1.26	1.48	1.75	1.72	1.15	-0.18	-0.47	-1.56	-0.05	-0.49	2.16

Panel B: Incentive Fee Call Option (per $1,000,000 of Net Assets)

Year	Jan.	Feb.	March	April	May	June	July	August	Sep.	Oct.	Nov.	Dec.
2008	$26,004.77	$14,252.17	$ 1,142.64	$ 697.07	$ 1,027.04	$ 1,248.24						
2007	62,489.45	66,072.50	71,137.83	69,803.68	80,023.77	75,866.86	$ 67,915.07	$ 54,473.80	$ 67,217.40	$ 84,791.45	$ 71,516.66	$ 65,614.69
2006	44,239.46	49,423.02	59,815.40	62,288.44	67,268.19	64,062.27	68,151.56	74,741.01	78,969.49	78,368.52	84,474.34	91,663.00
2005	21,352.02	17,022.03	9,907.29	2,184.33	709.15	911.87	1,307.53	1,188.87	1,900.23	690.00	77.02	0.00
2004	27,716.29	27,685.97	32,904.74	33,995.65	23,904.40	15,729.84	17,602.36	18,205.08	14,881.68	9,715.47	13,791.02	15,798.66
2003	43,538.48	53,906.18	61,376.92	74,696.15	86,312.43	79,895.54	72,349.94	64,881.73	76,939.41	91,574.47	99,576.68	108,270.48
2002	37,213.56	35,570.20	39,431.96	46,437.03	50,821.90	51,369.85	38,223.32	39,639.58	55,687.09	65,569.34	86,315.06	100,446.08
2001	86,872.66	92,417.18	107,045.22	115,400.85	118,207.28	113,854.84	118,601.46	128,536.78	132,076.23	138,647.28	142,331.49	139,759.19
2000	70,143.58	88,651.24	107,005.93	121,513.25	132,409.37	144,056.84	147,504.67	157,918.03	165,841.08	166,157.28	155,602.37	150,978.32
1999	65,423.25	61,646.91	78,314.90	102,376.01	114,723.89	122,038.56	130,521.26	131,552.81	134,828.40	135,002.29	141,598.76	149,003.16
1998	70,342.36	78,577.73	95,751.70	104,638.93	105,546.87	102,750.88	104,778.33	71,290.34	56,685.47	47,944.50	74,552.01	88,500.19
1997	60,017.44	63,951.75	70,375.53	72,895.29	85,171.88	98,296.62	111,987.86	120,023.32	127,616.96	136,295.72	133,278.62	133,727.13
1996	70,231.58	73,706.23	83,782.57	99,181.25	114,787.20	115,078.12	108,604.26	119,526.50	128,166.63	137,606.84	147,923.28	150,909.83
1995	21,353.38	22,350.67	34,988.10	45,290.21	58,071.72	73,374.16	88,526.30	92,326.04	101,171.22	108,284.45	117,910.59	125,462.03
1994	38,829.21	36,694.20	21,624.03	6,678.00	5,824.80	4,678.59	8,185.98	9,178.35	6,806.07	3,746.35	282.69	0.00
1993	42,934.68	45,963.90	68,247.97	81,553.95	93,445.10	102,054.91	115,270.80	127,472.17	135,574.32	146,701.22	150,572.37	156,145.58
1992	62,778.92	66,492.27	76,494.34	80,903.42	96,467.08	99,788.96	116,342.97	130,242.77	141,876.81	152,298.78	157,195.61	165,935.00
1991	67,939.49	72,340.49	85,387.62	93,919.35	99,528.46	104,367.33	117,395.82	134,468.74	143,055.70	151,394.68	163,899.70	176,537.17
1990	$59,777.44	$40,506.72	$ 51,177.49	$ 59,255.30	$ 73,402.81	$ 84,407.53	$ 91,109.50	$ 82,641.76	$ 71,033.22	$ 50,382.01	$ 43,527.45	$ 32,794.17

Source: Based on data from Hedge Fund Research, Inc.

Exhibit 16.4 HFRI merger arbitrage index monthly returns and incentive fee call option

Panel A: Monthly Net Returns (in Percent)

Year	Jan.	Feb.	March	April	May	June	July	August	Sep.	Oct.	Nov.	Dec.	YTD
2008	-1.78	0.88	-0.88	2.30	1.08	0.48	-0.76	0.37	0.98	1.89	-1.46	-0.28	2.04
2007	1.86	1.12	0.33	1.27	1.87	-0.29	0.76	0.68	-0.30	1.49	0.92	1.47	7.05
2006	3.12	1.16	1.97	1.41	-0.07	0.82	1.12	0.71	0.63	-1.57	1.29	1.82	14.24
2005	-0.03	0.72	0.12	-1.42	1.62	1.14	-1.02	0.20	0.59	0.54	1.62	1.10	6.26
2004	1.02	0.59	0.07	-0.85	-0.14	0.32	0.71	0.69	0.63	0.72	0.29	0.69	4.08
2003	0.15	-0.01	-0.10	1.29	1.76	0.43	0.93	0.69	0.63	0.72	0.59	0.52	7.48
2002	0.86	-0.36	0.56	-0.04	-0.25	-1.23	-1.90	0.50	-0.44	0.36	0.23	0.78	-0.86
2001	1.10	0.44	-0.75	0.23	1.69	-0.84	1.19	0.87	-2.72	0.84	1.20	1.16	2.76
2000	1.63	1.88	0.82	2.47	1.51	1.58	1.38	1.34	1.44	0.48	2.23	0.46	18.02
1999	0.71	0.25	1.05	1.31	2.04	1.61	-0.57	0.52	1.25	0.69	2.23	1.94	14.34
1998	0.96	1.89	1.05	1.59	-0.60	0.50	1.60	-5.69	1.74	2.14	2.33	1.90	7.23
1997	1.04	0.39	1.05	-0.70	1.92	2.13	0.81	1.04	2.13	0.84	2.02	1.37	16.44
1996	1.57	1.29	1.51	1.62	1.46	0.78	1.35	1.64	0.81	1.23	1.38	1.37	16.61
1995	0.86	1.45	1.49	0.35	1.26	2.47	0.68	1.35	1.63	0.91	2.13	1.31	17.86
1994	1.50	-0.41	1.37	-0.25	1.22	0.89	1.54	1.99	0.59	-0.26	-0.22	1.48	8.88
1993	2.12	1.64	0.49	1.30	1.17	2.25	1.45	1.67	1.85	2.05	0.86	1.65	20.24
1992	1.96	0.96	1.34	0.14	0.00	0.30	1.44	0.12	1.34	0.40	-2.22	1.91	7.90
1991	0.01	1.59	2.30	2.83	1.55	1.12	1.44	0.64	1.10	1.41	1.38	1.20	17.86
1990	-6.46	1.71	2.90	0.98	2.28	0.73	0.02	-0.82	-4.58	0.73	2.19	1.21	0.44

Panel B: Incentive Fee Call Option (per $1,000,000 of Net Assets)

Year	Jan.	Feb.	March	April	May	June	July	August	Sep.	Oct.	Nov.	Dec.
2008	$25,404.78	$23,906.86	$15,836.13	$27,136.41	$34,221.87	$37,067.35	$83,243.11	$82,858.83	$88,943.64	$105,375.45	$88,438.72	$82,828.30
2007	68,430.16	72,671.21	76,252.48	84,928.23	101,493.94	93,621.48	121,875.88	125,565.43	118,999.98	130,966.21	136,672.34	148,029.99
2006	72,386.27	80,024.17	102,470.41	114,281.67	111,586.70	116,360.49	53,419.27	59,237.10	63,918.35	46,723.21	56,089.63	73,410.46
2005	28,702.62	32,506.03	33,810.23	22,317.04	34,559.55	43,190.91	16,087.16	15,836.33	18,087.72	20,337.90	36,378.68	47,532.06
2004	29,560.54	32,813.77	32,558.94	25,208.13	23,086.12	23,858.70	29,670.07	33,774.77	37,989.89	43,828.03	45,756.62	51,534.24
2003	14,839.11	12,818.49	11,512.44	15,773.30	24,724.70	25,991.30	5,383.86	5,293.60	2,616.87	1,866.19	1,241.67	0.00
2002	32,952.68	27,284.85	30,253.70	28,025.85	24,699.00	15,024.89	51,090.12	57,103.78	28,410.49	32,173.32	31,100.71	36,448.92
2001	70,023.12	62,111.16	52,109.29	45,804.34	58,371.12	44,820.16	144,981.28	154,627.50	164,853.53	165,767.73	173,113.09	180,081.34
2000	67,669.72	82,337.55	90,752.08	112,627.02	125,383.52	136,311.91	112,559.20	114,668.97	124,160.46	128,088.29	147,277.04	148,377.45
1999	51,844.29	48,103.68	58,657.04	68,021.34	87,361.26	100,401.19	77,246.11	21,307.21	30,448.02	45,599.93	63,177.34	80,975.93
1998	60,974.92	72,660.37	83,973.68	95,417.58	86,528.99	85,801.28	105,781.12	112,822.02	130,974.83	136,042.65	152,628.62	167,872.71
1997	60,982.83	57,276.75	68,185.56	57,003.28	74,479.87	92,112.24	121,868.54	135,078.06	139,290.71	148,207.74	158,198.68	168,180.62
1996	68,062.61	73,797.43	87,325.03	99,867.81	112,628.72	116,504.10	125,930.38	135,228.48	147,065.71	152,493.21	169,620.56	178,690.79
1995	62,195.25	70,925.68	87,150.24	85,484.01	95,302.45	115,807.02	76,361.84	94,844.51	97,917.61	92,684.98	87,068.22	99,019.38
1994	49,073.11	41,683.85	55,761.49	51,960.41	64,114.55	71,091.31	129,097.14	143,835.97	159,951.32	178,145.50	184,400.47	198,141.84
1993	55,607.90	66,845.32	71,389.00	82,377.87	93,445.15	114,731.89	84,729.93	82,603.35	93,588.28	95,614.13	72,699.37	87,735.86
1992	61,743.50	65,463.46	78,939.31	76,126.17	73,245.74	72,063.61	142,036.33	144,104.40	150,488.13	160,640.90	170,276.25	178,660.54
1991	63,907.89	67,863.93	90,274.18	112,721.44	124,554.81	130,704.32	57,546.12	42,923.41	4,568.20	3,382.19	7,866.39	10,264.06
1990	$22,035.22	$23,624.56	$43,761.67	$44,431.07	$63,181.15	$63,303.51	$57,546.12	$42,923.41	$4,568.20	$3,382.19	$7,866.39	$10,264.06

Source: Based on data from Hedge Fund Research, Inc.

In a recent paper, Kazemi and Li[6] show that hedge fund managers may manage the volatility of their return processes in order to balance several risks and incentives. On one hand, the incentive fee has properties that make it similar to a call option on a portion of the funds profit, where the strike price is zero. As discussed, the manager has the incentive to increase the fund's volatility, especially if the option is about to expire out-of-the-money (i.e. the fund's NAV is below its high-water mark). However, higher volatility increases the probability that the fund may experience negative performance. This can negatively affect the manager's welfare for four reasons: (1) the manager may have her own capital invested in the fund and therefore will have to share in the losses; (2) negative performance means that the fund's NAV will be further below the high-water mark, making it less likely that the manager can collect incentive fees in future; (3) negative performance could lead investors to redeem their capital, reducing the asset management fees of the fund for current and future periods; and (4) negative performance along with higher volatility could damage the fund manager's reputation, reducing her future income. Kazemi and Li empirically test the impact of all these incentives on the behavior of hedge managers. They show that a manager tends to increase the fund's return volatility if: (1) the incentive option is at-the-money; (2) the fund's NAV has spent a significant amount of time under the high-water mark; and (3) the fund's assets are liquid enough to allow the manager to adjust the fund's volatility. Further, they show that small and young funds tend not to adjust their volatility. They argue that these managers could easily lose their assets, and, because they are just trying to establish their reputation, they are reluctant to manage the volatility of their funds.

CONCLUSIONS AND IMPLICATIONS

This chapter examined the option-like payout accruing to hedge fund managers for incentive fees. Hedge fund managers share in the upside of the hedge fund net asset value, but not in the downside. The binary nature of this payout is the same as the payout to a call option at maturity. We used the Black-Scholes Option Pricing Model to determine an approximate value of this option for three hedge fund strategies, and found that the option has considerable value.

There are several implications for how this option analysis can affect hedge fund manager behavior. First, an important implication of this analysis is that hedge fund managers can increase the value of their incentive fee call options by increasing the volatility of hedge fund net asset values. The holder of a call option will always prefer more variance in the value of the underlying asset, because the greater the variance, the greater the probability that the asset value will exceed the strike price at maturity of the option.

This establishes a key distinction between investors in the hedge fund and the hedge fund manager. Investors in the hedge fund own the underlying partnership units, and receive payoffs offered by the entire distribution of return outcomes associated with the hedge fund net asset value. They are generally risk averse and dislike higher volatility.

In contrast, the hedge fund manager is the holder of a contingent claim (the incentive fee call option) on the value of the underlying partnership units. The hedge fund manager, as the owner of the option, receives payoffs only from the tails of the hedge fund return distribution. The contingent claim nature of the incentive fee call option makes higher volatility in the net asset value of the hedge fund desirable to the hedge fund manager.

The irony is that investors in the hedge fund actually provide the incentive to the hedge fund manager to increase the volatility of the return distribution for the hedge fund. Furthermore, the

---

[6] Hossein Kazemi and Ying Li, "Managerial Incentives and Shift of Risk-Taking in Hedge Funds," working paper, Isenberg School of Management, University of Massachusetts, Amherst, 2008.

higher the percentage of profit sharing (e.g. a 30% profit-sharing fee versus a 20% profit-sharing fee), the greater the incentive for the hedge fund manager to increase the volatility of the hedge fund's returns.

A second important implication of hedge fund manager behavior is how hedge fund managers react when their incentive fee call option is far out-of-the-money. This happens when the hedge fund net asset value has declined significantly below the high-water mark. Then the strike price for the incentive fee option is significantly higher than the net asset value of the hedge fund.

When an option is out-of-the-money, the hedge fund manager has two choices to increase the value of the option. The first is to increase the volatility of the underlying asset. As the Black-Scholes Model demonstrates, one way to increase the value of the option is to increase the volatility of the underlying asset; for example, increase the volatility of the hedge fund net asset value. This means that the hedge fund manager is encouraged to increase the volatility of the hedge fund's trading strategy to enhance the value of the incentive fee call option.

Another strategy for a hedge fund manager to pursue is to reprice the option when it is out-of-the-money. However, it is unlikely that the hedge fund manager's current investors will allow the hedge fund manager to lower the high-water mark for the hedge fund manager back to the current (below the high-water mark) hedge fund value. Therefore, the only way to reprice the incentive fee call option back to being at-the-money is to start a new hedge fund. The incentive fee call option is automatically priced at-the-money at the start of any new hedge fund. Unfortunately, this is a growing phenomenon in the hedge fund world. Hedge fund managers that have their incentive fees struck out-of-the-money often start new hedge funds. The existing investors from the old hedge fund are out of luck when the hedge fund manager starts a new hedge fund and diverts his time and attention to the new fund where the incentive fee call option is more valuable than in the old hedge fund.

17

Hedge Fund Collapses

In this chapter we conduct postmortems on recent hedge fund blowups. This chapter is an anecdotal form of risk management. Sometimes history does repeat itself, and the lessons of history are valuable tools for due diligence in the future. While this is not a scientific risk management approach, we think that a brief discussion of some of the recent disasters will provide some insights into what can go wrong. These stories serve as a history lesson but are also a good supplement to Chapter 12 on due diligence.

AMARANTH HEDGE FUND

Amaranth was a self-described multistrategy hedge fund, investing across asset classes and strategies. As we have discussed in previous chapters, multistrategy hedge funds employ a variety of investment strategies. However, Amaranth's fall from glory came from an extremely concentrated bet in the energy markets.[1]

Although Amaranth was technically a multistrategy hedge fund with positions across asset classes, by 2006 it had devoted a large fraction of its risk capital to natural gas trading. Amaranth Advisors, LLC was founded in 2000 by Nicholas Maounis and was headquartered in Greenwich, Connecticut. The founder's original expertise was in convertible bonds, but the fund later became involved in merger arbitrage, long/short equity, leveraged loans, and energy trading. As of June 30, 2006, energy trades accounted for about half of the fund's capital and generated about 75% of its profits.

While Amaranth was based in Greenwich, Connecticut, its star trader, Brian Hunter, was based in Calgary, Alberta. The *Wall Street Journal* reported that Amaranth's head energy trader sometimes held "open positions to buy or sell tens of billions of dollars of commodities."[2] Mr. Hunter saw that a surplus of natural gas in the summer of 2007 could lead to low prices, but made bets that natural gas prices would increase if there was a severe winter or a disruption in supplies. He was also willing to buy natural gas in even further-away years, but this was a much more risky bet because of the lack of trading activity in natural gas for faraway years.

Natural gas trading requires some background. The key economic function for natural gas is to provide for heating demand during the winter in the northern states of the United States, although natural gas is also a key energy source for air-conditioning demand during the summer. There is a long so-called injection season from the spring through the fall in which natural gas is injected and stored in caverns for later use during the long winter season. By the end of February 2006, the fund held nearly 70% of the open interest in the November futures contracts on the New York Mercantile Exchange (NYMEX) and nearly 60% in the futures for January.

That size led to its collapse. Amaranth made a huge bet that natural gas spreads, or the difference between two monthly futures contracts, would rise, and it kept pumping more money into that bet. When natural gas prices fell in August and September 2006, Amaranth found itself on the wrong side of the market and could not recoup its losses.

---

[1] See Ann Davis, Gregory Zuckerman, and Henny Sender, "Hedge Fund Hardball," *Wall Street Journal*, January 30, 2007. This is an excellent article on the Amaranth meltdown.

[2] Ibid.

But Amaranth's fall did not happen overnight. By the end of May, at least some of Amaranth's traders and officers were aware of the firm's predicament (it had lost approximately $1 billion in that month alone). Still, Amaranth continued to put more money into its natural gas bets. By the end of August, Amaranth was still pumping in more money to hold its position, but the market had taken a different direction. After starting 2006 with $7.5 billion, the fund soared to $9.2 billion and eventually tumbled to less than $3 billion.

After the Amaranth crash, the U.S. Senate conducted an extensive investigation on the collapse of the hedge fund.[3] The Senate report confirmed what had already been suspected in the financial markets: that Amaranth had engaged in massive trading in natural gas calendar spreads and that these trades turned dramatically against the hedge fund. During its run, Amaranth was one of the largest traders in natural gas futures contracts, holding as many as 100,000 natural gas contracts in a single month, representing 1 trillion cubic feet of natural gas. This is 5% of all natural gas consumed in the United States in a single year.[4]

Amaranth engaged in a commodity futures strategy where it would go long winter delivery contracts for natural gas (typically the March contract), and go short the non-winter contract (typically the April contract). In particular, Amaranth's largest bet was on the spread between natural gas futures prices for March 2007 and April 2007.[5] Amaranth's bet was that this spread would increase when natural gas inventories stopped being drawn down due to the winter months and began to build up in the spring.

However, instead of this spread increasing, it collapsed. The spread between the March 2007 natural gas futures contract and the April 2007 contract declined from $2.50 down to 75 cents. This resulted in massive losses by Amaranth; for example, it lost $560 million on Thursday, September 14, 2006.

This led Amaranth to scramble to transfer its natural gas futures contracts to third-party financial institutions over the weekend of September 16 to 17. Initially, Merrill Lynch agreed to take on 25% of Amaranth's positions for a payment of about $250 million.[6]

Amaranth lost another $800 million on Tuesday, September 19, 2006.

The next day, on September 20, 2006, the fund succeeded in transferring its remaining energy positions to Citadel Investment Group and to its clearing broker, JPMorgan Chase, at a $2.15 billion discount to their mark-to-market value on just the day before. In total, Amaranth lost $6.6 billion in a matter of months.

It should be noted that prime brokers generally treat hedge funds as their most favored clients (MFCs). But when it comes to a quickly eroding hedge fund, the MFC status can turn on a dime and a hedge fund can find that prime brokers exacerbate the hedge fund's problems rather than alleviate them.

This appears to be part of the story for Amaranth. On Monday, September 18, just when Amaranth thought it had a rescue plan negotiated with Goldman Sachs, its prime broker, JP Morgan, refused to release the collateral that Amaranth had deposited with JP Morgan. This effectively killed any potential bailout of Amaranth.

---

[3] See U.S. Senate Permanent Subcommittee on Investigations, "Excessive Speculation in the Natural Gas Market," June 25, 2007.

[4] See U.S. Senate Permanent Subcommittee on Investigations.

[5] See Gretchen Morgenson and Jenny Anderson, "A Hedge Fund's Loss Rattles Nerves," *New York Times*, September 19, 2006.

[6] See Hilary Till, "The Amaranth Collapse: What Happened and What Have We Learned Thus Far?" EDHEC Risk and Asset Management Research Center White Paper, August 2007.

As our prior chapter on the hedge fund incentive fee call option feature demonstrated, Amaranth had a big incentive to take big bets. This is detailed in the *Wall Street Journal* article by Davis, Zuckerman, and Sender.

> At Amaranth, star energy trader Brian Hunter won an estimated $75 million bonus after his team produced a $1.26 billion profit in 2005. Like many others at the fund, he had to keep about 30% of his pay in the fund. The fund's chief risk officer, Robert Jones, got a bonus of at least $5 million for 2005, say people familiar with the bonuses. Nicholas Maounis—founder, majority owner, and chief executive of the Amaranth management firm—got an estimated $70 million cut of 2005 management fees, plus some of Amaranth's $200 million-plus in performance fees. He kept much of his compensation in the fund.[7]

What are the lessons to be learned here? First, hedge funds are well known to operate in an unregulated fashion. This was compounded by the fact that the trading schemes of Amaranth were conducted in the complex and uncoordinated world of natural gas markets. For example, the U.S. regulatory umbrella covering energy trading has had a noteworthy gap in coverage. The exchange-traded futures markets are explicitly regulated by the Commodity Futures Trading Commission (CFTC), and the physical natural gas markets are explicitly regulated by the Federal Energy Regulatory Commission (FERC). However, over-the-counter energy derivatives trading has not been subject to the same regulatory scrutiny. It was on such platforms that Amaranth carried out a substantial fraction of its trading.

Even more to the point, Amaranth traded many of its natural gas positions on the Intercontinental Exchange (ICE) as opposed to the New York Mercantile Exchange (NYMEX). Both exchanges trade natural gas contracts. However, under what is known as the "Enron Loophole," electronic exchanges like the ICE are not regulated, whereas physical exchanges like the NYMEX are.

Clearly, Amaranth exploited this loophole to establish large positions in natural gas futures contracts. In fact, the U.S. Senate established that once the NYMEX directed Amaranth to reduce its positions, the hedge fund simply moved its contracts over the ICE.[8]

Second, commodity derivatives markets are relatively small compared to global asset values. As this story indicates, it is possible for one large hedge fund to overwhelm these markets.

Last, prime broker relationships are paramount to the successful implementation of a hedge fund's trading strategy. As this story indicates, the cold hearts at JPMorgan effectively shut down a bailout by Goldman Sachs of Amaranth's positions, effectively guaranteeing that Amaranth would collapse.

PELOTON PARTNERS HEDGE FUND

Peloton's collapse caught the hedge fund community off-guard. Unlike Amaranth Advisors, which teetered on the brink of collapse for months before finally selling its assets and winding down operations, Peloton's collapse was swift. Making the story more poignant and fascinating is the fact that the destruction of Peloton, which had been founded in 2005, came just a few months after it had won a Hedge Fund Manager of the Year award at the prestigious *EuroHedge* magazine annual awards dinner.[9] Peloton had made a substantial bet in 2007 that the mortgage bond market would collapse. It did, and the fund earned an 87% annual return for which it received its hedge fund manager award.

---

[7] Davis, Zuckerman, and Sender, "Hedge Fund Hardball."

[8] See the U.S. Senate Permanent Subcommittee on Investigations.

[9] See Roddy Boyd, "Mortgage Mess Socks Ex Goldman Sachs Stars," *Fortune*, February 29, 2008.

However, Peloton reversed this bet and the $1.8 billion fund collapsed after a series of trades betting that the mortgage market would rebound dropped sharply in value, leading to margin calls from creditors that the firm was unable to meet.

In 2007, Peloton had taken short positions on investments backed by pools of subprime mortgages, meaning it bet that their values would fall. While other hedge funds like Paulson & Co. also bet short on mortgage bonds, Peloton did something more complicated: It wagered that slices of the same bond portfolio with different ratings would diverge sharply in price, a strategy known as capital structure arbitrage. Peloton took long positions on AAA-rated mortgage bonds and gambled that BBB-rated subprime bonds would fall in value. That calculation paid off big when the fund's short position fell 75% as a result of the subprime mortgage meltdown, while its AAA-rated positions declined much less in value.

This all changed in early 2008. The fund had about $16 billion in long positions versus $3.2 billion in shorts. The short positions, which had been so profitable in 2007, declined modestly in value, while the continued angst in the credit and mortgage markets drove the value of the massive long positions down an average of between $15 and $25 per bond in about a month. The fund suffered insurmountable losses as a result.

Compounding Peloton's problems was the fact that most investment banking creditors were in the same boat as Peloton. Their balance sheets had been under attack since the summer of 2007, caught up in the same liquidity crisis that destroyed Lehman Brothers, AIG, Washington Mutual, and others. As a consequence, the large banks did not have the resources to absorb the hit on behalf of the fund and instead demanded additional collateral from Peloton—collateral calls that Peloton was unable to meet. Finally, the consortium of Peloton's lenders (its prime broker Goldman Sachs, Citadel Group, and Och-Ziff Capital Management) declined to buy its portfolio. Peloton had no choice but to liquidate its fund.

Also, in early 2008, Peloton told investors that it was suspending redemptions in a second portfolio, a $1.6 billion multistrategy fund that finished 2007 up 27%. According to a letter sent to clients in March 2008, the multistrategy fund had a very large position in Peloton's flagship asset-backed securities fund, and the severe decline in the flagship fund had a "serious negative impact" on the multistrategy fund. In an amazing fall from grace, Peloton went from Hedge Fund Manager of the Year in January 2008 to being out of business by April of the same year.

So where did Peloton go wrong? First, there was a quick and sudden drop in the market value of highly rated mortgage securities. Second, there was a move by banks to significantly tighten margin lending requirements for hedge funds. Third, Peloton was highly leveraged and banks such as UBS and Deutsche Bank started demanding more collateral as the value of Peloton's investments fell. Peloton had an estimated $10 billion in outstanding positions but only $2 billion in assets in the fund.

If this story sounds familiar, it should. Ten years earlier, Long-Term Capital Management (LTCM) suffered a similar fate. LTCM bet on convergence trades, that two similar securities that were priced differently would converge over time. This is a common form of arbitrage among hedge fund strategies. A credit crisis started by the Russian bond default led to a divergence of pricing, not a convergence, and LTCM's arbitrage strategy failed to work. The failure of the arbitrage trades to work, combined with massive leverage on losing trades, led to its swift demise.

Similarly, Peloton's mortgage bond arbitrage strategy failed to work. Its long positions in AAA-rated slices of the mortgage market declined far more than its short positions in more risky mortgage slices. This was made all the more lethal by the large amount of leverage that Peloton employed. When it came time to face its margin calls, Peloton found its prime broker and bankers to be most unsympathetic, and Peloton's portfolios were liquidated.

CARLYLE CAPITAL CORPORATION

Another swift and stunning reversal of fortune was experienced by Carlyle Capital Corporation (CCC), a listed hedge fund that also traded in the mortgage market. The demise of CCC in March 2008 was a surprise to many. Its parent company, the Carlyle Group, is one of the most successful alternative asset franchises in the world, managing over $81 billion in assets for the world's most sophisticated clients. In 2006 and 2007 it returned $18 billion in profits and equity to clients.

The fund's demise came just eight months after it listed on Euronext Amsterdam in 2007. Similar to Peloton, CCC's collapse was another casualty of a liquidity crisis that led to over $50 billion in losses at major investment banks. CCC was created as part of the Carlyle Group's efforts to diversify its business and to give public shareholders a way to get exposure to some of its funds. Partners of the Carlyle Group retained a 15% ownership in CCC. However, within weeks of its July 2007 public listing, the Carlyle Group was forced to make its first bailout of the fund with additional injected capital.

CCC's dire funding problems first emerged on March 5, 2008, when it said it had been unable to meet margin calls from four banks on short-term repurchase agreements. Just two days earlier, Chief Executive John Stomber had told investors on a conference call that the fund wasn't seeing increased margin pressure from its lenders. Within a week, the margin calls had reached more than $400 million, and lending banks had seized about three-quarters of CCC's assets. Efforts to put in place a standstill agreement with banks holding the remaining assets failed late in the week of March 10.

CCC's strategy was not fraught with complex derivatives or secretive black-box trading schemes. Its strategy was simple: borrow at low short-term interest rates and invest this borrowed capital in long-term AAA-rated mortgage bonds issued by Freddie Mac and Fannie Mae. CCC's investment strategy was to make money on the difference between the cost of funding the AAA-rated mortgage securities and the interest received on them, with an aim of paying out an annual dividend of around 10%.

Freddie Mac and Fannie Mae securities are considered to be almost certain to be repaid by their issuers, but their value plummeted dramatically in February and March 2008 as investors worldwide shunned risk of any type and as the U.S. housing market continued to suffer. Furthermore, CCC was vulnerable to losing money if its investment strategy turned against it because of the highly leveraged nature of its investment strategy. For every $1 in capital it raised from investors, it borrowed about $31 to accumulate a portfolio of securities issued by the U.S. housing agencies. Carlyle Capital used about $670 million in cash equity to finance its $21.7 billion portfolio of securities issued by Freddie Mac and Fannie Mae.

The significant decline in value of Fannie Mae and Freddie Mac securities came to a head in early March 2008 when margin calls from Deutsche Bank, JPMorgan Chase, and other lenders reached more than $900 million. At that point, the lenders began to seize the fund's collateral and its chief assets, AAA-rated mortgage-backed securities.

The share price for CCC declined swiftly, dropping from its public offering price of $20 in July 2007 to $0.31 in March 2008. During the week of March 10, 2008, CCC declared that it would wind up its operations and further stated that there would not be any money left for shareholders. In the middle of March 2008, CCC announced that it had received default notices on funding lines for its entire $21.7 billion portfolio of mortgage-backed securities, and that its liabilities exceeded its assets; it was bankrupt. After the fund defaulted on more than $16 billion in assets, shares in CCC stock dropped 93%, closing at 35 cents on March 16.

The lesson here? Except for U.S. Treasury bonds, which rallied dramatically through the mortgage and liquidity crisis of 2007–2008 (the yield on 10-year U.S. Treasury bonds declined from 5.5%

to 3.5% during this time as Treasury bond prices soared), no security is safe from a liquidity crisis. The securities purchased by CCC were from Fannie Mae, Freddie Mac, and Ginny Mae, U.S. government-sponsored companies with either an explicit or an implicit guarantee by the U.S. government. But as the credit crisis took hold, even these safe investments declined significantly in value. Indeed, as history played out later in 2008, Fannie and Freddie were taken over by the U.S. government and the implicit guarantee of their bonds was finally made explicit.

A second lesson to be learned is that of protecting number one. Even the Carlyle Group, with its clout and reputation, could not negotiate a grace period from its bankers to save CCC. Prime brokers and bankers have no humor or compassion when it comes to declining collateral values.

BAYOU MANAGEMENT

In what is surely the most imaginative of all hedge fund frauds, we have Bayou Management. Bayou Management started out as a legitimate hedge fund but quickly degenerated into outright fraud. The two principals, founder Samuel Israel III and CFO Daniel Marino, were both sentenced to over 10 years in prison.[10]

The story of Bayou begins in 1996 when, within a few months after the Bayou Fund opened and started trading, Bayou sustained trading losses and began lying to customers about the fund's profits and losses. In fund performance summaries, Bayou concealed the volatile swings of its trading gains and losses by fabricating the results. In 1997, the profits of the Bayou Fund fell short of the amount principals had projected. To cover the difference between actual and projected profits, and to keep clients and attract new ones, Bayou transferred back into the fund a portion of the trading commissions that the fund had paid to Bayou Securities during that year. Bayou Securities was a separate broker that Bayou Capital had set up to process the trades from the fund—earning a commission on the Bayou Fund's losing trades.

Bayou did not disclose to its clients that the fund's performance was being bolstered by these rebates. Consequently, Bayou clients were left with a false impression that the Bayou Fund had made a profit. Trading losses continued into 1998, when Bayou Fund sustained a net loss of millions of dollars from trading. Over the course of the year, Israel and Marino concealed their losses by making material misstatements to clients about the Bayou Fund's performance and their clients' capital balances. Israel, Marino, and a former Bayou principal concocted false investment returns to report to their clients, and applied those false results to create false year-end financial statements.

By December 1998, the Bayou Fund's mounting losses could not withstand an independent audit. So Bayou decided to dismiss the fund's independent auditing firm and manufacture fictional auditor's reports, financial statements, and performance summaries. Marino, a certified public accountant, agreed to fabricate the annual audit of the Bayou Fund in order to conceal the trading losses. He created a fictitious accounting firm, Richmond-Fairfield Associates, to pose as the independent auditor of the Bayou Fund. But Marino was the sole principal of Richmond-Fairfield, and the firm had no other clients. From this firm, fraudulent financial statements were prepared.

In 1999, the Bayou Fund again lost a material amount of money. Bayou again concealed the loss by creating and distributing to the fund's investors false performance summaries and a false financial statement that purportedly had been audited by Richmond-Fairfield Associates. In the year-end financial statements, Israel and Marino again fabricated the Bayou Fund's results in order to make it appear that the fund was earning trading profits and achieving earnings targets. The trading losses continued to mount and fictional financial statements and summaries continued to be

---

[10] See Amanda Cantrell, "CEO Israel, Finance Chief Marino Face Potentially Long Jail Terms for Stealing Investors' Money," *CNNMoney.com*, September 29, 2005.

issued through the years 2000 to 2002 to create the appearance of modest, steady, and believable growth. The performance summaries sent out by Bayou indicated that clients were earning 1% to 2% in net profits each month.

Throughout this time, Bayou actively solicited both new and current investors and raised tens of millions of dollars of additional capital. In January 2003, defendants liquidated the Bayou Fund and created the four successor funds, Accredited, Affiliates, No Leverage, and Superfund, in order to attract more investors and capital. While investor deposits peaked in 2003 at more than $125 million, the reorganization did not improve profitability. The new funds lost even more money through trading. In 2003, Bayou Superfund took in more than $90 million in investments, but lost approximately $35 million through trading. However, according to its 2003 annual statement, Bayou Superfund had earned more than $25 million. Also, throughout this time period, the Bayou funds continued to collect profit-sharing fees on the fraudulent gains and Bayou Securities continued to earn millions of dollars of trading commissions.

By 2004, Israel and Marino had stopped trading and had transferred the rest of Bayou's assets to Israel and other non-Bayou entities but still sent periodic statements to investors describing profitable trades. Things began to unravel for Bayou when, in May 2005, $100 million was seized by legal authorities from the State of Arizona.

At the time, the Arizona authorities were investigating an unrelated financial fraud and became suspicious when they found that huge sums of money had been shifted around different accounts in rapid fashion, moving from London to the Wachovia bank in the United States and then to Wachovia's Hong Kong unit. Unbeknownst to Arizona authorities, they had stumbled onto what became one of the most spectacular hedge fund frauds ever. The extent of the fraud was later confirmed in a several-page suicide note drafted by Marino. He never did commit suicide, but his suicide dissertation pieced together the extent and blatancy of the fraud. The $100 million recovered by Arizona authorities, ultimately in a New Jersey bank account, was all that remained of the massive Bayou.

The lesson here? Some people are just out-and-out liars and charlatans with no scruples whatsoever. However, when a hedge fund uses a small outside audit firm, in fact, one that was unknown outside of its Bayou purpose, red flags should go up all around. As we noted in our chapter on due diligence, contacting and interviewing the outside auditors for a hedge fund is a must step of any due diligence. The only employee of the Richmond-Fairfield accounting firm was Marino. Gee, do you think that this was a clue?

As a final and bizarre postscript to this whole mess, Samuel Israel went missing on Monday, June 9, 2008, one day before he was to begin serving his 20-year prison sentence. His car was found near the Bear Mountain Bridge over the upper Hudson River in New York State. On the dust of his car's hood was written the message "Suicide is painless," a reference to the theme song from the movie and TV show $M*A*S*H$. He was later captured at a trailer park where he had been driven by his girlfriend after leaving his car at the bridge. He is now serving his 20-year jail sentence.

MARIN CAPITAL

Marin Capital was a well-known hedge fund manager performing a legitimate hedge fund strategy: convertible bond arbitrage. Convertible bonds are hybrid securities, a mixture of debt and equity. This hybrid nature can lead to mispricing in the market as traditional investors have a difficult time valuing securities that span asset classes. This is where convertible bond hedge fund managers jump in to buy convertible bonds and hedge out the expensive component of the bond, keeping what is undervalued. At its peak, Marin Capital had $2.2 billion in assets under management.

Generally, convertible bond arbitrage is considered a safe, conservative strategy. This strategy involves buying convertible corporate bonds (bonds with an attached call option that allows the bonds to be exchanged or converted into stock at what amounts to a specified price) and hedging out the value of the call option by short selling the stock. The amount of stock sold short depends on the exercise price or conversion ratio, the sensitivity of the option's value with respect to changes in the stock price (known as the delta risk), and the sensitivity of the delta with respect to the stock price (measured by a statistic called gamma). The strategy generates low-risk income if the option's value of the convertible bond is underpriced in the market and because the practice of hedging the option's value results in systematically selling the stock when the price is high and buying when it is low.

The strategy of convertible bond arbitrage worked well until the summer of 2006 when two bond-rating agencies cut the investment-grade status of both Ford's and General Motors' corporate bonds. GM was cut two notches to BB and Ford was cut one notch down to BB+. Although this represented just a couple of steps down the credit grade ladder, it meant that these two corporate giants had crossed the threshold from investment grade to junk status. Falling from the status of investment grade meant that pension funds and some other managed funds might be prevented from investing in their bonds. As a result, the price effects of this downgrade were larger than would otherwise result from a single- or double-step downgrade.

To put this in perspective, another reason that this downgrade was atypical was that GM and Ford were a major share of the corporate debt market. GM had $290 billion in outstanding debt and Ford had another $160 for a total of $450 billion, several times over the size of Argentina's debt, which suffered a default several years ago.

To make matters worse, at the same time that GM's and Ford's bonds were being downgraded to junk status, an unsolicited bid to buy GM came from billionaire financier Kirk Kerkorian. Mr. Kerkorian announced he would acquire a large stake in GM, causing a price spike in the stock of GM and other related companies like Ford.

This was a one-two punch against convertible bond managers. Recall that the strategy of convertible bond arbitrage is to buy a convertible bond, short the stock component of the bond, and hold what is usually a relatively safe straight piece of debt. So hedge fund managers like Marin Capital were especially hard hit because they had shorted the common stock of GM and held long positions in the underlying bonds. When the bonds got downgraded, hedge fund managers were forced to try to sell into a market with no buyers. Meanwhile, the hedge fund managers were forced to cover their short stock sales by purchasing GM and Ford stock that had appreciated in value. It was a double whammy effect; convertible bond hedge fund managers lost on both sides of their strategy. Instead of being hedged, convertible bond hedge fund managers like Marin Capital lost money on their equity hedging strategy as well as their long bond positions, and this was all the more exacerbated by the leverage that they employed.

BERNIE MADOFF

This name struck fear into the hearts of many investors and hedge funds of funds in December 2008. Early that month, Bernie Madoff allegedly confessed to running a giant hedge fund Ponzi scheme. He finally broke down and reportedly admitted to his family that his business was "all just one big lie," and basically a giant Ponzi scheme.[11] Along the way, Mr. Madoff managed to defraud high net worth investors, fund of hedge fund managers, movie producers, movie stars, and university endowments. All told, the scheme was reputed to have grown to $50 billion before being unmasked.

---

[11] See Kevin McCoy, "Pursuer of Madoff Blew a Whistle for Nine Years," *USA Today*, February 12, 2009.

What is amazing about this fraud is that questions, if not outright accusations, had been put forward since 2000. That year, Harry Markopolos, a Rampart Investment Management portfolio manager, and Neil Chelo, his top assistant, examined the performance numbers of Madoff Investments. They suspected some trickery because Madoff's performance rose at a nice 45-degree angle year after year, market cycle after market cycle. The consistency of Madoff's performance was too good to be believed.

Mr. Markopolos and his assistant studied the strategy supposedly used by Bernie Madoff, called split-strike conversion. This is an options strategy that should be limited in risk and provide limited rewards. What made Mr. Markopolos suspicious was that he had tried a similar strategy but did not produce the results that Madoff claimed to have earned.

So Mr. Markopolos went to the SEC with his conclusions. He approached the Boston, Massachusetts office of the SEC first in 2000 and then again in 2001. Unfortunately, these initial visits did not lead to SEC action. Frank Casey, a co-worker of Mr. Markopolos, tried to help by mentioning Madoff's amazing performance to a reporter from *MarHedge*, a publication that covers the hedge fund industry. Both *MarHedge* and *Barron's* subsequently published stories calling into question the remarkable results produced by Bernie Madoff. But these stories did not bring any additional scrutiny.

In 2005, Mr. Markopolos contacted the SEC's New York office. He sent a 21-page report to the SEC's branch chief explaining why he had concluded that Madoff's business was "the world's largest Ponzi scheme."[12] He continued to send warnings to the SEC in 2006 and 2007 but no action followed. The SEC chairman at the time, Christopher Cox, later stated that he was "gravely concerned by the apparent multiple failures over at least a decade to thoroughly investigate these allegations."[13] Unfortunately, the grave concern came much too late.

Bernie Madoff was arrested by federal agents on December 11, 2008, after being turned in to the authorities by his sons. It was then that Mr. Madoff allegedly made his comments about his business being all one big lie. In June 2009, three months after being incarcerated, a federal judge gave Madoff the maximum sentence of 150 years in prison.

CONCLUSION

So what can we learn from all of this? First, a consistent theme across most of our anecdotes was the use of large amounts of leverage. Hedge fund managers often employ strategies that allow them to pick up nickels and dimes off the street through reasonably straightforward arbitrage trades. They then increase these nickels and dimes into half-dollars and dollars through the use of leverage. But leverage is truly a two-edged sword. It can gear up your profits but also lead to large losses when trades turn against the hedge fund manager.

We also witnessed the cold-hearted way that banks and prime brokers act when it comes to protecting their collateral. As Amaranth, Peloton, and CCC indicate, when the value of a hedge fund manager's assets begins to decline, they will receive very little sympathy from their prime brokers. Hedge fund managers can go from rock stars to bums in the blink of an eye. There is no love lost on Wall Street. Again, as mentioned in our chapter on due diligence, documenting the prime broker relationships of the hedge fund manager is a key step in building the file on the hedge fund manager before you invest.

---

[12] Ibid.

[13] Ibid.

Last, the large fees of the hedge fund world attract geniuses, as well as charlatans. It is difficult but not impossible to detect fraud. Every fraud has some fatal flaw. In the case of Bayou, the partners created a fictional accounting firm. A small amount of detective work could have revealed this hole in their armor.

The case of Bernie Madoff was a bit more unusual. There were so many warning bells and printed stories and appeals for investigation that one is left scratching one's head as to how the fraud continued for so long. Furthermore, it is amazing how many institutional investors, wealthy individuals, and hedge funds of funds continued to give their money to Mr. Madoff even with the warning bells sounding like klaxons. Go figure.

18

Top Ten Hedge Fund Quotes

We turn now to a little humor surrounding the hedge fund industry. Throughout the course of my career at CalPERS and Hermes, I have visited with and have spoken to hundreds of hedge fund managers. As I have gone through these meetings on due diligence visits, I have asked the questions that were laid out in our chapter on due diligence. The responses from the hedge fund managers are not always what you would expect. So, I decided to compile my own "Top Ten" list of quotes from hedge fund managers to provide a humorous insight into the hedge fund industry.

At the outset, it should be realized that these quotes are not indicative of the whole industry. Rather, they demonstrate some of the chaff out there that has to be separated from the wheat. However, should you ever run across one of these quotes in your due diligence, proceed with caution. With no further ado, here we go.[1]

NUMBER 10: "IF WE DON'T CHARGE 2 AND 20, NOBODY WILL TAKE US SERIOUSLY."

A while back a brand-new hedge fund manager passed through CalPERS' investment offices looking to raise money. The two principals of the hedge fund knocked on our door through a contact well-known to CalPERS. They had successful track records investing in traditional long-only securities, but had never started a hedge fund before.

When I inquired as to where they learned to short, their response was that they had not previously shorted securities in their investment program. I then inquired why these two novice hedge fund managers with no prior hedge fund experience should be worthy of a 2% management fee and a 20% profit-sharing fee. And the response that I received was this quote.

Let's take a moment to analyze their response. These two start-up hedge fund managers did not take the time to justify their fees based on their investment acumen. Rather, they responded that their fee structure was what the market would bear—indeed, what the market expected from a hedge fund manager. There was no attempt to justify their fee structure based on their investment skill set.

Well, that may be what the market will bear, but it's not what CalPERS will bear. As a well-known investor in the hedge fund community, CalPERS is sometimes a bellwether indicator of what the market will accept, and in this case, we decided that we would not pay a 2 and 20 fee structure for neophyte hedge fund managers. Beware of hedge fund managers trying to justify their fees based on what they think the market will bear.

NUMBER 9: "WE CHARGE 3 AND 30 BECAUSE THAT IS THE ONLY WAY WE CAN KEEP OUR ASSETS BELOW SEVERAL BILLION DOLLARS."

Top Ten quote number 9 is the mirror image of Top Ten quote number 10. A few years back a very well known and successful hedge fund manager visited CalPERS headquarters. In the middle of

---

[1] This top ten list is based on the personal experiences of the author in his due diligence of hedge fund managers.

their presentation, I asked what his fee structure was. He initially responded, "Three and 30," which was followed by dead silence for about 30 seconds until he came back with this quote.

Let's analyze this statement a bit more. First, this gets back to an argument about what the market will bear. The hedge fund manager did not attempt to justify his fee structure based on his skill, investment acumen, or financial market insights. Rather, he justified it in terms of market demand.

Second, this manager was all about fee generation, not wealth generation. There is nothing in his statement that indicates that he is earning/making value for his clients. Granted, his statement does indicate some attempt to limit the capacity of his fund and he should be given some credit for that. Still, this is a statement more about making the hedge fund manager rich than it is about making his clients wealthy. Beware of hedge fund managers who focus on fees first and client wealth second.

NUMBER 8: "WE ARE 75% CASH BECAUSE WE CANNOT FIND SUFFICIENT INVESTMENTS."

This statement is bad on so many levels that it is hard to decide where to begin. First, this hedge fund manager billed himself as an equity long/short investor. The key word there is *equity*, not *cash*. His job is to find long/short investment opportunities in the U.S. equities market. Further, the cash he had in his account was not generated by short rebates held at the prime broker; it was capital that had not been put to work.

This manager sat on cash during 2001 and 2002. Why? Because he had changed his stripes from an equity long/short investor to a market timer. In 2001 and 2002, the best way to outperform the U.S. equity market when it declined by double digits was to sit on cash. It was easy to generate significant profits compared to the U.S. equity market during the three-year bear period of 2000 to 2002 and, in turn, to earn generous incentive fees.

Second, when CalPERS or Hermes hires a manager, we expect our investment capital to be put to full use. Cash is our decision, and we manage our cash position at monthly asset allocation meetings. We expect our external managers to put to work fully the investment capital that they have been allocated. If an external manager decides to sit on cash in a Hermes account, it introduces an unintended bet into the portfolio. Managers that cannot find sufficient investments should return the capital to their investors.

Third, neither CalPERS nor Hermes is willing to pay a 2% management fee for a manager to sit on cash. Hedge fund managers that sit on cash are the most expensive cash managers on the face of the earth. At the beginning of 2006, with overnight money earning 4.5% in the United States less a 2% hedge fund manager fee, cash balances held by hedge fund managers earn investors only 2.5%, you are better off putting this money to work in short-term U.S. Treasury bills.

NUMBER 7: "WE DON'T INVEST IN CROWDED SHORTS."

I cannot count the number of times that I have heard this statement from hedge fund managers. First, what does the term **crowded shorts** mean? This refers to a situation where a large group of hedge fund managers collectively short the same stock in expectation that it will decline in value. The shorting becomes crowded because all of the hedge fund managers rush to their prime brokers and request the same stock to borrow for their shorting strategies.

There are two problems with crowded short positions. First, crowded short positions can lead to the phenomenon of beta expansion. This is the case where the stock price becomes even more sensitive to the movements of the stock market, its beta expands to reflect a greater covariance with the stock market than an investor would normally expect. We showed a demonstration of this in our chapter on risk management. This can contribute to additional volatility in the stock price, as well as a covariance with the broader stock market that is temporarily out of balance.

The second issue is one of a short squeeze. Short squeezes occur when hedge fund managers have to cover their short sales by purchasing in the market the underlying stock that they had previously shorted. This now puts upward pressure on the stock price, reducing the profits to the shorting strategy. The last few hedge fund managers to evacuate their short position as the stock price increases are squeezed and see their profits from the short position erode dramatically. This phenomenon is all the more exacerbated the more crowded the short position.

Yet all of this should not be a problem if hedge fund managers never invest in crowded shorts. In fact, based on the number of times that I have heard hedge fund managers claim that they do not invest in crowded shorts, this phenomenon does not exist at all. Therefore, the associated phenomena of beta expansion and short squeezes are really just figments of our overheated investor imaginations!

Come on, we all know that crowded shorts exist and we have all seen the phenomena of beta expansion and short squeezes. This Top Ten quote demonstrates that you sometimes have to take what hedge fund managers tell you with a large grain of salt.

NUMBER 6: "I HAVEN'T SHORTED BEFORE, BUT I DO HAVE MY CAIA."

Again, we have the example of an inexperienced hedge fund manager who came from the world of traditional long-only investing. While it is commendable that this new hedge fund manager has his Chartered Alternative Investment Analyst (CAIA) designation, this alone does not qualify him to be an expert in shorting stocks.

Shorting securities is very different from traditional long-only investing. First, there is unlimited downside with a shorted security. With a long position the maximum amount an investor can lose is the dollar amount invested, as the long position can decline no further than zero. However, for a short position, in theory, the loss can be unlimited because the stock price has no bounds on how high it can go.

Second, as we just discussed with regard to Top Ten quote number 7, the phenomena of beta expansion and short squeezes are new challenges to hedge fund managers that do not occur in the world of long-only management.

Third, there is an additional skill set of knowing from which prime brokers to borrow general collateral (easy-to-borrow stocks) versus hard-to-borrow stocks, and how to negotiate with the prime broker the short rebate received from the short sales.

While the CAIA program is indeed a respected and rigorous alternative investment learning process, it is no substitute for developing short-selling skills. Bottom line, an investor has to ask himself: Does he want to pay 2 and 20 fees to a hedge fund manager to allow that hedge fund manager to get an education on shorting stock with the investor's capital?

NUMBER 5: "HEDGE FUNDS ARE BETTER INVESTMENTS THAN MANAGED FUTURES BECAUSE MANAGED FUTURES IS A ZERO-SUM GAME."

Excuse me? Aren't all alpha-generating ideas zero-sum games? For every winner there has to be a loser. Regardless of whether the alpha-generating idea makes a profit for a hedge fund manager or a managed futures manager, someone has to lose money on the other side.

Now, there can be reasons why investors on the other side of the trade might be willing to give up some gain. For example, in the managed futures world, Commodity Trading Advisors (CTAs) may be able to capture a return premium for providing risk transference services to commodity producers or commodity purchasers who wish to hedge the price risk of their commodity sales or purchases. Another example might be merger arbitrage, where investors may be willing to forgo the premium associated with a merger transaction because they do not wish to underwrite the risk of the deal collapsing. Still, there must be a balance where every gain has its counterpart in a commensurate loss.[2]

The fact that this hedge fund manager tried to promote his hedge fund over managed futures products by using this argument reflects a fundamental lack of understanding about the financial markets. This statement was all the more surprising because it was made at an alpha conference in front of a room of intelligent and sophisticated investors. Go figure.

NUMBER 4: "WHAT'S A MASTER TRUST?"

Several years ago a brand-new hedge fund based in Texas passed through the doors of CalPERS. The group contained some well-known characters from the great state of Texas. They brought with them their top attorney, a partner from a well-known and respected Texas law firm. In the course of our discussions with this new hedge fund I asked them whether they intended to have an onshore hedge fund and an offshore hedge fund. They assured me that given the success they anticipated, they would have both types of funds.

When I then asked their top attorney how they would resolve the inevitable conflicts of interest for trade allocation between the onshore and offshore hedge funds, he responded with "That's a good question." This alone should have qualified for the Top Ten list, but it gets better.

When I suggested to the lawyer that he might wish to consider a master trust and master feeder structure for the onshore and offshore hedge funds, his response was "What's a master trust?" But it gets better.

As I began to explain how a master trust and feeder structure worked, the top lawyer from this well-known law firm opened up his briefcase, pulled out the classic lawyer's legal pad and began to take notes as I lectured.

Now, what's wrong with this picture? First, a hedge fund manager that intends to run both an onshore and an offshore hedge fund had better have his infrastructure in place before rushing forward. Even better, why should CalPERS pay fees of 2 and 20 to a hedge fund manager when we were the ones to give them an education about how onshore versus offshore hedge funds work? In my mind, given the lessons learned that day by that hedge fund manager, they should have paid CalPERS 2 and 20, not the other way around.

NUMBER 3: "YOUR HEAD OF EQUITY DOES NOT UNDERSTAND OUR HEDGE FUND STRATEGY."

This is the same bunch of Texans as in Top Ten quote number 4. According to this group, in one hedge fund they were going to demonstrate their expertise in (and I quote here): convertible arbitrage, merger arbitrage, managed futures, equity long/short, and corporate governance.

---

[2] Note that there can be many other reasons why one investor might be willing to accept a loss. Different levels of risk aversion, time horizons, expectations about the risk and return of an underlying investment, and access to asset classes can all lead to a transfer of gains and losses among investors.

Putting aside for the moment that this Texas group did not have a clue about a master trust account or how to resolve conflicts of interest between onshore and offshore accounts, their statement about their five areas of expertise does stretch one's credibility a bit.

First, each of their five purported areas of expertise requires just that: considerable experience and expertise to invest successfully. For example, convertible arbitrage and merger arbitrage are very different strategies. As we discussed previously, convertible arbitrage is the search for cheap beta exposure among four primary systematic risk exposures, while merger arbitrage is a form of financial market insurance sales (e.g. the sale of put options). These are very different investment programs with very different risk profiles that require significantly different skill sets to perform well. Throw on top of these two strategies purported additional expertise in managed futures, equity long/short investing, and corporate governance, and this really strains the levels of credibility.

Further, consider that CalPERS itself is an expert in corporate governance and the strategy suggested by this hedge fund manager group did not even begin to make sense to the CalPERS investment staff, and you wonder even more.

Therefore, I turned down an investment in this hedge fund. At the time I was head of global equity for CalPERS. I explained to this group that I thought that their strategy lacked focus, that they needed to figure out their infrastructure between onshore and offshore hedge fund management, and last, I did not think that their corporate governance strategy really fit in with a hedge fund. When I spoke with this group and told them politely that I had declined to invest in their hedge fund, they were shocked. In their minds, a check for $100 million was virtually in their pocket.

So shocked and disappointed were the Texans that they immediately drafted a letter to the chief investment officer (CIO) of CalPERS with the opening line of the letter stating: "Your Head of Equity does not understand our hedge fund strategy."

There was only one problem with this letter. By the time they drafted their letter and mailed it to the CalPERS CIO, the former CIO for CalPERS had resigned and I had been promoted to be the new CIO of CalPERS; therefore, I was the recipient of their letter. I wonder how those guys ever made out, I have not heard from them since.

NUMBER 2: "BASICALLY I LOOK AT SCREENS ALL DAY AND GO WITH MY GUT."

As part of the due diligence with any hedge fund manager, I follow the three basic questions outlined in Chapter 12 on due diligence. Bottom line: I try to find out what makes the hedge fund manager so smart. How does he generate his trade ideas, what is his investment process, and where does he find good investments?

One day about two years ago while visiting a hedge fund manager in London, I asked the basic question: How do you generate your trade ideas? I never expected to get the response that I received, Top Ten quote number 2.

Humor aside, how do you document such a process? What happens if the hedge fund manager decides to take a vacation? Who will watch the screens then? Whose gut will substitute for the hedge fund manager's gut while he is away? What happens if the hedge fund manager's gut gets indigestion? The questions are endless. Bottom line: There is no process other than the random thoughts and ideas that bounce around in the hedge fund manager's head and the intuition of his gut. While he may be a gutsy investor, there is simply too much process risk associated with this hedge fund manager to make a credible investment. However, as a postscript, this hedge fund manager had about 200 million pounds sterling under management, so at least there was a sizable portion of investors willing to trust his gut.

AND THE NUMBER 1 TOP TEN QUOTE:
"HE WILL BE WITH YOU IN JUST A MINUTE,
SIR—HE'S STILL MEETING WITH HIS ARCHITECT."

Let me lay out the scene for you. Several years ago I went to visit a hedge fund manager in Greenwich, Connecticut. I had an appointment and showed up promptly at the agreed-upon hour. However, I was kept waiting in the reception area for a while. Five minutes passed, then 10, 15, and finally 20 minutes passed after our meeting time.

I began to wonder about the hedge fund manager, is he in the middle of a dynamic trade? Is he trying to negotiate an exotic swap agreement? Is he tied up in an important conference call? Finally, after 20 minutes, I went up to the receptionist and asked what the delay was. I received this quote.

This statement told me everything I needed to know about the hedge fund manager. He was more interested in building his new house than he was in meeting with a potential client.

Now, it is indeed everyone's right to have a nice home to live in, but when the design of a hedge fund manager's new home supersedes his business, it is time to cash out. A good friend of mine, Mark Yusko of Morgan Creek Capital, calls this the "red Ferrari syndrome." Simply, when a hedge fund manager begins to overly indulge in the pleasures of life, it is more than likely that the hedge fund manager has become risk averse and will now worry more about the preservation of his wealth than the generation of capital appreciation. This is a red flag (or Ferrari) and it is a good time to cash out of the hedge fund.

CONCLUSION

This chapter is not meant to discourage readers from pursuing hedge funds as a viable investment. Indeed, I am a committed investor to hedge funds; CalPERS, Hermes, and Nuveen have strong hedge fund programs. However, it does serve as a humorous reminder that hedge fund managers sometimes lose focus on generating wealth for their clients. This lack of focus may occur because of a shift in emphasis toward fee generation instead of wealth generation, or an overindulgence in the good things in life, or a lack of focus on their single best investment strategy.

My final thought is that I would never have developed a Top Ten list if I did not ask questions. Keep asking questions, and you will find some pretty interesting answers from hedge fund managers, some might even make your own personal Top Ten list.

References

Ackermann, Carl, Richard McEnally, and David Ravenscraft. 1999. The performance of hedge funds: Risk, return, and incentives. *Journal of Finance* (June): 833–874.

Agarwal, Vikas, Noveen Daniel, and Narayan Naik. 2006. Role of managerial incentives and discretion in hedge fund performance. *Journal of Finance*, forthcoming (last revised October 11, 2008).

Agarwal, Vikas, and Jayant Kale. 2007. On the relative performance of multi-strategy and funds of hedge funds. *Journal of Investment Management* 5.

Agarwal, Vikas, and Narayan Naik. 2000. Multi-period performance persistence analysis of hedge funds. *Journal of Financial and Quantitative Analysis* (September): 327–342.

Aggarwal, Rajesh, Galin Georgiev, and Jake Pinato. 2007. Detecting performance persistence in fund managers: Book benchmark alpha analysis. University of Minnesota working paper, Winter.

Amenc, Noel, Sina el Bied, and Lionel Martellini. 2003. Predictability in hedge fund returns. *Financial Analysts Journal* (September/October).

Ammann, Manuel, and Patrick Moerth. 2008. Impact of fund size and fund flows on hedge fund performance. *Journal of Alternative Investments* 11.

Anderson, Jenny. 2006. As leaders, hedge funds draw insider scrutiny. *New York Times,* October 16.

Ang, Andrew, Matthew Rhodes-Kropft, and Rui Zhao. 2008. Do funds-of-funds deserve their fees-on-fees? NBER Working Paper W13944, April.

Anson, Mark. 1999. Maximizing expected utility with commodity futures. *Journal of Portfolio Management* (Summer): 86–94.

Anson, Mark. 2001. Maximizing utility with private equity. *Journal of Investing* (Summer): 17–25.

Anson, Mark. 2002. Financial market dislocations and hedge fund returns. *Journal of Alternative Assets* (Winter).

Anson, Mark. 2006. *Handbook of alternative assets.* 2nd ed. Hoboken, NJ: John Wiley & Sons.

Anson, Mark, Ho Ho, and Kurt Silberstein. 2007. Building a hedge fund portfolio with skewness and kurtosis. *Journal of Alternative Investments.*

Barry, Ross. 2002. Hedge funds: A walk through the graveyard. MFAC Research Paper 25, September 20.

Bernardo, Antonio, and Oliver Ledoit. 2000. Gain, loss, and asset pricing. *Journal of Political Economy* 108.

Billio, Monica, Mila Getmansky, and Loriana Pelizzon. 2007. Dynamic risk exposure in hedge funds. Yale Working Paper 07-14, September.

Black, Fischer, and Myron Scholes. 1973. The pricing of options and corporate liabilities. *Journal of Political Economy* 81:637–654.

Blume, Marshall. 1970. Portfolio theory: A step toward its practical application. *Journal of Business* (April).

Boyd, Roddy. 2008. Mortgage mess socks ex Goldman Sachs stars. *Fortune,* February 29.

Brav, Alon, Wie Jiang, Frank Partnoy, and Randall Thomas. 2008. Hedge fund activism, corporate governance and firm performance. *Journal of Finance* 63:1729.

Brown, Stephen, Thomas Fraser, and Bing Liang. 2008. Hedge fund due diligence: A source of alpha in hedge fund portfolio strategy. NYU working paper, January 21.

Brown, Stephen, William Goetzmann, and Roger Ibbotson. 1999. Offshore hedge funds: Survival and performance, 1989–1995. *Journal of Business* 72 (1): 91–117.

Brown, Stephen, William Goetzmann, and Bing Liang. 2004. Fees on fees. Yale working paper, June 14.

Brown, Stephen, William Goetzmann, Bing Liang, and Christopher Schwarz. 2008. Estimating operational risk for hedge funds: The W-score. Yale Working Paper 08-08, May.

Brown, Stephen, William Goetzmann, and James Park. 2000. Hedge funds and the Asian currency crisis. *Journal of Portfolio Management* (Summer): 95–101.

Cantrell, Amanda. 2005. CEO Israel, finance chief Marino face potentially long jail terms for stealing investors' money. *CNNMoney.com*, September 29.

Christory, Corentin, Stéphane Daul, and Jean-René Giraud. 2006. Quantification of hedge fund default risk. *Journal of Alternative Investments* (Fall).

Cox, John, Stephen Ross, and Martin Rubinstein. 1979. Options pricing: A simplified approach. *Journal of Financial Economics* (September): 229–263.

CrossBorderCapital. 1999. Choosing investment styles to reduce risk. *Hedge Fund Research* (October).

Davies, Ryan, Harry Kat, and Sa Lu. 2004. Fund of hedge funds portfolio selection: A multiple objective approach. Working paper, ISMA Centre, Business School for Financial Markets, University of Reading.

Davis, Ann, Gregory Zuckerman, and Henny Sender. 2007. Hedge fund hardball. *Wall Street Journal,* January 30.

Edwards, Franklin, and Mustafa Onur Caglayan. 2001. Hedge fund performance and manager skill. *Journal of Futures Markets.*

Edwards, Franklin, and Jimmy Liew. 1999. Hedge funds versus managed futures as asset classes. *Journal of Derivatives* (Summer): 45–64.

Elton, Edwin, Martin Gruber, and Joel Rentzler. 1987. Professionally managed, publicly traded commodity funds. *Journal of Business* (April): 175–199.

Fama, Eugene. 1976. *Foundations of finance*. New York: Basic Books.

Feffer, Stuart, and Christopher Kundro. 2003. Understanding and mitigating operational risk in hedge funds. Working paper, Capital Markets Company Ltd., 2003.

Fung, William, and David Hsieh. 1997. Empirical characteristics of dynamic trading strategies: The case of hedge funds. *Review of Financial Studies* 10 (Summer): 275–302.

Fung, William, and David Hsieh. 1999. A primer on hedge funds. *Journal of Empirical Finance* 6, no. 3 (September): 309–331.

Fung, William, and David Hsieh. 2000a. Measuring the market impact of hedge funds. *Journal of Empirical Finance* 7.

Fung, William, and David Hsieh. 2000b. Performance characteristics of hedge funds and commodity funds: Natural versus spurious biases. *Journal of Financial and Quantitative Analysis* 25:291–307.

Fung, William, and David Hsieh. 2002a. Asset-based style factors for hedge funds. *Financial Analysts Journal* (September/October): 16–27.

Fung, William, and David Hsieh. 2002b. Hedge-fund benchmarks: Information content and biases. *Financial Analysts Journal* (January/February): 22–34.

Fung, William, and David Hsieh. 2004. Hedge fund benchmarks: A risk-based approach. *Financial Analysts Journal* (September/October): 65–80.

Fung, William, and David Hsieh. 2006. Hedge funds: An industry in its adolescence. *Federal Reserve Bank of Atlanta Economic Review*, May.

Getmansky, Mila, Andrew Lo, and Igor Makarov. 2004. An econometric model of serial correlation and illiquidity in hedge fund returns. *Journal of Financial Economics* 74.

Goetzmann, William, Jonathan Ingersoll Jr., and Stephen Ross. 2001. High-water marks and hedge fund management contracts. Working paper presented at the Berkeley Program in Finance, March.

Goetzmann, William, Jonathan Ingersoll Jr., Matthew Spiegel, and Ivo Welch. 2002. Sharpening Sharpe ratios. NBER Working Paper W9116, August.

Goldman, Sachs & Co. and Financial Risk Management Ltd. 1999. The hedge fund 'industry' and absolute return funds. *Journal of Alternative Investments* (Spring).

Goldman, Sachs & Co. and Financial Risk Management Ltd. 2000. Hedge funds revisited. *Pension and Endowment Forum* (January).

Grinold, Richard, and Ronald Kahn. 2000. *Active portfolio management*. New York: McGraw-Hill.

Gupta, Anurag, and Bing Liang. 2005. Do hedge funds have enough capital? A value-at-risk approach. *Journal of Financial Economics* 77, no. 1 (July).

The hedge fund industry creates a dinosaur: The macro manager. 2000. *New York Times,* May 6.

Hedge Fund Research, Inc. 2009. Record number of hedge funds liquidate in 2008. March 18.

Henker, Thomas. 1998. Naive diversification for hedge funds. *Journal of Alternative Assets* (Winter): 33–38.

Ibbotson, Roger, and Roger Chen. 2006. The A, B, C's of hedge funds: Alphas, betas and costs. Yale working paper, September.

Ineichen, Alexander. 2002. The alpha in fund of hedge funds. UBS Warburg white paper, February.

International Association of Financial Engineers. 2001. Report of the operational risk committee: Evaluating operational risk controls. November.

Jacobs, Bruce, and Kenneth Levy. 1995. The law of one alpha. *Journal of Portfolio Management* (Summer).

Jorion, Philippe. 2000. Risk management lessons from Long-Term Capital Management. Working paper, University of California at Irvine, January.

Kat, Harry. 2003. 10 things that investors should know about hedge funds. *Journal of Wealth Management* (Spring).

Kazemi, Hossein, and Ying Li. 2008. Managerial incentives and shift of risk-taking in hedge funds. Working paper, Isenberg School of Management, University of Massachusetts, Amherst.

Khandani, Amir, and Andrew Lo. 2007. What happened to the quants in August 2007? MIT working paper, November 4.

Lamm, R. McFall, Jr. 1999. Portfolios of alternative assets: Why not 100% hedge funds? *Journal of Investing* (Winter).

Lhabitant, Francois-Serge. 2004. *Hedge funds: Quantitative insights.* West Sussex, UK: John Wiley & Sons.

Lhabitant, Francois-Serge, and Michelle Learned. 2002. Hedge fund diversification: How much is enough? *Journal of Alternative Investments* (Winter): 23–49.

Liang, Bing. 1999. On the performance of hedge funds. *Financial Analysts Journal* (July/August): 72–85.

Liang, Bing. 2000. Hedge funds: The living and the dead. *Journal of Financial and Quantitative Analysis* 35, no. 3 (September): 309–326.

Liang, Bing. 2001. Hedge fund performance: 1990–1999. *Financial Analysts Journal* (January/February): 11–18.

Liang, Bing. 2003. Hedge fund returns: Auditing and accuracy. *Journal of Portfolio Management* 29.

Loomis, Carol. 1966. The Jones nobody keeps up with. *Fortune*, April, 237–247.

London Business School. 2009. Hedge funds 2009—Assets under management fell by nearly 30% in 2008. BizResearch, April 7.

Malkiel, Burton. 1995. Returns from investing in equity mutual funds 1971 to 1991. *Journal of Finance* 50 (2): 549–572.

Markowitz, Harry. 1952. Portfolio selection. *Journal of Finance* 7 (March).

McCoy, Kevin. 2009. Pursuer of Madoff blew a whistle for nine years. *USA Today,* February 12.

Moix, Pierre-Yves. 2000. The measurement of market risk. PhD dissertation, University of St. Gallen.

Nicholas, Joseph G. 2000. *Market neutral investing.* Princeton, NJ: Bloomberg Press.

Niederhoffer, Victor. 1998. *The education of a speculator.* New York: John Wiley & Sons.

Park, James, Stephen Brown, and William Goetzmann. 1999. Performance benchmarks and survivorship bias for hedge funds and commodity trading advisors. *Hedge Fund News*, August.

Park, James, and Jeremy Staum. 1998. Fund of funds diversification: How much is enough? *Journal of Alternative Investments* (Winter): 39–42.

Park, James, and Jeremy Staum. 1999. Performance persistence in the alternative investment industry. Working paper.

Permanent Subcommittee on Investigations, Committee on Homeland Security and Government Affairs, United States Senate. 2007. Excessive speculation in the natural gas market. Staff report, June 25.

Peskin, Michael, Michael Urias, Satish Anjilvel, and Bryan Boudreau. 2000. Why hedge funds make sense. *Morgan Stanley Dean Witter Quantitative Strategies*, November.

Purcell, David, and Paul Crowley. 1999. The reality of hedge funds. *Journal of Investing* (Fall): 26–44.

Reddy, Girish, Peter Brady, and Kaitik Patel. 2007. Are fund of funds simply multi-strategy managers with extra fees? *Journal of Alternative Investments* 10.

Rendleman, Richard, and Clifford Smith. 1979. Two-state option pricing. *Journal of Finance* (December): 1093–1110.

Schneeweis, Thomas. 1998. Evidence of superior performance persistence in hedge funds: An empirical comment. *Journal of Alternative Investments* (Fall): 76–80.

Schneeweis, Thomas, George Martin, Hossein Kazemi, and Vassilos Karavas. 2005. The impact of leverage on hedge fund risk and return. *Journal of Alternative Investments* (Spring).

Schneeweis, Thomas, and Richard Spurgin. 1998. Multifactor analysis of hedge fund, managed futures, and mutual fund return and risk characteristics. *Journal of Alternative Investments* (Fall): 1–24.

Securities and Exchange Commission. 2004. Registration under the Advisers Act of certain hedge fund advisers. 17 CFR, parts 275 and 279, 69 Federal Register 72054, December 10.

Segal, David. 1997. Market's crash destroys trader: A risky bet brings down a millionaire money manager. *Washington Post,* November 17, A1.

Shake-up continues at Soros's hedge-fund empire. 2000. *Wall Street Journal,* May 1, C1.

Sharpe, William. 1990. Asset allocation. In *Managing Investment Portfolios: A Dynamic Process,* ed. John Maginn and Donald Tuttle. New York: Warren, Gorham and Lamont.

Sharpe, William. 1992. Asset allocation: Management style and performance measure. *Journal of Portfolio Management* (Winter): 7–19.

Spurgin, Richard. 2001. How to game your Sharpe ratio. *Journal of Alternative Investments* 4 (Winter).

Stefanini, Filippo. 2006. *Investment strategies of hedge funds.* Hoboken, NJ: John Wiley & Sons.

Strasburg, Jenny. 2008. Smaller hedge funds struggle as money pipeline dries up. *Wall Street Journal,* October 4–5, B1.

U.S. Senate Permanent Subcommittee on Investigations. 2007. Excessive speculation in the natural gas market. June 25.

Weisman, Andrew, and Jerome Abernathy. 2000. The dangers of historical hedge fund data. Working paper.

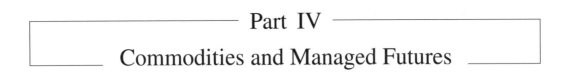

Part IV

Commodities and Managed Futures

19

Introduction to Commodities

In Chapter 1 we discussed how most alternative asset classes are really alternative investment strategies within an existing asset class. This statement applies to hedge funds and private equity, for example. However, it does not apply to commodities. Commodities are a separate asset class.

As the next four chapters demonstrate, investment in this asset class can be achieved through various products. Some will take passive positions in physical commodities (e.g. most commodity indexes) and earn the risk premium that is associated with this asset class. Other products, however, actively trade both physical and financial commodities and generate a rate of return that is both a function of the risk premium embedded in this asset class and the trading skills of the manager (e.g. managed futures invest in both physical commodities as well as financial futures).

Capital assets such as stocks and bonds can be valued on the basis of the net present value of expected future cash flows. Expected cash flows and discount rates are prime ingredients used to determine the value of capital assets. Conversely, commodities do not provide a claim on an ongoing stream of revenue in the same fashion as stocks and bonds.[1] For this reason, they cannot be valued on the basis of net present value, and interest rates have only a small impact on their value.

Commodities generally fall into the category of consumable or transformable assets. You can consume a commodity such as corn either as feedstock or as food stock. Alternatively, you can transform commodities like crude oil into gasoline and other petroleum products. Consequently, they have economic value, but they do not yield an ongoing stream of revenue.

Another distinction between capital assets and commodities is the global nature of commodity markets. Worldwide, commodities markets are mostly dollar-denominated. However, as other economies such as China and India grow and become the major source of demand for most commodities, other currencies may become increasingly important in determining the value of these commodities. Regardless, the value of a particular commodity is dependent on global supply and demand imbalances rather than regional imbalances. Consequently, commodity prices are determined globally rather than regionally.

This is very different from the equity markets, where, for instance, you have the U.S. stock market, foreign developed stock markets, and emerging markets. Foreign stock markets will reflect economic developments within their own regions compared to the United States.

Consider Exhibit 19.1. In this exhibit we provide the correlation coefficients between changes in the S&P 500 and the FTSE 100 stock indexes for the period 2000 to 2008. We can see that the stock price changes in the two countries are less than perfectly correlated, with a correlation coefficient of 0.86.

Compare this to the correlation coefficient associated with the change in prices of crude oil listed on the New York Mercantile Exchange and the International Petroleum Exchange in London.[2] The correlation is 0.94. The changes in crude oil prices in London and New York move in closer lockstep

---

[1] An exception to this rule is precious metals such as gold, silver, and platinum, which can be lent out at a market lease rate.

[2] In order to make a fair comparison of the correlation coefficients associated with the stock market returns of the United States and the UK and the crude oil markets in the United States and the UK, I converted FTSE prices into dollars. This removes any currency effects that might confound our analysis. Therefore, the correlation coefficients presented in Exhibit 19.1 are based on changes in dollar-denominated prices. I am indebted to Peter Nguyen for pointing this out to me.

Exhibit 19.1   Correlation coefficients, 2000–2008

	S&P 500	FTSE	New York Crude	London Crude
S&P 500	1.00	0.86	0.00	0.06
FTSE	0.86	1.00	0.10	0.08
New York Crude	0.00	0.10	1.00	0.94
London Crude	0.06	0.084	0.94	1.00

than stock prices in London and New York. This is because crude oil prices are determined by global economic factors, whereas stock markets, despite the ease of moving capital around the globe, still retain regional factors.[3]

Note also that the changes in the U.S. and UK stock market indexes have very low correlations with changes in the price of crude oil. These low correlations demonstrate that crude oil prices are driven by economic fundamentals different from the systematic risk factors for the stock market.

Finally, commodities do not conform to traditional asset pricing models such as the capital asset pricing model (CAPM). Under the CAPM there are two components of risk: market or systematic risk and company-specific or unsystematic risk. The CAPM teaches us that investors should be compensated only for systematic risk or market risk, because unsystematic risk (company-specific risk) can be diversified away. The CAPM uses a linear regression model to determine beta, a measure of an asset's exposure to systematic or market risk. The financial markets compensate investors for assuming market risk by assigning a market risk premium above the risk-free rate.

Bodie and Rosansky[4] and Dusak[5] find that commodity betas are not consistent with the CAPM. The reason is twofold. First, under the CAPM, the market portfolio is typically defined as a portfolio of financial assets such as stocks and bonds, and commodity returns map poorly onto financial market returns. Consequently, distinctions between market/systematic risk and unsystematic risk cannot be made. Second, commodity prices are dependent on global supply and demand factors, not what the market perceives to be an adequate risk premium for this asset class.

There may still be a natural risk premium in commodities if changes in supply and demand factors are correlated with sources of systematic risks in the economy. According to the CAPM, the only source of systematic risk in the economy is correlation with the market portfolio. However, more advanced versions of the CAPM (e.g. multibeta CAPM or arbitrage pricing theory) claim that there may be multiple sources of risk in the economy. Therefore, even though commodity prices may not be highly correlated with the return on the market portfolio, they may be highly correlated with other sources of risk and may therefore incorporate a risk premium that could be earned through a passive investment strategy. For example, gold may be highly correlated with a factor that represents political and liquidity risks. If this risk cannot be diversified away, then an asset whose return is correlated with this risk will command a risk premium. The premium need not be positive. That is, if gold can be used to hedge a systematic risk, then it will command a negative risk premium. By the same token, copper is usually perceived to be highly correlated with global economic growth factors. Again, since fluctuations in global economic growth represent a source of risk that cannot

---

[3] Of course, another reason is that the FTSE and the S&P 500 do not represent the same companies or even the same industries. The high correlation between oil prices in the U.S. and the UK is due to the fact that the global market for some energy products is highly integrated (e.g. natural gas, by contrast, is less integrated because it is expensive to move and store).

[4] See Zvi Bodie and Victor Rosansky, "Risk and Return in Commodity Futures," *Financial Analysts Journal* (May/June 1980), 27–39.

[5] K. Dusak, "Futures Trading and Investor Returns: An Investigation of Commodity Market Risk Premiums," *Journal of Political Economy* (November–December 1973), 1387–1406.

be diversified away, the movements in the price of copper would incorporate a risk premium that could be earned through passive investment in copper.

This brief introduction is meant to establish commodities as an asset class separate from stocks, bonds, and real estate. However, like stocks and bonds, there are different investment strategies within this asset class. In this chapter we describe the physical commodities markets in more detail and provide an overview of their pricing and underlying economics.

EXPOSURE TO COMMODITIES

Most investors do not include commodities in their investment portfolios. Part of the reason is lack of familiarity with this asset class. Another issue is how to gain exposure to commodity assets. There are six ways to obtain economic exposure to commodity assets: through the commodity itself, shares in a commodity-related firm, futures contracts, commodity swaps/forward contracts, commodity-linked notes, or exchange-traded funds (ETFs).

Purchase of the underlying commodity

An investor can purchase the underlying commodity to gain economic exposure. Actual ownership of physical commodities can be problematic, however. Storage and transportation costs associated with direct investments in commodities make this an unattractive alternative for most investors. Most investors are not familiar with the storage issues of physical commodities, let alone willing to bear the storage costs of ownership associated with physical commodities.

However, there are parts of the world where physical ownership of commodities is still the major form of economic wealth. India, for example, is the second largest consumer of precious metals in the world, after the United States. The reason is that many parts of India are geographically remote, far removed from the financial services and products that are commonplace in the United States. Stocks, bonds, mutual funds, and even bank savings accounts are the exception, not the rule. Consequently, some of the people in these remote regions may denominate their wealth in gold, silver, and platinum.

Natural resource companies

Another way to gain exposure to commodities is to own the securities of a firm that derives a significant part of its revenues from the purchase and sale of physical commodities. For instance, purchasing shares of Exxon Mobil Corporation might be considered a pure play on the price of oil since three-fourths of Exxon Mobil's revenues are derived from the exploration, refining, and marketing of petroleum products.

However, there are several reasons why this pure play might not work. First, part of the value of the stock in Exxon Mobil is dependent on the movement of the general stock market. This is the CAPM, discussed earlier, and as a result an investment in the stock of any company will result in exposure to systematic (market) risk, as well as firm-specific risk.

Systematic risk is measured by the beta of a stock. Beta measures the amount of market risk associated with a given security. A beta equal to 1.0 indicates the same level of systematic risk as the overall market, while a beta less than 1.0 indicates less risk than the market, and a beta greater than 1.0 indicates more risk than the market.

Consider Exhibit 19.2, which lists correlation coefficients and the betas associated with the stock returns of four large petroleum companies compared to the S&P 500 (the stock market). We also

Exhibit 19.2   Beta coefficients and correlation coefficients, 2000–2008

	Stock Market Beta	Stock Market Correlation Coefficient	Crude Oil Beta	Crude Oil Correlation Coefficient
ExxonMobil	0.82	0.57	0.17	0.28
Chevron/Texaco	0.80	0.53	0.22	0.33
Conoco/Phillips	0.84	0.49	0.32	0.40
BP Amoco	0.80	0.53	0.20	0.31

include correlation coefficients and betas for the stock returns of the four oil companies compared to the changes in the price of crude oil.

First, we can see that the oil companies all have high betas with respect to the S&P 500. This indicates that oil companies have significant stock market risk. Furthermore, the correlation coefficients between the stock returns of these four companies and the S&P 500 are very large. We can conclude that oil companies have considerable exposure to the general stock market.

The analysis changes when we examine the returns of these four companies compared to the prices of crude oil. Exhibit 19.2 indicates that the betas associated with crude oil prices are very low. In this case we define the market as the current price of crude oil traded in New York City. In addition, the correlation coefficients between the oil company stock prices and crude oil stock prices are all lower than their correlation with the stock market. We can conclude that the stock prices of oil companies are much more dependent on the movement of the stock market than they are on the movement of crude oil prices. Therefore, investing in an oil company as a pure play on crude oil prices provides an investor with significant stock market exposure and a relatively low crude oil exposure.

Second, when an investor invests with an oil company (or any company, for that matter) the investor assumes all of the idiosyncratic risks associated with that company. Consider the example of Texaco when in the 1980s it attempted an illfated merger with the Getty Oil Company despite the Getty Oil Company having an outstanding bid from Pennzoil. The result was massive litigation resulting in a several-billion-dollar verdict against Texaco, forcing the company to seek Chapter 11 bankruptcy protection. Further, in the 1990s, Texaco was the subject of a race discrimination lawsuit by many of its workers. This litigation cost Texaco several hundred million dollars.

Neither of these lawsuits, however, had anything to do with the price of oil. They were instead part of the idiosyncratic risk associated with the management practices of Texaco. Most investors seeking a pure play on oil would be disappointed to receive lengthy and expensive lawsuit exposure.

In addition, there are other operating risks associated with an investment in any company. A company's financing policies, for example, affect the price of its stock. Exxon Mobil has a debt/equity ratio of about 1.25. This is a little above average for the oil industry. There is also operating leverage (i.e. the ratio of fixed to variable expenses). Oil companies tend to have high variable costs associated with their exploration, refining, and marketing programs. While financial and operating leverage affect the price of a stock, they have nothing to do with the price of oil.

Finally, even if all of the other risks associated with an investment in an oil company are accepted, the investor might find that the oil company has hedged away its oil exposure. Most large oil and energy companies maintain their own trading desks. One main goal of these trading desks is to hedge the risk associated with the purchase and sale of petroleum products in order to reduce variability of corporate earnings. The reason is that oil companies, like most companies, prefer to smooth their annual earnings rather than be subject to large swings due to changes in the price of oil. The same issue arises in the context of mining companies. Many of them may choose to hedge against fluctuations in the price of the commodity they produce, and as a result their equities generally do not provide the same exposure that investments in commodities would provide.

The proof is demonstrated in Exhibit 19.2, where oil companies have low betas with respect to the price of crude oil. This is consistent with the fact that oil companies hedge away a considerable amount of their exposure to oil price risk.

Commodity futures contracts

Perhaps the easiest way to gain exposure to commodities is through commodity futures contracts. Futures contracts offer several advantages. First, these contracts are traded on an organized exchange. Therefore, they share the same advantages as stock exchanges: a central marketplace, transparent pricing, clearinghouse security, uniform contract size and terms, and daily liquidity.

Second, the purchase of a futures contract (i.e. taking a long position) does not require automatic delivery of the underlying commodity. An offsetting futures position can be initiated that will close out the position of the initial futures contract. In this way an investor can gain exposure to commodities without worrying about physical delivery. In fact, only about 1% of all commodity futures contracts result in the actual delivery of the underlying commodity.

Third, futures contracts can be purchased without paying the full price for the commodity. When a futures contract is purchased, a deposit is required. This deposit is called the **initial margin**. This margin requirement is a small percentage of the full purchase price of the underlying commodity, usually less than 10%. The initial margin is a good faith deposit to ensure full payment upon delivery of the underlying commodity. In the futures markets, the investor does not need to put up the total price for the underlying commodity unless she takes physical delivery of the commodity.

Futures accounts also have two other margin requirements. On a day-by-day basis, the value of the futures contract will fluctuate. Fluctuation of prices in the futures markets will cause the value of the investor's margin account to increase or decrease. This is called the **variation margin**. If the price of the futures contract increases, the holder of a long futures position will accrue positive variation margin. This adds to the equity in the futures margin account and may be withdrawn by the investor. Conversely, for an investor who has a short futures position, the increase in the price of the futures contract will result in a negative variation margin.

The **maintenance margin** is the minimum amount of equity that a futures margin account may have and is usually set at 75% to 80% of the initial margin. If subsequent variation margins reduce the equity in an investor's account down to the maintenance margin level, the investor will receive a margin call from the futures commission merchant. A **margin call** is a demand for additional cash to be contributed to the account to bring the equity in the account back over the maintenance margin level. If the investor cannot meet the margin call, the futures commission merchant has the right to liquidate the investor's positions in the account.

There can be some disadvantages to taking positions in futures contracts. First, if an investor wishes to maintain her exposure to commodity prices without taking physical delivery of the underlying contract, she will have to continually close out her existing futures position and reestablish a new position by entering into a new futures contract. This rolling of futures contracts can be costly, depending on the term structure of the futures prices. We discuss this in more detail in the next chapter.

Second, as we noted earlier, once a long futures position is established, there may be ongoing margin calls if the futures contract declines in value. Conversely, if an investor's futures contracts increase in value, she may withdraw the additional equity from her account. Nonetheless, managing the contributions and withdrawals from a futures account may require more activity than is required by a traditional long-only security account. Futures accounts may be opened only with licensed futures commission merchants who are registered with the National Futures Association and the Commodity Futures Trading Commission.

Commodity swaps and forward contracts

Close economic cousins to commodity futures contracts are commodity swaps and forward contracts. Commodity swaps and commodity forward contracts perform the same economic function as commodity futures contracts. However, there are some key structural differences.

- Commodity swaps and forward contracts are custom made for the individual investor. While this provides precise tailoring of the commodity exposure desired by the investor, it also makes commodity swaps and forward contracts less liquid because what works for one investor will not work for all investors. Typically, if an investor wishes to terminate a commodity swap or forward position prior to maturity, the investor will negotiate with the counterparty who sold the swap or forward contract to the investor.
- Commodity swaps and forward contracts are not traded on an exchange. Again, this impacts liquidity. Exchange-traded products with standardized terms and public pricing provide much greater liquidity than customized commodity swaps or forward contracts.
- Counterbalancing the lack of liquidity, a key advantage is that commodity swaps and forward contracts are private contracts that trade outside the public domain of an exchange. To the extent an investor wishes to be discreet about its investment strategy for commodities, commodity swaps and forward contracts provide a degree of privacy not afforded by the public markets.

Commodity-linked notes

Another way an investor can gain exposure to the commodity markets is through a commodity-linked note. This is where financial engineering and the commodities markets intersect. In its simplest form, a commodity-linked note is an intermediate-term debt instrument whose value at maturity will be a function of the value of an underlying commodity futures contract or basket of commodity futures contracts.

Commodity-linked notes are not a new invention. In 1863, the Confederacy of the South issued a 20-year bond denominated in both pounds sterling and French francs. Also, at the option of the bondholder, the bond could be converted into bales of cotton. This was a dual-currency, commodity-linked bond.[6]

Commodity-linked notes have several advantages. First, the investor does not have to worry about the rolling of the underlying futures contracts. This becomes the problem of the issuer of the note who must roll the futures contracts to hedge the commodity exposure embedded in the note.

Second, the note is, in fact, a debt instrument. While investors may have restrictions on investing in the commodities markets, they can have access to commodity exposure through a debt instrument. The note is recorded as a liability on the balance sheet of the issuer, and as a bond investment on the balance sheet of the investor. In addition, the note can have a stated coupon rate and maturity just like any other debt instrument. The twist is that the investor accepts a lower coupon payment than it otherwise could receive in exchange for sharing in the upside of the commodity prices.

Last, the holder of the note does not have to worry about any tracking error issues with respect to the price of a single commodity or basket of commodities. Once again, this problem remains with the issuer.

In practice, commodity-linked notes are tied to the prices of commodity futures contracts or commodity options. Consider Exhibit 19.3 and the following example. Suppose that a pension fund

---

[6] See S. Warte Rawls III and Charles Smithson, "The Evolution of Risk Management Products," in *The New Corporate Finance*, 2nd ed., ed. Donald H. Chew Jr. (New York: Irwin/McGraw-Hill, 1999).

Exhibit 19.3 Structured note with a GSCI call option: total return for various GSCI levels

GSCI	900	1,000	1,100	1,200	1,300
Principal	$1,000,000	$1,000,000	$1,000,000	$1,000,000	$1,000,000
Option value	$0	$0	$0	$90,909	$181,818
Coupon	$20,000	$20,000	$20,000	$20,000	$20,000
Total payment	$1,020,000	$1,020,000	$1,020,000	$1,110,909	$1,201,818
Total return	2%	2%	2%	11.09%	20.18%

is not allowed to trade commodity futures directly but wishes to invest in the commodity markets as a hedge against inflation. To diversify its portfolio, the fund purchases at par value from an investment bank a $1 million structured note tied to the value of the Goldman Sachs Commodity Index (GSCI). The GSCI is a diversified basket of physical commodity futures contracts.

The note has a maturity of one year and is principal guaranteed; at maturity, the pension fund will receive at least the face value of the note. However, if the GSCI exceeds a certain level at maturity of the note, the pension fund will share in this appreciation. Principal repayment therefore depends on the settlement price of the GSCI index at the note's maturity. The pension fund has, in fact, a call option embedded in the note. If the GSCI exceeds a predetermined level (the strike price) at the maturity date, the pension fund will participate in the price appreciation.

The embedded call option on the GSCI is costly. The pension fund will pay for this option by receiving a reduced coupon payment (or no coupon) on the note.[7] The closer the call option is to the money, the lower will be the coupon payment. Assume that the strike price for a GSCI call option is set at 10% out-of-the-money and that the coupon on the note is 2%.

Under normal circumstances, a plain-vanilla note from the issuer would carry a coupon of 6%. Therefore, the pension fund is sacrificing 4% of coupon income for the price of the call option on the GSCI. Assume that at the time the note is issued, the GSCI is at the level of 1,000. Therefore, the strike price on the call option (set 10% out-of-the-money) is 1,100. If at maturity of the note the value of the GSCI is above 1,100, the investor will receive its 2% coupon plus the appreciation of the GSCI. Otherwise, the investor will receive the coupon only. Therefore, the return contingent of the value of GSCI is:

$$[1 + \max(0, (GSCI_T - GSCI_x)/GSCI_x)] \times \$1,000,000 + 20,000$$

where

$GSCI_T$ = is the value of the GSCI index at maturity of the note
$GSCI_x$ = is the strike price for the call option embedded in the note
$20,000$ = 2% coupon × $1,000,000 face value note

If the option expires out-of-the-money (the GSCI is less than or equal to 1,100 at maturity), then the investor receives the return of its principal plus a 2% coupon. Exhibit 19.3 presents the possible payoffs to the structured note.

From Exhibit 19.3 we can see that the pension fund shares in the upside but is protected on the downside. The trade-off for principal protection is a lower coupon payment and only a partial sharing in the upside (above the call strike price).

With respect to the issuer of the note, it will purchase a one-year call option on the GSCI index with a strike price equal to 1,100. If the option matures in-the-money, the issuer will pass on the price

---

[7] It is assumed that the bond is sold at par.

Exhibit 19.4   Structured note with a GSCI futures contract: total return for various GSCI levels

GSCI	900	1,000	1,100	1,200	1,300
Principal	$1,000,000	$1,000,000	$1,000,000	$1,000,000	$1,000,000
Futures value	−$100,000	$0	$100,000	$200,000	$300,000
Coupon	$50,000	$50,000	$50,000	$50,000	$50,000
Total payment	$950,000	$1,050,000	$1,150,000	$1,250,000	$1,350,000
Total return	−5%	5%	15%	25%	35%

appreciation to the pension fund. In this way, the issuer maintains the commodity call option on its balance sheet, not the pension fund, but the pension fund gets the benefit of the option's payout.

Structured notes do not have to be principal protected. The pension fund can share fully in the upside as well as the downside. Consider Exhibit 19.4 and a second note also with a $1 million face value. However, this note shares fully in the change in value of the GSCI from the date the note is purchased. The trick here is that the change in value can be positive or negative. This is a commodity note linked to a futures contract instead of an option contract.

The note will pay a 5% coupon at maturity. Recall that the pension could otherwise purchase a regular one-year note from the same issuer (without commodity exposure) with a 6% coupon. The 1% difference in coupon payments reflects the issuer's transaction and administration costs associated with the commodity-linked note. Compared to the prior example, a commodity-linked note with an embedded futures contract is less costly to issue than a note with an embedded commodity option.

The terms of the note state that at maturity the issuer will pay to the investor:

$$[1 + (GSCI_T - GSCI_0)/GSCI_0] \times \$1,000,000 + \$50,000$$

where

$GSCI_T =$ is the value of the GSCI index at maturity of the note
$GSCI_0 =$ is the value of the GSCI index at the purchase date of the note

The payout for this second note is presented in Exhibit 19.4. Notice the difference between Exhibits 19.3 and 19.4. In Exhibit 19.4 we can see that the pension fund shares in a linear payout stream: if the GSCI increases in value, the pension gains; if the GSCI declines in value, the pension fund loses. However, in Exhibit 19.3, the pension fund shares only in the gains; it does not share in the losses. This is a demonstration of the protected principal or nonlinear payout function associated with a commodity option. In contrast, a commodity note linked to a futures contract will provide an investor with a linear payout function—sharing in both the upside and the downside of commodity price movement.

Last, note that the pension fund has the opportunity for a much greater gain with the commodity note linked to a futures contract. However, in return for this upside potential, the pension fund must bear the risk of loss of capital should the GSCI decline below its initial level of 1,000.[8] Another way of stating this is that with a commodity note linked to an option, the pension fund sacrifices some upside potential for the preservation of capital.

---

[8] The issuer of the note will purchase one-year futures contracts on the GSCI sufficient to cover the face value of the note. If the futures contracts increase in value, the issuer passes on this value to the pension fund. If the futures contracts decline in value, the issuer will close out its position at a loss. However, the issuer will be reimbursed for these losses because it does not have to return the full principal value of the note to the pension fund.

The financial engineering demonstrated in Exhibits 19.3 and 19.4 would not be necessary if the pension fund could invest directly in commodity futures and options. Engineering becomes necessary because of the pension fund's prohibition against purchasing commodities directly.

Commodity-linked notes are transparent because these notes utilize exchange-traded commodity futures and options contracts with daily pricing and liquidity or commodity swaps that are tied to the prices of commodity futures. Furthermore, the equation used to calculate their value is specified as part of the note agreement. As a result, pension funds, insurance companies, endowments, and other institutional investors may participate in viable securities that offer transparent exposure to a new asset class without a direct investment in that asset class.

In these examples, it was assumed that the issuer was a large commercial bank that purchased the commodity futures or options and passed on either the gains or the losses to the investor. However, commodity producers are also likely issuers of such notes.

Consider an oil producer that would like to reduce its cost of debt financing. One way to lower the coupon rate on its debt would be to issue calls on crude oil attached to its bonds. As we demonstrated in Exhibit 19.3, if a commodity-linked note is tied to a call option, the coupon payment will be lower than what the issuer would otherwise offer. From the oil producer's perspective, any cash outflows as a result of the call option being exercised should be offset by the lower cost of financing it receives. Furthermore, the oil producer can even use the commodity-linked note to hedge its oil exposure, in effect, getting its cake (cheaper debt financing) and eating it, too (hedging the commodity exposure from its income statement). From the investor's perspective, it trades a lower coupon payment on the note for the potential to share in the price appreciation of crude oil.

Commodity exchange-traded funds

One of the easiest ways to invest in a commodity is through an exchange-traded fund (ETF). An ETF is very similar to a passively managed mutual fund or closed-end fund. The ETF can be purchased through organized exchanges throughout the trading hours.

A commodity ETF may provide exposure to one commodity or a group of commodities. For example, USO, the oil ETF traded in the United States, seeks to reflect the performance, less expenses, of the spot price of West Texas Intermediate (WTI) light, sweet crude oil. The fund underlying the ETF invests in futures contracts for WTI light and other petroleum-based fuels that are traded on exchanges. Conversely, an investor may want a broader commodity exposure across the several sectors of the commodities markets. GSG is the iShares ETF that tracks the GSCI Excess Return Index. Similarly, DJP is an exchange-traded note (ETN) that tracks the Dow Jones AIG Total Return Commodity Index. There are now 23 different commodity ETFs and ETNs traded in the United States and on the London Stock Exchange.

RELATIONSHIP BETWEEN FUTURES PRICES AND SPOT PRICES

As we noted earlier, one of the easiest ways to gain exposure to commodities is through **commodity futures contracts**. These contracts are transparent, are denominated in standard units, are exchange traded, and have daily liquidity; and their value is highly correlated to the spot prices of the underlying commodity. The last point, the relationship between spot and futures prices, must be developed to understand the dynamics of the commodity futures markets.

A futures contract obligates the seller of the futures contract to deliver the underlying asset at a set price at a specified time. Conversely, the buyer of a futures contract agrees to purchase the underlying asset at the set price at a specified time. If the seller of the futures contract does not wish to deliver the underlying asset, he must close out her short futures position by purchasing an offsetting futures contract. Similarly, if the buyer of the futures contract does not wish to take delivery of the underlying asset, he must close out his long futures position by selling an offsetting futures contract. Only a very small percentage of futures contracts (usually less than 1%) result in delivery of the underlying asset.

There are three general types of futures contracts regulated by the Commodity Futures Trading Commission: financial futures, currency futures, and commodity futures. Commodity Trading Advisors and Commodity Pool Operators invest in all three types of futures contracts.

Additionally, many hedge fund managers apply arbitrage strategies with respect to financial and currency futures. The following examples demonstrate these arbitrage opportunities. We begin with financial futures, but the same principles apply to commodity futures as well.

Financial futures

Financial futures include U.S. Treasury bond futures, eurodollar certificate of deposit (CD) futures, and stock index futures. In the United States, these contracts are traded on the Chicago Board of Trade, the Chicago Mercantile Exchange, and the Intercontinental Exchange.

Consider the example of a financial asset that pays no income. In the simplest case, if the underlying asset pays no income, then the relationship between the futures contract and the spot price is:

$$F = Se^{r(T-t)} \tag{19.1}$$

where

> F = the price of the futures contract
> S = the spot price of the underlying asset
> e = the base of natural logarithm ($\sim$2.718), used to calculate continuous compounding
> r = the risk-free rate
> $T - t$ = the time (in years) until maturity of the futures contract

In words, the price of the futures contract depends on the current price of the underlying financial asset, the risk-free rate, and the time until maturity of the futures contract. Notice that the price of the futures contract depends on the risk-free rate and not the required rate of return for the financial asset. This is the case because of arbitrage opportunities that exist for speculators such as hedge funds.

Consider the situation where $F > Se^{r(T-t)}$. A hedge fund manager could make a profit by applying the following three-step strategy:

1. Borrow cash at the risk-free rate, r, and purchase the underlying asset with the borrowed funds at current price S.
2. Sell the underlying asset for delivery at time T and at the futures price F.
3. At maturity, deliver the underlying asset, pay the interest and principal on the cash borrowed, and collect the futures price F.

Exhibit 19.5 demonstrates this arbitrage strategy. Two points about Exhibit 19.5 must be noted. First, to initiate the arbitrage strategy, no net cash is required. The cash outflow matches the cash inflow. This is one reason why arbitrage strategies are so popular.

Second, at maturity (time T), the hedge fund manager receives a positive net cash payout of $F - Se^{r(T-t)}$. How do we know that the net payout is positive? It's simple: We know at the initiation of the arbitrage strategy that $F > Se^{r(T-t)}$. Therefore, $F - Se^{r(T-t)}$ must be positive.

Exhibit 19.5 Financial asset arbitrage when $F > Se^{r(T-t)}$

Time	Cash Inflow	Cash Outflow	Net Cash
t (initiate the arbitrage) T (maturity of the futures contract)	S (cash borrowed) F (price for future delivery)	S (to purchase the asset) $Se^{r(T-t)}$ (pay back principal and interest)	$S - S = 0$ $F - Se^{r(T-t)}$

Exhibit 19.6 Financial asset arbitrage when $F < Se^{r(T-t)}$

Time	Cash Inflow	Cash Outflow	Net Cash
t (initiate the arbitrage) T (maturity of the futures contract)	S (asset is sold short) F (receive principal and interest)	S (to purchase the asset) F (price paid for the asset at maturity of the futures contract)	$S - S = 0$ $Se^{r(T-t)} - F$

If the reverse situation were true at time t, $F < Se^{r(T-t)}$, then a reverse arbitrage strategy would make the same amount of profit: Buy the futures contract and sell short the underlying asset. This is demonstrated in Exhibit 19.6.

Exhibit 19.6 demonstrates the arbitrage profit $Se^{r(T-t)} - F$. How do we know this is a profit? Because we started with the condition that $Se^{r(T-t)} > F$. At maturity of the futures contract, the hedge fund manager will take delivery of the underlying asset at price F and use the delivery of the asset to cover the short position.

In general, futures contracts on financial assets are settled in cash, not by physical delivery of the underlying security.[9] However, this does not change the arbitrage dynamics just demonstrated. The hedge fund manager will simply close out the short asset position and long futures position at the same time and net the gains and losses. The profit will be the same as that demonstrated in Exhibit 19.6.

Most financial assets pay some form of income. Consider stock index futures contracts. A stock index tracks the changes in the value of a portfolio of stocks. The percentage change in the value of a stock index over time is usually defined so that it equals the percentage change in the total value of all stocks comprising the index portfolio. However, stock indexes are usually not adjusted for dividends. In other words, any cash dividends received by an investor actually holding the stocks are not reflected in measuring the change in value of the stock index.

There are futures contracts on the S&P 500, the NASDAQ-100 index, the Russell 1000 index, and the Dow Jones Industrial Average.[10] By far the most popular contract is the S&P 500 futures contract (SPX) traded on the Chicago Mercantile Exchange.

Consider the S&P 500 futures contract. The pricing relationship as shown in Equation 19.1 applies. However, Equation 19.1 must be adjusted for the fact that the holder of the underlying stocks receives cash dividends, while the holder of the futures contract does not.

In Exhibit 19.5 we demonstrated how an arbitrage strategy may be accomplished by borrowing cash at the risk-free rate to purchase the underlying financial asset. With respect to stocks, the hedge

---

[9] However, certain futures exchanges allow for a procedure known as *exchange for physicals* where a holder of a financial asset can exchange the financial asset at maturity of the futures contract instead of settling in cash.

[10] There is even a Mini S&P 500 contract index, which has the same mechanics as the regular S&P 500 futures contract with the exception that every point movement of the Mini S&P is worth $50 instead of $250 per point in the main S&P 500 contract.

fund manager receives the benefit of cash dividends from purchasing the stocks. The cash dividends received reduce the borrowing cost of the hedge fund manager. This must be factored into the futures pricing equation. We can express this relationship as:

$$F = Se^{(r-q)(T-t)} \tag{19.2}$$

where the terms are the same as before, and q is equal to the dividend yield on the basket of stocks.

The dividend rate, q, is subtracted from the borrowing cost, r, to reflect the reduction in carrying costs from owning the basket of stocks. Consider the example of a three-month futures contract on the S&P 500. Assume that the index is currently at 1,000, that the risk-free rate is 6%, and that the current annual dividend yield on the S&P 500 is 2%. Using Equation 19.2, the fair price for a three-month futures contract on the S&P 500 is:

$$F = 1,000e^{(.06-.02)(0.25)} = 1,010$$

Notice again that the futures price on stock index futures does not depend on the expected return on stocks. Instead, it depends on the risk-free rate and the dividend yield. Expected asset returns do not affect the pricing relationship between the current asset price and the future asset price, because any expected return that the underlying asset should earn will also be reflected in the futures price. Therefore, the difference between the futures price and the spot price should reflect only the time value of money, adjusted for any income earned by the financial asset over the term of the futures contract.

Suppose that instead of a price of 1,010, the three-month futures contract for the S&P 500 was priced at 1,015. Then a hedge fund could establish the following arbitrage: borrow cash at an interest rate of 6% and purchase a basket of S&P 500 stocks worth $250,000 ($250 $\times$ 1,000, where each point of the S&P 500 is worth $250 in the underlying futures contract), and sell the S&P 500 futures at a price of 1,015. At the end of three months, the hedge fund would earn the following arbitrage profit:

Futures price received for the S&P 500 stocks $= 1,015 \times \$250 = \$253,750$
Plus dividend yield on stocks $= \$250,000 \times \left(e^{(.02)\times(0.25)} - 1\right) = \$1,253$
Less repayment of the loan plus interest $= \$250,000 \times e^{(0.06)\times(0.25)} = \$253,778$
Equals arbitrage profits: $1,225

Exhibit 19.7 demonstrates the stock index arbitrage flowchart. A reverse arbitrage similar to Exhibit 19.6 can be implemented when $F < Se^{(r-q)(T-t)}$. That is, short the stocks, invest the cash at the risk-free rate, and buy the futures contract.

Currencies

A foreign currency may be considered an income-producing asset. The reason is that the holder of the foreign currency can earn interest at the risk-free rate prevailing in the foreign country. We define

Exhibit 19.7 Stock index arbitrage when $F > Se^{(r-q)(T-t)}$

Time	Cash Inflow	Cash Outflow	Net Cash
t (initiate the arbitrage)	S (cash borrowed)	S (to purchase the asset)	$S - S = 0$
T (maturity of the futures contract)	F (price for future delivery)	$Se^{(r-q)(T-t)}$ (pay back principal and interest less dividends received)	$F - Se^{(r-q)(T-t)}$

this foreign risk-free rate as f. Considered in this context, the relationship between a futures contract on a foreign currency and the current spot exchange rate can be expressed as:

$$F = Se^{(r-f)(T-t)} \qquad\qquad (19.3)$$

where the terms are defined as before, and f is the risk-free interest rate in the foreign country.

Equation 19.3 is similar to Equation 19.2 because a foreign currency may be considered analogous to an income-producing asset or a dividend-paying stock. Equation 19.3 also expresses the well-known **interest rate parity theorem**. This theorem states that the exchange rate between two currencies will depend on the differences in their interest rates.

Consider the exchange rate between the U.S. dollar and the Japanese yen. Assume that the current U.S. risk-free rate is 6% while that for the yen is approximately 1%. Also, assume that the current spot rate for yen to dollars is 100 yen per U.S. dollar, or 0.01 dollars per yen. A three-month futures contract on the yen/dollar exchange rate would be:

$$F = Se^{(.06-0.01)(0.25)} = 0.010126$$

The futures price on Japanese yen for three months is 0.010126 dollars per yen, or 98.76 yen per dollar.

To demonstrate a currency arbitrage when $F > Se^{(r-f)(T-t)}$, consider a hedge fund manager who can borrow 10,000 yen for three months at a rate of 1%. In three months' time, the hedge fund manager will have to repay $10,000 \times e^{(0.01)\times(0.25)} = 10,025$ yen. The manager converts the yen borrowed today into dollars at the spot exchange rate of 100 yen/\$1 = \$100. This \$100 can then be invested at the U.S. risk-free rate of interest for three months to earn $100 \times e^{(0.06)\times(0.25)} = 101.51$ dollars. If the three-month currency futures price on Japanese yen were the same as the spot exchange rate of 100 yen/\$1, the hedge fund manager would need to sell $10,025/100 = 100.25$ dollars to repay the yen loan. Since the manager receives 101.51 dollars back from her three-month investment in the United States, she will pocket the difference of $\$101.51 - \$100.25 = \$1.26$ in arbitrage profits.

Exhibit 19.8 demonstrates that 125 yen of arbitrage profits may be earned if the futures contract price does not take into account the differences in the interest rates between the foreign and domestic currencies. The 125 yen of arbitrage profit may be converted back to dollars: 125 yen/100 = \$1.25. Therefore, to prevent arbitrage, the currency futures price for Japanese yen must be 98.76 yen per U.S. dollar. Then the amount of cash inflow received will be exactly equal to the cash outflow necessary to pay back the Japanese yen loan: $\$101.51 \times (98.76 \text{ yen}/\$1) = 10,025$ yen.

In practice, arbitrage opportunities do not occur as obviously as in our example. Currency prices may be out of balance for only a short period of time. It is the nimble hedge fund manager that can take advantage of pricing discrepancies. Further, more famous hedge fund managers engage in currency speculation as opposed to currency arbitrage. In currency speculation, the hedge fund manager takes an unhedged position on one side of the market. Cash is committed to establish the

Exhibit 19.8 Currency arbitrage when $F > Se^{(r-f)(T-t)}$

Time	Cash Inflow	Cash Outflow	Net Cash
t (initiate the arbitrage)	10,000 yen borrowed at 1%	10,000 yen converted and invested in \$ at 6%	0
T (maturity of the futures contract)	\$101.51 from interest-bearing account	10,025 yen to repay the loan	(101.50×100) $- 10,025$ yen $= 125$ yen

position. The best example of this has been George Soros's bet against the British pound sterling in 1992.

Commodity futures

Commodities are not financial assets. Nonetheless, the pricing dynamics between spot prices and futures prices are similar to those for financial assets. However, there are important distinctions that will affect the pricing relationship.

First, as we discussed earlier, there are storage costs associated with physical commodities. These storage costs must be factored into the pricing equation. **Storage costs** can be considered as negative income. In other words, there is a cash outflow associated with holding the physical commodity. This is in contrast to financial assets discussed earlier. With financial assets, we demonstrated that income earned on the underlying asset will defray the cost of purchasing that asset. With physical commodities, however, there is both the cost of financing the purchase of the physical commodity and the storage cost associated with its ownership. This relationship may be expressed as:

$$F = Se^{(r+c)(T-t)} \tag{19.4}$$

where the terms are defined as before, and c is the storage cost associated with ownership of the commodity.

In Equation 19.4, the cost of storage, c, is added to the cost of financing the purchase of the commodity. For example, consider a one-year futures contract on crude oil. Assume that (1) it costs 2% of the price of crude oil to store a barrel of oil and the payment is made at the end of the year, (2) the current price of oil is \$100, and (3) the risk-free rate of interest is 6%.[11] Then the future value of a one-year crude oil futures contract is:

$$F = \$100e^{(0.06+.02)\times 1} = 108.33$$

A second difference between commodity futures and financial futures is the **convenience yield**. Consumers of physical commodities feel that there are benefits from the ownership of the commodity that are not obtained by owning a futures contract—that it is convenient to own the physical commodity. A benefit might be the ability to profit from temporary or local supply-and-demand imbalances, or the ability to keep a production line in process. Alternatively, the convenience yield for certain metals can be measured in terms of lease rates. Gold, silver, and platinum can be leased (lent) to jewelry and electronics manufacturers with the obligation to repay the precious metal at a later date.

Taking both the cost of storage and the convenience yield into account, the price of a futures contract may be stated as:

$$F = Se^{(r+c-y)(T-t)} \tag{19.5}$$

where the terms are defined as before and y is the convenience yield.

Notice that the convenience yield is subtracted from the risk-free rate, r, and the storage cost, c. Similar to financial assets, the convenience yield, y, reduces the cost of ownership of the asset.

Consider the following example. The current price of an ounce of gold is \$800, the risk-free rate is 6%, the cost of storage is 2% of the purchase price, and the lease rate to lend gold is 1%. A six-month futures contract on gold will be:

$$F = \$800e^{(0.06+0.02-0.01)(0.5)} = \$828.50$$

---

[11] If the storage costs are expressed as a dollar amount, then the appropriate equation is $F = (S + C)e^{(r-y)(T-t)}$, where C represents the present value of all storage costs incurred during the life of the futures contract.

Exhibit 19.9   Commodity futures arbitrage when $F > Se^{(r+c-y)(T-t)}$

Time	Cash Inflow	Cash Outflow	Net Cash
t (initiate the arbitrage)	S (cash borrowed)	S (to purchase the asset)	$S - S = 0$
T (maturity of the futures contract)	$F + S\left(e^{y(T-t)} - 1\right)$ (price for delivery of the asset plus income)	$Se^{(r+c)(T-t)}$ (pay back principal and interest on loan plus storage cost)	$F - Se^{(r+c-y)(T-t)} > 0$

Assume that $F > Se^{(r+c-y)(T-t)}$. Then an investor can earn an arbitrage profit by borrowing S to purchase the underlying commodity and selling the futures contract, F. This arbitrage is detailed in Exhibit 19.9.[12]

Exhibit 19.9 demonstrates the payment received from the arbitrage. At maturity of the futures contract, the investor receives a positive cash flow where $Se^{(r+c)(T-t)}$ represents the cash that must be paid back for the loan, interest on the loan, and storage costs.

This arbitrage cannot work in reverse if the investor does not already own the commodity. Except for precious metals, commodities are difficult to borrow. Consequently, they cannot be shorted in the same fashion as financial assets. Furthermore, companies that own the underlying commodity do so for its consumption value rather than its investment value.

ECONOMICS OF THE COMMODITY MARKETS: NORMAL BACKWARDATION VERSUS CONTANGO

With this pricing framework in place, we turn to the economics of commodity consumption, production, and hedging. Commodity futures prices exhibit a term structure similar to that of interest rates. This curve can be downward sloping or upward sloping. The reasons for the different curves will be determined by the actions of hedgers and speculators.

Consider a petroleum producer such as Exxon Mobil Corporation. Through its exploration, developing, refining, and marketing operations, this company is naturally long crude oil exposure. This puts Exxon Mobil at risk to declining crude oil prices. To reduce this exposure, it will sell crude oil futures contracts.[13]

From Exxon Mobil's perspective, by selling crude oil futures contracts it can separate its commodity price risk from its business risk (i.e. the ability to find crude oil, refine it, and market it to consumers). By hedging, Exxon Mobil can better apply its capital to its business risks rather than holding a reserve of capital to protect against fluctuating crude oil prices. Simply stated, hedging allows for the more efficient use of Exxon Mobil's invested capital. In fact, we demonstrated this very point in Exhibit 19.2, where we show that Exxon Mobil's stock price has only a small economic link to fluctuating oil prices. However, there must be someone on the other side of the trade to bear the price risk associated with buying the futures contract. This is the speculator.

If Exxon Mobil transfers its risk to the speculator, the speculator must be compensated for this risk. The speculator is compensated by purchasing the futures contract from the petroleum producer at less than the expected future spot price of crude oil. That is, the price established in the commodity futures contract will be below the expected future spot price of crude oil. The speculator will be

---

[12] In practice, storage costs may be quoted in dollar terms rather than as a percentage of the commodity's value, while convenience yields are quoted as a percentage of the commodity's value. Consider the case where C is equal to the present value of the storage costs that must be paid over the life of the futures contract. Then Equation 19.5 many be expressed as: $F = Se^{(r-y)(T-t)} + Ce^{r(T-t)}$.

[13] As we discussed before, oil producers have energy trading desks to hedge their long crude oil exposure. Another way that Exxon Mobil hedges this risk is through long-term delivery contracts where the price of crude oil is fixed in the contract.

compensated by the difference between the futures price and the expected spot price. This may be expressed as:

$$E(S_T) > F_T \tag{19.6}$$

where

$E(S_T)$ = the expected spot price of the underlying commodity at time T (the maturity of the futures contract)

F_T = the agreed-upon price in the futures contract to be paid at time T

If the inequality of Equation 19.6 remains true at the maturity of the futures contract, the speculator will earn a profit of $S_T - F_T$. However, nothing is certain, as commodity prices can fluctuate. It might turn out that the price agreed on in the futures contract exceeds the spot price at time T. Then the speculator will lose an amount equal to $F_T - S_T$.

This is the risk that the petroleum producer transferred from its income statement to the speculator's. Therefore, to ensure that the speculator is compensated more often than not for bearing the commodity price risk, it must be the case that agreed-on futures price F_T is sufficiently discounted compared to the expected future spot price S_T. This condition of the futures markets is referred to as **normal backwardation**, or simply, backwardation.

The term backwardation comes from John Maynard Keynes. Keynes was the first to theorize that commodity producers were the natural hedgers in the commodity markets and therefore would need to offer risk premiums to speculators in order to induce them to bear the risk of fluctuating commodity prices. This risk premium is represented by the difference of $E(S_T) - F_T$. Conversely, hedgers, because they are reducing their risks, are willing to enter into contracts where the expected payoff is slightly negative, effectively, the cost of hedging.[14]

Backwardated commodity markets have downward-sloping futures curves. The longer-dated the futures contract, the greater must be the discount compared to the expected future spot price to compensate the speculator for assuming the price risk of the underlying commodity for a longer period of time. Therefore, longer-dated futures contracts are priced more cheaply than shorter-term futures contracts.

The reverse situation of a backwardated commodity market is a contango market. In a contango market, the inequality sign in Equation 19.6 is reversed; the expected future spot price, S_T, is less than the current futures price, F_T.

A contango situation will occur when the most likely hedger of the commodity is naturally short the underlying commodity. Consider the aircraft manufacturer Boeing. The single largest raw material input in the construction of any jet aircraft is aluminum for the superstructure of the plane. Boeing is a major consumer of aluminum, but it does not own any aluminum mining interests. Therefore, it is naturally short aluminum and must cover this short exposure by purchasing aluminum to meet its manufacturing needs.

This puts Boeing at risk to rising aluminum prices. To hedge this risk, Boeing can purchase aluminum futures contracts.[15] However, a speculator must be lured to the market to sell the futures contract to Boeing and to take on commodity price risk. To entice the speculator, Boeing must be

---

[14] Although the term *backwardation* is used to describe generally the condition where futures prices are lower than the current spot price, the term *normal backwardation* refers to the precise condition where the expected future spot price is greater than the current futures price. I am indebted to Ray Venner, PhD, of the CalPERS investment staff for this important distinction.

[15] This is but one way that Boeing hedges its short exposure to aluminum. It can enter into long-term contracts to purchase aluminum at fixed prices. These are essentially custom-tailored futures contracts, or forward contracts.

willing to purchase the futures contract at a price F_T that is greater than the expected future spot price:

$$F_T > E\left(S_T\right) \tag{19.7}$$

Boeing is willing to purchase the futures contract at an expected loss in return for eliminating the uncertainty over aluminum prices. The speculator will sell the futures contract and expect to earn a profit of $F_T - E\left(S_T\right)$.

Of course, the speculator might earn more or less (or even lose money), depending on the actual spot price of aluminum at maturity of the futures contract. If the inequality in Equation 19.7 remains true at maturity of the aluminum futures contract, then the speculator will earn $F_T - S_T$.

The reader might ask why the speculator is necessary. Why doesn't Boeing negotiate directly with aluminum producers in fixed-price contracts to lock in the price of aluminum and eliminate its commodity price exposure? To the extent it can, Boeing does. In fact, to the extent that commodity producers and commodity consumers can negotiate directly with one another, price risk can be eliminated without the need for speculators. However, the manufacture of aluminum does not always match Boeing's production cycle, and Boeing will have short-term demands for aluminum that will expose it to price risk. Speculators fill this gap.

Similarly, Exxon Mobil has a nondiversified exposure to crude oil. It can reduce the price risk associated with oil by selling its production forward. Yet in many cases there may not be a willing consumer to purchase the forward production of crude oil. Therefore, Exxon Mobil must sell its future production at a discount to entice the speculator/investor into the market.

Contango futures markets have an upward-sloping price curve. That is, the longer dated the futures contract, the greater must be the futures price that the speculator receives from selling the futures contract to the hedger. Higher prices reflect the additional risk that the speculator accepts over the longer period of time.

Backwardated versus contango markets also depend on global supply and demand of the underlying commodity. When there is excess demand for a commodity, the futures price curve will be backwardated—downward sloping. Consider crude oil. Excess demand will pump up the price of crude oil currently available, whereas crude available at a later date will be less valued. Conversely, when there is an excess supply of crude oil, it will depress the current price.

Markets can also reflect who bears the most risk of commodity price changes at any given time. For example, suppose the risk of commodity price changes is felt squarely by oil consumers instead of oil producers. Oil consumers are naturally short crude oil, and they might bear more risk regarding the future price of crude oil than the oil producers because of potential adverse supply shocks that could disrupt the oil market. When the greater risk is price shocks/disruption of oil supplies, a contango market will result, where oil consumers will need to compensate speculators by purchasing crude oil futures contracts at a futures price that is greater than the expected future spot price.

The reverse is true when there is an excess supply of oil. When Organization of Petroleum Exporting Countries (OPEC) members cheat, there is always the potential for more supply to come to market. When this is the case, an oil producer must be willing to sell its oil at a futures price that is lower than the future expected spot price. The oil producer is willing to take a small loss (the cost of hedging) in order to entice the speculator to bear the risk of declining oil prices. Let's look at a couple of examples.

The year 2008 was certainly a roller coaster of a ride—mostly down. We started the year coming off a modest gain in the equity markets for 2007; the S&P 500 was up about 5.6%. Global growth was still positive at the start of 2008. As a result, current demand for oil at the beginning of 2008 was still high. This led to the backwardated crude oil market displayed in Exhibit 19.10. We can see that the prices

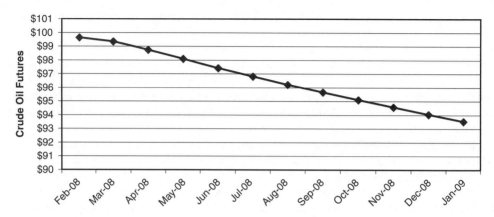

Exhibit 19.10   Backwardated market for crude oil futures, January 2009

of futures contracts in January 2008 were downward sloping. Current economic demand propped up the futures prices in the nearer futures months compared to longer-dated crude oil futures contracts.

However, as 2008 progressed, a global financial meltdown occurred the likes of which had not been seen since the Great Depression. By the third quarter of 2008, the world was slipping into a recession and the demand for crude oil dissipated quickly. Crude oil prices peaked in June 2008 at $150 per barrel but then declined rapidly as demand declined and supply increased. Exhibit 19.11 shows the crude oil futures curve as of November 2008. At that time, the market was in **contango**, an upward-sloping futures curve. The crude oil market in the space of just a few months swung from a backwardated market with excess demand to a contango market with excess supply. This was a demonstration of the swiftness with which the financial meltdown eroded economic growth and built up a supply of crude oil.

Commodity markets are backwardated most of the time. In fact, the crude oil market is in backwardation approximately 70% of the time. The reason is that backwardated markets encourage commodity producers to produce. Consider Exhibit 19.10. In January 2008, Exxon Mobil had a choice: It could produce crude oil immediately and sell it at a price of $99.62 per barrel or it could wait 12 months and sell it at an expected price of $93.54. The choice is easy; Exxon Mobil would prefer to produce today and sell crude oil at a higher price rather than produce tomorrow and sell it

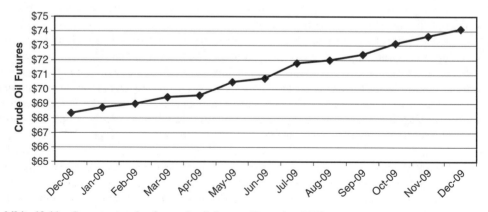

Exhibit 19.11   Contango market for crude oil futures, November 2009

at a lower price. Therefore, backwardation is a necessary condition to encourage current production of the underlying commodity.

However, economic slowdowns, recessions, and financial meltdowns can lead to a reduction in economic output and demand for energy products. When this occurs, commodity futures markets can reverse their natural course and flip between backwardation and contango. In addition, a contango market can develop when the risk bearing shifts from commodity producers to commodity consumers. This is the contango market in Exhibit 19.11. The global financial crisis led to an inevitable slowdown in gross domestic product (GDP) growth worldwide and a significant decline in the demand for crude oil. This in turn led to a buildup in crude oil surplus and a contango curve.

Exhibits 19.10 and 19.11 also highlight another useful point: the role of the speculator. The speculator does not care whether the commodity markets are in backwardation or contango; he is agnostic. All the speculator cares about is receiving an appropriate premium for the price risk he will bear. If the market is backwardated, the speculator is willing to purchase the futures contract from the hedger, but only at a discount. If the commodities market is in contango, the speculator will sell the futures contract, but only at a premium.

One last important point must be made regarding Exhibits 19.10 and 19.11. The speculator/investor in commodity futures can earn a profit no matter which way the commodity markets are acting. The conclusion is that the expected long-term returns to commodity investing depend on the long-term commodity price trends. As we just demonstrated, the speculator is agnostic with respect to the current price trend of crude oil. Investment profits can be earned whether the market is in backwardation or in contango. Therefore, profits in the commodity markets are determined by the supply of and demand for risk capital, not the long-term pricing trends of the commodity markets.

COMMODITY PRICES COMPARED TO FINANCIAL ASSET PRICES

In this section, we compare commodity prices to financial asset prices. As we stated at the beginning of the chapter, financial asset prices reflect the long-term discounted value of a stream of expected future revenues. In the case of stock prices, this future revenue stream may be eternal. In the case of a bond, the time is finite but can be very long, 10 to 20 years of expected cash flows. Investors in financial assets are compensated for the risk of fluctuating cash flows, and this risk is reflected in the interest rate used to discount those cash flows.

Thus, long-term expectations and interest rates are critical for pricing financial assets. Conversely, speculators and investors in commodities earn returns for bearing short-term commodity price risk. By bearing the price risk for commodity producers and commodity consumers, commodity investors and speculators receive exposure to the hedger's short-term earnings instead of its long-term cash flows. This point is all the more illuminated by how quickly the commodity markets can flip-flop between a contango market and a backwardated market. Exhibits 19.10 and 19.11 demonstrate that the nature of risk bearing can shift dramatically from producers to consumers of commodities.

This short-term exposure to a hedger's earnings illustrates that commodities will be priced very differently from financial assets. Long-term expectations and interest rates have only a minimal impact on commodity prices. Therefore, commodity prices can react very differently from financial asset prices when short-term expectations and long-term expectations diverge. This divergence occurs naturally as part of the course of the business cycle.

For instance, at the bottom of a recession, the short-term expectation of the economy's growth is negative. Commodity prices will decline to reflect this lower demand for raw inputs. However, it is at the bottom of a recession when discount rates are low and when long-term earnings expectations are revised upward that stocks and bonds begin to perform well. The converse is true at the peak of an expansion. Commodity prices are high, but long-term earnings expectations decline.

The different reactions to different parts of the business cycle indicate that commodities tend to move in the direction opposite to that of stocks and bonds. This has important portfolio implications that we discuss in the following chapters. For now it is sufficient to understand that commodity prices follow pricing dynamics different from the pricing dynamics of financial assets.

CONCLUSION

In this chapter we established commodity futures as a separate asset class distinct from financial assets. Commodity futures contracts are important tools not only for hedgers but also for speculators. Many hedge funds make use of the futures markets either for arbitrage opportunities or to earn risk premiums.

We also laid the groundwork in terms of pricing dynamics and discussed the economics of commodity futures markets. In the next two chapters we demonstrate how commodity futures can be added to a diversified portfolio to improve the overall risk-return profile of that portfolio.

20

Investing in Commodity Futures

In Chapter 19 we presented an introduction to the commodity markets and the methods by which investors access those markets. In this chapter we expand the discussion to cover the strategic reasons for investing in commodity futures.

We begin by developing the economic case for commodity futures. We then review the existing literature on the diversification benefits of commodity futures. Last, we examine several investable benchmarks that have been developed for the commodity futures markets.

Our discussion in this chapter focuses on the class of physical commodity futures. These commodity futures are sometimes referred to as **real assets**, assets that increase in value with inflation.[1] Real assets may also be defined by the tangible nature of their existence. A stock or a bond is represented by a piece of paper, but a real asset has a physical presence such as gold, oil, cattle, or wheat.[2] Some real assets such as gold or oil produce no income until the asset is sold, whereas others, such as real estate, produce income. Different approaches should be adopted in valuation of these two types of real assets. Income-producing assets may be valued in the same manner that stocks and bonds are valued based on the discounted value of their cash flows. Of course, adjustments must be made to reflect lack of liquidity in real estate investments. The market values of non-income-producing real assets are mostly functions of demand and supply factors of these assets.

ECONOMIC RATIONALE

We previously stated that commodities are an asset class distinct from stocks and bonds. In this section we clarify that distinction and demonstrate where and why commodity prices react differently from capital asset prices.

Commodities and the business cycle

In Chapter 19 we demonstrated that commodity prices are not as directly impacted by changes in discount rates as stocks and bonds are. We also discussed how commodity prices are not determined by the discounted value of future cash flows. Instead, commodity prices are determined by the current supply and demand of the underlying commodity. Since commodity prices are driven by different economic fundamentals than stocks and bonds, they should be expected to have little correlation or even negative correlation with the prices of capital assets.

There are three arguments as to why commodity prices should, in fact, be negatively correlated with the prices of stocks and bonds. The first is the relationship that commodity futures prices have with inflation. Inflation is well documented to have a detrimental impact on the values of stocks and bonds. However, inflation is expected to have a positive impact on commodity futures prices for two reasons.

---

[1] See Kenneth Froot, "Hedging Portfolios with Real Assets," *Journal of Portfolio Management* (Summer 1995), 60–77.

[2] Under this definition, real estate also qualifies as a real asset because there is a tangible nature to the investment (i.e. a building, a shopping center, or an apartment complex).

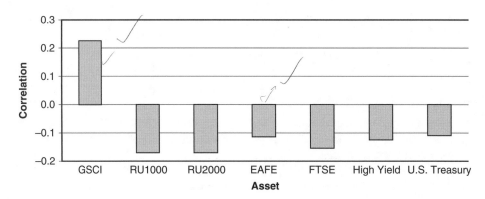

Exhibit 20.1   Correlation of stocks, bonds, and commodities with U.S. inflation, 1990–2008

First, prices of physical commodities such as oil are an underlying source of inflation. As the cost of raw materials increases, so does the producers' price inflation and the consumers' price inflation. In fact, commodity prices are a component of the producer price index (PPI) and the consumer price index (CPI). Therefore, higher commodity prices mean higher inflation.

Also, higher inflation means higher short-term interest rates. This also has a beneficial impact on commodity futures investments because of their collateral yield. As we discussed in the prior chapter, commodity futures contracts can be purchased with a down payment known as the initial margin. The initial margin can be contributed in the form of cash or U.S. Treasury bills. This means that one component of return from an investment in commodity futures is the interest that is earned on the margin deposit that supports the futures contract.[3] Higher inflation therefore means a higher interest rate on the margin on deposit, and a higher return from investing in commodity futures contracts.

Exhibit 20.1 documents the relationship between inflation, commodity futures, and stocks and bonds. This chart plots the correlation of monthly returns between large-cap stocks (the Russell 1000), small-cap stocks (the Russell 2000), international stocks (MSCI EAFE and FTSE indices) high-yield bonds (the Salomon Smith Barney High Yield Cash Pay Index), U.S. Treasury bonds, and commodities (as represented by the Goldman Sachs Commodity Index) with the rate of inflation. The time period is from 1990 through 2008.[4]

As can be seen, commodity futures prices are positively correlated with inflation. Conversely, capital assets such as stocks and bonds are negatively correlated with inflation. Therefore, throughout the course of the business cycle, as inflation increases, capital asset values decrease, but commodity futures values increase. The reverse is also true, as inflation decreases, capital asset prices increase, but commodity futures prices decrease.

Notice that the Financial Times/Stock Exchange Index (FTSE) of the 100 largest stocks traded on the London Stock Exchange and the MSCI EAFE index (Europe, Australasia, and the Far East) are also negatively correlated with the U.S. inflation rate. This is important to note because an investor seeking international diversification as a means to escape the ravages of domestic inflation does not find it in foreign stocks.

---

[3] If the futures margin is deposited in cash, then the futures broker may pay a higher interest rate on that deposit. Alternatively, if the futures margin is deposited in Treasury bills, as the T-bills mature, newer, higher-yielding T-bills may be used to replace them.

[4] We use the Goldman Sachs Commodity Index as our proxy for commodity prices. There are, in fact, several commodity indices that we discuss later in the chapter.

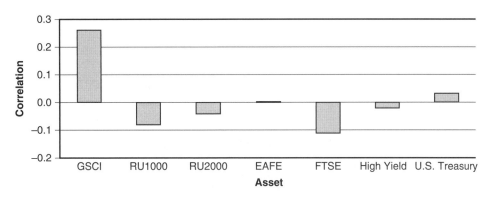

Exhibit 20.2   Correlation of stocks, bonds, and commodities with changes in U.S. inflation, 1990–2008

Even more important, commodity futures prices are positively correlated with the change in the inflation rate, whereas capital assets are negatively correlated with changes in the rate of inflation.[5] This is important because changes in the rate of inflation tend to reflect inflation shocks (i.e. unanticipated changes that force investors to revise their expectations about future inflation). A positive change in the inflation rate means that investors' expectations regarding future inflation rates will increase. Stock and bond prices react negatively to such revised expectations, whereas commodity futures prices react positively.

Exhibit 20.2 demonstrates the reaction of capital assets and commodities to changes in the rate of inflation. We see that commodities remain highly correlated with changes in the inflation rate. In fact, commodities have a stronger correlation to changes in the inflation rate than to the absolute inflation rate. Conversely, stocks and corporate bonds do not respond well to changes in inflation, the correlation coefficient is negative (except for MSCI EAFE, where it is close to zero). Last, we note that U.S. Treasury bonds respond positively to changes in inflation.

A second reason why commodity price changes may be negatively correlated with the returns to stocks and bonds is that commodity futures prices are impacted by short-term expectations, whereas stocks and bonds are affected by long-term expectations. For example, in a strong economy financial assets may decline over fears of increased inflation or sustainability of economic growth. These are long-term concerns. Conversely, commodity prices will react favorably because they are influenced by the high demand for raw materials under the current market conditions. The result is that commodity futures prices and stock and bond prices can react very differently at different parts of the business cycle. Exhibit 20.3 diagrams these different cyclical price moves.

This countercyclical movement between commodity futures and stocks and bonds is demonstrated by research conducted by Goldman Sachs & Co.[6] When the economy is below capacity (as measured by long-run GDP), equity returns have been at their highest, but commodity prices have been at their lowest. This occurs at the bottom of an economic cycle. As economic growth accelerates, stock prices begin to decline but commodity prices increase. When the economy heats up and exceeds long-run GDP, the return to commodity futures exceeds that for stocks. In sum, rising and falling commodity prices coincide with the current state of the economic cycle, whereas stocks and bonds are priced based on their future cash flows and not the current state of the economy.

---

[5] See Philip Halpern and Randy Warsager, "The Performance of Energy and Non-Energy Based Commodity Investment Vehicles in Periods of Inflation," *Journal of Alternative Assets* (Summer 1998), 75–81.

[6] See Goldman Sachs & Co., "The Strategic Case for Using Commodities in Portfolio Diversification," Goldman Sachs Research Series on Commodities as an Asset Class, July 1996.

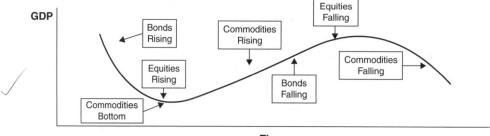

Exhibit 20.3   The business cycle and stock, bond, and commodity prices

The point of Exhibit 20.4 is that stocks and bonds are anticipatory in their pricing, whereas commodities are priced based on the state of current economic conditions. The value of stocks and bonds is derived from expectations regarding long-term earnings and coupon payments. Consequently, they perform best when the economy appears the worst but the prospects for improvement are the highest.

Real assets, however, show the opposite pattern. Commodity prices are determined not so much by the future prospects of the economy, but by the level of current economic activity. Consequently, commodity prices are at their lowest when economic activity is at its lowest, and at their highest when economic activity is at its highest. Exhibit 20.4 demonstrates that commodity returns are negative when economic activity is negative. The most recent example is the credit crisis and recession of 2008.

A third argument for the negative correlation between commodity prices and capital assets is based on economic production.[7] Consider the three primary inputs to economic production: capital, labor, and raw materials. The returns to these three factors should equal the price of production. In the short to intermediate term, the cost of labor should remain stable. Therefore, for any given price level of production, an increase in the return to capital must mean a reduction in the return to raw materials, and vice versa. The result is a negative correlation between commodity prices and the prices of capital assets.

In sum, commodity price changes are expected to be at the very least uncorrelated with the returns to stocks and bonds. Additionally, there are three reasons to expect commodity prices to be negatively correlated with stocks and bonds. First, inflation has a positive impact on commodity prices but a negative impact on stocks and bonds. Second, commodity prices are impacted by a different set of expectations than that for stocks and bonds. Last, in the production process there is a trade-off between the returns to capital and the returns to raw materials.

Event risk

In our chapters on hedge funds, we demonstrated how financial assets and hedge fund strategies are exposed to significant event risk. For example, our analysis of the returns to hedge funds around the financial turmoil of 2008 indicated that most hedge fund strategies experienced significant negative returns. Additionally, we demonstrated that most arbitrage strategies have exposure to event risk, which can result in significant negative returns.

---

[7] See Robert Greer, "Institutional Use of Physical Commodity Indices," in *Commodity Derivatives and Finance*, ed. Kathleen Tener Smith and Pam Kennison (London: Euromoney Books, 1999).

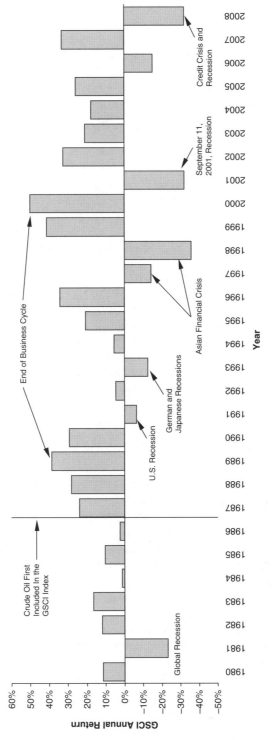

Exhibit 20.4 Commodity returns are coincident with the state of the economic cycle

333

Commodities, by contrast, tend to have positive exposure to event risk. The reason is that the surprises that occur in the commodities markets tend to be those that unexpectedly reduce the supply of the commodity to the market. Events such as Organization of Petroleum Exporting Countries (OPEC) agreements to reduce the supply of crude oil, a cold snap in winter, war, or political instability can drive up energy prices. Similarly, events such as droughts, floods, and crop freezes all reduce the supply of agricultural products. Last, strikes and labor unrest can drive up the prices of both precious and industrial metals. Shocks that would unexpectedly reduce demand significantly tend to be rare. However, shocks in terms of unexpectedly large buildups in inventories that may lead to significant price declines do occur. At least historically more commodity prices appear to have a positive exposure to various event risks.

These patterns of unexpected shocks to the commodity prices should provide a pattern of positively skewed returns. In our examination of hedge funds, we demonstrated that many hedge fund strategies have positively skewed distributions, that is, more return observations to the right of the median (positive) than to the left of the median (negative). Positively skewed return distributions will have a beneficial impact to a diversified portfolio because they can provide an upward return bias to the portfolio.

We examine the distribution of commodity futures returns later in this chapter. For now, it is sufficient to say that these patterns of returns demonstrate a positive skew to commodity futures prices indicating a bias for upside returns instead of downside returns.

Furthermore, these patterns of commodity shocks are expected to be uncorrelated. For example, OPEC agreements to cut oil production should be uncorrelated with droughts in the agricultural regions around the world[8] or with labor strikes affecting metals mining. The point is that the global supply and demand factors for each individual commodity market that determine the price of each commodity are very different. The primary factors that determine the supply and demand for oil, and the price of oil, are very different from those that affect the price of wheat, gold, or aluminum.[9] Consequently, we would expect the price patterns of commodities to be uncorrelated with each other. This has important implications for commodity indices.

Equally important is that shocks to the commodities markets are expected to be at least uncorrelated with the financial markets, and more likely to be negatively correlated with the financial markets. The reason follows from our prior discussion—most shocks to the commodity markets tend to reduce the supply of raw materials to the market. The sudden decrease of raw materials should have a positive impact on commodity prices, but a negative impact on financial asset prices, whose expected returns will be reduced by the higher cost of production inputs.

Consider Exhibit 20.5. This exhibit demonstrates several years where there were significant shocks to the supply and demand of physical commodities. Again, we use the GSCI as a benchmark for commodity returns. In the early and mid-1970s there was a series of oil price shocks. This was a boon for commodity prices, but disastrous for financial asset prices. In contrast, 1981 was a year of severe recession for the United States. Financial asset prices declined, but so did prices of commodities, as there was simply insufficient demand both for finished goods and for raw materials to support either financial asset prices or commodity prices. Next, 1990 was the year of the Iraqi invasion of Kuwait. This political instability had a negative impact on financial asset prices, but a positive impact on commodity prices. Conversely, in 1998, there was a glut of cheap crude oil and petroleum

---

[8] Since oil is a major input to the agricultural sector of the economy in the form of fuel and fertilizers, significant contraction in this sector may have a negative impact on oil prices.

[9] Due to the expansion of ethanol use in recent years, we have since seen an increased correlation between prices of some agricultural products (e.g. corn) and oil prices.

Exhibit 20.5 Annual returns in years of market stress

Year	S&P 500	Commodities
1973	−14.69%	74.96%
1974	−26.47	39.51
1977	−7.16	10.37
1981	−4.92	−23.01
1987	5.25	23.77
Oct. 1987	−21.54	1.05
1990	−3.10	29.08
1998	28.58	−35.75
2000	−9.10	49.74
2001	−11.89	−31.93
2002	−22.10	32.07
2008	−37.98	−32.02

products in the market. In late 1997, OPEC voted to increase production just as the Southeast Asian economies were slipping into a steep recession. In addition, under the United Nations Oil-for-Food Program, new oil production came on line from Iraq. Further, an extremely mild winter (recall El Niño) resulted in a buildup of petroleum inventories around the world. The result, in 1998, was plenty of cheap raw materials, which in turn translated to strong stock market gains in the United States.

Next came the three-year equity bear market following the bursting of the technology bubble. Note that in 2001 when the economy slid into a brief recession, commodity prices and stock prices moved in the same direction. Another example of when commodity prices and financial prices move in the same direction is during a global financial and economic meltdown. The credit and financial crisis of 2008 led to a deep recession around the world, and commodity prices declined significantly as a result of negative global GDP. Otherwise, commodities have not been correlated with the stock market movements during bear markets. Also, during severe liquidity shocks most commodity prices tend to decline because of lower leverage and availability of capital for commodity trading.

In conclusion, commodity price shocks tend to favor supply disruptions rather than sudden increases in supply. These disruptions provide positive returns for commodities at the same time that they provide negative returns for financial assets. Therefore, the event risk associated with commodities tends to favor investors in the commodity markets while detrimentally impacting investors in the financial markets. In the next section we discuss the empirical literature that supports the place of commodities within a diversified portfolio.

EMPIRICAL EVIDENCE SUPPORTING COMMODITY FUTURES AS AN ASSET CLASS

While commodities within an investment portfolio are considered to be a new phenomenon, organized commodity trading has been in existence far longer than stock and bond trading. The first commodity exchange was the Osaka rice exchange that began trading in Japan in the 1400s. By contrast, the New York Stock Exchange did not begin organized trading until the early 1800s (trading did take place in lower Manhattan under the buttonwood tree as early as the 1790s). Nonetheless, commodity futures investing is relatively new compared to stock and bond investing.

In his seminal paper more than 30 years ago, Robert Greer introduced the idea of investing in commodity futures as a portfolio diversification tool.[10] He proposed that an unleveraged index of commodity futures prices be used as an inflation hedge for a stock portfolio. He demonstrated that a combination of a commodity futures index and large-capitalization stocks provided a better risk and return profile than a portfolio constructed solely of stocks.

Five years later, Zvi Bodie examined how commodity futures contracts can supplement a portfolio of stocks and bonds to improve the risk and return trade-off in an inflationary environment.[11] Studying the period of 1953 to 1981, he found that the inclusion of commodity futures shifted the efficient frontier up and to the left (providing higher expected returns and lower risk). He concluded that a portfolio of stocks, bonds, Treasury bills, and commodity futures improved the risk and return more than an investment portfolio constructed without commodity futures.

In more recent research, Ankrim and Hensel,[12] Lummer and Siegel,[13] Kaplan and Lummer,[14] Gibson,[15] Anson,[16] and Gorton and Rouwenhorst[17] all examine adding commodity futures to an investment portfolio through an investment in a passive commodity futures index. All five studies conclude that an investment in a passive commodities futures index provides a good diversifier for stocks and bonds as well as an effective hedge against inflation.

Satyanarayan and Varangis extend the investment analysis of commodity futures to an international portfolio.[18] They find that commodity futures returns are negatively correlated with the returns to all developed markets and with three of six emerging markets. One reason why all developed markets are negatively correlated with changes in commodity futures' prices is that developed markets are the primary consumers of commodity inputs. Conversely, emerging markets tend to be net suppliers of commodity inputs. Consequently, it is not surprising to find that some emerging markets are positively correlated with commodity futures prices.

Anson extends the analysis of commodity futures to utility theory. He finds that the marginal utility of commodity futures investing increases with an investor's level of risk aversion. That is, the more risk averse the investor, the greater the utility from investing in commodity futures.[19]

Froot compares three classes of real assets: real estate, commodity futures, and the stocks of companies that are commodity producers.[20] He finds that when commodity futures are the initial hedge in a portfolio, this renders the other real assets ineffective. Yet, when commodity futures

---

[10] See Robert Greer, "Conservative Commodities: A Key Inflation Hedge," *Journal of Portfolio Management* (Summer 1978).

[11] See Zvi Bodie, "Commodity Futures as a Hedge against Inflation," *Journal of Portfolio Management* (Spring 1983), 12–17.

[12] Ernest Ankrim and Chris Hensel, "Commodities in Asset Allocation: A Real Asset Alternative to Real Estate?" *Financial Analysts Journal* (May/June 1993), 20–29.

[13] Scott Lummer and Laurence Siegel, "GSCI Collateralized Futures: A Hedging and Diversification Tool for Institutional Investors," *Journal of Investing* (Summer 1993), 75–82.

[14] Paul Kaplan and Scott Lummer, "GSCI Collateralized Futures as a Hedging and Diversification Tool for Institutional Investors: An Update," working paper, Ibbotson Associates (November 1997).

[15] Roger Gibson, "The Rewards of Multiple Asset Class Investing," *Journal of Financial Planning* (March 1999), 50–59.

[16] Mark Anson, "Spot Returns, Roll Yield, and Diversification with Commodity Futures," *Journal of Alternative Investments* (Winter 1998), 16–32.

[17] Gary Gorton and K. Geert Rouwenhorst, "Facts and Fantasies about Commodity Futures," *Financial Analysts Journal* (March/April 2006).

[18] See Sudhakar Satyanarayan and Panos Varangis, "Diversification Benefits of Commodity Assets in Global Portfolios," *Journal of Investing* (Spring 1996), 69–78.

[19] See Mark Anson, "Maximizing Utility with Commodity Futures," *Journal of Portfolio Management* (Summer 1999), 86–94.

[20] See Kenneth Froot, "Hedging Portfolios with Real Assets," *Journal of Portfolio Management* (Summer 1995), 60–77.

are added to the portfolio as a secondary hedge after other real assets have already been added, commodity futures still remain a significant portfolio diversifier. However, he concludes that the same cannot be said for real estate. Once commodity futures have been added to an investment portfolio, real estate does little to reduce portfolio volatility. The same conclusion is reached for commodity-based equity. In other words, commodity futures provide a more effective hedge against unexpected inflation than do either real estate or the stocks of commodity-producing companies.

New research by Erb and Harvey casts some doubt on the value of commodity futures as a strategic asset class and as an inflation hedge.[21] They find that the long-term returns to commodity futures depend on the construction of the commodity index. Those indices that overweight commodities with historically backwardated yield curves generate positive roll yield and positive long-term returns. However, they find that an equally weighted index of commodity futures does not provide significant long-term positive returns. In contrast to Exhibit 20.2 in this chapter, they did not find commodities to provide a hedge against unexpected inflation. However, they do make a case for using commodities on a tactical basis when using the term structure of the commodity futures curve or investing in commodities based on a momentum strategy.

In conclusion, most of the empirical studies have found commodity futures to have significant diversification potential for financial assets. All of the studies to date have found that the addition of commodity futures to a portfolio of stocks and bonds has the ability to reduce the risk of the portfolio for a given level of return (we note that the Erb and Harvey study reach this conclusion based on a tactical application of commodity futures). Further, each of these studies used an investable commodity futures index to reach its conclusions.

COMMODITY FUTURES INDICES

In this section we review several investable commodity futures indices, analyze their construction, and consider their application to a diversified portfolio.

Description of a commodity futures index

The first commodity indices were designed to reflect price changes either in the cash/spot markets or in the futures markets. However, these indices did not reflect the total return that can be earned from commodity futures contracts. Therefore, they were not investable. An example of a price change index was the Commodity Research Bureau (CRB) Commodities Index. However, this index was taken over by Reuters and Jefferies & Company in 2005 and is now an investable index.

A commodity futures index should represent the total return that would be earned from holding long-only positions in unleveraged physical commodity futures. Financial futures should not be included because, as we demonstrated in Chapter 19, financial futures contracts are economically linked to the underlying financial assets. Therefore, there is no diversification benefit from adding long positions in financial futures to a portfolio of financial assets.

In Chapter 19 we also described how a futures contract may be purchased by depositing only a small portion of the total price of the underlying commodity, called the initial margin. The initial margin typically represents 5% to 10% of the futures price. Therefore, futures contracts are purchased with leverage. For example, a 10% initial margin requirement translates into a leverage ratio of 10 to 1. This means that for every dollar invested in a commodity futures contract, the investor would receive $10 of commodity price exposure. The application of leverage can enhance an investor's

---

[21] See Claude Erb and Campbell Harvey, "The Tactical and Strategic Value of Commodity Futures," *Financial Analysts Journal* (2006).

return, but at the same time can also exacerbate an investor's losses. Therefore, the leverage associated with a futures contract can increase the volatility of the investment.

In contrast, commodity futures indices are constructed to be unleveraged. The face value of the futures contracts is fully supported (collateralized) either by cash or by Treasury bills. Futures contracts are purchased to provide economic exposure to commodities equal to the amount of cash dollars invested in the index. Therefore, every dollar of exposure to a commodity futures index represents one dollar of commodity price risk.

For example, the current initial margin for gold is $1,500. With gold selling at $930 per ounce in July 2009 and 100 ounces of gold being the size of the contract, one futures contract has an economic exposure to gold of $93,000. A managed futures account would typically pay the initial margin of $1,500 and receive economic exposure to gold equivalent to $93,000. The percentage of equity capital committed to the futures contract is equal to $1,500/$93,000 = 1.61%. In contrast, a commodity futures index will fully collateralize the gold futures contract. This means $93,000 of U.S. Treasury bills will be held to fully support the face value of the gold futures contract. In fact, the face value of every futures contract included in a commodity index will be fully collateralized by an investment in U.S. Treasury bills.

In this way, an unleveraged commodity futures index represents the returns an investor could earn from continuously holding a passive long-only position in a basket of commodity futures contracts. The passive index must reflect all components of return from commodity futures contracts: price changes, collateral yield, and roll yield (the last source of return will be explained later).

Finally, we note that a commodity futures index has several differences compared to a managed futures account. **Managed futures accounts** represent the returns that can be earned from the active investment style of a Commodity Trading Advisor (CTA) or a Commodity Pool Operator (CPO). In a managed futures account the CTA or CPO has discretion over the trading positions taken.

First, managed futures accounts are just that (actively managed accounts), whereas **commodity futures indices** are designed to provide passive exposure to the commodity futures markets. Second, CTAs and CPOs, including financial futures as well as commodity futures in their investment portfolios, tend to invest across the spectrum of the futures markets. Third, CTAs and CPOs may invest both long and short in futures contracts. In fact, many CTA/CPO trading programs are designed to have simultaneous long and short positions so as to have as little net market exposure as possible. Commodity futures indices, in contrast, invest in long-only positions. Last, managed futures accounts tend to apply leverage in the purchase and sale of commodity futures contracts. We will have more to say about the managed futures industry in a future chapter.

Sources of index return

The total return from an unleveraged commodity futures index comes from three primary sources: changes in spot prices of the underlying commodity, the interest earned from the Treasury bills used to collateralize the futures contracts, and the roll yield. Each component can be an important part of the return of a commodity index in any given year.

Spot prices

As we indicated in Chapter 19, spot commodity prices are determined by the supply and demand characteristics of each commodity market as well as the current level of risk aversion between consumers and producers of commodities. We demonstrated, for example, how the price of crude oil plummeted in 1998 due to overproduction by OPEC members, extra production by Iraq, and the slow-down in Southeast Asia due to the Asian contagion of late 1997. This supply imbalance drove crude oil prices down. However, in early 1999, OPEC members reached an agreement to cut production and restrict the supply of crude oil into the marketplace. This changed the supply-and-demand equilibrium from one of excess supply to one of excess demand, and crude oil prices rose significantly.

These price changes in the spot market are reflected directly in the commodity futures markets. Recall the following equation from Chapter 19:

$$F = Se^{(r+c-y)(T-t)} \tag{20.1}$$

where

F = the futures price
S = the current spot/cash price of the underlying commodity
r = the risk-free rate of return
c = the cost of storage
y = the convenience yield
$T - t$ = the time to maturity of the contract

Other factors remaining equal (storage cost, risk-free rate, and convenience yield), when the spot price of the underlying commodity increases in value, so will the futures price. The reverse is also true: as spot prices decline, so will the futures price. Therefore, changes in the current cash price of a commodity flow right through to the futures price.

This is important to understand, because as we discussed above, most of the shocks with respect to physical commodities tend to be events that reduce the current supply. That is, physical commodities have positive event risk. Supply and demand shocks to the physical commodity markets result in positive price changes for both the spot market and the futures market.

Collateral yield

As we discussed earlier, a commodity futures index is unleveraged. It is unleveraged because the economic exposure underlying the basket of futures contract is fully collateralized by the purchase of U.S. Treasury bills. Therefore, for every $1 invested in a commodity futures index, the investor receives $1 of diversified commodity exposure plus interest on $1 invested in U.S. Treasury bills.

The interest earned on the Treasury bills used as collateral is called the **collateral yield**, and it can be a significant part of the total return to a commodity futures index. Further, changes in inflation rates will be reflected in the yield on Treasury bills. This is another way that a commodity futures index can hedge against inflation.

Roll yield

Roll yield is the least obvious source of return for commodity futures. Roll yield is derived from the shape of the commodity futures term structure. Recall our discussion from Chapter 19 that commodity futures markets can either be in backwardation, where futures prices are below the spot price, or contango, where futures prices are above the current spot price for the underlying commodity.

When the futures markets are in backwardation, a positive return will be earned from a simple buy-and-hold strategy. The positive return is earned because as the futures contract gets closer to maturity, its price must converge to that of the spot price of the commodity. Since the spot price is greater than the futures price, this means that the futures price must increase in value. This convergence is known as rolling up the yield curve, or simply **roll yield**. A demonstration should help.

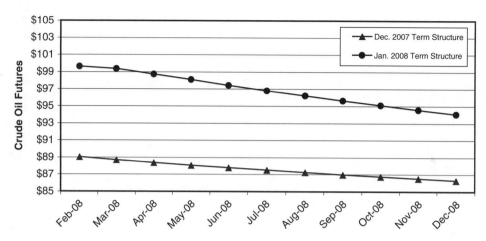

Exhibit 20.6   Term structure for crude oil futures

Consider Exhibit 20.6. This exhibit demonstrates the term structure for crude oil futures contracts in December 2007 and January 2008. Notice that the futures prices decline the longer the maturity of the futures contract. Therefore, the term structure is downward sloping. This is a demonstration of backwardation, the futures prices are below the current spot price for crude oil.

Recall that a backwardated market indicates that producers of commodities are willing to hedge their commodity price risk by selling their future production at lower prices than the current spot price of the commodity. The farther out in time that they sell their future production, the greater the discount they must offer to investors to entice them to purchase the futures contracts. As a futures contract gets closer to maturity, less price risk remains, and an investor will harvest part of the price discount as profit by rolling up the futures yield curve. Rolling up the term structure results in profit harvesting.

In January 2008 the futures term structure is significantly above the crude oil term structure that existed in December 2007, reflecting a sharp increase in crude oil spot prices of $9.87. The increase in spot prices shifted the whole term structure upward. In addition to the price appreciation, the owner of a long crude oil futures contract can earn the roll yield.

Exhibit 20.7 calculates the roll yield associated with each futures contract over the one-month holding period of December 2007 to January 2008. As a futures contract approaches maturity, there

Exhibit 20.7   Calculation of the roll yield for crude oil futures

Contract Month	Price as of January 2008	Less Price at December 2007	Less Change in Spot Price	Equals Roll Yield
Feb-08	$99.62	$89.04	$9.87	$0.71
Mar-08	99.33	88.69	9.87	0.77
Apr-08	98.74	88.36	9.87	0.51
May-08	98.09	88.06	9.87	0.16
Jun-08	97.42	87.76	9.87	−0.21
Jul-08	96.80	87.49	9.87	−0.56
Aug-08	96.22	87.23	9.87	−0.88
Sep-08	95.65	86.99	9.87	−1.21
Oct-08	95.10	86.76	9.87	−1.53
Nov-08	94.57	86.53	9.87	−1.83
Dec-08	94.05	86.31	9.87	−2.13

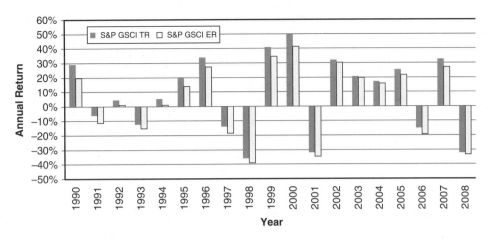

Exhibit 20.8   GSCI total return and excess return

is less price risk, and therefore less of a discount is required to entice buyers into the market. Therefore, part of the price discount can be harvested by rolling up the yield curve.

Exhibit 20.7 demonstrates the calculation of the roll yield. For example, suppose an investor purchased the February 2008 crude oil futures contract in December 2007. The price of the Feb-08 contract in December 2007 was $89.04. One month later, in January 2008, the Feb-08 crude oil futures contract was priced at $99.62. The increase in value of $10.58 can be split into two components. The first is the increase in spot prices over this one-month holding period. Crude oil prices shot up by $9.87 a barrel in January due to a surge in demand and limited supply. The remainder of the price increase of $0.71 was due to roll yield.

As can be seen, the roll yield is greater the closer the futures contract is to maturity. This is because a greater amount of uncertainty is reduced the closer the futures contract is to maturity. The farther out on the term structure an investor goes, the less uncertainty can be resolved as a futures contract rolls up the curve. Consequently, as an investor moves farther out on the term structure, the roll yield declines and can even be negative.

How large can this roll yield be? A study of crude oil futures prices found that a long position in the first nearby futures contract (the contract closest to maturity) earned an average annual roll yield of 9% over the period 1987 to 1995.[22] The study also found that the roll yield was greatest for commodity futures contracts that were closer to maturity.

Notice that the roll yield can also be negative. In a contango market, when futures prices are greater than spot prices, the futures prices will roll down the term structure, resulting in lost value as the futures price converges to the spot price. Recall from Chapter 19 that in a contango market, commodity consumers are the natural hedgers, and they purchase futures contracts. Investors who sell short the futures contracts to the commodity consumers will collect the futures premium as the futures contract rolls down the term structure.

Comparing the components of a commodity index

To give the reader some sense of how the different components of a commodity index work, Exhibit 20.8 presents the returns to the GSCI Excess Return Index and the GSCI Total Return Index. The

---

[22] See Daniel Nash, "Relative Value Trading in Commodities," working paper, July 15, 1996.

GSCI Excess Return Index measures the return from investing in the nearby GSCI futures contract and rolling this contract forward each month. It captures the roll yield as well as the movement in the underlying commodity prices over the prior month. The GSCI Total Return Index captures all the effects associated with investing in commodity futures: roll yield, collateral yield, and commodity price changes. Notice that the GSCI Total Return is always greater than the GSCI Excess Return. This reflects the additional yield associated with Treasury bills posted as collateral against the futures positions. Unfortunately, you cannot add the return to Treasury bills (the collateral yield) directly to the GSCI Excess Return to get the GSCI Total Return, because this ignores the impact of the reinvestment of Treasury bill collateral yield gains back into commodity futures as well as gains/losses from commodity futures back out of or into Treasury bills. Therefore, the difference between the Total Return Index and the Excess Return Index is only an estimate of what the collateral yield was in any given year.

Also, note that the total return is larger than the excess return in years when interest rates are higher. For example, in 1999 and 2000 when the economy was peaking and short-term interest rates were high, the total return was significantly greater than the excess return. Conversely, when interest rates are low, such as in the economic recession year of 2008, there is only a slight advantage to the GSCI Total Return versus the GSCI Excess Return.

There is one last point to note about the returns to commodity indices. Not only are commodity indices excellent diversification tools vis-à-vis stocks and bonds, but they also have excellent diversification with respect to their sources of return. Commodity indices earn returns from spot prices, roll yield, and collateral yield. This provides a diversification of return sources that enhances the probability of a positive return in any given month or year.

During 2007 and 2008 we saw that these potential diversification benefits may come with a significant cost in terms of volatility and drawdown. Also, as more investors increase their allocations to commodities, we may see increased correlation between commodity prices and stock and bond prices. The reason is that in response to changes in the economic environment investors would adjust their portfolio holdings.

Investable commodity futures indices

It may surprise investors that there are several commodity futures indices in existence. These indices have all the benefits of a stock index: They are transparent, they are liquid, you can trade in the underlying component parts of the index, and they are investable. Even if an investor, such as a pension plan, cannot invest directly into commodity futures indices, it may still gain exposure through a commodity-linked note of the type described in Chapter 19.

An investment manager can use commodity futures indices in two ways. First, a commodity futures index can be used to implement a specific view on the expected returns from commodities as an asset class. This is a tactical bet by the investment manager that commodities will outperform stocks and bonds given the current position of the business cycle.

Alternatively, commodity futures indices can be used to provide passive portfolio diversification. Exhibit 20.3 demonstrated that commodity prices peak and bottom out at different parts of the business cycle than do financial assets. Within this context, commodities have a strategic purpose: to diversify the investment portfolio's risk and return, without any view as to the current state of the business cycle.

Unlike equity stock indices, where an investor can maintain her positions almost infinitely, commodity futures contracts specify a date for delivery. In order to maintain a continuous long-only position, expiring futures contracts must be sold and new futures contracts must be purchased. This provides the roll yield discussed earlier.

Standard & Poor's Goldman Sachs Commodity Index

The GSCI is designed to be a benchmark for investment in the commodity markets and as a measure of commodity market performance over time. It is also designed to be a tradable index that is readily accessible to market participants. It is a long-only index of physical commodity futures. Not only is the GSCI comprised of physical commodity futures contracts, but a futures contract trades on the index itself. In other words, investors can purchase a futures contract tied to the future expected spot value of the GSCI.

The GSCI was introduced in 1991. Although the GSCI was not published prior to that time, Goldman Sachs has calculated the historical value of the GSCI and related indices dating back to January 1970, based on historical prices of futures contracts and using the selection criteria and index construction established in 1991. The GSCI has been normalized to a value of 100 on December 31, 1969.

The GSCI is composed only of physical commodity futures. Financial futures contracts (on securities, currencies, or interest rates) are not included. The limitation to only physical commodity futures focuses the construction of the index on real assets that are the inputs to the global production process. Additionally, the GSCI is composed of the first nearby futures contract in each commodity (the futures contract that is closest to maturity).

The GSCI is a production-weighted index that is designed to reflect the relative significance of each of the constituent commodities to the world economy while preserving the tradability of the index by limiting eligible futures contracts to those with adequate liquidity. The use of production weighting is designed as an economic indicator. The GSCI assigns the appropriate weight to each commodity in proportion to the amount of that commodity that flows through the global economic engine. The GSCI is constructed using five-year averages of a particular commodity's contribution to world production. This is done to mitigate the effect of any aberrant year with respect to the production of a commodity.

The GSCI is constructed with 24 physical commodities across five main groups of real assets: precious metals, industrial metals, livestock, agriculture, and energy. Exhibit 20.9 presents the weights of these five commodity groups in the GSCI as of December 2008. Energy is the largest component of the index. This reflects the importance of energy products in the global production process, as well as the global surge in energy prices into the first half of 2008. Clearly, at almost 72% of the total index as of the end of 2008, energy was the most dominant component of the worldwide production cycle. The next largest component of the index was agriculture—not surprising given the need to feed the growing worldwide population. Precious metals, by contrast, represent the smallest

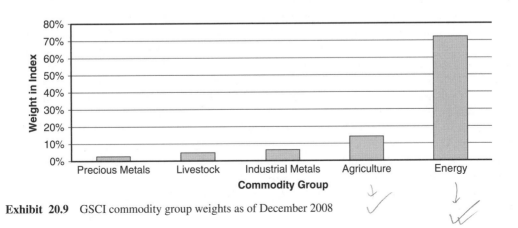

Exhibit 20.9 GSCI commodity group weights as of December 2008

component of the GSCI. While precious metals may be held as a store of value, they are a smaller input to global production.

The GSCI physical weights are set once a year (in January) and then the dollar percentage values are allowed to float for the remainder of the year. There is no limit to the weight any one commodity may attain in the index and no minimum weight for any commodity. Value-weighted indices such as the GSCI represent a momentum investment strategy, because those commodity futures contracts that do well represent an increasing portion of the index.

Last, we consider the distribution of returns associated with the GSCI. In Exhibit 20.10 we plot the monthly return distribution for the GSCI over the period 1990 to 2008. First, note the wide dispersion of monthly returns to the GSCI. These returns vary from −29% at one end to +23% at the other end of the return distribution. In addition, the mass of the distribution is not concentrated to the same extent as hedge fund returns. For example, the mass of the GSCI return distribution in the 0% to 2% range is only 14.6%. This dispersion is further evidenced by the very high standard deviation of monthly returns of 6.12%. Compare this with the return mass associated with hedge funds. In Chapter 13 we showed how the return mass for hedge funds is frequently concentrated in the 0% to 2% range up to 75% of the time. Clearly, the GSCI generates much less consistent returns than certain hedge fund strategies. Overall, the average monthly return to the GSCI is 0.65% with a monthly standard deviation of 6.12%. This results in a Sharpe ratio of 0.05.

The GSCI has a slight negative skew of −0.14 and a positive kurtosis of 2.39. From our discussion in prior chapters, we know that this condition of leptokurtosis means that commodity returns experience large outlier returns more frequently than might be expected with a normal distribution. Indeed, when we look at Exhibit 20.10 we can visually discern these outlier data points. This indicates that commodity futures are exposed to event risk: the risk of sudden shocks to the global supply and demand for physical commodities. From our discussion of commodity event risk being mostly shocks that reduce the supply of commodities, we expect that exposure to event risk to have a beneficial impact on commodity returns. Interestingly, we find a slightly negative skew, indicating a small (almost negligible) downward bias to these shocks. The negative skew observed here may be due to the fact that GSCI and other investable commodity indices are not entirely passive investments; the positions in futures contracts have to be managed, and because of this the return may demonstrate properties not shared by a passive investment in the underlying commodity.

Dow Jones–AIG Commodity Index

The **Dow Jones–AIG Commodity Index (DJ-AIGCI)** is designed to provide both liquidity and diversification with respect to physical commodities.[23] It is a long-only index composed of futures contracts on 20 physical commodities. These include petroleum products (crude oil, heating oil, and unleaded gasoline); natural gas; precious metals (gold and silver); industrial metals (copper, aluminum, zinc, and nickel); grains (wheat, corn, and soybeans); livestock (live cattle and lean hogs); vegetable oil (soybean oil); and the soft commodities (coffee, cotton, cocoa, and sugar). The DJ-AIGCI is composed of commodities traded on U.S. commodity exchanges and also on the London Metals Exchange (LME). Contracts on the LME provide exposure to industrial metals such as aluminum, nickel, and zinc.

Unlike the GSCI, to determine the weightings of each commodity in the index, the DJ-AIGCI relies primarily on liquidity data. This index considers the relative amount of trading activity associated with a particular commodity to determine its weight in the index. Liquidity is an important indicator

---

[23] Information on the DJ-AIGCI can be found at the Dow Jones web site (www.dj.com) and by using the Dow Jones Web links to the DJ-AIGCI.

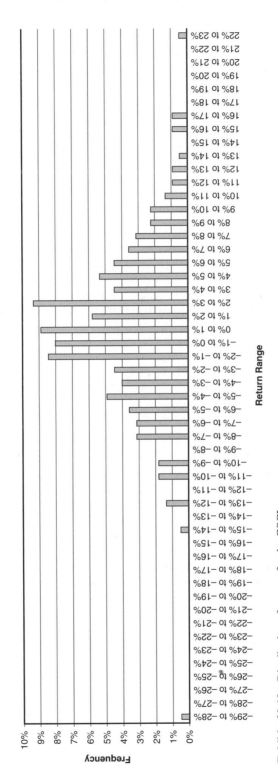

Exhibit 20.10 Distribution of returns for the GSCI

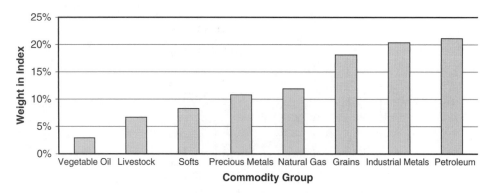

Exhibit 20.11   Dow Jones–AIG Commodity Index weights in December 2008

of the interest placed on a commodity by financial and physical market participants. The index also relies to a lesser extent on dollar-adjusted production data to determine index weights. Therefore, the index weights depend primarily on endogenous factors in the futures markets (liquidity), and secondarily on exogenous factors to the futures markets (production).

The component weightings are also determined by several rules to ensure diversified commodity exposure. Disproportionate weighting to any particular commodity or sector could increase volatility and negate the concept of a broad-based commodity index. Therefore, the DJ-AIGCI index also applies two important diversification rules:

1. No related group of commodities (e.g. energy products, precious metals, livestock, or grains) may constitute more than 33% of the index weights.
2. No single commodity may constitute less than 2% of the index.

The DJ-AIGCI is reweighted and rebalanced every January. Rebalancing and reweighting are designed to reduce the exposure of the index to commodities that have appreciated in value and to increase the index's exposure to commodities that have underperformed. During the course of the year, commodity weights are free to increase or decrease as their values increase or decrease, subject to the two limits imposed. This represents a momentum type of index.

Exhibit 20.11 presents the weights as of December 2008 associated with the DJ-AIGCI. Notice that the combination of natural gas at 11.9% plus petroleum products at 21.1% is at the 33% limit for any commodity sector (in this case, energy).

Exhibit 20.12 presents a frequency distribution of the monthly returns to the DJ-AIGCI over the time period from 1991 to 2008.[24] Similar to the GSCI, this distribution of returns demonstrates a small negative skew of −0.71, indicating that there is a slight bias toward negative returns occurring more frequently than positive returns. In addition, we see a value of kurtosis of 3.52 that is greater than that for the S&P GSCI, indicating a bias toward more outlier events and fatter tails. Visually, like the GSCI, we can see that there are occasionally very large positive and negative returns for the DJ-AIG Commodity Index.

Notice that the dispersion of returns to the DJ-AIGCI is much less than that for the GSCI. At 4.14% the standard deviation of the DJ-AIGCI is about one-third less than the monthly standard deviation for the S&P GSCI. However, the average return is also less at 0.57% per month. This is due to the

---

[24] The Dow Jones–AIG Commodity Index has been in operating existence only since 1998. Therefore, to calculate returns prior to 1998, Dow Jones and AIG had to calculate index returns back in time using the index construction rules currently in place. The returns are calculated back to 1991.

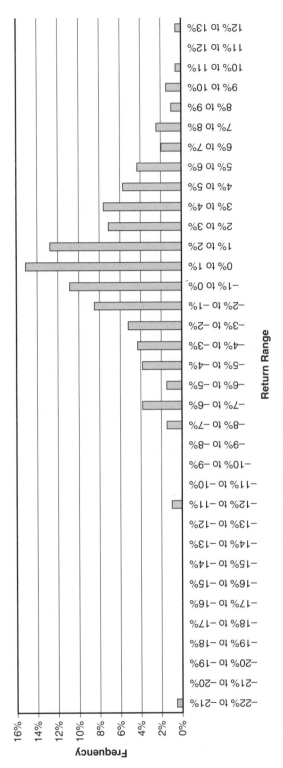

Exhibit 20.12 Distribution of Returns for the Dow Jones–AIG Commodity Index

construction rules for the DJ-AIGCI that expressly limit the exposure to any one commodity group at 33%. Compare this to the exposure of the GSCI to energy at 72%. This limitation ensures broader diversification among the different physical commodities; the index cannot become top-heavy in any one commodity group. However, the S&P GSCI generates a higher monthly average return than the DJ-AIGCI, so the Sharpe ratios for the two indices are not materially different: 0.05 for the S&P GSCI versus 0.06 for the DJ-AIGCI.

Which is the better commodity index? Like everything else in life, there are pros and cons. On the one hand, the DJ-AIGCI is less volatile. On the other hand, the GSCI provides exposure to the very large price shocks (both positive and negative) that affect commodity prices. The choice of an index is really a matter of preference.

Commodity Research Bureau Index

The Reuters/Jefferies **Commodity Research Bureau (CRB) Index** is the oldest of commodity indices. It was first calculated by Commodity Research Bureau, Inc. in 1957 and has been published since 1958. Originally, the index construction was a simple arithmetic average of a basket of commodity prices. The index was renamed the Reuters/Jefferies CRB Index in 2005 and its index construction changed as well. The index is currently made up of 19 commodities quoted on the New York Mercantile Exchange (NYMEX), Chicago Board of Trade (CBOT), London Metals Exchange (LME), Chicago Mercantile Exchange (CME), and Commodity Exchange of New York (COMEX).

Today, the index uses a four-tiered grouping system of commodities designed to more accurately reflect the significance of each commodity. Tier I has 33% of the index weight and includes only petroleum products: crude oil, heating oil, and unleaded gasoline. These are selected for both their liquidity and their economic importance to global economic development. Tier II commodities represent 42% of the index and consist of markets that are highly liquid: natural gas, corn, soybeans, live cattle, gold, aluminum, and copper. Tier III commodities provide 20% of the index weight and are included to provide diversification and broad representation for the index. Last, Tier IV commodities represent only 5% of the index but provide meaningful diversification for the Reuters/Jefferies CRB Index. Exhibit 20.13 shows the index construction.

Exhibit 20.14 provides the distribution of returns for the CRB Index. Again, we see a trade-off of risk profiles. For example, the Reuters/Jefferies CRB Index has the lowest monthly standard deviation of the three commodity indices at 3.48% it also has the most negative skew at −1.23 and

Exhibit 20.13 Composition of the Reuters/Jefferies CRB Index

Tier I		Tier III	
Crude oil	23%	Sugar	5%
Heating oil	5	Cotton	5
Unleaded gas	5	Cocoa	5
Total	**33%**	Coffee	5
		Total	**20%**
Tier II			
Natural gas	6%	**Tier IV**	
Corn	6	Nickel	1%
Soybeans	6	Wheat	1
Live cattle	6	Lean hogs	1
Gold	6	Orange juice	1
Aluminum	6	Silver	1
Copper	6	**Total**	**5%**
Total	**42%**		

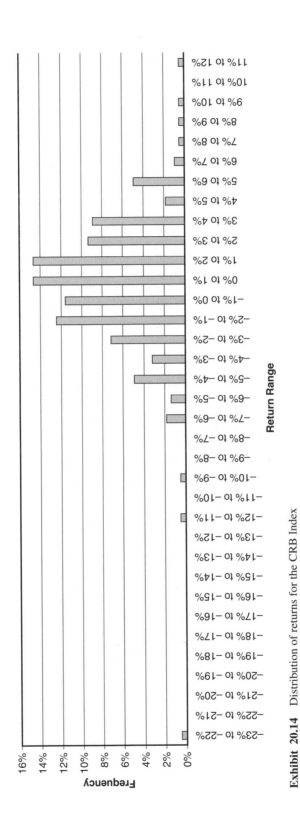

Exhibit 20.14 Distribution of returns for the CRB Index

Exhibit 20.15   Composition of the Mount Lucas Management Index

Commodities (25%)	Currencies (32.5%)	Global Bonds (42.5%)
Crude oil	Australian dollar	Canadian government bond
Heating oil	British pound	Euro bund
Natural gas	Canadian dollar	Japanese government bond
Unleaded gas	Euro currency	Long gilt
Corn	Japanese yen	U.S. 10-Year bond
Soybeans	Swiss franc	
Wheat		
Copper		
Gold		
Live cattle		
Sugar		

the largest value of kurtosis at 8.07. This demonstrates a sizable downside tail associated with this commodity index. Also, the Reuters/Jefferies CRB Index has the lowest average monthly return at 0.32%, which leads to a Sharpe ratio of virtually zero.

Mount Lucas Management Index

Mount Lucas Management introduced the **Mount Lucas Management Index (MLMI)** in 1988.[25] It is a passive index designed to capture the returns to active futures investing. The MLMI represents the return to a specific commodity trading strategy and therefore differs significantly from the previously discussed futures indices in three ways.

First, the MLMI is designed to be a trend-following index. The MLMI uses a 12-month look-back window for calculating the moving average unit asset value for each futures market in which it invests. Once a month, on the day prior to the last trading day, the algorithm examines the current unit asset value in each futures market compared to the average value for the prior 12 months. If the current unit asset value is above the 12-month moving average, the MLMI purchases the futures contract. If the current unit asset value is below the 12-month moving average, the MLMI takes a short position in the futures contract.

This highlights the second difference associated with the MLMI. This index can be both long and short futures contracts, whereas the GSCI, DJ-AIGCI, and CRB Index take only long positions in futures contracts.

The theory behind the MLMI is that the mismatch in commercial firms' futures positions is greatest, and investors can profit the most, when the underlying futures market is moving broadly from one price level to another, either up or down. The object of this index construction is to capture the potential profits represented by such broad market trends.

The last difference with respect to the MLMI is that it invests in physical commodity, financial, and currency futures. There are 22 commodity futures contracts in the three categories. Exhibit 20.15 provides the details of the component parts of the MLMI.[26]

The MLMI has three different categories to the index: commodities at a 25% weighting, currencies at a 32.5% weighting, and global fixed income at 42.5% weighting. Within each category, the

---

[25] Information regarding the MLMI was provided by Raymond Ix at Mount Lucas Management.

[26] There is one additional difference with respect to the MLMI. Two versions of the index are calculated. One version is unleveraged, and one version is three times leveraged.

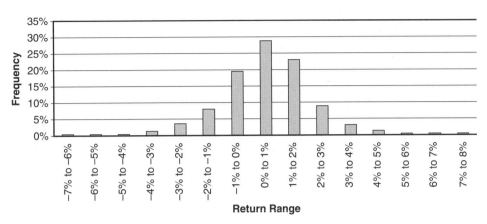

Exhibit 20.16   Distribution of returns for the MLMI

physical or financial futures contracts are equally weighted. The purpose of its construction is to capture the pricing trend of each commodity without regard to its production value or trading volume in the market. Therefore, the price trend for each futures contract in the index is given the same consideration. Given its trend-following design, the MLMI rebalances every month based on the prior 12-month moving average.

In Exhibit 20.16, we present the probability distribution for the returns of the MLMI index. The results are generally better than for the three physical-commodity-only indices. First, the monthly standard deviation, at 1.73% is much lower than that for the three commodity indices and the average monthly return is 0.54% which leads to the highest Sharpe ratio at 0.13. In addition, there is a slight positive skew of 0.06 and a value of kurtosis of 2.76, indicating a slight bias to the upside. Furthermore, in Exhibit 20.16 we can see that there is a much more symmetrical distribution with fewer outliers than the commodity indices. Also, a greater portion of the mass (52%) is centered in the 0 to 2% range, demonstrating much more consistent returns compared to the commodity indices.

Comparison of commodity futures indices

It is worthwhile to summarize some of the differences between the commodity indices just discussed. The GSCI, for example, is economically weighted. The weights in the index are determined solely by exogenous economic data (e.g. production values for the global economy). The argument for constructing such an index is analogous to that for the capitalization-weighted S&P 500; the most economically important commodities should influence a portfolio tracking an index.[27]

In contrast, the DJ-AIGCI is primarily activity weighted. Those commodities that are most actively traded determine its construction. This index relies on endogenous variables (trading volume and liquidity) to determine its weights. This approach assures maximum liquidity for portfolios tracking the index.

The Reuters/Jefferies CRB Index provides yet another weighting scheme. It should be noted that for most of its history it was an equally weighted index. This changed in 2005. The R/J CRB Index now follows a hybrid weighting scheme based on a four-tier system. Each tier has a different total weight in the index. However, within each tier, the weights to individual commodities are fixed and the index is rebalanced monthly to maintain the constant weights. We note that the S&P GSCI, the

---

[27] See Greer, "Institutional Use of Physical Commodity Indices."

DJ-AIGCI, and the R/J CRB all have negative skews and large positive values of kurtosis. This demonstrates a bias to the downside with large, fat downside tails. While the negative values of skew are small for the S&P GSCI and the DJ-AIGCI, they are larger for the R/J CRB Index. The R/J CRB also has the largest value of kurtosis, demonstrating the largest downside tail. This is different from the situation a few years ago, when small, positive skews were observed for the commodity indices. The additional three years of commodity futures return data (2006 to 2008) has produced this change in skew.

Conversely, The MLMI is the only futures index that has a positive skew associated with it. This value indicates a positive bias to event risk. In addition, The MLMI has much smaller dispersion in its returns than the other three indices. The standard deviation of the MLMI returns is 72% less than that for the GSCI, 58% less than that for the DJ-AIGCI, and 50% less than that of the CRB Index. This should be expected given the construction of the MLMI. Its trend-following strategy should reduce its exposure to extreme outlier events. In addition, the MLMI has the largest Sharpe ratio of the four commodity futures indices. The MLMI not only has the best risk-return trade-off, but it also provides the best exposure to positive outlier events.

The DJ-AIGCI specifically limits the exposures of commodity sectors so the index does not become top-heavy with respect to any particular commodity or sector (particularly the energy sector). This cap may reduce the exposure of outlier events within the DJ-AIGCI compared to the GSCI. This cap, in fact, acts like a short call option position that truncates the distribution of returns above the allowable percentage limit in the index. Truncating a return distribution will reduce an investor's exposure to large outlier returns. This reduces the volatility of the DJ-AIGCI compared to the S&P GSCI, but surprisingly, we get a larger value of kurtosis for the DJ-AIGCI than for the S&P GSCI. Similarly, the monthly rebalancing of the R/J CRB Index reduces the volatility still further compared to the S&P GSCI and the DJ-AIGCI, but the value of kurtosis continues to increase. This is a surprising outcome that we have difficulty explaining. Last, we note that the MLMI provides a good risk-return trade-off while maintaining a more tightly bunched return distribution (i.e. there are fewer outliers).

CONCLUSION

This chapter was designed to introduce the reader to the economic rationale behind investing in commodity futures. Its second purpose was to introduce several commodity futures indices that can be used for performance benchmarking.

In this sense, commodity futures investing has developed further than the hedge fund industry, because several well-defined and transparent benchmarks have been invented to track the performance of commodity futures investing. However, investment capital committed to commodity futures is considerably smaller than that invested with hedge funds. Estimates are in the range of $500 billion, considerably less than the almost $2 trillion invested in hedge funds.

One reason is the lack of understanding of the product. Therefore, this chapter was designed to provide an introduction to commodity futures investing. A second reason is the perceived view that commodity futures are extremely risky investments, best left to cowboy speculators and flamboyant floor traders. In the next chapter we disarm this myth and consider whether commodity futures have a place within an investment portfolio.

However, as large institutional investors have sought greater diversification in their investment portfolios, commodities investing has grown to meet the demand. Commodities offer another form of beta—a new systematic risk factor to be included within a broad diversified portfolio to distribute risk more evenly. It is expected that the demand for commodities investing and other real assets will grow into the baby boomer retirement years.

21

Commodity Futures in a Portfolio Context

In the prior two chapters we first identified commodity futures as a distinct asset class and then we discussed the economics associated with the pricing of commodity futures. In addition, we indicated that commodity futures prices are influenced by factors different from those for financial assets. This led us to the conclusion that commodity futures have the potential to be excellent diversifying agents for a stock and bond portfolio.

In this chapter we consider commodity futures within a portfolio context. First, we compare the economic statistics of commodity futures to those for stocks and bonds. Next we build portfolios of commodity futures, stocks, and bonds and observe the risk and return of these portfolios compared to those constructed without commodity futures. Last, we examine commodity futures as a defensive investment. Our analysis concludes that commodity futures are indeed valuable diversification tools.

ECONOMIC SUMMARY OF COMMODITY FUTURES

In this section we briefly review the inflation protection offered by commodity futures. We also compare the risk and return profile of commodity futures to that of stocks and bonds over a long period of time.

Inflation protection

Bonds are a contingent claim on the earning power of a corporation. They have a senior claim on revenue earned by a corporation. However, bonds perform poorly when the purchasing power of money declines in an inflationary environment.

Conversely, stocks, as the residual claim on the physical assets of a corporation, provide better purchasing power protection. However, stocks also represent a claim on the future earning potential of the corporation. When this earning power is eroded due to inflationary concerns, stocks also decline in value.

Real assets such as commodity futures can hedge this decline in value due to inflation. In the prior chapter we introduced four investable commodity futures indices, the S&P GSCI, the DJ-AIGCI, the MLMI,[1] and the Reuters/Jefferies CRB Index.

Exhibit 21.1 presents the correlation of the four indices with domestic U.S. inflation over the time period from 1990 to 2008. We also include the S&P 500 for domestic stocks; EAFE (Europe, Australasia, and Far East) and FTSE (Financial Times Stock Index) for international stocks; and the 10-year U.S. Treasury bond and high-yield bonds for fixed income exposure. Exhibit 21.1 demonstrates that, with the exception of high-yield bonds (odd, but we have no good explanation for this), all classes of stocks and bonds are negatively correlated with the rate of inflation. Higher inflation means lower returns to stocks and bonds, and vice versa. Conversely, three out of the four commodity indices (the MLMI being the lone exception) are positively correlated with inflation.

---

[1] As discussed in the previous chapter, the MLMI is not a true commodity index; rather, it represents the return to a specific systematic trading strategy. It is generally not used as a benchmark for measuring return to commodities, but rather as a benchmark for performance evaluation of Commodity Trading Advisors (see the next chapter).

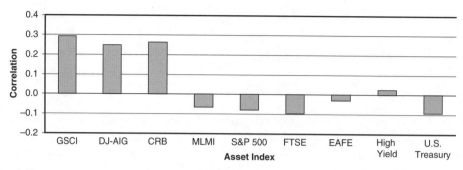

Exhibit 21.1   Correlation with inflation, 1990–2008

Higher inflation means higher returns to commodity futures, and lower inflation means lower returns. Therefore, commodity futures offer the potential for good inflation protection for financial assets.

Note also that the returns earned by international stocks experience the same level of negative correlation with the U.S. inflation rate. One reason is that price increases of raw materials affect foreign economies just as much as they affect the U.S. economy. Consequently, an investor seeking a hedge against domestic inflation would not find it by diversifying into foreign stocks.

An argument might be made that an investor could purchase TIPS as a hedge against inflation. It is true that the cash flows accruing to TIPS are adjusted to maintain their value in an inflationary environment. However, TIPS do not offer inflation protection for other assets in the portfolio.

Treasury Inflation-Protected Securities (TIPS) are designed to have the coupon rate increase so that the price of a TIPS does not decline when inflation increases. This preserves or maintains the value of the TIPS investment. However, the preservation of TIPS value does not offer relief for other assets in the portfolio. In contrast, commodity futures increase in value when inflation goes up. This increase in value can be used to shelter some of the decline in value suffered by financial assets in the portfolio.

Commodity futures are often perceived to be extremely volatile, with large price swings up and down. We expect commodity futures to be riskier than U.S. Treasury bonds, but we also expect the return to be greater to compensate for the additional risk.

We might also expect commodity futures to have greater volatility than large-capitalization stocks because futures prices are subject to short-term fluctuations based on supply and de-mand imbalances. In turn, we expect commodity futures to earn an average rate of return greater than stocks for this additional volatility. These expectations are summarized in Exhibits 21.2 and 21.3.

Exhibit 21.2 shows that the returns to the S&P GSCI, the DJ-AIGCI, and the MLMI are comparable to stock and bond returns during the period from 1990 to 2008. We note that the returns in Exhibit 21.2 are influenced by the credit crisis and financial market meltdown that occurred in 2007 and 2008. As a result, no asset class earned an average annual return in excess of 9% during this time period. Also, the global financial crisis has equalized the long-term returns across many asset classes. The two lowest-yielding classes over this time period are the DJ-AIGCI and the MSCI EAFE, both providing a return about equal to the rate of U.S. inflation.

In Exhibit 21.3 we look at the other side of the equation: risk. We find the S&P GSCI to have the highest annual volatility at 21%, while the MLMI has the lowest volatility of all of the asset classes at 6% even lower than U.S. Treasury bonds, which have an annual volatility of 6.8%. Exhibit 21.4 summarizes the risk and return trade-off in terms of the Sharpe ratio. The MLMI has the highest

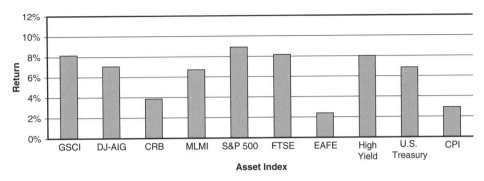

Exhibit 21.2   Average returns for stocks, bonds, and commodities, 1990–2008

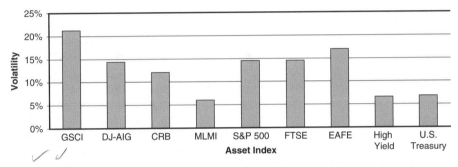

Exhibit 21.3   Volatility of stocks, bonds, and commodity returns, 1990–2008

Sharpe ratio (0.53) among the commodity indices, while high-yield bonds have the highest Sharpe ratio (0.68) among the financial asset classes.

With mixed results for return and risk, we turn to the third criterion for determining whether commodities might be a valuable addition to a stock and bond portfolio: diversification. Exhibit 21.5 shows the correlation of the commodity indices with stocks and bonds. All four commodity indices have either very low positive correlation or negative correlation with the financial asset classes. The MLMI consistently has negative correlations with each of the financial asset classes, demonstrating the best potential for portfolio diversification.

Exhibit 21.4   Annual Sharpe ratios

Asset Class	Sharpe Ratio
S&P GSCI	0.22
DJ-AIGCI	0.25
R/J CRB Index	0.03
MLMI	0.53
S&P 500	0.37
FTSE 100	0.32
EAFE	−0.07
High-Yield	0.68
U.S. Treasury Bonds	0.49

Exhibit 21.5   Correlation of stocks, bonds, and commodities with inflation

	GSCI	DJ-AIG	CRB	MLMI	S&P 500	FTSE	EAFE	High-Yield	U.S. Treasury	CPI
GSCI	1.00									
DJ-AIG	0.90	1.00								
CRB	0.75	0.89	1.00							
MLMI	0.09	0.03	−0.05	1.00						
S&P 500	0.04	0.18	0.18	−0.29	1.00					
FTSE	0.05	0.17	0.16	−0.20	0.76	1.00				
EAFE	0.14	0.34	0.30	−0.18	0.70	0.70	1.00			
High-Yield	0.15	0.26	0.27	−0.20	0.60	0.49	0.48	1.00		
U.S. Treasury	0.03	0.03	−0.04	0.08	0.02	−0.08	−0.03	0.18	1.00	
CPI	0.29	0.25	0.26	−0.07	−0.08	−0.10	−0.03	0.02	−0.09	1.00

Any asset that is less than perfectly correlated with stocks and bonds will provide diversification to a stock and bond portfolio, and commodities demonstrate distinctly favorable diversification properties.

Therefore, an investment in commodity futures should not be analyzed in a vacuum. Instead, commodity futures are best considered within a portfolio context, where their diversification potential can be achieved. In the next section, we consider commodity futures as part of a diversified portfolio.

On a final note, it is worthwhile to repeat that the S&P GSCI, DJ-AIGCI, and R/J CRB indices are all positively correlated with inflation. This demonstrates a good opportunity to hedge against inflation with real assets. Unfortunately, the MLMI has a negative correlation with inflation, just as stocks and bonds are also negatively correlated with inflation. Therefore, the GSCI, DJ-AIGCI, and R/J CRB demonstrate an excellent inflation hedge to provide protection to a traditional portfolio of stocks and bonds.

COMMODITY FUTURES AND THE EFFICIENT INVESTMENT FRONTIER

Having established commodity futures as a distinct new asset class in the prior chapters, we consider how this asset class performs in a diversified portfolio of stocks and bonds. In this section, we construct efficient frontiers for stocks, bonds, and passive commodity futures.

The **efficient frontier** is a graphical depiction of the trade-off between risk and return. It provides a range of the risk and return that can be achieved in a balanced portfolio of investable assets. First, we graph the efficient frontier using domestic stocks and bonds to provide a benchmark of risk and return data points that can be achieved without commodity futures. We then add commodity futures to the investment portfolio and observe how the efficient frontier changes with the addition of this new asset class.

Exhibit 21.6 presents the initial frontier using stocks and bonds. At the highest return point on the frontier, the portfolio consists of 100% stocks. At the lowest return point, the portfolio consists completely of U.S. Treasury bonds. In between, the portfolio mix of assets ranges from 90% stocks and 10% bonds to 10% stocks and 90% bonds.

The efficient frontier in Exhibit 21.6 indicates that higher return may be achieved only at the cost of assuming more risk. Along the efficient frontier, there is no other combination of stocks and bonds that will yield a higher return for a given level of risk, or a lower level of risk for a given level of

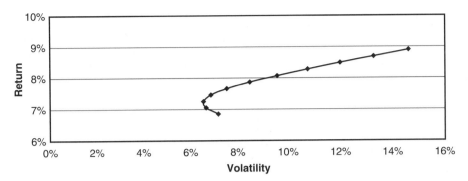

Exhibit 21.6   Efficient frontier for stocks and bonds

return. This is why the frontier is efficient: it provides a graphical description of the best portfolios that may be achieved using stocks and bonds.

The efficient frontier changes when commodity futures are added to the mix. Exhibit 21.7 demonstrates the efficient frontier with commodity futures included in the stock and bond portfolio. Initially, we use the S&P GSCI to represent an asset allocation to commodity futures.

Again, the two end points of the graph are defined by 100% stocks at the highest return level and 100% bonds at the lowest return level. In between, the allocation to commodity futures remains constant at 10%, with a 5% less allocation to stocks and a 5% less allocation to bonds. For example, in Exhibit 21.6, we plot risk and return data points at 90% stocks and 10% bonds, 80% stocks and 20% bonds, and so on. With commodity futures in Exhibit 21.7, the data points become 85% stocks, 5% bonds, and 10% commodity futures; 75% stocks, 15% bonds, and 10% commodity futures; and so forth.

In Exhibit 21.7, the new efficient frontier including commodity futures is above and to the left of the original frontier plotted in Exhibit 21.6. We include the original frontier from Exhibit 21.6 in Exhibit 21.7 for comparison. The original efficient investment frontier without commodity futures clearly lies below the efficient frontier with commodity futures. In other words, the addition of commodity futures into the investment portfolio pushes the investment frontier up and to the left into a more efficient risk and return area of the graph. This demonstrates that commodity futures improve the risk-return trade-off for the investment portfolio.

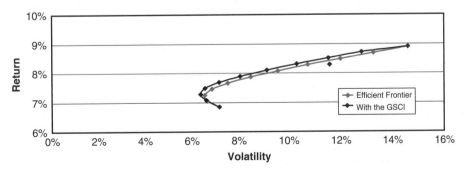

Exhibit 21.7   Efficient frontier with the GSCI

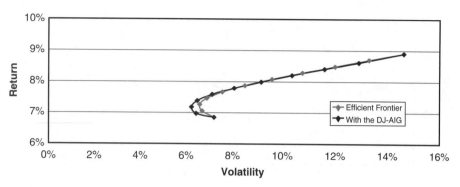

Exhibit 21.8   Efficient frontier with the DJ-AIG

Reflect back for a moment to Exhibit 21.3. The GSCI had the highest volatility of returns of the major commodity indices presented. At first glance, an investor may discount the value of investing in commodity futures because of the higher volatility associated with the GSCI compared to the S&P 500. Such a comparison ignores the negative correlation of the returns to the GSCI with the returns to stocks and bonds. The impact of this negative correlation can be achieved only within a diversified portfolio. As a stand-alone investment, the diversification potential of commodity futures vis-à-vis stocks and bonds cannot be observed. It can be appreciated only within a portfolio context.

In Exhibit 21.8, we again present both the efficient frontier, but this time with the DJ-AIG and without commodity futures. We also see an improvement in the efficient frontier, although not as dramatic as for the S&P GSCI. The DJ-AIGCI pushes out the efficient frontier at the lower ranges of risk and return. Still, this is an improvement over the original efficient frontier. Efficient frontiers are a useful point from which to discuss utility theory. In modern portfolio theory it is assumed that investors are rational utility maximizers. This means that investors realize that life is full of trade-offs: invest today to consume tomorrow or seek more return but only with the assumption of greater risk.

Maximizing utility with commodity futures is an important concept because the greater the risk aversion of the investor, the greater the benefit of investing in commodity futures. This point may seem counterintuitive because commodity futures are often perceived as risky investments. However, the returns to commodity futures are negatively correlated with the returns to financial assets. Therefore, when considered within a portfolio context, commodity futures provide positive utility to a risk-averse investor. In fact, Anson demonstrates that the greater the risk aversion of the investor, the greater will be the marginal utility of investing in commodity futures.[2]

Exhibit 21.9 plots the efficient frontier with a 10% constant allocation to commodity futures represented by the CRB. Unfortunately, we do not see an improvement in the efficient frontier when we use the R/J CRB Index as our proxy for commodity returns. This is undoubtedly due to the low annual average return of 3.9% displayed in Exhibit 21.2. We also note that in Exhibit 21.4 the R/J CRB Index has the lowest Sharpe ratio of the four commodity indices. Its average annual return is sufficiently less than stocks and bonds that adding it to a portfolio of stocks and bonds does not improve the efficient frontier.

Last, Exhibit 21.10 presents the efficient frontier for a portfolio of stocks, bonds, and 10% futures as represented by the MLMI. The MLMI also improves the efficient frontier but mostly at the lower

---

[2] See Mark Anson, "Maximizing Utility with Commodity Futures," *Journal of Portfolio Management* (Summer 1999), 86–94.

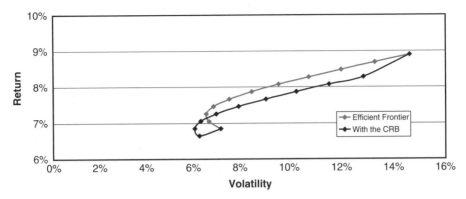

Exhibit 21.9   Efficient frontier with the CRB

end of the risk-return spectrum. Given the negative correlation of the MLMI with stocks and bonds, we would expect a larger improvement in the efficient frontier. However, the average annual return for the MLMI is less than that for U.S. stocks and U.S. Treasury bonds; consequently, there is little room for improvement in the efficient frontier at the higher return levels with the addition of the MLMI.

It is important to note again that the four commodity indices are all investable commodity futures indices. Three of these indices represent relatively passive long-only investments in commodities, while the MLMI represents the performance of a systematic trend-following trading strategy. All four indices are designed with the investor in mind, and an investor can allocate a portion of her portfolio assets to any of these three indices just as she might make an allocation to emerging market stocks, for instance. Therefore, each index is an appropriate proxy for investing in the commodity futures markets (again, unlike the other three, MLMI takes both long and short positions in commodities).

The preceding discussion was intended to demonstrate that commodity futures are best analyzed within a portfolio context. Only then can their full investment benefit be appreciated. The ability of commodity futures returns to move in the opposite direction of the returns to stocks and bonds provides a powerful tool for portfolio diversification. This is consistent with our discussion in the prior chapter regarding how commodity futures react differently from stocks and bonds to different parts of the economic cycle. Exhibits 21.7 through 21.10 translate this business cycle concept into

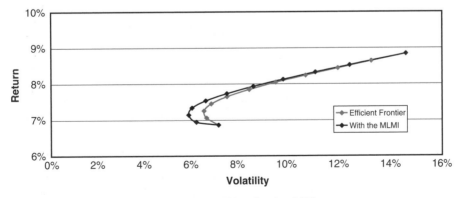

Exhibit 21.10   Efficient frontier with the MLMI, 1990 to October 2008

portfolio construction. In the next section, we consider another useful element of commodity futures investing: downside risk protection.

COMMODITY FUTURES AS A DEFENSIVE INVESTMENT

It is an unfortunate fact of life that when things "hit the fan," they tend to do it all at the same time. For example, a number of studies have examined the correlation of the U.S. domestic and international equity markets during periods of market stress or decline. The conclusion is that the equity markets around the world tend to be more highly correlated during periods of economic stress.[3] This means that international equity markets tend to decline at the same time as the U.S. stock market. Therefore, international equity diversification may not provide the requisite diversification when a U.S. domestic investor needs it most—during periods of economic turmoil or decline.

One reason why international equity investments might not provide suitable diversification for a U.S. stock portfolio is that almost all traditional assets react in similar fashion to macroeconomic events. A spike in oil prices, for example, will be felt across all economies, and inflation fears will be uniform around the globe. In fact, Exhibit 21.1 demonstrates that both domestic and international equity markets are negatively impacted by the domestic inflation rate. Further, international equity markets are becoming increasingly linked for four reasons.

First, policy makers from major industrial nations regularly attend economic summits where they attempt to synchronize fiscal and monetary policy. The Maastricht Treaty and the birth of the European Union is an example. Second, corporations are expanding their operations and revenue streams beyond the site of their domestic incorporation. Third, the increased volume of international capital flows means that economic shocks will be felt globally as opposed to being country specific. Last, nations such as Japan have undergone a so-called Big Bang episode where domestic investors have greater access to international investments. This provides for an even greater flow of capital across international boundaries. As a result, the equity markets are becoming a single, global asset class and distinctions between international and domestic stocks are beginning to fade.

This is one reason why skill-based investing has become so popular with investors. Hedge funds and other skill-based strategies might be expected to provide greater diversification than international equity investing because the returns are dependent on the special skill of the manager rather than any broad macroeconomic events or trends.

Yet diversification need not rely on active skill-based strategies. Diversification benefits can be achieved from the passive addition of a new asset class such as commodity futures.

The greatest concern for any investor is downside risk. If equity and bond markets are becoming increasingly synchronized, international diversification may not offer the protection sought by investors. The ability to protect the value of an investment portfolio in hostile or turbulent markets is the key to the value of any macroeconomic diversification.

Within this framework, an asset class distinct from financial assets has the potential to diversify and protect an investment portfolio from hostile markets. Commodity futures make a good choice for downside risk protection.

To demonstrate this downside risk protection, we start with a standard portfolio of stocks and bonds. We begin with a portfolio that is 60% the S&P 500 and 40% U.S. Treasury bonds. In Exhibit 21.11 we provide a frequency distribution of the monthly returns to this portfolio over the time period

---

[3] See Claude Erb, Campbell Harvey, and Tadas Viskanta, "Forecasting International Equity Correlations," *Financial Analysts Journal* (November/December 1994), 34–35; and Rex Sinquefield, "Where Are the Gains from International Diversification?" *Financial Analysts Journal* (January/February 1996), 8–14.

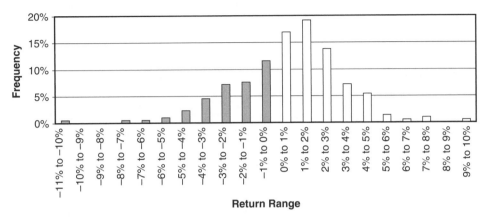

Exhibit 21.11 Distribution of returns for 60/40 stocks/bonds

1990 to 2008. This exhibit shows the return pattern for monthly returns to a 60%/40% stock/bond portfolio over this time period.

Our concern is the shaded part of the return distribution. This shows where the returns to the stock and bond portfolio were negative. That is, the shaded part of the distribution shows both the size and the frequency with which the combined portfolio of 60% S&P 500 plus 40% U.S. Treasury bonds earned a negative return in a particular month. It is this part of the return distribution that an investor attempts to avoid or limit.[4]

We find that the average monthly return to a 60/40 stock/bond portfolio in the shaded part of the distribution of Exhibit 21.11 is a negative 2.12%. In other words, when the standard stock/bond portfolio earned a negative return in any given month, on average the magnitude of that return was −2.12%. Seventy-nine months experienced negative returns.

These negative returns are exactly the returns that investors want to reduce through diversification. We consider how this shaded part of the curve changes when we add in commodity futures.

In Exhibit 21.12 we change the standard stock/bond investment portfolio by providing a 10% allocation to commodity futures. The resulting portfolio is 55% S&P 500 stocks, 35% U.S. Treasury bonds, and 10% S&P GSCI. Exhibit 21.12 plots the frequency distribution for returns to this portfolio.

Once again, we are concerned with the shaded part of the frequency distribution of returns to this stock/bond/commodities portfolio. Although the distribution looks similar, it has in fact changed significantly from Exhibit 21.11. The average monthly return to the 55/35/10 stock/bond/commodities portfolio in the shaded part of Exhibit 21.12 is reduced to −2.01%. In other words, when the stock/bond/commodities portfolio earned a negative return in any given month, on average the magnitude of the return was −2.01%. In addition, there were only 77 months of negative returns, two less than in the stock/bond portfolio.

Exhibit 21.13 provides a frequency distribution for a portfolio that consists of 55% S&P 500, 35% U.S. Treasury bonds, and a 10% allocation to the DJ-AIGCI. The average negative return in the shaded part of Exhibit 21.12 is −2.04%. In addition, the number of months with negative returns again declines to 77.

---

[4] See Steve Strongin and Melanie Petsch, "Managing Risk in Hostile Markets," *Goldman Sachs Commodities Research*, April 24, 1996.

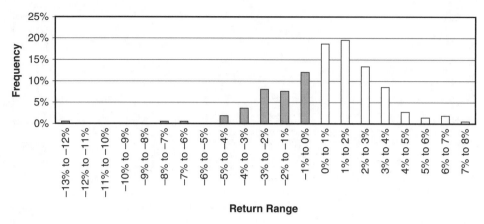

Exhibit 21.12   Return distribution for 55/35/10 stocks/bonds/GSCI

Exhibit 21.14 provides the same analysis for the Reuters/Jefferies CRB Index. The average return in the shaded part of the distribution is −2.04% and the number of negative months again declines to 77.

Exhibit 21.15 plots the frequency distribution for a portfolio consisting of 55% S&P 500, 35% U.S. Treasury bonds, and 10% MLMI. The MLMI provides the greatest downside protection by reducing the average return to −1.93% in down months, and the number of down months declines to 76.

Let's look at the impact of commodity allocation depicted in Exhibits 21.12 through 21.15. These graphs demonstrate that a small allocation of commodity futures benchmarked to a passive futures index can provide a degree of protection against downside exposure. This downside exposure is summarized in Exhibit 21.16. We perform a simple calculation to determine the amount of **downside risk protection** offered by each commodity index. The calculation is:

Number of downside months of the 60/40 stock/bond portfolio
× Average downside month return
− Number of downside months in the 55/35/10 stock/bond/commodity portfolio (21.1)
× Average downside month return

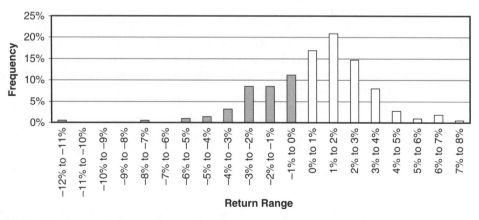

Exhibit 21.13   Return distribution for 55/35/10 stocks/bonds/DJ-AIG

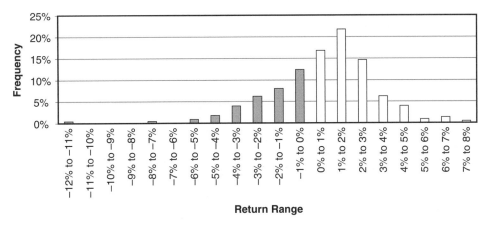

Exhibit 21.14 Return distribution for 55/35/10 stocks/bonds/CRB

The results are summarized in Exhibit 21.16. Using our calculation, we get a total downside risk protection for the S&P GSCI of 12.71%. Similar downside protection is shown for the other commodity indices.

Finally, we consider the downside protection of international stocks. We indicated earlier that the equity markets are becoming less distinct and resembling more of a global asset class. This reduces the diversification potential of international stocks. To demonstrate this idea, we build a portfolio consisting of U.S. stocks, U.S. bonds, and foreign stocks. The exact allocation is 55% S&P 500, 35% U.S. Treasury bonds, and 10% EAFE.[5]

Exhibit 21.17 provides the frequency distribution for this portfolio. Again, we concentrate on the shaded part of the distribution. The average monthly return to the downside portion of this distribution is −2.27%. That is, a 10% allocation to international stocks provided an additional exposure to downside risk of −15 basis points. Therefore, an allocation to international stocks did not diversify an investment portfolio comprised of domestic stocks and bonds. In fact, a

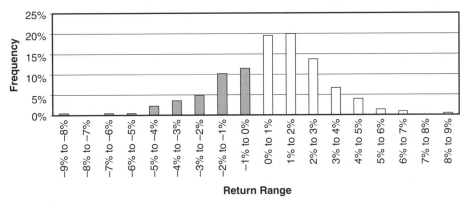

Exhibit 21.15 Return distribution for 55/35/10 stocks/bonds/MLMI

[5] EAFE (Europe, Australasia, and Far East) is an international stock index developed and maintained by Morgan Stanley Capital International.

Exhibit 21.16   Summary of downside protection for commodities

Portfolio	Average Return	Standard Deviation	Skew	Kurtosis	Sharpe	Number of Negative Months	Average Return Negative Month	Downside Risk Protection
60/40 S&P 500/U.S. Treasury	0.65	2.65	−0.41	1.37	0.13	79	−2.12	N/A
55/35/10 S&P 500/Bonds/GSCI	0.65	2.52	−0.73	2.98	0.13	77	−2.01	12.71
55/35/10 S&P 500/Bonds/DJ-AIG	0.64	2.52	−0.66	2.44	0.13	77	−2.04	10.40
55/35/10 S&P 500/Bonds/CRB	0.62	2.50	−0.69	2.57	0.12	77	−2.04	10.40
55/35/10 S&P 500/Bonds/MLMI	0.64	2.38	−0.33	1.07	0.14	76	−1.93	20.80
55/35/10 S&P 500/Bonds/EAFE	0.61	2.76	−0.61	1.64	0.10	80	−2.27	−14.12

10% allocation to international stocks increased the exposure to downside risk. Indeed, adding international stocks to the 60/40 U.S. stock/U.S. bond portfolio provided a total additional downside risk of 14% (not a very good portfolio diversifier).

We also consider what might be sacrificed to achieve this downside protection. It is possible that in protecting against some downside exposure, an investor must accept a reduction in positive returns in the nonshaded (positive) part of the return distributions. We examine this possibility in Exhibit 21.16.

The expected monthly return to the standard 60/40 stock portfolio over this period was 0.65%. Compare this to the expected monthly return to a 55/35/10 stock/bond/commodity futures portfolio in Exhibit 21.16. The expected return for a portfolio with the GSCI is 0.65% per month, the same as the stock/bond portfolio. Therefore, a passive exposure to commodity futures represented by the GSCI resulted in significant downside protection without sacrificing any upside return. The other futures indices provide only a slight decline in the monthly expected return.[6]

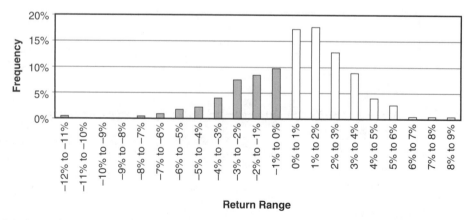

Exhibit 21.17   Return distribution for 55/35/10 stocks/bonds/EAFE

---

[6] The DJ-AIG cannot be compared precisely to the GSCI, CRB, or MLMI because it has a shorter track record.

Finally, we compare the Sharpe ratios for the standard 60/40 stock/bond portfolio to those portfolios including commodity futures and international equity. We find that the MLMI increases the Sharpe ratio, whereas an allocation to international stocks significantly decreases the Sharpe ratio.

CONCLUSION

Our prior chapters were concerned with the introduction to commodity futures as an asset class distinct from financial assets such as stocks and bonds. In this chapter we considered the diversification value of this new asset class.

The greatest value of commodity futures is achieved within a portfolio context. Analyzing commodity futures as a stand-alone investment ignores the fact that the returns to commodity futures tend to be negatively correlated with the returns to financial assets. We discussed in Chapter 20 that the returns to commodity futures tend to peak and reach a trough at different parts of the economic cycle than stocks and bonds. This countercyclical effect provides the potential for portfolio diversification.

This diversification potential was revealed in two separate ways. First, we demonstrated how a 10% allocation of commodity futures provided an efficient investable frontier that improved the efficient frontier that was achieved with stocks and bonds alone. Second, we demonstrated how a 10% allocation to commodity futures provided significant downside protection in hostile markets. In contrast, we found that international stocks provided no downside exposure and, in fact, increased the exposure to hostile markets for a standard 60/40 stock/bond portfolio.

22

Managed Futures

The term **managed futures** refers to the active trading of futures and forward contracts on physical commodities, financial assets, and currencies. The purpose of the managed futures industry is to enable investors to profit from changes in futures prices through active management by a trader. The goal here is not necessarily diversification, but instead added value.

The managed futures industry provides a skill-based style of investing. Investment managers attempt to use their special knowledge and insight in buying and selling futures and forward contracts to extract a positive return. These futures managers tend to argue that their superior skill is the key ingredient in deriving profitable returns from the futures markets.

There are three ways to access the skill-based investing of the managed futures industry: public commodity pools, private commodity pools, and individual managed accounts. **Commodity pools** are investment funds that pool the money of several investors for the purpose of investing in the futures markets. They are similar in structure to hedge funds and are considered a subset of the hedge fund marketplace.

Every commodity pool must be managed by a general partner. In the United States, typically, the general partner for the pool must register with the Commodity Futures Trading Commission (CFTC) and the National Futures Association (NFA) as a Commodity Pool Operator (CPO). However, there are exceptions to the general rule. Registrations are also discussed in Chapter 12.

Public commodity pools are open to the general public for investment in much the same way that a mutual fund sells its shares to the public. Public commodity pools must file a registration statement with the Securities and Exchange Commission (SEC) before distributing shares in the pool to investors. An advantage of public commodity pools is the low minimum investment and the frequency of liquidity (the ability to cash out).

Private commodity pools are sold to high-net-worth investors and institutional investors to avoid the lengthy registration requirements of the SEC and sometimes to avoid the lengthy reporting requirements of the CFTC. Otherwise, their investment objective is the same as that of a public commodity pool. Advantages of private commodity pools are usually lower brokerage commissions and greater flexibility to implement investment strategies and extract excess returns from the futures markets.

Commodity Pool Operators (for either public or private pools) typically hire one or more Commodity Trading Advisors (CTAs) to manage the money deposited with the pool. CTAs are professional money managers in the futures markets.

Like CPOs, CTAs must register with the Commodity Futures Trading Commission (CFTC) and the National Futures Association (NFA) before managing money for a commodity pool. In some cases a managed futures investment manager is registered as both a CPO and a CTA. In this case, the general partner for a commodity pool may also act as its investment adviser.

Last, wealthy and institutional investors can place their money directly with a CTA in an **individually managed account**. These separate accounts have the advantage of narrowly defined and specific investment objectives as well as full transparency to the investor.

Commodity Trading Advisors may invest in both exchange-traded futures contracts and forward contracts. A forward contract has the same economic structure as a futures contract with one difference: it is traded over the counter. Forward contracts are private agreements that do not trade on a futures exchange. Therefore, they can have terms that vary considerably from the standard terms of exchange-listed futures contracts. Forward contracts accomplish the same economic goal as a futures contract but with the flexibility of custom-tailored terms.

In this chapter, we examine the managed futures industry. First, we provide a brief history of the managed futures industry. We then review the prior empirical research regarding the benefits to investing in managed futures. Next, we examine the distribution of managed futures returns. Last, we conduct an analysis of downside risk protection for managed futures within a portfolio context.

HISTORY OF MANAGED FUTURES

Organized futures trading began in the United States in the 1800s with the founding of the **Chicago Board of Trade (CBOT)** in 1848. It was founded by 82 grain merchants, and the first exchange floor was above a flour store. Originally, it was a cash market where grain traders came to buy and sell supplies of flour, timothy seed, and hay.

In 1851, the earliest futures contract in the United States was recorded for the forward delivery of 3,000 bushels of corn, and two years later, the CBOT established the first standard futures contract in corn. Since then, the heart and soul of the CBOT has been its futures contracts on agricultural crops grown primarily in the Midwestern states: corn, wheat, and soybeans. Therefore, commodity futures exchanges were founded initially by grain producers and buyers to hedge the price risk associated with the harvest and sale of crops.

Other futures exchanges were established for similar reasons. The **Chicago Mercantile Exchange (CME)**, for example, lists futures contracts on livestock. Chicago was once famous for its stockyards where cattle and hogs were herded to the market. Ranchers and buyers came to the CME to hedge the price risk associated with the purchase and sale of cattle and hogs.

Other exchanges are the **New York Mercantile Exchange (NYMEX)**, where futures contracts on energy products are traded. The Commodity Exchange of New York (now the COMEX division of the NYMEX) lists futures contracts on precious and industrial metals. The New York Coffee, Sugar, and Cocoa Exchange lists futures contracts on (what else?) coffee, sugar, and cocoa. In January 2007, the Coffee, Sugar, and Cocoa Exchange was merged into the InterContinental Exchange. The ICE also took over the New York Cotton Exchange and now trades cotton and frozen concentrated orange juice. The Kansas City Board of Trade lists futures contracts on wheat.

Over the years, certain commodities have risen in prominence while others have faded. For instance, the heating oil futures contract was at one time listed as inactive on the NYMEX for lack of interest. For years, heating oil prices remained stable and there was little interest or need to hedge the price risk of heating oil. Then along came the Arab oil embargo of 1973, and this contract quickly took on a life of its own, as did other energy futures contracts.

Conversely, other futures contracts have faded away because of minimal input into the economic engine of the United States. For instance, rye futures traded on the CBOT from 1869 to 1970, and barley futures traded from 1885 to 1940. However, the limited importance of barley and rye in finished food products led to the eventual demise of these futures contracts. For a while in the 1990s there was even a contract on shrimp futures to hedge the prices of shrimp harvested from the Gulf of Mexico.

As the wealth of the United States has grown, a new type of futures contract has gained importance: financial futures. The futures markets changed dramatically in 1975 when the CBOT introduced the first financial futures contract on Government National Mortgage Association (GNMA—Ginnie Mae) mortgage-backed certificates. This was followed two years later in 1977 with the introduction of a futures contract on the U.S. Treasury bond. Today this is the most actively traded futures contract in the world.

The creation of a futures contract that was designed to hedge financial risk as opposed to commodity price risk opened up a whole new avenue of asset management for traders, analysts, and portfolio managers. Now, it is more likely that a financial investor will flock to the futures exchanges to hedge her investment portfolio than that a grain purchaser will trade to hedge commodity price risk. Since 1975, more and more financial futures contracts have been listed on the futures exchanges. For instance, in 1997 stock index futures and options on the Dow Jones Industrial Average were first listed on the CBOT. The S&P 500 stock index futures and options (first listed in 1983) are the most heavily traded contracts on the CME. In addition, futures contracts tied to the NASDAQ-100 stock index are listed on the CME while Russell 1000 and Russell 2000 stock index futures are listed on the ICE. Additionally, currency futures were introduced on the CME in the 1970s (originally listed as part of the International Monetary Market).

With the advent of financial futures contracts, more and more managed futures trading strategies were born. However, the history of managed futures products goes back more than 50 years.

The first public futures fund began trading in 1948 and was active until the 1960s. This fund was established before financial futures contracts were invented, and consequently traded primarily in agricultural commodity futures contracts. The success of this fund spawned other managed futures vehicles, and a new industry was born.

The managed futures industry has grown from just $1 billion under management in 1985 to $150 billion of funds invested in managed futures products in 2008. The stock market's return to more rational pricing in 2000 helped fuel increased interest in managed futures products. Still, managed futures products are a fraction of the estimated size of the hedge fund marketplace of $1.8 trillion. Yet, issues of capacity are much less of an issue in the managed futures industry than in the hedge fund marketplace, where the best hedge funds are closed to new investors.

Similar to hedge funds, CTAs and CPOs charge both management fees and performance fees. The standard 2 and 20 (2% management fee and 20% incentive fee) are equally applicable to the managed futures industry, although management fees can range from 0% to 3% and incentive fees from 10% to 35%.

Unfortunately, until the early 1970s, the managed futures industry was largely unregulated. Anyone could advise an investor about the merits of investing in commodity futures or form a fund for the purpose of investing in the futures markets. Recognizing the growth of this industry and the lack of regulation associated with it, in 1974 Congress promulgated the **Commodity Exchange Act (CEA)** and created the **Commodity Futures Trading Commission (CFTC)**.

Under the CEA, Congress first defined the terms Commodity Pool Operator and Commodity Trading Advisor. In addition, Congress established standards for financial reporting, offering memorandum disclosure, and bookkeeping. Further, Congress required CTAs and CPOs to register with the CFTC. Last, upon the establishment of the **National Futures Association (NFA)** as the designated self-regulatory organization for the managed futures industry, Congress required CTAs and CPOs to undergo periodic educational training.

Today, there are four broad classes of managed futures trading: agricultural products, financial and metal products, currency products, and diversified trading strategies (across all futures markets). Before examining these categories, we review the prior research on the managed futures industry.

PRIOR EMPIRICAL RESEARCH

There are two key questions with respect to managed futures: (1) Will an investment in managed futures improve the performance of an investment portfolio? (2) Can managed futures products produce consistent returns?

The case for managed futures products as a viable investment is mixed. Elton, Gruber, and Rentzler, in three separate studies, examine the returns to public commodity pools.[1] In their first study, they conclude that publicly offered commodity funds are not attractive either as stand-alone investments or as additions to a portfolio containing stocks and/or bonds. In their second study, they find that the historical return data reported in the prospectuses of publicly offered commodity pools are not indicative of the returns that these funds actually earn once they go public; in fact, they conclude that the performance discrepancies are so large that the prospectus numbers are seriously misleading. In their last study, they do not find any evidence that would support the addition of commodity pools to a portfolio of stocks and bonds and that commodity funds do not provide an attractive hedge against inflation. They also find the distribution of returns to public commodity pools to be negatively skewed; therefore, the opportunity for very large negative returns is greater than for large positive returns. Three additional studies (Irwin, Krukemyer, and Zulauf;[2] Schneeweis, Savanayana, and McCarthy;[3] and Edwards and Park[4]) also conclude that public commodity funds offer little value to investors as either stand-alone investments or as an addition to a stock and bond portfolio. However, Irwin and Brorsen find that public commodity funds provide an expanded efficient investment frontier.[5]

For private commodity pools, Edwards and Park find that an equally weighted index of commodity pools has a sufficiently high Sharpe ratio to justify it either as a stand-alone investment or as part of a diversified portfolio.[6] Conversely, Schneeweis et al. conclude that private commodity pools do not have value as stand-alone investments, but they are worthwhile additions to a diversified stock and bond portfolio.[7]

With respect to separate accounts managed by CTAs, McCarthy, Schneeweis, and Spurgin find that an allocation to an equally weighted index of CTAs provides valuable diversification benefits to a portfolio of stocks and bonds.[8] In a subsequent study, Schneeweis, Spurgin, and Potter find that a portfolio allocation to a dollar-weighted index of CTAs results in a higher portfolio Sharpe ratio.[9] Edwards and Park find that an index of equally weighted CTAs performs well both as a stand-alone investment and as an addition to a diversified portfolio.[10]

An important aspect of any investment is the predictability of returns over time. If returns are predictable, then an investor can select a commodity pool or a CTA with consistently superior performance. Considerable time and effort have been devoted to studying the managed futures

---

[1] See Edwin Elton, Martin Gruber, and Joel Rentzler, "Professionally Managed, Publicly Traded Commodity Funds," *Journal of Business* 60, no. 2 (1987), 175–199; "New Public Offerings, Information, and Investor Rationality: The Case of Publicly Offered Commodity Funds," *Journal of Business* 62, no. 1 (1989), 1–15; "The Performance of Publicly Offered Commodity Funds," *Financial Analysts Journal* (July–August 1990), 23–30.

[2] See Scott Irwin, Terry Krukemyer, and Carl Zulauf, "Investment Performance of Public Commodity Pools: 1979–1990," *Journal of Futures Markets* 13, no.7 (1993), 799–819.

[3] See Thomas Schneeweis, Uttama Savanayana, and David McCarthy, "Alternative Commodity Trading Vehicles: A Performance Analysis," *Journal of Futures Markets* 11, no. 4 (1991), 475–487.

[4] See Franklin Edwards and James Park, "Do Managed Futures Make Good Investments?" *Journal of Futures Markets* 16, no. 5 (1996), 475–517.

[5] See Scott Irwin and B. Wade Brorsen, "Public Futures Funds," *Journal of Futures Markets* 5, no. 3 (1985), 463–485.

[6] See Edwards and Park, "Do Managed Futures Make Good Investments?"

[7] See Schneeweis, Savanayana, and McCarthy, "Alternative Commodity Trading Vehicles."

[8] See David McCarthy, Thomas Schneeweis, and Richard Spurgin, "Investment through CTAs: An Alternative Managed Futures Investment," *Journal of Derivatives* (Summer 1996), 36–47.

[9] See Thomas Schneeweis, Richard Spurgin, and Mark Potter, "Managed Futures and Hedge Fund Investment for Downside Equity Risk Management," in *The Handbook of Managed Futures: Performance, Evaluation and Analysis*, ed. Carl C. Peters and Ben Warwick (New York: McGraw-Hill, 1997).

[10] Edwards and Park, "Do Managed Futures Make Good Investments?"

industry to determine the predictability and consistency of returns. Unfortunately, the results are not encouraging.

For instance, Edwards and Ma find that once commodity funds go public through a registered public offering, their average returns are negative.[11] They conclude that prior pre-public-trading performance for commodity pools is of little use to investors when selecting a public commodity fund as an investment. The lack of predictability in historical managed futures returns is supported by the research of McCarthy, Schneeweis, and Spurgin;[12] Irwin, Zulauf, and Ward;[13] and the three studies by Elton, Gruber, and Renzler.[14] In fact, Irwin et al. conclude that a strategy of selecting CTAs based on historical good performance is not likely to improve upon a naive strategy of selecting CTAs at random. The problem of selecting an investment manager based on past performance is not confined to CTAs. Most available evidence suggests that selecting asset managers in hedge funds and the long-only segment of the equity and fixed income industry solely based on their past performance does not guarantee positive alpha in future.

In general, the empirical research supports the use of managed futures in a diversified portfolio context. These potential benefits may not exist if the investments take place through CPOs that manage a pool of CTAs. The second layer of fees charged by these CPOs effectively eliminates most of the benefits associated with this asset class. In the next section we provide an overview of several managed futures benchmarks and their potential for portfolio diversification.

Review of managed futures benchmarks

In this section, we examine the construction, inflation hedging ability, and risk-return profiles of several managed futures indices.

To begin with, in Exhibit 22.1 we list several managed futures indices and their construction techniques. One thing we can quickly note is that even though managed futures trading has been around for several decades, industry benchmarks to track the industry are relatively new; approximately one-half have been developed since 2000. Those with the longest historical track records are the Barclay CTA Index; the Center for International Securities and Derivatives Markets (CISDM, at the University of Massachusetts) indices; and the Mount Lucas Management Index (MLMI).

We can also see that, similar to hedge fund indices, some of these benchmarks are equally weighted while others are asset weighted. In addition, there is at least one investable managed futures index, the CSFB Investable Managed Futures Index.

One way to measure whether managed futures can have a beneficial impact on a diversified portfolio is to examine their inflation hedging potential. Exhibit 22.2 presents the case for managed futures as an inflation hedge. Unfortunately, all of the managed futures indices have a negative correlation with inflation, indicating that they are not an effective hedge against inflation. That is, their values tend to decline as inflation increases. This is in contrast to the positive inflation hedging potential of commodity futures that we demonstrated in the prior chapter. However, the correlation values are generally not very large, and certainly not as negative as we observed for stocks and bonds

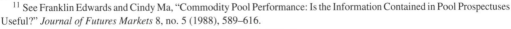

[11] See Franklin Edwards and Cindy Ma, "Commodity Pool Performance: Is the Information Contained in Pool Prospectuses Useful?" *Journal of Futures Markets* 8, no. 5 (1988), 589–616.

[12] McCarthy, Schneeweis, and Spurgin, "Investment through CTAs."

[13] Scott Irwin, Carl Zulauf, and Barry Ward, "The Predictability of Managed Futures Returns," *Journal of Derivatives* (Winter 1994), 20–27.

[14] Elton, Gruber, and Rentzler, "Professionally Managed, Publicly Traded Commodity Funds," "New Public Offerings, Information, and Investor Rationality," and " Performance of Publicly Offered Commodity Funds."

Exhibit 22.1 Summary of CTA fund indices

Index Provider	Provides a Single Index	Data History	Number of Subindices	Number of Funds	Equal or Asset Weighted	Investable or Noninvestable	Net of Fees	Web Site
Bloomberg BAIF HF CTA MGD FUT	Yes	2006	0		Equal	No	Yes	www.bloomberg.com
Barclay Trader CTA Index	Yes	1980	6	491	Equal	No	Yes	www.barclayhedge.com
BBOTTOM 50 Barclay U.S. Managed Futures Index	Yes	1987	0	50	Equal	Yes	Yes	www.barclayhedge.com
CASAM/CISDM CTA Asset Weighted Index	Yes	1979	7	500	Asset	No	Yes	www.casamhedge.com
CASAM/CISDM CTA Equal Weighted Index	Yes	1979	7	500	Equal	No	Yes	www.casamhedge.com
CSFB/Tremont Investable Managed Futures Index	Yes	2003	0	6	Asset	No	Yes	www.hedgeindex.com
CSFB/Tremont Managed Futures Index	Yes	1994	0	31	Asset	Yes	Yes	www.hedgeindex.com
EDHEC-Risk CTA Global*	Yes	2006	0	5*	Other	No	Yes	www.edhec-risk.com
Eurekahedge Global CTA/Managed Futures Index	Yes	2000	0	351	Equal	No	Yes	www.eurekahedge.com
MLM Index†	Yes	1988	0	N/A	Other	Yes	No	www.mtlucas.com
RBC Hedge 250 Managed Futures	Yes	2005	0	16	Equal	Yes	Yes	www.rbchedge250.com

*Index of indices.
†Managed futures replication index.

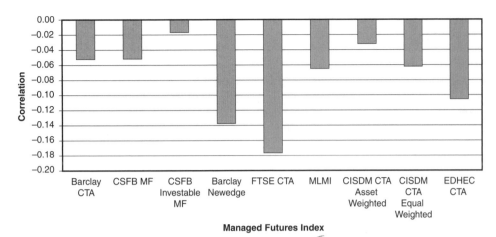

Exhibit 22.2 Managed futures index correlations with inflation, 1990 to October 2008

in the prior chapter. Still, our analysis suggests that commodity futures investing is a better inflation hedge than managed futures investing.

Our next stage of review includes studying the risk and return properties of managed futures. Exhibit 22.3 presents the annual expected return, annual standard deviation, Sharpe ratio, skewness, and kurtosis for each of the managed futures indices. First, we can see that all of the indices have a positive Sharpe ratio, demonstrating a positive risk-return trade-off. Another point to consider is that the volatility of managed futures, as measured by the return standard deviation, is very low compared to that for commodity futures indices, approximately one-half of that observed for commodity futures in our prior chapters. Expected returns are lower, too, but overall, the Sharpe ratios are higher than those for commodity futures indices.

We also note that most of the managed futures indices have a positive skew and a small but positive value of kurtosis, indicating a small but positive bias to larger upside returns. This, too, is in contrast to what we found for commodity futures indices, where the skews tended to be negative but the kurtosis was positive, indicating a bias to large downside returns. One significant caveat to this conclusion is the result presented for the CSFB Investable Managed Futures Index. We can see that this index is the only one with a negative skew, that is, a return distribution with a tendency toward larger negative returns and smaller positive returns. This is a good reality check on the benefits

Exhibit 22.3 Managed futures index performance, 1990 to October 2008

	Average Return	Annualized Standard Deviation	Sharpe Ratio	Skewness	Kurtosis
Barclay CTA	7.14%	8.62%	0.43	0.39	0.55
CSFB MF	7.65%	11.95%	0.35	0.01	0.12
CSFB Investable MF	6.21%	11.88%	0.23	−0.19	−0.66
Barclay Newedge	8.02%	9.59%	0.48	0.16	0.47
FTSE CTA	9.64%	13.56%	0.46	0.44	0.00
MLMI	6.69%	6.01%	0.54	0.06	2.76
CISDM CTA Asset Weighted	10.91%	9.59%	0.78	0.64	1.99
CISDM CTA Equal Weighted	9.84%	9.36%	0.69	0.52	0.60
EDHEC CTA	8.62%	8.92%	0.58	0.10	−0.17

of managed futures because this index produces results that an investor can reasonably expect to access by investing in managed futures. We also note that the Sharpe ratio for the CSFB Investable Managed Futures Index is the lowest of all of the managed futures indices presented. Again, this is another good reality check as to the returns that can reasonably be expected to be achieved through a managed futures program. Last, we note that this index has a negative value for kurtosis. This is very rare to achieve in a return distribution. It demonstrates a return distribution with thinner tails (less exposure to outliers) than a normal distribution. This is good for risk management purposes because a smaller value of kurtosis means fewer shocks to the portfolio (both positive and negative) and indicates a more consistent return process.

Next, in Exhibit 22.4, we plot the return and risk for all of the managed futures indices. One thing that might strike the reader right away is the consistency of the risk and return for all of these indices. They are tightly grouped to the upper right-hand corner of the chart. The returns are generally in the 7% to 10% range with volatility in the 9% to 12% range. This merely demonstrates a greater consistency of returns associated with managed futures returns than, for instance hedge funds. If readers turn back to our chapters on hedge funds, they will find a similar chart for the many hedge fund indices. A key difference between the two is that there is much more variation in risk and return for hedge funds than for managed futures.

Last, in Exhibit 22.5 we examine the correlation coefficients between the returns to managed futures indices and the returns to stocks and bonds. First, we note that the correlation coefficients between managed futures and U.S. and international stocks are consistently negative across the spectrum. Managed futures demonstrate consistently good diversification properties for domestic and international stocks. We find similar diversification properties for high-yield bonds; the correlation coefficients are also negative across all of the managed futures. This is not surprising given that high-yield bonds trade with considerable stock market risk compared to interest rate risk. We can see that managed futures are mostly positively correlated with Treasury bond returns, showing less diversification potential than with stocks. Still, the correlation coefficients with Treasury bonds are low, significantly less than 1.0, which demonstrates an ability to diversify some of the interest rate risk. In the last column we include once more the correlation coefficients for managed futures associated with inflation. Again, we see that these correlation coefficients are all negative. Rather than diversify away from inflation we, in fact, want a positive correlation with inflation. The reason is that the most effective hedge against inflation is to find an asset class that moves in tandem with

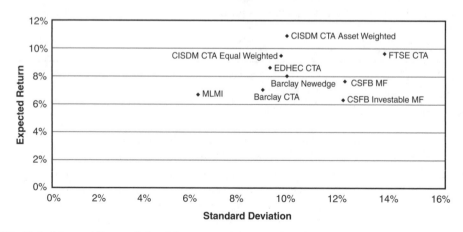

Exhibit 22.4 Managed Futures Index risk return trade-off, 1990 to October 2008

Exhibit 22.5 Managed futures index correlations, 1990 to October 2008

Correlations	S&P 500	FTSE 100	EAFE	10-Year U.S. Treasury	High-Yield Bonds	Inflation
Barclay CTA	−0.14	−0.19	−0.10	0.24	−0.14	−0.05
CSFB MF	−0.15	−0.12	−0.02	0.24	−0.17	−0.05
CSFB Investable MF	0.03	−0.02	0.05	−0.09	−0.13	−0.02
Barclay Newedge	−0.22	−0.18	−0.06	0.22	−0.22	−0.14
FTSE CTA	−0.16	−0.14	−0.08	0.26	−0.15	−0.18
MLMI	−0.29	−0.20	−0.18	0.08	−0.20	−0.06
CISDM CTA Asset Weighted	−0.09	−0.17	−0.07	0.24	−0.09	−0.03
CISDM CTA Equal Weighted	−0.15	−0.19	−0.09	0.24	−0.15	−0.06
EDHEC CTA	−0.15	−0.13	−0.06	0.31	−0.17	−0.11

inflation. Unfortunately, managed futures moves in the opposite direction from inflation. This is another way to say that inflation erodes the returns of managed futures just as it does those of stocks and bonds.

RETURN DISTRIBUTIONS OF MANAGED FUTURES

Similar to our analysis for hedge funds and passive commodity futures, we examine the distribution of returns for managed futures. We use several of the managed futures indices displayed in Exhibit 22.1.

Managed futures products may be good investments if the pattern of their returns is positively skewed. One way to consider this concept is that it is similar to owning a Treasury bill plus a lottery ticket. The investor consistently receives low but positive returns. However, every once in a while an extreme event occurs and the CTA is able to profit from the movement of futures prices. This would result in a positive skew. To get a full range of managed futures return distributions, we use the following indices for our frequency distributions:

- Barclay Trader CTA Index.
- CSFB/Tremont Managed Futures Index.
- CSFB/Tremont Investable Managed Futures Index.
- Barclay Newedge CTA Index.
- FTSE Hedge CTA Index.
- MLM Index.
- CISDM CTA Asset Weighted Index.
- CISDM CTA Equal Weighted Index.
- EDHEC-Risk CTA Global Hedge Index.

Managed futures traders have one goal in mind: to capitalize on price trends. Most CTAs are considered to be trend followers, while there is also a large number of discretionary CTAs. Trend-following CTAs represent the dominant group because it is easier for investors to perform due diligence on this group and the source of return is better defined. Further, discretionary CTAs tend not to be as diversified as trend-following CTAs and therefore are perceived to be more risky.

Typically, trend-following CTAs look at various moving averages of commodity prices and attempt to determine whether the price will continue to trend up or down; they then trade accordingly.

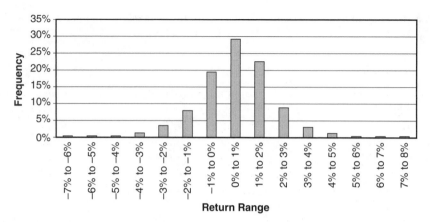

Exhibit 22.6   Return distribution for MLM Index, 1990 to October 2008

Therefore, it is not the investment strategy that is the distinguishing factor in the managed futures industry, but rather the markets in which CTAs and CPOs apply their trend-following strategies.[15]

In this chapter we use the Mount Lucas Management Index (MLMI) as a benchmark by which to judge CTA performance. Recall from our discussion in the prior chapter that the MLMI represents the return to a systematic trend-following strategy. The strategy is simple enough to be replicated by an unskilled investor who has sufficient capital, because it applies a mechanical and transparent rule for capitalizing on price trends in the futures markets. It does not represent active trading. Instead, it applies a consistent rule for buying or selling futures contracts depending on the current price trend in any particular commodity futures market. In addition, the MLMI invests across agricultural, currency, financial, energy, and metal futures contracts. Therefore, it provides a good benchmark by which to examine the four managed futures strategies.

Exhibit 22.6 demonstrates the frequency distribution for monthly returns for the MLMI. The first thing we can observe is that the MLMI is amazingly symmetrical. This is a balanced distribution— while there are outliers, they are almost equally balanced between large positive returns and large negative returns. The large positive and negative returns in the tails of the distribution lead to the rather large (compared to the other managed futures indices) value of kurtosis of 2.76. In fact, the MLMI has the largest value of kurtosis among the managed futures indices. However, the skew of the distribution is very low at 0.06. While this is a very slight positive skew—which is a good thing—the skew is effectively zero, which demonstrates a well-balanced distribution with no preference for either positive or negative returns, just like a normal distribution. Also, we observe that 52% of the returns are grouped in the 0 to 2% range, which is a demonstration of significant mass in the center of a positive return distribution. This concentrated mass contributes to a positive expected return of 6.7% on an annual basis. Last, looking back at Exhibit 22.3, we can see that the MLMI has a strong Sharpe ratio, indicating a good risk-return trade-off. In reviewing the distribution of returns for managed futures strategies, we keep in mind that the returns are generated from active management. As we indicated in our discussion of hedge funds, one demonstration of skill is the ability to shift a distribution of returns from a negative skew to a positive skew. Therefore, if CTAs do in fact have skill, we would expect to see distribution of returns with a positive skew.

 In conclusion, the MLMI offers a symmetrical distribution where the positive returns and negative returns are almost perfectly balanced. There is a high level of kurtosis, and we can see from

---

[15] In fact, one article has noted that the managed futures industry suffers because too many CTAs are using similar trend-following strategies. See Daniel Collins, "A New Life for Managed Futures," *Futures* (April 1, 2001).

Exhibit 22.6 that the tails of the distribution extend out in both positive and negative directions. We will use the MLMI to compare the active managed futures indices.

Active Futures Indices

In Exhibit 22.7 we provide the return distribution for the full Barclay Managed Futures CTA Index over the time period 1990 to 2008. This index contains 400 actively traded commodity futures programs across currencies, financials, metals, agriculture, and diversified strategies.

We note in Exhibit 22.3 that the expected annual return for the Barclay CTA Index is similar to that for the MLMI index at 0.07 (more precisely, 7.14% versus 6.69%). However, the Barclay CTA Index has a larger positive value of skew of 0.39 compared to a small value for the MLMI. Therefore, actively traded managed futures provide a bias toward large positive returns as compared to large negative returns. As we discussed in our prior chapters on hedge funds, the ability to shift the distribution of returns from a negative skew to a positive skew is a demonstration of skill. If we use the MLMI as our market indicator for actively managed futures trading, Exhibit 22.7 demonstrates a skill level where large positive returns are produced with greater frequency than large negative returns.

There is, however, a trade-off for this demonstration of skill. The Barclay CTA Index has higher volatility compared to the MLMI: 8.62% versus 6.01%. In other words, there are no free lunches. While actively managed futures provide a bias to the upside similar to that of the MLMI, it does so with higher return volatility that results in a lower Sharpe ratio than that of the MLMI.

CSFB Indices

Exhibit 22.8 presents the CSFB/Tremont Managed Futures Index. At first glance, this index looks more stretched out than that of the MLMI. For example, in the 0% to 2% range, only 22% of the mass of the distribution is contained. Surprisingly, the skew of this distribution is virtually zero at 0.01 (from Exhibit 2.3). In addition, the kurtosis is very close to zero at 0.12. This symmetry comes at a price, higher volatility. The CSFB/Tremont Managed Futures Index has the second highest volatility measure at almost 12%. This results in a lower Sharpe ratio of 0.35 compared to the MLMI's Sharpe ratio of 0.54.

Exhibit 22.9 examines the CSFB/Tremont Investable Managed Futures Index. At first glance, it is hard to draw any conclusions from this frequency distribution as the returns seem to be scattered

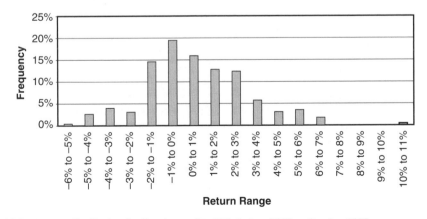

Exhibit 22.7   Return distribution for Barclay trader CTA Index, 1990 to October 2008

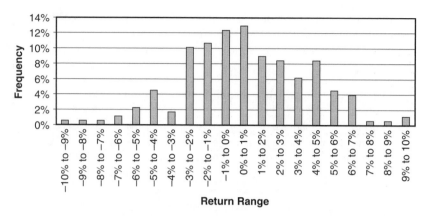

Exhibit 22.8   Return distribution for CSFB/Tremont Managed Futures Index, 1994 to October 2008

without any discernible pattern. Certainly the symmetry that we observed for the MLMI is not to be found in this pattern of returns. This is where statistics can be helpful for making sense of an otherwise random arrangement of returns.

As we noted earlier, this is the one index that has a negative skew of −0.19. It also has the lowest Sharpe ratio of 0.23. This is a good lesson to be learned. What an investor believes she can earn from an asset class by observing the returns to a benchmark or index may not be the same as the return that is actually achieved when cash is invested. Give credit to CSFB/Tremont for providing an index that mirrors what investors can actually expect to earn from the managed futures industry. Unfortunately, skill is less evident in this investable index than otherwise indicated from the other managed futures indices examined in this chapter.

Barclay Newedge CTA Index

Exhibit 22.10 presents the Barclay Newedge CTA Index. This is a newer index for Barclay with data from 2000 on. Again, we see that the mass of the distribution is spread out across the return range;

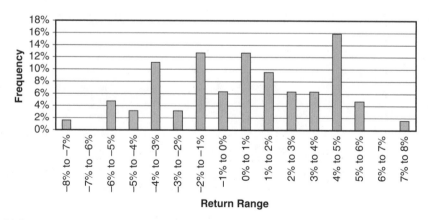

Exhibit 22.9   Return distribution for CSFB/Tremont Investable Managed Futures Index, August 2004 to October 2008

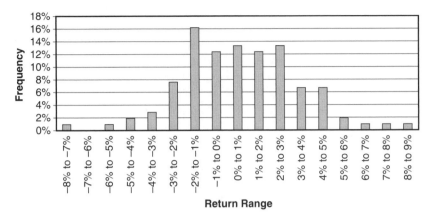

Exhibit 22.10 Return distribution for Barclay Newedge CTA Index, February 2000 to October 2008

only 25% of the monthly returns are in the 0% to 2% range. Consistency of return is not as great as in the case of the MLMI.

In addition, we see a slightly positive skew of 0.16, demonstrating some ability to shift the return distribution of managed futures more to the positive side than to the negative side. Recall that a positive skew demonstrates a return distribution that has more positive returns above the median return than negative returns below the median. This is a desirable quality to have with any return distribution. As we saw in prior chapters, domestic and international stocks as well as high-yield bonds have negative skews. Therefore, any asset class than can help shift the portfolio skew more toward the positive side is a valuable addition to a well-diversified portfolio. Last, we see from Exhibit 22.3 that the Barclay Newedge CTA Index has a Sharpe ratio of 0.48; there is a positive risk and return trade-off.

FTSE CTA Index

In Exhibit 22.11 we examine the FTSE CTA index. This return distribution also shows returns strung out more than the MLMI. Only 16% of the distribution mass is concentrated in the 0 to 2% range. Surprisingly, the kurtosis for the distribution is virtually zero at −0.002. This simply indicates that

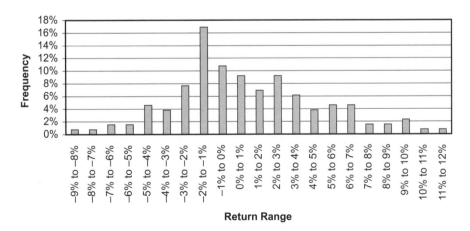

Exhibit 22.11 Return distribution for FTSE hedge CTA Index, 1998 to October 2008

very little of the mass of the distribution is pushed into the tails of the distribution. Also, there is a positive skew of 0.44. This can be observed in Exhibit 22.11 where we see that more of the mass of the distribution is shifted toward positive returns than negative returns. Last, the Sharpe ratio is respectable at 0.46. There is a spike in negative returns in the −1% to −2% range of the distribution, amounting to 17% of the return mass. This is puzzling, and we have no good explanation for this spike within the distribution. Still, even with this unusual concentration of negative returns at this point of the distribution, it is not sufficient to create a negative skew.

CISDM CTA Indices

Exhibit 22.12 presents the return distribution for the CISDM Asset Weighted CTA Index. The first thing we can observe from this chart is that there is a clear shift toward positive returns. This is borne out by the largest positive skew in our study of managed futures indices at 0.64. This return distribution also has a higher value of kurtosis of 1.99, which is brought on by the one monthly observation in the 14% to 15% range.

This shows that you cannot rely wholly on statistics; you have to look at the picture from time to time. A good lesson to be learned here is that if we were to remove this one return observation from our return distribution, it would reduce the kurtosis to 0.5 and the positive skew to 0.35. Nonetheless, we have to take our data as we find it even though common sense tells us that it is unlikely that we would observe another monthly return in the 14% to 15% range.

Exhibit 22.13 again presents the CISDM CTA index, but this time the index is equally weighted among the CTA managers in the index. This distribution also shows a clear shift to the right, or positive return territory, resulting in a positive skew value of 0.52. We also observe a lower kurtosis value of 0.60. Last, with the equal weighting of the index, we see that there is still a large positive outlier return but now it is in the 11% to 12% range. Clearly this large positive return was generated by a large CTA manager, which is why it is even more of an outlier return in the asset-weighted CISDM index. Another way to say this is that equal weighting of a managed futures index has the advantage of ensuring that no one active CTA manager exerts too much influence on the return pattern of the index.

This is also demonstrated by the difference in the expected returns between the two CISDM indices. The asset-weighted index produces an expected annual return of 10.91% compared to 9.84% for the

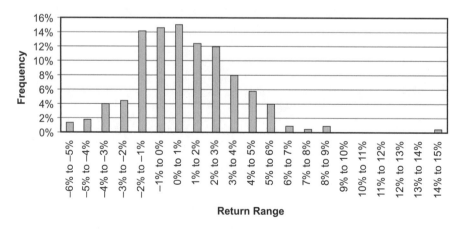

Exhibit 22.12   Return distribution for CISDM CTA Asset Weighted Index, 1990 to October 2008

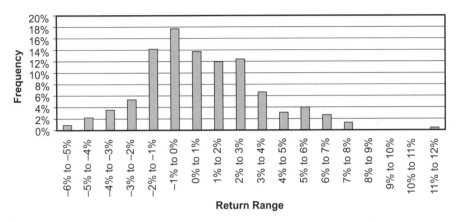

Exhibit 22.13 Return distribution for CISDM CTA equal weighted index, 1990 to October 2008

equally weighted index. This also results in a lower Sharpe ratio for the equal-weighted index (0.69) compared to the asset-weighted index (0.78).

EDHEC-Risk CTA Global Index

Our final managed futures index is presented in Exhibit 22.14, the EDHEC-Risk CTA Global Index. This index also demonstrates a good symmetry, with a skew of 0.10 and kurtosis of −0.17. Both statistics indicate a return pattern very similar to a normal distribution. The central mass of the returns is still spread out a bit more than that for the MLMI, but visually, a reasonable symmetry can be observed from Exhibit 22.14.

We also note that the EDHEC CTA index has one of the lower risk profiles, with an annual volatility of 8.92%. This risk combined with an expected return of 8.62% produces a good Sharpe ratio of 0.58.

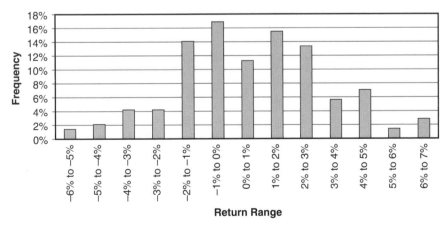

Exhibit 22.14 Return distribution for EDHEC-Risk CTA Global Index, 1997 to October 2008

MANAGED FUTURES IN A PORTFOLIO CONTEXT

Similar to the analysis that we conducted in Chapter 21 on commodity futures and the efficient frontier, we add managed futures to a stock and bond portfolio to see if there are diversification benefits. Just as in Chapter 21, we blend a 10% allocation to managed futures into our stock and bond portfolio, and then observe whether there is any improvement along the efficient frontier. The results of our analysis are presented in Exhibits 22.15 through 22.18. The indices chosen for this part of our analysis were selected because of their longer track records. A longer track record provides us with a higher level of confidence that managed futures can provide long-term portfolio diversification benefits.

We begin with the MLMI as our initial case for adding managed futures to a diversified portfolio. We start with this index for two reasons. First, the MLMI is an investable index, so it is a very good indicator of the portfolio diversification that an investor can actually achieve with managed futures. Second, the MLMI is a passive index. As we previously discussed, the MLMI follows an established trend-following rule designed to mimic the trading patterns of CTAs and CPOs in the managed futures business.

In Exhibit 22.15 we show the results when we blend a 10% allocation into the MLMI. The original efficient frontier with a 60/40 stock/bond allocation is the lightly shaded line marked with triangles for data points. Above this line is a darker shaded line denoted by squares for data points: this is the efficient frontier with a 55/35/10 allocation to stocks/bonds/MLMI. We can see that the efficient frontier shifts up and to the left when the investor makes an allocation to the MLMI. The efficient frontier with the MLMI is more efficient because more return is achieved for the same level of risk; alternatively, less risk is needed to achieve the same level of return. We can see that the

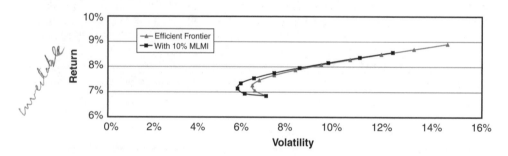

Exhibit 22.15   Efficient frontier with 55/35/10 stocks/bonds/MLMI

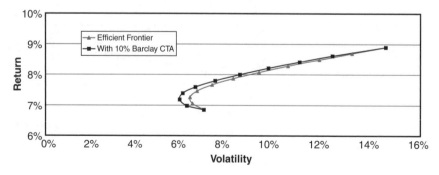

Exhibit 22.16   Efficient frontier with 55/35/10 stocks/bonds/Barclay CTA

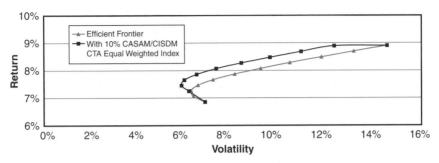

Exhibit 22.17 Efficient frontier with 55/35/10 stocks/bonds/CISDM CTA equal weighted

MLMI improves the efficient frontier at the lower range of risk, but there is not much improvement when the risk (volatility) of the portfolio is above 8%. Therefore, an allocation to the MLMI will be most beneficial for those investors who are very risk averse and unwilling to seek higher returns by accepting a larger amount of volatility.

Exhibit 22.16 shows similar results for the Barclay CTA Index. Once again, the darker line marked by squares shows the efficient frontier when managed futures are added to the asset allocation. The greatest improvement is at the lower range of volatility. However, there is improvement in the efficient frontier along all points of the range of volatility, although the improvement diminishes at higher levels of volatility.

Last, we include the two CISDM managed futures indices, one asset weighted by a CTA manager and one equally weighted. Exhibit 22.17 shows the CISDM CTA Equal Weighted Index. Here, we can see considerable improvement of the efficient frontier all along the frontier and volatility range. This demonstrates that investors using the CISDM index for asset allocation would apply managed futures no matter what their level of risk aversion or tolerance. Along each data point, at both high and low volatility levels, the CISDM index shows a marked improvement in the efficient frontier.

Last, we turn to Exhibit 22.18, the CISDM CTA Asset Weighted Index. Again, the efficient frontier using this index is marked by the darker line and data points marked by squares. This index shows the greatest improvement in efficient frontier among all of our managed futures indices. If we used assets under management as a proxy for successful performance, then investing with a better managed futures manager makes a significant difference in portfolio performance.

As we conclude this section, we offer one significant caveat. Most of these indices are not investable, and therefore an investor cannot expect to achieve the same level of performance and

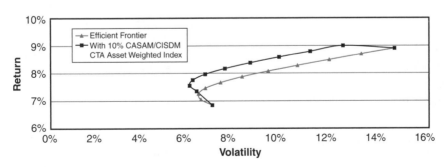

Exhibit 22.18 Efficient frontier with 55/35/10 stocks/bonds/CISDM CTA asset weighted

portfolio diversification as these exhibits demonstrate. The one exception, of course, is the MLMI: this index is designed to be investable. Notably, while the MLMI did improve the efficient frontier, it provided the least improvement out of the four managed futures indices studied.

MANAGED FUTURES AS DOWNSIDE RISK PROTECTION FOR STOCKS AND BONDS

This section is similar to that presented in Chapter 21 for passive commodity futures. As we discussed in Chapter 21, the greatest concern for any investor is downside risk. If equity and bond markets are becoming increasingly synchronized, international diversification may not offer the protection sought by investors. The ability to protect the value of an investment portfolio in hostile or turbulent markets is the key to the value of any macroeconomic diversification.

Within this framework, an asset class distinct from financial assets has the potential to diversify and protect an investment portfolio from hostile markets. We saw in Chapter 21 that commodity futures have the ability to diversify a stock and bond portfolio. They provide strategic diversification. We now face the question of whether skill-based strategies like managed futures can provide the same amount of downside protection as commodity futures.

Exhibit 22.19 presents our results for downside risk protection. As a brief review, we first construct a portfolio of 60% stocks/40% bonds. We then measure the number of months with a negative return and the average negative return in a downside month. We then blend in a 10% allocation to managed futures and count the number of months with negative returns and the average return in a downside month.

Exhibit 22.19 presents our results. First, we note that across all of the managed futures indices, each provided downside risk protection, similar to commodity futures. Unfortunately, not all of the managed futures indices have as long a tenure as the Barclay, MLMI, and CISDM indices. As a result, these latter indices show the most downside risk protection because we can track their downside protection back to 1990. The more recently constructed indices also provide downside risk protection, but their cumulative protection is less because of their shorter track records.

Nonetheless, the results are very encouraging for each index. If we used the Barclay CTA Index, we can see that the number of downside months decreases from 79 to 76 and the average return in a downside month decreases from -2.12% to -1.97%. The total downside return protection provided over the past 18 years is 17.76%, or about 1% per year. We observe even better downside return protection using the MLMI and the CISDM indices.

Providing a 1% downside protection (or better) per year does not seem like a lot. However, as of the writing of this book in 2009, we are in a significant negative return environment where stocks, high-yield bonds, real estate, and senior loans have deteriorated by 20% to 40%, so any amount of downside risk protection would be beneficial.

The downside risk protection demonstrated by managed futures products is consistent with the research of Schneeweis, Spurgin, and Potter and of Anson.[16] Specifically, they find that a combination of 50% S&P 500 stocks and 50% CTA managed futures outperforms a portfolio comprised of the S&P 500 plus protective put options. Unfortunately, our research indicates that only in limited circumstances do managed futures products offer financial benefits greater than those offered by a passive commodities futures index. Further, it is highly unusual to find an institutional portfolio with a large allocation to CTAs.

---

[16] See Thomas Schneeweis, Richard Spurgin, and Mark Potter, "Managed Futures and Hedge Fund Investment for Downside Equity Risk Protection," *Derivatives Quarterly* (Fall 1996), 62–72. See also Mark Anson, "Managing Downside Risk in Return Distributions Using Hedge Funds, Managed Futures and Commodity Futures," *CTA Reader* (2004).

Exhibit 22.19 Summary of downside risk protection for managed futures, 1990 to October 2008

Portfolio	Average Monthly Return	Monthly Standard Deviation	Skewness	Kurtosis	Sharpe Ratio	Number of Negative Months	Average Return Negative Month	Downside Risk Protection
60/40 S&P 500/U.S. Treasury	0.65%	2.65%	-0.41	1.37	0.13	79	-2.12%	N/A
55/35/10 S&P 500/Bonds/Barclay CTA	0.64	2.41	-0.29	1.34	0.14	76	-1.97	17.76%
55/35/10 S&P 500/Bonds/CSFB MF	0.59	2.41	-0.44	0.88	0.11	63	-1.97	9.45
55/35/10 S&P 500/Bonds/CSFB Investable MF	0.30	2.01	-1.88	6.48	-0.01	22	-1.68	9.68
55/35/10 S&P 500/Bonds/Newedge CTA	0.19	2.26	-0.61	2.20	-0.05	41	-1.94	7.38
55/35/10 S&P 500/Bonds/FTSE CTA	0.37	2.40	-0.49	1.25	0.02	53	-1.88	12.72
55/35/10 S&P 500/Bonds/MLMI	0.64	2.38	-0.33	1.07	0.14	76	-1.93	20.78
55/35/10 S&P 500/Bonds/CISDM CTA Asset Wtd	0.67	2.43	-0.26	1.35	0.15	75	-1.98	19.08
55/35/10 S&P 500/Bonds/CISDM CTA Equal Wtd	0.66	2.41	-0.25	1.27	0.14	77	-1.92	19.83
55/35/10 S&P 500/Bonds/EDHEC CTA	0.48	2.48	-0.46	1.04	0.07	54	-1.97	8.10

CONCLUSION

In this chapter we examined the benefits of managed futures products. Prior empirical research has not resolved the issue of whether managed futures products can add value either as stand-alone investments or as part of a diversified portfolio.

On a stand-alone basis, our review indicates that managed futures products mostly outperformed in total return a naive trend-following index represented by the MLMI. The MLMI is a transparent commodity futures index that mechanically applies a simple price trend-following rule for buying or selling commodity futures. However, the MLMI outperformed many of the managed futures indices on a risk-adjusted basis when measured by a Sharpe ratio. We also note that because the MLMI is an investable index, the results achieved by this index are a good indication of what investors may actually obtain in their portfolios.

One of the biggest advantages of the MLMI is its symmetry. This was evident from Exhibit 22.16, which showed a nice bell curve shape, albeit with larger tails than a normal distribution. Also, the mass of the distribution for the MLMI was much more concentrated than that for many of the managed futures indices. This pushing together of the return pattern results in more consistent results. This was evidenced by the lower volatility of the MLMI compared to all of the managed futures indices. A study of managed futures in a portfolio context found that managed futures can improve the risk-return trade-off in a diversified portfolio. We studied four managed futures indices that had sufficiently long data histories to provide us with an analysis in which we have a high degree of confidence. We found that all four managed futures indices significantly expanded the efficient frontier for investors, with the CISDM equal-weighted and asset-weighted indices having the greatest ability to improve the efficient frontier.

Last, we found that all of the managed futures indices provided significant downside risk protection. Each index not only lowered the average negative return in a downside month, but also reduced the number of months with a negative return. After an absolutely brutal year in the financial markets in 2008, investors might wish to seek out some downside risk protection.

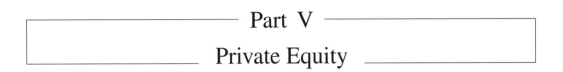

Part V
Private Equity

23

Introduction to Venture Capital

The private equity sector purchases the private stock or equity-linked securities of nonpublic companies that are expected to go public or provides the capital for public companies (or their divisions) that may wish to go private. The key component in either case is the private nature of the securities purchased. Private equity, by definition, is not publicly traded. Therefore, investments in private equity are illiquid. Investors in this marketplace must be prepared to invest for the long haul; investment horizons may be as extended as 5 to 10 years.

Private equity is a generic term that encompasses four distinct strategies in the market for private investing. First, there is venture capital (VC), the financing of start-up companies. Second, there are leveraged buyouts (LBOs), where public companies repurchase all of their outstanding shares and turn themselves into private companies. Third, there is **mezzanine financing**, a hybrid of private debt and equity financing. Last, there is **distressed debt**, private equity investments in established (as opposed to start-up) but troubled companies.

Private equity is as old as Columbus' voyages. Queen Isabella of Spain sold her jewelry to finance Columbus' small fleet of ships in return for whatever spoils Columbus could find in the New World. The risks were great but the potential rewards were even greater. This in a nutshell summarizes the private equity market: a large risk of failure but the potential for outstanding gains. More generally, private equity provides the long-term equity base of a company that is not listed on any exchange and therefore cannot raise capital via the public stock market. Private equity provides the working capital that is used to help private companies grow and succeed. It is a long-term investment process that requires patience, due diligence and hands-on monitoring.

In this chapter we focus on the best known of the private equity categories: venture capital. **Venture capital** is the supply of equity financing to start-up companies that do not have a sufficient track record to attract investment capital from traditional sources (e.g. the public markets or lending institutions). Entrepreneurs that develop business plans require investment capital to implement those plans. However, these start-up ventures often lack tangible assets that can be used as collateral for a loan. In addition, start-up companies are unlikely to produce positive earnings for several years. Negative cash flows are another reason that banks and other lending institutions as well as the public stock market are unwilling to provide capital to support the business plan.

It is in this uncertain space where nascent companies are born that venture capitalists operate. Venture capitalists finance these high-risk, illiquid, and unproven ideas by purchasing senior equity stakes while the firms are still privately held. The ultimate goal is to make a buck. Venture capitalists are willing to underwrite new ventures with untested products and bear the risk of no liquidity only if they can expect a reasonable return for their efforts. Often, venture capitalists set expected target rates of return of 33% or more to support the risks they bear. Successful start-up companies funded by venture capital money include Cisco Systems, Google, Microsoft, and Genentech.

We begin with a brief history of venture capital. We then consider the role of a venture capitalist in a start-up company raising a venture capital fund. Next we review the heart of the venture capital industry, the business plan. We then review the current structure of the industry. This is followed by a review of the different stages of venture capital financing. Last, we conclude with a case study of a start-up company financed with venture capital.

HISTORY OF VENTURE CAPITAL

While the history of private equity can be traced back to the days of Columbus discovering the New World, the formal process of private equity investing can be traced back to the 1800s in the United Kingdom. In the 1800s, the developed nations of the world were undergoing a significant economic change. Previously, wealth had been defined in terms of the amount of real estate an individual owned. Land barons were aptly named.

However, starting in the 1800s, economic society began to transform itself from an agricultural society to an industrial one. Instead of ownership of land, ownership of goods and services became the new denominator of wealth. Wealthy land barons began to finance the companies of entrepreneurs by purchasing equity ownerships in these companies. Private equity came of age.

The first modern venture capital firm was American Research and Development. It was formed in 1946 as a publicly traded closed-end fund. Its investment objective was to finance companies in growth industries. At that time, these were broadcasting, aerospace, and pharmaceuticals.

Over the next 12 years, a small number of venture capital firms (less than 20) were established. Most were structured as closed-end funds like American Research and Development. In 1958 two new developments were introduced into the venture capital industry.

First, Congress created the Small Business Investment Companies (SBICs). SBICs are licensed and regulated by the Small Business Administration. These are government-backed but privately owned investment companies that provide both management assistance and venture financing for start-up companies. These companies include Citicorp Venture Capital and Clinton Capital. SBICs have provided financing to successful household names such as Apple Computer, Federal Express, and Intel Corporation. Today, there are an estimated 300 SBICs in the United States, concentrated in states with high levels of entrepreneurial talent such as California, Massachusetts, New York, and Texas.[1]

The second development in 1958 was the formation of the first venture capital limited partnership, Draper, Gaither, and Anderson. Limited partnerships have become the standard tool for investing in venture capital by wealthy and institutional investors. Although imitators soon followed, limited partnerships accounted for a small number of the venture capital vehicles throughout the 1960s and 1970s. Furthermore, the annual flow of money into venture capital limited partnerships or closed-end funds never exceeded a few hundred million dollars during this time period.[2]

A third important watershed in the development of the venture capital industry was a change in the so-called **prudent person** standard in the rules governing the pension fund industry in the 1970s. Since 1974, corporate pension plans have been governed by the Employee Retirement Income Security Act of 1974 (ERISA), which was established to ensure proper investment guidelines for the mounting pension liabilities of corporate America.

Initially, ERISA guidelines prohibited pension funds from investing in venture capital funds because of their illiquid and high-risk status. In 1979, the Department of Labor (which oversees ERISA) issued a clarification of the prudent person rule to indicate that venture capital and other high-risk investments should not be considered on a stand-alone basis, but rather on a portfolio basis. In addition, the rule clarified that the prudent person test is based on an investment review process and not on the ultimate outcome of investment results. Therefore, as long as a pension fund investment fiduciary follows sufficient due diligence in considering the portfolio effects of investing in venture capital, the prudent person test is met. The change in the prudent person rule allowed pension funds for the first time to wholly endorse venture capital investing.

---

[1] See W. Keith Schilit, "Structure of the Venture Capital Industry," *Journal of Private Equity* (Spring 1998), 60–67.

[2] See Paul Gompers and Josh Lerner, "The Use of Covenants: An Empirical Analysis of Venture Partnership Agreements," *Journal of Law and Economics* (October 1996), 463–498.

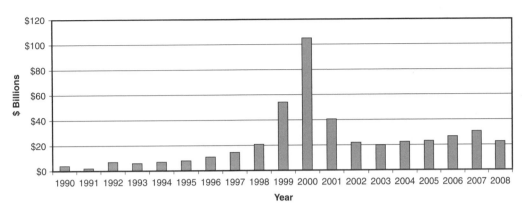

Exhibit 23.1   Venture capital investing, 1990–2008

Source: Thomson Financial Venture Economics.

The 1980s saw yet another new development in the venture capital industry: the **gatekeeper**. Although many pension funds and wealthy investors access the venture capital industry through investment funds or limited partnerships, few investors have devoted resources to evaluate and monitor these investments. Investors' lack of experience and expertise in venture capital led to the birth of **investment advisers** to fill this gap.

In the 1980s, investment advisers came to prominence to advise pension funds and wealthy investors on the benefits of venture capital investing. These gatekeepers got their name because venture capital funds and limited partnerships could no longer access pension fund investment staffs directly. Venture capitalists now had to go through the investment adviser to get a capital commitment from a pension fund. In turn, gatekeepers pooled the resources from their clients and became a dynamic force in the venture capital industry. By 1991, up to one-third of all pension fund commitments to venture capital and one-fifth of all venture money raised came through a gatekeeper.[3]

Venture capital financing increased steadily in the 1980s from about $1.5 billion in commitments in 1980 to over $5 billion in commitments in 1987. During this time, the number of active venture capital investment vehicles increased fourfold. However, the stock market crashes in 1987 and 1989 as well as the recession of 1990 to 1991 reduced the capital commitments to about $2.5 billion by 1991. The 1990s saw the longest economic growth cycle ever experienced in the United States. For many years after the U.S. recession ended in 1991 the economy sustained strong growth with a minimum of inflation. This was the perfect environment for venture capital to blossom.

Exhibit 23.1 demonstrates the growth of investment capital committed to venture capital from 1990 through 2008. For the first half of the 1990s, the annual commitments to venture capital generally ranged from $5 billion to $7 billion. However, starting in 1996, the venture capital industry experienced exponential growth. The average annual growth rate of venture capital commitments between 1995 and 2000 was 82%. From 1990 through 1999, investing in venture capital increased ninefold. The frenzy of venture capital investing peaked in the year 2000 with over $100 billion committed to the venture capital industry in one year. This one year virtually equaled all of the venture capital that had been committed over the previous decade. However, with the bursting of the technology bubble in 2000, the amount of capital committed to venture capital declined rapidly. The market began to recover after 2002, but then the bottom fell out in the global market meltdown in 2008.

This growth was fueled by three factors: robust returns in the stock market in the United States, a strong initial public offering (IPO) market, and low inflation. These three factors allowed investors to

---

[3] Ibid.

simultaneously increase their risk tolerance and extend their investment horizons. Increased risk tolerance allowed investors to bear the high risks of start-up companies. Extended investment horizons allowed investors to accept the long lock-up periods associated with venture capital investing.

Returns to venture capital

Venture capital returns are accessed by way of limited partnerships. These are investment funds that pool the capital of large sophisticated investors to fund new and start-up companies.

Each venture capital fund is managed by a general partner. The general partner is typically a corporation—the venture capital firm that raised the capital for the fund. The general partner sources investment opportunities for the fund, reviews business plans, performs due diligence, and, once an investment is made, typically takes a seat on the board of directors of the start-up company and works with the management of the company to develop and implement the business plan.

Two important keys to successful venture capital investing are to access the top-tier venture capital managers and to achieve vintage-year diversification. We demonstrate these points next.

First, we start with a broad review of venture capital returns. It must be recognized that venture capital investing is a high-risk business. Many start-up companies fail and are dissolved. Furthermore, investors in venture capital limited partnerships are typically required to invest their capital for 10 years or longer. Venture capital is a very illiquid investment class. For these reasons, investors should expect to earn a return premium for investing in venture capital compared to the public equity markets.

Exhibit 23.2 demonstrates the returns to venture capital compared to the S&P 500 over 3-, 5-, 10-, and 20-year investment horizons (1988–2008). Early stage venture capital (VC) funds invest in companies that have a business plan for a product or service but typically have minimal or no revenues. As these start-up companies begin to mature, they produce revenues and establish a customer base. These companies then become suitable for **late stage** or **expansion** venture capital funds. **Balanced VC funds** have a blend of early and late stage companies in their portfolios. We include the returns for late stage, early stage, and balanced venture capital funds. The first column (dark outline) shows the returns for early stage VC, followed by balanced VC (light shading), late stage VC (dark shading), and the S&P 500 (diagonal lines). We can see that over longer time horizons (10 years and 20 years), the returns to venture capital dominate those of the S&P 500. A several hundred basis point premium is demonstrated across each stage of venture capital. Even the five-year

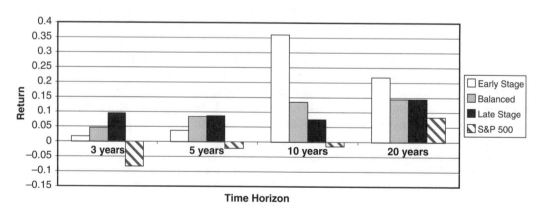

Exhibit 23.2   Returns to venture capital versus S&P 500

Source: National Venture Capital Association.

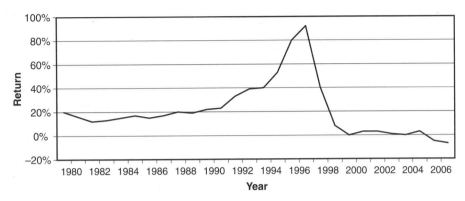

Exhibit 23.3   Vintage-year internal rates of return

Source: National Venture Capital Association.

returns to venture capital show a premium over the public stock market, but these returns include the disastrous public equity year of 2008. Recent venture capital returns (three-year performance) also shows a premium of venture versus public markets.[4]

The old saying that "what's good for the goose is good for the gander" is particularly true for the public and private equity markets. When the public equity markets provide solid investment returns, the opportunity for venture capital investments to be harvested at excellent rates of return is even better. Conversely, a weak public stock market can be the kiss of death to venture capital returns.

This "goose and gander" analogy is demonstrated in Exhibit 23.3. These are vintage-year internal rates of return (IRRs) on venture capital funds. This chart demonstrates the average return to venture capital funds started in different years. Although not separated out in this exhibit, vintage years are a way to compare venture capital funds on equal footing. Different economic circumstances and business cycle years can affect the returns to a venture capital fund depending on the year in which it was started. Vintage-year analysis corrects this problem by looking at venture capital funds that were started in the same year.

As shown in Exhibit 23.3, there was a significant increase in vintage-year IRRs toward the end of the 1990s. This was due to the tech bubble and the dot-com frenzy that built up around anything associated with the Internet. Remember when the clicks were going to take over the bricks? In any event, the tech bubble burst, and since then, vintage-year IRRs have yielded significantly lower results.

Exhibit 23.4 plots the value of the NASDAQ Composite index compared to the S&P 500 and the Dow Jones Industrial Average from the beginning of 1995 through the end of 2006.[5] The thick line represents the value of the NASDAQ, while the thin line is the S&P 500 and the dashed line represents the Dow Jones Industrial Average. As can be seen, the NASDAQ closely tracked the valuations of the S&P 500 and the Dow until the beginning of 1999. Then valuations began to diverge, with the NASDAQ soaring in value compared to the S&P 500 and the Dow. This created a valuation bubble fueled by the belief that technology stocks would take over the world and create a new economic paradigm that would defy basic principles of cash flows and valuation. However, the bubble burst in 2000 when new technology companies failed to produce the earnings and revenue growth forecast by

---

[4] See Keith Ambachtsheer, "How Should Pension Funds Managed Risk?" *Journal of Applied Corporate Finance* (Summer 1998), 1–6.

[5] To compare the values of these stock indices, we measure the value of $1,000 invested in each index over the period January 1995 through December 2005.

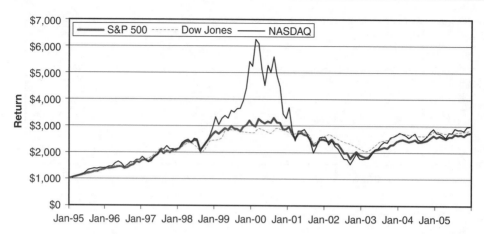

Exhibit 23.4   The technology bubble

Source: Bloomberg Finance, L.P.

optimistic Wall Street analysts. By the beginning of 2001, these three stock indices had converged back to similar values. As Exhibit 23.4 shows, the bubble quickly deflated, and by 2001, the valuations of technology companies listed on the NASDAQ had converged back to similar valuations for more traditional companies comprising the Dow Jones Industrial Average as well as for the S&P 500. Last, we mentioned previously that access to top-tier managers is a key to successful venture capital investing. Simply, success breeds success. The difference between top-quartile venture capital managers and bottom quartile managers is large, up to 20% annually. Notice that the returns in Exhibit 23.3 peak before those in Exhibit 23.4. This may seem a bit odd, so it is important to remember that Exhibit 23.3 is based on vintage-year returns. That is, vintage-year returns are based on the full 10-year investment cycle of the venture capital fund. For example, the vintage-year returns peak in 1997 in Exhibit 23.3. This reflects the 10-year IRRs earned by venture capital funds started in 1997, not just the venture capital returns from the year 1997. Similarly, venture capital funds started in 1998 will reflect the IIRs for the full 10 years of their investment cycle through 2007, and so on. Those venture capital funds with vintage years in the mid-1990s did the best because they were able to exit their investments at the height of the tech bubble and reap the most rewards. That is why vintage-year returns in Exhibit 23.3 peak before the popping of the tech bubble shown in Exhibit 23.4.

Exhibit 23.5 plots the returns to the different stages of venture capital and the returns to top-quartile performers, median performers, and bottom-quartile performers. The difference or delta

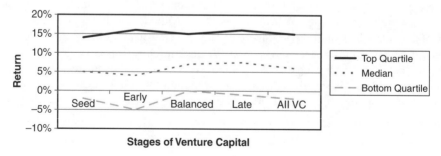

Exhibit 23.5   Top-quartile, bottom-quartile, and median VC returns

Source: National Venture Capital Association.

between top-quartile and bottom-quartile performers ranges from 15% for balanced VC funds to 21% for early stage VC funds.

It has been documented that return performance is very persistent in the private equity industry. Venture capital managers that perform well in one VC fund tend to perform well in their next VC fund.[6]

This return persistence is very different from that of other asset classes like large-cap public equities or fixed income, where the marketplace is much more liquid and competitive. Quite a bit of this performance persistence can be explained by the reputation of the general partner that manages the venture capital fund. The best venture capital firms attract the very best entrepreneurs, business plans, and investment opportunities. The most successful venture capital firms have an established track record of getting start-up companies to an initial public offering (IPO) of stock. This allows them to attract investment capital from their limited partners as well as proprietary deal flow from start-up companies seeking venture capital. The general partner of a better-performing venture capital fund is more likely to raise a follow-on fund and to raise larger funds than a venture capital firm that performs poorly.

ROLE OF A VENTURE CAPITALIST

Venture capitalists have two roles within the industry. Raising money from investors is just the first part. The second is to invest that capital with start-up companies. Venture capitalists are not passive investors. Once they invest in a company, they take an active role either in an advisory capacity or as a director on the board of the company. They monitor the progress of the company, implement incentive plans for the entrepreneurs and management, and establish financial goals for the company. Besides providing management insight, venture capitalists usually have the right to hire and fire key managers, including the original entrepreneur. They also provide access to consultants, accountants, lawyers, investment bankers, and, most important, other businesses that might purchase the start-up company's product. In this section we focus on the relationship between the venture capitalist and his investors. In the next section we consider the process by which a venture capitalist selects investments.

Relationship of the venture capitalist to her investors

Before a venture capitalist can invest money with start-up ventures, she must go through a period of fund-raising with outside investors. Most venture capital funds are structured as limited partnerships where the venture capitalist is the general partner and the investors are limited partners. Each venture capital fund first goes through a period of fund-raising before it begins to invest the capital raised from the limited partners.

The venture capitalist, or her company, is the general partner of the venture capital fund. All other investors are limited partners. As the general partner, the venture capitalist has full operating authority to manage the fund as he pleases, subject to restrictions placed in the covenants of the fund's documents.

As the venture capital industry grew and matured through the 1980s and 1990s, sophisticated investors such as pension funds, endowments, foundations, and high-net-worth individuals began to demand that contractual provisions be placed in the documents and subscription agreements that establish and govern a private equity fund. These covenants ensure that the venture capitalist sticks

---

[6] See Steven Kaplan and Antoinette Schoar, "Private Equity Performance: Returns, Persistence, and Capital Flows," *Journal of Finance* 60 (August 2005), 1791–1823.

to her knitting and operates in the best interest of the limited partners who have invested in the venture capital fund.

These protective covenants can be broken down into three broad classes of investor protections: (1) covenants relating to the overall management of the fund, (2) covenants that relate to the activities of the general partner, and (3) covenants that determine what constitutes a permissible investment.[7]

Restrictions on the management of the venture capital fund

Typically, the most important covenant is the size of an investment by the venture capital fund in any one start-up venture. This is typically expressed as a percentage of the capital committed to the venture capital fund. The purpose is to ensure that the venture capitalist does not commit too much capital to a single investment. In any venture capital fund, there will be start-up ventures that fail to generate a return. This is expected. By diversifying across several venture investments, this risk is mitigated.

Other covenants may include a restriction on the use of debt or leverage by the venture capitalist. Venture capital investments are risky enough without the venture capitalist gearing up the fund through borrowing.

In addition, there may be a restriction on co-investments with prior or future funds controlled by the venture capitalist. If a venture capitalist has made a poor investment in a prior fund, the investors in the current fund do not want the venture capitalist to throw good money after bad. Furthermore, there is usually a covenant regarding the distribution of profits. It is optimal for investors to receive the profits as they accrue. Distributed profits reduce the amount of committed capital in the venture fund, which in turn reduces the fees paid to the venture capitalist. It is in the venture capitalist's economic interest to hold on to profits, while investors prefer to have them distributed as they accrue.

Restrictions on the activities of the general partner

Primary among restrictions on the general partner's activities is a limit on the amount of private investments the venture capitalist can make in any of the firms funded by the venture capital fund. If the venture capitalist makes private investments on her own in a select group of companies, these companies may receive more attention than the remaining portfolio of companies contained in the venture fund.

In addition, general partners are often limited in their ability to sell their general partnership interest in the venture fund to a third party. Such a sale would likely reduce the general partner's incentive to monitor and produce an effective exit strategy for the venture fund's portfolio companies.

Two other covenants relate to keeping the venture capitalist's eye on the ball. The first is a restriction on the amount of future fund-raising. Fund-raising is time-consuming and distracting; less time is spent managing the investments of the existing fund. Also, the limited partners typically demand that the general partner spend substantially all of his time on managing the investments of the fund; outside interests are limited or restricted.

Restrictions on the type of investments

Generally, these covenants serve to keep venture capitalists focused on investing in those companies, industries, and transactions where she has the greatest experience. So, for instance, there may be restrictions or prohibitions on investing in leveraged buyouts, other venture capital funds, foreign securities, or companies and industries outside the realm of the venture capitalist's expertise.

---

[7] See Josh Lerner, *Venture Capital and Private Equity* (New York: John Wiley & Sons, 2000).

Venture capital fees

Venture capitalists have the potential to earn two types of fees: a management fee and an incentive fee (percentage of the profits earned by the venture fund). Management fees can range anywhere from 1% to 3.5% with most venture capital funds in the 2% to 2.5% range. Management fees are used to compensate venture capitalists while they look for attractive investment opportunities for their venture capital funds.

A key point to remember is that the management fee is assessed on the amount of committed capital, not invested capital. Consider the following example: The venture capitalist raises $100 million in committed capital for her venture fund. The management fee is 2.5%. To date, only $50 million of the raised capital has been invested in start-ups. The annual management fee that the venture capitalist collects is $2.5 million, 2.5% × $100 million, even though not all of the capital has been invested. Investors pay the management fee on the amount of capital they have agreed to commit to the venture fund whether or not that capital has actually been invested.

Consider the implications of this fee arrangement. The venture capitalist collects a management fee from the moment that an investor signs a subscription agreement to invest capital in the venture fund, even though no capital has actually been contributed by the limited partners yet. Further, the venture capitalist then has a call option to demand, according to the subscription agreement, that the investors contribute capital when the venture capitalist finds an appropriate investment for the fund. This is a great deal for the venture capitalist; he is paid a large fee to have a call option on the limited partners' capital: not a bad business model. We will see later that this has some keen implications for leveraged buyout funds.

The second part of the remuneration for a venture capitalist is in the form of profit-sharing or incentive fees. This is really where venture capitalists make her money. Incentive fees provide the venture capitalist with a share of the profits generated by the venture fund. The typical incentive fee is 20% but the better-known venture capital funds can charge up to 35%. That is, the best venture capitalists can claim over one-third of the profits generated by the venture fund.

Similar to our discussion of hedge fund incentive fees, the incentive fees for venture capital funds represent a free option. If the venture capitalist generates profits for the venture fund, he can collect a share of these profits. If the venture fund loses money, the venture capitalist does not collect an incentive fee, but loses nothing beyond reputational damage. This binary fee payout can be described as:

$$\text{Payout on incentive fee} = \text{Max}(i \times \text{Profits}, 0) \qquad (23.1)$$

where

$i =$ the percent of profit sharing by the venture capitalist (e.g. 20%)
Profits $=$ the profits generated by the venture fund

Equation 23.1 is the basic equation for the payout on a call option. Similar to our option pricing model for hedge fund incentive fees, this option has significant value to the venture capitalist. Further, valued within an option context, venture capital profit-sharing fees provide some interesting incentives to the venture capitalist.

For example, one way to increase the value of a call option is to increase the volatility of the underlying asset. This means that the venture capitalist is encouraged to make riskier investments with the pool of capital in the venture fund to maximize the value of his incentive fee.

This increased risk may run counter to the desires of the limited partners to maintain a less risky profile. Further, it is fascinating to realize that this incentive fee is costless to the venture capitalist, he does not pay any price for the receipt of this option. Indeed, the venture capitalist gets paid a management fee in addition to this free call option on the profits of the venture fund. As we noted earlier, this is not a bad business model for the venture capitalist.

Fortunately, there is a check and balance on incentive fees in the venture capital world. Most, if not all, venture capital limited partnership agreements include some restrictive covenants on when incentive fees may be paid to the venture capitalist. The three primary covenants used are as follows:

First, most venture capital partnership agreements include a **clawback** provision. A clawback covenant allows the limited partners to claw back previously paid incentive fees to the venture capitalist if, at the end/liquidation of the venture fund, the limited partners are still out of pocket some costs or have lost investment capital. This prevents the venture capitalist from earning an incentive fee if the limited partners do not earn a profit.

Second, there is often an escrow agreement where a portion of the venture capitalist incentive fees are held in a segregated escrow account until the fund is liquidated. Again, this ensures that the venture capitalist does not walk away with any profit unless the limited partners also earn a profit. Only after a profit has been earned by every limited partner are the escrow proceeds released to the venture capitalist.

Last, there is often a prohibition on the distribution of profit-sharing fees to the venture capitalist until all committed capital is paid back to the limited partners. In other words, the limited partners must first be paid back their invested capital before profits may be shared in the venture fund. Sometimes, this covenant may stipulate that all management fees must also be recouped by the limited partners before the venture capitalist can collect his incentive fees.

Just as a side observation, it is interesting to note that these types of profit-sharing covenants are seldom incorporated into hedge fund limited partnership agreements.

THE BUSINESS PLAN

The venture capitalist has two constituencies: investors on the one hand, and start-up portfolio companies on the other. In the prior section we discussed the relationship between the venture capitalist and her investors. In this section we discuss how a venture capitalist selects her investments for the venture fund.

The most important document on which a venture capitalist will base her decision to invest in a start-up company is the business plan. The business plan must be comprehensive, coherent, and internally consistent.

It must clearly state the business strategy, identify the niche that the new company will fill, and describe the resources needed to fill that niche. This is not the time to fake it—the business plan must include not only the potential financial rewards, but also the risks and competitive challenges facing the start-up company. Keep in mind that the business plan has two key objectives: (1) to secure financing from a venture capitalist and (2) to serve as an internal game plan for the development of the start-up company.

The business plan also reflects the start-up management team's ability to develop and present an intelligent and strategic plan of action. Therefore, the business plan not only describes the business opportunity but also gives the venture capitalist an insight into the overall strength of the management team.

Last, the business plan must be realistic. One part of every business plan is the assumptions about revenue growth, cash burn rate, additional rounds of capital injection, and expected date of profitability and/or IPO status. The financial goals stated in the business plan must be achievable. Additionally, financial milestones identified in the business plan can become important conditions for the vesting of management equity, the release of deferred investment commitments, and the control of the board of directors.

In this section we review the key elements of a business plan for a start-up venture. This is the heart and soul of the venture capital industry—it is where new ideas are born and capital is committed.

Executive summary

The executive summary is the opening statement of any business plan.

In this short synopsis, the management team must clearly define the unique selling point of the start-up venture. Is it a new product, distribution channel, manufacturing process, design, or consumer service? Whatever it is, it must be spelled out well enough for a nontechnical person to understand.[8]

The executive summary should quickly summarize the nine main parts of the business plan:

1. The market.
2. The product or service.
3. Intellectual property rights.
4. The management team.
5. Operations and prior operating history.
6. Financial projections.
7. Amount of financing.
8. Schedule.
9. Exit opportunities.

We next discuss briefly each part of the business plan.

The market

The key issue here is whether there is a viable commercial opportunity for the start-up venture. The first question is whether there already is an existing market. If the answer is yes, this is both good and bad. It is good because the commercial opportunity has already been demonstrated by someone else. It is bad because someone else has already developed a product or service to meet the existing demand.

This raises the issue of competition. Virtually every new product already has some competition at the outset. It is most unlikely that the product or service is so revolutionary such that there exists no form of competition. Even if the start-up venture is first to market, there must be an explanation on how this gap in the market is currently being filled with existing (but deficient) solutions.

An existing product makes a prima facie case for market demand, but then the start-up venture must describe how its product/service improves upon the existing market solution. Further, if there is an existing product, the start-up venture should make a direct product comparison, including price, quality, length of warranty, ease of use, product distribution, and target audience.

In addition to a review of the competition, the start-up venture must describe its marketing plan. This should encompass three elements: pricing, product distribution, and promotion.

Pricing is clear enough. If the product is first to market, it may be able to command a price premium, initially at least. But in today's electronic markets for example, pricing power can erode rapidly. The start-up venture must describe its initial expected margins, but also how those margins will likely be impacted over time as technology advances.

Product distribution is simply a description of how the start-up venture will get its product to market. Will it use wholesalers, retailers, the Internet, or direct sales? Is a sales force needed? Is a 24-hour help desk required? Also, different distribution channels may require different pricing. For

---

[8] See British Venture Capital Association, "A Guide to Private Equity," white paper, October 2004.

instance, wholesalers will need price discounts to be able to make a profit when they sell to retailers, or the start-up company may wish to offer a discount to those that order the product directly from the start-up venture.

Last, the start-up venture must describe its promotion strategy, including a discussion of trade shows, the Internet, mass media, and tie-ins to other products. The start-up venture should indicate whether its product will be marketed to a targeted audience or whether it has mass appeal. Finally, the cost of promotional materials and events must be evaluated as part of the business plan.

The product or service

A description of the product or service should be done along every dimension that establishes the start-up venture's unique selling point. Furthermore, this discussion must be done in plain English without psychobabble or the jargon that normally creeps into the explanation of technology products.

In fact, the key objective of this section of the business plan is to clearly delineate the unique selling point of the product or service. Is it new to the market, available at a lower price, of higher quality, produced more efficiently or rapidly, provided with better customer service, smaller in size, and/or easier to operate? Each of these points can provide a competitive advantage on which to build a new product or service.

One-shot, single products are a concern for a venture capitalist. The upside will inevitably be limited as competition is drawn into the market. Therefore, business plans that address a second generation of products are generally preferred.

Intellectual property rights

The third essential part of the business plan is a discussion of intellectual property rights. To illustrate the importance of this part of the business plan, let us take a look at Exhibit 23.6, which provides a view of the industries to which venture capital flowed in 2008. The majority of beneficiaries came from the technology sector, such as computer software, telecommunications, biotechnology, and semiconductors, although health care and medical devices represented two other growth industries.

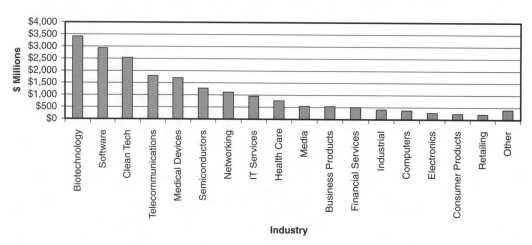

Exhibit 23.6   Uses of venture capital, 2008

Source: PricewaterhouseCoopers/MoneyTree.

Most start-ups in the technology and other growth sectors base their business opportunity on the development and ownership of proprietary technology. It is very important that a start-up's claim and rights to that intellectual property be absolute. Any intellectual property owned by the company must be clearly and unequivocally assigned to the company by third parties (usually the entrepreneur and management team). A structure where the entrepreneur still owns the intellectual property but licenses it to the start-up company is disfavored by venture capitalists because license agreements can expire or be terminated, leaving the venture capitalist with a shell of a start-up company.

Generally, before a venture capitalist invests with a start-up company, it will conduct patent and trademark searches, seek the opinion of a patent counsel, and possibly ask third parties to confidentially evaluate the technology owned by the start-up company. Additionally, the venture capitalist may require key employees to sign noncompetition agreements, where they agree not to start another company or join another company operating in the same sector as the start-up for a reasonable period of time. Key employees may also be asked to sign nondisclosure agreements to further protect a start-up company's proprietary technology.

The start-up management team

Venture capitalists invest in ideas and people. Once the venture capitalist has reviewed the start-up venture's unique selling point, he will turn to the management team. Ideally, the management team should have complementary skill sets: marketing, technology, finance, and operations. Every management team has gaps. The business plan must carefully address how these gaps will be filled.

The venture capitalist will closely review the resumes of every member of the management team. Academic backgrounds, professional work history, and references will all be checked. Most important to the venture capitalist will be the professional background of the management team. In particular, a management team that has successfully brought a previous start-up company to the IPO stage will be viewed most favorably.

In general, a great management team with a good business plan will be viewed more favorably than a good management team with a great business plan. The best business plan in the world can still fail from inability to execute. Therefore, a management team that has previously demonstrated the ability to follow and execute a business plan will be seen as more likely to succeed than an unproven management team, even one with a great business opportunity. However, this is where a venture capitalist can add value. Recognizing a great business opportunity but a weak management team, the venture capitalist can bring his or her expertise to the start-up company as well as additional, outside seasoned management professionals. While this often creates some friction with the original entrepreneur, the ultimate goal is to make money. Egos often succumb when there is money to be made.

In addition to filling in the gaps of the management team, the venture capitalist will need to round out the board of directors of the start-up venture. At a minimum, one seat on the board will be filled by a member of the venture capitalist's own team. However, other directors may be added to fill in some of the gaps found among the management team, such as distribution expertise. The venture capitalist may also ask an executive from an established company to sit on the board of the start-up to provide contacts with potential strategic buyers. In addition, a seasoned board member from a successful company can lend credibility to a start-up venture when it decides to go public (see our case study on CacheFlow/Blue Coat at the end of this chapter).

Last, the management team will need a seasoned chief financial officer (CFO). This will be the person primarily responsible for bringing the start-up company public. The CFO will work with the investment bankers to establish the price of the company's stock at the initial public offering. Since an IPO is often the exit strategy used by venture capitalists as well as founders and key employees, it is critical that the CFO have IPO experience.

Operations and prior operating history

The operations section of the business plan discusses how the product will be built or the service delivered. This will include a discussion of production facilities, labor requirements, raw materials, tax incentives, regulatory approvals, and distribution. In addition, if a prototype has not yet been developed, then the business plan must lay out a cost-estimate and time line for its production. Cost of production must be discussed because this will feed into the gross margin discussion underlying the financial projections (see the next subsection). Last, barriers to entry should be described. While there might be a higher cost of production at the outset, it may also prevent competition from entering the market later.

Venture capitalists are not always the first investors in a start-up company. In fact, they may be the third source of financing for a company. Many start-up companies begin by seeking capital from friends, family members, and business associates. Next they may seek a so-called angel investor: a wealthy private individual or an institution that invests capital with the company but does not take an active role in managing or directing the strategy of the company. Then come the venture capitalists.

As a result, a start-up company may already have a prior history before presenting its business plan to a venture capitalist. At this stage, venture capitalists ensure that the start-up company does not have any unusual history such as a prior bankruptcy or failure.

The venture capitalist will also closely review the equity stakes that have been previously provided to family, friends, business associates, and angel investors. These equity stakes should be clearly identified in the business plan, and any unusual provisions must be fully understood and documented. Equity interests can include common stock, preferred stock, convertible securities, rights, warrants, and stock options. There must still be sufficient equity and upside potential for the venture capitalist to invest. Finally, all prior security issues must be properly documented and must comply with applicable securities laws.

The venture capitalist will review the company's articles of incorporation to determine whether it is in good legal standing in the state of incorporation. Further, the venture capitalist will examine the company's bylaws and the minutes of any shareholder and board of directors meetings. The minutes of the meetings can indicate whether the company has a clear sense of direction or is mired in indecision.

Financial projections

The previous discussion on operations and production costs leads right into the financial projections. A comprehensive set of financial statements is required, including income statement, balance sheet, and cash flow projections. These projections must be realistic but at the same time attractive enough to the venture capitalist to warrant the investment of capital.

First, the income statement must show in which year breakeven will be achieved. Most business plans show a profit being turned by the third year after initial financing. The income statement should include realistic sales forecasts, allowances for discounts, clear numbers for the cost of goods sold, and reasonable estimates of marketing and other overhead costs. Both gross and net margins must meet the return requirements of the venture capitalist.

The balance sheet is an important determinant of when to add debt and other forms of financing to the capital structure of the start-up venture. Also, the balance sheet should accurately reflect receivables from the sale of the product as well as reasonable assumptions about the timing and collection of those receivables.

Last, the cash flow statement provides the venture capitalist with a realistic burn rate for the cash on hand. Initially, all firms require infusions of capital to fund their working capital. However, at some point in time, the start-up venture must become self-financing such that its operating and expansion capital needs can be drawn solely from the sale of its products.

All of these financial projections need to be tested under a variety of possible scenarios. What happens if a new competitor comes to the market quickly or the economy falls into recession? Generally, the forecasts should include a base case, a pessimistic case, and an optimistic case for projected sales growth.

Amount of financing

This section of the business plan gets down to brass tacks: How much money is the start-up venture requesting? This ties in neatly with the financial projections. As part of the assessment of cash flows, the start-up company needs to estimate its burn rate. The **burn rate** is simply the rate at which the start-up venture uses cash on a monthly basis. The amount of financing requested must be equal to the burn rate over the time horizon anticipated by the start-up venture.

Schedule

Sometimes this is included in the section on financing, but other times it appears as a stand-alone part of the business plan. In any event, the entrepreneur must establish a schedule of product development that parallels the stages of financing. How long will it take to go from a beta product to a fully marketable/salable product? And what will be the stages of financing along the way? A business plan for a service typically requires fewer stages of financing. Conversely, product development may need a first, second, and third stage of financing before becoming marketable.

The schedule can be as finely parsed as monthly or quarterly. Included might be a timetable for the completion of prototypes, stages of beta testing, early sales hurdles, the timing of key personnel hires, expansion of plant capacity, and the necessary infusions of capital.

Exit plan

Eventually, the venture capitalist must liquidate her investment in the start-up company to realize a gain for herself and her investors. When a venture capitalist reviews a business plan, he will keep in mind the timing and probability of an exit strategy.

An exit strategy is another way the venture capitalist can add value beyond providing start-up financing. Venture capitalists often have many contacts within established operating companies. An established company may be willing to acquire the start-up company for its technology as part of a strategic expansion of its product line. Alternatively, venture capitalists maintain close ties with investment bankers. These bankers will be necessary if the start-up company decides to seek an IPO. In addition, a venture capitalist may ask other venture capitalists to invest in the start-up company. This helps to spread the risk as well as provide additional sources of contacts with operating companies and investment bankers.

Venture capitalists almost always invest in the convertible preferred stock of the start-up company. There may be several rounds (or series) of preferred stock financing before a start-up company goes public. Convertible preferred shares are the favored manner of investment because they are senior to common stock in terms of dividends, voting rights, and liquidation preferences. Furthermore, venture capitalists have the option to convert their shares to common stock when exiting via an IPO.

Other investment structures used by venture capitalists include convertible notes or debentures that provide for the conversion of the principal amount of the note or bond into either common or preferred shares at the option of the venture capitalist. Convertible notes and debentures may also be converted upon the occurrence of an event such as a merger, an acquisition, or an IPO. Venture capitalists may also be granted warrants to purchase the common equity of the start-up company as well as stock rights in the event of an IPO.

Other exit strategies used by venture capitalists are redemption rights and put options. Usually, these strategies are used as part of a company reorganization. Redemption rights and put options are generally not favored because they do not provide as large a rate of return as an acquisition or IPO. These strategies are often used as a last resort when there are no other viable alternatives. Redemption rights and put options are typically negotiated at the time the venture capitalist makes an investment in the start-up company (often called the registration rights agreement).

Usually, venture capitalists require no less than the minimum return provided for in the liquidation preference of a preferred stock investment. Alternatively, the redemption rights or put option might be established by a common stock equivalent value that is usually determined by an investment banking appraisal. Last, redemption rights or put option values may be based on a multiple of sales or earnings. Some redemption rights take the highest of all three valuation methods: the liquidation preference, the appraisal value, or the earnings or sales multiple.

In sum, there are many issues a venture capitalist must sort through before funding a start-up company. These issues range from identifying the business opportunity to addressing legal and regulatory issues. Along the way, the venture capitalist must assess the quality of the management team, prior capital infusions, status of proprietary technology, operating history (if any) of the company, and timing and likelihood of an exit strategy.

CURRENT STRUCTURE OF THE VENTURE CAPITAL INDUSTRY

The structure of the venture capital industry has changed dramatically over the past 20 years. We focus on three major changes: sources of venture capital financing, venture capital investment vehicles, and specialization within the industry.

Sources and uses of venture capital financing

The structure of the venture capital marketplace has changed considerably since 1985. What is most notable is the change in leading sources of venture capital financing. For example, over the period 1985–1990, the leading source of venture capital financing was pension funds. This came as a result of the revisions to the prudent person standard for pension fund investing in 1979. Over the 1985–1990 period, pension funds accounted for nearly 70% of all venture capital funding. Endowments and intermediaries were a smaller source of venture capital funds. Also, from 1985 to 1990, government agencies accounted for about 11% of the total source of venture capital funds.[9]

By 2008, however, the landscape of venture capital financing had changed considerably. Funding by pension funds had dropped from 70% to less than 50%. Government agencies supplied almost no venture capital in 2008, having been squeezed out by private sources. The federal and state governments no longer needed to support the venture capital industry. Virtually all money now comes from institutional and other investors willing to take the risk of start-up companies in return for sizable gains.

To replace the decline of pension funds and government agencies, three new sources of venture capital funds have grown over the past 20 years: endowments and foundations, intermediaries, and family offices. Endowments, with their perpetual investment horizons, are natural investors for private equity. Also, as the wealth of the United States has grown, wealthy individuals have allocated a greater share of their wealth to venture capital investments. In addition, a new and powerful player

---

[9] See Steven Lipin, "Venture Capitalists 'R' Us," *Wall Street Journal*, February 22, 2000, C1.

has entered into the venture capital world over the past decade: the sovereign wealth fund (SWF). SWFs have grown in importance, from Middle Eastern state plans with funding from oil revenues to funds of prosperous nations like the Government Investment Corporation of Singapore. Last, intermediaries such as private equity funds of funds, consultants, and yes, even hedge funds, have entered the venture capital market.

Exhibit 23.7 demonstrates the changing sources of venture capital financing in the United States. Exhibit 23.6, presented earlier, demonstrates another trend in the venture capital industry, the surge in financing of Internet-related companies. In 2008 alone, nearly $20 billion flowed into internet-related start-up ventures. Exhibit 23.6 is the complement to Exhibit 23.7; it presents the uses of venture capital financing.

Technology-related companies still receive the lion's share of venture capital financing, but clean technology and medical devices are two fast-growing sectors of the venture capital industry. In general, the bursting of the Internet bubble saw the venture capital industry return to funding legitimate business plans.

Venture capital investment vehicles

As the demand for venture capital investments has increased, venture capitalists have responded by creating new financing vehicles. These include limited partnerships, limited liability companies, corporate venture funds and venture capital funds of funds.

Limited partnerships

The predominant form of venture capital investing in the United States is the limited partnership. Most venture capital funds operate as either as 3(c)(1) or 3(c)(7) funds to avoid registration as an investment company under the Investment Company Act of 1940. The same regulatory exemptions apply to venture capital funds.

As a limited partnership, all income and capital gains flow through the partnership to the limited partner investors. The partnership itself is not taxed. The appeal of the limited partnership vehicle has increased since 1996 with the "check the box" provision of the U.S. tax code.

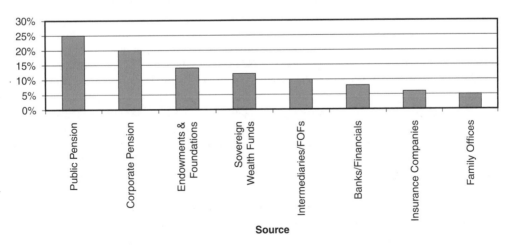

Exhibit 23.7   Sources of venture capital commitments

Source: Pricewaterhouse Coopers/MoneyTree.

Previously, limited partnerships had to meet several tests to determine whether their predominant operating characteristics resembled a partnership more than a corporation. Such characteristics included, for instance, a limited term of existence. Failure to qualify as a limited partnership would mean double taxation for the investment fund, first at the fund level and second at the investor level.

This changed with the U.S. Internal Revenue Service's decision to let entities simply decide their own tax status by checking a box on their annual tax form as to whether they wished to be taxed as a corporation or as a partnership. "Checking the box" greatly encouraged investment funds to establish themselves as limited partnerships.

Limited partnerships are generally formed with an expected life of 10 years with an option to extend the limited partnership for another one to five years. The limited partnership is managed by a general partner who has day-to-day responsibility for managing the venture capital fund's investments as well as general liability for any lawsuits that may be brought against the fund. The general partner is typically the venture capital firm that put together the venture capital fund. Limited partners, as their name implies, have only a limited (investor) role in the partnership. They do not take part in the management of the fund nor do they bear any liability beyond their committed capital.

All partners in the fund agree to commit a specific investment amount at the formation of the limited partnership. However, the limited partners do not contribute money to the fund until the money is called down or "taken down" by the general partner. Usually, the general partner will give one to two months' notice of when it intends to make additional capital calls on the limited partners. Capital calls are made when the general partner has found a start-up company in which to invest. The general partner can make capital calls up to the amount of the limited partners' initial commitments.

An important element of limited partnership venture funds is that the general partner/venture capitalist has also committed investment capital to the fund. This assures the limited partners of an alignment of interests with the venture capitalist. Typically, limited partnership agreements specify a percentage or dollar amount of capital that the general partner must commit to the partnership.

Limited liability companies

Another financing vehicle in the venture capital industry is the limited liability company (LLC). Similar to a limited partnership, all items of net income or loss as well as capital gains are passed through to the shareholders in the LLC. Also, like a limited partnership, an LLC must adhere to the safe harbors as defined by the Investment Company Act of 1940. In addition, LLCs usually have a life of 10 years with possible options to extend for another one to five years.

The managing director of an LLC acts like the general partner of a limited partnership. The managing director has management responsibility for the LLC, including the decision to invest the committed capital of the LLC's shareholders in start-up companies. The managing director of the LLC might itself be another LLC or a corporation. (The same is true for limited partnerships, the general partner need not be an individual; it can be a legal entity like a corporation.)

In sum, LLCs and limited partnerships accomplish the same goal, the pooling of investor capital into a central fund from which to make venture capital investments. The choice depends on the type of investor sought. If the venture capitalist wishes to raise funds from a large number of passive and relatively uninformed investors, the limited partnership vehicle is the preferred venue. However, if the venture capitalist intends to raise capital from a small group of knowledgeable investors, the LLC is preferred.

The reason is twofold. First, LLCs usually have more specific shareholder rights and privileges. These privileges are best utilized with a small group of well-informed investors. Second, an LLC structure provides shareholders with control over the sale of additional shares in the LLC to new shareholders. This provides the shareholders more power with respect to the twin issues of increasing the LLC's pool of committed capital and controlling who will commit that capital.

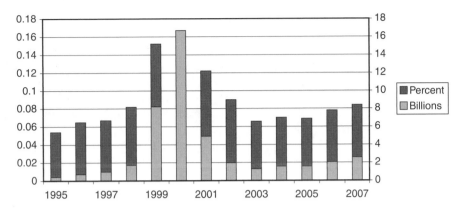

Exhibit 23.8   Corporate venture capital programs

Corporate venture capital funds

With the explosive growth of technology companies in the late 1990s, many found themselves flush with large cash balances. Microsoft, for example, had current assets (cash, cash equivalents, and receivables) of over $43.2 billion and generated a free cash flow of over $21.6 billion in 2008. These companies needed to invest this cash to earn an appropriate rate of return for their investors.

A corporate venture capital fund is an ideal use for a portion of a company's cash. First, venture capital financing is consistent with Microsoft's own past; it was funded with venture capital over 25 years ago. Second, Microsoft can provide its own technological expertise to help a start-up company. Last, the start-up company can provide new technology and cost savings to Microsoft. In a way, financing start-up companies allows Microsoft to think outside of the box without committing or diverting its own personnel to the task.

Corporate venture capital funds are typically formed only with the parent company's capital; outside investors are not allowed to join. In addition to Microsoft, other corporate venture funds include Xerox Venture Capital, Hewlett-Packard Co. Corporate Investments, Intel Capital, and Amoco Venture Capital. Investments in start-up companies are a way for large public companies to supplement their internal research and development budgets. In addition to accessing new technology, corporate venture capital funds also gain the ability to generate new products, identify new or diminishing industries, acquire a stake in a future potential competitor, derive attractive returns from excess cash balances, and learn the dynamics of a new marketplace. Exhibit 23.8 shows the amount invested by corporate venture capital programs from 1999 to 2007. It shows both the total dollars invested and the percentage of total venture capital dollars invested in each year. The lightly shaded part of each bar shows the total dollar amount, while the dark-shaded part of the bar shows the percentage of all venture capital invested by corporate programs. Thus in 2000 the percentage invested was just over 16% and the dollar amount was just over $16 billion.

Perhaps the best reason for the existence of corporate venture capital funds is to gain a window on new technology. Consider the case of Supercomputer Systems of Wisconsin. Steve Chen, the former CEO of Cray Research, left Cray to start his own supercomputer company. Cray Research is a supercomputer company that was itself a spin-off from Control Data Corporation, which in turn was an outgrowth of Sperry Corporation. When Steve Chen founded his new company, IBM was one of his first investors even though IBM had shifted its focus from large mainframe computers to laptop computers, personal computers, and service contracts.[10]

---

[10] See Schilit, "Structure of the Venture Capital Industry."

Exhibit 23.9   Intel Capital's venture capital program

Fund	Amount (Millions)
Intel Capital China Technology Fund II	$500
Intel Communications Fund	500
Intel Capital India Technology Fund	250
Intel Digital Home Fund	200
Intel Capital Brazil Technology Fund	50
Intel Capital Middle East and Turkey Fund	50
Total	**$1,550**

Source: www.intel.com/capital/news.

Another example is Intel Capital, Intel Corporation's venture capital subsidiary.[11] The goal of Intel Capital is to develop a strategic investment program that focuses on making equity investments and acquisitions to grow the Internet economy, including the infrastructure, content, and services in support of Intel's main business, which is providing computer chips to power personal and laptop computers. To further this goal, Intel Capital has provided venture capital financing to companies like Peregrine Semiconductor Corporation, a start-up technology company that designs, manufactures, and markets high-speed communications integrated circuits for the broadband fiber-optic, wireless, and satellite communications markets.

Since its founding in 1991, Intel Capital has invested more than $7.5 billion in approximately 1,000 companies in more than 45 countries. Of these 1,000 companies, 212 portfolio companies have been acquired and another 168 have gone public on exchanges around the world, a combined success rate of 38% for start-up ventures. Intel Capital's program is sufficiently mature now that Intel has six separate funds from which to seed start-up ventures. These are presented in Exhibit 23.9.

There are, however, several potential pitfalls to a corporate venture capital program. These may include conflicting goals between the venture capital subsidiary and the corporate parent. In addition, the 5- to 10-year investment horizon for most venture capital investments may be a longer horizon than the parent company's short-term profit requirements. Further, a funded start-up company may be unwilling to be acquired by the parent company. Still, the benefits from corporate venture capital programs appear to outweigh these potential problems. As of 2008, there were almost 100 corporate venture capital subsidiaries in the United States alone.

Another pitfall of corporate venture capital funds is the risk of loss. Just as every venture capitalist experiences occasional losses in portfolio of companies, so too will the corporate venture capitalist. This can translate into significant losses for the parent company. While the Intel Capital program has been very successful, not every corporate venture capital program has been as successful. Take the case of Dell, which took a charge of $200 million in the second quarter of 2001 as a result of losses from Dell Ventures, the company's venture capital fund. In June 2001, Dell reported that its investment portfolio had declined in value by more than $1 billion.[12] Eventually, Dell decided to exit the venture capital business altogether. It sold the remainder of its venture capital portfolio to Lake Street Capital, a San Francisco private equity firm, for $100 million in 2005.

Perhaps the most extreme case of nonperforming corporate venture capital investments is that of Comdisco Inc. Comdisco sought bankruptcy protection in July 2001 after making $3 billion in loans to start-up companies that were unable to repay most of the money.[13] The company wrote off

---

[11] See the Intel web page at www.intel.com/capital/news.

[12] See Joseph Menn, "Tech Giants Lose Big on Start-Up Ventures," *Los Angeles Times,* June 11, 2001.

[13] See Jeff St. Onge, "Comdisco Seeks Bankruptcy Protection from Creditors," *Bloomberg News*, July 16, 2001.

$100 million in loans made by its Comdisco Ventures unit, which leases computer equipment to start-up companies. In addition, Comdisco also took a $206 million reserve against earnings from investments in those ventures.

Venture capital fund of funds

A venture capital fund of funds is a venture pool of capital that, instead of investing directly in start-up companies, invests in other venture capital funds. The venture capital fund of funds is a relatively new phenomenon in the venture capital industry. The general partner of a fund of funds does not select start-up companies in which to invest. Instead, she selects the best venture capitalists with the expectation that they will find appropriate start-up companies to fund.

A venture capital fund of funds offers several advantages to investors. First, the investor receives broad exposure to a diverse range of venture capitalists and, in turn, a wide range of start-up investing. Second, the investor receives the expertise of the fund of funds manager in selecting the best venture capitalists with whom to invest money. Last, a fund of funds may have better access to popular, well-funded venture capitalists whose funds may be closed to individual investors. In return for these benefits, investors pay a management fee (and, in some cases, an incentive fee) to the fund of funds manager. The management fee can range from 0.5% to 2% of the net assets managed.

Fund of funds' investing also offers benefits to the venture capitalists. First, the venture capitalist receives one large investment (from the venture fund of funds) instead of several small investments. This makes fund-raising and investor administration more efficient. Second, the venture capitalist interfaces with an experienced fund of funds' manager instead of several (potentially inexperienced) investors.

Life cycle of a venture capital fund

A venture capital fund is a long-term investment. Typically, investors' capital is locked up for a minimum of 10 years—the standard term of a venture capital limited partnership. During this long investment period, a venture capital fund will normally go through five stages of development.

The first stage is the fund-raising stage where the venture capital firm raises capital from outside investors. Capital is committed—not collected. This is an important distinction noted earlier. Investors sign a legal agreement (typically a subscription) that legally binds them to make cash investments in the venture capital fund up to a certain amount. This is the committed, but not yet drawn, capital. The venture capital firm/general partner will also post a sizable amount of committed capital.

Fund-raising normally takes six months to a year. However, the more successful venture funds such as Kleiner, Perkins, Caufield and Byers typically raise funds in just a few months.

The second stage consists of sourcing investments, reading business plans, preparing intense due diligence on start-up companies, and determining the unique selling point of each start-up company. This period begins the moment the fund is closed to investors and normally takes up the first five years of the venture fund's existence.

During the first two stages, no profits are generated by the venture capital fund. In fact, quite the reverse: the venture capital fund generates losses because the venture capitalist continues to draw annual management fees (which can be up to 3.5% a year of the total committed capital). These fees generate a loss until the venture capitalist begins to extract value from the investments of the venture fund at a later stage.

Stage three is the investment of capital. During this stage, the venture capitalist will determine how much capital to commit to each start-up company, at what level of financing, and in what form of investment (convertible preferred shares, convertible debentures, etc.). At this stage the venture capitalist will also present capital calls to the investors in her venture fund to draw on the capital of the limited partners. Note that no cash flow is generated yet; the venture fund is still in a deficit. It might surprise many investors that they should expect that the value of their investment in a VC fund will drop over the first three to five years. This is because the organizational expenses of the venture capital partnership are deducted immediately before any capital call is made. In addition, management fees are charged as the committed capital is drawn down by the venture capital general partner. All of this means that investors must be braced for a loss on their investment for the first three to five years of a venture capital fund's life. Truly, venture capital is for the long-term investor.

Stage four begins after the funds have been invested and lasts almost to the end of the term of the venture capital fund. During this time the venture capitalist works with the portfolio companies in which the venture capital fund has invested. The venture capitalist may help to improve the management team, establish distribution channels for the new product, refine the prototype product to generate the greatest sales, and generally position the start-up company for an eventual public offering or sale to a strategic buyer. During this time period, the venture capitalist will begin to generate profits for the venture fund and its limited partner investors. These profits will initially offset the previously collected management fees until a positive net asset value is established for the venture fund.

The last stage of the venture capital fund is its windup and liquidation. At this point, all committed capital has been invested and now the venture capitalist is in the harvesting stage. Each portfolio company is either sold to a strategic buyer, brought to the public markets in an initial public offering, or liquidated through a Chapter 7 bankruptcy liquidation process. Profits are distributed to the limited partners, and the general partner/venture capitalist now collects her incentive/profit-sharing fees.

These stages of a venture capital firm lead to what is known as the **J-curve effect**. Exhibit 23.10 demonstrates the J-curve. We can see that during the early life of the venture capital fund, it generates negative revenues (losses); but eventually profits are harvested from successful companies and these

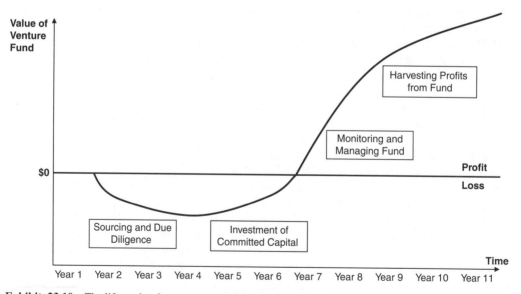

Exhibit 23.10   The life cycle of a venture capital fund

Source: Mark Anson, *Handbook of Alternative Assets*, 2nd ed. (Hoboken, NJ: John Wiley & Sons, 2006). Reprinted with permission of John Wiley & Sons, Inc.

cash flows overcome the initial losses to generate a net profit for the fund. Clearly, given the initial losses that pile up during the first four to five years of a venture capital fund, this type of investing requires patience.

Specialization within the venture capital industry

Like any industry that grows and matures, expansion and maturity lead to specialization. The trend toward specialization in the venture capital industry exists along two dimensions: industry and stage of financing. Specialization is the natural by-product of two factors. First, the enormous amount of capital flowing into venture capital funds has encouraged venture capitalists to distinguish themselves from other funds by narrowing their investment focus. Second, the development of many new technologies over the past decade has encouraged venture capitalists to specialize in order to invest most profitably.

Specialization by industry

Specialization by entrepreneurs is another reason why venture capitalists have tailored their investment domain. Just as entrepreneurs have become more focused in their start-up companies, venture capitalists have followed suit. The biotechnology industry is a good example.

The biotech industry came into being on October 14, 1980, when the stock of Genentech, Inc. went public. On that day, the stock price went from $39 to $85 and a new industry was born. By 2009, Genentech was a Fortune 50 company with a market capitalization of $85 billion. Other successful biotech start-ups include Cetus Corporation, Biogen, Inc., Amgen Corporation, and Centacor, Inc.

The biotech paradigm has changed since the days of Genentech. Genentech was founded on the science of gene mapping and splicing to cure diseases. However, initially it did not have a specific product target. Instead, it was concerned with developing its gene mapping technology without a specific product to market.

Compare this situation to that of Applied Microbiology, Inc. of New York. It has focused on two products with the financial support of Merck and Pfizer, two large pharmaceuticals.[14] One of its products is an antibacterial agent to fight gum disease; a mouthwash containing this agent is to be marketed by Pfizer. Specialized start-up biotech firms have led to specialized venture capital firms. For example, ARCH Venture Partners invests in life science companies that are pioneering in the fields of biopharmaceuticals, bioinformatics, gene therapy, medical devices, and other life science breakthrough technologies. ARCH grew out of the University of Chicago but now is a stand-alone venture capital firm with over $1 billion committed to early stage biotechnology companies.

STAGES OF FINANCING

While some venture capital firms classify themselves by geography or industry, by far the most distinguishing characteristic of venture capital firms is the stage of financing. Some venture capitalists provide first stage or seed capital, while others wait to invest in companies that are further along in their development. Still other venture capital firms come in at the final round of financing before the IPO. A different level of due diligence is required at each level of financing because the start-up venture has achieved another milestone on its way to success. In all, there are five discrete stages of venture capital financing: angel investing, seed capital, first stage capital, second stage/expansion capital, and mezzanine financing. We discuss each of these separately.

---

[14] See W. Keith Schilit, "The Nature of Venture Capital Investments," *Journal of Private Equity* (Winter 1997), 59–75.

Angel investing

Angel investors often come from "F & F": friends and family sometimes venture capitalists include a third "F" for fools. At this stage of the new venture, typically there is a lone entrepreneur who has just an idea, possibly sketched out at the kitchen table or in the garage. There is no formal business plan, no management team, no product, no market analysis, just an idea.

In addition to family and friends, angel investors can also be wealthy individuals who dabble in start-up companies. This level of financing is typically done without a private placement memorandum or subscription agreement. It may be as informal as a cocktail-napkin agreement. Yet, without the angel investor, many ideas would wither on the vine before reaching more traditional venture capitalists.

At this stage of financing, the task of the entrepreneur is to begin the development of a prototype product or service. In addition, the entrepreneur begins drafting a business plan, assessing the market potential and possibly even assembling some key management team members. No marketing or product testing is done at this stage.

The amount of financing at this stage is typically very small, $50,000 to $500,000. Any more than that would strain family, friends, and other angels. The money is used primarily to flesh out the concept to the point where an intelligent business plan can be constructed. Perhaps the single greatest demonstration of angel investing was the initial capital given to Google. Google began as a research project in January 1996 by Larry Page, a Ph.D. student at Stanford University, together with a close friend, Sergey Brin (also a Stanford Ph.D. student). The two transformed a Ph.D. research project into the world's greatest search engine. But first, they needed capital.

Google's first capital infusion came in August 1998. Andy Bechtolsheim, a co-founder of Sun Microsystems, wrote a check to a corporation that did not even exist yet. Although Larry Page and Sergey Brin had put a name to their company, they did not incorporate Google, Inc. until the following month, September 1998. Meanwhile, the check they received from Andy Bechtolsheim had to wait to be cashed until Google could establish a corporate bank account.

Seed capital

Seed capital is the first stage where venture capital firms invest their capital. At this stage, a business plan is completed and presented to a venture capital firm. Some members of the management team will have been assembled at this point, and a market analysis and other parts of the business plan as discussed previously in this chapter will be addressed by the entrepreneur and his small team. Financing is provided to complete the product development and possibly begin initial marketing of the prototype to potential customers. This phase of financing usually raises $1 million to $5 million.

At this stage of financing, a prototype is developed and product testing begins. This is often referred to as **beta testing**, whereby a prototype is sent to potential customers free of charge to get their input into the product's viability, design, and user-friendliness.

Very little, if any, revenue has been generated at this stage, and the company is definitely not profitable. Venture capitalists invest in this stage based on their due diligence of the management team, their own market analysis of the demand for the product, the viability of getting the product to market while there is still time and no other competitor, the additional management team members who will need to be added and the likely timing for additional rounds of capital from the same venture capital firm or from other venture capital funds. Unfortunately, seed capital venture capital firms are not numerous; thus the entrepreneur might have to rely on angel investors through this stage as well.

Examples of seed financing companies are Technology Venture Investors of Menlo Park, California; Advanced Technology Ventures of Boston; and Onsent, located in Silicon Valley.[15]

---

[15] Schilit, "Nature of Venture Capital Investments."

Seed capital venture capitalists tend to be smaller firms because large venture capital firms cannot afford to spend the endless hours with an entrepreneur for a small investment of often no greater than $1 million to $2 million.

Early stage venture capital

The start-up company should now have a viable product that has been beta tested. The next step is to begin **alpha testing**. This is the testing of the second-generation prototype with potential end users. Typically, a price is charged for the product or a fee for the service. Revenues are being generated, and the product/service is now demonstrating its commercial viability. Early stage venture capital financing is usually $2 million and more.

Early stage financing is typically used to build out the commercial-scale manufacturing services. The product is no longer being produced out of the entrepreneur's garage or out of some vacant space above a grocery store. The company is now a going concern with an initial, if not complete, management team. At this stage, there will be at least one venture capitalist sitting on the board of directors of the company. In addition, the business and marketing plans will be refined, manufacturing will have begun, and initial sales will have been established.

The goal of the start-up venture is to achieve market penetration with its product. Some of this will have been accomplished with the beta and alpha testing of the product. However, additional marketing must now be completed. In addition, distribution channels should be identified by now and the product should be established in these channels. Reaching a break-even point is the financial goal.

Late stage/expansion venture capital

At this point the start-up company may have generated its first profitable quarter, or be just at the point of breaking even. Commercial viability is now established. Cash flow management is critical at this stage, as the company is not yet at the level where its cash flows alone can sustain its own growth.

Late stage/expansion capital fills this void. Sometimes late stage/expansion capital is broken down into finer stages called second and third stage venture capital. This level of venture capital financing is used to help the start-up company get through its cash crunch. The additional capital is used to tap into distribution channels, establish call centers, expand manufacturing facilities and attract the additional management and operational talent necessary to make the start-up company a longer-term success. Because this capital is earmarked for expansion, financing needs are typically greater than for seed and early stage capital. Amounts may be in the $5 million to $25 million range.

At this stage, the start-up venture enjoys the growing pains of all successful companies. The future is bright but working capital is short. Sales are snowballing and receivables are growing, but the receivables have not yet been translated into a solid and stable cash flow. The start-up may need additional working capital because it has focused on product development and product sales, but now finds itself with a huge backload of accounts receivable from customers that it must now collect. Inevitably, start-up companies are very good at getting the product out the door but very poor at collecting receivables and turning sales into cold, hard cash. Also, at this stage, market penetration will have been established and the company will have met some initial sales goals. A break-even point will have been achieved, and the company will now start to generate profits even though its cash will still be lagging.

Again, this is where expansion capital can help. Late stage venture financing helps the successful start-up get through its initial cash crunch. Eventually, the receivables will be collected and sufficient internal cash will be generated to make the start-up company a self-sustaining force. Until then, one more round of financing may be needed.

Mezzanine stage

Mezzanine venture capital is the last stage before a start-up company goes public or is sold to a strategic buyer. At this point a second-generation product may already be in production if not distribution. The management team is together and solid, and the company is working on improving its cash flow management. Manufacturing facilities are established, and the company may already be thinking about expanding internationally. Amounts vary depending on how long the bridge financing is meant to last but generally are in the range of $5 million to $25 million.

The financing at this stage is considered bridge or mezzanine financing to keep the company from running out of cash until the IPO or strategic sale. At this stage the company is a proven winner with an established track record. However, the start-up company may still have a large inventory of uncollected accounts receivable that need to be financed in the short-term. Profits are being recorded, but accounts receivable are growing at the same rate as sales.

Mezzanine financing may be in the form of convertible debt. In addition, the company may have sufficient revenue and earning power to qualify for a traditional loan. This means that the start-up company may have to clean up its balance sheet as well as its statement of cash flows. Commercial viability is more than just generating sales; it also requires turning accounts receivable into actual dollars. In addition, mezzanine financing may be used to buy out earlier investors and pay for other costs incurred before going public.

THE J CURVE FOR A START-UP COMPANY

Exhibit 23.11 presents the J curve for a start-up company. Similar to the J curve for a venture capital fund, the initial years of a start-up company generate a loss. Money is spent turning an idea into a prototype product and from there beta testing the product with potential customers. Little or no revenue is generated during this time. It is not until the product goes into alpha testing that revenues may be generated and the start-up becomes a viable concern.

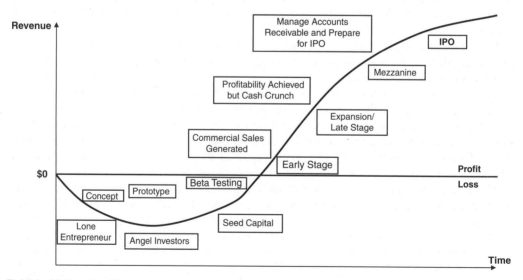

Exhibit 23.11   The life cycle of a start-up company

Source: Mark Anson, *Handbook of Alternative Assets*, 2nd ed. (Hoboken, NJ: John Wiley & Sons, 2006). Reprinted with permission of John Wiley & Sons, Inc.

Once a critical mass is generated—where sales are turned into profits and accounts receivable is turned into cash—then it becomes a matter of timing until the start-up company achieves a public offering. Additional rounds of financing may be needed to get the company to its IPO nirvana. At this point commercial viability is established, but managing the cash crunch becomes critical.

VENTURE CAPITAL CASE STUDY: CACHEFLOW INC./BLUE COAT SYSTEMS

As an example of how different venture capital firms invest at different points of a start-up company life cycle, consider the example of CacheFlow Inc.[16] CacheFlow was founded in 1996 by Michael Malcolm, a renowned computer scientist and former professor at the University of Waterloo in Canada. Malcolm and his team quickly realized that the Internet is inherently slow. Therefore, CacheFlow was founded to produce the first Internet accelerator to speed up applications on the World Wide Web. Internet accelerators allow data to be stored and updated frequently at popular web sites so that users can get them quickly from a cache of data rather than from an original computer server. Thus, CacheFlow was started to produce network caching equipment that would enable the Internet pipeline to flow more efficiently.

CacheFlow started operations with $1 million in seed capital raised from a dozen angel investors in March 1996. From this initial angel investment, CacheFlow was quickly able to assemble a business plan and to seek more formal rounds of venture capital.

In October 1996, only six months after it was funded with angel capital, CacheFlow received its first venture capital infusion, selling 3.2 million shares of Series A convertible preferred stock at 87.5 cents per share ($2.8 million) to Benchmark Capital Partners for a 25% stake in the company. In December 1997, CacheFlow raised a middle round of venture capital financing from U.S. Ventures. U.S. Ventures paid $6 million for Series B convertible preferred stock for 17% of the company. Next, in March 1999, CacheFlow received $8.7 million in late stage venture capital from Technology Crossover Ventures. This venture capital group paid $4.575 a share for Series C convertible preferred stock for 7% of the company. Finally, in November 1999, just before its initial public offering, CacheFlow sold 280,953 shares of Series D preferred stock at a price of $11.04 per share for $3.1 million.

This final sale was an important capstone for CacheFlow before going public. The sale was to one individual, Marc Andreessen, one of the original founders of Netscape and a well-known Silicon Valley entrepreneur. He purchased all of the Series D convertible preferred stock and also joined the CacheFlow board of directors. This provided a significant boost to CacheFlow's public offering.

CacheFlow recorded its first revenue in January 1998. Its products were initially sold to Internet service providers, and later to Fortune 500 companies seeking to improve the functionality of their rapidly growing web sites. At the time of its public offering, CacheFlow had an accumulated deficit of $26.2 million and had lost more than $6 million in its most recent quarter on sales of only $3.6 million.

CacheFlow went public on November 18, 1999, at a price of $24 a share. Its stock price exploded on the first day of trading and closed at $126\frac{3}{8}$ a share, a one-day price increase of $102\frac{3}{8}$ or 427%.

---

[16] For a great case history on a start-up company, see Suzanne McGee, "Venture Capital 'R' Us: CacheFlow: The Life Cycle of a Venture-Capital Deal," *Wall Street Journal* (February 22, 2000), C1. See also "Corporate Profile for CacheFlow," *Business Wire*, May 21, 1999; Mike Strathdee, "Internet Equipment Company, Started by UW Professor, Goes Public," *Toronto Star*, October 6, 1999; Matt Krantz, "CacheFlow IPO Rockets 428%," *USA Today*, November 22, 1999; "CacheFlow Completes Strategic Transition to Web Security Business by Becoming Blue Coat," *Bloomberg News* (August 21, 2002); "Blue Coat Directors Approve One for Five Reverse Stock Split," *Bloomberg News* (September 13, 2002); and "Blue Coat Achieves #1 Market Share in New Security," *Bloomberg News* (July 8, 2003).

Not bad for one day's work. The first day's closing price for CacheFlow gave it a market value approaching $3 billion. Based on the purchase prices for the different series of convertible preferred stock, by the end of the first day of trading, Series A stockholders had a return of over 14,000%, Series B stockholders had a gain of over 5,400% and Series C stockholders had a gain of over 2,600%. The Series D stock had a much smaller gain, only a 1,150% gain, but the holding period from purchase of Series D through the IPO was only two and a half weeks.

CacheFlow's stock price reached a peak of $165 at the end of November 1999. Its success, unfortunately, was short-lived. The popping of the technology bubble affected CacheFlow as it did virtually every other Internet company. CacheFlow's stock price had declined 51% by November 2000 when its revenue growth failed to please analysts and investors. In addition, CacheFlow announced in February 2001 that its third quarter revenues were only about $21 million, less than half of what analysts had projected. The company announced that it was restructuring to reduce costs and was aggressively managing its head count. By the end of 2001, its stock price had declined to pennies on the dollar.

With its stock price trading below $1, CacheFlow had to reinvent itself. First, it changed its business model and product development. Instead of providing caching services to speed up the Internet, CacheFlow found that its security applications were more valuable to customers. Consequently, CacheFlow changed its product delivery to being a strategic provider of security appliances that protect and control enterprise web site infrastructures. CacheFlow developed security applications to combat the increased assault on web site locations by hackers and other mischief makers. Instead of providing speed to the World Wide Web, it now provided Internet security.

Second, CacheFlow changed its name to reflect its new technology and business model. On August 21, 2002, CacheFlow renamed itself Blue Coat Systems, Inc. (NASDAQ: BCSI). The new name reflected a culmination of CacheFlow's strategic evolution to an Internet security provider. As of

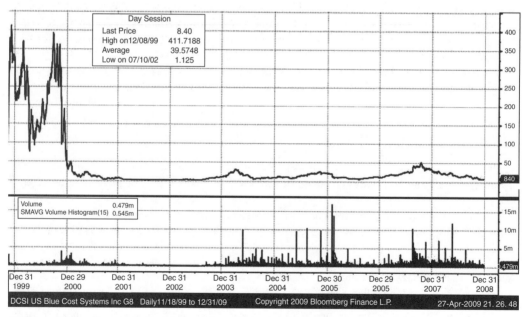

Exhibit 23.12   Blue Coat/CacheFlow—November 1999 IPO to December 2008

Source: Bloomberg Finance, L.P.

2009, Blue Coat Systems has become the leader in content security gateway appliances. Virtually all companies use some form of Internet security gateway solutions because there is an explosive growth in the number, variety, and volume of bugs, viruses, spam, and irritating direct marketing programs that can come through the World Wide Web. Blue Coat delivers this security through its Application Delivery Network infrastructure.

Shortly after changing the name of the company, in September 2002, the board of directors implemented another change—a reverse stock split. The board approved a one-for-five reverse stock split that decreased the number of shares outstanding and thereby increased the share price of the company above $1.

The company is now a viable concern. For the 12 months that ended April 30, 2009, Blue Coat's earnings before interest, taxes, depreciation, and amortization (EBITDA) were −$8.1 million, and it had revenues of $444.75 million. It is a successful company with a track record of earnings, but still below the $3 billion market capitalization that it achieved with its IPO. However, on a reverse-split adjusted basis from its IPO price, its stock price was around $1 in 2009. Exhibit 23.12 demonstrates the rise and fall of Blue Coat's share price.

CONCLUSION

The venture capital industry has grown tremendously over the past 50 years, but the fundamental concept remains unchanged: investing private capital with promising but untested business opportunities in order to reap long-term returns that offer a significant premium above the general stock market.

The long bull market of the 1990s, combined with the greatest period of economic expansion in U.S. history, helped to fuel extraordinary growth in the venture capital industry. However, a slowdown in the technology sector as well as the U.S. and global economies has cooled the return expectations of venture capitalists and investors alike. As a result, commitments to venture capital funds declined significantly in the years 2001 to 2008 compared to the year 2000. In addition, the vintage-year returns achieved by VC funds in the late 1990s will probably never be seen again. This was an extraordinary time of market hype, so-called new paradigm thinking, and outright delusion. Long-term investors should expect to earn a premium from venture capital that is about 400 to 800 basis points over the public stock market, depending on the venture capital stage of financing. The rewards are excellent, but patience, prudence, and sensibility are required.

24

Introduction to Leveraged Buyouts

Leveraged buyouts (LBOs) are a way to take a publicly traded company private, or a way to put a company in the hands of the current management, sometimes referred to as **management buyouts (MBOs)**. This is a form of mergers and acquisitions (M&A) activity. LBOs use the assets or cash flows of the company to secure debt financing either in bonds issued by the corporation or in bank loans, in order to purchase the outstanding equity of the company. In either case, control of the company is concentrated in the hands of the LBO firm and management, and there is no public stock outstanding. Typically, the loans and bonds issued to purchase the outstanding public equity are secured by the underlying assets of the company being acquired. The term leveraged is used to indicate that, after the buyout, the debt-to-equity ratio is much greater than before the acquisition. In fact, the debt-to-equity ratio can be as high as 9 to 1, where the capital structure of the company after the buyout is 90% debt and 10% equity.

Leveraged buyouts represent a mechanism for increasing the value of a corporation. They can be a way to unlock hidden value, maximize the borrowing capacity of a company's balance sheet or exploit existing but underfunded opportunities. In addition, professional management is often added by the private equity managers. Specifically, the private equity managers raise capital in specialized intermediaries called limited partnerships from institutional investors and then use this capital as the new equity to be infused into a leveraged buyout.

We begin this chapter with a brief history of the LBO market. Next we provide a theoretical example of how LBOs work. We then discuss how LBOs add value, using short case histories of successful buyout transactions as examples. As successful as LBO transactions have been, there are risks and we examine these risks in light of the large leverage ratios used to fund buyouts. We also examine the fee structures and other methods by which LBO funds make money. Last, we consider some of the corporate governance advantages to using LBOs.

HISTORY OF LBOs

Although LBOs began after World War II, it was not until the 1970s that the investment value of LBOs became apparent. The very first LBO was the purchase of the Pan-Atlantic Steamship Co. by McLean Industries in 1955. McLean issued $7 million in preferred stock and borrowed $42 million in bank loans to purchase Pan-Atlantic. Soon after the closing of the deal, McLean turned around and used $20 million in cash and other liquid assets on the balance sheet of Pan-Atlantic to pay down the $42 million loan. Right after World War II, the Great Depression was still fresh in the minds of the investing public and corporate America. In fact, at the nadir of the Depression, corporate bond defaults across all credit qualities (investment grade and non-investment grade) hit a high of 14%. Consequently, debt was viewed negatively and was underutilized. Concurrent with the limited use of debt was the development of the conglomerate, large companies with widely scattered business units across multiple industries. Management ranks began to grow with the advent of MBA programs, and inefficiencies began to creep into these large conglomerates. As a result, profitability began to slide.

In 1976 a new investment firm was created on Wall Street, Kohlberg Kravis Roberts & Company (KKR).[1] The founders of KKR had previously worked at Bear Stearns and Company, where they helped pioneer the LBO transaction as early as 1968. No firm has had a greater impact on the leveraged buyout market than KKR. Indeed, many of the transactions discussed in this chapter were originated by KKR.

KKR began with just $3 million of its own funds to invest, but soon raised enough capital from other investors to finance the buyout in 1977 of A.J. Industries, a small manufacturing conglomerate. The transaction was for $94 million and consisted of $62 million in bank debt and $32 million of KKR and investor equity. At that time, there were no investors willing to provide subordinated debt to finance an LBO transaction.

This changed with KKR's buyout of Houdaille Industries in 1979. This transaction was financed with 86% debt in the form of senior and subordinated notes. The Houdaille deal demonstrated to the market that there were many investors willing to purchase the debt of an LBO in addition to providing the equity.

The 1980s witnessed the rise of another key element of LBOs: the junk bond. **Junk bonds** are subordinated debt typically with little in the way of collateral protection. These bonds are just one step above equity, often have a low credit rating and trade much like equity. Junk financing is popular because the bond terms can be flexible, just as with private bank financing, but the potential investor base is often far broader.

Michael Milken became famous for developing Drexel Burnham Lambert's junk bond business. By the mid-1980s, Michael Milken was one of the most powerful men on Wall Street (despite operating out of the Beverly Hills, California, office of Drexel Burnham Lambert). The deals that Milken and KKR put together demonstrated that a company's cash flows and the strength of its management team were more creditworthy assets than traditional forms of collateral such as property, plant, and equipment.[2]

Fed by junk bond financing, LBO deals reached an initial peak in 1989 when KKR bought the giant food conglomerate RJR Nabisco Inc. for $31 billion in a deal that was documented in the book and movie titled *Barbarians at the Gate*. This LBO would stand as the largest LBO for many years, until KKR outdid itself in 2006 with its bid for TXU Corporation.

In the 1990s, LBO transactions ran into two obstacles. First was the U.S. recession of 1990–1991, which briefly pushed credit spreads out to unfriendly levels and thus put a lid on junk bond financing for buyouts. By the end of 1991, 26 of 83 large LBOs completed between 1985 and 1989 had defaulted on their debt financing. Second, in 1998, came the default by the Russian government on its bonds which once again sent credit spreads spiraling upward. Whereas debt had accounted for as much as 95% of some LBO deals during the previous decade, by the end of the 1990s debt loads of over 75% were viewed as unattractive.

The new millennium started quietly for the LBO market. After hitting a peak of over $100 billion in 2000, fund-raising trailed off, slowed down by the recession of 2001–2002. However, easy money soon came back to Wall Street and elsewhere, leading to an unparalleled boom in leveraged buyouts from 2003 into early 2007, culminating in the largest buyout ever: the $45 billion buyout of TXU Corporation. Once again, KKR was at the heart of negotiating this record-setting LBO. But by late 2007, the leverage and liquidity bubble had burst, leading to the credit crisis of 2008 and the swift decline of the LBO market. Exhibit 24.1 shows the growth of committed capital. There have been two LBO bubbles: the first peaked in 2000 coincident with the tech bubble bursting, and the second

---

[1] Their offices are actually in midtown Manhattan.

[2] Michael Milken was subsequently arrested, indicted, and convicted of securities fraud for the role he played in financing several corporate takeovers in the 1980s. The subsequent securities scandal resulted in the demise of Drexel Burnham Lambert.

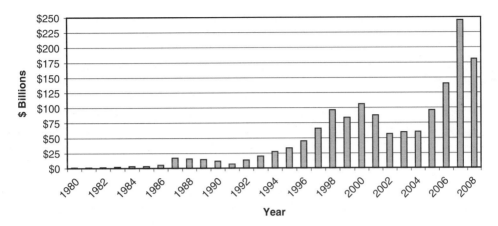

Exhibit 24.1 Leveraged buyouts committed capital

Source: Thomson Financial Venture Economics.

in 2007 after the tremendous build-up in LBO commitments fueled by ample investor funding and easy bank credit.

The sheer number of LBO firms seeking investor capital helped spur this growth. Whereas in the 1970s only two firms dominated the market, KKR and Forstmann Little & Co., there were now well over 1,000 LBO funds competing for money and companies. The growth of this market has led to mixed returns for investors.

The bursting of the technology bubble as well as the economic recession that followed put the brakes on LBO activity early in the new millennium. For example, in the year 2000, the biggest LBO deal was Donaldson, Lufkin & Jenrette Inc.'s $3.8 billion attempted buyout of U.S. meat producer IBP Inc. (formerly known as Iowa Beef Processors), which eventually lost out to a higher bid from Tyson Foods. However, as the decade progressed, larger and larger buyouts came back into vogue. For example, the largest LBO in 2005 was the buyout of Hertz Corporation from Ford Motor Company by the Carlyle Group and Clayton Dublier & Rice for $15 billion. This was followed in 2006 and 2007 by several deals that topped $20 billion.

Currently, the major challenge facing LBO firms is finding sufficient deals in which to invest their capital. The large pool of industrial conglomerates in the 1980s that were ripe to buy out, strip down, and then resell has shrunk. This was a ready-made pipeline for LBO transactions but has dried up as more and more companies now specialize within their core competencies instead of diversifying into wayward industries. However, the flow of money into the leveraged buyout industry has allowed private equity firms to direct their attention toward supersized buyouts. Whereas just a few years ago a mega buyout was considered to be any deal greater than $10 billion, there have now been several "super mega" buyouts in excess of $20 billion. Exhibit 24.2 lists the largest buyout deals in 2006 and 2007. Leveraged buyouts in excess of $20 billion became routine with easy credit available. However, as the credit markets came crashing down in 2008, so, too, did the size of buyouts. The largest buyout in 2008 was the Trans Alta Canadian electric utility. The buyout was estimated at $10.2 billion in U.S. dollars.

Another interesting insight into the LBO industry is the amount of equity contributed to a leveraged buyout. In 1990, the average equity contributed to the buyout was about 13% of the bid price. But by the end of the 1990s, buyout funds were putting more equity into their deals. In 1999, the average equity contribution reached 36%, and peaked in 2001 at 40%. Not surprisingly, this peak was coincident with the onset of the recession of 2001. However, after that recession, the capital markets experienced massive infusions of liquidity from banks and other investors. (We will have

Exhibit 24.2   Largest leveraged buyouts in 2006 and 2007

Target Company	Year	Price	Acquirers
TXU Corp.	2007	$45 billion	KKR, Texas Pacific Group, Goldman Sachs
Equity Office Properties	2006	$39 billion	Blackstone
HCA Corp.	2006	$32.7 billion	Bain Capital, KKR, Merrill Lynch
Alltel Corp.	2007	$27.5 billion	TPG, Goldman Sachs
Harrah's Entertainment	2006	$27.4 billion	Apollo Advisors, TPG
Clear Channel Communications	2006	$25.7 billion	Bain Capital, Thomas H. Lee Partners
First Data Corp.	2007	$25.6 billion	KKR

much more to say about this in our chapters on credit derivatives.) Suffice it to say that cheap and easy financing drove down equity levels yet again, bottoming out in 2007 around 25%, on average. However, the collapse of the credit markets in 2008 drove the required equity commitment back up toward 40%. Exhibit 24.3 demonstrates the average equity component of buyouts.

As larger LBO deals were pursued, larger buyout funds became the norm. Mega funds in excess of $10 billion are becoming more common. In 2006, Texas Pacific Group raised $14.25 billion for its most recent LBO fund. This was later topped by the $21.7 billion buyout fund raised by the Blackstone Group in 2007.

Performance of leveraged buyouts

As discussed earlier, there are several economic motivations for private equity. Most private equity limited partnerships require investors to lock up their capital for as long as 10 years. In return for this lack of liquidity, there has to be a value proposition for a private equity manager's limited partners:

- Improve application of the balance sheet capacity of the acquired company.
- Bring active equity ownership to the private company.
- Acquire representation on the board of directors.
- Replace the existing management team—bring professional management to the acquired company.
- Direct the company's cash flows toward the equity holders instead of unnecessary projects.
- Redirect the acquired company's business plan to the creation of value for the equity owners instead of the managers.
- Align management compensation with long-term equity value creation.

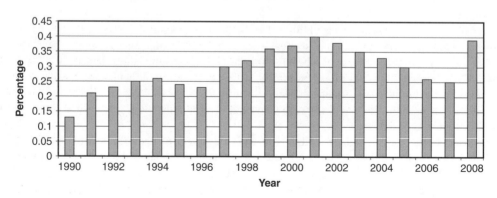

Exhibit 24.3   Equity percentage in LBO deals

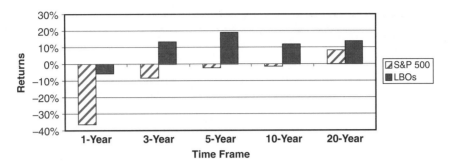

Exhibit 24.4   Average annual returns to leveraged buyouts

An investor in a private equity limited partnership should expect to receive a premium to what she might achieve in the public markets.

Exhibit 24.4 presents the returns for leveraged buyouts on 1-year, 3-year, 5-year, 10-year, and 20-year time frames through 2008, compared to the S&P 500. The dark bar represents the returns to buyouts, while the striped, lightly shaded bar represents the return to the S&P 500. We can see that over every time period, the return to private equity exceeded that of the public markets.

It is expected that private equity should earn a return premium to the public markets to reflect the special skill set of the private equity managers, the application of leveraged capital, and a return premium for the illiquid (private) nature of these investments. However, the returns presented in Exhibit 24.4 must be taken with two very large grains of salt.

First, 2008 was a year of a global financial meltdown. The S&P 500 was down more than 35% and this negative return also bled into the 3-year, 5-year, and 10-year returns for the S&P 500. Second, private equity firms still have considerable discretion on the marking of their portfolios. Even with the advent of FAS 157 in the United States (the accounting rule that requires quarterly mark-to-market accounting), the inputs into fair market valuations for illiquid investments are still at the discretion of private equity managers. Therefore, it is likely that the decline in value for private equity investments will lag those witnessed in the public markets as private equity managers come to grips about how to apply FAS 157.

The results in Exhibit 24.4 are presented for all private equity firms; it is an average of the worst-performing, top-performing, and average private equity managers. However, there is a significant dispersion in private equity returns between top-quartile performers and bottom-quartile performers. This emphasizes that one of the keys to success for investors in private equity is to gain access to the best-performing managers.

Performance persistence among the best private equity managers is the most important key to successful private equity investing. Private equity firms whose private equity funds outperform the industry in one fund are likely to outperform the industry in their next fund. This is different from other asset classes such as active public equity investing, where performance persistence is much less evident. Performance persistence has been identified to exist across funds raised by individual private equity firms (as opposed to large asset management conglomerates). The returns also improve with partnership experience. Better-performing funds are more likely to raise new funds and larger funds than those private equity firms that perform poorly.[3] Much of the persistence in private equity returns can be traced to the reputation of the firm's general partners and team members, and their

---

[3] See Steven Kaplan and Antoinette Schoar, "Private Equity Performance: Returns, Persistence, and Capital Flows," *Journal of Finance* 60 (August 2005), 1791–1823.

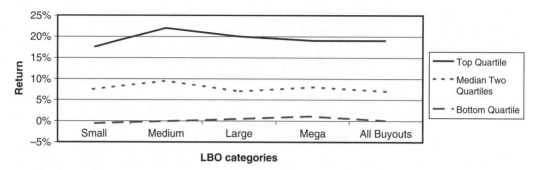

LBO categories

Exhibit 24.5   Returns for top and bottom quartile LBO firms, as well as the median return for all LBO firms

ability to attract capital, the best entrepreneurs, and the best buyout opportunities. Those private equity firms that have a history of success can establish a proprietary deal flow that increases their competitive advantage.

Exhibit 24.5 demonstrates the advantage of performance persistence in the LBO market. We can see that there is a very large difference of between 18% and 22% in the returns of top-quartile versus bottom-quartile performers. Even the difference between the top quartile and median return remains a significant 10% to 12%.[4]

THEORETICAL EXAMPLE OF A LEVERAGED BUYOUT

In a perfect world, everyone makes money and no one is disappointed. But in reality, the results can vary dramatically, as previously noted. We will discuss some spectacular LBO failures later. In the meantime, we describe how a theoretical LBO should work. Imagine a company with an equity market value of $500 million and a debt face value of $100 million. The company generates **earnings before interest, taxes, depreciation, and amortization (EBITDA)** of $80 million. EBITDA represents the free cash flow from operations that is available for the owners and debtors of the company. This equates to a 13.3% return on capital for the company's shareholders and debt holders.

An LBO fund offers $700 million to purchase the equity of the company and to pay off the outstanding debt. The debt is paid off at a face value of $100 million, while the remaining $600 million (e.g. a 20% premium over current market value) is offered to the equity holders to entice them to tender their shares to the LBO fund. The $700 million LBO is financed with $600 million in debt (with a 10% coupon rate) and $100 million in equity. Thus, the company must pay $60 million in annual debt service to meet its interest payment obligations. After the LBO, the management of the company improves operations, streamlines expenses and implements better asset utilization. As a result, the cash flow of the company improves from $80 million to $120 million a year.[5] By forgoing dividends and using the free cash flow to pay down the remaining debt, the management of the company can own the company free and clear in about seven years.

---

[4] In fact, this performance disparity is likely even greater, because it does not take into account survivorship bias—the numbers do not include the performance of funds that have failed and are no longer in business.

[5] Studies of LBOs indicate that corporate cash flows increase 96% from the year before the buyout to three years after the buyout. See Michael Jensen, "The Modern Industrial Revolution, Exit, and the Failure of Internal Control Systems," in *The New Corporate Finance*, 2nd ed., ed. Donald H. Chew Jr. (New York: Irwin/McGraw-Hill, 1999).

This means that, after seven years, the LBO firm can claim the annual cash flow of $120 million completely for itself. Assuming a long-term growth rate of 2% per year and a discount rate of 12%, this cash flow is worth:

$$\$120 \text{ million}/(0.12 - 0.02) = \$1.2 \text{ billion}$$

Therefore, assuming that the management of the company can own the company free and clear in seven years the total return on the investment for the LBO transaction would be:

$$(\$1.2 \text{ billion}/\$100 \text{ million})^{1/7} - 1 = 42.6\%$$

The total return of 42.6% represents the annual compounded return for this investment. Notice the impact that leverage has on this transaction. The company is financed with a 6:1 debt-to-equity ratio. This is a very high leverage ratio for any company.

However, the cash flows generated by the company are used to pay down the debt to a point where the company is completely owned by the equity holders. The equity holders receive a very high return because the debt used to finance the transaction is locked in at a 10% coupon rate. This means that any operating efficiencies and capital gains generated from the business will accrue to the benefit of the equity holders. This is a keen incentive for the equity holders to improve the operations of the company.

As this example demonstrates, the returns to LBO transactions can be quite large, but the holding period may also be commensurately long. At the end of seven years, the management of the company can reap the $1.2 billion value through one of six methods:

1. *Sale to a strategic buyer.* This is the most common **exit strategy**. The management can sell the company to a competitor or another company that wishes to expand into the industry. For example, in November 2007, Goldman Sachs and Texas Pacific Group (TPG) purchased the wireless telephone company Alltel Corporation and took it from public to private in a $27.5 billion LBO. This was the largest (and still is the largest) buyout in the telecommunications industry. At the time of the LBO, it was speculated that Goldman Sachs and TPG would eventually sell Alltel to a bigger competitor, possibly Verizon. Sure enough, less than a year later (only eight months, actually), Goldman Sachs and TPG sold Alltel to Verizon for $28.1 billion. While the price appreciation, $27.5 billion to $28.1 billion, does not seem that large, the actual return on equity was larger. Goldman and TPG committed $4.6 billion in equity capital in the buyout of Alltel and received back net cash of $5.9 billion from Verizon, for a net profit of $1.3 billion. This equates to a 28% return on equity over an 8-month holding period—not bad!
2. *Initial public offering (IPO).* Consider the example of Gibson Greetings. This company was purchased from RCA for $81 million with all but $1 million financed by bank loans and real estate leasebacks. When Gibson Greetings went public, the 50% equity interest owned by the LBO firm was worth about $140 million, equal to a compounded annual rate of return of over 200%.
3. *Another LBO.* In another example, the management of a company doubled its value from $600 million to $1.2 billion. They can now refinance the company in another LBO deal where debt is reintroduced into the company to compensate management for their equity stake. In fact, the existing management may even remain as the operators of the company with an existing stake in the second LBO transaction, providing them with the opportunity for a second go-round of leveraged equity appreciation.
4. *Straight refinancing.* This is similar to the preceding example where a company takes on debt to pay out a large cash dividend to its equity owners.
5. *A buyout-to-buyout deal.* Increasingly in the private equity industry, a private equity firm will sell one of its portfolio companies to another buyout firm. This type of transaction is called a

buyout-to-buyout deal. The second buyout firm believes that it can create a second leg of growth after the original buyout firm sells the company. It is estimated that almost one-third of private equity deals are now buyout-to-buyout deals.

6. Any combination of the previous five methods.

Consider the case of Hertz Corporation, the rental car company. Hertz has been renting cars since 1918 and was owned by the Ford Motor Company. With the problems in the U.S. auto industry, Ford decided to sell Hertz to raise cash and to open up more debt capacity on Ford's balance sheet.

A consortium of Clayton, Dubilier & Rice, the Carlyle Group, and Merrill Lynch won the bidding war for Hertz with a leveraged buyout price of $15 billion in December 2005. In the deal, the private equity firms agreed to assume $9.4 billion in debt and to pay Ford $5.6 billion in cash. The amount of equity put up by the three private equity firms was $2.3 billion. The other $2.2 billion came from additional bank financing.

The three private equity firms quickly secured new bank and junk bond financing for Hertz that reduced its overall borrowing costs and increased net cash flows.

In June of 2006, just six months after the deal closed, Hertz negotiated an additional loan facility of $1 billion that was used to pay a special dividend to the three private equity firms. This was quickly followed by an IPO for Hertz in November 2006, less than one year after being taken over in the leveraged buyout.

Hertz raised $1.32 billion in its IPO. Of this, $900 million was used to pay off the special loan taken out in June 2006, the proceeds of which had been used to pay the $1 billion dividend to the private equity firms. The remaining $420 million of the IPO proceeds was used to pay a second dividend to Clayton, Dubilier & Rice, the Carlyle Group, and Merrill Lynch's private equity group. The IPO represented a sale of 28% of the company to the public.

Hertz then had a secondary offering for its stock seven months later in June 2007, raising $1.2 billion. Hertz did not receive any of the proceeds of this secondary offering; it all went to the three private equity firms. The secondary offering reduced the three private equity firms' stake in the company to 58%. By June 2007, only one and a half years after acquiring Hertz, the three private equity firms had received $2.52 billion in cash and still owned a 58% stake of the company valued at about $2.9 billion. Given their initial equity investment of $2.3 billion in the leveraged buyout, in a very short period of time the buyout firms had made 2.3 times their money invested—not a bad deal for their investors.

Kaplan and Stromberg have documented the frequency of LBO exit strategies.[6] Their findings are presented in Exhibit 24.6. The sale of a buyout company to a strategic buyer remains one of the most common strategies to exit an LBO. However, sales to financial buyers and other LBO firms have grown in frequency. From 2006 to 2007, this category had grown to represent 36% of all exits, versus only 35% for sales to a strategic buyer. IPOs, by comparison, have declined significantly as an exit strategy, whereas recapitalizations have grown in importance. Given the easy bank financing available from 2006 through 2007, it is not surprising that recapitalizations became a more favored exit strategy as compared to IPOs.

The appeal of a leveraged buyout

Leverage buyouts have a number of appealing characteristics to corporate management and investors alike. From the perspective of corporate management, the benefits of a buyout are:

- The use of leverage where interest payments are tax deductible.
- Less scrutiny from public equity investors.

---

[6] See Steven Kaplan and Per Stromberg, "Leveraged Buyouts and Private Equity," National Bureau of Economic Research, Working Paper 14207, July 2008.

Exhibit 24.6   Frequency of LBO Exit Strategies

LBO Exit Strategy	1970 to 2007	2006 to 2007
Sale to strategic partner	38%	35%
Financial sale/buyout-to-buyout	30	36
IPO	14	1
Recapitalization/other	11	24
Bankruptcy	6	3
Sold to management	1	1
	100%	100%

Source: Steven Kaplan and Per Stromberg, "Leveraged Buyouts and Private Equity," National Bureau of Economic Research, Working Paper 14207, July 2008.

- Freedom from a distracted (and potentially distracting) corporate parent.
- The potential of company management to become significant equity holders and thereby benefit directly from building the business.

From the shareholders' side of the equation, they typically respond favorably to a leveraged buyout because the bid price for their shares is typically at a large premium compared to the market price. Consequently, they also share in a portion of the upside potential of the LBO when they tender their shares at a premium to initiate the buyout transaction.

More to the point, leveraged buyout firms often target companies that have a depressed stock price. This is one of the leading criteria for an LBO target (which we will discuss in more detail later). Consequently, shareholders often welcome an LBO bid because it typically reflects superior pricing to what they can currently receive for their shares in the marketplace.

Financing a leveraged buyout

As our simple example demonstrated, a leveraged buyout will be financed with a combination of debt and equity, with debt being the large majority of the financing. Generally in LBO deals there are three tranches of financing: senior debt, mezzanine debt, and equity. Senior debt typically entails financing from banks, credit/finance companies and insurance companies. Mezzanine debt is purchased by mezzanine debt funds (another form of private equity that we discuss in the next chapter), insurance companies, and other institutional investors. Last is the equity tranche, which will be held by the LBO firm that has taken the company private, the management of the company, and often includes some form of **equity kicker** from the mezzanine debt tranche. Exhibit 24.7 lays out the layers of LBO financing.

As an example of recent financing for a large buyout deal, Exhibit 24.8 shows the financing for the $26.4 billion leveraged buyout of First Data Corporation (FDC), a credit card and payment processor that was spun out of American Express in 1992. This transaction was financed with $15 billion in bank loans split between a term loan and a revolving credit facility (a revolver), $9 billion in junk bonds split among a senior unsecured offering of $3.75 billion, a senior pay-in-kind toggle bond (the bond can pay interest in cash or in additional bonds) of $2.75 billion, and a $2.5 billion subordinated tranche. Last, $2.4 billion in equity was contributed by the buyout firm, KKR. The equity in this deal was less than 30%, an indication of the easy liquidity that existed from bank financing into 2007.

HOW LBOs CREATE VALUE

The theoretical example given earlier is a good starting point for describing an LBO transaction, but there is no standard format for a buyout. Each company is different, and every LBO deal has

Exhibit 24.7   Tranche Financing for a Leveraged Buyout

Financing Tranche	Percentage of Transaction	Expected Return	Financing Parameters	Source of Funding
Senior debt	40% to 60%	4% to 5% over LIBOR	4- to 6-year payback 2× to 3× EBITDA	Commercial banks Finance companies Insurance companies
Mezzanine debt	20% to 30%	12% to 14% coupon 17% to 20% total return	5- to 7-year payback 1× to 2× EBITDA Equity kickers to boost total return	Mezzanine debt funds Insurance companies Institutional investors Investment banks
Equity	20% to 40%	25% to 40%	5- to 7-year exit	LBO firm Management of company Equity kickers for mezzanine debt

different motivations. However, there are five general categories of LBOs that illuminate how these transactions can create value.

LBOs that improve operating efficiency

A company may be bought out because it is shackled with a noncompetitive operating structure. For large public companies with widespread equity ownership, the separation of ownership and management can create agency problems with ineffective control mechanisms. Management may have little incentive to create value because it has a small stake in the company, and monitoring of management's actions by a diverse shareholder base is likely to be just as minimal.

Exhibit 24.8   Financing tranches for the First Data Corporation buyout

Financing Tranche	Dollar Amount (Billions)	Percentage of Transaction	Financing Parameters	Source of Funding
Senior bank loans	$13 $ 2	49.24% 7.58%	7-year term loan at LIBOR + 2.75% Revolving credit at LIBOR + 2.75%	7-bank consortium led by Credit Suisse and Citigroup
Total bank loans	$15	56.82%		
Junk bond/ Mezzanine debt	$3.75 $2.75 $2.50	14.20% 10.42% 9.47%	Senior unsecured at 10.75% Senior pay-in-kind unsecured Subordinated unsecured	Insurance companies and CDO funds CDO funds Mezzanine debt funds
Total junk bond financing	$9.00	34.09%		
Equity	$2.40	27.27%	Collects the benefits of any capital gains and residual cash flows	KKR
Total	**$26.4**	**100%**		

Under these circumstances, management is likely to be compensated based on revenue growth. This may result in excessive expansion and operating inefficiencies. These examples often occur in mature industries with stable cash flows. Consider the following case history.

Safeway, Inc.

In 1986, KKR took Safeway, a grocery/supermarket chain, private at a cost of $4.8 billion. The transaction was financed with 86% debt financing. At the time Safeway had an expensive cost structure that was not competitive with the rest of the supermarket food industry. Its employees earned wages that were 33% above the industry average. In sum, Safeway had stores that were losing money due to inefficient inventory controls and other poor operating procedures. At the time, Safeway's managers were compensated based on revenue growth, not profitability.

Drastic measures were implemented, including renegotiations with unions, employee layoffs, and store closings. For example, Safeway sold its worst-performing division in Salt Lake City to Borman's Supermarkets for $75 million, and sold all 121 stores in its Dallas division to different grocery chains. Within two years, all divisions lacking wage parity with Safeway's competitors had been divested. This resulted in the sale of over 1,000 stores and a 40% reduction in employees.

In addition, regional managers were compensated not by how much they generated in sales (the prior incentive scheme), but instead by how much their operations earned on the market value of capital employed. As a result, managers worked hard to keep costs in line, closed underperforming stores, and expanded the business only when it appeared profitable.

The freedom to cut costs and the necessity to meet high debt service forced the management of Safeway to think of profits first and expansion second. It worked, and KKR eventually took the company public again after it had improved its operations and profitability. The LBO investors earned an annualized return approaching 43%.

Safeway is an example of where value creation came not from entrepreneurial input, but rather from greater operating efficiencies. The grocery chain industry is a mature industry. New innovations are rare; it is a high-volume, low-margin business. Margin expansion comes not from brilliant insights into new strategies, but rather from increasing operating efficiencies. As a result, Safeway is best categorized as an efficiency buyout.[7] Efficiency buyouts often lead to a reduction in firm assets and revenue with the goal of eventually increasing firm profits.

Such a buyout introduces more concentrated ownership and a better incentive scheme to mitigate agency problems. Management is given a stake in the company with an incentive scheme tied not to increasing revenues, but to increasing operating margins and equity value. In addition, a high leverage ratio is used to ensure that management has little discretion to pursue inefficient projects. Last, the LBO firm replaces the diverse shareholder base and provides the active oversight that was lacking with the prior (widespread) equity owners.

Unlocking an entrepreneurial mind-set

LBOs can also create value by helping to free management to concentrate on innovations. One frequently used strategy focuses on the unwanted (or neglected) operating division. Often an operating division of a conglomerate is chained to its parent company, which may impede its ability to implement an effective business plan. An LBO can free the operating division to control its own destiny.

---

[7] See Robert Hoskisson, Mike Wright, and Lowel W. Busenitz, "Firm Rebirth: Buy-Outs as Facilitators of Strategic Growth and Entrepreneurship," *Academy of Management Executive* (February 2001).

Duracell Corporation

Duracell was a division of Kraft Foods, a consumer products company, but different from the consumer foods (cookies, macaroni and cheese, etc.) primarily produced by Kraft. Duracell was too small and too different from its parent company to warrant much attention. The buyout of Duracell was led by its managers in a management buyout (MBO) because they felt that they could increase Duracell's value if they were freed from a bureaucratic parent company.

Duracell was taken private in 1988. The goal of management was not to sell assets and shrink the company (although it did consolidate its production by eliminating small plants). Rather, the company increased its budget for research and development, which resulted in the production of batteries that were not only longer lived but also more environmentally friendly. Additionally, management pursued an overseas expansion plan aimed at becoming a dominant supplier around the globe. Finally, management implemented an aggressive marketing and advertising campaign.

In short, unshackled from its corporate parent, Duracell was free to pursue its expansion plans with capital that had previously been unavailable. However, this capital was costly and, in the absence of a corporate parent with deep pockets to bail it out, forced management to focus on cash flows and more efficient use of existing assets.

In response to the pressure to manage its debt service and increase the value of equity, Duracell adopted the concept of **economic value added** (EVA®). EVA is a method for evaluating projects and performance by including a charge against profits for the cost of capital that a company employs.[8] The capital charge under EVA measures the return that investors could expect to earn by investing their money in a portfolio of stocks with similar risk as the company.

The EVA approach to value creation has gained popular attention because it reflects economic reality rather than accounting conventions such as earnings per share or return on equity. Accounting-based measures can be distorted by noncash charges, early revenue recognition, and other accounting conventions. This may lead to a temptation by management to manipulate accounting-based performance measures such as earnings per share. Conversely, EVA measures the opportunity cost of capital based on the risk undertaken to achieve a revenue stream. As a result, EVA redirects management's focus from accounting numbers to equity value creation.

Duracell was a success story. It managed to increase its cash flows from operations at an annual rate of 17% from 1989 through 1995. Eventually, KKR negotiated the sale of Duracell to the Gillette Company in 1996, resulting in a compound annual return of 40%. Management's shares were valued in excess of $45 compared to the price of $5 a share at the time of the buyout.[9]

Duracell is a prime example of an entrepreneurial LBO. Once freed from Kraft Foods, Duracell was able to implement new innovations such as mercury-free alkaline batteries. Not only was the production process cheaper, but its new environmentally-friendly batteries also appealed to the public. Duracell also developed rechargeable nickel hydride batteries for use in laptop personal computers. Last, rather than build new production facilities as it had done previously, Duracell

---

[8] The formula for EVA is: Net operating profits after tax − (Cost of capital × Total capital employed). See Al Ehrbar, *EVA: The Real Key to Creating Wealth* (New York: John Wiley & Sons, 1998). Many firms have adopted EVA as a way to measure their performance, including Coca-Cola, Briggs & Stratton, and Boise Cascade. In addition, the California Public Employees' Retirement System (CalPERS) uses EVA in its annual review of corporate governance of corporations based in the United States.

[9] For more details on the Safeway and Duracell buyouts, see George Baker and George David Smith, "Leveraged Management Buyouts at KKR: Historical Perspectives on Patient Equity, Debt Discipline and LBO Governance," in *Private Equity and Venture Capital: A Practical Guide for Investors and Practitioners*, ed. Rick Lake and Ronald Lake (London: Euromoney Books, 2000).

formed manufacturing joint-ventures in Germany, Japan, India, and China. This helped Duracell to expand internationally while deploying its capital more efficiently under the principles of EVA.

It is important to note that in an entrepreneurial LBO, the leverage ratio cannot be as high as for an operating efficiency LBO. The reason is that there must be sufficient flexibility for the managers/entrepreneurs to pursue their new initiatives. Whereas in the Safeway example management's actions needed to be restricted, in the Duracell example management's actions needed to be indulged. A moderate amount of leverage is usually required (50% to 70%), which provides sufficient discipline but still allows for innovative flexibility. As a postscript, Gillette Company was purchased by the Procter & Gamble Corporation in 2005 in one of the largest mergers ever: $57 billion.

The overstuffed corporation

One of the mainstream targets of many LBO firms are conglomerates. Conglomerates consist of many different divisions or subsidiaries, often operating in completely different industries. Wall Street analysts are often reluctant to follow or cover conglomerates because they do not fit neatly into any one industrial category. As a result, these companies can be misunderstood by the investing public, and therefore undervalued. Consider the following case history.

Beatrice Foods

In yet another KKR deal, Beatrice Foods (a food processing conglomerate) was bought out via an LBO in 1986 for $6.2 billion. This represented a 45% premium over the company's market value one month earlier.

Over the next two years, with KKR's assistance, the management of the company sold off $7 billion of assets, reaping an $800 million gain over the initial LBO price. In addition to all of its food brands, Beatrice Foods owned Avis Rent a Car and Playtex underwear, as well as children's clothing lines. This is a clear demonstration of the market and Wall Street analysts undervaluing a company. The LBO transaction paid for itself in the asset sales alone. This is all the more impressive when one recalls that KKR's $6.2 billion purchase price was at a 45% premium to the company's stock price. Beatrice Foods represents an excellent example of an undervalued conglomerate.

As might be expected, sales for the streamlined company declined from $11.4 billion to $4.2 billion after the $7 billion of asset sales. Yet profits increased from about $300 million to almost $1 billion. Finally, after the sale of assets, the total debt of Beatrice Foods rose only slightly, from $300 million to $376 million. The annual compounded return on this transaction was in excess of 40%. Eventually, KKR sold Beatrice Foods to Conagra for $1.4 billion.

The Beatrice Foods example is similar in some respects to the Safeway example. In each case, entrepreneurial insight was not required. Instead, strong operating management was the key to a successful LBO. In Safeway's case, the management's job was to eliminate inefficient and unprofitable divisions. Safeway sold off these divisions and made them someone else's problem.

Similarly, Beatrice Foods' management also pared down its assets, not necessarily to improve operations, but instead to give the company a better focus and identity. Beatrice was overstuffed with too many products across too many markets, resulting in a lack of coverage by the investment community and a lack of understanding of its core value.

Last, what Safeway and Beatrice needed was strong monitoring by their shareholders. In their public form this was difficult to do for both companies because of their widespread shareholder base. However, in the LBO format, the equity of each company was concentrated in the hands of the LBO fund. This resulted in closer monitoring of company operations. What these companies needed was not more growth, but rather a business plan that focused on streamlining and improving core divisions.

Buy-and-build strategies

Another LBO value creation strategy involves combining several operating companies or divisions through additional buyouts. The LBO firm begins with one buyout and then acquires more companies and divisions that are strategically aligned with the initial LBO portfolio company. The strategy seeks to benefit from synergies realized through the combination of several different companies into one. In some respects, this strategy is the reverse of that for conglomerates. Rather than strip a conglomerate down to its most profitable divisions, this strategy pursues a **buy-and-build** approach. This type of strategy is also known as a **leveraged build-up**.

Berg Electronics

The buyout firms of Hicks, Muse, Tate & Furst and Mills & Partners jointly purchased Berg Electronics from E.I. du Pont de Nemours and Company in 1993 for a price of $335 million. At that time, DuPont's evaluation of Berg indicated that it generated about $18 million in profit on revenue of $380 million. Berg manufactured computer connectors as well as socket and cable assembly products for the telecommunications industry.

Berg Electronics was used as a platform for further leveraged transactions in the same industry. Over the next five years, Berg Electronics made eight acquisitions under the direction of Hicks, Muse and Mills & Partners, including the acquisition of AT&T's connector business and Ericsson AB's connector division. By 1997, Berg had sales of $785 million and profits of over $180 million and employed 7,800 workers in 22 countries.

In early 1998, the buyout firms distributed shares in Berg to their investment partners and retained 20% of the firm for themselves. In August 1998, Framatome Connectors International, based in France and the third largest maker of electrical connectors, purchased Berg Electronics for $35 a share, for a total of $1.85 million, a 41% gain in purchase price before including the effects of leverage. Based on the initial equity contributed, the Berg Electronics transaction earned an estimated return in excess of 1,000%.[10]

LBO turnaround strategies

The U.S. economic recession of 2007 and 2008 highlighted another form of LBO: the turnaround LBO. Unlike traditional buyout firms that look for successful, mature companies with low debt-to-equity ratios and stable management, turnaround LBO funds look for underperforming companies with excessive leverage and poor management. The targets for turnaround LBO specialists come from two primary sources: (1) ailing companies on the brink of Chapter 11 bankruptcy and (2) underperforming companies in another LBO fund's portfolio. In some cases, the private equity firm will not buy out the complete company but instead will make a large equity contribution at a discounted price to the public market price of the stock and will also take seats on the target company's board of directors.

Washington Mutual

The credit crisis of 2007–2008 hurt many banks. One of them was Washington Mutual, Inc. (known as WaMu). WaMu was founded in 1889 in Seattle, Washington, and was one of the oldest savings and loan banks in existence. Unfortunately, like many banks in the United States, WaMu pushed its loan portfolio into riskier mortgages at the height of the housing boom. WaMu was the second biggest provider of payment-option adjustable-rate mortgages (ARMs), with over $50 billion of

---

[10] See Hoskisson, Wright, and Busenitz, "Firm Rebirth."

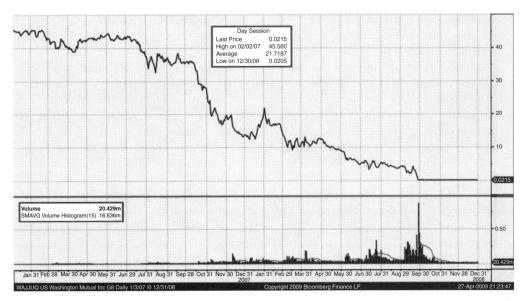

Exhibit 24.9   Stock Price of WaMu, 2007–2008

Source: Bloomberg Finance, L.P.

these mortgages in its portfolio in 2008. Option ARMs allow borrowers to skip part of their payment and add that sum to the principal. Essentially, this is a way for home buyers to dig themselves into a deeper hole and a way for banks to lose staggering amounts of money.

In April 2008, Texas Pacific Group (TPG), one of the largest buyout firms in the world, led a $7 billion investment in WaMu, buying shares at $8.75 when the public market price was $13.15. This represented a 33% discount to the public market price. The news of TPG's investment caused the stock price to rally to $14. TPG thought it was protected because it negotiated a clause that required WaMu to buy back TPG's shares at the original price of $8.75 a share if WaMu were subsequently sold for a price lower than $8.75. In addition, TPG founder David Bonderman gained a seat on WaMu's board of directors. TPG became WaMu's largest shareholder.

Unfortunately, over the summer of 2008, the losses accruing to WaMu's bad mortgages continued to mount. In June 2008, WaMu disclosed that it expected to lose $21.7 billion from its mortgage loans, far more than the $12 billion to $15 billion the company had forecasted. By the end of the summer, WaMu's stock price had declined to $2, resulting in a run on the bank as depositors withdrew $17 billion in deposits during one week in September alone. By the middle of September 2008, WaMu was on the ropes and desperate to find a buyer. Finally, on September 17, TPG agreed to waive its $8.75 protection clause, which allowed WaMu to put itself up for sale.

WaMu and TPG were too late. Federal banking regulators seized control of WaMu on September 25, 2008 in the biggest bank failure in U.S. history. In the end, U.S. banking regulators sold what was left of WaMu to JPMorgan Chase for $1.9 billion. Equity holders in WaMu had their interests wiped out, among them TPG. Exhibit 24.9 shows the stock price of WaMu.

THE FAILED LBO

Failed LBOs are becoming much more common. In particular, the credit and liquidity crisis of 2007 to 2008 contributed to the collapse of several high-profile deals. At the center of these failures is a contractual clause called a **material adverse change (MAC) clause**.

MAC clauses are an escape hatch for private equity firms. It allows them to scuttle the deal if there is some unforeseen and negative change to the business of the target company. An example may help clarify the process.

In April 2007, a private equity consortium led by JC Flowers offered a $25 billion buyout offer for the SLM Corporation (previously known as Sallie Mae). SLM is the leading provider of student loans in the United States. Despite the credit crisis, there is a fast-growing and lucrative business in providing loans for higher education and private education. College tuition in the United States has continued to increase every year, allowing SLM to grow its business.

The JC Flowers consortium offered $60 a share, a 33% premium over the share price of $45 before the offer. The offer also included a $900 million breakup fee if JC Flowers walked away from the deal.

Unfortunately, legislation passed by the U.S. Congress threatened to curtail some of SLM's business. Congress issued new student loan legislation under a College Cost Reduction and Access Act that called for a subsidy reduction of 2% for lenders in certain federally insured programs, like the ones run by SLM, and a 55 basis point cut to a special allowance that contributed to SLM's college lending margins. Effectively, the new law significantly reduced a subsidy that SLM had previously received from the U.S. government. JC Flowers claimed that this was a material adverse change to the core business of SLM, and sought to kill the buyout. What happened next was open warfare in the courts. Lawsuits were filed by both parties and the SLM buyout began to break apart.

The deal was finally put to rest in January 2008 when SLM and JC Flowers signed a breakup agreement that allowed each side to drop its litigation and walk away from the deal. The two sides reached an agreement and SLM gave up its claim on the $900 million breakup fee. Exhibit 24.10 shows the price of SLM. It closed the year 2008 at a share price of $11.50.

Another recent failed deal was the LBO for BCE, Canada's largest telecom company (the former Bell Canada). Announced in July 2007, this LBO was to be the largest LBO in the telecom industry at a whopping U.S. $41 billion. The deal collapsed in December 2008 based on a report from the

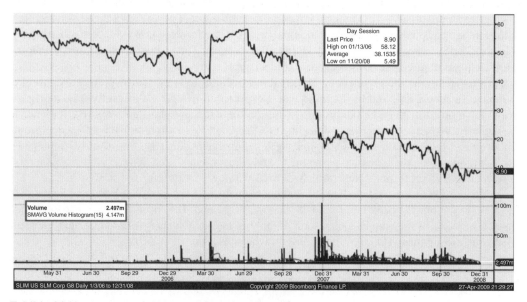

Exhibit 24.10   Stock price of SLM corporation, 2006–2008

Source: Bloomberg Finance, L.P.

accounting firm KPMG. The terms of the buyout required the company to receive a clean financial bill of health from its outside auditors. However, in November 2008, KPMG issued a report stating that the additional leverage, up to $39 billion in debt, would make BCE insolvent once the deal closed. In a last-ditch effort to save the buyout, BCE hired a second set of accountants in December 2008, the firm of PricewaterhouseCoopers, to help persuade KPMG to reverse its view that the company would be insolvent after the additional LBO debt. But KPMG held its ground and the deal collapsed.

Immediately after the deal collapsed, both sides to the agreement entered into litigation over the $1 billion breakup fee. BCE sought the breakup fee claiming that the Ontario Teachers Pension Plan and its private equity partners had withdrawn from the LBO prematurely, a mere 24 hours ahead of the deadline for the transaction's completion. For their part, the private equity firms claimed that the KPMG opinion represented a MAC, allowing them to withdraw. As of the date of this book, the lawsuit remains unresolved.

LBO FUND STRUCTURES

In this section we discuss how LBO funds are structured. While LBO funds are very similar to venture capital funds in design, they can be much more creative in structuring their fees.

Fund design

Almost all LBO funds are designed as limited partnerships. This is very similar to the way hedge funds and venture capital funds are established. In fact, many LBO funds have the name "Partners" in their title.

Every LBO fund is run by a general partner. The general partner is typically the LBO firm, and all investment discretion as well as day-to-day operations vest with the general partner. Limited partners, as their name implies, have a very limited role in the management of the LBO fund. For the most part, limited partners are passive investors who rely on the general partner to source, analyze, perform due diligence, and invest the committed capital of the fund.

Some LBO funds have advisory boards comprised of the general partner and a select group of limited partners. The duties of the advisory board are to advise the general partner on conflicts of interest that may arise as a result of acquiring a portfolio company or collecting fees, to provide input as to when it might be judicious to seek independent valuations of the LBO fund's portfolio companies, and to discuss whether dividend payments for portfolio companies should be in cash or in securities.

Similar to hedge funds and venture capital funds, LBO funds must be aware of the regulatory restrictions that apply to the offering of interests in their funds. To avoid being deemed an investment company, LBO funds take advantage of the 3(c)(1) and 3(c)(7) provisions of the Investment Company Act of 1940. These provisions were discussed at length with respect to hedge funds and apply equally to LBO funds.

Fees

If there was ever an investment structure that could have its cake and eat it too, it would be an LBO firm. LBO firms have any number of ways to make their money.

First, there are the annual management fees charged by LBO firms. These range from 1.25% to 3%. Consider the recent Blackstone Fund that raised $12 billion. The management fee on this fund is reported to be around 2%. 2% times $12 billion equals $240 million in annual management fees. And these fees are collected before any profits are recorded, indeed, even before any investments are made.

In addition, LBO firms share in the profits of the investment pool. These incentive fees usually range from 20% to 30%. Incentive fees are profit-sharing fees. For instance, an incentive fee of 20% means that the LBO firm keeps one dollar out of every five earned on LBO transactions. This incentive fee is a so-called free option, just as we discussed with respect to the incentive fees for venture capital funds and hedge funds.

For arranging and negotiating the transaction, LBO firms may also charge fees to the corporation that it is taking private of up to 1% of the total selling price. As an example, KKR earned $75 million for arranging the buyout of RJR Nabisco, and $60 million for arranging the buyout of Safeway, Inc. These transaction fees are divided up differently by various LBO firms; there is no standard practice. Some LBO firms keep all of these fees for themselves rather than sharing them with the limited partner investors. Other LBO firms split the transaction fees, with the percentage kept by the LBO firm ranging from 25% to 75%. Still other LBO firms include all of these fees as part of the profits to be split up between the general partner and the limited partners.

Not only do LBO firms earn fees for arranging deals; they can also earn breakup fees if a deal craters. Consider the Donaldson, Lufkin & Jenrette LBO of IBP Inc. This $3.8 billion buyout deal, first announced in October 2000, was subsequently topped by a $4.1 billion takeover bid from Smithfield Foods Inc. in November 2000. This bid was in turn topped by a $4.3 billion takeover bid from Tyson Foods Inc. in December 2000. Despite losing out on the buyout of IBP, as part of the LBO deal terms DLJ received a $66.5 million breakup fee from IBP because it was sold to another bidder.

In addition to earning fees for arranging the buyout of a company or for losing a buyout bid, LBO firms may also charge a divestiture fee for arranging the sale of a division of a private company after the buyout has been completed. Further, an LBO firm may charge director's fees to a buyout company if managing partners of the LBO firm sit on the company's board of directors after the buyout has occurred. As you can see, there are any number of ways for an LBO firm to make money on a buyout transaction.

The debate over private equity fees has intensified in recent years. As larger and larger buyout funds have grown, the management fees of the funds have not been adjusted downward. When the buyout industry started, the 1% to 2% management fee was necessary to pay the expenses of the private equity general partner. This fee covered travel expenses, utility bills, and the salaries of the general partner's staff. In short, the management fee was originally used to keep the private equity manager afloat until the incentive fee/carried interest could be realized, which often took several years.

Now, however, private equity funds have grown to immense size. $10 billion funds are common, and the Blackstone Group recently raised a record-breaking $21 billion fund. However, as private equity funds have grown, the management fee percentage has not been adjusted downward. A considerable amount of profit is now earned by the private equity manager from its management fees as opposed to its incentive fee/carried interest. This could blunt the incentive of the private equity manager to seek only the most potentially profitable private equity opportunities.

Let's take a simple example. Assume private equity Firm A raises a $10 billion buyout fund and charges a management fee of 1.5%. This is an annual fee of $150 million for the life of the fund. If we assume a 10-year life for the fund and an 8% discount rate for the time value of money, the present value of the management fees to the private equity firm is $1.006 billion. With management fees like this, there could be a disincentive to generate profits.

Let's take the example a step further. Typically, the private equity firm will put up 3% of the fund value, or $300 million in our example. So the private equity firm puts up $300 million to earn over the life of the fund a present value stream of management fees worth $1.445 billion. The IRR on this investment by the private equity firm is 49%, not a bad IRR on the management fee alone. Buyout firms typically say that they target a return of 20% for their investors. In our example, it is better to be private equity Firm A (the general partner of the fund) than it is to be a limited partner investor in Firm A's private equity fund.

In summary, LBO firms are "Masters of the Universe" when it comes to fee structures. It is no wonder that they have become such popular and profitable investment vehicles.

Terms of private equity funds

Every private equity fund has a contractually set lifetime, typically 10 years with provisions to extend the limited partnership for one to two more years. During the first five years of the partnership, deals are sourced and reviewed, and partnership capital is invested. After companies are taken private, the investments are managed and eventually liquidated. As the portfolio companies are sold, taken public, or recapitalized, distributions are made to the limited partners, usually in cash but sometimes in securities (as is often the case in an IPO). Generally, private equity firms begin to raise capital for a new fund once the investment phase for the prior partnership has been completed.

Fund-raising should occur about every three to five years in a normal private equity cycle. However, during the easy money years of 2002 through 2007, private equity firms greatly accelerated their fund-raising, starting new funds on an almost annual basis. This came to a screeching halt with the credit crisis of 2008.

Portfolio management

A private equity limited partnership typically invests in 10 to 30 portfolio companies. This translates to approximately two to six companies a year being sourced, reviewed, and purchased. Supplying the capital for the fund are the limited partners and the general partner, the private equity firm that manages the buyout fund. The number of limited partners in a private equity fund is not fixed. Most private equity funds have 20 to 50 limited partners, but some have as few as five and others more than 50.

In a buyout, the private equity fund will take seats on the board of directors. The new directors are supplied by the private equity firm, the general partner, which manages the private equity fund. The general partner will usually pick one to four of its partners to sit on the private company's board. As directors, the private equity firm interacts with the management of the private company on a weekly, if not daily, basis. The private equity firm will assist the private company in developing a new business plan. This plan might entail expansion or contraction, adding new employees or deleting part of the workforce, introducing new products, and cutting off unproductive and distracting product development. In a majority of cases, the private equity firm will get the private company to streamline its workforce, reduce its expenses, and increase its balance sheet capacity for more leverage. The theory is that the cost savings from workforce reduction and operating efficiencies will be more than enough to offset the increase in debt expenses. Over time, the higher cash flows pay down the debt, and the company increases its worth.

The J-curve effect

In the prior chapter on venture capital, we described the J-curve effect for a venture capital fund. The same effect applies to leveraged buyout funds. LBO funds go through the same stages as a venture capital fund: fund-raising, due diligence, investment, and harvesting of profits.

Recall from our previous discussion that a private equity fund will provide negative returns in the early part of its life. This is because the firm draws management fees from its limited partners to finance the sourcing of deals, to conduct due diligence of potential investment candidates and to monitor the portfolio companies once an investment is made. In the early part of the LBO fund's life, the fund will thus generate a negative cash flow reflecting the cost of management fees. However,

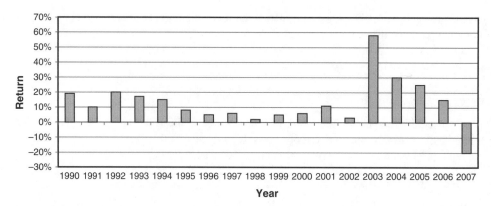

Exhibit 24.11   J-curve for LBOs—cumulative IRRs by vintage year

Source: Thomson Financial Venture Economics.

as the fund matures and portfolio companies are sold to generate the fund's investment returns, it is expected that the investment profits will more than compensate for the initial management fees charged, and eventually reward LBO investors with positive cash flows.

Exhibit 24.11 demonstrates the J-curve effect from another angle, the concept of **vintage year**. The vintage year is a way to compare private equity funds based on their year of formation. For example, it would be unfair to compare an LBO fund in its first year of operations with an LBO fund it its eighth year of operations, because the former fund is just getting started with the sourcing of private equity deals and due diligence, while the latter fund is in the profit-harvesting stage. To make an apples-to-apples comparison, it is only fair to compare a fund of one vintage year to other funds of the same vintage year; these funds have all left the starting gate at the same time.

Exhibit 24.11 shows the return by vintage year (year of formation). Notice that the most recent year shows the most negative returns. This is an application of the J-curve effect. More recent vintage year funds are still in their sourcing, due diligence, investment, and monitoring phases. They tend to have lower rates of return because they have not had sufficient time to implement their business plans and harvest profits from their portfolio companies. Note that 2003 was a remarkable year as the bear market came to an end, money was easy, and valuations became rich. However, we can see that vintage-year internal rates of return (IRRs) began to slow down in 2004. The liquidity crisis of 2007–2008 may result in some very low vintage-year IRRs for funds started during this time period. (There are no vintage-year returns for 2008 yet because the capital raised in 2008 by new LBO funds has not yet been invested such that it could produce an IRR.)

PROFILE OF AN LBO CANDIDATE

We now turn to how LBO firms find good buyout candidates. What makes a good LBO candidate? In this section we examine the profile of a public company that has been bandied about as a potential candidate.

In 2007, Kimberly-Clark (K-C), a large consumer goods maker, became the target of several buyout rumors.[11] When looking for LBO candidates, buyout firms look at both financial characteristics and

---

[11] See "Kimberly-Clark's Share Price May Attract Buyout, *Barron's* Says," *Bloomberg News*, January 14, 2007; and Leslie Wines, "Kimberly-Clark Could Be a Takeover Play," MarketWatch, January 8, 2007.

operating characteristics. Not surprisingly, financial reviews focus on cash flows and the ability to support large amounts of debt on the balance sheet. Specifically, LBO firms look for:

- A history of profitability and stable profit margins.
- Strong free cash flows to service additional debt levels.
- A balance sheet that is not already overburdened with a high debt level and existing debt that is A-rated or better.
- A strong balance sheet with a large cash/current asset balance.
- An undervalued stock price.

Exhibits 24.12 and 24.13 demonstrate many of the financial characteristics that LBO firms look for. First, the operating and net margins for K-C are 15 and 10 respectively and it has an EBITDA margin of 19.5%. These are respectable margins and enough to generate interest from LBO firms. Furthermore, K-C has been a consistent profit maker, generating operating profits of between $2.2 billion to $2.75 billion every year for the past five years. In addition, its balance sheet is solid, with a debt-to-equity ratio of 1.75 to 1. As we observed, in 2007 the average amount of equity in an LBO was 23%, which translates to a debt-to-equity ratio of 77% to 23%, or 3.35 to 1. Clearly, there is a lot of debt capacity left on K-C's balance sheet.

Furthermore, the ratio of operating cash flow (EBITDA) of $3,558 million to K-C's interest expense of $264 million is a whopping 13.5 to 1. In addition, K-C's debt-to-EBITDA multiple is 3.3. Most LBOs have debt-to-EBITDA multiples in the 5 to 7 range. This demonstrates a considerable capacity to finance the additional debt burden required for a leveraged buyout. Also, the free cash flow after interest expense and taxes is almost $2.5 billion a year, which is a lot of cash for an LBO to absorb. The only hesitancy in pursuing K-C (and probably why K-C has not received an LBO bid) is that its stock price was trading at the historical high point of around $70 per share at the beginning of 2007. However, as its stock price dropped in 2008 the buyout rumors started anew. Exhibit 24.13 shows that K-C's stock price did decline throughout 2007 and 2008, but it was down only 24% compared to the broader stock market decline of 41%, perhaps not enough to make private equity firms bite.

On the operating side of the equation, LBO firms look for:

- A mature firm with a strong brand name and competitive market position.
- Products that are not subject to technological obsolescence.
- A diversified customer base that generates recurring revenues.
- A management team that might require some improvement to increase operating efficiency.

Kimberly-Clark is considered the second largest player in the health care, personal hygiene, and cleaning products category. K-C makes everything from Huggies diapers to Scott paper towels to Kleenex tissues. It is smaller than its giant rival, Procter & Gamble.

With its many brand names managed in separate divisions, K-C could make an attractive takeover or LBO candidate because its individual pieces may be worth more than the whole company. In addition, consumer products companies tend to perform better than the broader stock market during a decline. Given the deep recession that the United States entered into in December 2007 (according to the National Bureau of Economic Research), K-C might offer a good value play for LBO firms looking to buy companies that are not as exposed to the U.S. business cycle. Also, K-C has a demonstrated record of stable and consistent cash flows.

In addition, K-C has a great corporate culture that was documented in the book *Good to Great*.[12] In his book, Jim Collins analyzed the motivation and leadership of K-C that enabled it to become one of

---

[12] See Jim Collins, *Good to Great* (New York: HarperCollins, 2001).

Exhibit 24.12 Kimberly-Clark financial data

Income Statement	($ Millions)	Balance Sheet	($ Millions)	Operating Cash Flow	($ Millions)
Net Sales	$18,266	Current Assets	$6,096	Operating Income	$2,752
Less: Cost of Goods Sold	12,472	Noncurrent Assets	12,343	Depreciation & Amortization	806
Less: Selling & Admin.	3,042				
Operating Income	$2,752	Total Assets	$18,439	EBITDA	$3,558
Less: Interest Expense	$264	Current Liabilities	$4,928	Free (Net) Cash Flow	
Less: Nonoperating Expenses	2	Noncurrent Liabilities	6,799		
Less: Income Tax	536	Total Debt	$11,727	Net Income	$1,822
Less: Minority Interests	128			+ Depreciation & Amortization	806
Net Income	$1,822	Shareholders' Equity	$6,712	+ Other Noncash Adjustments	129
				− Change in Noncash Capital	−329
				Net Cash from Operations	$2,428

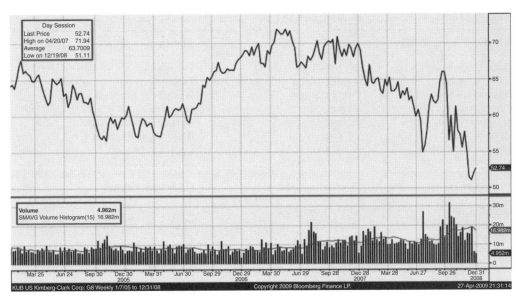

Exhibit 24.13   Stock price of Kimberly-Clark, 2005–2008

Source: Bloomberg Finance, L.P.

the world's best consumer products companies. With its strong corporate culture and management, a big piece of the LBO puzzle is already in place.

If we consider our checklist from before, consumer health care/personal care products are not subject to great changes in technology. In addition, K-C has a stable and recurring customer base with well-recognized brand names in the consumer goods category. In sum, K-C has a balance sheet with plenty of capacity for additional debt, stable and consistent cash flows, good brand-name products, and a strong corporate culture. Its strong stock price is perhaps the one key deterrent to an LBO bid.

VENTURE CAPITAL VERSUS LEVERAGED BUYOUTS

Venture capital and leveraged buyouts are two sides of the capital markets coin. Whereas venture capital funds target nascent, start-up companies, leveraged buyouts target established, mature companies. They operate at opposite ends of the life cycle of a company. Every corporation experiences three stages in its life: a start-up stage, a growth stage, and a stable or mature stage. Different financing needs are required for these different stages, and different product technology is found in each stage. For example, as a start-up, venture capital is necessary to get a prototype product or service out the door. Conversely, in a leveraged buyout the capital is necessary not for product development but to take the company private so that it can concentrate on maximizing operating efficiencies.

Despite their differences, both venture capital and leveraged buyouts contribute to managed entrepreneurship. Both types of private equity seek to apply capital with activist equity ownership to improve the underlying company's chances for success. A summary of the differences between start-up companies and the venture capital they need compared to the companies targeted by LBO firms is presented in Exhibit 24.14.

In terms of company characteristics, start-up companies generally have a new or innovative technology that can be exploited with the right amount of capital. The management of the company

Exhibit 24.14   Venture capital versus leveraged buyouts—start-up versus mature

Company Characteristic	Start-Up	Mature
Market environment	Developing	Developed
Product demand	Undiscovered	Established
Customer base	Early adopter	Widespread acceptance
Management type	Entrepreneur	Seasoned
Management skills	Idea generation	Operations management
Revenues	Just beginning	Recurring and predictable
Capital consumption	Ravenous	Conservative
Competitive advantage	New technology	Distribution, marketing, production
Financing Characteristics	**Venture Capital**	**Leveraged Buyout**
Target IRR	40% to 50%	20% to 30%
Shareholder position	Minority	Control of company
Board seats	One or two	All
Valuation	Compare to other companies	Discounted cash flow model
Use of debt	Nonexistent	Majority of financing
Investment strategy	Finance innovation	Improve operating efficiency
Time to exit	2 to 5 years	4 to 7 years
Exit options	IPO, acquisition	IPO, acquisition, or recapitalization

is typically idea driven rather than operations driven. A proven revenue model may not yet be established, and the capital consumption is likely high.

Conversely, with an LBO there is an established product, if not in fact an established industry. The management of the company is driven not by idea generation but by operating efficiency. Revenues are established, recurring, and fairly predictable. Also, a mature company generally has self-sustaining cash flows that allow it to fund growth internally.

It is also interesting to compare the equity stake venture capitalists acquire to that of leveraged buyout firms. A venture capital firm will typically acquire a significant but minority position in the company. Control is not absolute. Conversely, in a leveraged buyout all of the equity is acquired, and control is absolute. In addition, venture capitalist and LBO firms target different internal rates of return. While both are quite high, not surprisingly venture capital targets are higher. The reason is simple: There is more risk funding a nascent company with brand-new technology than an established company with regular and predictable cash flows.

The last significant difference between venture capital and leveraged buyouts is the investment strategy. Venture capitalists finance new, but unproven, technologies. These technologies may be so revolutionary in concept or design that they define a new industry, like the Sony Walkman of the early 1980s or the Apple iPod of the early 2000s. Conversely, leveraged buyouts look to see where they can add operating efficiencies or expand product distribution. New technology or innovation is not the cornerstone of their investment philosophy. They take an existing product and refine it through improvements to the production process, or by developing new and/or expanding existing distribution channels. The product is established; LBO firms seek only to improve upon it.

RISKS OF LEVERAGED BUYOUTS

Leveraged buyouts have less risk than venture capital deals for several reasons. First, the target corporation is already a seasoned company with public equity outstanding. Indeed, many LBO targets are mature companies with undervalued assets.

Second, the management of the company has an established track record. Therefore, assessment of the key employees is easier than assessment of a new team in a venture capital deal.

Third, the LBO target usually has established products or services and a history of earning profits. However, management of the company may not have the freedom to fully pursue their initiatives. An LBO transaction can provide this freedom.

Last, the eventual exit strategy of a new IPO is much more feasible for a buyout than for a venture capital deal. This is because the buyout company already had publicly traded stock outstanding. A prior history as a public company, demonstrable operating profits, and a proven management team make an IPO for a buyout firm much more feasible than an IPO for a start-up venture.

The obvious risk of LBO transactions is the extreme leverage used. This will leave the company with a high debt-to-equity ratio and a very large debt service. The high leverage can provide large gains for the equity owners, but it also leaves a very small margin for error. If the company cannot generate enough cash flow to service the interest payments demanded by its bondholders, it may end up in bankruptcy, with little left over for its equity investors. "Leveraged fallouts" are an inevitable fact of life in the LBO marketplace.

Consider the example of Robert Campeau's buyout of the department store chain Allied Stores in December 1986. Campeau bid $3.6 billion for the stores, a 36% premium over the common share price at that time. With such a high offer, shareholders quickly tendered their shares and the company became private. The deal was highly leveraged. Of the $3.6 billion, $3.3 billion was financed by callable senior and subordinated notes. Upon completion of the LBO, Campeau quickly sold a large portion of Allied Stores' assets for $2.2 billion and paid down the outstanding debt. As a result, sales of Allied Stores declined from $4.2 billion in 1986 to $3.3 billion in 1988. In addition to asset sales, employment declined significantly from 62,000 employees in 1986 to 27,000 in 1988. As a result, the Allied Stores, which lost $50 million in 1986, turned a profit in 1988.

Unfortunately, the debt-to-equity ratio of Allied Stores remained high, and the company could not generate sufficient cash flow to meet its debt service. The chain filed for bankruptcy in 1990.

Another example of a retailing LBO is the management buyout of Macy's Department Stores in 1986. Unlike the Allied Stores example, the management of Macy's attempted to keep the company intact rather than sell off chunks of assets. Macy's was purchased for $3.5 billion, about a 20% premium over the existing stock price at that time. Over the next two years, sales increased from $4.7 billion to $5.7 billion as Macy's management pursued a course of expansion rather than contraction. Unfortunately, the cost of expansion as well as the high debt service turned Macy's from a profitable company to a money-losing venture. By 1988, Macy's debt service was $570 million.[13] That is, its interest payments (not the face value of debt) totaled almost $600 million. By the end of 1991, Macy's had over $5.4 billion of debt on its balance sheet. The large debt ratio plus the recession of 1991 forced Macy's into Chapter 11 bankruptcy protection in January 1992.

Although high debt levels eventually forced Allied Stores and Macy's into bankruptcy, there are several advantages to using large leverage ratios. First, high levels of debt financing allow equity investors, with only a small amount of committed capital, to realize large gains as debt levels are paid down. Second, a high debt level means a small equity level, and this allows the management of a buyout company to purchase a significant equity stake in the company. This "carrot" provides for a proper alignment of management's interests with that of the LBO investment firm. Last, high debt levels and debt service payments are a useful "stick" to keep management operating at peak levels of efficiency to ensure that the debt is paid down at timely intervals.

---

[13] See W. Keith Schilit, "The Nature of Venture Capital Investments," *Journal of Private Equity* (Winter 1997), 59–75.

CORPORATE GOVERNANCE AND LBOs

One of the interesting by-products of an LBO transaction is the development of strong corporate governance principles. **Corporate governance** is the process by which the managers of a corporation align their interests with the equity owners of the business (the shareholders). Corporate governance plays a key part in a successful LBO transaction. We briefly describe the corporate governance issue and then consider how LBOs address this problem.

Agency costs and firm management

The objectives of senior management may be very different from those of a corporation's equity owners. For instance, management may be concerned with keeping their jobs and presiding over a large empire. Conversely, shareholders want value creation. In a large company, equity ownership may be so widely dispersed that the owners of the company cannot make their objectives known to management, or even control management's natural tendencies.

In a corporation, senior management is the agent for the shareholders. Shareholders, as the owners of the company, delegate day-to-day decision-making authority to management with the expectation (or hope) that management of the company will act in the best interests of the shareholders.[14] The separation of ownership and control of the corporation results in agency costs.

Agency costs come in three forms. First, there is the cost to properly align management's goals with the value-creation goal of shareholders. Alignment usually is achieved in the form of incentives for management that may include stock options, bonuses, and other performance-based compensation. Second, there is the cost of monitoring management. This may include auditing financial statements, shareholder review of management perquisites, and independent reviews of management's compensation structure. Last, agency costs can include the erosion of shareholder value from management-led initiatives that are not in the best interests of value creation.

In a well-known study, Jensen and Meckling demonstrate that the agents of a company (management) will act in the best interests of the principals (shareholders) only if appropriate incentives are given to the agents and the agents are monitored.[15] This is where LBO firms come in.

LBO firms replace a disperse group of shareholders with a highly concentrated group of equity owners. The concentrated and private nature of the shareholders allows the management of the buyout firm to concentrate on maximizing cash flows, not earnings per share. Management no longer has to account to outside analysts or the media regarding its earnings growth. Further, the management of the now private company is often given a significant equity stake in the company. This provides for an exact alignment of interests between the management/agents of the company and its principals/shareholders. As the company's fortunes increase, so will the personal fortunes of the management.

With a majority of the remaining equity of the once public/now private company concentrated in the hands of the LBO firm, the interaction between equity owners and management becomes particularly important. After a company is taken private, LBO firms maintain an active role in guiding and monitoring the management of the company. They are active, not passive shareholders. In addition, the LBO firm will often establish incentive goals for the management of the company, including the terms and conditions governing bonus payments.

---

[14] At CalPERS, reference is often made to "shareowners" rather than "shareholders."

[15] See Michael Jensen and William Meckling, "Theory of the Firm: Managerial Behavior, Agency Costs and Ownership Structure," *Journal of Financial Economics* (October 1976), 305–360.

After a transaction is complete, an LBO firm remains in continuous contact with company management. As the majority equity owner, the LBO firm has the right to monitor the progress of management, ask questions, and demand accountability. Often an LBO firm will ask for detailed monthly reports from either the CEO or the CFO of the company so that the LBO firm can monitor the progress management has made toward implementing the business plan. A constant dialogue between the management of a company and its equity investors is the essence of corporate governance.

Establishing a new business plan

For an LBO to succeed, it is imperative that the management of the company and the LBO firm agree on the business plan for the company going forward. This is very different from how a public corporation operates. Rarely does a public company submit its business plan to its shareholders for approval. The reason is twofold. First, the shareholder base is normally so disparate as to make it unlikely you could achieve consensus. Second, most shareholders are not sufficiently knowledgeable to fully assess the business plan.

The corporate governance paradigm changes with an LBO company. As the supermajority shareholder of the private company (up to 90% of the equity may be owned by the LBO firm, the remainder by management), the LBO firm is able to provide clear and complete direction to its agents (the management of the company). Although the specific business plans vary from LBO company to company, there are three common goals.

First, the management of the company and the LBO firm must come up with a plan to unlock the intrinsic value of the company. This might mean shedding marginally profitable divisions or subsidiaries and concentrating on the company's core strength. It might mean cutting back on expansion plans in order to focus on improving the profitability of existing operations. It might mean streamlining operations by reducing the existing workforce and cutting back on overhead. In sum, there must be some economic rationale for pursuing the LBO.

Second, a plan must be implemented to meet and pay down the outstanding debt. This is a key control over the management of the company. If the debt cannot be paid down, there will be no appreciation of the equity of the company, and bankruptcy may result. Management is forced to focus on maximizing profits and utilizing assets most efficiently. It is not in management's best interest to be wasteful or to pursue empire building if this means that their equity stake in the private company will depreciate.

Last, the management and the LBO firm must work together to develop the long-term value of the equity in the company. Since management of the company also has an equity stake, its interests are perfectly aligned with those of the LBO firm. LBO transactions take time to come to fruition—the average length of investment is between six and seven years. During this time, the value of the equity position must be increased and an exit strategy must be fulfilled. It is not enough to unlock the hidden value of a company; both the management and the LBO firm must be able to extract this value.

Ideally, LBO firms should not interfere with management's implementation of the business plan, but rather should act as a sounding board or consultant for management's ideas. LBO firms can bring their prior experience to the management of a company as well as their access to investment bankers, lawyers, consultants, accountants, and other professionals.

Spillover of corporate governance to the public market

The principles of corporate governance that LBO firms apply to their private companies have three important benefits for the public market. First, the strong governance principles that an LBO firm implements in its private firms should remain when those firms are taken public again. Proper management incentives and monitoring mechanisms have already been established. Even if the private company is sold to another corporation (possibly a public company), the robust corporate governance principles should have an impact on the acquiring company's bottom line.

Second, LBO transactions are a warning to management of public companies. If a company has a poor incentive scheme and minimal shareholder monitoring, it may be ripe for an LBO acquisition. Further, there is no guarantee that the existing management of a public company will remain after the LBO transaction. The LBO firm will have the final say as to who remains and who departs. This threat may provide an incentive for the management of public companies to adopt strong corporate governance principles that increase shareholder value.

Last, the incentive and monitoring schemes implemented by LBO firms for their portfolio companies provide guidance to management and shareholders alike. Management of public companies can view how new concepts such as EVA can increase shareholder value while providing for fair performance compensation. In addition, the principle of enhancing shareholder wealth has now become firmly established in corporate America. Empire building by corporate executives is no longer rewarded. Instead, executive management and shareholders alike focus on cash flows and share prices, not revenues and conglomerates. Furthermore, if they can concentrate their power at a shareholder meeting, shareholders can observe the impact that they, as owners of the business, have on the company's performance. Shareholder power is a powerful tool, and LBOs have used this tool most effectively.

THE DISMANTLING OF CONGLOMERATES

We indicated earlier that conglomerates can be popular targets for LBO firms, although there are very few left. As business schools churned out tens of thousands of MBA graduates in the 1960s, 1970s, and 1980s, diversification became all the rage. "Don't put all your eggs in one basket," a lesson learned in business school, became a mantra for many companies as they bought unrelated businesses in an attempt to diversify their operating risks.

Examples (in the 1980s) include Mobil Corporation's purchase of the retail store chain Montgomery Ward and Exxon Corporation's establishment of a personal computer division, Exxon Information Systems. Homogeneous, single-industry firms were discouraged; diversification was the new game in town.

Unfortunately, diversification at the corporate level is unnecessary and redundant for investors, who could just as easily purchase shares of Mobil and Montgomery Ward if they wished to diversify their portfolios with oil and retailing stocks, or Exxon Corporation and Hewlett-Packard if they wanted oil and personal computer exposure. In addition, corporations on a diversification binge had to pay large premiums to the market in expensive tender offers.

Ultimately, this led to depressed share prices of the conglomerates. The large premiums they paid represented corporate waste because there was no reason to pay a large premium for something shareholders could already do themselves, and at a cheaper price. As a result, the share prices of conglomerates languished because there were no synergies to be gained by wanton diversification.

However, this is where LBO firms were able to add value. Not only did they buy out conglomerates by the bucketful, but they also paid top dollar, thereby returning to shareholders of the conglomerates some of the prior corporate waste from diversification. Further, they streamlined the conglomerates, spinning off unrelated divisions into pure plays. This added value for the LBO firms' investors as well as for the new shareholders of the pure-play spin-offs.

Last, more than any other factor, LBO firms stopped the unnecessary diversification of large corporations. The pickings were just too easy for LBO firms, and eventually conglomerates faded away to a corporate form of the past.

MERCHANT BANKING

As a final discussion, we take a moment to briefly describe merchant banking. Merchant banking is a first cousin of leveraged buyouts. Sometimes it is difficult to distinguish between the two.

Merchant banking is the practice whereby financial institutions purchase nonfinancial companies. Most investment banking companies and large money-center banks have merchant banking units. These units buy and sell nonfinancial companies for the profits that they can generate for the shareholders of the merchant bank. In some cases the merchant banking units establish limited partnerships similar to LBO funds. At that point there is very little distinction between a merchant banking fund and the LBO funds discussed earlier.

Merchant banking started as a way for Wall Street investment banks and midtown money-center banks to take a piece of the action that they helped to fund. If a bank lent money to an LBO group to purchase a company, the merchant banking unit of the bank would invest some equity capital and get an equity participation in the deal. Soon the merchant banking units of investment banks established their own buyout funds and created their own deals.

While merchant banking is designed to earn profits for the investment bank, it also allows the bank to leverage its relationship with the buyout company into other money-generating businesses such as underwriting, loan origination, merger advice, and balance sheet recapitalization. All of this ancillary business translates into fee generation for the investment bank.

Two of the largest merchant banking firms are DLJ Merchant Banking Partners (a division of Credit Suisse Asset Management) and Goldman Sachs. For example, DLJ Merchant Banking Partners, along with the Morgans Hotel Group, purchased the Hard Rock Hotel & Casino in Las Vegas for $770 million in February 2007.[16] Morgans Hotel Group put up $57.5 million in equity for a one-third interest in the hotel and casino while DLJ supplied $115 million for a two-thirds ownership interest. The remainder of the purchase price was financed with a mortgage loan from a consortium of banks.

The risk of merchant banking is that an investment bank will continue to throw good money after bad to fund a company owned by its merchant banking unit. An example is Goldman Sachs's purchase of AMF Bowling Inc. Goldman led a $1.37 billion leveraged buyout of the bowling company in 1996 along with buyout firms Kelso & Co. and the Blackstone Group.[17]

Goldman Sachs subsequently brought AMF Bowling public again in November 1997 in an IPO that raised about $263 million at a share price of $19.50. After the IPO, Goldman Sachs remained the majority shareholder with about 54% of the company. A year later, in December 1998, Goldman Sachs paid almost $48 million for $343 million face value of zero-coupon convertible debentures. At that time, AMF's share price had declined over 80% to the $4 to $5 range.[18]

From the time of its buyout, AMF went on a buying spree, increasing its bowling centers from about 300 in 1996 to over 500 by 1998. Unfortunately, AMF expanded just at a time when customer demand for its bowling equipment, accessories, and bowling center packages declined. The leverage

---

[16] See "Morgans Hotel Group and DLJ Merchant Banking Partners Complete Acquisition of Hard Rock Hotel & Casino," Business Wire, February 5, 2007.

[17] See Gregg Wirth, "Bum Deals: As a Buyout Binge Looms, Will Wall Street Learn from Its Merchant Banking Mistakes?," *Investment Dealers' Digest* (February 12, 2001).

[18] In July 1999 AMF repurchased approximately 45% of its outstanding debentures.

from the buyout and its acquisition binge quickly pushed AMF's total debt to over $1.2 billion. Eventually, AMF's debt burden, combined with its operating losses, became so large that AMF Bowling Worldwide, the main operating subsidiary of AMF Bowling Inc., filed for Chapter 11 bankruptcy in July 2001. It is estimated that the cost to Goldman through its equity and bond purchases was at least $400 million.[19] However, the bankruptcy of AMF ushered in another chapter in its private equity life. Distressed debt investors, sometimes known as vulture investors, bought AMF's debt for 20 to 25 cents on the dollar, about $250 million total, and became its new owners. The new owners were Farallon Capital, Angelo Gordon & Co., Satellite Asset Management, and OakTree Capital Management, all distressed debt investors. In 2003 the distressed investors began looking for a sale of the company to start the public/private equity cycle all over again. AMF was sold to the private equity firm Code Hennessy Simmons in 2004 for $670 million, a little more than double what the distressed managers paid for AMF.

CONCLUSION

Over the past 25 years, leveraged buyouts have become a mainstream investment product. Most institutional investors now commit some component of their portfolios to leveraged buyouts. Indeed, the primary investors in LBO funds are pension and endowment funds. The State of Oregon's $1 billion commitment to KKR's Millennium Fund is a good indication of the institutional level of interest in buyouts.

Leveraged buyout funds rival venture capital funds in the amount of money committed for investment. Over the period of 1990 to 2008 the amount of capital committed to leveraged buyout funds was $1.4 trillion.[20] There are two reasons for this swell of investment into buyout funds. First, LBOs are less risky than venture capital investments because they target established companies with existing profits. Second, LBO firms have been able to generate positive returns comparable to those of venture capital.

The average returns to large and mega buyout deals have surpassed those for the S&P 500 over the longer term (20 years). But the average return premium for all buyout funds has been only 100 to 200 basis points above the S&P 500. However, these average returns mask the disparity between top-quartile private equity managers and bottom-quartile private equity managers. The return difference between the top and bottom quartiles can be 19% to 20%. Clearly, there is a keen advantage to investing with top-quartile private equity managers. Academic research has also indicated that there is significant performance persistence with top-quartile private equity managers; success breeds more success. Mostly, this is due to the most successful private equity firms having access to proprietary deal flow and supportive bank financing.

However, the LBO industry has begun to mature as an investment industry. The best indication of this is the club deals of private equity firms pooling their resources together as they get into bidding wars against other clubs. Large buyouts tend to attract teams of private equity firms rather than the tradition of a single private equity firm taking a company private. For example, the $45 billion purchase of TXU Corporation combined KKR, TPG, Goldman Sachs, and Lehman Brothers. With club deals, no buyout is too large.

---

[19] See Wirth, "Bum Deals."

[20] As reported in *Venture Economics* and the National Venture Capital Association. Over the same time period, there was a total of $447 billion in venture capital commitments.

25

Debt as Private Equity Part I: Mezzanine Debt

In this chapter we discuss mezzanine debt, a form of private equity that appears as debt on an issuer's balance sheet. Mezzanine debt is closely linked to the leveraged buyout (LBO) market, and the strategy can result in a significant equity stake in a target company. In addition, like venture capital and LBOs, mezzanine debt provides an alternative investment strategy within the equity asset class.

It is important to recognize that mezzanine debt investing can be distinguished from traditional long-only investing. The reason is that this form of private equity attempts to capture investment returns from economic sources that are mostly independent of the economy's long-term macroeconomic growth. While the direction of the stock market and the health of the overall economy may have some influence on a company, it is more likely that the fortunes of the company will be determined by its capital structure.

OVERVIEW OF MEZZANINE DEBT

Mezzanine debt is often hard to classify because the distinction between debt and equity can blur at this level of financing. More often than not, **mezzanine debt** represents a hybrid, a combination of debt and equity. Mezzanine financing gets its name because it is inserted into a company's capital structure between the "floor" of equity and the "ceiling" of senior secured debt. It is from the in-between nature of this type of debt that mezzanine debt derives its name.

Typically, mezzanine financing is constructed as an intermediate-term bond with some form of equity participation, or kicker, thrown in as an additional enticement to the investor. The equity portion provides the investor with an interest in the upside of the company, while the debt component provides for a steady payment stream.

The most common form of mezzanine financing is an intermediate-term note, which is typically unsecured and coupled with stock warrants to purchase the stock of the acquiring company. The coupon payments on the note may be in cash or as payment in kind (PIK). **Payment in kind** means that instead of paying cash on the mezzanine debt, the company distributes more notes to the investor. This increases the company's leverage, as well as the investor's equity stake in the company (through the receipt of more warrants). Typically, PIK bonds are called PIK toggle bonds because the issuer has the choice to pay the coupon either in cash or in more notes. When this is the case, the coupon payment for cash is usually less than the coupon payment in kind.

However, mezzanine financing need not be in the form of debt. In some cases it will be in the form of preferred stock. In such circumstances, the preferred stock has a set dividend payment, as well as a conversion right into the common stock. The main point is that mezzanine finance provides the filler between the senior debt of the company and its bottom-line common equity holders.

The equity kicker often contained in mezzanine financing is some form of option, warrant, or conversion feature that allows the mezzanine investor to convert or receive some portion of the equity interest in the underlying company. Frequently, mezzanine financing will include some form of cash or PIK coupon plus the equity kicker. Exhibit 25.1 provides a general view of the capital structure of a company. This exhibit illustrates the many forms that mezzanine financing can take

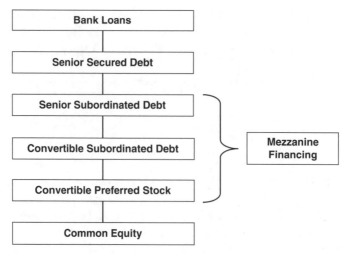

Exhibit 25.1   Overview of corporate capital structure

between senior debt and common equity. Therefore, the gap that mezzanine finance might fill can be quite large, and can include several tranches of junior debt or preferred equity.

Mezzanine financing is not used to provide cash for the day-to-day operations of a company. Instead, it is used during transitional periods in a company's life. Frequently, a company is in a situation where its senior creditors (banks) are unwilling to provide any additional capital and the company does not wish to issue additional stock. Mezzanine financing can fill this void.

Mezzanine debt has become increasingly popular for two reasons. First, after the 2001–2002 recession in the U.S. economy, banks and other senior debt lenders became less aggressive about providing capital. Second, there are now fewer lending institutions in the bank market. The credit and liquidity crisis of 2007 and 2008 resulted in many bank failures and mergers (Washington Mutual/JPMorgan Chase, Wachovia/Wells Fargo, Merrill Lynch/Bank of America, etc.). As a result, by 2009 there were fewer than 25 players in the syndicated loan market.

Still, mezzanine financing is a niche market, operating between so-called story credits and the junk bond market. **Story credits** are private debt issues that have a good story to sell them. Generally, these are senior secured financings with good credit. However, not all firms have good credit or interesting stories. Mezzanine debt may be their best or only source of financing.

Mezzanine financing is often described as a "middle market" vehicle. This refers to companies that are not as large as those companies that have ready access to the financial markets but larger than companies seeking venture capital. Companies in this middle market category form the broad backbone of any economy, and generally have a market capitalization in the range of $200 million to $2 billion. These middle market companies often use mezzanine financing in the range of $5 million to $50 million to complete small acquisitions.

Some investors, such as insurance companies, view mezzanine financing as a traditional form of debt. Insurance companies are concerned with the preservation of capital, the consistency of cash flows, and the ability to make timely interest payments. Other investors, such as mezzanine limited partnerships, LBO firms, and commercial banks, focus on the capital appreciation or equity component of mezzanine debt. Often these firms demand that an equity kicker be attached to the mezzanine debt. This kicker is usually in the form of equity warrants to purchase stock at a discounted strike price. Mezzanine finance, by definition, defies generalization. There is no typical or standard deal structure. Each financing consists of unique terms and conditions that depend on the preferences of the user and provider and that emerge from a highly negotiated process. The mezzanine piece can be structured as debt or equity, depending on how much capital the owner wants and how much control the owner wants to cede to the mezzanine partner. The flexibility of mezzanine financing is what makes it so popular with borrowers and investors alike. Both sides can tailor the mezzanine tranche to fit their borrowing and investment criteria. Mezzanine financing is the ultimate in flexible term negotiations.

Return expectations for mezzanine financing

Mezzanine financing provides a greater risk profile to an investor than senior debt because of its unsecured status, lower credit priority, and equity kicker. Typically, the total return sought by investors in mezzanine financing is in the range of 15% to 20%.

However, this return range is significantly below that for venture capital and leveraged buyouts. The reduced return reflects a lower risk profile compared to other forms of private equity. The reason is twofold. First, mezzanine financing does not necessarily translate into control of the company compared to a leveraged buyout. Mezzanine financing is much more passive than an LBO. Second, mezzanine financing is appropriate for those companies that have a reliable cash flow. This is in contrast to venture capital where the start-up company does not have sufficient cash flows to support debt.

The largest piece of the total return is the coupon rate on the mezzanine security, usually 10% to 14%. Further, this coupon payment may be divided between a cash payment and a payment in kind. The remainder of the upside comes from the equity kicker—either warrants or some other equity conversion. The equity kicker can provide an additional 5% to 10% return to the mezzanine finance provider.

Exhibit 25.2 presents the returns to mezzanine financing funds over the years from 1990 to 2008. As can be seen, the returns are quite variable, reflecting the higher risk associated with this type of investment. Although returns are mostly in the low to middle teens, the returns can be as high as 30%.

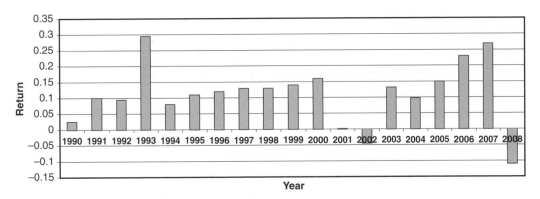

Average   11.12%   Std. Dev.   9.79%   Sharpe   0.64

Exhibit 25.2   Returns to mezzanine debt

In general, however, this asset class has not lived up to its return expectations. The average return over this period has only been about 12%, below the target returns for mezzanine financing as an asset class.

Mezzanine debt and the J-curve

In previous chapters we discussed the J-curve effect for private equity. Essentially, in the early years of a private equity fund, the fund experiences a negative return because it incurs management fees while investing the fund's capital. It generally takes four to five years before the general partner for the private equity fund begins to harvest profits from the initial investments. Until then, the fund experiences a negative cash flow to pay the assessed management fees.

However, with a mezzanine fund, the J-curve effect is not a factor. One of the distinct advantages of mezzanine financing is its immediate cash-on-cash return. Mezzanine debt bears a coupon that requires twice-yearly interest payments to investors. As a result, mezzanine financing funds can avoid the steep negative returns associated with venture capital or leveraged buyout funds.

Simple example of mezzanine debt

Exhibit 25.3 lays out how mezzanine capital can lower the capital costs for a company. Bank debt is cheap and equity is expensive. Unfortunately, a bank may only be willing to loan up to 60% of the total capital structure of the company. Equity must fill the remaining capital gap unless mezzanine debt can be used to help fill the gap.

In Exhibit 25.3, we show a simple capital structure for a company faced with a 60% bank loan/40% equity capital structure. We then replace half of the equity capital with mezzanine debt with a coupon of 15%. At the bottom of the exhibit we calculate the weighted cost of capital for the company. Without mezzanine debt, the cost of capital is 16.8%. But when mezzanine debt is added to the capital structure, the weighted average cost of capital declines to 13.8%.

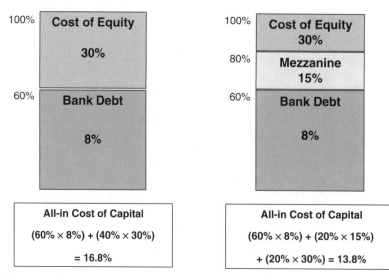

Exhibit 25.3   Mezzanine Financing and the Cost of Capital

Mezzanine compared to other forms of financing

Not only does mezzanine financing fill a gap in a company's capital structure, it also fills a gap in the capital markets. Increasingly, high-yield financing is not available to middle market companies. High-yield issues now tend to start at $400 million and continue up. The same is true for leveraged loans. Generally, it is large public companies that tap the high-yield or leveraged-loan market. Conversely, mezzanine financing generally seeks amounts below $400 million.

Mezzanine financing is highly negotiated and can be tailored to any company's situation. The flip side is that the level of tailoring makes mezzanine debt illiquid. Any trading usually involves a lengthy negotiation process with the company that issued the mezzanine debt to buy back its securities or with a secondary private equity investor. In both cases, mezzanine debt is often sold at a large discount in the secondary market.

Mezzanine debt is typically provided by mezzanine debt funds raised by private equity firms. Mezzanine financing stands behind senior debt and is usually applied on an earnings before interest, taxes, depreciation, and amortization (EBITDA) multiple basis. While bank loans/senior loans generally require a loan-to-EBITDA multiple of 2 to 2.5, mezzanine debt typically allows for a higher multiple of 4 to 4.5. Mezzanine debt is unsecured financing as compared to senior loans that are typically secured by the assets of the underlying company. Because mezzanine debt is not backed by collateral, it carries a higher coupon payment than senior debt.

Mezzanine debt is generally medium-term money, usually five to seven years in length. Typically mezzanine financing requires only payment of interest up until maturity. There is no amortization of the underlying debt. Mezzanine debt often includes a PIK toggle application that allows the underlying company to choose whether it will pay cash or more mezzanine bonds in kind.

Last, mezzanine financing is typically unique to the situation. It is custom tailored to meet a specific need of the underlying company. This makes mezzanine financing the least liquid part of a company's capital structure.

In Exhibit 25.4, we compare mezzanine debt to leveraged loans and high-yield debt. Notice that leveraged loans have the strictest debt covenants, which lead to greater protection from default, but

Exhibit 25.4 Comparison of leveraged loans, high-yield bonds, and mezzanine debt

	Leveraged Loans	High-Yield Bonds	Mezzanine Debt
Seniority	Most senior	Contractual and structural subordination	Lowest priority
Type of security	First lien on assets	Unsecured	Unsecured
Credit rating	Required	Required	Not required
Loan covenants	Extensive	Less comprehensive	Minimal—typically related only to payment of coupons
Term	5 years	7 to 10 years	4 to 6 years
Amortization	Installments	Bullet payment	Bullet payment
Coupon type	Cash/floating	Cash/fixed	Cash/PIK/fixed
Coupon rate	LIBOR + 300 to 450 bps	8% to 12%	12% to 15%
Prepayment penalty	Usually none	High—usually the company must pay a call premium	Moderate—sometimes equity conversion is forced
Equity kicker	None	Sometimes	Almost always—usually equity warrants
Recovery if default	60% to 100%	40% to 50%	20% to 30%
Liquidity	High	Low	Minimal

also to a lower return. Further, leveraged loans do not contain any type of equity kicker, so they do not share in any upside of the company. Also, a credit rating is required before a bank will lend credit through a leveraged loan, whereas this is not necessary for mezzanine debt. In addition, leveraged loans typically have a floating interest rate tied to the London Interbank Offered Rate (LIBOR), while mezzanine debt has a fixed coupon. Additionally, mezzanine financing typically has some PIK provision with respect to its coupon payments, whereas leveraged loans never have such a provision.

One last point is that mezzanine investors focus on the total return from mezzanine financing, including future equity participation through a convertible security or warrants attached to the mezzanine debt. This is distinctly different from bank loans, which focus exclusively on the cash yield. High-yield debt falls somewhere between these two forms of financing.

EXAMPLES OF MEZZANINE FINANCING

As noted earlier, mezzanine financing fills either a gap in a company's financial structure or a gap in the supply of capital in the financial markets. This makes mezzanine financing extremely flexible. The examples that follow demonstrate this flexibility. Note that while mezzanine financing is mostly the domain of smaller companies in the middle market, large companies are not excluded from its use, as the First Data Corporation example demonstrates. There are seven basic transactions to which mezzanine debt is applied:

1. Management buyouts
2. Growth/expansion
3. Acquisitions
4. Recapitalizations
5. Real estate financing
6. Leveraged buyouts
7. Bridge financing

Mezzanine financing for a management buyout

In March 2005, the senior management team for the bakery and coffee restaurant chain Au Bon Pain led a $90 million management buyout (MBO) of the chain from its parent company, Compass Group PLC. Au Bon Pain is an operator and franchisor of fast, casual bakery cafes throughout the United States.

The $90 million deal was financed with $82 million in debt, $20 million of which was supplied by PNC Mezzanine Capital of Pittsburgh, Pennsylvania. The $20 million of mezzanine financing was broken down into:

- $10 million of senior subordinated debt with equity warrants.
- $4.7 million of junior PIK subordinated debt with warrants.
- $5.3 million of convertible preferred stock.

The strengths of the mezzanine financing were:

- Support the management in its buyout of the company from the parent.
- Structure a debt facility to support the growth of the company.
- Provide flexibility to accommodate the seller's equity rollover in the MBO.
- Provide an additional equity-like cushion for the senior lenders.
- Provide the management of the company with substantial equity incentives.[1]

---

[1] See PNC Capital, "Investment Case Studies," www.pncmezzaninecapital.com/investmentprofiles.

Mezzanine financing for growth and expansion

T2Systems, a software manufacturing and service company based in Indianapolis, Indiana, could not raise traditional bank financing. T2Systems provides software, hardware, and outsourcing solutions for parking management, permits, enforcement, control, and collection. It needed capital to expand its customer service and R&D departments.

Petra Capital Partners provided a $3 million mezzanine contribution in 2007 to T2Systems. The capital was used to hire 35 additional staff and to support the rollout of T2System's parking solutions package beyond its existing customer base.

The debt will mature in five years and is structured as preferred equity. As such, T2Systems must make monthly dividend payments for five years. At maturity, the company is required to repay the debt completely and make good on the attached warrants. T2Systems estimates that the additional capital will enable it to grow by 150% year over year.[2]

Mezzanine debt for an acquisition

In 2005, Brockway Moran & Partners purchased the Woodstream Corporation from Friend Skoler & Company LLC. Woodstream is a maker of wild animal cages, traps, rodent control devices, and pesticides. The purchase price was $100 million.

Of the purchase price, $17 million was provided by CIT Private Equity and Denali Advisors LLC as a subordinated note. This mezzanine debt had the following terms:

- Subordinated to a $58 million senior bank facility.
- 7% cash interest.
- 7% PIK interest.
- Warrants to purchase up to 5% of Woodstream's equity at a price of $0.05 per share.
- Repayment of the mezzanine debt in five years or at an exit event.[3]

Mezzanine debt to recapitalize a company

In June 2007, American Capital, one of the largest players in the private equity and mezzanine debt space, provided $548 million to Exstream Software to recapitalize the company's balance sheet. American Capital's investment took the form of a senior term loan, senior subordinated mezzanine debt, junior subordinated mezzanine debt, convertible preferred stock, and common equity. In fact, American Capital's investment is almost a perfect demonstration of a complete capital structure investment similar to that shown in Exhibit 25.1. American Capital's investment in Exstream Software is shown in Exhibit 25.5. Apparently this recapitalization worked. Hewlett-Packard purchased Exstream in 2008 for an estimated $1 billion.

Mezzanine finance in real estate

Mezzanine financing in real estate has grown in popularity as a result of the increased securitization of real estate and the packaging of pools of loans for sale into the secondary market. Mezzanine capital fills the gap between the first mortgage financing, which usually has a loan-to-value ratio of 40 to 75%, and the equity contributed to the project. Typical equity contributions for real estate are

---

[2] See Gary Stern, "Is Mezzanine Financing Good for Your Business?," www.smallbusinessreview.com, 2008; and "Petra Capital Partners Invests in T2 Systems, Inc.," Business Wire, June 25, 2007.

[3] See Ian Giddy, "Woodstream's Mezzanine Debt: An Exercise in Leveraged Finance," www.pages.stern.nyu.edu/igiddy/cases/woodstream.

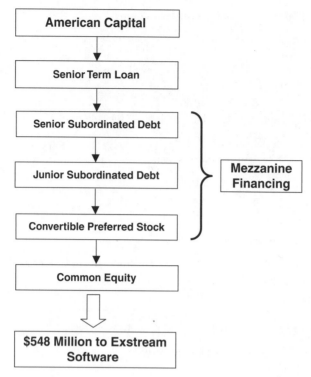

Exhibit 25.5   Example of mezzanine debt to recapitalize a company

in the 10% to 15% range. It is in between bank loans and equity that you'll find mezzanine financing, supplying historically 10% to 40% of the project's capital structure.

Mezzanine financing can take several forms in real estate. Often it involves extending credit to the partners or other equity holders of a borrower in exchange for a pledge of such parties' equity interests. These pledges include the rights to share in the distribution of income. Conversely, the mezzanine debt provider may take a preferred equity position. This entitles the mezzanine debt investor to distributions of excess cash flow after debt service, but ahead of the borrower's principals. A combination loan structure may also be used to mix a first mortgage loan with mezzanine financing at an aggregate loan-to-value ratio of 90 to 95%. This blend of financing may contain a shared appreciation or contingent feature, or an exit fee paid by the borrower, or sometimes both.

For example, on March 24, 2006, W Financial successfully provided a $4,297,779 mezzanine loan subordinate to a $20,000,000 first mortgage construction loan for the development of a 12-unit mixed-use property in downtown Manhattan. W Financial is an investment company that specializes in special situation financing for commercial real estate projects. The finished building, located in the trendy neighborhood of TriBeCa, consists of retail space, offices, and residential condominium units.

Mezzanine financing in a leveraged buyout

Mezzanine financing is an established component of many leveraged buyouts. The large amount of debt frequently used in a leveraged buyout (leverage, after all, implies a lot of debt is to be issued in the buyout) often requires a tiering of the capital structure. Not all debt can be senior. A significant amount of the financing may come from mezzanine investors.

Also, bank lenders will not be willing to provide the full debt capacity needed to finance an LBO. It goes back to the saying that "not all debt can be senior." Banks look for junior or subordinated debt as an additional so-called loss tranche below their bank loans in the event of bankruptcy. The greater the amount of junior debt backing an LBO, the more comfortable the bank lenders will be because they know that there will be more than enough assets to cover those loans that have first call on the company's assets if the LBO doesn't work.

An example of this is the LBO of First Data Corporation by Kohlberg Kravis Roberts & Company (KKR) in 2007. KKR paid $26.5 billion for First Data. First Data had been spun off from the American Express Company and had gone public in 1992. It provides electronic commerce solutions such as credit card, debit card, check and prepaid payment processing and collections.

As part of the First Data buyout, KKR, along with its bankers, put together one of the largest financing packages ever, $25 billion in loans and subordinated debt. This was to be used to finance the buyout and the redemption of some of First Data's outstanding debt. The whole packaged consisted of:

- $13 billion in senior secured term loans, distributed across several tranches.
- $2 billion in a senior secured revolver.
- $3.75 billion in senior unsecured cash-pay term loans.
- $2.75 billion in senior unsecured PIK term loans.
- $2.5 billion in a senior subordinated unsecured term loan.
- $1 billion in senior unsecured PIK notes.

The full details of the First Data Corporation buyout financing are presented in Exhibit 25.6. Note that there are several tranches of mezzanine debt in this capital structure, starting with the $3.75 billion senior unsecured cash-pay term loan. Again, we can see the value of mezzanine debt: it is flexible, can be structured to fit any situation, and can plug many gaps. In addition, we can see that mezzanine financing commands a higher coupon rate, often denoted in payment-in-kind coupons.

Mezzanine financing as bridge financing

As the prior buyout example illustrates, mezzanine financing can be very creative to ensure that sufficient debt is raised to finance the buyout. Often, a good portion of the initial LBO debt is raised as bridge financing.

Bridge financing is a method of debt financing that is used to maintain liquidity while waiting for an anticipated and reasonably expected inflow of cash. In the case of an LBO, bridge financing is used as another form of gap financing. The private equity firm finances part of the LBO purchase price with bridge loans from banks. The loans are then converted to mezzanine debt after a short period of time. Another example will help.

Once again, KKR, with TPG, took center stage in 2007 with the mega $45 billion buyout of TXU Corporation. This buyout was so big that it required over $35 billion in debt financing alone. Initially, however, KKR and TPG were not able to issue mezzanine debt to finance the acquisition, so they turned to their banks for bridge loans. In all, $35.75 billion in total debt was raised, broken down into two big chunks:

1. $24.5 billion in senior bank loans at a cost of LIBOR +3.50%.
2. $11.25 billion in bridge loans to be converted to mezzanine debt as soon as possible.

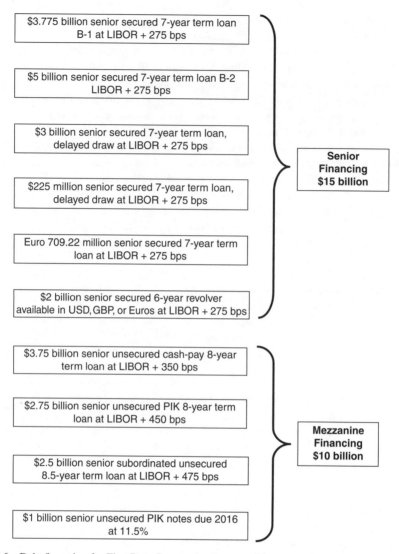

Exhibit 25.6 Debt financing for First Data Corporation leveraged buyout

The LBO closed in October 2007 with the senior and bridge loans in place. Starting in December 2007, TXU, now called Energy Future Holdings, began to refinance the bridge loans with mezzanine debt. Eventually, all of the bridge loans were replaced with mezzanine debt by June 2008. Exhibit 25.7 shows the initial bridge loans for TXU and the subsequent conversion into mezzanine notes.

Mezzanine total return

Mezzanine debt is valued on a total return basis, including the return of the potential equity participation in the underlying company. This equity participation can come from a conversion feature of the mezzanine debt or from equity warrants attached to the mezzanine debt.

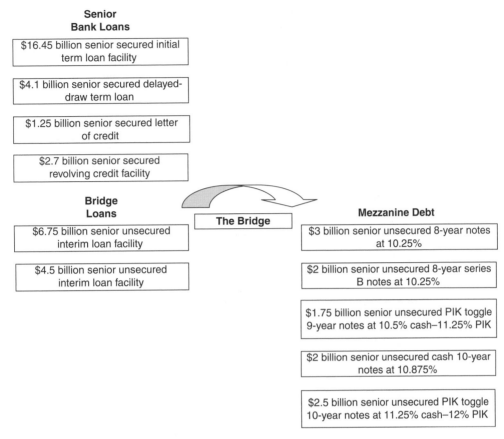

Exhibit 25.7   Bridge financing for TXU leveraged buyout

Therefore, the typical exit strategy for mezzanine debt occurs when the underlying company goes public, or through a large equity issuance by the underlying company. In addition, the borrower can be sold or recapitalized. When one of these events happens, the mezzanine debt provider gets back the face value of the mezzanine debt plus the sale of stock from the conversion rights or sale of warrants attached to the mezzanine debt. This equity kicker is what kicks up the total return of the mezzanine debt beyond its coupon payment.

INVESTORS IN MEZZANINE DEBT

In the preceding section, we reviewed the uses of mezzanine debt. In this section we review the investors in mezzanine debt. In addition, we consider the advantages of mezzanine financing to both the investor and the issuer.

Mezzanine funds

Mezzanine funds must pay attention to the same securities laws as hedge funds, venture capital funds, and buyout funds. This means that mezzanine funds must ensure that they fall within either the 3(c)(1) or the 3(c)(7) exemptions of the Investment Company Act of 1940. These safe harbor provisions ensure that mezzanine funds do not have to adhere to the filing, disclosure, record-keeping, and reporting requirements of mutual funds.

There are two key distinctions between venture capital funds and mezzanine funds. The first is the return expectations. Mezzanine funds seek total rates of return in the 15% to 20% range. Compare this to LBO funds that seek returns in the 20% and 30% range and venture capital funds that seek returns in the 30% to 50% range. This puts mezzanine funds at the lower end of the private equity risk-return spectrum.

Exhibit 25.8 shows the risk-return spectrum for the four basic forms of private equity: venture capital, leveraged buyouts, distressed debt (discussed in the next chapter), and mezzanine financing. Mezzanine financing is the least risky of the private equity strategies. Part of this comes from the fact that mezzanine debt is not subject to the J-curve effect, unlike venture capital and leveraged buyouts, and is not faced with a distressed situation.

For example, senior bank debt in a private equity transaction is usually priced at 200 to 300 basis points over LIBOR, while mezzanine financing usually bears a coupon rate of 400 to 600 basis points over LIBOR. In addition, mezzanine financing often contains some form of equity kicker that can raise the total return toward 20%.

Mezzanine financing is the most expensive form of debt because it is the last to be repaid. It ranks at the bottom of the creditor totem pole, just above equity. As a result, it is expected to earn a rate of return only slightly less than common equity. Exhibit 25.2 demonstrates that rates of return are quite favorable: generally in the 12% to 15% range, but as high as 30% in one year. Given the highly leveraged nature of companies that use mezzanine debt, the return can, in fact, resemble that of equity returns.

Second, mezzanine funds are staffed with different expertise than a venture capital fund. Most venture capital funds have staff with heavy technology-related experience, including former senior executives of software, semiconductor, and Internet companies. In contrast, mezzanine funds are inundated with financial engineers, experienced at structuring and negotiating loans incorporating the use of equity kickers and/or warrants.

Mezzanine funds have not attracted the same flow of investor capital as venture capital funds or leveraged buyout funds. However, mezzanine funds have enjoyed steady growth throughout the

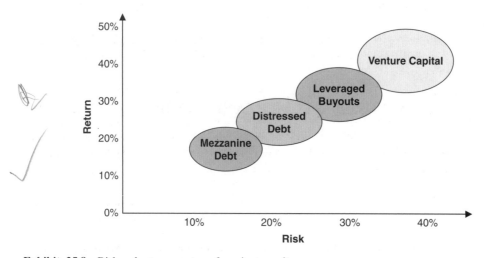

Exhibit 25.8   Risk and return spectrum for private equity

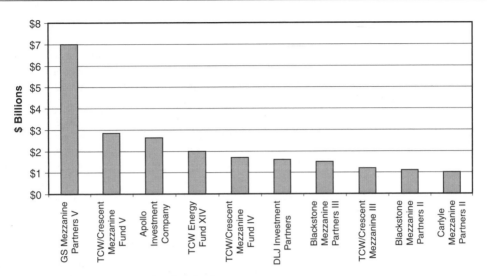

Exhibit 25.9   Ten largest mezzanine debt funds

1990s. Exhibit 25.9 shows the 10 largest mezzanine funds.[4] Note that these funds are considerably smaller than the gargantuan ($20 billion plus) leveraged buyout funds. This reflects the fact that mezzanine financing is distinctly a middle market phenomenon and cannot support mega funds of the type commonly associated with leveraged buyouts.

Another reason for the relatively small size of the mezzanine market as reflected by the funds in Exhibit 25.9 is that with a robust economy throughout most of the 1990s, the demand for mezzanine debt was not so great. Also, mezzanine financing tends to be small, generally in the $20 million to $300 million range. Last, mezzanine debt, while it can yield greater returns than junk bonds, cannot compete with the returns earned by venture capitalists and leveraged buyout funds.

Mezzanine funds look for businesses that have a high potential for growth and earnings, but do not have a sufficient cash flow to receive full funding from banks or other senior creditors. Banks may be unwilling to lend because of a short operating history or a high debt-to-equity ratio. Mezzanine funds look for companies that, over the next four to seven years, can repay the mezzanine debt through a debt refinancing, an initial equity offering, or an acquisition.

Mezzanine funds are risk lenders. This means that in a liquidation of the company, mezzanine investors expect little or no recovery of their principal. Mezzanine debt is rarely secured. As the last rung of the financing ladder (see the earlier First Data example) it is often viewed as a form of equity by the more senior lenders. Consequently, mezzanine investors must assess investment opportunities outside of conventional banking parameters. Existing collateral and short-term cash flow are less of a consideration. Instead, mezzanine investors carefully review the management team and its business plan to assess the likelihood that future growth will be achieved by the issuing company. In sum, similar to stockholders, mezzanine debt investors assume the risk of the company's success or failure.

Investors in mezzanine funds are generally pension funds, endowments, and foundations. These investors do not have the internal infrastructure or expertise to invest directly in the mezzanine market. Therefore, they enter this alternative investment strategy as limited partners through a

---

[4] See Sree Vidya Bhaktavatsalam and Jason Kelly, "Mezzanine Funds Gain an Edge in Credit Market Turmoils," Thinkingmoose.blogspot.com, December 14, 2007.

mezzanine fund. Mezzanine funds also tend to charge a similar fee structure as venture capital and LBO funds: a management fee in the 1% to 2% range and a profit-sharing fee of 20%.

Similar to hedge funds, venture capital funds, and LBO funds, mezzanine funds are managed by a general partner who has full investment discretion. Many mezzanine funds are managed by merchant banks that have experience with gap financing or by mezzanine professionals who previously worked in the mezzanine departments of insurance companies and banks.

Other mezzanine lenders

Pension and endowment funds are not the only investors in mezzanine debt. The high coupon rates plus the chance for some upside potential also appeal to more conservative investors.

Insurance companies

As previously noted, insurance companies are a major source of mezzanine financing. They are natural providers of mezzanine debt because the durations of their liabilities (life insurance policies and annuities) are best matched with longer-term debt instruments.

These investors take more of a fixed income approach and place a high value on the scheduled repayment of principal. Insurance companies are more concerned with a higher coupon payment than with the total return represented by equity warrants. Therefore, insurance companies act more like traditional lenders than like equity investors. They provide mezzanine financing to higher-quality credit names and emphasize the preservation versus appreciation of capital.

Traditional senior lenders

Interestingly, banks and other providers of senior secured debt often participate in mezzanine financing. This financing takes the form of so-called stretch financing where a bank lends more money than it believes is prudent given existing assets. This excess advance of debt beyond the collateral value of a company's business assets is the stretch part of the financing, and is often called an "airball."[5]

Stretch financing may be provided, for instance, when an LBO firm agrees to put up more equity for a buyout deal. Generally, the amount looked for is 30% or more equity in the LBO. In addition, the senior lender may ask for an equity kicker such as warrants to compensate it for stretching its financing beyond the assets available.

Traditional venture capital firms

When the economy softens, venture capital firms look for ways to maintain their stellar returns. In addition, the large flow of capital into venture funds makes it necessary to expand their investment horizons resulting in a greater interest in mezzanine financing.

Furthermore, mezzanine financing and venture capital frequently go hand in hand, with mezzanine debt serving as the bridge. In this case, the bridge is the last round of private financing before a start-up company goes public.

As an example, consider Mimosa systems. Mimosa helps other companies store and archive e-mails. The kind of comprehensive archiving that Mimosa offers is necessary for the e-discovery process, the process of searching through a company's electronic archives, primarily e-mails. With the

---

[5] See Bailey Barnard, "Mezzanine Financing Demystified," www.caltius.com/pdfs/DemistMezz.PDF, January 2002.

growing number of legal requests, primarily as a result of Sarbanes-Oxley, litigation and Securities and Exchange Commission (SEC) records requests, there has been a lot of money looking to invest in this field. Consequently, by 2008, Mimosa was able to raise $51 million in various rounds of venture capital financing.

In May 2008, it entered into a last round of financing before its IPO. This round was called the mezzanine round, and it was financed by venture capital firms such as Focus Ventures, August Capital, Clearstone Venture Partners, JAFCO Ventures, and the Mayfield Fund.

As the preceding example demonstrates, the lines between mezzanine financing and different forms of private equity can become blurred. With respect to pre-IPO companies, it is difficult to distinguish where venture capital ends and mezzanine financing begins. Also, as we noted earlier, mezzanine financing can be used as the last leg in the capital structure of a start-up company before it goes public. This bridge financing allows the company to clean up its balance sheet before its IPO.

Advantages of mezzanine debt to the investor

Mezzanine debt is a hybrid. It has debt-like components but usually provides for some form of equity appreciation. This appeals to investors who are more conservative but like to have some spice in their portfolios.

High equity-like returns

The high returns to mezzanine debt compared to senior debt appeal to traditional fixed income investors who look for a little extra yield. Mezzanine debt typically has a coupon rate that is 200 to 300 basis points over that of senior secured. In the First Data and TXU examples, the mezzanine debt was priced at a premium of 100 to 200 basis points compared to the senior debt, and for mezzanine notes, the coupon rate was 300 to 350 basis points more than the senior debt. While insurance companies and similar investors in this market generally eschew riskier equity-like assets, given their long-term investment horizon, they may be less concerned with short-term earnings fluctuations associated with this hybrid vehicle.

Further, mezzanine debt often has an equity kicker, typically in the form of warrants. These warrants may have a strike price as low as $0.01 per share. The number of warrants included is inversely proportional to the coupon rate. The higher the coupon rate, the fewer the warrants that need to be issued.

Nonetheless, the investor receives both a high coupon payment plus participation in the up-side of the company should it achieve its growth potential. The equity component can be significant, representing 5% to 20% of the outstanding equity of the company. For this reason, mezzanine debt is often viewed as an investment in the company as opposed to an unsecured lien on assets.

Priority of payment

Although mezzanine debt is generally not secured by collateral, it still ranks higher than equity and may be ranked higher than other unsecured creditors (e.g. trade creditors). For example, in the TXU mezzanine financing case, all of the mezzanine notes issued were labeled "senior unsecured." This raises the potential for more notes to be issued that would be subordinated to the senior notes.

Schedule of repayment

Like senior secured debt, mezzanine debt usually has a repayment schedule. This schedule may not start for several years as senior debt is paid off, but it provides some certainty of when a return of capital is expected.

Instant returns

Unlike other forms of private equity, mezzanine debt provides instant returns through the coupon payment on the debt. This provides investors with a high level of current return instead of waiting for returns along the J-curve. However, these instant returns can be in the form of payment-in-kind interest, not really a cash flow but the issuance of more debt.

Board representation

A subordinated lender generally expects to be considered an equity partner. In some cases, mezzanine lenders may request board observation rights, while in other cases, the mezzanine lender may insist on a seat on the board of directors with full voting rights.

Restrictions on the borrower

Although mezzanine debt is typically unsecured, it still may come with restrictions on the borrower. The mezzanine lender may have the right to approve or disapprove of additional debt and require that any new debt be subordinated to the original mezzanine debt. The lender may also enjoy final approval over any contemplated acquisitions, changes in the management team, or payment of dividends.

Advantages provided to the company/borrower

Mezzanine debt is a tool for plugging holes in a company's business plan. It can be shaped and molded to meet the company's business needs. Its malleability appeals to corporate issuers.

Flexibility

There are no set terms to mezzanine financing. Subordinated debt comes in all shapes, maturities, and sizes. The structure of mezzanine debt can be as flexible as needed to accommodate the parties involved. For example, the repayment of principal is usually deferred for several years and can be tailored to fit the borrower's cash flow projections. Further, mezzanine debt can be structured so that no interest payments begin for two to three years. Alternatively, mezzanine debt can be structured so that interest is due and payable only in the first two to three years.

Semi-equity

Mezzanine lenders focus on the total return of the investment over the life of the debt. Therefore, they are less concerned with collateral or short-term earnings fluctuations. In fact, subordinated unsecured debt resembles a senior class of equity, and most senior lenders consider a company to have strengthened its balance sheet by adding this layer of capital.

Lengthening of maturity

The borrower can improve its cash flow by lengthening the maturity of the debt repayment associated with mezzanine financing. This is because the payback of the mezzanine debt is often delayed until the fifth or sixth year, and is usually executed as a lump-sum or bullet payment.

No collateral

The borrower does not have to pledge any collateral for mezzanine debt.

Payment in kind

As discussed previously, mezzanine debt coupons are often structured so that some form of the coupon is not required to be paid in cash but can be paid in kind. This means that the holder of the mezzanine debt receives additional issuances of debt as part of the coupon payment on the debt. This can provide the issuer of the mezzanine debt considerable flexibility if there is a crunch regarding the cash flows of the company. Even more flexibility can be built into mezzanine financing with PIK toggle notes. The TXU example is a good demonstration of PIK toggle notes. TXU (now Energy Future Holdings) has a choice in how it wishes to make coupon payments. It can pay in cash at a lower coupon rate (e.g. 10.5%), or it can pay out interest in the form of PIK but at a higher cost of 11.5%.

Less equity dilution

The borrower has not immediately diluted the equity of its outstanding shares. True, mezzanine debt almost always comes with some form of equity kicker that will eventually dilute the number of outstanding common shares. However, this kicker may not kick in for several years, affording the company a chance to implement its business plan and improve its share price before it is subject to dilution. Additionally, the company can refinance the mezzanine debt at a later date with traditional bonds before the equity kickers come into play.

Cheaper than common equity

Even though senior lenders may consider mezzanine financing to be a form of equity, it does not carry all the risks of equity. Therefore, it does not need to yield the same total return as expected by shareholders. Exhibit 25.10 shows a typical term sheet for a mezzanine debt offering.

Negotiations with senior creditors

The subordination of mezzanine debt is typically accomplished in an agreement with the company's existing creditors. The agreement is usually called an **intercreditor agreement**. The intercreditor agreement may be negotiated separately between the senior creditors and the mezzanine investor, or it may be incorporated directly into the loan agreement between the mezzanine investor and the company. In either case, this agreement places certain restrictions on both the senior creditor and the mezzanine investor.

Exhibit 25.10   Hypothetical terms for a mezzanine debt offering

Company	Company XYZ
Debt amount	$50 million
Security on debt	None
Interest rate	12% coupon with up to 4% of coupon as PIK
Maturity	6 years
Amortization	6-year bullet
Subordination	Subordinated to bank loans and senior notes
Conversion rights	None
Warrants	10 warrants per $1,000 face value detachable and exercisable at $0.50
Exercise period for warrants	1 year from the date of issuance until maturity
Tag-along rights	Holders of warrants have the right to participate in any sale of common stock by the issuer
Drag-along rights	Company may require debt holders to sell their warrants in the sale of a controlling interest of the company
Board representation	None
Registration	None: sold as an exempt offering under Rule 144A of the Securities Act of 1933

Subordination

The subordination may be either a blanket subordination or a springing subordination.[6] A **blanket subordination** prevents any payment of principal or interest to the mezzanine investor until after the senior debt has been fully repaid. A **springing subordination** occurs when the mezzanine investor receives payments while the senior debt is still outstanding. However, if a default occurs or a covenant is violated, the subordination "springs" up to stop all payments to the mezzanine investor until the default is cured or fully repaid.

Acceleration

The violation of any covenant may result in the senior debt lender accelerating the senior loan. This means that the senior lender can declare the senior debt due and payable immediately. This typically forces a default and allows the senior lender to enforce the collateral security.

Drawdown

The order of drawdown is important to senior lenders. Because senior lenders often view mezzanine capital as a form of equity financing, they will require that mezzanine debt be fully drawn before lending the senior debt.

Restrictions to amending credit facility documents

Intercreditor agreements usually restrict amendments to the credit facility so that the terms of the intercreditor agreement cannot be circumvented by new agreements between the individual lenders and the borrower.

---

[6] See Chapman Tripp and Sheffield Young, "Mezzanine Finance: One Person's Ceiling Is Another Person's Floor," *Finance Law Focus* (November 1998).

Assignment

Senior lenders typically restrict the rights of the mezzanine investor to assign its interests to a third party. Generally, senior lenders will allow an assignment providing the assignee executes a new intercreditor agreement with the senior lender.

Insurance proceeds

Mezzanine lenders typically want any insurance proceeds to be deployed to purchase new assets for the borrower and not to repay senior debt. The reason for this is found in the equity-like nature of mezzanine financing. Mezzanine investors consider their debt to be a long-term investment in the company where a significant return component depends on the operations of the company appreciating in value.

Takeout provisions

A **takeout provision** allows the mezzanine investor to purchase the senior debt once it has been repaid to a certain level. This is one of the most important provisions in an intercreditor agreement and goes to the heart of mezzanine investing. By taking out the senior debt, the mezzanine investor becomes the most senior level of financing in the company and, in fact, can take control of the company. At this point the mezzanine investor usually converts the debt into equity (through either convertible bonds or warrants) and becomes the largest shareholder of the company.

From the preceding discussion, it can be seen that intercreditor agreements are a matter of give-and-take between senior secured lenders and mezzanine investors. Mezzanine investors are willing to grant senior lenders certain provisions that protect the capital at risk of the senior lenders. In return, mezzanine investors have the ability to buy out the senior debt and then assert their equity rights in the company.

CONCLUSION

In this chapter we identified a form of debt investing that is really a variation on private equity investing. Mezzanine financing is the epoxy of the financing world. It fits in where traditional debt and equity cannot. Like epoxy, mezzanine financing is thoroughly flexible. Its shape and size depends on the specifics of the financing needed. In addition, mezzanine financing can strengthen a debtor company's balance sheet by providing the glue between debt and equity.

Borrowers like mezzanine capital because it provides an inexpensive way to raise money without immediately diluting the outstanding equity of the company. Investors, in turn, like the high yields offered by mezzanine debt plus the ability to share in some of the appreciated value of the debtor company. Both like the ability to tailor mezzanine financing to the needs of the borrower and the investment requirements of the lender. Like epoxy, mezzanine debt is extremely malleable.

The returns to mezzanine financing, however, are decidedly mixed. Despite target return ranges of 15% to 20% and the presence of equity kickers, the average mezzanine fund over the 19 year period of 1990–2008 achieved a rate of return between 11 and 12%. This return exceeded U.S. Treasury bonds and was close to the return of the stock market. This is generally the target range for mezzanine debt. Recall from Chapter 24 that the 20-year average return to the S&P 500 through 2008 is only 8.32%.

26

Debt as Private Equity Part II:
Distressed Debt

Distressed debt investing is the practice of purchasing the debt of troubled companies. These companies may have already defaulted on their debt, may be on the brink of default, or may be seeking bankruptcy protection. Now, a company seeking protection from its creditors does not seem like a very appealing investment, but, beneath the distress of the company, investment opportunities may well exist. Like the other forms of private equity previously discussed, this form of investing requires a longer-term horizon and the ability to accept the lack of liquidity for a security where often no trading market exists.

Similar to mezzanine debt discussed in the previous chapter, the returns to distressed debt depend less on the overall performance of the stock market. This is because the value of the debt of a distressed or bankrupt company is more likely to rise and fall with the fortunes of the individual company. In particular, the company's negotiations with its creditors will have a much greater impact on the value of the company's debt than will the performance of the general economy.

The key to distressed debt investing is to recognize that the term distressed has two meanings. First, it means that the issuer of the debt is troubled: its liabilities may exceed its assets or it may be unable to meet its debt service and interest payments as they become due. Therefore, distressed debt investing almost always means that some workout, turnaround, or bankruptcy solution must be implemented for the bonds to appreciate in value.

Second, distressed refers to the price of the bonds. Distressed debt often trades for pennies on the dollar. This affords a savvy investor the opportunity to make a killing if she can identify a company with a viable business plan but a short-term cash flow problem.

In this chapter we begin with a short discussion on the growth of the distressed debt marketplace. We then describe the nature of investors that seek value in distressed debt. Next, we provide a brief overview of the bankruptcy process and how this can influence the value of distressed debt. We examine the different ways that distressed debt can be used to generate superior returns either through an equity stake in the company or through more opportunistic methods. Last, we discuss the risks of distressed debt investing.

GROWTH OF THE DISTRESSED DEBT MARKET

Exhibit 26.1 presents the market value and face value of all distressed portfolios over the time period of 1990 to 2007. Distressed debt represents the outstanding liabilities of companies that are under financial strain, in bankruptcy, or undergoing a corporate reorganization. Another simple definition of distressed debt is any liability that trades at less than 50 cents on the dollar. As can be seen, the distressed market has grown dramatically. Several factors influenced this growth.

First, many more types of commercial loans are available for resale. In addition to the traditional industrial loans that are routinely bought and sold, there are many new types of charge-off loan portfolios that include auto deficiencies, credit card paper, medical and health care receivables, personal loans, retail sales agreements, and insurance premium deficiencies, as well as aviation, boat, and recreational vehicle loans.

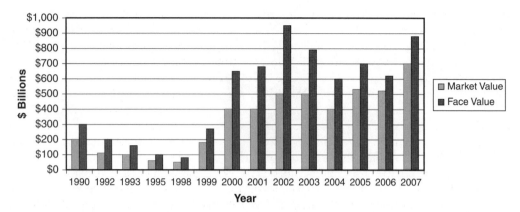

Exhibit 26.1   Size of the defaulted and distressed debt market

Source: Edward Altman, New York University Salomon Center.

Second, many more banks and other lenders are managing their assets from a global portfolio perspective as opposed to an account level basis. Proactive risk management techniques are being applied that prune or groom the portfolio to achieve a desired risk and return balance. The result is that banks are selling nonperforming and subperforming loans in the market at attractive discounts to get them off their books.

Third, debt loads continue to grow. Commercial and industrial loans reached almost $2 trillion in 2008, double the amount from 1999. In addition, the volume of low-quality debt, defined as B– or below, as a percentage of total high-yield bond issuance has grown significantly in recent years.

Exhibit 26.2 shows the growth of low-quality debt issuance over the period 1993 to 2007. Notice that during the U.S. recession of 2001 to 2002, the percentage of low-quality debt decreased significantly, only to pick up again during the growth years of 2003 to 2007.

This relationship is important to note because there has been a historical relationship between the issuance of high-yield bonds in one year and the incidence of bond defaults a few years later.

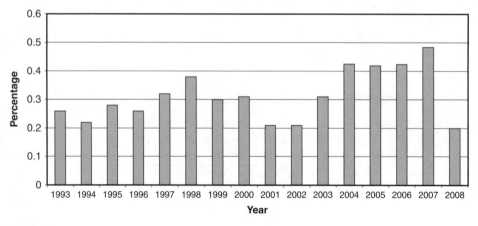

Exhibit 26.2   Low-quality debt as a percentage of total high-yield bonds

Source: Standard & Poor's.

During the recession of 1990 and 1991, the default rate for corporate bonds was 10% each year. This led to a tightening of credit standards by banks, rating agencies, and investors. Consequently, after the 1990 to 1991 recession, bond defaults declined significantly partly due to an upbeat U.S. economy, but also because of tighter credit standards. However, bond issuance rose significantly in the late 1990s, based on "irrational exuberance," resulting in an overabundance of low-quality debt that quickly became distressed debt in 2001 to 2002. The reader can see now that a new generation of distressed debt is being incubated with the high level of low-quality debt issued in the years 2004 to 2007. With the global recession of 2008 to 2009 well under way at the time this book is being written, one can anticipate a significant slowdown of economic activity sufficient to transform much of this low-quality debt to distressed status.

Fourth, the robust U.S. economy through most of the 1990s spawned thousands of new companies, not all of which were successful. This, too, added to the supply of distressed debt. These new companies were prime candidates for the distressed debt market during the recession of 2001 and 2002. In Exhibit 26.3 we show the default rates for all outstanding U.S. corporate bond debt from 1991 through 2008 as well as their associated recovery rates. First, we can see that during recessionary periods (1990 to 1991 and 2001 to 2002) default rates spiked, not surprisingly. Default rates quickly climbed in 2008 to 4.2% and we wait to see what the default rate will be in 2009; current estimates are in excess of 10%. We can also see that default rates and recovery rates are inversely correlated. The higher the default rate, the lower the recovery rate. Notice that during the recessionary periods of 1990 to 1991 and 2001 to 2002 recovery rates fell to below 30%. Also, in 2008, default rates rose again while recovery rates declined significantly.

Covenant-light loans

Another factor in the growth of the distressed market is the explosion of **covenant-light loans** (cov-lite). The distressed market grew as a result of the increase in very debtor-friendly and creditor-unfriendly loan market terms. The erosion of covenant protection in leveraged loans increased the risk for the holders of bank loans. Differential covenant protection has been a hallmark of the leveraged loan market. However, tremendous market liquidity through the year 2007 expanded risk tolerances and diminished creditor influence, which led to a greater dispersion in losses in the secured bank loan market and an increased supply of distressed debt. Exhibit 26.4 shows the decline in the leveraged loan default rate up to the year 2007, followed by a sharp increase.

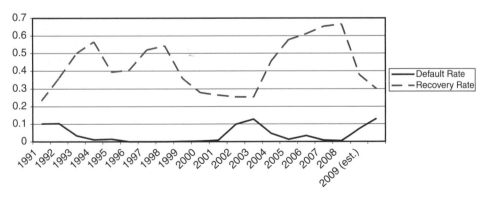

Exhibit 26.3   Default and recovery rates for corporate bonds

Source: Moody's Investors Service.

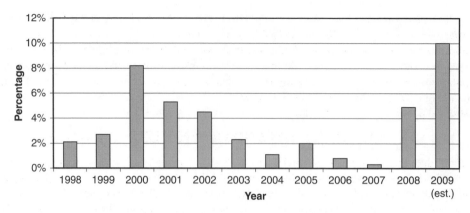

Exhibit 26.4   Leveraged loan default rate

The best way to explain cov-lite loans is that they have bondlike incurrence covenants, much like high-yield bonds. Incurrence covenants are much less severe and restrictive than maintenance covenants, the historical norm for bank loans.

Incurrence covenants typically require that if a borrower takes a specific action such as issuing more debt, it would still need to be in compliance with specific thresholds established in the loan covenant. For example, if the incurrence covenant states that the borrower must maintain a limit on total debt of five times EBITDA, the borrower would only be able to take on more debt as long as it was still within this constraint. If the borrower breached this covenant by incurring more debt, it would be in default of the covenant and the bank loan. However, if the borrower found itself above the five times EBITDA limit simply because its earnings and cash flow had deteriorated, it would not be in violation of the incurrence covenant and would not be in default.

Compare this to a maintenance covenant. Under the same debt limit of five times EBITDA, the borrower must pass this test each and every quarter regardless of whether it added more debt or its earnings/cash flow deteriorated. In other words, the maintenance covenant requires the borrower to remain within the five times EBITDA debt limit regardless; thus the covenant would be triggered if the borrower's earnings and cash flows eroded. Clearly, maintenance covenants are much stronger than incurrence covenants.

Traditionally, maintenance covenants were associated with bond issuance. However, the excessive liquidity available to borrowers, including leveraged buyout (LBO) firms, from 2002 to 2007 resulted in banks making loans with incurrence covenants instead of maintenance covenants. The key point is that without maintenance covenants, lenders lost their ability to step in at an earlier stage to reprice risk, restructure the loan, or shore up collateral provisions.

Mergers and acquisitions: the other side of distressed debt

Another leading factor in the growth of the distressed debt market is the growth of the mergers and acquisitions (M&A) and buyout market. In the cycle of life, many acquisition and LBO deals go bad and turn into distressed debt situations. This is why many of the LBO firms have also started distressed debt funds: Apollo Management, the Carlyle Group, Blackstone, and Kohlberg Kravis Roberts & Company (KKR).

Consider the acquisition of Lyondell Chemical Company by Basell in 2007. The terms of the deal resulted in a purchase price of almost $20 billion. To finance the deal, a total of $20 billion of first, second, and third lien loans were issued by a variety of large banks, including Goldman Sachs, Citigroup, ABN Amro, UBS, Royal Bank of Scotland, and others.

Unfortunately, the global economic slowdown led Lyondell to file for Chapter 11 bankruptcy less than two years later in January 2009. At that time, Lyondell loans were trading at 21 to 25 cents on the dollar. As a result, Citigroup, for example, wrote down the value of its loan to Lyondell from $2 billion to $600 million, a 70% haircut on its debt.

VULTURE INVESTORS AND HEDGE FUND MANAGERS

Distressed debt investors are often referred to as "**vulture investors**," or just "**vultures**," because they pick the bones of underperforming companies. They buy the debt of troubled companies, including subordinated debt, junk bonds, bank loans, and obligations to suppliers. Their investment plan is to buy the distressed debt at a fraction of its face value and then seek improvement of the company.

Sometimes this debt is used as a way to gain an equity investment stake in the company should the vultures agree to forgive the debt they own in return for stock in the company. At other times, the vultures may help the troubled company get back on its feet, thus earning a significant return as their distressed debt recovers in value. At still other times, distressed debt buyers may help impatient creditors to cut their losses and wipe a bad debt off their books. The vulture, in return, waits patiently for the company to correct itself and for the value of the distressed debt to recover.

There is no standard model for distressed debt investing; each distressed situation requires a unique approach and solution. As a result, distressed debt investing entails mostly company selection. There is a low covariance with the general stock market.

The returns for distressed debt investing can be very rewarding. Distressed debt obligations generally trade at levels that yield a total return of 20% or higher. For example, by the beginning of 2001 an estimated 15% to 20% of all leveraged bank debt loans traded at 80 cents on the dollar or less.[1]

Exhibit 26.5 presents the year-by-year returns to distressed investing over the period from 1991 to 2008. As shown, these returns can exceed 30% in any given year. The average annual return over this time was 13% but this included the disastrous year of 2008 when even first lien bank loans returned a negative 25%. Notice, however, that even with the miserable year of 2008, the average return to distressed debt exceeds that for mezzanine debt (measured in Chapter 25) by 200 basis points.

In fact, 2008 is a perfect example of the protection afforded senior loans compared to junior bank loans. In a nutshell, 2008 was a miserable year for any type of debt instrument (except U.S. Treasury bonds). Bank loans were affected just as much as corporate bonds. However, depending on where the loan fell in the seniority scale of bank debt, it may have suffered less.

Exhibit 26.6 demonstrates the returns to bank loans based on their seniority. Although every bank loan category suffered negative returns in 2008, it is clear that the lower the loan was in the seniority schedule, the more negative were the returns. For example, first lien bank loans were down 25%, while third lien bank loans suffered a 44.5% decline, almost 20 percentage points less return as one worked one's way down the capital structure.

Distressed debt is an inefficient and segmented market

One reason why the distressed debt market is attractive to vulture and other investors is that it is an inefficient market. First, distressed debt is not publicly traded like stocks. Further, most distressed

---

[1] See Riva D. Atlas, "Company in Trouble? They're Waiting," *New York Times*, January 21, 2001.

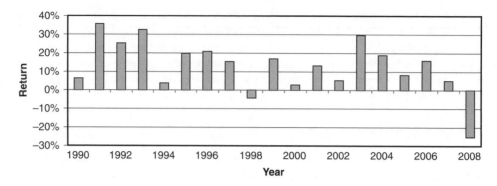

Exhibit 26.5   Returns to distressed debt

Note: Average 12.96%; Standard Deviation 14.17%; Sharpe ratio 0.63.

bonds were issued in a private offering under Rule 144A of the Securities Act of 1933, which allows companies to sell their bonds directly to institutional investors instead of retail investors. These bonds lack liquidity from the outset, and what little liquidity exists dries up even more when the company becomes distressed. This lack of liquidity may lead to bonds trading at steep discounts to their true value.

A second reason that the distressed debt market is inefficient is that it is a segmented market. Segmented markets exist when certain classes of investors deselect themselves from the market. For example, many pension funds are banned by their charters from investing in below-investment-grade debt. So when a company becomes distressed, the fund must sell the bonds regardless of their true value, often at depressed prices. Another form of segmentation occurs with banks. Banks are in the business of lending credit and may not have the patience or risk appetite required during the tedious workout process of a bankruptcy situation. Consequently, they may sell their nonperforming loans at prices that offer a considerable discount to vulture investors who have greater experience at working out a plan of reorganization for a company. Last, trade creditors are in the business of producing

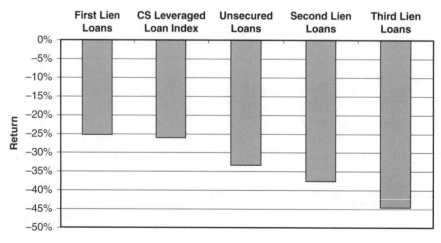

Exhibit 26.6   2008 Returns to bank loans

Exhibit 26.7   Recovery rates for corporate bonds and bank loans

	Bonds		
Rating	BBB	BB	B
Senior secured	51%	52%	52%
Unsecured	44	45	45
Subordinated	19	19	19
	Loans		
	BBB	BB	B
Senior secured first lien	67%	70%	70%
Senior secured first lien cov-lite	60	63	63
Senior unsecured	46	48	48
Subordinated	22	22	22

goods, not managing a distressed debt portfolio. They also may sell their claims at depressed prices.

Take the example of Barneys clothing stores. This is one of the most successful brand names in retail clothing, with shops that sell high-end merchandise beyond most people's pocketbooks. In the late 1990s Barneys expanded too rapidly, leading to a distressed situation where Barneys had overextended itself. Subsequently, Barneys filed for bankruptcy under Chapter 11. At that point, its trade claims sold for as little as 30 cents on the dollar. Barneys was, and is, a solid business that experienced a temporary distress situation. Barneys was subsequently purchased out of bankruptcy in 2000 by Bay Harbour Management and Whippoorwill Associates for approximately $240 million. They sold Barneys to Jones Apparel in 2004 for $400 million. Jones Apparel, in turn, sold Barneys to the private equity arm of the Dubai government in 2007 for $825 million.

Another way to consider the distressed debt market is to examine recovery rates. Once a company becomes distressed or declares bankruptcy, that does not mean the value of the debt is completely wiped out. In almost all instances, there is some amount of recovery value: not the full face value of the debt, to be sure, but some amount is offered to the debt holder.

Exhibit 26.7 demonstrates recovery rates for both bonds and bank loans. Bank loans are typically senior to bond financing in a company's capital structure. This is reflected in the recovery rate for bank loans compared to corporate bonds: the recovery rate is generally twice as high for bank loans as for corporate bonds. We note that the lower down the capital structure (the greater the subordination), the lower the recovery rate. Ironically, though, recovery rates tend to improve slightly with lower-quality credits. The reason for this is that lenders for lower-quality credits tend to overcollateralize their loans, ensuring a greater chance of recovery in a default situation.

DISTRESSED DEBT AND BANKRUPTCY

Distressed debt investing and the bankruptcy process are inextricably intertwined. Many distressed debt investors purchase the debt while the borrowing company is currently in the throes of bankruptcy. Other investors purchase the debt before a company enters into bankruptcy proceedings with the expectation of gaining control of the company. In either case, a brief summary of Chapter 11 bankruptcy is appropriate to understanding distressed debt investing.

Overview of Chapter 11

Chapter 11 of the U.S. Bankruptcy Code recognizes the corporation as a going concern.[2] It therefore affords a troubled company protection from its creditors while the company attempts to work through its operational problems. Only the debtor company can file for protection under Chapter 11. Chapter 11 was introduced by the Bankruptcy Code of 1978 and provided the many changes that impact the distressed debt marketplace. One of the key purposes of the Code was to favor reorganization over liquidation. This shifted the focus from asset valuation to going concern valuation.

Generally, under a Chapter 11 bankruptcy, the debtor company proposes a plan of reorganization that describes how creditors and shareholders are to be treated under the new business plan. The claimants in each class of creditors are entitled to vote on the plan. If all impaired classes of security holders vote in favor of the plan, the bankruptcy court will conduct a confirmation hearing. If all requirements of the bankruptcy code are met, the plan is confirmed and a newly reorganized company will emerge from bankruptcy protection. The process of Chapter 11 bankruptcy is illustrated in Exhibit 26.8.

Classification of claims

Under the bankruptcy code, a reorganization plan may place a claim in a particular class only if such claim is substantially similar to the other claims in that class. For instance, all issues of subordinated debt by a company would constitute one class of creditor under a bankruptcy plan. Similarly, all secured bank loans (usually the most senior of creditor claims) are usually grouped together as one class of creditor. Finally, at the bottom of the pile is common equity, the last class of claimants in a bankruptcy.

Plan of reorganization

The debtor has an exclusive right to file a plan of reorganization within 120 days of seeking Chapter 11 bankruptcy protection.[3] If the debtor company files a plan during this 120-day window, it has another 60 days to lobby its creditors to accept the plan. During this time (120 days plus 60 days), no other party in interest may file a competing reorganization plan.[4] This harks back to the main purpose of the bankruptcy code: to favor reorganization over liquidation. By giving the debtor company 120 days to propose its reoganization plan and another 60 days to coerce creditors, the code puts the debtor in the driver's seat, at least initially.

After the exclusive period ends, any claimant may file a reorganization plan with the bankruptcy court. At this point the gloves come off and senior and subordinated creditors can petition the bankruptcy court to have their reorganization plan accepted. Marquis of Queensbury rules[5] need not be recognized.

This is the interesting part of a bankruptcy process, and it can become very acrimonious. In the Federated/Macy's case discussed later in this chapter, the negotiations became so intense that the bankruptcy court appointed Cyrus Vance, the former U.S. secretary of state, to mediate the discussions.

---

[2] See 11 U.S.C., Section 101 and the following sequence.

[3] See 11 U.S.C., Section 1121(b).

[4] However, the bankruptcy court may increase or reduce this exclusive period "for cause."

[5] Fair stand-up boxing rules.

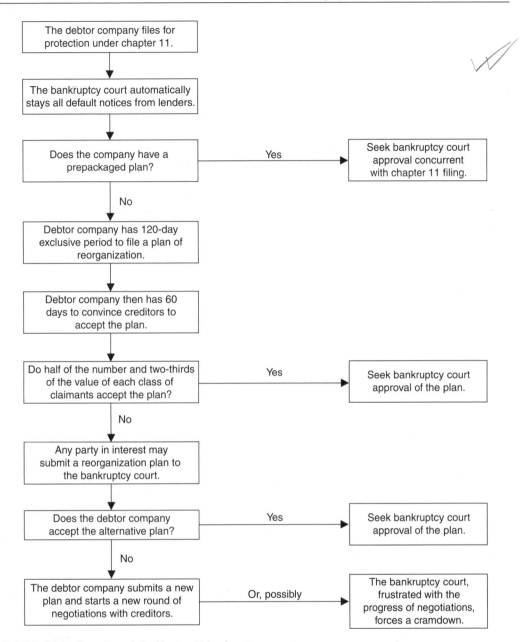

Exhibit 26.8   Overview of the Chapter 11 bankruptcy process

Source: Mark Anson, *Handbook of Alternative Assets*, 2nd ed. (Hoboken, NJ: John Wiley & Sons, 2006). Reprinted with permission of John Wiley & Sons, Inc.

A plan is accepted when all classes of claimants vote in favor of the plan. This is an important point because any one class of creditors can block a debtor's plan of reorganization.

Evolution of debt to own

As just described, the bankruptcy code favors reorganization over liquidation. However, this means that the bankrupt company must reduce its debt, and the most common and obvious way to do this is to convert the old, defaulted debt into equity. This in turn dilutes or eliminates the prior equity holders. It also reduces the debt to a level that allows the company to survive and emerge from Chapter 11 proceedings. Consequently, the new equity holders of the reorganized company are typically the former creditors. But the former creditors may not want to be the new equity holders. They may be restricted by their business model (banks) or their investment policies (institutional investors). This puts even more downward pressure on the bankrupt company's distressed debt, driving its price down for the vulture investors or distressed debt funds to snap up.

Prepackaged bankruptcy filing

Sometimes a debtor company agrees in advance with its creditors on a plan of organization before it formerly files for protection under Chapter 11. Creditors usually agree to make concessions up front in return for equity in the reorganized company. The company then files with the bankruptcy court, submits its already negotiated plan of reorganization, and quickly emerges with a new structure. A good example of a prepackaged bankruptcy is Station Casinos.

Station Casinos was a publicly traded company that was taken private in an LBO in 2007 for $8.8 billion. At the time of the buyout, Station's 6.625% notes due in 2018 were trading at 92.25 cents on the dollar.[6] Unfortunately, its large debt load and a dramatic slowdown of the economy forced Station into bankruptcy. Station quickly organized a prepackaged bankruptcy where holders of its senior notes received $400 in face value of new senior notes plus $100 cash for each $1,000 in principal amount of the old senior notes. In short, Station's old bondholders received about 50 cents on the dollar.

Station's subordinated bondholders fared even worse. They received $70 in face value of new subordinated notes plus $30 in cash for every $1,000 in face value of old senior notes. Simply, old subordinated debt holders of Station Casinos received 10 cents on the dollar for their old debt.

Voting within a class

To constitute an acceptance of a plan of reorganization, either (1) the class must be completely unimpaired by the plan (i.e. the class will be paid in full) or (2) one-half in number and two-thirds in dollar amount of claims in the class must vote in favor of the reorganization plan.

All claims within a class must receive the same treatment. If the members of a class vote in favor of a reorganization less than unanimously, and any dissenting claimants in the class would receive at least what they would have obtained in a Chapter 7 liquidation plan, the dissenters are bound to receive the treatment under the reorganization plan. The reason is that the dissenters are no worse off than they would be under a liquidation of the company, and may be better off if the reorganized company is successful.

---

[6] See Heather Burke and Carol Wolf, "Station Casinos Agrees to Be Bought for $8.8 Billion," *Bloomberg News*, February 26, 2007.

Blocking position

A single creditor can block a plan of reorganization if it holds one-third of the dollar amount of any class of claimants. Recall that acceptance of a plan is usually predicated on a vote of each class of security holders, which requires support of two-thirds of the dollar amount of the claims in each class of creditors. Therefore, a single investor can obtain a blocking position by purchasing one-third of the debt in any class. A blocking position forces the debtor company to negotiate with the blocking creditor.

The cramdown

Under Section 1129(b) of the bankruptcy code, a reorganization plan may be confirmed over the objection of any impaired class that votes against it so long as the plan (1) does not unfairly discriminate against the members of that class, and (2) is fair and equitable with respect to the members of that class.[7] This provision of the bankruptcy court is called the cramdown because it empowers the bankruptcy court judge to confirm a plan of reorganization over the objections of an impaired class of security holders (the plan is crammed down the throats of the objecting claimants).

Cramdowns are usually an option of last resort if the debtor and creditors cannot come to an agreement. Bankruptcy courts have considerable discretion to determine what constitutes "unfair discrimination" and "fair and equitable" treatment for members of a class. In practice, cramdown reorganizations are rare. Eventually, the debtor and creditors come to some resolution.

Absolute priority

A plan of reorganization must follow the rule of priority with respect to its security holders. Senior secured debt holders, typically bank loans, must be satisfied first. The company's bondholders come next. These may be split between senior and subordinated bondholders. The company's shareholders get whatever remains. As the company pie is split up, it is usually the case that senior secured debt is made whole and that subordinated debt receives some payment less than its face value, while the remainder of the company's obligation is transformed into equity in the reorganized company. Last, the original equity holders often receive nothing. Their equity is replaced by that converted from the subordinated debt.

It may seem unfair that the original equity holders are wiped out, but this is the residual risk that is borne by every shareholder in every company. As the U.S. Supreme Court has stated, "one of the painful facts of bankruptcy is that the interests of shareholders become subordinated to the interests of creditors."[8]

Throughout the bankruptcy process, the debtor company's outstanding debt may be freely bought and sold. This allows distressed debt investors the opportunity to purchase undervalued debt securities with the anticipation that the debtor company will implement a successful reorganization.

The ability in the bankruptcy process to wipe out the ownership of existing shareholders and to transform the debt of senior and subordinated creditors into the company's new equity class is a key factor in distressed debt investing. The examples that follow demonstrate how distressed debt investors may gain control of a company through Chapter 11 bankruptcy proceedings.

---

[7] See 11 U.S.C., Section 1129(b)(1).

[8] See *Commodity Futures Trading Commission v. Weintraub*, 471 U.S. 343, at 355 (1985).

Debtor-in-possession financing

With the advent of the credit meltdown in 2008, more and more secured lenders faced the decision of whether to extend credit to a debtor company. This is commonly known as **debtor-in-possession (DIP) financing**. The borrower's desire in seeking DIP financing is clear: without additional credit, the borrower might not continue in business and would then shut down.

Creditors are often willing to grant DIP financing for a number of reasons. First, it keeps the debtor company afloat and gives it a chance to work out from under its debt load. Second, under bankruptcy law, DIP loans get priority over any forms of debt or financing incurred by the debtor before filing for bankruptcy under Chapter 11.

Once a debtor files for Chapter 11 bankruptcy protection, creditors are divided into two broad classes: pre-petition lenders and post-petition lenders. DIP lenders are the post-petition lenders.

Another reason that lenders may be willing to provide DIP financing is the ability to roll up their pre-petition loans. In the case where a DIP lender also holds pre-petition claims against the borrower, the DIP lender will often try to cross-collateralize its pre-petition loans and post-petition loans so that the pre-petition claims will be secured with the collateral pledged post-petition. This is especially favorable for an undersecured creditor who can convert their undersecured loan into a fully secured post-petition loan. Cross-collateralization is not always allowed by the bankruptcy court, and it remains a controversial maneuver in the management of distressed debt.

However, roll-up financing is being increasingly allowed in the bankruptcy process. In a roll-up, secured lenders get to convert their pre-petition debt into post-petition debt with better priority and security.

Roll-ups come in two basic forms. In the first structure, in addition to the new funding advanced to finance the debtor's operating needs, the post-petition loan facility also contains a loan that is applied to pay off the pre-petition loan. This has the effect of leaving the same amount of debt outstanding, by converting all of the creditor's loan to the debtor to post-petition debt.

In the second type of roll-up, the creditor requires that for each dollar of post-petition funding received, the debtor must apply a dollar of proceeds of collateral sales first to pay off the pre-petition loans until all of the pre-petition loans are fully rolled up into the post-petition loan.

The advantage of using DIP financing with a roll-up provision is that it is a more subtle way to achieve cross-collateralization. Even if a lender's pre-petition loan is fully secured, roll-up financing allows the secured lender to move up the priority chain by becoming a secured post-petition lender. This is a much more secure position under Chapter 11.

Chapter 7 bankruptcy

If a plan of reorganization cannot be accepted by the creditors of the company, the company may liquidate its assets. This is a Chapter 7 bankruptcy process. Under Chapter 7, the company is no longer considered a going concern. Chapter 7 results in a liquidation of the company's assets for the benefit of its debt holders. Essentially it shuts down its operations and parcels out its assets to its creditors.

DISTRESSED DEBT INVESTMENT STRATEGIES

There are three broad categories of investing in distressed debt securities. The first approach is an active approach with the intent to obtain control of the company. In this strategy, the investors intend to assume an active role in the management and direction of the company. These investors typically purchase distressed debt to gain control through a blocking position in the bankruptcy process with a subsequent conversion into the equity of the reorganized company. Often, these investors purchase the more junior debt that is most likely to be converted into the equity of the reorganized company; these are sometimes referred to as fulcrum securities.

This strategy will also seek seats on the board of directors, and even the chairmanship of the board. This is the most risky and time-intensive of the distressed investment strategies. Returns are expected in the 20% to 25% range, consistent with those for leveraged buyouts, where control of a company is also sought.

The second general category of distressed debt investing seeks to play an active role in the bankruptcy and reorganization process but stops short of taking control of the company. Here, the principals may be willing to swap their debt for equity or for another form of restructured debt. An equity conversion is not required, because control of the company is not sought. These investors participate actively in the creditors' committee to ensure the most beneficial outcome for their debt. They may accept equity kickers such as warrants with their restructured debt. Their return target is in the 15% to 20% range, very similar to mezzanine debt investors.

Last, there are passive or opportunistic investors. They often do not take an active role in the reorganization and rarely seek to convert their debt into equity. These investors buy debt securities that no one else wants. They might be the purest of the vulture investors because they have no goal other than to pick at the scraps that other investors leave behind. These vultures receive their scraps from several sources:

- Banks and other financial institutions that do not have the time or inclination to participate in the bankruptcy reorganization.
- High-yield mutual funds that are restricted in their ability to hold distressed securities: there may be limits to the amount of distressed securities they can hold in their portfolios.
- Investors that invested in high-yield bonds for their high coupon payments, but do not want to convert a high cash yield into an equity position in the company.

Exhibit 26.9 provides an overview of both active and passive distressed debt investment strategies.

Using distressed debt to recycle private equity

Leveraged buyout (LBO) firms are a great source for distressed debt. So-called leveraged fallouts occur frequently, leaving large amounts of distressed debt in their wakes. However, this provides an opportunity for distressed debt buyers to jump in, purchase nonperforming bank loans and subordinated debt cheaply, eliminate the prior private equity investors, and assert their own private equity ownership.

Consider Regal Cinemas Inc., the largest U.S. theater chain. Regal was originally taken private in 1998 through the combined efforts of Hicks, Muse, Tate & Furst and KKR. The two buyout firms each put up about $500 million in equity to purchase the firm for $1.5 billion. Over the next two years, Regal added $1.2 billion to its balance sheet in bank debt and subordinated notes.

Unfortunately, too many movie theaters, a slowing U.S. economy, and fewer blockbuster movies resulted in a loss of $167 million for Regal in the first nine months of 2000. In December 2000, bank lenders refused to let the company pay interest to its subordinated bondholders because it would violate loan covenants. Regal's debt officially became distressed. Regal's bad year of 2000 was followed by an even worse year in 2001 when it racked up net losses of $366 million.

Distressed debt buyers Philip Anschutz and Oaktree Capital Management stepped in. Together, they purchased 65% of Regal's outstanding bank debt and 95% of its subordinated debt. It was

Exhibit 26.9   Distressed debt investment strategies

Active Seeking Control	Active Not Seeking Control	Passive
Often seeks one-third of a class of debt to block and control the Chapter 11 bankruptcy process.	May seek one-third of a debt class to obtain a blocking position.	Goal is to purchase debt securities that are undervalued and trading significantly below their face value.
Control of the company is expressly sought through an equity-for-debt conversion.	Will take an active role in the restructuring process. Will be an active participant in the creditors' committee.	Various strategies may include credit arbitrage among different levels of seniority or fire sale purchases.
Control is also sought through board seats and even the chairmanship.	Typically, will not seek control but may be willing to accept an equity-for-debt conversion. If not a full conversion, may seek equity kickers.	Buy securities from more risk-averse investors who cannot commit the time required for a bankruptcy reorganization.
Investors play a direct role in restructuring both the capital structure of the company and its business plan.	Exit time frame is one to three years.	Holding period is up to one year.
Additional equity infusions might be made after the equity-for-debt conversion.	Return expectation is 15% to 20%.	Return expectation is 12% to 15%.
Exit time frame is two to four years.		
Return expectation is 20% to 25%.		

reported that this debt cost them 19 to 21 cents per dollar of debt purchased.[9] In September 2001, Regal announced a prepackaged bankruptcy plan where holders of Regal's bank debt would receive all of the equity in the reorganized company.[10]

In effect, Anschutz and Oaktree Capital replaced the private equity ownership of KKR and Hicks, Muse in Regal Cinemas with their own private equity stake. In fact, in 2001, KKR and Hicks, Muse both had already written off their respective investments of almost $500 million in Regal Cinemas. The purchase of Regal debt on the cheap by Anschutz and Oaktree proved to be a very savvy investment. Regal Cinemas' balance sheet was quickly cleaned up. The overcapacity was reduced, and by May 2002 Regal Cinemas was ready to go public again in an IPO.

Regal Cinemas raised $342 million in its IPO in May 2002. After the IPO, Anschutz owned a 77% stake in Regal valued at about $1.5 billion while Oaktree's stake was valued at about $435 million. The market value of Regal more than doubled their initial investment for a holding period of less than one year. By the beginning of mid-2009, Regal Cinemas' market value had increased from $342 million at its IPO to $2.2 billion.

Distressed buyouts

A wonderful example of a distressed buyout is the Long Term Credit Bank of Japan. When the Japanese stock market bubble burst in 1990 and the economy fell into a decade-long recession, many Japanese banks were stuffed with nonperforming loans (NPLs). Japanese banks stayed in

---

[9] See David Fox, "Creditors Gain Control of Knoxville-Based Regal Cinemas, TheDeal.com Says," *NashvillePost.com*, May 29, 2001.

[10] See "Regal Movie Chain Shares Rise 14% after $342 Million IPO," *Bloomberg News*, May 9, 2002.

business but stopped making loans. Eventually, the NPLs caught up with the Long Term Credit Bank of Japan and it finally collapsed in 1998.

Two American buyout firms, Ripplewood Holdings and JC Flowers, came in and purchased the Long Term Credit Bank from the Japanese government in 2000. Under the terms of the buyout, Ripplewood and JC Flowers purchased the outstanding common equity for only $10 million and a promise to subscribe to $1.1 billion more equity in the future. In return, the Japanese government agreed to take $37 billion of bad loans off of the books of the Long Term Credit Bank.

Ripplewood and JC Flowers renamed the bank Shinsei (New Life), improved its balance sheet (with the help of the Japanese government), streamlined operations, and took the bank public in an IPO in 2004. Ripplewood and JC Flowers sold a one-third stake in the bank for $1.8 billion. The LBO firms followed up with a second offering the following year. Ripplewood and JC Flowers sold another one-third of the bank for $2.8 billion. At that time, the remaining one-third of the bank owned by the buyout firms was worth roughly $2.7 billion.

In all, Ripplewood and JC Flowers had to contribute $1.1 billion. In return, they received cash of $4.2 billion and owned a remaining stake in the bank worth $2.7 billion. This distressed deal generated approximately a $7\times$ payback.

Converting distressed debt to private equity in a prepackaged bankruptcy

In February 2001, Loews Cineplex Entertainment Corporation, the largest publicly traded U.S. movie theater chain and one of the largest movie theater chains in the world, filed for Chapter 11 bankruptcy. At the same time, it signed a letter of intent with Oaktree Capital Management, LLC and the Onex Corporation to sell Loews Cineplex and its subsidiaries to the investor group. This was a prepackaged bankruptcy where the debtor agrees in advance to a plan of reorganization before formally filing for Chapter 11 bankruptcy.

The letter of agreement proposed that Onex and Oaktree convert their distressed debt holdings of about $250 million of senior secured bank debt and $180 million of unsecured company bonds into 88% of the equity of the reorganized company. Unsecured creditors, including subordinated debt holders, would receive the other 12% of equity.[11] All existing equity interests would be wiped out by the reorganization. Last, the remaining holders of bank debt would receive new term loans as part of the bankruptcy process equal in recovery to about 98% of the face amount of current debt.

In this prepackaged example, Onex and Oaktree became the majority equity owners of Loews by purchasing its bank and subordinated debt. Furthermore, their bank debt was converted to a private equity stake because all public shares of Loews were wiped out through the bankruptcy proceedings. Loews' two largest shareholders, Sony Corporation (40% equity ownership) and Vivendi Universal SA (26%) lost their complete equity stakes in Loews. In effect, the bankruptcy proceeding transformed Loews from a public company to a private one. Onex paid approximately $320 million for a 60% share of Loews, making the total invested capital about $533 million.[12]

The deal turned out to be a very good one for Onex and Oaktree. They subsequently sold Loews two years later to the buyout group of Bain Capital, the Carlyle Group, and Spectrum Equity for $1.5 billion, approximately three times their invested capital.

However, the story of Loews was not yet finished. In June 2005, AMC Entertainment, another movie theater chain owned by JP Morgan Partners and the private equity firm of Apollo Management,

---

[11] Oaktree Capital also owned about 60% of Loews' senior subordinated notes.

[12] "Onex Completes Acquisition of Loews Cineplex Entertainment; Loews Cineplex Entertainment Emerges from Bankruptcy," *Business Wire*, March 22, 2002.

merged with Loews. JP Morgan and Apollo received 60% of the merged company, while Bain Capital, the Carlyle Group, and Spectrum Equity received 40% of the combined movie theater company.

Since then, the new company, called AMC Entertainment Holdings, has tried to go public twice. The first time was in December 2006, but investors balked at a $17 share price and the company withdrew its IPO in May 2007. AMC tried to go public again in 2008 but again withdrew its offering when preliminary investor interest seemed lackluster. One drawback was the fact that the company was going to receive very little, if any, of the proceeds from the IPO. The existing private equity investors intended to use the IPO to sell their shares, not reduce the still high debt load of AMC. As of January 2009, AMC Entertainment Holdings remains a private company.

Using distressed debt for a takeover

As a good example of how a corporation can use distressed debt to take control of another company, consider the merger of Federated Department Stores and R.H. Macy & Company. Federated was able to gain control of Macy's with an initial investment in distressed debt of only $109 million.

Federated itself was a victim of the leveraged fallouts of the late 1980s and early 1990s. Federated was taken private in an LBO by Robert Campeau in 1988, the same gentleman who took Allied Department Stores private in 1986. Campeau's vision was to create a huge retailing empire anchored by two separate retailing chains: Allied and Federated. Unfortunately, the high debt burden of both buyouts forced the two companies into Chapter 11 bankruptcy in January 1990. Federated Department Stores emerged from bankruptcy in February 1992 after creditors agreed to swap $4.8 billion in claims for equity in the reorganized company. This helped to reduce Federated's debt from $8.3 billion to $3.5 billion thereby reducing its interest payments from $606 million to $259 million. The connection to Robert Campeau was severed. In an ironic twist of fate, Federated emerged from bankruptcy just nine days after Macy's filed for Chapter 11 bankruptcy protection. Macy's was yet another victim of a leveraged fallout.

Soon after the Macy's bankruptcy filing, Federated made overtures to acquire its longtime rival. This was another twist of fate because Macy's had bid against Robert Campeau in 1988 for control of Federated. Macy's rebuffed Federated's inquiries because it believed that the company could be better served if it remained independent.[13]

With Macy's mired in negotiations with its senior creditors regarding a plan of reorganization and a takeover out of the question (there was no equity to take over), Federated decided to become one of Macy's creditors. In January 1994, Federated purchased half of Macy's most senior secured debt from the Prudential Insurance Company of America, Macy's largest creditor. Prudential held a senior loan of $832.5 million that was secured by 70 of Macy's best stores. With accrued interest, the total amount of the distressed debt was $1 billion, representing one-sixth of Macy's total debt.[14]

Federated paid Prudential $109.3 million up front and promised to pay the remainder in three years. In addition, Federated received an option from Prudential to purchase the remaining half of Prudential's senior loan within three years. Overnight, Federated became Macy's largest and most senior creditor.

Given its new standing as a senior secured creditor, Federated received permission from the bankruptcy court to (1) challenge Macy's plan of reorganization (Federated now had a blocking

---

[13] See Richard Siklos, "Macy's Holiday Revival," *Financial Post*, December 24, 1994.

[14] See "Federated Buys Large Share of Macy Debt," *Facts on File World News Digest*, January 6, 1994.

position within the senior secured class of creditors); (2) propose a competing plan to the bankruptcy court; and (3) obtain nonpublic financial information regarding Macy's business prospects.

Federated proposed to convert Macy's bank debt into equity and assume it's existing liabilities. Macy's continued to resist. Specifically, Macy's director Laurence A. Tisch teamed up with counsel for bondholders holding $1.2 billion in subordinated debt and demanded a reorganization plan valued at least $4 billion.[15] Meanwhile, Federated received support from Fidelity Management & Research Company, which signed a lockup letter stating that it would only support a plan that gave the banks full recovery in return for the banks' support of Federated's plan.[16] The lockup letter worked, and Federated was able to merge the two companies in December 1994 when it agreed to convert its senior loan to equity and to assume $4.1 billion in outstanding Macy's debts.[17]

Distressed debt as an undervalued security

Distressed debt is not always an entrée into private equity; it can simply be an investment in an undervalued security. In this instance, distressed debt investors are less concerned with an equity stake in the troubled company. Instead, they expect to benefit by the company implementing a successful turnaround strategy.

Consider the case of CalPine Corporation, the operator of power plants from Maine to California. Calpine, based in California, operated 88 power plants in 21 U.S. states. However, it fell into trouble in 2005 as a jump in natural gas prices (used to heat steam generators for electricity generation), an aggressive and debt-laden growth strategy, and an excess supply of power left it unable to pay interest on almost $20 billion in debt. More than half of its generation capacity remained idle as power generation costs exceeded prices paid for power generation. As a result, in 2005 it filed for the largest Chapter 11 bankruptcy protection to date.

At the time of its bankruptcy filing in December 2005, the rating on CalPine's outstanding debt was cut to D by Standard & Poor's. Calpine's debt was trading at just 20 cents on the dollar. Exhibit 26.10 shows the price for Calpine's 8.625% bonds due in 2010.

However, Calpine quickly turned its fortunes around as the so-called spark spread—the spread between the cost of power generation and the revenues received for power—improved throughout 2006 and 2007. By June 2006, the price of Calpine's bonds had increased to 44 cents on the dollar, and by the end of 2007 Calpine had become profitable again. Its plan for reorganization was approved in December 2007, and Calpine emerged from bankruptcy in January 2008. Calpine returned to the public markets with so much strength that it received an unsolicited takeover offer from NRG Corporation for $11 billion in May 2008.

Exhibit 26.10 depicts the price history of Calpine's bonds. It was a wild ride for the bondholders. However, those investors who recognized that Calpine's problems were temporary and were able to buy Calpine's bonds on the cheap made a huge profit. Eventually, the bonds were called at their $110 call price, quite a gain from the 20 cents on the dollar price at the time of the bankruptcy filing.[18]

---

[15] See Karen Donovan, "Macy Merger Squeezes Out Weil Gotshal; Bankruptcy Judge Approves Federated's Takeover Plan," *National Law Journal* (December 19, 1994).

[16] Ibid.

[17] There was significant legal maneuvering before the deal was completed, including the appointment of Cyrus R. Vance, the former U.S. secretary of state, to mediate the discussions among Macy's, Federated, and other outstanding creditors.

[18] See Edward Klump, "Calpine Rises after Confirming Takeover Bid from NRG," *Bloomberg News*, May 22, 2008; Mark Pittman, "Calpine Bonds Rally Six Months after Bankruptcy," *Bloomberg News*, June 30, 2006; and Christopher Scinta and Jim Polson, "Calpine Emerges from Bankruptcy, Cuts Debt by Half," *Bloomberg News*, January 31, 2008.

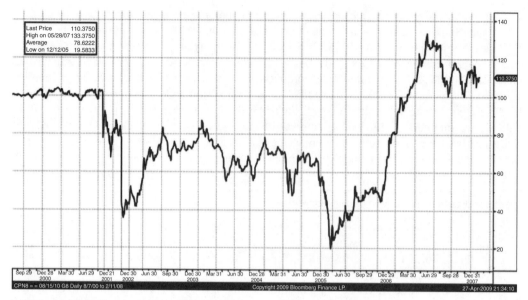

Exhibit 26.10   Price of Calpine's 8.625% bonds due in 2010

Source: Bloomberg Finance, L.P.

Distressed debt in a fire sale

Although a majority of distressed debt comes from companies that are under financial stress, there are many other sources of distressed financing. Consider the case of Lone Star Capital's purchase of distressed debt from Merrill Lynch in July 2008.

Throughout 2007 and 2008 Merrill Lynch was rocked by distressed assets on its balance sheet leading to almost $30 billion in losses, costing John Thain his CEO job at Merrill, and forcing Merrill into the arms of the Bank of America in a merger of distressed partners. The bulk of Merrill's problems arose from collateralized debt obligations (CDOs) that it maintained on its balance sheet as part of its structured products group.

In one of the more fascinating sales of the year, Merrill agreed to sell $30.6 billion of its CDO loans to the Lone Star Funds for just $6.7 billion, about 22 cents on the dollar. Even more astounding was that Merrill agreed to finance 75% of the purchase price paid by Lone Star! In effect, Lone Star put up only about $1.67 billion of its own money to get access to over $30 billion of face value CDOs.

Merrill Lynch was under pressure to clean up its balance sheet, and many CDOs were viewed as toxic; that is, they were viewed as potentially racking up significant defaults and losses. Merrill was determined to remove as much of this distressed debt as possible, even to the point of financing the purchase by Lone Star. As far as bargain hunting goes in the distressed market, this was the biggest, and possibly best, deal of 2008.[19]

---

[19] See Heather Landy, "After Merrill's Sale of Bad Debt, Few Have Followed," *Washington Post*, August 26, 2008; and Walden Siew and Dane Hamilton, "Lone Star to Buy Merrill Debt," Reuters, July 29, 2008.

RISKS OF DISTRESSED DEBT INVESTING

There are two main risks associated with distressed debt investing. First, business risk still applies. Just because distressed debt investors can purchase the debt of a company on the cheap does not mean it cannot go lower. This is the greatest risk to distressed debt investing, i.e. that a troubled company may ultimately prove to be worthless and unable to pay off its creditors. While creditors often convert their debt into equity, the company may in the end not be viable as a going concern. If the company cannot develop a successful plan of reorganization, it will simply continue its downward spiral.

It may seem strange, but creditworthiness doesn't apply. The reason is that the debt is already distressed because the company may already be in default and its debt thoroughly discounted. Consequently, failure to pay interest and debt service may have already occurred.

Instead, vulture investors consider the business risks of the company. They are concerned not with the short-term payment of interest and debt service, but rather with the ability of the company to execute a viable business plan. From this perspective, it can be said that distressed debt investors are truly equity investors. They view the purchase of distressed debt as an investment in the company as opposed to a lending facility.

Consider the case of Global Crossing (GC). Global Crossing was a spectacular failure. Built up during the heyday of the telecom/tech bubble, it grew tremendously and then flamed out just as brilliantly.

While GC was a highflier in the 1990s, overcapacity in fiber-optic cables and huge debt loads began to take its toll. By the summer of 2001, GC's 8.7% notes due in 2007 were trading at 50 cents on the dollar. Distressed and vulture investors swooped in, buying the debt on the cheap.

Unfortunately, matters only got worse for GC. On top of the bad industry economics, shady accounting practices soon came to light. In addition, a recession in the United States diminished overall demand for the company's products. Together, these problems ultimately forced GC into bankruptcy in 2002.

In a nutshell, GC was a mess. Lawsuits ran thick and fast. Citigroup was sued by multiple investors for overstating GC's financial health. GC and its founder, Gary Winnick, were also sued by investors for using improper accounting practices to inflate revenues. Last, GC's auditing firm (Arthur Andersen—who else?) was sued for failing to detect GC's accounting fraud.

At the time of GC's bankruptcy in 2002, its 8.7% notes due in 2007 were trading for just 7 cents on the dollar. This implied a yield to maturity on the notes of 100%.

Distressed investors lost a significant amount of money due not to credit risk, but to business risk. What ultimately doomed GC were its fraudulent accounting practices. The discovery of this risk pushed GC's bonds down precipitously and virtually wiped out the company. Exhibit 26.11 shows the price of GC's stock. Effectively, by 2001, GC's stock flatlined to zero.

Unfortunately, distressed investors in GC lost a lot of money. Ultimately, GC was sold for only $407 million in 2002, about 1% of its $39 billion market value just three years earlier. Under the reorganization plan, GC's bondholders received only $25 million in new notes and equity worth virtually nothing. It is estimated that bondholders recovered only about 3.5 cents on the dollar from the GC bankruptcy.[20]

The second main risk is the lack of liquidity. The distressed debt arena is a fragmented market, dominated by only a few players. Trading out of a distressed debt position may mean selling at a

---

[20] See "Global Crossing Wins Approval of Bankruptcy Plan," *Bloomberg News*, December 17, 2002; Jef Feeley and Gregory Cresci, "Citigroup Reaches $75 Million Global Crossing Settlement," *Bloomberg News*, March 2, 2005; Jef Feeley, "Global Crossing to Pay $325 Million to Settle Lawsuits," *Bloomberg News*, March 19, 2004.

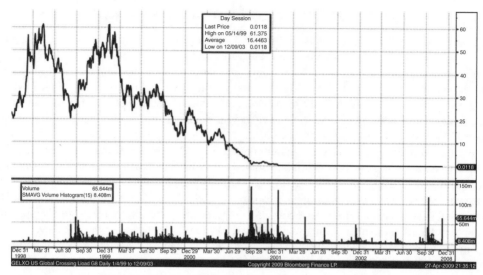

Exhibit 26.11   Global Crossing's Stock Price, 1998–2003

Source: Bloomberg Finance, L.P.

significant discount to the book value of the debt. For example, at the time of the Loews bankruptcy filing, its senior subordinated notes were trading at an offer of 15, but with a bid of 10, a gap of 5 cents or $50 for every $1,000 face value of the security.

In addition, purchasers of distressed debt must have long-term investment horizons. Workout and turnaround situations do not happen overnight. It may take several years for a troubled company to correct its course and appreciate in value.

CONCLUSION

Distressed debt investing is often seen as representing one side of a coin, with the buyout world representing the other. In this chapter we demonstrated how distressed debt investing and leveraged buyouts often go hand in hand. In fact, the excessive leverage used in LBOs in 2007 and 2008 led to many distressed financing situations and several bankruptcies to boot.

Distressed debt rarely occurs because of some spectacular event that renders a company's products worthless overnight. Rather, a company's financial condition typically deteriorates over a period of time due to inefficient or tired management. The management of a company that was once established in the marketplace may become lacking in energy or rigid, unable or unwilling to cope with new market dynamics. As a result, the company fails to execute its business plan or, worse still, tries to implement an obsolete business plan.

This is where private equity managers earn their bread and butter. Revitalizing companies and implementing new business plans are their specialty. The adept distressed investor is able to spot these tired companies, identify their weaknesses, and bring a fresh approach to the table. By purchasing the debt of the company, the distressed debt investor creates a seat for herself at the table and the opportunity to turn the company around.

27

Trends in Private Equity

There have been a number of changes in the private equity market commencing with the new millennium. First, with respect to leveraged buyouts (LBOs), what was previously thought to be a segmented, inefficient marketplace has turned into an efficient, auction-driven asset class. This has resulted in many secondary sales of private equity portfolios. Second, the efficiency of the LBO market has forced private equity investors to look to new forms of private equity investments such as leveraged loans and private investments in public equity (PIPEs). We review the growth of the LBO industry and observe some interesting trends. We also consider some of the more esoteric segments of the private equity market. Last, we draw some conclusions.

INDUSTRY GROWTH AND MATURATION

It may seem unusual to think of it in this way, but the private equity marketplace is a growth industry, along the lines of health care, biotech, and semiconductors. Exhibit 27.1 displays the growth of the leveraged buyout industry since 1980. From 1991 to 2000 the commitments to private equity funds increased 20-fold. More recently, in the short period from 2004 through 2007, we have seen commitments to private equity increase fourfold. Commitments declined in 2008 as the global credit and liquidity crisis affected every part of the investment management industry. The year 2008 notwithstanding, the primary growth driver was the fact that private equity went from being a cutting-edge investment for institutional investors to being a core holding in any long-term investor's portfolio. Pension funds now include an average allocation to private equity equal to 5%, while endowments and foundations go as high as 15%.

An auction market

Whenever such a large sum of capital enters an investment market, inefficiencies begin to erode. This has led to two new developments in the private equity market. The first is an **auction market** environment.

In the past, private equity deals were sourced by a single private equity firm without any competitive bidding from other private equity firms. The traditional model of private equity was one where a single private equity firm approached a stand-alone public company about going private, or approached a parent company with respect to spinning off a subsidiary. In this model, the lone private equity firm would work with the executive management of the public company (or parent company) to develop a financing plan for taking the public company or a subsidiary private. This process might take months or years to bring a deal to fruition as the private equity firm worked on building its relationship with the senior management of the company.

But the rules have changed. Single-sourced deals are a thing of the past. Now, when a parent company decides to sell a subsidiary in a leveraged buyout format, it almost always hires an investment banker to establish a bidding process among several private equity firms. Each private equity firm is pitted against other private equity firms in a bidding contest where the highest bid wins. But this competitive bidding process can often result in less upside for the private equity investor.

489

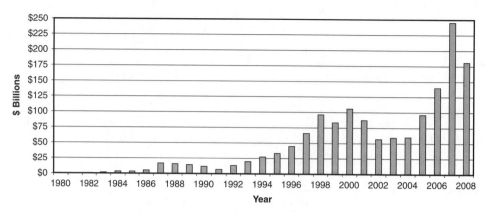

Exhibit 27.1 Committed capital for leveraged buyouts, 1980–2008

The auction process reflects the maturation of the private equity industry. It is part of the natural evolution of any industry: as more capital is attracted to that industry, inevitably competition follows. More competition means erosion of returns on invested capital. In fact, an auction market is one indicator of an efficient market.

Ironically, in some cases, auctions in the private equity marketplace can be less efficient than a single-sourced deal. In a private equity auction, a private equity firm has less time to review the target company's financial statements and operations. In an auction, the bidding process is compressed in time, the opposite of a single-sourced deal where a private equity firm works with the executive management of a company over a long period of time before taking the company private. The shorter time frame simply means that there is less time for a private equity firm to conduct thorough due diligence. Finally, in an auction market, the private equity firm may meet with senior management only two or three times. Contrast this with a single-sourced deal where the private equity firm meets extensively with senior management before taking the company private.

Club deals

Another recent development in the private equity market, particularly as it relates to LBO firms, is the club deal. In the past, LBO firms worked on exclusive deals, one-on-one with the acquired company. However, the large inflow of capital into the private equity market has forced LBO firms to work together in so-called clubs. In a **club deal**, two or more LBO firms work together to share costs, present a business plan, and contribute capital to the deal. There is considerable debate about whether club deals add or subtract value. On the one hand, some have expressed concern that club deals could depress acquisition prices by reducing the number of firms bidding on target companies. However, others have posited that club deals could increase the number of potential buyers by enabling firms that could not individually bid on a target company to do so through a club. In addition, sellers of target companies, as well as potential buyers, can initiate club deals.

A recent report by the U.S. General Accountability Office found that 493 LBOs, or about 16% of all LBOs completed in the United States from 2000 to 2007, were club deals. These club deals accounted for $463.1 billion, or about 44%, of the $1.05 trillion in total LBO deal value. Exhibit 27.2 displays how club deals have grown substantially in both number and value since 2000.[1]

---

[1] See "Private Equity: Recent Growth in Leveraged Buyouts Exposed Risks That Warrant Continued Attention," U.S. General Accountability Office Report GAO-08-885, September 2008.

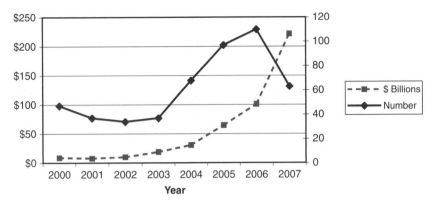

Exhibit 27.2 Club deals in the United States, 2000–2007

One of the principal reasons cited by private equity firms in support of club deals is that they enable firms to participate in buying companies that, individually, they would not have sufficient capital to purchase alone. A second key reason is that private equity firms may be restricted from investing more than a specified portion of their capital in a single deal. For example, a common restriction found in many limited partnership agreements limits private equity funds from investing more than 25% of their total capital in any one deal. For some of the very large buyouts discussed in this book, club deals are necessary. Another benefit of club deals is that they allow private equity firms to pool resources for the prebuyout due diligence research, which can often be quite costly. In addition, club deals allow one private equity firm to get a second opinion about the value of a potential acquisition.

It is interesting to note that while club deals are relatively new to the LBO world, venture capital firms have been using them for years. Witness the earlier example of CacheFlow/Blue Coat Systems in Chapter 23 on venture capital. Each stage of this start-up company was financed by a different venture capital firm. Venture capital firms long ago learned that by bringing in different levels of expertise, one can add significantly to the long-term prospects of the company.

As noted earlier, buyout firms have caught on to the many benefits of combining intelligence with their competitors. Exhibit 27.3 shows the largest club deals since 2005. Note that just about every blue-chip private equity firm now participates in club deals. It is no longer a stigma to invite

Exhibit 27.3 Largest private equity club deals since 2005

Deal	Size	Club Members	Year
TXU Corp.	$43.8 billion	TPG, Goldman Sachs, KKR	2007
HCA Corp.	$32.7 billion	Bain Capital, KKR, Merril Lynch PE	2006
Alltel Corp.	$27.9 billion	Goldman Sachs, TPG	2007
Harrah's Entertainment	$27.4 billion	TPG, Apollo Advisors	2008
Kinder Morgan	$21.6 billion	AIG, Carlyle/Riverstone Partners, Carlyle Group, Goldman Sachs	2007
Freescale Semiconductor	$17.6 billion	Carlyle Group, TPG, Blackstone, Permira	2006
Hertz Company	$15 billion	Clayton Dubilier & Rice, Carlyle Group, Merrill Lynch Global Private Equity	2005
Univision TV	$13.6 billion	Saban Capital, Thomas H. Lee, TPG, Madison Dearborn, Providence Equity	2007
SunGard Data Systems	$11.3 billion	Silver Lake Partners, TPG, Thomas H. Lee, Blackstone Group, KKR, Providence Equity	2005

another private equity firm to the party—to the contrary, it is a sign of strength when two or more well-known private equity firms collaborate on a buyout deal.

The argument against club deals is that they reflect a lack of opportunities in the market for the amount of capital that the LBO firms have to put to work. This is the old argument of too much money chasing too few deals. In addition, there is the concern that too many cooks in the corporate kitchen can spoil the dinner. In a club deal, it is less clear who will take the lead in the business plan, which private equity firm will sit on the board of directors of the private company, who will be responsible for monitoring performance, and who will negotiate with outside lenders to provide the debt financing for the LBO. Last, club deals may allow for the participation of a private equity firm that has no real deal flow itself if not for other private equity firms.

SECONDARY PRIVATE EQUITY MARKET

Another indicator of market efficiency is a market with active secondary trading. In the public stock market, secondary trading takes place on an exchange: the New York Stock Exchange (NYSE), the NASDAQ, the London Stock Exchange, or the Deutsche Bourse, for example. Secondary trading is an indication of investor interest and increases liquidity in the market. In the past there was no secondary market for private equity, but now that has changed at both the private equity firm level and the investor level.

Secondary buyouts

Increasingly, private equity firms are selling to one another as an exit strategy. Private equity firms, flush with capital commitments from investors, are now looking at their competitors for sourcing of deals or as an exit strategy.

Rather than finding new deals, private equity firms are looking at existing private deals, another potential symptom of too much capital in the private equity industry. This is in contrast to the traditional exit strategies of a public offering, recapitalization, or sale of the private company to a strategic buyer (a corporation in the same or a related industry).

Initially, secondary buyouts were rare. Private equity firms were reluctant to sell a portfolio company to another private equity firm in a buyout-to-buyout deal. There was a stigma of failure associated with not being able to take a company public or selling it to a strategic partner.

As an example of a buyout-to-buyout deal, consider the case history of Jostens Inc. Jostens, a maker of high school and college class rings and yearbooks, was initially taken private by Investcorp of Bahrain for $227 million in May 2000. Investcorp subsequently sold Jostens in 2003 to CSFB Private Equity in a private-to-private deal worth $500 million. This translates to a 30% internal rate of return (IRR) for Investcorp of Bahrain.

Jostens was not done yet. CSFB had previously acquired Von Hoffman Corporation and Arcade Marketing, two other specialty printers, for its private equity portfolio. For Von Hoffman, CSFB paid $106 million in equity, while for Arcade Marketing, CSFB paid $90 million. CSFB then sold all three printing companies to Kohlberg Kravis & Roberts (KKR) for $2.2 billion in July 2004. This represented an IRR for CSFB of approximately 20% to 25%.

Now it was KKR's turn. KKR contributed $256 million in equity and the remainder in new debt. It then merged the three printing companies together to form a new company called Visant. Further, in anticipation of a later public offering, Visant filed an annual 10-K report with the Securities and Exchange Commission (SEC) in which it reported 2005 sales of $1.5 billion and total earnings before interest, taxes, depreciation, and amortization (EBITDA) of $293 million.

But KKR was just beginning. In May 2007, KKR sold the Von Hoffman division of Visant to R.R. Donnelley & Sons for $412 million. In July 2007, KKR hired Goldman Sachs and Credit Suisse to explore strategic options for Visant. Meanwhile, Visant's earnings continued to grow. While no buyer has been found for Visant as of February 2009, the value of the company has increased significantly. Adjusted EBITDA for the full year 2008 was $340 million. Media and publishing companies sell in the range of a 10 to 12 multiple of EBITDA. Using the lower multiple of 10, the current value of Visant at the beginning of 2009 was approximately $3.4 billion. When you include the $412 million in cash from the sale of Von Hoffman, the total return to KKR for its investment is: ($412 million + $3.4 billion) ÷ $2.2 billion = 1.73, or a 73% return over its four-year holding period. If we use the $256 million of contributed equity as the denominator in the equation, then the holding period return for equity (after taking into account about $1.8 billion of debt that would need to be repaid) is: $3.8 billion in total value creation minus $1.8 billion in debt = $2 billion in equity value creation, and $2 billion ÷ $256 million equity = 781% return on equity.

Exhibit 27.4 summarizes the buyout-to-buyout-to-buyout deal for Jostens.

Sometimes a firm goes from an LBO to an exit strategy and then back to another LBO. Consider the case of the bakery and restaurant chain Au Bon Pain. In 1998, the private equity firm of Bruckmann, Rosser, Sherrill & Company purchased the company in a leveraged buyout from its parent company, Panera Bread Company.

Au Bon Pain did not stay private very long. It was sold to British food and catering company Compass Group PLC in 2000 for $108 million. Au Bon Pain was then the subject of a management buyout in 2005. Compass sold 75% of the bakery/cafe chain to its senior management for $90 million; $82 million of the buyout was financed by CapitalSource Finance and PNC Mezzanine Capital. Au Bon Pain remains private as of 2009.

There is, however, one large problem with private-to-private deals.

Along the way, at each sale point, incentive fees are earned. Consequently, part of the value associated with an operating company is pulled out by each private equity firm along the private-to-private food chain. Another way to look at this is that each private-to-private equity sale incurs transaction costs in the form of incentive fees, and each time fees are earned, this erodes the value of the operating company to the ultimate investor just a little more.

The investor secondary market

In a similar vein, more investors are rationalizing their private equity investments and selling portions of their limited partnership interests in the secondary market. A limited partnership (LP) interest in a private equity fund is a security for purposes of the securities laws of the United States. However, these LP interests are unregistered; that is, they are privately negotiated and traded securities, not listed on an exchange and not required to be registered with the SEC. The lack of registration makes the purchase and sale of LP interests less liquid than public market stock or other registered securities.

There are three primary reasons why a private equity investor may need to sell part of the portfolio:

1. To raise cash for funding requirements. For example, three million Americans are expected to retire by 2012. This will put pressure on public and corporate pension plans to generate cash to fund retirement benefits.
2. To trim the risk of the investment portfolio. During the credit and liquidity crisis of 2007–2009, many large investors decided that they needed to strategically adjust the risk profiles of their investment portfolios.

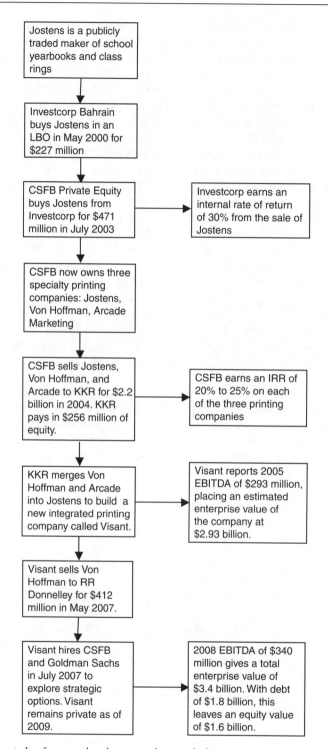

Exhibit 27.4 Case study of a secondary buyout-to-buyout deal

3. To <u>rebalance the portfolio</u> from time to time. This is a form of active portfolio management, mainly for institutional investors, where allocations to asset classes sometimes are decreased, resulting in a partial liquidation of an asset class. Without a secondary market, this would not be possible.

A key risk, however, is that once a limited partner sells its stake in a private equity fund in a secondary market transaction, it is most unlikely that the general partner of the fund will invite that limited partner to join in future private equity funds sponsored by the general partner. General partners usually do not like to see their investors sell their limited partnership interests to outside third parties.

The three reasons cited are about the strategy and the structure of the selling investor. The motivation to sell secondary private equity interests is typically not about the value of the underlying investment. From a buyer's perspective, there are several advantages to a secondary purchase.

- The investor gains exposure to a portfolio of companies with a vintage year that is different from his existing portfolio.
- Secondary interests typically represent an investment with a private equity firm that is further along in the investment process than a new private equity fund and may be closer to harvesting profits from the private portfolio, thereby shortening the J-curve process.
- Purchasing the secondary interest of a limited partner who wishes to exit a private equity fund may be a way for another investor to gain access to future funds offered by the general partner. The buyer may see greater potential for cash flows from the secondary portfolio than current primary investments. Simply stated, this is opportunistic buying.

The Venture Capital Fund of America, founded in 1982 by Dayton Carr, was probably the first investment firm to begin purchasing private equity interests in existing venture capital, leveraged buyout, and mezzanine funds, as well as direct secondary interests in private companies. Another early pioneer in the secondary market was Jeremy Coller. In the years immediately following the dot-com crash, many investors sought an early exit from their outstanding commitments to the private equity asset class, particularly venture capital. As a result, the nascent secondary market grew to become an increasingly active sector within private equity during this period. Secondary transaction volume increased from historical levels of 2% or 3% of private equity commitments to 5% of the market.

The surge in activity in the secondary market between 2004 to 2007 prompted new entrants to the market. It was during this time that the market evolved from what had previously been a relatively small niche into a functioning and important area of the private equity industry. Prior to 2004, the market was still characterized by limited liquidity and distressed prices, with private equity funds trading at significant discounts to fair value. From 2004 to 2007, the secondary market developed into a more efficient market in which assets began to trade at or above their estimated fair values and liquidity increased dramatically. During these years, the secondary market evolved from a niche subcategory in which the majority of sellers were distressed to an active market with an ample supply of assets and numerous market participants.

With the credit and liquidity crisis in global markets in 2008, more sellers entered the market, including endowments, foundations, and pension funds. Many sellers were facing significant overcommitments to their private equity programs, and in certain cases significant unfunded commitments to new private equity funds were prompting liquidity concerns. Simply, the private equity firms were making capital calls on their limited partner investors at the very time when those investors could ill afford to meet the capital calls. This resulted in a dramatic increase in the number of distressed sellers entering the market at the same time, causing prices in the secondary market to fall

Exhibit 27.5   Secondary sales

Seller	Buyer	Amount	Type of Secondary	Year
CalPERS	Oak Hill, Conversus Capital, Coller Capital, Lexington Partners, HarbourVest, Pantheon Ventures	$2.1 billion	LP interests	2007
Bank of America	Conversus Capital	$1.925 billion	LP interests and directs	2007
Harvard University	Unknown	$1.5 billion (est.)	LP interests	2009
ABN Amro	Goldman Sachs, AlpInvest, CPP	$1.5 billion	Directs	2008
Mellon Financial Corp.	Goldman Sachs	$1.4 billion	LP interests and directs	2006
Dresdner Bank	AIG	$1.4 billion	LP interests and directs	2005
American Capital Strategies	HarbourVest, Lexington Partners, Partners Group	$1 billion	LP interests	2006
Ohio Bureau of Workers' Compensation	Panoma Partners	$400 million	LP interests	2007
MetLife	CSFB Strategic Partners	$400 million	LP interests	2007

rapidly. In these transactions, sellers were willing to accept major discounts of up to 50% to current valuations. The valuations, of course, were set by the private equity firms making the capital calls. Limited partner investors were faced with the prospect of further asset write-downs in their existing portfolios. Consequently, many investors had to achieve liquidity within a limited amount of time. This put tremendous price pressure on secondary interests of private equity. Exhibit 27.5 provides a list of the largest sales of secondary interests from 2005 to 2009. Exhibit 27.6 indicates the growth in secondary funds. The largest players are Coller Capital, Lexington Partners, and Goldman Sachs. Notice how the size of these secondary funds has increased in a very short period of time.

Secondary sale of direct interests

This category is sometimes called **direct secondaries**. It refers to the sale of portfolios of direct investments in operating companies rather than the sale of limited partnership interests described in the preceding subsection. These portfolios have traditionally originated from either corporate development programs or large financial institutions. There are three general categories of direct secondaries.

1. *Secondary direct.* This is the sale of a captive portfolio of direct private equity investments in portfolio companies. The buyers will either manage the investments themselves or arrange for a new manager of the portfolio companies. The sale of the Dresdner Bank portfolio is a good example.

Exhibit 27.6   Largest secondary buyout funds

Fund	Amount	Year
Goldman Sachs Vintage Fund IV	$3 billion	2007
Coller Capital Fund IV	$2.6 billion	2002
Lexington Partners V	$2 billion	2003
Goldman Sachs Vintage Fund III	$1.5 billion	2004

Exhibit 27.7 Leveraged buyout performance (through 2007)

	3-Year	5-Year	10-Year	20-Year
Small funds	7.30%	8.10%	4.20%	11.90%
Medium funds	12.80	12.00	9.40	12.60
Large funds	11.40	15.00	7.90	12.80
Mega funds	15.10	16.50	9.10	12.30
All buyout funds	14.00	15.50	8.60	12.40
S&P 500	8.60	12.80	5.90	11.80

Source: Thomson Financial Venture Economics.

2. *Synthetic secondary/spinout.* In this transaction, secondary investors acquire an interest in a new limited partnership that is formed specifically to hold a portfolio of direct investments. An example of this is the Conversus Capital purchase of the Bank of America private equity portfolio in 2007.
3. *Tail end.* This category refers to the sale of the remaining assets in a private equity fund that is approaching or has exceeded its anticipated lifetime. A tail-end transaction allows the private equity manager to wrap up a fund quickly and achieve liquidity for its limited partners.

Exhibit 27.5, discussed previously, lists some of these direct secondary offerings. Note that many of the directs originate with banks and other financial institutions.

Impact on returns

With the private equity market becoming more efficient and driven by an auction process with a growing secondary market, returns are expected to suffer. Traditionally, private equity firms aimed for hurdle rates in excess of 20%. However, the competitive nature of this market has trimmed these return expectations down to 20% or less.

Exhibit 27.7 presents the 3-, 5-, 10-, and 20-year returns earned by buyout firms through 2007 (the S&P 500 has been added as a benchmark). Most private equity firms expect to earn a premium of 400 to 500 basis points above the public markets to compensate investors for the lack of liquidity and the concentrated portfolios of private equity firms. For the most part, the 3-, 5-, and 10-year results show a return premium to private equity over the S&P 500, but less so on a 20-year basis. Still, there is evidence of superior returns, if not in fact the expected 400 to 500 basis points of outperformance compared to the public stock market. LBO funds, in particular, flush with cash, will need to find new ways to put this investment capital to work. These results do not yet include the horrible year of 2008, which is, in fact, better. The global meltdown in 2008 was an aberration and could distort the long-term relationship between private equity and the public markets. Therefore, the long-term return premium for private equity observed in Exhibit 27.7 is a better indicator of what an investor can expect to receive compared to the public markets.

NEW TRENDS IN PRIVATE EQUITY

To maintain performance, private equity firms have turned to other avenues to gather assets and generate returns. At the same time, private equity firms now receive competition for deals from some unexpected sources.

Hedge funds and private equity

Hedge funds have begun to compete with private equity firms in the purchase of corporate assets. A recent case is the bidding competition for Texas Genco in its sale by its parent company, Center-Point Energy. The bidding war for this energy-generation company pitted Seneca Capital, Caxton Associates, and Cerberus Capital Management, three hedge funds, against the private equity firms of KKR, Texas Pacific Group (TPG), Hellman and Friedman, and the Blackstone Group. It was fascinating to see not only a club deal of private equity firms joining together for these assets, but competing against a club of hedge funds, the most secretive and competitive of investment vehicles. The private equity consortium eventually won the auction for the assets, but this is an indication of things to come.

This creates the third new strategy for private equity: if you cannot beat hedge funds, join them. For example, Texas Pacific Group, the large U.S.-based private equity firm, announced in 2005 that it intended to start a new hedge fund called TPG-Axon Capital, with plans to raise up to $3 billion. This is on top of TPG's 2006 $12 billion buyout fund. The Blackstone Group already has a successful fixed income arbitrage hedge fund called Blackstone Bridge, as well as a $9 billion hedge fund of funds business. Bain Capital, another well-known private equity manager, has run the Brookside Capital hedge fund for several years with almost $4 billion of assets under management.

The attraction of hedge funds to private equity firms is easy to see. The advantages, compared to the typical deal terms of a private equity firm, are many:

- Hedge funds offer another source of fund-raising and fee generation.
- Fund-raising for hedge funds was estimated at $125 billion in 2005.
- Hedge fund incentive fees are front-loaded.
- Hedge fund incentive fees are based on changes in net asset value, not realized profits like private equity funds.
- Hedge fund incentive fees are collected on a regular basis, either quarterly or semiannually.
- Investor capital does not need to be returned first to collect incentive fees.
- Management fees do not need to be recouped before incentive fees are paid.
- Hedge funds have no provisions for the clawback of management or incentive fees.

In sum, the deal terms for a hedge fund are much more favorable than those for a private equity funds. Another consideration is that hedge funds have lower hurdle rates than private equity funds. Most private equity funds target returns in the 20% range, while hedge funds aim to beat a cash index plus some premium (e.g. LIBOR plus 6%). This provides hedge funds with a competitive advantage against private equity firms when bidding for operating assets. Lower hurdle rates allow hedge funds to bid more aggressively than private equity firms.

Growth of leveraged loans

Another asset class that private equity firms have moved into is leveraged loans: the market for syndicated bank loans to non-investment-grade borrowers. Loans made by banks to corporations can be divided into two general classes: those made to companies with investment-grade credit ratings and leveraged loans. A **leveraged loan** is made to a corporate borrower that is leveraged: that is, a company that is not investment grade, often due to excess leverage on its balance sheet. Generally, a loan is considered leveraged if:

- The company has outstanding debt that is rated below BBB– by S&P or lower than Baa by Moody's.

- The loan bears a coupon that is in excess of 150 basis points over LIBOR.
- The loan has a second lien interest after other senior secured loans: the term second lien loan market is often used synonymously with the leveraged loan market.

In many respects, leveraged loans are similar to high-yield debt/junk bonds in terms of credit rating and corporate profile. In fact, many non-investment-grade corporations have both high-yield bonds and leveraged loans outstanding. Since private equity firms are used to dealing with banks and other fixed income investors to finance their buyouts, leveraged loans provide a natural extension of their financing business.

This is apparent when considered in light of the secondary trading of leveraged loans. Exhibit 27.8 demonstrates the growth of the institutional leveraged loan market. Institutional investors have an increasing focus on active total return management. This has led to an increase in the secondary trading for leveraged loans as an absolute return product. As a result, the rate of issuance of leveraged loans has surpassed that of high-yield financing. This is an important development because banks were once reluctant to lend to below-investment-grade companies, but this has changed. With the entry of institutional investors into this space, through private equity vehicles, leveraged loans have become an accepted form of investing. And who better to invest in leveraged loans than LBO firms that for years have sought high-yield financing for their buyout targets?

Secondary trading of leveraged loans improved significantly with the introduction of credit ratings by recognized rating agencies. For example, Moody's Investors Service began to assign credit ratings to bank loans in 1995. Moody's recognized the growing importance of institutional loan investors, and the increase in active management practiced by commercial banks in managing their credit exposure. Today, Moody's rates over $1.5 trillion of bank loans. The distribution of Moody's ratings on U.S. bank loans is definitely skewed toward the leveraged loan market. Exhibit 27.9 shows the distribution of bank loan ratings provided by Moody's. Approximately 78% of the rated bank loans fall into the sub-investment-grade categories (Ba, B, and Caa to C).

Unfortunately, the leveraged loan market has not produced stellar returns. Exhibit 27.10 shows the returns to B-rated leveraged loans over the period 2001 to 2008. The best year was 2003 as the United States came out of a recession. The worst year has been 2008 in the midst of the global liquidity and credit crisis.

Notice in Exhibit 29.11 that banks (U.S., Asian, Canadian, and European) account for only 28% of the leveraged loan market. Going back to the 1990s, most of the leveraged loans issued by banks were

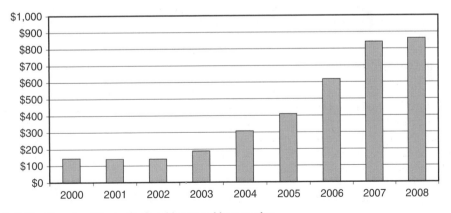

Exhibit 27.8   Growth of the institutional leveraged loan market

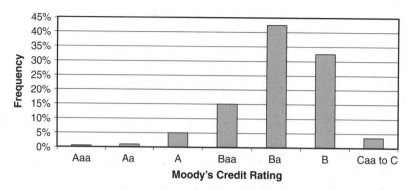

Exhibit 27.9   Distribution of bank loan ratings by Moody's Investors Service

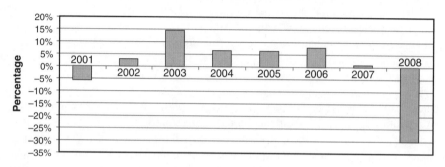

Exhibit 27.10   Returns to B-rated leveraged loans, 2001–2008

held on their balance sheets. Currently, banks have learned that their primary skill is in assessing credit risks (including lending capital and collecting loan origination fees), but not necessarily holding those credit risks on their balance sheets. Consequently, a large portion of leveraged loans made each year (over 70%) are sold in the secondary market to investors who are much better at assessing the investment risk of holding a leveraged loan for three to five years. Exhibit 27.11 demonstrates this shift.

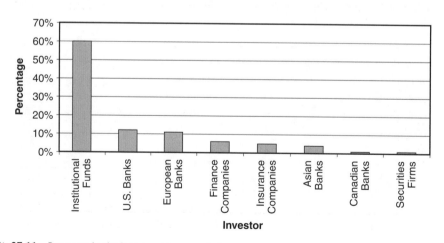

Exhibit 27.11   Investors in the leveraged loan market

Stated differently, large commercial banks have changed their business model from that of a traditional lender where the bank loans are kept on their balance sheets to that of an originator and distributor of debt. Commercial banks are in the fee generation business, not the asset management business. Origination and distribution of bank loans allow banks to both collect fees and manage their credit risk. In short, commercial banks capitalize on their strengths: lending money and collecting loan fees. The subsequent management of the asset (the leveraged loan) is increasingly left up to institutional investors.

PRIVATE INVESTMENTS IN PUBLIC EQUITY (PIPEs)

Private investment in public equity (PIPE) transactions involve privately issued equity or equity-linked securities that are done outside of a public offering. Typically, these securities are exempt from registration under Regulation D of the Securities Act of 1933. In a PIPE transaction, investors purchase the securities directly from a publicly traded company in a private transaction. These transactions are undertaken by companies that already have common stock that is publicly traded. PIPE issuers can be anything from small companies listed in the over-the-counter (OTC) market to NYSE-listed companies.

PIPEs form a crossover strategy between venture capital and LBOs. While many PIPE transactions involve small, nascent corporations of the type that interests venture capitalists, other PIPE transactions involve established public companies, the domain of the LBO market. Thus, venture capitalists and leveraged buyout firms might find themselves side by side on a PIPE deal because it has elements of start-up capital along with private financing for more established companies. The PIPE boom rode the stock market of the 1990s. Although the PIPE market hit a temporary peak in 2002 before declining, it has resumed its growth through the remainder of the decade, hitting a record $253 billion worth of transactions in 2008. Exhibit 27.12 documents the growth of the PIPEs market.

Most PIPE transactions are designed for small capital infusions, in the range of $10 million to $50 million. However, some PIPE transactions can be $500 million or more. The typical profile is a company with a market capitalization of under $500 million that seeks an equity infusion of $10 million to $75 million. Clearly, smaller PIPE transactions appeal to venture capitalists who take much smaller bets on companies, while the larger PIPEs appeal to LBO firms that have a much greater quantity of capital to invest. PIPE transactions may be issued in a variety of forms, such as

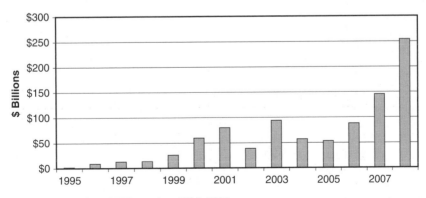

Exhibit 27.12   Growth of the PIPEs market, 1995–2008

unregistered common stock or a convertible security such as preferred stock or notes. The following are the four types of PIPEs.

1. *Registered common stock.*   This is common stock issued under an existing and effective registration statement filed with the SEC. However, instead of a broad public marketing of the stock, the common equity is sold to a select investor universe. The security offers the investor the benefits of receiving registered shares right away. However, typically there is only a small (if any) discount to the current trading price of the stock.

2. *Privately placed common stock.*   This is common equity issued without a registration statement, so it is not publicly tradable. Generally, the issuing company commits to register the shares within a short time frame after the offering, generally three to six months. Because the stock is not registered and cannot be publicly traded, it is offered at a discount to the investors.

3. *Convertible preferred shares or convertible debt.*   This is an equity-linked security structured as either preferred stock or convertible debt. The security is issued as a private placement with an agreement to register the underlying shares at some point after the close of the offering. The advantage to investors is that they have a senior position compared to the outstanding common shareholders. In addition, a liquidity discount must be provided because these are privately issued securities without the benefit of a registration statement and public trading. The advantage to the issuer is the broad flexibility to structure the transaction consistent with its financial situation.

4. *Equity line of credit (ECL).*   This is a contractual agreement between an issuer and an investor that enables the investor to purchase a formula-based quantity of stock at set intervals of time (e.g. quarterly). An effective registration must be maintained by the issuer to allow drawdowns to be completed on the ECL.

The single greatest advantage for a company is that it can quickly raise capital without the need for a lengthy registration process. An SEC registration process can take up to nine months, whereas a PIPE transaction can be completed in just a few weeks. Initially, PIPEs were used by small, growing companies that were strapped for cash because their initial public offerings did not raise sufficient capital for their operations. However, larger companies view PIPEs as a cheaper process for raising capital quickly, especially from a friendly investor. Further, the management of the company does not need to be distracted with a prolonged road show that typically precedes every public offering of stock. Management can remain focused on the operations of the business while receiving an equity infusion that strengthens the balance sheet. Last, the documentation required for a PIPE is relatively simple compared to a registration statement. Typically, all that is needed is an offering memorandum that summarizes the terms of the PIPE, the business of the issuer, and the intended uses of the PIPE proceeds.

The advantage for the investor is that it can acquire a block of stock at a discount to the public market price. This is particularly appealing for private equity firms that have large chunks of cash to commit to companies. The greater the illiquidity, the greater the discount for the PIPE. Also, conversion prices embedded in preferred stock and convertible debt tend to be lower than the conversion prices on the publicly traded instruments. In addition, the issuer of the PIPE usually commits to register the equity securities with the SEC within the next six months. This feature is particularly appealing for private equity firms: They get to purchase cheap equity with a ready-made exit strategy, a public registration in six months' time.

PIPEs fall into two broad categories: traditional and structured. Traditional PIPEs are straightforward private purchases of common equity and preferred stock with a fixed conversion into common shares. Traditional PIPEs have a single conversion price, fixed at a premium to the current market price of the outstanding public stock, which is maintained throughout the life of the PIPE.

We will discuss structured PIPEs in a moment. However, the large majority of PIPE transactions are traditional PIPEs.

Example of a traditional PIPE

Traditional PIPEs can take any one of the four forms discussed earlier, but they all have a standard feature: The sale of the common stock is done at a fixed price. The traditional PIPE is still typically sold at a discount from the public market price of the issuer's stock to reflect the lack of liquidity. Most traditional PIPE transactions are done with convertible preferred stock or debt, but at a fixed conversion price. This limits the amount of dilution to existing shareholders. Also, the convertible preferred stock or debt may provide the investor with dividends and other rights in a sale, merger, or liquidation of the company that are superior to the residual claims of the existing stockholders.

Consider the PIPE transaction issued by Level 3 Communications. Level 3 is an international communications and information services company. It is one of the largest providers of wholesale dial-up service to Internet service providers in North America, and it is a primary provider of Internet connectivity for broadband subscribers.

In 2005, Level 3 entered into a PIPE transaction worth $880 million with several investment companies. The PIPE was structured as a 10% convertible senior note due in 2011. The notes had a fixed conversion price of $3.60 and could be converted after January 1, 2007.

Exhibit 27.13 shows the investors in the Level 3 Communications PIPE. Unfortunately, the fortunes of Level 3 have continued to deteriorate. As of 2009, Level 3's stock was trading at $0.90, well below the conversion price. Exhibit 27.14 shows the stock price of Level 3 from the beginning of 2005 through 2008.

Toxic PIPEs

Structured PIPEs include the more exotic investments such as floating rate convertible preferred stock, convertible resets, and common stock resets. These PIPEs have a floating conversion price, which can change depending on the price of the publicly traded common stock. They are sometimes referred to as floating convertibles because the conversion price of the convertible preferred or debt floats up or down with the company's common stock price. This can lead to the financial situation of a toxic PIPE or a so-called **death spiral**. Floating convertibles got their bad reputation because, unlike standard convertible bonds or preferred stock, which get converted at a fixed conversion price, the conversion price for these securities adjusts downward whenever the underlying common stock price declines. The drop in stock price leads to a drop in the conversion price, which can lead to a significant dilution of shareholder value.

Exhibit 27.13   Investors in Level 3 Communications PIPE

Investor	Amount
Southeastern Asset Management	$400 million
Davis Selected Advisers	$100 million
Fairfax Financial Holdings	$100 million
Legg Mason Opportunity Trust	$100 million
MSD Capital	$100 million
Torray Companies	$50 million
Markel Corporation	$30 million

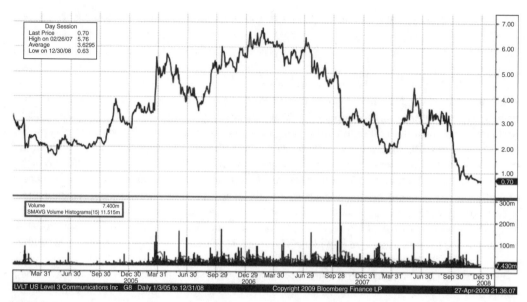

Exhibit 27.14   Stock price of Level 3 Communications, 2005–2008

Source: Bloomberg Finance, L.P.

Under a structured PIPE, if the stock price of the issuer declines in value, the PIPE investor receives a greater number of shares to convert into, or the conversion price declines commensurately with the outstanding stock price. This can lead to a situation that is potentially poisonous to the company's financial health. A **toxic PIPE** works as follows:

- A company goes public before it has a chance to fully establish its business strategy.
- The company quickly burns through its IPO cash and needs more capital to continue its growth.
- Due to the company's unstable balance sheet and uncertain cash flows, the public stock market is closed to further public offerings of its common stock.
- Private equity investors agree to provide more capital in return for PIPEs that can be converted into stock at a floating conversion rate and at a discount to the common stock price.
- Either the private equity investors short the stock of the company or the company's fortunes decline (or both). This is the catalyst turning the structured PIPE into a toxic PIPE.
- The downward pressure on the company's common stock price triggers larger and larger conversion ratios for the PIPE investors, resulting in greater and greater dilution of the common stock of the company.
- The company must reduce the conversion ratio for the PIPEs into common stock at lower and lower prices, which continues to drive down the common stock price, resulting in an even lower conversion price for the PIPEs.
- The PIPE investors either sell their converted shares or take control of the company through their lopsided conversion ratio for the company's common stock.

While this scenario sounds improbable, more than one PIPE transaction has led to poisonous results for a company. Consider the case of Log On America Inc. Log On America was a provider of high-speed Internet access. In February 2000, Log On issued $15 million of convertible preferred shares to Promethean Asset Management LLC of New York, Citadel Limited Partnership of Chicago, and Marshall Capital Management Inc., a unit of Credit Suisse First Boston. The preferred shares were structured so that they were convertible into more shares of common stock if the price of Log On's common shares fell. The lower the price of Log On's common shares, the greater the conversion ratio for the preferred shares.

Shortly after the PIPE transaction, Log On's stock price fell significantly. In a lawsuit filed in the U.S. District Court in New York City in August 2000, Log On alleged that three investment firms drove down its stock price through short sales of the company's stock so that they could convert preferred shares they held into more common shares. According to the lawsuit, the decline in Log On's stock was sufficient to result in the conversion of the preferred stock into 8 million shares of common stock, equal to roughly 50% of the company's equity. The lawsuit contended that the firms planned to acquire enough shares to take control of the company. Unfortunately for Log On, a federal judge did not agree and the lawsuit was dismissed in December 2001.

However, Log On's problems did not stop there. Shortly thereafter, Log On's common shareholders filed a class action lawsuit alleging, among other things, that the company issued materially false and misleading information regarding its revenues and its expected profitability. Unfortunately, Log On could not execute its business plan and filed for Chapter 11 bankruptcy protection in July 2002. Moreover, Log On's bankruptcy reorganization plan failed to gain bankruptcy court approval. As a result, Log On's Chapter 11 filing was turned into a Chapter 7 liquidation plan in 2003 and Log On went out of business. Exhibit 27.15 shows the demise of Log On America.

Using PIPEs to take control

One reason why private equity firms are interested in PIPEs is that they allow the private equity firm to gain a significant stake in the company, even control, at a discount. This is very enticing to private equity firms, which normally have to pay a premium for a large chunk of a company's equity.

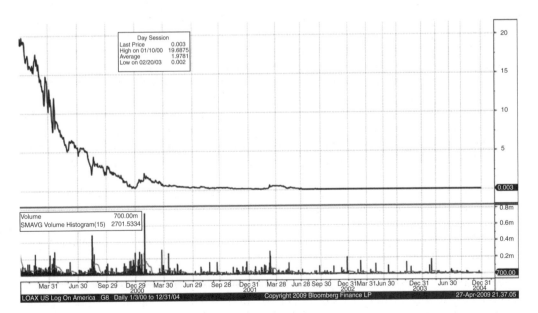

Exhibit 27.15 A PIPE gone bad: Log On America

Source: Bloomberg Finance, L.P.

Consider the case of MoneyGram International. MoneyGram is a leading global payment services company that conducts money transfers, money orders, and payment processing solutions for financial institutions and retail customers. Strapped for cash in March 2008, MoneyGram turned to private equity investors Thomas H. Lee Partners and Goldman Sachs.

The investors agreed to purchase $760 million of Series B and Series B-1 preferred stock that was convertible into 79% of the common equity of MoneyGram at a fixed conversion price of $2.50 per share. In addition, the convertible preferred stock received a nice coupon rate of 10%. In effect, Thomas H. Lee and Goldman Sachs now own MoneyGram, and get a nice dividend to boot.

Unfortunately, MoneyGram's shareholders did not react favorably to the sale of the company to Thomas H. Lee and Goldman Sachs at a discount. MoneyGram's stock price quickly dipped below $5.00 once the PIPE was announced, and by the time the transaction was completed, the stock price had slipped below $2.50, as shown in Exhibit 27.16. As of February 2009, the stock was trading at $1.29 a share.

The risks of PIPEs for investors

We have reviewed the risk of PIPEs from the viewpoint of the issuing company: namely, the toxicity of PIPEs. However, the investor also takes considerable risk that the stock price will trade down after the PIPE transaction is completed.

Consider the case of MBIA Inc. MBIA is a leading financial guarantor in the municipal bond as well as other debt markets. Unfortunately, MBIA got into trouble when the collateralized debt obligation (CDO) and collateralized loan obligation (CLO) markets crashed. MBIA was a significant guarantor of these structures and consequently incurred huge charges and losses when the market imploded. By late 2007, MBIA was in trouble.

In stepped Warburg Pincus to the rescue in two PIPE agreements. In the first agreement, struck in December 2007, Warburg Pincus agreed to purchase 16.1 million shares of MBIA common stock

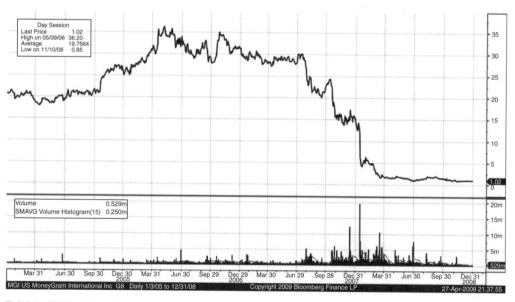

Exhibit 27.16   MoneyGram's stock price

Source: Bloomberg Finance, L.P.

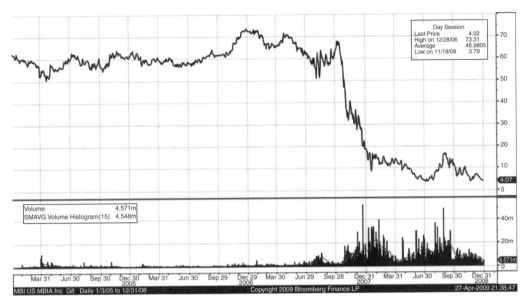

Exhibit 27.17 MBIA's stock price

Source: Bloomberg Finance, L.P.

at a price of $31, which was a 3% premium to the closing price of MBIA's shares on the New York Stock Exchange at the time. In addition, Warburg Pincus received warrants to purchase an additional 8.7 million of MBIA shares at a fixed price of $40 per share. Further, Warburg Pincus agreed to be a backstop to a shareholder rights offering of up to potentially another $500 million by MBIA. In return for the backstop, Warburg Pincus received a second set of warrants to purchase 7.4 million shares of MBIA common stock at $40 a share. The term of each set of warrants was for seven years through 2014.

Unfortunately, the global credit crisis worsened in 2008, and MBIA's fortunes further deteriorated. MBIA's stock price tumbled swiftly from $30 in December 2007 to around $16 by February 2008. This led Warburg Pincus and MBIA to revise their PIPE agreement in February 2008.

Under their second agreement, Warburg Pincus would no longer purchase the common shares of MBIA, but instead would purchase $750 million of convertible preferred shares. The preferred shares can be converted at a fixed conversion price of $12.15. In addition, Warburg Pincus received B warrants to acquire between 4 million and 8 million of MBIA common shares at a fixed strike price of $16.20. The warrants have a tenure of seven years.

The misfortunes of MBIA continued through 2008. By June 2008, MBIA's stock was trading around $5 a share and it was reported that Warburg Pincus had already taken a write-down of $215 million on its stake in MBIA.[2]

Exhibit 27.17 shows the quick demise of MBIA's stock value. Unfortunately for Warburg Pincus, it was a bit like throwing good money after bad. Even though it quickly revised its PIPE transaction with MBIA in February 2008, it could not stop the declining fortunes of MBIA. At a current stock price of around $4.40 in July 2009, Warburg's convertible preferred stock and warrants remain significantly out-of-the-money.

---

[2] See Mark DeCambre and Zachery Kouwe, "Warburg Takes a Bath on MBIA Stake," *New York Post*, July 8, 2008.

CONCLUSION

The competitive environment for private equity firms has changed significantly. What was once an inefficient, almost secretive, deal-driven market where private relationships were the principle source of deal flow has now become a considerably more public market where club deals and auctions have become much more the norm.

This has forced private equity firms to seek new sources of revenues and businesses. While this can have its advantages, there are several risks involved. Particularly troubling is the crossover between hedge funds and private equity. Hedge fund managers are now bidding for operating assets in open competition with private equity firms. The current size of the hedge fund industry is estimated in the $1.5 trillion range. If just 10% of these assets, $150 billion, competed with private equity firms for deals, there would be an even larger inflow of funds than that presented in Exhibit 27.1. This means more money chasing the same number of deals.

PIPE deals offer another way for private equity firms to spread their overabundance of capital around. These transactions appeal to both venture capital and LBO firms and are another form of a crossover strategy.

While toxic PIPEs garner a lot of headlines, these are much more the exception than the rule. Most PIPE transactions are traditional PIPEs, which means that they have fixed conversion rates, rather than floating conversion rates. This prevents excessive dilution of the common equity. The PIPEs market is alive and well, as demonstrated in Exhibit 27.12. However, the risks of investing in PIPEs are not trivial, as highlighted in our MBIA example.

28

The Economics of Private Equity

The prior chapters have been descriptive in nature. We have provided a fundamental depiction of each class of private equity investing: venture capital, leveraged buyouts, mezzanine debt, and distressed debt. In addition, we have highlighted recent changes or trends in each, and noted their causes. In this chapter we consider the risks and returns associated with private equity investing.

Consistent with our prior analysis of hedge funds and commodities, we begin with an examination of how these classes of private equity have performed relative to the broader stock market. We also review the distribution of returns associated with the different classes of private equity. Last, we consider private equity within a portfolio context.

PERFORMANCE OF PRIVATE EQUITY

In this section we look at the performance of each class of private equity relative to that of the S&P 500. Our purpose is simply to determine how private equity returns have compared to public equity returns over the period 1990 to 2008.

Venture capital

Most venture capitalists seek to earn a long-term rate of return in excess of 5% above that of the public stock market. This risk premium can be viewed as providing compensation for three main risks. First, there is the business risk of a start-up company. Although many start-ups successfully make it to the initial public offering (IPO) stage, many more do not succeed. Venture capitalists must anticipate earning a return that sufficiently compensates them for bearing the risk of potential corporate failure. Although public companies can also fail (see Chapter 26 on distressed debt), venture capital is unique in that the investor takes on this business risk before a company has had the opportunity to fully implement its business plan.

Second, there is significant liquidity risk. There is no public market for trading venture capital interests. What secondary trading exists is generally limited to other private equity investors.

This is a fragmented and thus inefficient market. The tailored nature of a venture capitalist's holdings is unlikely to appeal to more than a very select group of potential buyers. Consequently, the sale of an interest in a venture capital fund is not an easy task. Further, another venture capital firm may not have the time or ability to perform as thorough a due diligence as the initial investing firm. Thus, effecting a secondary sale often requires a significant pricing discount.

Third, there is an additional risk due to the lack of diversification associated with a venture capital portfolio. The capital asset pricing model (CAPM) teaches us that the only risk investors should be compensated for is the risk of the general stock market, or systematic risk. This is because unsystematic or company-specific risk can theoretically be diversified away. However, the CAPM is predicated upon security interests being freely transferable. This is not possible in the venture capital marketplace. The lack of liquidity severely impairs transferability. Consequently, company-specific risk must be rewarded.

Also, the CAPM requires diversification, yet venture capital firms have become increasingly specialized. This specialization developed as a result of the intensive knowledge base required to

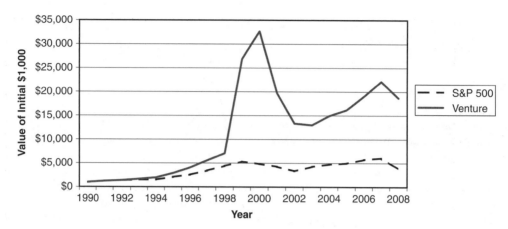

Exhibit 28.1   Value of venture capital and the S&P 500

invest in the technology, telecom, and biotech industries, and has expanded further to include the stage of investment in the life cycle of a start-up company. Unfortunately, specialization leads to concentrated portfolios, the very anathema of the CAPM.

Specialization might be the most important development in the venture capital world. Not only does specialization help private equity managers invest more efficiently; it also allows them to earn a higher return over the market. Another way to state this observation is that specialization may lead to a higher long-term risk premium over a market benchmark to reflect the increased risk associated with concentrated portfolios.

In light of these risks, we examine the returns to venture capital compared to the S&P 500 index, our proxy for the market return. We include all stages of venture capital (seed, early, and late) in our analysis. In Exhibit 28.1, we graph the value of $1,000 invested at the beginning of 1990 through the end of 2008. This 19-year period should be sufficient to reveal any long-term risk premium earned by venture capitalists.[1]

Not surprisingly, venture capital returns have exceeded those for the general stock market. For most of the 1990s, venture capital earned a steady excess return over the S&P 500. However, beginning in 1998, venture capital returns skyrocketed compared to the S&P 500. This aberration culminated in an average venture capital fund return of 280% in 1999.

Clearly, this was an unusual time, when many technology stocks traded beyond any bounds of rationality. Many newly minted Wall Street analysts outdid themselves with outrageous forecasts of performance and almost criminally deficient stock price projections. We demonstrated in our chapter on venture capital how this technology bubble burst with the NASDAQ Composite first soaring above the S&P 500 and the Dow Jones Industrial Average, and then crashing back down to earth. In hindsight, it is clear that many start-up companies were insanely overvalued.

It should be noted that venture capital returns are dependent on a healthy public stock market. A three-year bear market during 2000 to 2002 resulted in depressed public stock prices and discouraged IPOs for start-up companies. A strong public securities market supports the IPO market, the major exit strategy of most venture capitalists.

---

[1] For venture capital and leveraged buyouts, we use data from Cambridge Associates. For mezzanine debt, we use data from CitiGroup/Salomon Smith Barney. This information presents the average returns from reporting investment firms. For distressed debt, we use data from Hedge Fund Research, Inc.

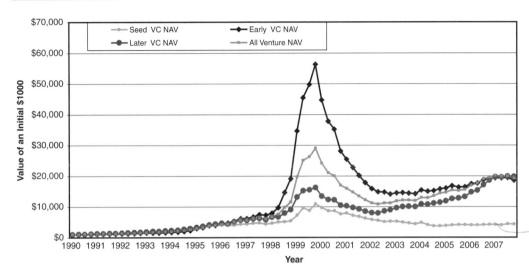

Exhibit 28.2 Value of $1,000 invested in different stages of venture capital

When the stock market weakened in 2001 and 2002, venture capital returns came tumbling down closer to earth. Still, venture capital has provided a healthy risk premium over the public markets even during this time period.

In Exhibit 28.2, we break down the returns to the venture capital industry by the stage of venture investing: seed, early, and late stage venture funds. We also include the return to all venture funds as a comparison. In Exhibit 28.2, from the bottom up, the first line is for seed capital, followed by late stage venture funds, all venture funds, and early stage venture funds at the top.

First, note that the returns (changes in NAV or net asset value) to the different stages of venture capital investing were similar through 1998. The valuation of $1,000 invested in 1990 remained very consistent across early stage, seed, and late stage venture capital. Then the outlier year of 1999 occurred when the returns to early stage venture capital funds earned over 400% in one year. However, these outsized returns (even for venture capital) quickly reversed with three years of negative returns. The largest bubble appears with respect to early stage venture capital funds. These funds inflated the most with the tech bubble before crashing back down to reality. As 2008 closed out, the returns to the different stages of venture capital were once again roughly equivalent.

The one exception was seed venture capital. This stage of investing earned smaller returns than late stage and early stage venture capital funds. This is interesting because, presumably, seed capital venture funds carry the greatest risk because they are typically the first investors in any start-up company. Nonetheless, seed capital venture funds did not participate as extensively in the outrageous returns of 1999 or the subsequent crash of the returns to venture capital funds in 2000 to 2002. In fact, the value of $1,000 invested in seed capital remains considerably below that for early or late stage venture capital at the end of 2008.[2]

---

[2] We note that for our venture capital analysis and for all of the analysis in this chapter, we use the full sample of data. This includes top-performing funds, worst-performing funds, and median funds. Our prior chapters on venture capital and buyouts demonstrated that there is a significant performance differential between top-quartile private equity managers and bottom-quartile managers.

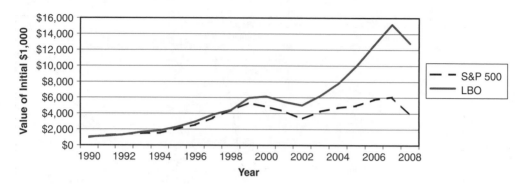

Exhibit 28.3   Value of leveraged buyout funds compared to the S&P 500

Leveraged buyouts

Like venture capital firms, leverage buyout firms also concentrate on company selection as opposed to market risk. However, leveraged buyout funds have less risk than venture capital funds for two reasons.

First, leveraged buyouts take private public companies that are considerably beyond their IPO stage (i.e. they buy out established operating divisions of public companies). The business risk associated with start-up companies does not exist. Typically, buyouts target successful but undervalued companies. These companies generally have long-term operating histories, generate a positive cash flow, and have established brand names and identities with consumers.

Second, LBO firms tend to be less specialized than venture capitalists. While LBO firms may concentrate on one sector from time to time, they tend to be more eclectic in their choices of targets. LBO target companies can range from movie theaters to grocery stores.[3] Therefore, although they maintain smaller portfolios than traditional long-only managers, they tend to have greater diversification than their venture capital counterparts.

Consequently, we can expect to see lower returns for LBO funds, but not below that earned by the broader stock market. In Exhibit 28.3 we present the value of a $1,000 investment in an average LBO fund versus that for the S&P 500 over the time period from 1990 to 2008.

First, we see that LBO firms in fact earn a lower return than venture capital firms. Second, we observe that the return to the average LBO fund followed that of the stock market through the 1990s. It was not until the new millennium that the performance of buyout funds exceeded that of the S&P 500. Starting in the year 2000, LBO funds really came into their own in terms of providing a return premium to the S&P 500. Except for the year 2008, when LBO funds returned roughly the same negative return as the S&P 500, buyout funds provided superior performance through the early 2000s. By the end of 2008, the value of $1,000 invested in LBO funds significantly exceeded the same dollar amount invested in the public stock market.

In Exhibit 28.4 we examine the different types of LBO funds. LBO funds distinguish themselves by the size of the companies that they take private. Generally, they classify themselves as investing in small-capitalization companies ($100 million to $1 billion in sales revenue), mid-capitalization companies ($1 billion to $5 billion in sales revenue), and large-capitalization firms ($5 billion and above in sales revenues). The large category of LBOs also includes the supersized or mega LBOs. In Exhibit 28.4 we include the returns to all LBO funds as a benchmark for comparison.

---

[3] For instance, at the time that KKR was writing down its investment in Regal Cinemas, it was racking up large gains from its investment in Randall's Food Markets, Inc.

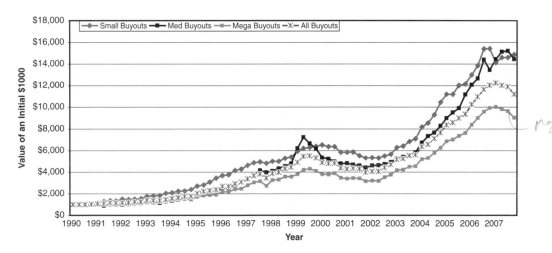

Exhibit 28.4   Value of $1,000 invested in different sizes of buyouts

Exhibit 28.4 shows that the three classifications of LBO funds tended to track each other closely through the 1990s but then began to show some dispersion in returns based on size as the new millennium began. In Exhibit 28.4, from the bottom up, the first line is for large/mega LBOs, followed by all buyouts, midsize buyouts, and small buyouts.

It is clear from Exhibit 28.4 that, in all but a few cases, small buyouts earned a consistent premium over the returns for both mega and midsize LBOs. In fact, the large/mega buyout category has been the clear laggard. By the end of 2008, there was a significant divergence of value between small and midsize LBOs and large/mega LBOs.

There are several potential reasons for the underperformance of the large/mega buyouts. One culprit could be the fact that many large deals are conducted in an auction process. Most large buyouts use an investment banker to attract the highest bid. This auction process leads to a more efficient market with less return potential. By contrast, small and midsize LBOs tend to be engaged in a one-on-one basis with the company going private. Auctions are more an exception and less the rule with smaller LBOs than for the larger deals. This makes the market less efficient and thus results in higher returns as compared to the large LBO deals. Another reason could be the club nature of large LBO deals. With club deals coming together and pooling their capital and expertise for large buyouts, the company being taken private can often demand a higher price given the increased efficiencies. Last, it could simply be the case that it is more difficult to squeeze economic efficiencies out of a large corporation than a small corporation, given their increased operational complexities.

Note also that there is much less variation among the different classes of LBO funds than among the different classes of venture capital funds. Exhibit 28.2 demonstrates much greater variation among the types of venture funds compared to the LBO funds displayed in Exhibit 28.4. The conclusion is that, from an investor's perspective, the choice of what class to invest in is much less critical for LBO funds than for venture capital funds.

Mezzanine debt

Recall our previous chapter on mezzanine debt. Mezzanine financing is a hybrid. It has debtlike components such as coupon payments and a fixed maturity date, but also provides for equity appreciation, usually in the form of warrants or an equity conversion factor. In addition, mezzanine debt often includes flexible features like pay-in-kind coupons and differential coupon rates. Consequently, we might expect it to under perform the equity investments of venture capital or

LBO firms. And, given its debt component, we might also expect it to under perform the S&P 500. Offsetting this however is the high fixed coupon associated with mezzanine debt which offers the potential for steady returns, with much less volatility than the stock market.

Exhibit 28.5 confirms our expectations. Mezzanine debt performed roughly the same as the S&P 500 through the mid-1990s. During this time, the large coupon payments on mezzanine debt plus some equity appreciation provided returns that were similar to the U.S. equity market. However, beginning in 1997, the returns to mezzanine debt began to fall behind those of the U.S. stock market, underperforming from 1997 through 1999. The debtlike nature of mezzanine financing held it back as the U.S. stock market surged through the buildup of the technology bubble. But, not surprisingly, when the bubble burst in 2000, mezzanine financing once again began to outperform the S&P 500.

This is principly due to the downside protection offered by debt over equity. Most of the outperformance for mezzanine financing compared to the U.S. equity market during the early 2000s comes from the fact that mezzanine values did not decline as precipitously as the public stock market over the 2001 to 2002 time period. The combination of debt and equity in most mezzanine financing provided superior downside protection vis a vis the U.S. public equity market. From 2003 through 2007, the returns to mezzanine debt once again mirrored those found in the public equity markets.

Distressed debt

Distressed debt investors are usually equity investors in debt's clothing. Most of the time, the vultures are looking to swoop in, purchase cheap debt securities, convert them to stock, turn the company around, and reap the rewards of appreciation. Consequently, they are less concerned with coupon payments, debt service, or repayment schedules. They are in it for the capital appreciation that can be squeezed out of distressed debt situations.

As we discussed in our chapter on distressed debt, the risks are large because in one way or another the underlying company is in some form of distress. Similar to venture capital, there is a large business risk associated with distressed debt investing. The management of the troubled company must arrest the company's decline and turn it around. Typically, management can stop a company's decline by seeking Chapter 11 bankruptcy protection. However, the harder challenge is coming up with a plan of reorganization that will reward senior and unsecured creditors. If such a plan is successful, distressed debt investors can reap a bonanza. Consequently, distressed debt

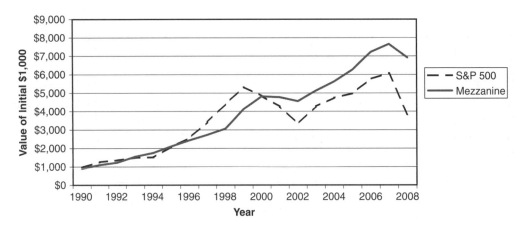

Exhibit 28.5   Value of mezzanine debt compared to the S&P 500

investors are exposed to event risk, either the event that the company will declare bankruptcy or the event that the company will not be able to emerge from bankruptcy protection.

Like LBO and venture capital funds, distressed debt investors also tend to run concentrated portfolios of companies. However, distressed debt investors tend to invest across industries as opposed to concentrating in a single industry. This may lead to better diversification than is found in venture capital funds.

Within the risk spectrum, distressed debt investors fall between mezzanine debt and LBO firms. Like LBO firms, distressed debt investors purchase securities of companies that have established operating histories. In most cases these companies have progressed far beyond their IPO stage. However, unlike LBO firms that target successful but stagnant companies, distressed investing targets troubled companies. These companies have declined past stagnation and may already be in bankruptcy proceedings. We also discussed in our prior chapter on distressed debt that there is a natural cycle between private equity and distressed debt investing. Since LBOs use a significant amount of debt to take a company private, sometimes this debt burden becomes too much to bear and the private company now enters into a distressed situation. Consequently, LBOs can be a good source of distressed debt.

Like venture capital and LBO funds, distressed debt investors assume considerable business risk. However, distressed debt investing is less risky than venture capital or LBOs because debt holders command higher seniority than equity investors in an LBO. The company's current problems might be due to poor execution of an existing business plan, an obsolete business plan, or simply poor cash management. These problems can be fixed, whereas a start-up company with a non-viable product cannot.

Exhibit 28.6 presents the value of distressed debt investing compared to the S&P 500. For much of the 1990s, distressed debt tracked the public stock market. However, in the new decade, distressed debt has added a significant return premium above the public stock market. This return premium is consistent with the extra business risk assumed for investing in the securities of troubled companies.

Consistent with our earlier discussion, while distressed debt outperformed the public stock market, it provided less value than LBOs or venture capital. In 2008, distressed debt earned a negative return of −25%. This return was worse than that for LBOs and venture capital. Also, if you compare Exhibit 28.6 to Exhibit 28.5, you can see that distressed debt has earned a return premium compared to mezzanine debt. This is consistent with distressed debt having a higher risk profile than mezzanine debt.

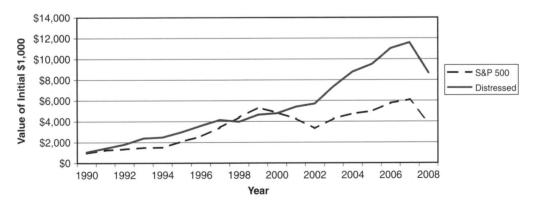

Exhibit 28.6 Value of distressed debt compared to the S&P 500

PRIVATE EQUITY RETURN DISTRIBUTIONS

In this section we perform the analysis that was previously deployed for hedge funds, commodities, and managed futures. Through the process of graphing the returns to private equity we try to understand the nature of the risks associated with this form of investing.

In previous chapters we introduced the concepts of skewness and kurtosis. These are statistical measures that help to describe the distribution of returns earned from an investment in an asset class. Recall that skewness and kurtosis are defined by the third and fourth moments of the distribution, respectively. A normal (bell-shaped) distribution has no skewness because it is a symmetrical distribution. The values of kurtosis in the following exhibits are measured relative to a normal, bell-shaped distribution. A positive value for kurtosis indicates a distribution with fatter than normal tails (a condition called leptokurtosis) whereas a negative value indicates a distribution with thinner than normal tails (platykurtosis).

Normal distributions can be defined exclusively by the first two moments of the distribution—the mean and the variance. Therefore, for a normal distribution, a Sharpe ratio is an appropriate measure for risk and return. However, if higher moments of the distribution are present, a Sharpe ratio may not capture the complete risk versus return trade-off.[4] By plotting the return distribution, we are able to observe if it exhibits nonnormal properties that might not be captured by a Sharpe ratio analysis.

We take the data contained in the Venture Economics database and recalibrate them to plot a frequency distribution of the returns associated with venture capital, LBOs, and mezzanine debt. This data is presented on a quarterly basis. For distressed debt investing, we use the return information in the Hedge Fund Research, Inc. (HFRI) database. The HFRI data is presented on a monthly basis. The following exhibits provide a graphical depiction of the range and likelihood of returns associated with private equity investing. We calculate the mean, standard deviation, skew, and kurtosis associated with each strategy.

Recall that in our chapters on hedge funds we also examined the returns to high-yield bonds. We found that the distribution of returns to high-yield bonds demonstrated a significant downside tail. This fat tail reflects the event risk of downgrades, defaults, and bankruptcies. Fat tails are the result of two distribution characteristics: a large positive value for kurtosis and a negative value for skewness. These two statistics describe the condition whereby a considerable amount of the mass of the distribution is located on the left side of the graph, this indicates a predilection for large negative returns, hence the fat tail. In our examination of high-yield bonds we found a negative skew of about −1.5 and a kurtosis of 7.65. These values indicated a significant downside fat tail.

A negative skew indicates that the mean of the distribution is to the left of (less than) the median of the distribution. This means that there are more frequent large observations to the left of the distribution (negative returns) and there are more small and midrange positive return observations to the right of the distribution. In other words, large negative outlying returns occur more frequently than large positive outlying returns, indicating a bias to the downside.

A positive skew indicates the reverse of a negative skew. It indicates that the mean of the distribution is located to the right of the median and that there are more frequent large positive returns than there are large negative returns. A positive skew demonstrates a bias to the upside.

---

[4] For a detailed examination of symmetric performance measures and asymmetric return distributions, see Mark Anson, "Symmetric Performance Measures and Asymmetric Trading Strategies: A Cautionary Example," *Journal of Alternative Investments* (Summer 2002), 81–85.

Venture capital

Exhibit 28.7 presents the frequency distribution for the quarterly returns to venture capital over the past 19 years. Using annualized data, we find an annual expected return of 19% with a standard deviation of about 22%. There are both positive and negative outliers, but it is clear just from a visual examination of Exhibit 28.7 that the outliers tend to be more positive than negative. This leads to a very large skew value of 2.88 and an astounding kurtosis of 32.81.

We must keep in mind that these results are literally skewed by the phenomenal returns enjoyed by venture capital in the years from 1998 to 2000 before the tech bubble burst. Although the period from the second half of 2000 through the end of 2002 was a period of significant negative returns for venture capital, it did not offset the positive returns enjoyed from 1998 through the first half of the 2000. The period from 2003 to 2007 once again produced positive returns but was subsequently followed by negative returns in 2008 as the financial crisis took hold.

Venture capital also has the highest standard deviation of the four classes of private equity. Clearly, this investment class is not for the fainthearted. Given that we are dealing with nascent companies that may or may not burst upon the scene (some just burst), a wide range of returns should be expected.

We do observe large outlier returns for venture capital, and a potential reason for these returns is the very nature of venture capital investing. When a company does well it can result in dramatic upside gains (a "20-bagger") for its venture capital investors.[5] Unfortunately, many start-up companies go bust resulting in the venture capitalists losing part or even all of their investments. This return pattern is ideal for posting a large positive skew with a large positive value of kurtosis. If a company goes bust, the most a venture capitalist can lose is the money invested. However, if the company is successful, the gains can be extraordinary.

This return pattern is similar to a call option. The venture capitalist has a simple binary choice with respect to every business plan: invest or don't invest. Investing in a start-up company is similar to the purchase of a call option. The price of the option is the capital that the venture capitalist invests in the start-up company. If the company fails, the venture capitalist forfeits the option premium, the capital invested. However, if the start-up company is successful, the venture capitalist shares in all of the upside—much like a call option.

The reverse of a long call option is a short put option. This is the pattern demonstrated by high-yield bonds. Investors in high-yield bonds effectively have sold a put option to other market participants. If the high-yield bond pays off, the investor collects a known amount (the face value of the bonds), just like collecting the premium from the sale of a put option. However, if the underlying company's fortunes evaporate, the high-yield investor is on the hook for whatever losses the bond incurs. This asymmetric payoff function results in a limited upside but a large downside risk. This again results in a large kurtosis value but this time with a negative skew.

Leveraged buyouts

Exhibit 28.8 presents the frequency distribution for LBOs. Interestingly, the return pattern to LBOs shows a much more symmetrical distribution of returns than the return pattern for venture capital. The values for skew (−0.29) and kurtosis (−0.08) are close to zero, indicating a normal or symmetrical distribution of returns.

---

[5] The terminology "20-bagger" comes from Peter Lynch, the former manager of the Fidelity Magellan Fund. He often referred to a stock in baseball terms. Therefore, a two-bagger was a stock that doubled your money, a three-bagger tripled your money, and so on. A 20-bagger indicates a company that appreciates in value 20-fold compared to the cost of the venture capital investment.

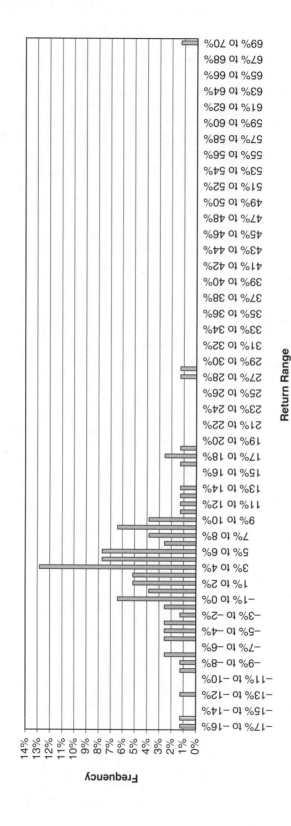

Exhibit 28.7 Frequency distribution for venture capital

Note: Annualized returns 1990–2008: Average Return 19%; Std. Dev. 21.80%; Skew 2.88; Kurtoisis 2.81; Sharpe ratio 0.7.

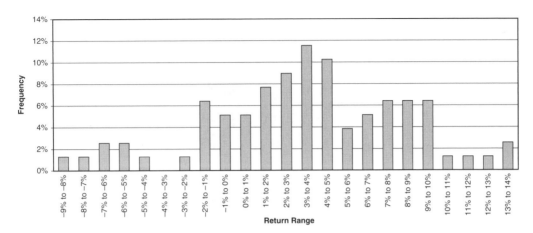

Exhibit 28.8   Frequency distribution for LBOs

Note: Annualized returns 1990–2008: Average Return 14.40%; Std. Dev. 9.70%; Skew −0.29; Kurtosis −0.08; Sharpe ratio 1.08.

Leveraged buyout firms have far less business risk than venture capital firms. LBO firms target successful, established but undervalued companies, whereas venture capitalists work with new and unproven companies. These firms have operating management in place, an established product and brand name, an operating history and a stable balance sheet. LBO firms then implement a better business plan that generates increased cash flow adding on leverage to boost the returns to equity.

As a result, the return pattern to LBOs resembles that of the public stock market more than venture capital. There is almost no skew and almost no kurtosis. The returns to LBO funds, in fact, demonstrates a remarkably symmetrical return pattern during the period 1990–2008E (estimated). Large downside returns occur with the same frequency as large positive returns. Overall, LBO firms generate an average annual return of 14.4% with a volatility that is much lower than that for venture capital at 9.7%. This return pattern results in a higher Sharpe ratio for LBOs of 1.08 compared to 0.7 for venture capital. Bottom line: LBO funds provide a better risk-return trade-off than do venture capital funds.

Last, it is interesting to note that the return distribution for LBO funds produces a negative kurtosis. Although very small, this demonstrates a condition whereby the tails of the distribution are thinner than the tails for a normal distribution. Simply, LBO funds do not demonstrate the same exposure to outlier events as do venture capital funds. This could be due to the fact that LBO funds look for well-established companies with stable cash flows. This might tend to reduce the exposure of LBO funds to outlier returns. Those investors looking for less risk in their portfolios would be more attracted to LBO funds than to venture capital funds.

Mezzanine debt

Given mezzanine debt's status as a hybrid, part debt and part equity, we would expect to see lower returns than for venture capital and LBOs, but also lower volatility of returns. Both cases are observed: mezzanine debt earns less than venture capital and LBOs, but there is also less risk. The result is a solid Sharpe ratio of 0.87: lower than that for LBOs but higher than venture capital. The empirical results can be found in Exhibit 28.9.

With respect to skewness and kurtosis, we observe a negative skew and a positive kurtosis. This is similar to the negative skew and positive kurtosis of high-yield bonds. However, junk bonds have a much larger negative skew and greater kurtosis, indicating a larger downside fat tail than mezzanine

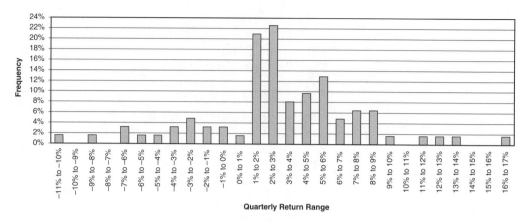

Exhibit 28.9 Frequency distribution for mezzanine financing

Note: Annualized returns 1990–2008: Average Return 11.20%; Std. Dev. 9.40%; Skew −0.16; Kurtosis 2.3; Sharpe ratio 0.87.

debt. This is reflective of the credit/event risk associated with high-yield bonds. From this analysis, we can conclude that mezzanine debt has much less exposure to event risk than high-yield bonds. This is due to the fact that mezzanine funds share in the upside of the company through some form of equity kicker. This provides a level of diversification away from mezzanine debt's exposure to credit events.

Distressed debt

Although distressed debt is a way to convert outstanding debt into equity, the investor must bear the event risk that the company will cease to function. As we discussed in the prior chapter, distressed companies may already be in Chapter 11 bankruptcy proceedings. However, Chapter 11 bankruptcy protection is not a panacea; the company could end up liquidating, similar to the Global Crossing case study presented in Chapter 26.

Consequently, credit risk still exists. From our prior discussions with respect to high-yield bonds, we know that event risk translates into a negative skew and large kurtosis. This is confirmed in Exhibit 28.10. In this exhibit we present two frequency distributions. The first is for the Merrill Lynch (ML) Distressed Debt index. This is a passive index that tracks the up-and-down price movement of the distressed debt market. We can see that the expected return over this period for a passive allocation to distressed debt resulted in a negative average annual return of −1.5%—not very encouraging with a high standard deviation of 12.27%. In addition, the Merrill Lynch index demonstrates a large negative downside tail. The value of the skew is −1.02 and kurtosis is 4.8. In general, the distressed debt market over the period 1990–2008E did not provide much upside and exposed the investor to significant downside risk.

However, in Exhibit 28.10 we also provide the frequency distribution for active distressed managers. The results are far more encouraging. First, the average annual return increases to 12.3% and the Sharpe ratio improves from −0.44 for the Merrill Lynch index to 1.26 for the active distressed debt managers. In fact, the distressed debt managers achieve the highest Sharpe ratio across the four types of private equity.

However, active management cannot eliminate the fat downside tail associated with distressed debt. In fact, the skew increases to −1.11 and the kurtosis expands to a very large 18.75. However, the standard deviation is much lower than the ML Index at 6.67%. In summary, while active distressed

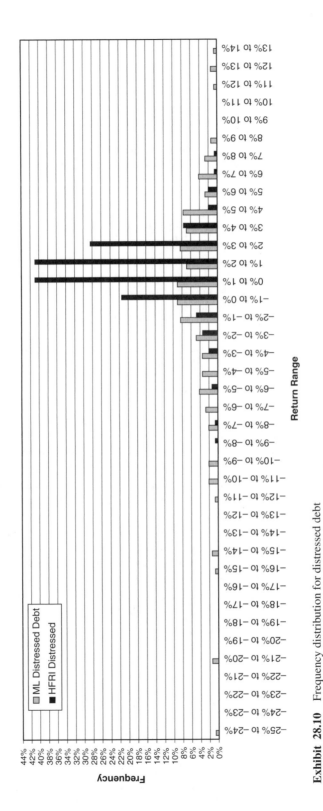

Exhibit 28.10 Frequency distribution for distressed debt

ML Index: Average Return –1.5%; Std. Dev. 12.27%; Skew –1.02; Kurtosis 4.8; Sharpe ratio –0.44.

Active Distressed Debt: Average Return 12.3%; Std. Dev. 6.67%; Skew –1.11; Kurtosis 18.75; Sharpe ratio 1.26.

debt management does lead to a strong Sharpe ratio, there is still the risk of very large negative returns that skews the return distribution toward a fat downside tail. In fact, active management appears to enlarge this downside tail risk rather than shrinking it.

Correlation of private equity returns

The preceding analysis considered each class of private equity in isolation. In this section we consider how the different classes of private equity work with each other. In other words, we check to see whether the different classes provide return patterns that are more or less correlated with each other are clustered.

Exhibit 28.11 provides a correlation matrix with the four classes of private equity as well as large-capitalization stocks (S&P 500), small-cap stocks (Russell 2000), high-yield bonds, and U.S. Treasury bonds. The results are revealing. First, the different classes of private equity investing have low correlations with each other. Venture capital, for example, has a correlation coefficient of only 0.54 with buyouts, a higher 0.69 with mezzanine financing, and a very low correlation of 0.17 with distressed debt. This indicates that each class of private equity can be a useful addition to a diversified portfolio of stocks and bonds because the returns to the different private equity classes do not double up on one another. We do note that buyouts have a higher correlation with mezzanine financing at 0.72 and distressed debt at 0.54. However, as we mentioned previously in our chapter, this is not surprising given that mezzanine financing is a key component of large buyout deals, while leveraged buyouts are often seen as a good source of distressed debt. In summary, both mezzanine debt and distressed debt feed off the buyout industry. LBOs are not the sole source of mezzanine and distressed debt, but they are a large source of these two debt forms.

Second, it can be seen from Exhibit 28.11 that the returns to private equity have low correlations with traditional asset classes. First, all four classes of private equity are negatively correlated with Treasury bonds. Also, the correlation coefficients with the public equities, while all positive, are less than 1.00, indicating some diversification potential. Surprisingly, the correlation coefficient between mezzanine financing and large-cap stocks (0.69) and small-cap stocks (0.72) is very consistent and large. Apparently, mezzanine financing picks up considerable stock market risk due to the convertible features built into most mezzanine debt. Recall, too, our description of how mezzanine debt is used by both large and small companies, hence its consistent correlation with both large-cap and small-cap stocks. Interestingly, the correlation coefficient of distressed debt compared to high-yield bonds is very high at 0.91, while the correlation coefficient between mezzanine debt and high-yield debt is much lower at 0.54. Apparently, the equity kickers contained in mezzanine debt are sufficient to diversify it away from the high-yield market.

Exhibit 28.11   Correlation table for different types of private equity

	S&P 500	RU2000	T-Bonds	High-Yield	Venture	Buyouts	Mezzanine	Distressed
S&P 500	1.00							
RU2000	0.83	1.00						
T-Bonds	−0.10	−0.16	1.00					
High-Yield	0.76	0.92	0.00	1.00				
Venture	0.39	0.29	−0.40	0.01	1.00			
Buyouts	0.79	0.65	−0.40	0.48	0.54	1.00		
Mezzanine	0.69	0.72	−0.26	0.54	0.69	0.72	1.00	
Distressed	0.65	0.87	−0.18	0.91	0.17	0.54	0.60	1.00

PRIVATE EQUITY WITHIN A DIVERSIFIED PORTFOLIO

The popularity of private equity investments has led to many studies on the value of investing in these vehicles.[6] Exhibit 28.11 indicates that the different classes of private equity have negative correlations with Treasury bonds and relatively low positive correlations with public equity. We examine these potential benefits next.

There are, however, concerns about the returns to private equity. First, Gompers and Lerner conclude that inflows to private equity funds have a substantial impact on the pricing of private equity investments.[7] The implication is that the positive valuations associated with private equity investments may in part be due to new capital inflows instead of real economic value.

Second, Gompers demonstrates that young venture capital firms bring private companies to the public market earlier than older venture capital firms in order to establish a positive reputation.[8] He concludes that this type of signaling causes real wealth losses in the form of underpriced IPOs (i.e. lower equity valuations), and that this loss is borne by the limited partners in the venture fund. We also note again that the performance data used in this chapter is for all funds in a category, including top-quartile performers, bottom-quartile performers, and median performers. This is important to note because of our prior discussions on performance persistence. Performance persistence is a consistent attribute of private equity investing. The better-performing funds of today and yesterday tend to be the better-performing funds of tomorrow. We documented in our chapters on venture capital and private equity that the differential performance between top-quartile performers and bottom-quartile performers can be upwards to 20% per annum.[9]

Third, as mentioned in our conclusions, with the advent of Financial Accounting Standard 157, new mark-to-market accounting rules do not allow the listing of private investments at cost. As a result, the reported volatility of private equity investments is expected to increase in coming years, thus offsetting the potential diversification benefits of investing in this asset class. Despite these potential caveats, empirical research indicates that private equity has favorable risk and return characteristics. Next we examine these properties within a portfolio framework.

Building a diversified portfolio with private equity

We now examine the ability of private equity to expand the investment opportunity set. Following the same analysis we performed for commodity futures and managed futures, we first build the efficient frontier using stocks and bonds. We then blend in a 10% allocation to each class of private equity. Our results are presented in Exhibits 28.12 to 28.16.

We start by building the efficient frontier with just stocks (S&P 500) and bonds (10-year U.S. Treasury bonds). This is the same frontier that we have used in other parts of this book. At the

---

[6] See Alon Brav and Paul Gompers. "Myth or Reality? The Long-Run Underperformance of Initial Public Offerings: Evidence from Venture and Non-Venture Capital-Backed Companies," *Journal of Finance* (December 1997), 1791–1821; Paul Gompers and Josh Lerner, "Money Chasing Deals? The Impact of Fund Inflows on the Valuation of Private Equity Investments," *Journal of Financial Economics* (2000), 281–325; Paul Gompers and Josh Lerner, "The Challenge of Performance Assessment," in *Private Equity and Venture Capital*, ed. Rick Lake and Ronald Lake (London: Euromoney Books, 2000); Paul Gompers, "Grandstanding in the Venture Capital Industry," *Journal of Financial Economics* (1996), 131–156; Steve Kaplan and Antoinette Schoar, "Private Equity Performance: Returns, Persistence, and Capital Flows," working paper, University of Chicago Graduate School of Business and MIT Sloan School of Management, 2006; Steve Kaplan and Per Stromberg, "Leveraged Buyouts and Private Equity," NBER Working Paper 14207, July 2008.

[7] See Gompers and Lerner, "Money Chasing Deals?"

[8] See Gompers, "Grandstanding in the Venture Capital Industry."

[9] See Kaplan and Schoar, "Private Equity Performance."

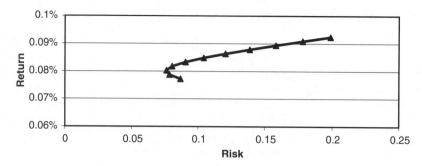

Exhibit 28.12   Efficient frontier with stocks and bonds

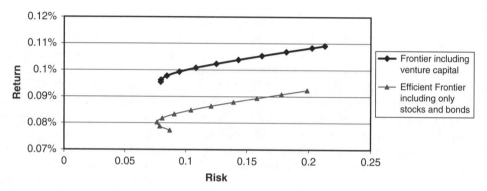

Exhibit 28.13   Efficient frontier with venture capital

left-hand side of the efficient frontier where returns and risk are the lowest is a 100% allocation of U.S. Treasury bonds. At the far right-hand side of the frontier is a 100% allocation to stocks. Between these two end points we have blended in different combinations of stocks and bonds to achieve the curve demonstrated in Exhibit 28.12.

Having established our initial efficient frontier, we now blend in different private equity components. Exhibit 28.13 demonstrates the efficient frontier when we blend in a 10% allocation to venture capital. That is, at every point along the efficient frontier we now have an allocation to 10% venture capital so that the starting point on the left represents 90% Treasury bonds and 10% venture capital,

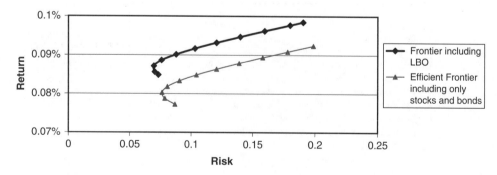

Exhibit 28.14   The efficient frontier with leveraged buyouts

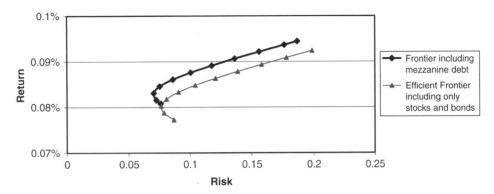

Exhibit 28.15   Mezzanine efficient frontier

while the end point on the right represents a 90% allocation to public equities and a 10% allocation to venture capital. In between these two endpoints we blend the three components together (85% bonds/5% public stocks/10% venture, 75% bonds/15% public stocks/10% venture, etc.). We can see that the efficient frontier with venture capital lies significantly above that of the original efficient frontier representing only stocks and bonds. Simply, the addition of venture capital into the portfolio results in a better risk-return trade-off than if we just had public equity and Treasury bonds.

A similar result, although less striking, is found with leveraged buyouts. Blending in a 10% allocation to LBOs to a public stock and bond portfolio results in an improved efficient frontier. In Exhibit 28.14, the frontier with LBOs lies above and to the left of the original frontier. This demonstrates a better risk-return trade-off when leveraged buyouts are added to the original stock and bond portfolio.

Exhibit 28.15 shows the efficient frontier with mezzanine debt added to the public stock and bond portfolio. We find similar results compared to leveraged buyouts. That is, a 10% allocation to mezzanine financing provides sufficient return diversification that it pushes the original efficient frontier up and to the left, indicating that a better risk-return trade-off is obtained at every point of the efficient frontier when we blend in mezzanine debt with public stocks and Treasury bonds.

Last, we examine distressed debt. Using the same technique of blending in a 10% allocation to distressed debt at every point along the efficient frontier, we find an improved frontier in Exhibit 28.16. The efficient frontier with distressed debt lies above and slightly to the left of the original frontier.

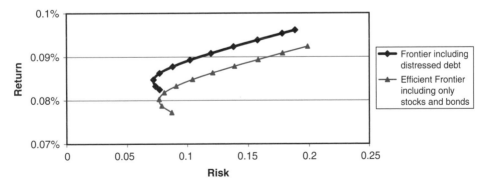

Exhibit 28.16   Distressed debt efficient frontier

Again, this demonstrates the beneficial diversification properties associated with distressed debt; it improves the risk-return trade-off from the original public stock and Treasury bond portfolio.

In our introductory chapters, we maintained that private equity is not really a different asset class but just one point along the equity investment spectrum. However, the results in Exhibits 28.13 to 28.16 demonstrate that the diversification properties of private equity compared to public equity and bonds provide a potential source of returns that can be viewed both for their excess returns and for their diversification properties.

CONCLUSION

This chapter was concerned with the economics of private equity. Initially, we observed that each form of private equity, venture capital, leveraged buyouts, mezzanine financing, and distressed debt, earned a premium in excess of the public stock market over the period from 1990 to 2008. Also, the Sharpe ratios for each form of private equity were in excess of what was achieved by the public stock markets over this same time period.

However, one caveat must be noted. Prior to 2008, private equity managers had unfettered ability to mark their private portfolios up or down. Often, private equity managers would leave the value of a private equity investment at cost until there was some market event. Leaving a portfolio investment marked at the same price quarter after quarter would have the effect of dampening volatility associated with the private equity portfolio. It was not because volatility was non-existent in private equity investments. Rather it was the fact that the private equity manager, using his or her discretion to mark up or down the value of the investments, could mask the volatility that existed.

However, with the advent of Financial Accounting Standard (FAS) 157, private equity managers must now apply new mark-to-market accounting rules. They can no longer keep a private investment listed at cost; they have to provide a market valuation on a quarterly basis. The result should be an increase in the volatility of private equity investments. This may reduce the gains that we saw with respect to the expansion of the efficient frontiers in Exhibits 28.13 to 28.16. This could potentially change our conclusions about the diversifying abilities of private equity portfolios. This is an area of private equity economics that bears keen watching over the next several years.

We found that the return distributions for the four classes of private equity were very different. Venture capital, for example, exhibited a large positive skew and huge kurtosis, indicating a large fat tail to the upside. This is consistent with our description of venture capital as a call option on the success of a start-up company. Essentially, venture capital is exposed to positive event risk. Conversely, distressed debt displayed a large negative skew and large kurtosis, indicating a fat downside tail. This is consistent with an asset class that is exposed to negative event risk: the risk of defaults and bankruptcies. Leveraged buyouts and mezzanine debt, however, displayed much more symmetrical returns.

Part VI
Credit Derivatives

29

Introduction to Credit Derivatives

Credit derivatives are financial instruments that are designed to transfer the credit exposure of an underlying asset or issuer between two or more parties. They are individually negotiated financial contracts that may take the form of options, swaps, forwards, or credit-linked notes where the payoffs are linked to, or derived from, the credit characteristics of the referenced asset or issuer. With credit derivatives, a financial manager can either acquire or hedge credit risk.

Many asset managers have portfolios that are very sensitive to changes in the interest rate spread between riskless and risky assets, and credit derivatives are an efficient way to hedge this exposure. Conversely, other asset managers may use credit derivatives to target specific exposures as a way to enhance portfolio returns. In each case, the ability to transfer credit risk and return provides a new tool for portfolio managers to improve performance.

Credit derivatives, therefore, appeal to financial managers who invest in high-yield bonds, bank loans, or other credit-dependent assets. The possibility of default is a significant risk for asset managers, and one that can be effectively hedged by shifting the credit exposure.

In their simplest form, credit derivatives may be nothing more than the purchase of credit protection. The ability to isolate credit risk and manage it independently of underlying bond positions is the key benefit of credit derivatives. Prior to the introduction of credit derivatives, the only way to manage credit exposure was to buy and sell the underlying assets. Because of transaction costs and tax issues, this was an inefficient way to hedge or gain exposure.

Credit derivatives, therefore, represent a natural extension of the financial markets to unbundle the risk and return buckets associated with a particular financial asset, such as credit risk. They offer an important method for investment managers to hedge their exposure to credit risk, because they permit the transfer of the exposure from one party to another. Credit derivatives allow for an efficient exchange of credit exposure in return for credit protection.

Before we can discuss credit derivatives, we must first review the underlying risk that these financial instruments transfer and hedge. We begin this chapter with a discussion of credit risk. We then review the credit risks inherent in four important financial markets: high-yield bonds, leveraged bank loans, sovereign emerging market debt, and distressed debt. The credit and liquidity crisis of 2007–2008 brought about by the subprime mortgage meltdown has provided a special highlight to the credit derivatives market.

THREE SOURCES OF CREDIT RISK

A fixed income debt instrument represents a basket of risks. There is the risk from changes in interest rates (duration and convexity risk); the risk that the issuer will refinance the debt issue (call risk); and last, the risk of defaults, downgrades, and widening credit spreads (credit risk). The total return from a fixed income investment such as a corporate bond is the compensation for assuming all of these risks. Depending on the credit rating on the underlying debt instrument, the return from credit risk can be a significant part of a bond's total return.

There are three important types of credit risk: default risk, downgrade risk, and credit spread risk. **Default risk** is the risk that the issuer of a bond or the debtor on a loan will not repay the outstanding debt in full. Default risk can be complete in that no amount of the bond or loan will be repaid, or

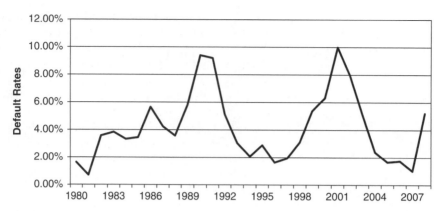

Exhibit 29.1   Default rates for high-yield bonds

it can be partial in that some portion of the original debt will be recovered. **Downgrade risk** is the risk that a national rating agency will lower its credit rating for an issuer based on perceived earnings capacity. **Credit spread risk** is the risk that the spread over a reference riskless rate will increase for an outstanding debt obligation. Credit spread risk and downgrade risk differ in that the latter pertains to a specific, formal credit review by an independent agency while the former is the financial markets' reaction to perceived credit deterioration.

A debtor is deemed to be in default when it fails to make a payment on its outstanding obligations. This can be as simple as the failure to make one scheduled coupon payment on an outstanding bond, or one interest payment on an outstanding loan. A bond or loan that has failed to make a scheduled payment is considered to be in default and the price of the asset declines accordingly.

In the following three exhibits we examine the three forms of credit risk. First, Exhibit 29.1 plots the default rates over the past 29 years for high-yield bonds, as tracked by the Moody's Investors Service rating agency. As Exhibit 29.1 indicates, default risk is a significant risk for high-yield bonds, particularly during periods of economic stress. The recession years of 1990, 1991, and 2001 show large spikes in default rates. The year 2008 also shows a dramatic increase in default rates as the credit crisis came into full bloom.

Exhibit 29.2 demonstrates the second source of credit risk: the risk of a credit downgrade. This happens when a **Nationally Recognized Statistical Rating Organization (NRSRO)** such as Moody's or Standard & Poor's lowers the credit rating on the outstanding debt of an issuer. The credit rating agencies call this "ratings migration."

Ratings migration can be both positive and negative. An increase in credit rating demonstrates an improvement in the financial health of a company, and investors normally react by bidding up the price of the company's related debt. Conversely, a downward ratings migration indicates a

Exhibit 29.2   Historical ratings migration for investment-grade and high-yield bonds

	Aaa	Aa	A	Baa	Ba	B	Caa	Ca to C	Default	Withdrawn
Single A	0.08%	2.93%	85.09%	5.30%	0.69%	0.11%	0.02%	0.01%	0.08%	5.70%
Single B	0.01%	0.05%	0.17%	0.63%	6.29%	71.46%	5.01%	0.50%	3.92%	11.96%

Note: Shaded areas represent positive migration.
Source: Bloomberg.

deteriorating financial condition and results in lower bond prices. In Exhibit 29.2 we plot the ratings migration from Moody's ratings matrix over the history of 1920 to 2007. We focus on bonds rated Baa (investment-grade) and B (high-yield).

Exhibit 29.2 demonstrates that rating migrations can cut both ways. For example, looking at single A-rated bonds, we can see that the long-term average annual positive migration from A-rated to Aa-rated is 2.93% while the long-run average negative rating migration to Baa is 5.3%. Similarly, for single B-rated bonds, the long-run average positive migration to Ba is 6.29% while a negative ratings migration to Caa rated is 5.01%. Note also that for single B-rated bonds, there is a long-run average migration to default status of 3.92% annually. The last column, "Withdrawn," stands for "withdrawn rating." The reader will occasionally see a bond with a "WR" rating. This means that the rating agency no longer rates the outstanding bond issue. WR ratings represent a combination of firms that no longer need to borrow or that roll over their debt with another lender and that debt is not rated.

Finally, in Exhibit 29.3, we graph the credit spread for high-yield bonds compared to U.S. Treasury bonds. U.S. Treasury bonds are regarded as default free. Therefore, the credit spreads for all other bonds are compared to U.S. Treasury bonds.

Credit risk is influenced by both macroeconomic events and company-specific events. For instance, credit risk typically increases during recessions or slowdowns in the economy. In an economic contraction, revenues and earnings decline across a broad swath of industries, reducing the interest coverage with respect to loans and outstanding bonds for many companies caught in the slowdown. This is demonstrated clearly in Exhibit 29.3 with respect to the U.S. recession of 2001–2002. Additionally, credit risk can be affected by a liquidity crisis when investors seek the haven of liquid U.S. government securities. Company-specific events are unrelated to the business cycle and impact a single company at a time. These events could be due to a deteriorating client base, an obsolete business plan, noncompetitive products, outstanding litigation, or any other reason that shrinks the revenues and earnings of a particular company.

There are two common methods of measuring credit risk. The first is a company's credit rating. NRSROs categorize corporations according to their credit risk. These rating firms include Standard & Poor's, Moody's Investors Service, and Fitch Ratings. Credit ratings are assigned on the basis of a variety of factors, including a company's financial statements and an assessment of management.

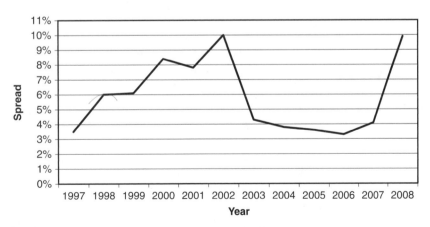

Exhibit 29.3   Credit spreads for high-yield bonds over U.S. treasury bonds
Source: Bloomberg.

Second, credit risk can be measured by the credit risk premium. This is the difference between the yield on a credit-risky asset and that of a comparable default-free U.S. Treasury security. The premium is the compensation that investors must be paid to hold the credit-risky asset.

As a company's credit quality deteriorates, a larger credit risk premium will be demanded to compensate investors for the risk of default. In fact, the non-U.S. Treasury fixed income market is often referred to as the **spread product** market. This is because all other fixed income products, such as bank loans, high-yield bonds, investment-grade corporate bonds, or emerging market debt, trade at a credit spread relative to U.S. Treasury securities.

Traditional methods of managing credit risk

Credit risk has been traditionally managed by underwriting standards, diversification, and asset sales.[1] First consider the underwriting standards used by a bank that is analyzing a corporate client for a bank loan. The bank will begin by considering the company's financial position, revenue growth, earnings potential, interest coverage, and operating leverage. Next the bank will consider the corporation's balance sheet, its ratio of debt to equity, and its ratio of short-term liabilities to long-term liabilities. Then the bank will review the industry in which the company operates. It will consider competitive pressures, consolidation, new products, and growth prospects. The bank will then set a limit on the amount it will lend and will consider the loan amount against the bank's total limit for the industry in which the company operates.

Diversification is the second traditional method of managing credit risk. Banks build loan portfolios consisting of commercial loans across several different industries. This reduces the likelihood that all of the loans will suffer defaults at the same time. It is simply an application of "don't put all of your loans in one basket."

Last, banks have sold their loan portfolios to reduce their exposure to certain industries or clients. While effective, this method can be difficult to implement. The reason is that banks build custom loan portfolios that match the particular balance sheet composite for the bank as well as its target audience of commercial borrowers. A loan portfolio for one bank will not perfectly suit another bank. Therefore, the sale of a loan portfolio usually entails a considerable discount.

However, this issue has largely been eliminated over the past decade with the increase in collateralized debt obligations (CDOs). These are notes that are securitized by a pool of bank loans. The loans are packaged together, and new securities are issued to outside investors. We discuss these securities at length in Chapter 30.

CREDIT-RISKY INVESTMENTS

Every bond that is not a U.S. Treasury bond is considered a credit-risky investment. However, in this section we consider four types of fixed income investments that are considered at the farther region of the credit-risky spectrum: high-yield bonds, leveraged loans, distressed debt, and emerging market bonds. In addition, it is these categories of credit-risky investments that form the primary collateral for CDOs, which we discuss in the next chapter.

To provide a brief introduction into the risk and return characteristics of these four classes of credit-risky investments, we include Exhibits 29.4 and 29.5. Exhibit 29.4 provides the average return, standard deviation, and Sharpe ratio for these four investments over the period 1993–2008. We also include the S&P 500 and 10-year U.S. Treasury bonds for comparison. Notice, for instance, that emerging market bonds have a very favorable risk-return trade-off compared to both the U.S.

---

[1] See Robert Neal, "Credit Derivatives: New Financial Instruments for Controlling Credit Risk," *Economic Review* (Federal Reserve Bank of Kansas City), Second Quarter 1996.

Exhibit 29.4 Mean returns, standard deviations (volatility), and Sharpe ratios (monthly data, 1993–2008)

	Leveraged Loans	Emerging Markets	High-Yield	Distressed Debt	Treasury Bonds	U.S. Stocks
Average	−0.61%	10.85%	6.85%	9.91%	5.89%	8.43%
Standard deviation	3.73%	14.14%	9.13%	28.29%	8.67%	17.98%
Sharpe ratio	−0.97	0.55	0.42	0.24	0.33	0.30

Source: Bloomberg.

stock market and U.S. Treasury bonds, while leveraged loans performed poorly during this period. Leveraged loans were particularly negatively impacted by the popping of the tech bubble, the 2001–2002 recession, and the credit and liquidity crisis of 2007 to 2009.

Exhibit 29.5 presents a correlation matrix for these four credit investments. Notice that these asset classes have low to medium correlations with the U.S. stock market, and almost no correlation with the U.S. Treasury bond market. In fact, distressed debt and leveraged loans have a slightly negative correlation with Treasury bonds. The key takeaway from Exhibit 29.5 is that credit risk provides a different risk and return exposure from stock market risk (the S&P 500) or interest rate risk (U.S. Treasury bonds). Therefore, these credit-risky investments provide an opportunity to diversify a portfolio of traditional stocks and bonds.

High-yield bonds

The high-yield bond market has become a large economic force in the capital markets. The term high-yield generally means those bonds that have a large credit risk premium relative to a comparable risk-free bond. High-yield bonds are generally considered to be those bonds that lack an investment-grade credit rating. This includes securities that are rated lower than BBB by Standard & Poor's and less than Baa by Moody's Investors Service.

The high-yield bond market is subject to considerable credit risk. Consider Exhibit 29.6. This is the distribution of monthly returns for high-yield bonds over the period 1993 to 2008. As we have previously discussed in other chapters, credit-risky assets have a negative skew and a large value of leptokurtosis. This leads to a condition generally called "fat tails," in which the probability mass of the return distribution is concentrated in outlier events (relative to the normal distribution). These two statistics indicate that high-yield bonds are subject to considerable downside exposure. That is, high-yield bonds have a large negative fat tail. This risk is translated in the form of defaults, downgrades, or increased credit spreads.

Exhibit 29.5 Correlation matrix (monthly data, 1993–2008)

	Leveraged Loans	Emerging Markets	High-Yield	Distressed Debt	Treasury Bonds	U.S. Stocks
Leveraged Loans	1.00					
Emerging Markets	0.29	1.00				
High-Yield	0.71	0.48	1.00			
Distressed Debt	0.64	0.45	0.76	1.00		
Treasury Bonds	−0.18	0.11	0.12	−0.26	1.00	
U.S. Stocks	0.42	0.36	0.69	0.31	0.07	1.00

Source: Bloomberg.

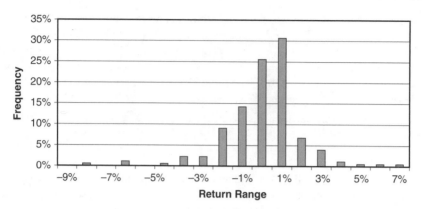

Exhibit 29.6   Frequency distribution for high-yield bonds (monthly data, 1993–2008)

Note: Average 0.56%; Std. Dev. 1.97% Skew −0.69; Kurtosis 4.02.
Source: Bloomberg.

Leveraged bank loans

The leveraged loan market is typically defined as bank loans that are made to companies that have below-investment-grade credit ratings, or loans that are priced at LIBOR plus 150 basis points or more. Similar to high-yield bonds, bank loans are subject to the risk that the borrower will pay down the loan faster than expected or refinance the loan (call risk), as well as the risk of default, downgrade, and increased credit spread.

The corporate bank loan market typically consists of syndicated loans to large and midsize corporations. They are floating-rate instruments, often priced in relation to LIBOR. Corporate loans may be either revolving credits (known as **revolvers**) that are legally committed lines of credit, or term loans that are fully funded commitments with fixed amortization schedules. Term loans tend to be concentrated in the lower-credit-rated corporations because revolvers usually serve as backstops for commercial paper programs of fiscally sound companies.

Term bank loans are repriced periodically. Because of their floating interest rate nature, they have reduced market risk resulting from fluctuating interest rates. Consequently, credit risk takes on greater importance in determining a commercial loan's total return.

The leveraged loan market rivals that of the high-yield bond market. Institutional investors in the bank loan market have grown rapidly from 1996 to 2008. Previously, leveraged loans were primarily the purview of the banks that lent the money to corporate borrowers. However, increasingly institutional investors have entered this market as a means of seeking consistent yield in their fixed income portfolios. Through the growth of the collateralized debt obligation and collateralized loan obligation market, institutional investors now account for almost 50% of this leveraged loan market.

This growth has been fueled by several factors. First, over the past several years, the bank loan market and the high-yield bond market have begun to converge. This is due partly to the relaxation of commercial banking regulations, which has allowed many banks to increase their product offerings, including high-yield bonds. In fact, the global financial crisis of 2007 to 2009 brought the unusual situation of investment banks and brokerage firms applying to the U.S. Federal Reserve System to become bank holding companies. At this point, the difference between deposit-gathering banks and investment banks is minimal.

In addition to banks and brokerage firms, insurance companies have become increasingly involved in the bank loan business, as demonstrated by the growth and subsequent demise of American

International Group (AIG). With regulatory barriers mostly broken down, there are fewer distinctions between commercial banks, brokerage firms, and insurance companies. Integration of these three branches of financial services firms has led to a greater expansion of the leveraged loan market.

A third reason is the acceptance of bank loans as a form of investment by institutional investors. Pension funds, endowment funds, mutual funds, and high-net-worth individuals have all entered the market for bank loan investing. Institutional investors seek bank loans because they meet their need for higher spreads and match up well against their liabilities. The entrance of the rating organizations into the bank loan market makes it easier for investors to classify bank loans by investment grade versus leveraged status. For example, as of the end of 2007, the total volume of rated bank loans by Moody's was over $1 trillion, of which approximately half were leveraged loans.

The entrance of institutional investors has led to a change in the structure of many syndicated loans. Where the tenor of a bank loan was previously in the two- to four-year range, longer-term loans are being arranged to meet the longer investment horizons of institutional investors. Often a syndicated loan will be offered with different tranches constructed not by differences in credit ratings but by differences in maturity. For example, Allied Waste's recent loan facility had three tranches. Tranche A was a $2.25 billion term loan with a five-year tenor, tranche B was for $1 billion maturing in six years, and tranche C was for $1.25 billion with a maturity of seven years. The tranches of these alphabet loans will have different pricing despite having the same credit quality. The different pricing reflects the different maturities of the tranches. The A tranche was usually priced in the range of LIBOR plus 150, with subsequent tranches priced at LIBOR plus 250 basis points and up. This tranching effect will continue because investors tend to segregate themselves by maturity of the debt. However, after the credit crisis of 2007 to 2009, debt tranches based on credit ratings are expected to be more significant.

Last, a new and more efficient capital market has emerged for bank loans. Many commercial banks have realized that their strength is best displayed in reviewing the creditworthiness of borrowers and originating new loans, but not necessarily holding those loans on their balance sheets. Consistent with the development of the collateralized loan obligation market, banks can now repackage these loans and sell them to other investors. In this way banks can better manage their risk capital and generate higher returns on equity.

Exhibit 29.7 provides a graphical review of the leveraged loan market. Despite their status of non-investment-grade, leveraged loans display very consistent returns. Notice that the distribution of returns is much tighter than for high-yield bonds. That is, there are fewer outlier returns; much of the probability mass of the leveraged loan return distribution is concentrated in the 0% to 2% range. Still, with a negative skew value of −1.58 and a value of kurtosis of 6.71, leveraged loans demonstrate the same downside fat tail as high-yield bonds. In fact, the tail is even fatter for leveraged loans than for high-yield bonds.

Although leveraged loans are at risk to the occasional large downside event, they tend to earn consistent returns. This is demonstrated in Exhibit 29.7, where 86% of the probability mass is concentrated in the 0% to 2% range. This credit-risky asset class offers the most consistent returns of the four credit risk categories examined. Unfortunately, the track record for leveraged loans has not been very good. The average monthly return over the time period is −0.05%. This reflects the absolutely miserable year of 2008 when the total return for leverage loans was a −34%. 2008 is responsible for the negative average monthly returns to leveraged loans.

Emerging markets debt

Credit risk is not unique to the domestic U.S. financial markets. When investing in the sovereign debt of a foreign country, an investor must consider two crucial risks. One is political risk—the risk that

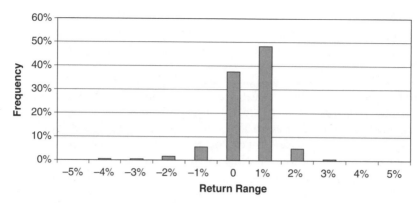

Exhibit 29.7   Frequency distribution for leveraged loans (monthly data, 1993–2008)

Note: Average 0.05%; Std. Dev. 0.81% Skew −1.58; Kurtosis 6.71.
Source: Bloomberg.

even though the central government of the foreign country has the financial ability to pay its debts as they come due, for political reasons (e.g. revolution, new government regime, trade sanctions), the sovereign entity may decide to forfeit (default on) payment. The second type of risk is credit risk, the same old inability to pay one's debts as they become due.

Many sovereign governments rely on essentially two forms of cash flows to finance its government programs and to pay its debts: taxes and revenues from state-owned enterprises. Taxes can come from personal income taxes, corporate taxes, import duties, and other excise taxes. State-owned enterprises can be oil companies, telephone companies, national airlines and railroads, and manufacturing enterprises.

In times of economic turmoil such as a recession, cash flows from state-owned enterprises decline along with the general malaise of the economy. Additionally, tax revenues decline as corporations earn less money, as unemployment rises, and as personal incomes decline. Last, with a declining foreign currency value, imports decline, reducing revenue from import taxes.

Exhibit 29.8 provides the return distribution for emerging market debt from 1993 through 2008. We can see that this distribution of returns has a long downside tail. This negative tail of the probability mass is even fatter than that for high-yield bonds or leveraged loans. With a skew value of −2.24 and a kurtosis value of 13.65, this distribution of returns has the fattest tail of the credit bunch. There is a distinct bias toward large negative returns.

Much of this downside bias, however, can be traced to three events. The first occurred in October 1997, when the Asian contagion hurt the emerging markets. In that month, the index declined by 10.5%. Second, in August 1998 the Russian government defaulted on its bonds, sending the index down by 27.4%. Last, we had the global financial market meltdown of 2007 to 2009 that adversely affected all credit-risky bonds.

For example, consider the Russian government 10% bond due in 2007. In July 1997 when this bond was issued, its credit spread over a comparable U.S. Treasury bond was 3.5%. However, by the time the Russian government defaulted on its bonds, the credit spread had increased to 53% (5,300 basis points) over comparable U.S. Treasury securities. This spread widening led to billions of dollars of losses as Russian bonds traded for just pennies on the dollar.[2]

---

[2] See "Financial Firms Lose $8 Billion So Far," *Wall Street Journal*, September 3, 1998, A2. This bond issue was subsequently refinanced at a loss.

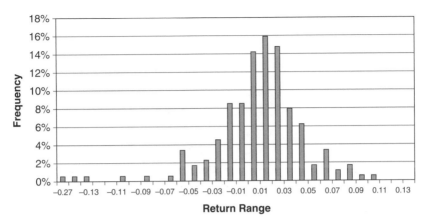

Exhibit 29.8   Frequency distribution for emerging market debt (monthly data, 1993–2008)

Note: Average 0.90%; Std. Dev. 4.05% Skew −2.24; Kurtosis 13.65.
Source: Bloomberg.

Once again, we note that credit risk is not all one-sided. Even though there was a rapid decline in the credit quality of emerging markets sovereign debt in 1997, such a steep retreat presented opportunities for credit quality improvement at the time of the Russian bond default, and the market recovered quickly. In fact, Exhibit 29.4 demonstrates that emerging markets bonds have the best risk-reward trade-off as measured by the Sharpe ratio.

Distressed debt

Our last category of credit-risky investments was previously discussed in our chapters on private equity. Some private equity managers play in the distressed debt arena for the potential to convert the debt into an equity stake in a reorganized company. In this section, we focus on the credit risk profile of distressed debt.

Distressed debt is generally considered debt that is impaired in some way or shape. This can be debt that is already in default through the missed payment of a bond coupon or loan interest; it can be bonds of a company that is undergoing a Chapter 11 bankruptcy reorganization; it can be the debt of a company that has good growth prospects but severe cash flow problems; or finally, it can be the debt of a company with a very low credit rating and a high probability of bankruptcy filing. Loans and bonds that meet the profile of one of these scenarios are all fair game for the distressed debt players.

Exhibit 29.9 displays the distribution of monthly returns for distressed debt from 1993 to 2008. Notice how spread out the returns are: from −33% to +22%. Distressed debt has by far the greatest dispersion of the credit-risky investments. This is evidenced by its high monthly standard deviation of returns of 6.24%. In fact, Exhibit 29.4 demonstrates that distressed debt has a higher annual volatility than even U.S. stocks: 28.29% versus 17.98%. Clearly, this is not an asset class for the faint of heart. In addition, distressed debt demonstrates the same large negative downside tail as other credit-risky investments. With a skew of −0.94 and a kurtosis of 6.31, the return distribution for distressed debt also suffers from large negative fat tails.

In summary, we can see with the four primary forms of credit risk that each has a significant negative skew and a large value of kurtosis. This leads to large negative fat tails—a key indication

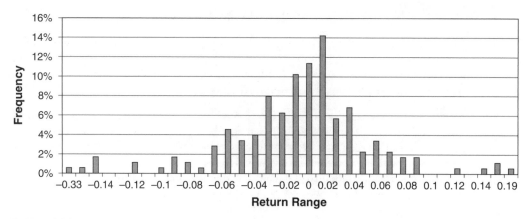

Exhibit 29.9   Frequency distribution for distressed debt (monthly data, 1993–2008)

Note: Average 0.74%; Std. Dev. 6.24% Skew −0.94; Kurtosis 6.31.
Source: Bloomberg.

of downside risk exposure. However, for the most part, this risk is rewarded. Exhibit 29.10 plots the values of these risky asset classes as well as the S&P 500 index and 10-year U.S. Treasury bonds over the period from 1994 to 2008. We assign each asset a value of 100 in 1994 and then observe how their values grow over the 15-year time frame.

The lines are ranked from best-performing to worst-performing. We see clearly that emerging markets bonds, despite having the fattest tail, outperformed all of the other assets. The performance of emerging markets bonds is followed by U.S. stocks and then high-yield bonds and distressed debt, earning an almost identical long-term return. After that are U.S. Treasury bonds, and last, leveraged loans. It is clear that with the exception of leveraged loans, each asset was rewarded with positive returns. Keep in mind that this 15-year period spans some very turbulent financial times: the tequila crisis, the Asian contagion, the Russian bond default (1998), the popping of the technology bubble (2000–2002), the recession of 2001, and the financial crisis of 2007 to 2009. In fact, this period of time is noted more for its economic difficulties than it is for its economic growth. This is all the more reason to begin our next section on the types and uses of credit derivatives.

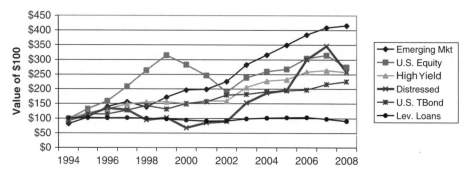

Exhibit 29.10   Performance of credit risky assets
Source: Bloomberg.

CREDIT OPTION DERIVATIVES

In the prior sections of this chapter we provided a demonstration of credit risk and its importance in determining asset value. In this section we review one of the basic credit derivatives structures: credit options. These instruments may be used for transferring or accumulating credit exposure.

Credit derivatives provide investors with several advantages:

- Credit derivatives isolate credit risk. This allows a more efficient management of credit risk than the buying and selling of credit-risky assets to increase or decrease an investor's credit exposure.
- Credit derivatives transfer credit risk. Again, this may be a more efficient way to gain or reduce credit exposure than buying and selling the underlying assets.
- Credit derivatives can provide liquidity to the market in times of credit stress.
- Through the purchase and sale of underlying credit collateral, credit derivatives provide more rigorous and transparent pricing.

Credit put option

In its simplest form, a credit option can be a binary option. With a binary credit option, the option seller will pay out a sum if and when a default event occurs with respect to a referenced credit (e.g. the underlying issuer is unable to pay its obligations as they become due). Therefore, a binary option represents two states of the world: default or no default; it is the clearest example of credit protection. At maturity of the option, if the referenced credit has defaulted, the option holder receives a payout. If there is no default at maturity of the option, the option buyer receives nothing and forgoes the option premium. A binary credit option could also be triggered by a ratings downgrade.

A European binary credit option pays out a sum only at maturity if the referenced credit is in default. An American binary option can be exercised at any time during its life. Consequently, if an American binary credit option is in-the-money (a default event has occurred), it will be exercised immediately because delaying exercise will reduce the present value of the fixed payment.

Consider an American credit put option that pays the holder of the option the difference between the strike price and the market value of the bond if a high-yield bond is in default.[3] If the bond is not in default, the payoff to the put option is zero. This option may be described as:

$$P[B(t)] = \begin{cases} X - B(t) \text{ if the bond is in default} \\ 0 \text{ otherwise} \end{cases}$$

where

$X =$ the strike price of the put option
$B(t) =$ the market value of the bond at default[4]

This type of credit derivative protects the investor only after default has occurred. The bond may have declined in price before the issuing company declares a default.

---

[3] Typically, the market price of the bond is fixed at some period of time after the default, such as one month from the default date. Also, the condition of default must be specified. This could be a failure to make a timely payment of interest or principal, or it may be triggered by a Chapter 11 bankruptcy filing.

[4] Mathematical formulas have been developed to determine the value of credit options. These equations can be quite complicated. Generally, they fall into two types of pricing methodologies: structural versus term structure. For more information regarding credit option pricing formulas, see Mark J.P. Anson, Frank J. Fabozzi, Moorad Choudhry, and Ren-Raw Chen, *Credit Derivatives: Instruments, Pricing, and Applications* (Hoboken, NJ: John Wiley & Sons, 2004).

Instead of waiting for an actual default to occur, the strike price of the option can be set to a minimum net worth of the underlying issuer below which default is probable. For instance, if the firm value of the referenced credit (assets minus liabilities) falls to $100 million, then the binary credit option will be in-the-money.

Alternatively, a binary credit put option may be based on credit ratings as the threshold or trigger. For instance, in January 1998 bondholders forced the International Finance Corporation of Thailand (IFCT) to redeem $500 million in bonds several years before their maturity. The bond issue contained a provision that allowed investors to put the bonds back to the issuer at face value should the sovereign credit rating of Thailand fall below investment grade.

This binary credit put option may be expressed as:

$$P[V(t); \$500 \text{ million}] = \begin{cases} \$500 \text{ million} - V(t) \text{ if credit rating is below} \\ \qquad\qquad \text{investment grade} \\ \$0 \text{ if credit rating is above investment grade} \end{cases}$$

Exhibit 29.11 demonstrates the payout to the credit put option on the IFCT bonds.

Credit call option

In addition to the binary put option just described, the IFCT bonds also provided that investors would receive an additional 50 basis points of coupon income should the credit rating of Thailand decline by two notches. Further, investors would receive 25 basis points of coupon income for every subsequent decline in credit rating thereafter. These call options were in effect until a below-investment-grade credit rating was reached. Then the bonds were putable as described earlier.

The ability to earn additional yield as the credit rating of Thailand declined is the same as a series of binary call options. These options may be expressed as:

$$C[CR(t); ICR] = \begin{cases} \$2,500,000 \text{ if } CR(t) \text{ is two grades below } ICR \\ \$0 \text{ if } CR(t) \text{ is not two grades below } ICR \end{cases}$$

where $CR(t)$ is the current credit rating for Thailand at time t, ICR is the initial credit rating of Thailand at the issuance of the bonds, and $\$2,500,000 = 0.005 \times \$500,000,000$.

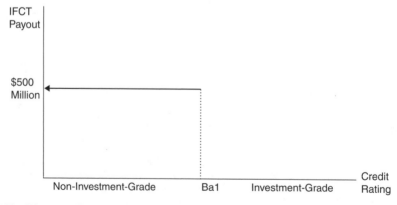

Exhibit 29.11   Binary credit put option on IFCT bonds

Source: Mark Anson, *Handbook of Alternative Assets*, 2nd ed. (Hoboken, NJ: John Wiley & Sons, 2006). Reprinted with permission of John Wiley & Sons, Inc.

The payout function for these binary credit call options is displayed in Exhibit 29.12. The bonds suffered three credit downgrades before they hit the non-investment-grade level and became putable.

The reader may question why the IFCT would issue bonds with attached binary credit options. The reason is one of cost. Options are not free. By attaching credit options to its bonds, the IFCT was in fact selling these options to its investors in return for paying a lower coupon rate. Through the sale of these credit options, the IFCT was able to initially lower its funding costs by 100 basis points. Unfortunately, the credit rating of Thailand deteriorated, ultimately resulting in a greater expense to the IFCT.

Credit-linked notes

Credit-linked notes (CLNs) are bonds issued with an embedded credit option. Typically, these notes can be issued with reference to a single corporation or to a basket of credit risks. The holder of the CLN is paid a coupon and the par value of the note at maturity if there is no default on the underlying referenced corporation or basket of credits. However, if there is some default, downgrade, or other adverse credit event, the holder of the CLN will receive either a lower coupon payment or only a partial redemption of the CLN principal value.

Why would an investor purchase a CLN? The reason is simple. By agreeing to bear some of the credit risk associated with a corporation or basket of other credits, the holder of the CLN will receive a higher yield on the CLN. In effect the holder of the CLN has sold some credit insurance to the issuer of the note. If a credit event occurs, the CLN holder must forgo some of his coupon or principal value to make the seller of the note whole. If there is no credit event, the holder of the CLN collects an insurance premium in the form of a higher yield. The investor in the CLN is, in fact, selling credit protection in return for a higher yield on the CLN. CLNs appeal to investors who wish to take on more credit risk but are either wary of stand-alone credit derivatives such as swaps and options or limited in their ability to access credit derivatives directly. In contrast, a CLN is just that, a coupon-paying note. They are on-balance-sheet debt instruments that any investor can purchase. Furthermore, they can be tailored to achieve the specific credit risk profile that the CLN holder wishes to target.

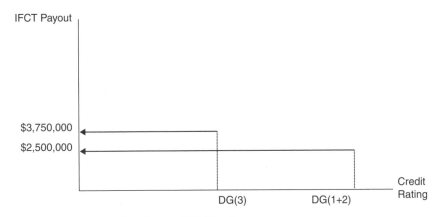

Exhibit 29.12   Binary credit call options on IFCT bonds

Source: Mark Anson, *Handbook of Alternative Assets*, 2nd ed. (Hoboken, NJ: John Wiley & Sons, 2006). Reprinted with permission of John Wiley & Sons, Inc.
DG(1+2) indicates the first two credit downgrades; DG(3) indicates the third downgrade.

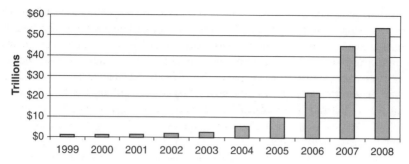

Exhibit 29.13   Growth of the credit derivatives market

Source: Bloomberg and International Swaps and Derivatives Association.

CREDIT DEFAULT SWAPS

By far the most important development in the credit derivative market is the **credit default swap (CDS)**. This credit derivative is primarily responsible for the amazing growth of the credit derivative market. Exhibit 29.13 demonstrates the explosive growth of this market over the past ten years. Notice that the notional amount of these contracts is now measured in the trillions of dollars.

A key component fueling this expansion is the growth of the synthetic collateralized debt obligations (CDOs). Synthetic CDOs use CDSs to gain exposure to credit risk. We discuss CDOs extensively in the next chapter.

A credit default swap is similar to the binary put options discussed earlier in that its primary purpose is to hedge the credit exposure to a referenced asset or issuer. In this sense, credit default swaps operate in a similar fashion to a standby letter of credit. A credit default swap is the simplest form of credit insurance. It is simply a bilateral contract where the credit protection buyer pays a periodic fee (or insurance premium) to the credit protection seller in exchange for a contingent payment if a credit event occurs with respect to an underlying credit-risky asset. A CDS may be negotiated on any one of the credit-risky investments discussed at the beginning of this chapter.

There are two types of credit default swaps. The first type, and by far the predominant CDS, is a bilateral contract where the credit protection buyer pays a periodic premium on a predetermined amount (the notional amount) in exchange for a contingent payment from the credit protection seller to reimburse the buyer for any losses suffered from a specified credit event.

Exhibit 29.14 demonstrates the predominant form of a credit default swap. In Exhibit 29.14, the credit risk of the underlying risky asset is transferred from the credit protection buyer to the credit protection seller.

Exhibit 29.14   Credit default swap with transfer of default risk

Source: Mark Anson, *Handbook of Alternative Assets*, 2nd ed. (Hoboken, NJ: John Wiley & Sons, 2006). Reprinted with permission of John Wiley & Sons, Inc.

A variation on the credit default swap is for the owner of the credit-risky asset to pass on the total return of the asset to the credit protection seller in return for a certain payment. The credit protection buyer gives up the uncertain returns of the credit-risky asset in return for certain payments from the credit protection seller. The credit protection seller now receives both the upside and the downside of the return associated with the credit-risky asset. This is really nothing more than a total return swap where the credit protection buyer passes on the credit protection seller all of the economic exposure associated with the credit-risky asset. The credit protection buyer takes on all of the economic risk of the underlying asset just as if that asset were on his balance sheet or in his investment portfolio. Exhibit 29.15 demonstrates this swap.

Large banks are the natural dealers for credit default swaps because it is consistent with their letter of credit business; not surprisingly, banks are the largest players in this market. Banks may sell credit default swaps as a natural extension of their credit lending business. Alternatively, a bank may use a credit default swap to hedge the credit exposure that exists on its balance sheet. For example, a bank may wish to reduce its exposure to a particular corporate borrower or to an industry that is geared for difficult times. The bank can reduce its exposure to its customer credit risk in most cases without the knowledge or consent of the bank's primary borrowers.

Credit default swaps are very flexible. For instance, a credit default swap may state in the contract the exact amount of insurance payment in the event of a credit event. Alternatively, a credit default swap may be structured so that the amount of the swap payment by the credit protection seller is determined after the credit event. Usually, this is determined by the market value of the referenced asset after the credit event has occurred.

Development of the credit default swap market

The CDS market has become very developed, with daily CDS quotes on most listed companies. For example, Exhibit 29.16 shows the spread over Treasuries for a 5-year Freddie Mac CDS. We can see that the spread for CDS for Freddie Mac spiked at 350 basis points with the U.S. government takeover of Freddie in the summer of 2008. This means that a CDS purchaser (a buyer of credit protection) for Freddie Mac would have to pay 350 basis points over a comparable U.S. Treasury bond to the credit protection seller to get protection against Freddie Mac outstanding bonds.

Exhibit 29.17 shows the CDS spread for Morgan Stanley before its announced decision to become a bank holding company in September 2008. The CDS rate spiked at more than 1,000 basis points over U.S. Treasuries, this for the second largest investment bank (after Goldman Sachs) on Wall Street. A firm that was rated investment grade at the time by both Moody's and Standard & Poor's was suddenly perceived to be very risky during the financial crisis of 2008. The spreads for Morgan Stanley CDSs quickly came down with its announced filing for bank holding company status.

The development of the CDS market has even led to indices of CDSs now available for trading. As the CDS market has grown in importance and to its current huge size, tradable CDS indices have been developed to allow investors and traders a broad spectrum of credit-risky assets at a lower cost.

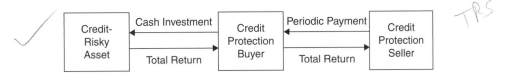

Exhibit 29.15   Credit default swap with transfer of total return

Source: Mark Anson, *Handbook of Alternative Assets*, 2nd ed. (Hoboken, NJ: John Wiley & Sons, 2006). Reprinted with permission of John Wiley & Sons, Inc.

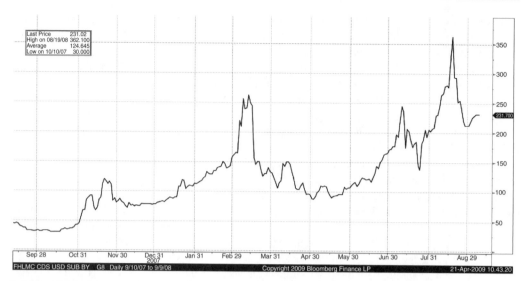

Exhibit 29.16   Five-year CDS for Freddie Mac, September 2007– September 2008

Source: Bloomberg Finance, L.P.

There are two CDS index families: the International Index Company's ITraxx index and the Dow Jones CDX index.

For example, Exhibit 29.18 shows the ITraxx CDS index for European investment-grade bonds, while Exhibit 29.19 shows the ITraxx CDS index for European high-yield debt. The investment-grade ITraxx index is composed of the 125 most liquid CDSs referencing European investment-grade credits. The ITraxx Europe Crossover index is comprised of the 50 most liquid CDSs in the sub-investment-grade credits. In Exhibit 29.20 we show the full range of CDS indices produced by ITraxx.

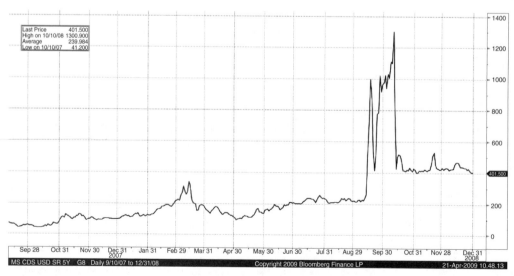

Exhibit 29.17   Five-year CDS for Morgan Stanley Debt, September 2007–December 2008

Source: Bloomberg Finance, L.P.

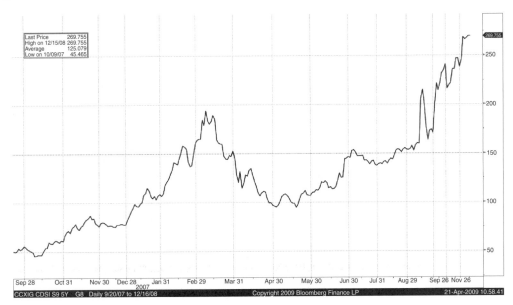

Exhibit 29.18   ITraxx Europe investment-grade CDS index, September 2007–December 2008

Source: Bloomberg Finance, L.P.

Mechanics of a credit default swap

The CDS market is contract driven. By this we mean each CDS is a privately negotiated transaction between the credit protection buyer and seller. Fortunately, the **International Swaps and Derivatives Association (ISDA)**, the primary industry body for derivatives documentation, has established standardized terms for CDSs. In this section we provide some detail on the standard ISDA agreement.

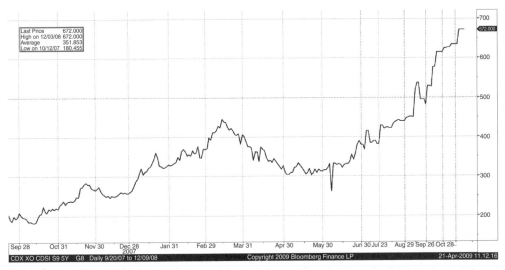

Exhibit 29.19   ITraxx Europe crossover (sub-investment-grade) CDS index, September 2007–December 2008

Source: Bloomberg Finance, L.P.

Exhibit 29.20   The Family of ITraxx European CDS Indices

Type	Index Name	Number of Entities	Description
Benchmark Indices	ITraxx Europe	125	Most actively traded investment-grade CDSs in the prior six months
	ITraxx Europe HiVol	30	Highest spread/riskiest names from the ITraxx Europe index
	ITraxx Europe Crossover	50	CDSs on the 50 most liquid sub-investment-grade credits
Sector Indices	ITraxx Nonfinancials	100	CDSs on nonfinancial credits
	ITraxx Financials Senior	25	CDSs on senior subordinated financial credits
	ITraxx Financials Sub	25	CDSs on junior subordinated financial credits
	ITraxx TMT	20	CDSs on technology, media, telecommunications
	ITraxx Industrials	20	CDSs on industrial credits
	ITraxx Energy	20	CDSs on energy credits
	ITraxx Consumers	30	CDSs on manufacturers of consumer goods
	ITraxx Autos	10	CDSs on auto industry credits

Source: Bloomberg.

CDS spread

The premium to be paid by the credit protection buyer is often called the spread and it is quoted in basis points per annum on the notional value of the CDS. CDS spreads are not credit yield spreads in the manner of Exhibit 29.3, but rather price quotes for buying credit insurance. Typically, the price of insurance is paid quarterly by the protection buyer.

Contract size

The ISDA does not impose any limits on size or length of term of a CDS; this is up to the negotiation of the parties involved. Most CDSs fall in the range of $20 million to $200 million with a tenor of three to five years.

Trigger events

This is the heart of every CDS transaction. Trigger events determine when the credit protection seller must make a payment to the credit protection buyer. As you might imagine, both sides to a CDS negotiate these terms intensely. The credit protection buyer wishes to have the trigger events defined as broadly as possible, while the credit protection seller wants to have these events construed as narrowly as possible.

The ISDA provides for six kinds of trigger events, but the parties to a CDS can add more, although the six events identified by the ISDA cover virtually all types of credit events. The six credit events are:

1. *Bankruptcy.* This pretty much says it all regarding a company's inability to pay its debt.
2. *Failure to pay.* While a company may not be in bankruptcy yet, it may not be able to meet its debt obligations as they come due.

3. *Restructuring.* This is any form of debt restructuring that is disadvantageous to the credit protection buyer. Restructuring is a fuzzy term, and ISDA attempts to clarify this part of the standard contract by offering four options for the parties to consider.

4. *Obligation acceleration.* All bond and loan covenants contain provisions that accelerate the repayment of the loan or bond if the credit quality of the borrower begins to deteriorate due to any number of events such as a failure to pay or a bankruptcy (which ISDA covers independently), or a ratings downgrade.

5. *Obligation default.* This is any failure to meet a condition in the bond or loan covenant that would put the borrower in breach of the covenant. It could be something like the failure to maintain a sufficient current ratio or a minimum interest earnings coverage ratio.

6. *Repudiation/moratorium.* This is most frequently associated with sovereign or emerging markets debt. It is simply a refusal by the sovereign government to repay its debt as it comes due or even an outright rejection of its debt obligations. As an example, the U.S. government takeover of Fannie Mae and Freddie Mac in September 2008 was determined to be a credit event triggering the payment of approximately $1.4 trillion of outstanding CDSs. This meant potentially $1.4 trillion of Fannie Mae and Freddie Mac bonds changed hands, with credit protection buyers cashing in their credit protection under the CDS and in turn delivering to the credit protection sellers Fannie Mae and Freddie Mac bonds. The credit protection sellers were then responsible for holding the Freddie Mac and Fannie Mae bonds. As of October 2008, Fannie Mae and Freddie Mac bonds were trading around 98 cents on the dollar. Therefore, while there was a credit event with the U.S. government takeover of Fannie and Freddie, the losses incurred under the CDSs were small.

Settlement

If a credit event occurs, settlement can be made either with a cash payment or with a physical settlement. In a cash settlement, the credit protection seller makes the credit protection buyer whole by transferring to the buyer an amount of cash to make up for the lost value of the underlying credit-risky bond.

Cash settlement does not occur as frequently as one might expect, because it is difficult to get a good market quote for a distressed asset. Therefore, most CDSs use physical settlement upon the occurrence of a credit event. Under physical settlement, the credit protection seller purchases at par value the impaired loan or bond from the credit protection buyer. The credit-risky asset is physically transferred to the credit protection seller's balance sheet, and now the seller has the incentive to get as much in recovery value as possible from the impaired asset.

Delivery

Within certain limits, the credit protection buyer has a choice of assets that she can deliver for physical settlement. This raises the issue of which is "cheapest to deliver." In yet another page from the Fannie Mae and Freddie Mac debacle, credit protection buyers of CDSs on Fannie and Freddie tried to deliver to the credit protection sellers principal-only Fannie and Freddie bonds. These bonds are like zero coupon bonds in that they pay no interest and pay only principal upon maturity. Because they do not pay interest, zero coupon bonds tend to be heavily discounted at any point in time.

This is a form of "cheapest to deliver" under a derivative contract. When a derivatives contract has to be settled with the physical delivery of a bond, the party that has to deliver the bond looks for the cheapest bond to deliver to minimize the delivery cost. In the case of Fannie Mae and Freddie Mac, these companies had principal-only bonds outstanding as well as typical bonds that paid both interest and principal. At the time of the U.S. government takeover of Fannie and Freddie, the principal-only bonds were discounted to 40 to 50 cents on the dollar whereas the standard bonds with coupon payments were trading in the 95 cents on the dollar range. The ISDA quickly ruled that principal-only bonds could not be delivered under CDSs tied to Freddie and Fannie.

In general, the credit protection seller can deliver the following:

- Direct obligations of the referenced entity such as corporate bonds or bank loans.
- Obligations of a subsidiary of the referenced entity if the subsidiary is at least 50% or more owned by the referenced entity (this is sometimes called **qualifying affiliate guarantees**).
- Obligations of a third party that the referenced entity may have guaranteed, known as **qualifying guarantees**.

Keep in mind that although ISDA provides standard terms, the parties to a CDS can negotiate any and all terms plus throw in a few of their own if they wish. The main point is that the standardization of CDS terms has provided the infrastructure for the huge growth of the credit derivative markets as demonstrated in Exhibit 29.13.

Risks of credit default swaps

While credit derivatives offer investors alternative strategies to access credit-risky assets, they come with specialized risks. These risks apply equally to credit options and to credit swaps.

First, there is operational risk. Operational risk is the risk that traders or portfolio managers could imprudently use credit swaps. Since these are off-balance-sheet contractual agreements, excessive credit exposures can be achieved without appearing on an investor's balance sheet. Without proper accounting systems and other back-office operations, an investor may not be fully cognizant of the total credit risk exposure.

Second, there is counterparty risk. Credit default swaps are individually negotiated, private transactions. They are illiquid investments with a very limited secondary market. Further, the legal documentation associated with a CDS may prevent one party from selling its share of the CDS without the other party's consent. This creates the risk that the counterparty to a swap agreement will default on its obligations. It is ironic that a credit protection buyer, for example, can introduce a new form of credit risk into her portfolio (counterparty credit risk) from the purchase of a credit default swap. For a credit protection buyer to suffer a loss, two things must happen: (1) there must be a credit event on the underlying credit-risky asset and (2) the credit protection seller must default on its obligations to the credit protection buyer.

Normally, counterparty credit risk is small. However, the liquidity and credit crisis of 2007 to 2008 claimed the lives of Bear Stearns, Lehman Brothers, Fannie Mae, Freddie Mac, and a host of large, well-known hedge funds. Under these stressful conditions, counterparty credit risk took on literally epic proportions. This required close monitoring of collateral and credit exposure with these previously safe but now much more risky counterparties.

Another source of risk is liquidity risk. Currently, there are no exchange-traded credit derivatives. Instead, they are traded over-the-counter as customized contractual agreements between two parties. The very nature of this customization makes credit derivatives illiquid. Credit derivatives will not suit all parties in the financial markets, and a party to a custom-tailored credit derivative contract may not be able to obtain the fair value of the contract if he tries to sell his position.

Last, there is pricing risk. As the derivative markets have matured, the mathematical models used to price derivative contracts have become increasingly complex. These models are dependent on assumptions regarding underlying economic parameters. Consequently, the pricing of credit derivatives is sensitive to the assumptions of the models.

Credit derivatives join together the world of traditional guarantees with financial derivatives. Financial guarantee pricing models traditionally were based on credit ratings and historical default and ratings migration rates. Conversely, the sophisticated nature of the derivatives market uses mathematical models instead of historical information to price the derivative instruments. The key point for the reader is to understand that history and math do not always work in harmony.

CONCLUSION

This chapter was designed to be a brief introduction to credit risk and new derivative products that may be used to access credit-risky assets. We saw visually that the four credit-risky asset classes (emerging markets bonds, high-yield bonds, distressed debt, and leveraged loans) have distinct downside fat tail risk, all the more encouragement for the development of a credit derivative market.

Credit derivatives provide new tools for banks, insurance companies, and institutional investors to buy, sell, diversify, and trade units of credit risk. In addition, credit derivatives allow investors to achieve favorable yields to match their outstanding liabilities.

Chief among the new credit derivatives is the credit default swap. According to ISDA, these instruments account for more than half the growth of the credit derivative market. Not only are they used for credit risk management as demonstrated in this chapter, but they also form the foundation for much of the growth of the CDO market described in the next chapter.

In our next chapter we introduce the collateralized debt obligation market. This market would not be as successful and large without the initial development of the credit derivative market. Wall Street and investors have embraced these alternative strategies to access credit return.

30
Collateralized Debt Obligations

Collateralized debt obligations (CDOs) are a form of asset-backed security (ABS) where a pool of fixed income instruments are repackaged into highly rated securities. These structures were born in the late 1980s as banks began to repackage high-yield bonds that they held on their balance sheets that were not the type of liquid assets that banks demand. These securities were called **collateralized bond obligations (CBOs)**, and they were backed by a portfolio of senior or subordinated bonds issued by a variety of corporate or sovereign issuers. CBOs are just another form of a debt instrument that is not backed by the credit of a single issuer, but instead is supported by the credit of many different issuers. Following on the heels of CBOs, banks began to realize that they had other assets on their balance sheets, leveraged loans, that could be repackaged into a collateral pool and sold to investors. Hence **collateralized loan obligations (CLOs)** were born in the early 1990s.

From these two streams of asset-backed securities, CDOs were born. A CDO is simply a security that is backed by a portfolio of bonds and loans together. In fact, the term CDO is often used broadly to refer to any CLO or CBO structure. In its simplest form, a CDO is a trust or **special purpose vehicle (SPV)** that purchases loans and bonds from banks, insurance companies, corporate issuers, and other sellers, and then issues new securities to investors where the new securities are collateralized by the bonds and loans contained in the trust.

In this chapter we provide an introduction to the CDO marketplace. We describe the various uses for CDOs as well as the risks and benefits. We also provide some examples of recent CDO structures. Last, we consider how CDO structures may be combined with other forms of alternative investment strategies such as private equity and hedge funds.

GENERAL STRUCTURE OF CDOs

As just explained, the term CDO can be used to broadly refer to any CBO or CLO. These two categories describe a large portion of the CDO marketplace. However, there are also investment vehicles that combine both bonds and loans into a single asset-backed pool. These structures are best referred to as CDOs because the underlying pool of collateral contains both bonds and loans. Therefore, the term CDO may also refer to a hybrid asset-backed structure where the supporting collateral is a combination of debt instruments, including bank loans, high-yield corporate bonds, emerging market sovereign debt, and even other CDO securities.

Size of the market for CBOs and CLOs

The first CDO was created in 1987 by bankers at the now-defunct Drexel Burnham Lambert for a savings and loan association called Imperial Savings Association. The transaction size was $100 million. From this simple beginning, the CDO market has grown to hundreds of billions of dollars.

Exhibit 30.1 shows the growth of the CDO market. As can be seen, CDO issuance grew rapidly through the first few years of the new millennium, peaking in 2006. As the first cracks of the credit

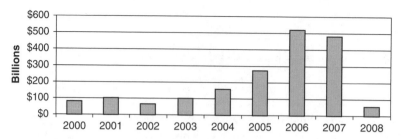

Exhibit 30.1   Growth of the CDO market—annual issuance
Source: Bloomberg.

crisis appeared in 2007, CDO issuance began to decline. Then, with the crisis in full panic mode in 2008, the CDO market collapsed to almost one-tenth of its former size.

Why the growth of CDOs?

CDOs are all about repackaging and transferring credit risk. The collateral underlying a CDO can be high-yield bonds, leveraged loans, distressed debt, emerging markets bonds, or real estate mortgages. The ability to pool together bonds, loans, or mortgages of different sizes and credit qualities to form a diversified pool of credit-risky assets and then to sell investment-grade notes that participate in this pool is a powerful financial tool for investors, banks, asset managers, and brokerage houses.

Most investors are underexposed to credit risk. Since there is a natural risk premium attached to this risk, investors would benefit from increasing exposure to it. As demonstrated in the prior chapter, credit-risky assets have low to medium correlations with the equity and Treasury instruments. This offers the opportunity to use credit exposure to earn a premium and to diversify the risk of an equity/Treasury portfolio.

CDOs provide investors with convenient access to a ready-made diversified pool of credit-risky assets. This is more efficient than if the investor had to construct a credit-risky portfolio on its own. Further, CDOs allow the investor to pick and choose among the different classes of credit-risky assets: high-yield bonds, bank loans, emerging markets debt, and so forth. There are CDO vehicles for every type and kind of credit-risky bond, loan, and mortgage out there.

Better still, CDOs issue multiple classes of securities against the credit-risky collateral pool, with each class or tranche of a CDO security having a different level of seniority and credit rating. This process is called **credit tranching**, and it allows an investor to even more finely tune her desired level of credit exposure. The investor chooses the risk attachment point to the underlying credit-risky collateral pool.

For banks, CDOs allow the bank to manage the credit risks of its balance sheet of loans. For asset managers, they of course collect asset management fees for managing the CDO structure. Without fees, there would be no incentive for asset managers to construct CDOs. Last, brokerage firms collect underwriting fees for selling CDO tranches to clients.

Balance sheet CDOs versus arbitrage CDOs

The asset-backed nature of CDO securities may be used to effect two main types of transactions: balance sheet CDOs and arbitrage CDOs. Banks and insurance companies are the primary sources of balance sheet CDOs. They use these structures to manage the assets on their balance sheets.

Frequently, balance sheet CDOs tend to be in the form of collateralized loan obligation structures. There are several goals of a balance sheet CDO:

- A bank or insurance company might wish to reduce its credit exposure to a particular client or industry. It transfers this risk to the CDO.
- The bank or insurance company might wish to reduce its regulatory capital charges. Selling a portion of its loan or bond portfolio to a CDO can free up regulatory capital required to support those credit-risky assets.
- The bank or insurance company might need a capital infusion.

Although CLO structures were invented in the late 1980s, it was not until the ROSE Funding No. 1 CLO in November 1996 that the value of CLOs to manage balance sheet risk became apparent. In that transaction National Westminister Bank sold $5 billion of high-quality commercial bank loans to the ROSE CLO. This sale represented 15% to 20% of Nat West's total loan book (about 2,000 corporate loans). The transaction not only provided new funding to Nat West, it also released up to $400 million of regulatory capital.[1]

Since the Nat West transaction, banks have realized that they can use the asset-backed securities market to manage their balance sheets. This is a vast improvement over the traditional way for a bank to manage its credit exposure: using its lending policies to cut back on its lending exposure in one industry while increasing its loan exposure in a different industry. The dramatic increase in technology and financial engineering in the 1990s allows banks to manage their credit risks more finely. In today's financial markets, many banks have concluded that their expertise lies in analyzing credit risk and originating loans to match that risk, but not necessarily in holding the loans on their balance sheets.[2]

In contrast to banks, money managers are the main suppliers of arbitrage CDOs. Initially, most arbitrage CDOs were in the form of a CBO structure because money managers tended to have more experience managing high-yield bonds than leveraged loans. However, arbitrage CDOs have expanded dramatically, and now contain bonds, mortgages, commercial loans, and even investments in other CDO structures. The ultimate goal is to make a profit instead of managing balance sheet risk. Arbitrage CDOs are designed to profit by capturing a spread for the equity investors in the CDO. The spread is captured between the higher-yielding securities that the CDO earns on its portfolio and the yield that it must pay out on its own securities issued to the CDO investors. Furthermore, money management firms earn fees on the amount of assets under management. By creating an arbitrage CDO, the firm can increase its income by increasing its assets under management.

Cash-funded versus synthetic CDOs

Within the two broad categories of balance sheet and arbitrage CDOs there are several subcategories that further segment the CDO marketplace. For instance, balance sheet CDOs can be either cash funded or synthetically constructed through the use of credit derivatives. Similarly, arbitrage CDOs can be funded with cash or through the use of credit derivatives. Exhibit 30.2 lays out the many different types of CDO structures.

A **cash CDO** involves the purchase of a portfolio of securities such as high-yield bonds, asset-backed securities, bank loans, mortgage-backed securities, and more. Physical ownership of the

[1] See Charles Smithson and Gregory Hayt, "Tools for Reshaping Credit Portfolios: Managing Credit Risk," *RMA Journal* (May 2001).

[2] See Kenneth E. Kohler, "Collateralized Loan Obligations: A Powerful New Portfolio Management Tool for Banks," *Securitization Conduit* (Summer 1998).

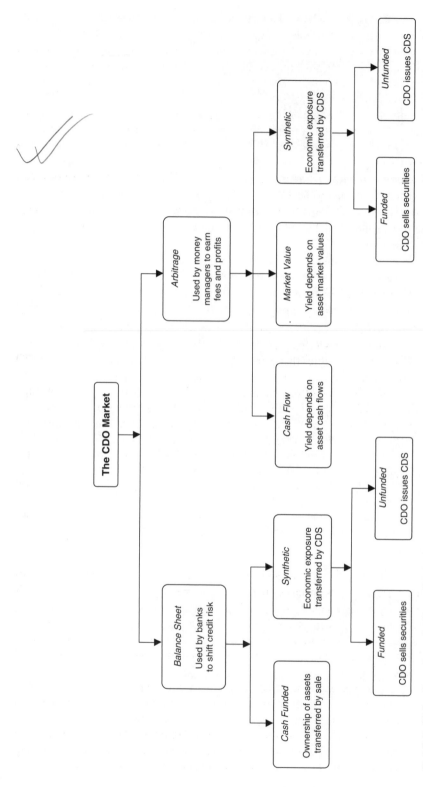

Exhibit 30.2 Overview of collateralized debt obligations

assets is acquired by the CDO. The CDO issues securities and receives cash inflows from its investors. These cash inflows are used to purchase the underlying assets of the CDO portfolio.

Conversely, in a **synthetic CDO**, the CDO does not actually own the underlying assets. Instead, a synthetic CDO gains its credit exposure through the use of a credit derivative such as a total return swap or a credit default swap. Physical ownership of the underlying basket of securities is not transferred to the CDO, only the economic exposure.

In effect, the CDO sells credit protection on a referenced basket of assets. For this protection, the CDO receives income in the form of CDS payments from the credit protection buyer. The credit protection payments are then divided up among the CDO's investors based on the seniority of the securities issued by the CDO.

Synthetic CDOs were initially very popular for balance sheet CDOs because the use of credit derivatives was a convenient way for banks to transfer risk from their balance sheets without actually selling their loan books. However, the ease of execution of the synthetic approach quickly appealed to money managers. Now, synthetic CDOs are equally likely to be constructed for either a balance sheet CDO or an arbitrage CDO.

Cash flow versus market value CDOs

Under the arbitrage CDO structure, there can be a further subdivision between cash flow CDOs and market value CDOs. In a cash flow CDO, the CDO issues securities the proceeds of which are used to purchase a portfolio of underlying credit-risky assets. Typically, there is a fixed tenor (maturity) for a cash flow CDO's liabilities that coincides with the maturity of the underlying CDO portfolio assets. More specifically, the CDO portfolio is managed to wind down and pay off the CDO's liabilities through the collection of interest and principal on the underlying CDO portfolio. Therefore, the focus of the CDO manager is on the credit quality of the underlying portfolio because the portfolio must liquidate with a minimum of defaults to redeem the liabilities issued by the CDO.

Conversely, in a market value CDO, the underlying portfolio is actively traded. The liabilities of the CDO are paid off through the trading and sale of the underlying portfolio. In a market value CDO, the portfolio manager is most concerned with the underlying volatility of the market values of the portfolio, because precipitous declines in values will reduce a market value CDO's ability to redeem its liabilities.

Funded versus unfunded CDOs

This category applies only to synthetic CDOs. Some synthetic CDOs issue regular classes of bonds just like **cash-funded CDOs**. In this instance, the CDO manager typically places the proceeds received from investors in low-risk securities, typically Treasury notes. The credit exposure for a synthetic CDO comes from credit derivatives, typically CDSs. Therefore, the CDO receives periodic fees from its CDSs as well as interest on the underlying portfolio of low-risk securities. This income is passed on to the CDO's investors in the priority ranking of their investment in the CDO (we will discuss this in a just a bit).

If a credit event did occur under one of the CDSs, the CDO would be required to make a credit protection payment. It would fund this payment by selling some of the low-risk collateral contained in the CDO portfolio. This would force some of the CDO's assets to decline.

Alternatively, some synthetic CDOs are unfunded. In an **unfunded CDO**, the CDO does not collect any proceeds from its investors. An investor in an unfunded CDO does not pay a purchase price for her tranche of the CDO. Instead, the CDO investor assumes the role of the credit protection seller. The investor receives payments from the CDO as a credit protection seller but must pay the CDO issuer, as the credit protection buyer, if the underlying referenced credit portfolio suffers losses above a specified level. In this case, the synthetic CDO is nothing more than an intermediary bringing together investors who wish to take on credit risk through a CDS and other asset owners who wish to hedge their credit exposure by purchasing credit protection through a CDS. The CDO manager simply brings these parties together under the synthetic CDO structure and collects a management fee for his efforts.

Special purpose vehicles

At the center of every CDO structure is a special purpose vehicle (SPV). This is a term to describe a legal entity that is established to accomplish a specific transaction such as a CDO structure. SPVs are usually set up as either a Delaware or Massachusetts business trust or as a special purpose corporation (SPC), usually Delaware based. In the case of a balance sheet CDO, the SPV will most often be established as a collateralized loan obligation (CLO) trust. The selling bank will be the sponsor for the trust, meaning that it will bear the administrative and legal costs of establishing the trust. In the case of an arbitrage CDO, the SPV is usually a collateralized bond obligation (CBO) trust and the sponsoring entity is typically a money manager.

SPVs are often referred to as **bankruptcy remote**. This means that if the sponsoring bank or money manager goes bankrupt, the CDO trust will not be affected. The trust assets remain secure from any financial difficulties suffered by the sponsoring entity.

The SPV owns the collateral placed in the trust, and issues notes and equity against the collateral it owns. These collateralized debt obligations may be issued in different classes of securities or tranches. Each tranche of a CDO structure may have its own credit rating. The most subordinated tranche of the CDO is usually called the equity tranche.

At the core of every SPV is the slicing and dicing of credit risk into different classes or tranches of securities. The SPV issues notes differentiated by their level of seniority in the SPV structure. Typically, there are three main tranches to every CDO: senior, mezzanine, and equity. The nomenclature of the CDO market parses these tranches out more finely into: supersenior tranche, senior tranche, senior mezzanine tranche, mezzanine tranche, and the equity tranche.

Typically, every tranche of notes issued by the CDO SPV receives an investment-grade rating by a Nationally Recognized Statistical Rating Organization (NRSRO) with the exception of the equity tranche. The equity tranche is the **first-loss tranche**. It is the last to receive any cash flows from the CDO collateral and is the first tranche on the hook for any defaults or lost value of the CDO collateral.

Usually the supersenior tranche is the largest tranche (up to 85% of the total SPV notes), followed by tranches of less seniority. Each class or tranche of SPV notes has different rights and priorities concerning payments generated by the CDO collateral. The seniorities of the tranches form a **waterfall** by which it is dictated how the proceeds from the CDO cash flows (both coupon receipts and liquidation sales) will first be used to meet the obligations owed to the most senior tranche of the SPV. After all of the claims of the supersenior tranche are fulfilled, then the CDO cash flows are used to meet the obligations of the senior tranche, and so forth. Exhibit 30.3 demonstrates the waterfall structure.

These securities are issued privately to institutional investors and high-net-worth individuals. The collateral held by the SPV produces cash flows that are used to pay interest and dividends on the notes and equity issued by the SPV. The majority of principal on the securities issued by the SPV is paid at the end of the life of the SPV, usually from final principal payoffs or the sale of the SPV assets.

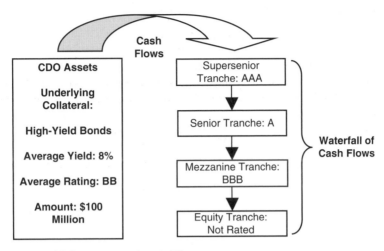

Exhibit 30.3   A basic CDO structure and waterfall

Source: Mark Anson, *Handbook of Alternative Assets*, 2nd ed. (Hoboken, NJ: John Wiley & Sons, 2006). Reprinted with permission of John Wiley & Sons, Inc.

BALANCE SHEET CDO STRUCTURES

Balance sheet CDO structures are typically constructed as collateralized loan obligations. Following Exhibit 30.2, we consider two examples of balance sheet CDO structures: cash funded and synthetic. We diagram how these structures work and discuss the benefits to a bank or other lending institution from sponsoring a CLO structure.

Cash-funded balance sheet CDO

In a balance sheet CDO, the seller of the assets is usually a bank that seeks to remove a portion of its loan portfolio from its balance sheet. The bank constructs a special purpose vehicle to dispose of its balance sheet assets into the CDO structure. Exhibit 30.4 demonstrates this type of CDO structure.

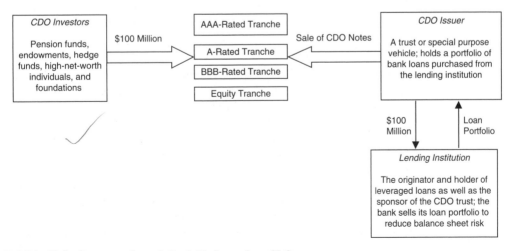

Exhibit 30.4   Structure of a cash-funded balance sheet CLO

Bank loan CDO trusts usually have a professional asset manager to manage the assets contained in the trust. This can be the selling bank, where the bank is hired under a separate agreement to manage the portfolio of loans that it sold to the CDO trust. Also, the CDO trust will have a trustee whose job it is to protect the security interests of the CDO investors in the trust's assets. Usually, this is not the bank or an affiliate because of conflict of interest provisions. Last, the CDO trust may purchase a credit enhancement from an outside insurance provider. The credit enhancement guarantees from a third party timely payment of interest and principal on the CDO securities up to a specified amount, and ensures that they will receive an investment-grade credit rating.

Many bank CDOs are self-liquidating. All interest and principal payments from the commercial loans are passed through to the CDO investors. Other balance sheet CDOs provide for the reinvestment of loan payments into additional commercial loans to be purchased by the CDO trust. After the initial reinvestment period, the CDO trust enters into an amortization period when the loan proceeds are used to pay down the principal of the outstanding CDO tranches.

Synthetic balance sheet CDO

Synthetic balance sheet CDOs differ from the cash-funded variety in several important ways. First, cash-funded CDOs are constructed with an actual sale and transfer of the loans or assets to the CDO trust. Ownership of the assets is transferred from the bank's balance sheet to that of the CDO trust. In a synthetic CDO, however, the sponsoring bank or other institution transfers the total return profile of a designated basket of loans or other assets via a credit derivative transaction, usually a credit default swap or a credit return swap. Therefore, the bank transfers its risk profile associated with its assets, but not the legal ownership of the assets.

Second, in a cash-funded CDO, the proceeds received from the sale of the CDO securities are used to purchase the collateral for the CDO trust. The cash flows from the collateral held by the CDO trust are then used to pay the returns on the CDO securities. Conversely, the cash proceeds from a synthetic balance sheet CDO are usually invested in U.S. Treasury securities. The interest received from these securities is an additional return to the CDO's investors.

Third, a synthetic balance sheet CDO can use leverage. The use of leverage can boost the returns received by the CDO investors, thereby increasing the attractiveness of the CDO securities.

Last, a synthetic balance sheet CDO is less burdensome in transferring assets. Certain commercial loans may require borrower notification and consent before being transferred to the CDO trust. This can take time, increase the administration costs, and lead to dissatisfaction on the part of the bank's loan customers.

Exhibit 30.5 demonstrates a synthetic balance sheet CDO. Assume that a bank establishes an SPV in the form of a trust for a balance sheet CDO. The bank wishes to reduce its exposure to a basket of loans on its balance sheet.[3]

The CDO trust issues medium-term notes to investors that the trust records on its balance sheet as a liability and the investors record on their balance sheets as privately issued 144A securities.[4] The proceeds from the sale of the CDO securities are used to purchase U.S. Treasury securities with the same maturity as the CDO securities. The CDO securities receive an investment-grade credit rating because they are backed by default-free U.S. Treasury securities.

---

[3] We omitted the asset manager and trustee from Exhibit 30.5 to make the diagram less cluttered. These two entities are still used, but are not crucial to our example.

[4] These private securities are typically offered in the form of SEC Rule 144A. Under this rule, the securities do not need to be registered with the SEC via a registration statement, but may be sold only to qualified institutional buyers.

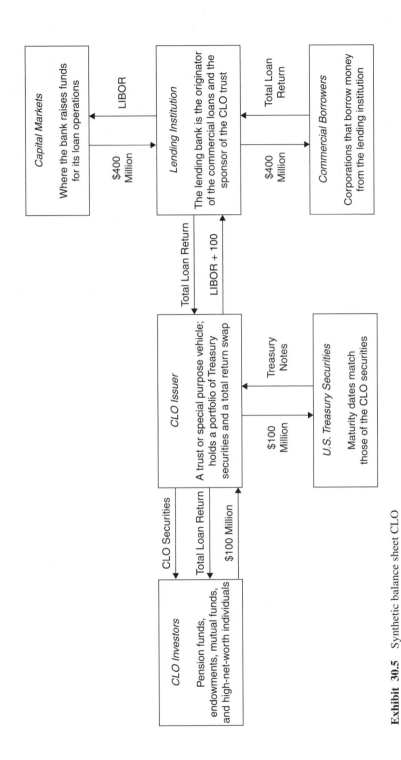

Exhibit 30.5 Synthetic balance sheet CLO

Source: Mark Anson, *Handbook of Alternative Assets*, 2nd ed. (Hoboken, NJ: John Wiley & Sons, 2006). Reprinted with permission of John Wiley & Sons, Inc.

Initially, most synthetic balance sheet CDOs used a total return swap to transfer the credit risk exposure from the bank to the CDO trust. However, now most synthetic balance sheet CDOs are constructed with a credit default swap (CDS).

Exhibit 30.6 shows a synthetic balance sheet CDO using a CDS. The key difference is in the payments between the bank and the CDO trust. Under the terms of the CDS, the bank now makes periodic payments to the CDO trust. These payments reflect the insurance premium that the bank must pay as the credit protection buyer. In effect, the CDO trust sells credit insurance to the bank for which the bank must make periodic payments—the CDO trust is the credit protection seller. The CDO trust, in turn, combines the periodic payments from the bank with the interest proceeds from the U.S. Treasury securities to make payments to the CDO note holders. Notice that the CDO investors are insulated from the derivative transaction with the bank. The CDO acts as the intermediary between the CDO investors and the bank so that the two sides do not need to negotiate separately.

In return for receiving periodic insurance premiums from the bank, the CDO trust now bears the risk of loss on the referenced bank loans that remain on the bank's balance sheet. The CDS requires the CDO trust to make payments to the bank upon any condition of default. Conditions of default are spelled out in the swap agreement between the bank and the CDO trust.

Another advantage of the structure in Exhibit 30.6 is the use of leverage. While the CDO investors put up $100 million of cash, the CDO can negotiate with the bank through the CDS for credit exposure greater than $100 million.

Assume that the bank is willing to pay 100 basis points for credit protection on a $500 million loan portfolio that currently yields the bank LIBOR plus 200 basis points. If the CDS is negotiated with the bank on the full loan portfolio of $500 million, the CDO investors will receive $5 million of CDS income on their $100 million investment—this is a 5% return. Plus the CDO investors earn

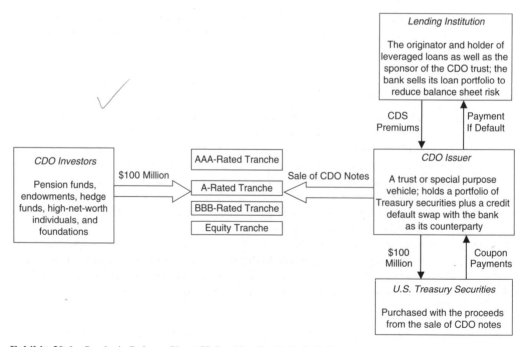

Exhibit 30.6   Synthetic Balance Sheet CDO with a Credit Default Swap

income from the U.S. Treasury securities held by the CDO. The ability of CDO investors to earn 500 basis points of income plus the yield on U.S. Treasury securities far exceeds the LIBOR + 200 return they could earn if they purchased the loans outright from the bank.

Note that the $100 million of U.S. Treasury securities serves as collateral for the CDO's side in honoring the credit default swap. If the basket of reference loans defaults, the Treasury securities will be liquidated to pay for this loss. Therefore, the CDO is considered the first-loss position for the bank—it will absorb the first $100 million in defaults on the bank loans. Any defaults after this will be borne by the bank. For this reason, the bank will receive regulatory capital relief on only the first-loss position.

Exhibit 30.6 also demonstrates that the CDO will issue several tranches of notes to investors. Typically, pension funds, endowments, and foundations purchase the investment-grade AAA and A tranches, while high-net-worth investors often purchase the B (mezzanine) tranche. Initially, the selling bank had to purchase some or all of the equity tranche to make the CDO attractive to other investors. However, hedge fund managers have quickly become the equity tranche investor of choice in many CDO structures—freeing banks to sponsor even more synthetic CDO deals.

Synthetic CDOs are often called **correlation products** because the CDS contract references the default of more than one bank loan or obligor. Investors in the CDO buy correlation risk. This is the joint default risk between several obligors. The job of the CDO manager is to structure the CDS so that the correlation risk is minimized. That is, the CDO manager does not want all defaults to occur at the same time.

The key point of this section is that the transfer of credit risk from the bank to the CDO trust through a synthetic balance sheet transaction is done primarily with CDSs. This has helped fuel the growth of the credit derivative market.

Benefits to banks from CDOs

Although there is a growing demand from investors for CDO structures, banks are equally motivated to build CDO trust structures. Risk reduction, as indicated earlier, is just one of several benefits to banks from CDOs.

Reducing risk-based/regulatory capital

Reducing risk-based/regulatory capital is the single most important motivation for a bank to form a CDO trust. Under the 1988 Basel Accord adopted by the G-10 group of industrialized nations, banks in these nations are required to maintain risk-based capital equal to 8% of the outstanding balance of commercial loans.[5] The 8% regulatory capital charge required for commercial loans is the highest percentage of capital required to be held against any asset type.

Using a CDO trust to securitize and sell a portfolio of commercial loans can free up regulatory capital that must be committed to support the loan portfolio. Consider a bank with a $500 million loan portfolio that it wishes to sell. It must hold risk-based capital equal to 8% × $500 million = $40 million to support these loans. If the bank sponsors a CDO trust where the trust purchases the $500 million loan portfolio from the bank and finds outside investors to purchase all of the CDO securities, the bank no longer has any exposure to the basket of commercial loans and now has freed $40 million of regulatory capital that it can use in other parts of its balance sheet.

---

[5] For a more detailed discussion on the Basel Accord and its impact on regulatory capital, see Mark Anson, *Credit Derivatives* (New Hope, PA: Frank J. Fabozzi Associates, 1999).

Unfortunately, sometimes the equity tranche of the CDO trust is unappealing to outside investors and cannot be sold. Under this circumstance, the sponsoring bank may have to retain an equity or first-loss position in the CDO trust. If this is the case, the regulatory capital standards require the bank to maintain risk-based capital equal to its first-loss position. For example, if the sponsoring bank had to retain a $10 million equity piece in the CDO trust to attract other investors, it must take a one-for-one regulatory capital charge for this first-loss position. This means that only $40 million minus $10 million = $30 million of regulatory capital will be freed by the CDO trust. However, with the arrival of hedge funds into the CDO market, this has become less of an issue.

Increasing loan capacity

In our earlier regulatory capital example, not only does the bank free up $40 million of regulatory capital, but it also receives cash proceeds from the sale of its loans to the CDO trust. The funds generated by the loan securitization can be used to originate additional commercial loans at either better rates or better credit quality or can be used to purchase different assets for the bank's balance sheet. Either way, the bank has generated a large cash inflow that it can use to strengthen its balance sheet.

Improving ROE and ROA measures

With its cash in hand, the bank can reduce its overall balance sheet by paying down its liabilities. In fact, if the bank can reduce its overall capital base and at the same time increase the proportion of higher-yielding assets, it will increase its return on equity (ROE) and return on assets (ROA).

Continuing with our example from before, assume that the bank's cost of funds is LIBOR and that the $500 million portfolio of loans earns on average LIBOR plus 100 basis points. Therefore, the bank earns $5 million per year on this loan portfolio. The required regulatory capital is $40 million for a ROE of $5 million ÷ $40 million = 12.5%.

The bank uses the $500 million received from the sale to the CLO trust to lend out in the residential mortgage market. The bank receives loan income of LIBOR plus 0.75% on the residential mortgages. However, the regulatory capital required to support residential mortgages is one-half of that for commercial loans, or $20 million. The bank's return on equity is now $3.75 million ÷ $20 million = 18.75%.

Reducing credit concentrations

The selling bank may be at the limit of its credit exposure to one industry or group of borrowers. It may find this industry profitable in terms of commercial loans, but cannot increase its exposure. By selling part of its loan portfolio, it has produced more "dry powder" to lend to that borrower or industry.

In addition to reducing credit concentrations, CDOs can help a bank manage its overall credit exposure to the leveraged loan market. Exhibit 30.7 shows the level of global loan defaults over the period 1996 to 2008 as followed by Moody's. As can be seen, during times of economic slowdown, like the U.S. recession of 2001–2002 or the financial crisis of 2007 to 2008, loan defaults increase. Therefore, when a bank expects a slowdown in the economic cycle of growth, CDO products can help it manage its credit risk.

Preserving customer relations

A bank is often in the uncomfortable position of accepting more exposure to a bank client that it wishes. In order to maintain its relationship with its borrower, the bank can reduce its exposure to

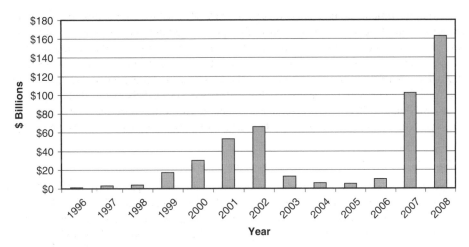

Exhibit 30.7   Global loan defaults

Source: Bloomberg.

the client by selling a portion of the bank's loan portfolio pertaining to the client to the CLO trust. In a CLO, the portfolio manager for the trust is often the bank so that the borrowing client need not even know that its loan has been sold to the CLO trust.

Competitive positioning

There is a large investor base of pension funds, endowments, mutual funds, insurance companies, and high-net-worth individuals that seek to invest in bank loans.[6] Institutional investor participation in bank loans now exceeds 50%. Simply, bank loans have come of age not just as a lending tool for banks and corporate borrowers, but as a mainstream investment for those that seek greater yield.

CLO trusts are the natural format for achieving this exposure. Furthermore, large banks desiring to position themselves in this increasingly competitive marketplace may wish to establish a program of CLO trusts in order to attract and maintain qualified investors for the CLO securities.

Credit enhancements

Most CLO structures contain some form of **credit enhancement** to ensure that the CLO securities sold to investors will receive an investment-grade rating. These enhancements can be internal or external. Generally, credit enhancements are made at the expense of lower coupon rates paid on the CLO securities. While we discuss credit enhancements with respect to CLO trusts, these provisions are equally applicable to all CDO structures.

Subordination

Subordination is the most common form of credit enhancement in a CDO transaction, and it flows from the structure of the CLO trust. This is an internal credit enhancement.

For instance, CLO trusts typically issue several class or tranches of securities. The lower level, or subordinated tranches, provides credit support for the higher-rated tranches. As we discussed

---

[6] See Smithson and Hayt, "Tools for Reshaping Credit Portfolios."

previously, the equity tranche in a CLO trust provides the first-loss position with respect to a basket of loans. This tranche provides credit enhancement for every class of CLO securities above it.[7]

Junior tranches of a CDO are rated lower than the senior tranches but in return receive a higher interest rate commensurate with their subordinated status and therefore greater credit risk. The payment structure of a CDO can vary, but it is usually in one of three forms: sequential pay, fast pay/slow pay, or pro rata.

In a sequential-pay CDO, the senior tranches must be paid in full before any principal is paid to the junior tranches. In a fast pay/slow pay CDO, the senior tranches are paid down faster than the junior tranches. Last, in a pro rata payment, the senior and junior tranches are paid down at the same rate. Most CDO structures go with a sequential-pay format.

This sequential payment structure is often referred to as the waterfall. As interest and principal payments are received from the underlying collateral, they flow down the waterfall, first to the senior tranches of the CLO trust and then to the lower-rated tranches. Subordinated tranches must wait for sufficient interest and principal payments to flow down the tranche structure before they can receive a payment. The concept of the waterfall was already demonstrated in Exhibit 30.3.

Overcollateralization

Overcollateralization results from the senior/junior nature of tranches in a CDO. For example, consider a CDO trust with a market value of collateral trust assets of $100 million. The CDO trust issues two tranches. Tranche A is the senior tranche and consists of $80 million of securities. Tranche B consists of $20 million of subordinated securities and is paid after the senior tranche is paid in full. The level of overcollateralization for the senior tranche is $100/$80 = 125%. The funds used to purchase the excess collateral come from the subordinated tranche; tranche B provides the overcollateralization to tranche A. Overcollateralization is an internal credit enhancement.

Spread enhancement

Another internal enhancement can be excess spread of the loans contained in the CLO trust compared to the interest promised on the CLO securities. The excess spread may arise because the assets of the CLO trust are of lower credit quality than the CLO securities, and therefore yield a higher interest rate than the rate paid on the CLO securities. A higher yield on the trust assets may also result from a different term structure. This excess spread may be used to cover any losses associated with the CLO trust loan portfolio. If there are no losses on the loan portfolio, the excess spread accrues to the equity tranche of the CLO trust.

Cash collateral or reserve account

Excess cash is held in highly rated instruments such as U.S. Treasury securities or high-grade commercial paper that provide security to the debt holder of the CLO trust. Cash reserves are often used in the initial phase of a cash flow transaction. During this phase, cash proceeds received by the trust from the sale of its securities are used to purchase the underlying collateral and the reserve account. Cash reserves are not the most efficient form of credit support, because they generally earn a lower rate of return than that required to fund the CLO securities. Therefore, there is a clear

---

[7] Most CLO structures are delinked. That is, there is no link with the selling bank; the CLO trust holds ownership over the loan assets. In this case the credit rating of the bank does not affect the CLO trust. In some cases, however, the CLO trust remains linked with the selling bank. In this case, the bank sells the risk to the CLO trust via a credit-linked note or a credit swap so that the CLO trust must depend on the creditworthiness of the selling bank to collect on the trust's assets.

trade-off: A higher cash **reserve account** means greater credit support but at the expense of lower interest payments on the CLO securities.

External credit enhancement

An **external credit enhancement** is provided by an outside third party in the form of insurance against defaults in the loan portfolio. This insurance may be a straightforward insurance contract, the sale of a put option, or the negotiation of a credit default swap to protect the downside from any loan losses. The effect is to transfer the credit risks associated with the CLO trust collateral from the holders of the CLO trust securities to the insurance company.

ARBITRAGE CDOs

An arbitrage CDO seeks to make a profit. The profit is earned by selling CLO/CBO securities to outside investors at a price that is higher than that paid for the assets placed into the CLO/CBO structure. In addition, arbitrage CDOs are typically set up by money managers who increase their assets under management and their corresponding management fees. Most often, an arbitrage CDO consists of bonds and other asset-backed securities purchased on the open market. These bonds are then placed into the CDO trust and the manager of the trust sells new securities (the CBOs) to new investors. An arbitrage profit is earned if the CDO trust can sell its securities at a lower yield than the yield received on the bond collateral contained in the trust. Exhibit 30.8 presents the structure for a CBO trust.

The key to understanding arbitrage CDOs is that they are driven by profit-making considerations. First, there is the arbitrage or excess spread income that can be earned. We will show a demonstration of this in a moment. In addition, asset managers—the primary sponsors of arbitrage CDOs—earn a management fee for managing the assets of the CDO trust. In the asset management business, the

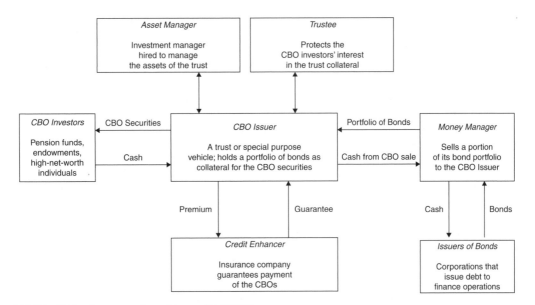

Exhibit 30.8   Structure of an arbitrage CDO/CBO

Source: Mark Anson, *Handbook of Alternative Assets*, 2nd ed. (Hoboken, NJ: John Wiley & Sons, 2006). Reprinted with permission of John Wiley & Sons, Inc.

game is all about accumulating assets under management, and a CDO trust is simply another way to apply an asset management fee to another pool of assets.

Cash flow arbitrage CDO

In a cash flow arbitrage CDO, the repayment of the CDO securities is dependent on cash flows from the underlying pool of bonds and loans. These structures typically invest in high-yield bonds but can also invest in bank loans, investment-grade corporate debt, mortgages, emerging markets bonds, and any other credit-risky security.

In a **cash flow CDO**, the trust holds the bonds and receives the debt service (principal and interest payments). The CDO trust securities are sold to match the payment schedules of the bonds held as collateral by the trust. As the collateral pays down, the CDO trust pays down its securities. Simply, the cash flows from the underlying assets are used to make payments to the CDO investors.

In some cases, the cash flow arbitrage CDO is static. This means that the collateral held by the CDO trust does not change; it remains static throughout the life of the trust. There is no active buying or selling of securities once the CDO trust is established. For static CDOs, the key is minimizing the default risk of the underlying assets, because it is the return of principal from the underlying CDO portfolio securities that is used to pay back the CDO investors.

However, most arbitrage CDOs are actively managed. This means that after the initial CDO portfolio is constructed, the manager of the CDO trust can buy and sell bonds that meet the CDO trust's criteria to enhance the yield to the CDO investors and reduce the risk of loss through default.

Cash flow arbitrage CDO trusts are dependent on default and recovery rates. For example, assume that a CDO trust has two tranches or classes of securities. Tranche A is the senior class and represents $100 million in CDO securities. Tranche B is the subordinated or equity class, and is $50 million of securities. Underlying the CDO trust is $150 million of high-yield bonds that pay income to the trust of LIBOR plus 4%.

The senior tranche is promised payments of principal plus LIBOR plus 1%, and the subordinate tranche receives whatever is left after the senior tranche is fully paid. For simplicity, we assume that the CDO trust is organized for one year with a bullet payment at the end of one year and that LIBOR is equal to 5%.

We demonstrate several scenarios: no default of high-yield bonds, a 1% default rate, a 2% default rate, and so on up to a 5% default rate. The historical recovery rate for defaulted high-yield debt is about 40%. Therefore, if 5% of the bonds default, the CDO trust would expect to recover 5% × 40% = 2%, resulting in a net loss of 3%.[8]

Under the no-default scenario, at maturity of the CDO trust, the subordinated equity tranche of the CDO trust will receive:

$$\$150 \text{ million} \times [1 + (\text{LIBOR} + 4\%)] - \$100 \text{ million} \times [1 + (\text{LIBOR} + 1\%)] = \$57.5 \text{ million}$$

On an original investment of $50 million, this is a return of 15%.

Under the next scenario, 1% ($1.5 million) of the high-yield bonds held by the CDO trust default. With a recovery rate of 40%, this is a net loss of $0.9 million that must be absorbed by equity tranche. Under this loss scenario, the equity tranche will receive:

$$\$148.5 \text{ million} \times [1 + (\text{LIBOR} + 4\%)] + \$0.6 \text{ million} - \$100 \text{ million} \times [1 + (\text{LIBOR} + 1\%)]$$
$$= \$56.465 \text{ million}$$

On an original investment of $50 million, this is a return of 12.93%.

---

[8] We also assume that recovery on any defaulted bond is made by the maturity of the CDO trust. In practice, recovery can take several years, stretching out the payments to the equity tranche of the CDO. Last, we assume that all accrued income is lost on defaulted debt, and that any recovery pertains only to the face value of the debt.

These scenarios can be used to generate a yield table of the equity tranche for this CDO structure. Exhibit 30.9 provides a graph of the default rate and the resulting yield to maturity for the equity tranche. As can be seen, the return to the equity tranche declines quickly as the default rate rises. At a default rate of 5%, the return to the equity tranche is less than 5%.

The important point to this example is that the return on investment for both tranches depends only on the cash flows received by the CDO trust. The critical factors associated with these cash flows are the default rate for the high-yield bonds held by the CDO trust and the recovery rate on those bonds once they default. At no time does the market value of the high-yield bonds affect the return to the CDO investors. Although the prices of the high-yield bonds may fluctuate up and down, this does not affect the returns to the CDO security holders as long as the underlying collateral pays its coupons and principal at maturity.

Market value arbitrage CDO

With these CDO structures, the return earned by investors is linked to the market value of the underlying collateral contained in the CDO trust. These structures are used when the maturity of the collateral assets purchased by the trust does not match precisely the maturity of the CDO securities. In fact, this is usually the case.

Consider the example of a CDO trust that buys high-yield bonds. It is unlikely that the trust will be able to sell securities that perfectly mimic the maturity of the high-yield bonds held as collateral. Therefore, the cash flows associated with a market value arbitrage CDO come from not only the interest payments received on the collateral bonds, but also from the sale of these bonds to make the principal payments on the CDO securities. Therefore, the yield on the CDO securities is dependent on the market value of the high-yield bonds at the time of resale.

Given the dependency on market prices, market value arbitrage CDOs use the total rate of return as a measure of performance. The total rate of return takes into account the interest received from the high-yield bonds as well as their appreciation or depreciation in value.

Let's use the same example as before for the cash flow CDO structure. There are two tranches, a $100 million tranche paying LIBOR plus 1% and an equity tranche. The CDO trust lasts for one year, and at the end of one year both tranches of securities receive a bullet payment. The difference is that at the end of one year, the CDO trust must sell its underlying high-yield bond portfolio to fund the redemption of the CDO trust securities.

Under this scenario, we assume not that there are defaults, but instead that the high-yield bond portfolio has suffered a decline in value of 0% to 5%. Under the 0% decline in value scenario, the

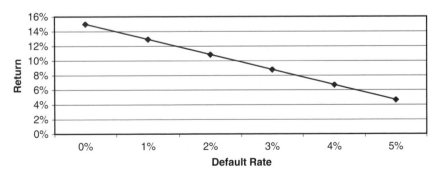

Exhibit 30.9   Projected return for equity in a cash flow arbitrage CDO

Source: Bloomberg.

return to the equity tranche in a market value CDO will be the same as under the cash flow example, 15%. Under a decline of value of 1%, the return to the equity tranche will equal:

$$\$150 \text{ million} \times [1 + (\text{LIBOR} + 4\%)] - \$100 \text{ million} \times [1 + (\text{LIBOR} + 1\%)] - \$1.5 \text{ million}$$
$$= \$56 \text{ million}$$

This equals a total return of 12%.

In Exhibit 30.10 we provide a graph similar to Exhibit 30.9 that plots the return to the equity tranche versus the decline in value of the high-yield bond portfolio. As we can see, a decline in market value results in a more precipitous decline (compared to a cash flow arbitrage CDO) in the return to the equity tranche of this CDO trust. The reason is that there is no opportunity for the trust collateral to recover the lost value. The high-yield bonds must be sold to fund the redemptions of the CDO securities. This decline in value is locked in at the time of the liquidation of the trust.

Practically, a market value CDO trust will also experience defaults just like cash flow CDO trusts. When this occurs, the market value trust must take into account defaults and recovery rates as well as changes in market value. In fact, it is likely that as default rates increase, the market value of the bond portfolio will decrease. These complementary effects can erode the return to the equity tranche even faster than indicated in Exhibits 30.9 and 30.10. Throughout 2008 and into 2009, market value CDOs declined significantly, leading to a rapid decline in the first loss, or equity, tranche of the CDO. Many CDO sponsors had to eat this loss and put up more capital to protect the more senior tranches from eroding in value. Going forward, it is much less likely that arbitrage CDOs will be structured as market value CDOs.

Synthetic arbitrage CDOs

Synthetic arbitrage CDOs simulate the risk transference similar to a cash sale of assets without any change in the legal ownership of the assets. The risk is transferred by a credit default swap or a total return credit swap.

Synthetic arbitrage CDOs are used by asset management companies, insurance companies, and other investment shops with the intent of exploiting a mismatch between the yield of underlying securities and the lower cost of servicing the CDO securities. These structures are less administratively burdensome when compared to cash-funded structures, particularly when attempting to transfer only a portion of a credit risk.

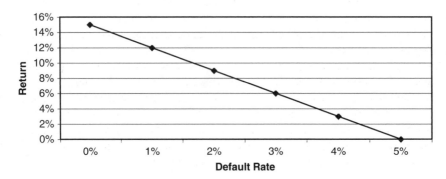

Exhibit 30.10   Expected return for the equity tranche of a market value CDO

Source: Bloomberg.

Synthetic CDO trusts can also be used to provide economic exposure to credit-risky assets that may be relatively scarce and difficult to acquire in the cash market. Last, synthetic CDO trusts can employ leverage. In Exhibit 30.5 we demonstrated a synthetic balance sheet CLO where the leverage ratio was 5 to 1.

The mechanics of a synthetic arbitrage CDO are similar to those demonstrated in Exhibit 30.5. The CDO trust enters into a swap agreement on a reference portfolio of fixed income securities. The portfolio may be fully funded or only partially funded at the time of the swap agreement (there is often a ramping-up period when credit-risky assets are selected for the reference portfolio). Under the swap agreement, the CDO trust will pay LIBOR plus a spread to the sponsoring money manager and, in return, receive the total return on the reference portfolio. The total return includes interest received from the securities in the reference portfolio as well as any price appreciation or depreciation. Alternatively, the CDO can use a credit default swap where the CDO receives periodic payments from the credit protection buyer and must make a payment if a default occurs. The reference portfolio is funded on the balance sheet of the sponsoring institution.

One key difference of a synthetic arbitrage CDO compared to a cash flow CDO is that the swap payments are made periodically, usually on a quarterly basis. Therefore, the underlying collateral must be marked to market each quarter to determine the total return on the credit swap. This exposes the CDO securities holder to market risk similar to a market value arbitrage CLO trust discussed earlier.

Profiting from an arbitrage CDO trust

We have mentioned several times that the motivation for an arbitrage CDO trust is to earn a profit. We provide an example of how this is done. Assume a money manager establishes an arbitrage CDO to invest in high-yield bonds. The trust will have a life of three years and raises $500 million by selling three tranches of securities. The security tranches issued by the trust are divided by credit rating. In tranche A, debt with the highest priority is issued against the highest credit quality bonds in the trust collateral. This senior debt tends to have a lower return and volatility than the composite bond portfolio return and volatility.

The second or mezzanine tranche is securitized with the average credit quality bond in the pool and the subordination of the equity tranche. Here, the credit rating of tranche B may not be any greater than that of the average high-yield bond owned by the CDO trust, but this tranche still has the advantage of a diversified pool of bonds and the seniority to the last CDO tranche. The final tranche is subordinated to the two other CDO tranches and is securitized with the lowest credit quality bonds in the trust portfolio. For this tranche, the risk is the highest, but the bonds securing it are also the highest yielding. The equity tranche also collects any residual income generated by the CDO collateral.

Exhibit 30.11 provides a more detailed example of this arbitrage CDO trust. Consider a money manager that has a portfolio of high-yield bonds with credit ratings of the underlying issuers equal to BB. The bonds pay an average coupon of 9%, and have a face value of $500 million and a current market value of $450 million. The money manager sells these bonds to the trust for a fee of 20 basis points ($900,000). In addition, the money manager charges an annual management fee of 50 basis points for managing the face value of the trust's assets: 50 basis points × $500 million = $2,500,000. Last, there is a fee for the trustee to oversee the indenture clauses of the CDO notes. This fee is $250,000.

In addition, the CDO trust buys a $50 million three-year U.S. Treasury note at an annual coupon of 5%. The Treasury note will be used to provide credit protection to tranche A and allow for an AA

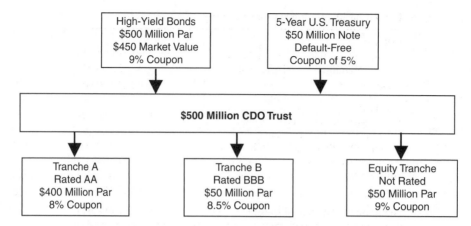

Exhibit 30.11 An arbitrage CDO structure

credit rating. The $50 million is the difference between the $500 million of notes sold by the CDO trust and the purchase price of the high-yield bonds of $450 million.

Tranche A has a $400 million face value and a coupon of 8%, and is rated AAA. This tranche gets the highest credit rating possible because it is partly principal protected by the three-year Treasury note and by the subordination of the other two tranches. However, the tranche A investors receive a higher coupon than U.S. Treasuries because they have a claim on a portion of the pass-through return earned from the high-yield bond portfolio.

The second tranche has a face value of $50 million and a stated coupon of 8.5%, and is rated BBB. This tranche has a higher rating than the underlying bonds because it has first-loss protection through the equity tranche. However, the first-loss protection covers only the first $50 million worth of defaulted bonds. After that, tranche B will lose dollar for dollar of defaulted bonds in the CDO collateral pool. Therefore, this tranche does not have the same principal protection as tranche A, and consequently receives a lower credit rating but has a higher coupon payment.

Tranche C is the equity tranche. It does not get paid until tranches A and B receive their payments. Consequently, this tranche bears all of the residual risk of the CDO trust, just as stockholders bear all of the residual risk in a corporation. This tranche has a face value of $50 million and a stated coupon of 9%, and is not rated. Effectively, this class has the same risk as the high-yield bonds in the collateral pool, or a BB credit rating.

Where does the trust get the money to pay for the money manager's annual fee of $2.5 million? It receives the money from the spread between the coupons collected from the CDO collateral pool of high-yield bonds and three-year Treasury note and the coupon payments it must pay out to the CDO note holders. Note that the stated coupon on each tranche is less than (or equal to) the average interest coupon on the high-yield bonds. The difference between the interest income earned on the high-yield bonds and that paid to the CDO security holders is spread income to the CDO trust. The trust uses this spread income to pay the management fee. Any residual income left over accrues to the tranche C security holders, which are the equity investors in the CDO trust.

It is often the case that the money manager will retain a portion of the equity in the CDO tranche. The manager purchases the equity tranche for two reasons. The first is to reap the excess spread income received from the CDO trust. The money manager can profit from the arbitrage it creates between the CDO collateral income and the coupon payments on the CDO notes. The second is to attract other investors who may not wish to bear the subordinated risk of the equity tranche.

Exhibit 30.12   Cash flows for an arbitrage CDO

Inflows	
9% on $500 million high-yield bonds	$45,000,000
5% on $50 million U.S. Treasury note	2,500,000
Total	**$47,500,000**
Outflows	
8% on $400 million tranche A notes	$32,000,000
8.5% on $50 million tranche B notes	4,250,000
9% on $50 million equity tranche	4,500,000
Annual management fee	2,500,000
Annual trustee fee	250,000
Total	**$43,500,000**
Net annual CDO trust income	**$ 4,000,000**

The spread income that can be earned in a CBO trust is demonstrated in Exhibit 30.12. Together, the Treasury note and the high-yield bonds generate $47,500,000 in annual income. The three CBO tranches and annual management and trustee fees, however, require only $43,500,000 of annual cash payments. The difference of $4,000,000 is the spread earned by selling CDO securities at a lower yield than earned by the high-yield bond portfolios. This residual income accrues to the equity tranche and results from the arbitrage between the receipt of income from the high-yield bonds and the payments required to the CDO note holders.

In summary, there are three ways to make a profit from an arbitrage CDO. First, the money manager can earn a transaction fee for selling its high-yield portfolio to the CDO trust. Second, the money manager, as an equity investor in the CDO trust, can earn the spread or arbitrage income from the CDO trust between the CDO collateral income and the payouts on the CDO notes. Last, the CDO sponsor usually is also the manager of the CDO trust and can earn management fees for its money management expertise.

CDO LIFE CYCLE

In most arbitrage CDOs there is a three-period life cycle. First, there is the ramp up period during which the CDO trust uses the proceeds from the CDO note sale to acquire the initial collateral pool. The CDOs trust documents will govern what type of assets may be purchased. The second phase is normally called the revolving period, during which the manager of the CDO trust actively manages the collateral pool for the CDO, buying and selling securities and reinvesting the excess cash flows received from the CDO collateral pool. The last phase is the amortization period. During this phase, the manager for the CDO stops reinvesting excess cash flows and begins to wind down the CDO by repaying the CDO debt securities. As the CDO collateral matures, the manager uses these proceeds to redeem the CDO's outstanding notes.

EXAMPLE OF A CDO STRUCTURE

As the previous discussion indicated, CDOs can come in all shapes and sizes. Frequently, these investment vehicles have several classes of securities outstanding and can invest in several different types of collateral. We provide an example of a recent CDO.

Exhibit 30.13   Highgate ABS CDO, Ltd.

Credit Tranche	Amount	Percent	Rating at Issuance	Rating at end of 2008
Class A-1 Notes	$601,200,000	80%	Aaa	Baa3
Class A-2 Notes	$71,918,000	9.57%	Aaa	B1
Class B Notes	$50,201,000	6.68%	Aa2	B3
Class C Notes	$9,018,000	1.20%	A2	C
Class D Notes	$8,642,000	1.15%	Baa2	C
Equity Tranche	$10,521,000	1.40%	no rating	no rating
Total	$751,500,000			

The Highgate ABS CDO, Ltd. is a CDO with a closing date of December 2005. Its sponsor and manager is Vanderbilt Capital Advisors, a registered investment adviser under the Investment Advisers Act of 1940 with more than $7 billion in fixed income assets under management.

The tranches of the CDO were sold by the Royal Bank of Canada Capital Markets and were rated by Moody's Investors Service. Exhibit 30.13 shows the structure of the credit tranches for the Highgate CDO. Class A-1 is the supersenior tranche, class A-2 is the senior tranche, class B is the senior mezzanine tranche, classes C and D are the mezzanine tranches, and last, the preference shares make up the equity tranche, which is not rated.

Underlying these CDO tranches is a pool of collateral that includes residential mortgage-backed securities, commercial mortgage-backed securities, notes from other CDO trusts, and synthetic securities. Exhibit 30.14 describes the underlying collateral of this pool. Exhibit 30.15 provides the weighted average rating for the CDO collateral. The weighted average collateral rating is often a covenant specified as part of the CDO trust indenture. This protects the CDO note holders by ensuring that the average rating of the underlying collateral does not fall below a certain credit rating.

Exhibit 30.15 shows that the average credit rating is Aa2. This is the same rating as the class B or senior mezzanine notes. Notice how the financial engineering of the CDO works in this example. Fully 80% of the notes issued by the Highgate CDO receive Moody's highest credit rating of Aaa even though the weighted average credit rating of the underlying collateral equals that of only the senior mezzanine tranche B notes. By repackaging credit risk, CDOs can neatly carve up the risk spectrum to provide investment opportunities at all levels of credit exposure. Unfortunately, with the meltdown in the real estate market, the Highgate ABS CDO has not fared very well. For example, in Exhibit 30.13, the most senior tranche, the Class A-1 notes, has been downgraded several notches by Moody's Investor Services from Aaa to Baa3, while the Class A-2 notes have fallen even further

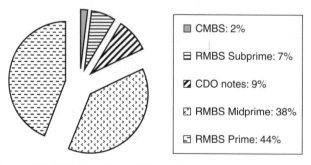

Exhibit 30.14   Highgate ABS CDO Underlying Collateral

Exhibit 30.15 Weighted average credit rating for the Highgate ABS CDO, Ltd.

Collateral Rating	Assign Credit Ranking	Percent of Collateral Pool	Weighted Average Rating
Aaa	1	34.02%	0.3402
Aa1	2	6.67	0.1334
Aa2	3	27.05	0.8115
Aa3	4	8.62	0.3448
A1	5	4.13	0.2065
A2	6	14.22	0.8532
A3	7	5.29	0.3703
Weighted Average Ranking			**3.0599**
Equals a Weighted Average Credit Rating			**Aa2**

from Aaa to B1: junk bond status. Further, as of the end of 2008, Moody's had every tranche of the Highgate ABS CDO on credit review for further downgrades. The credit ratings as of the end of 2008 are also presented in Exhibit 30.13. Using Exhibit 30.15, the current weighted average rating comes to B3.

CONCLUSION

This chapter was designed to introduce the reader to the basics of the collateralized debt obligation market. This is still a sizeable market, in spite of its collapse in 2008 in the midst of the global real estate and financial crisis.

Although commercial loans and high-yield bonds are the most popular form of assets for a CDO, just about any type of underlying asset can be used to collateralize a CDO trust. For instance, CDOs may now be backed by subprime mortgage-backed securities, credit card securities, emerging market debt, and other forms of assetbacked securities. In sum, the expanse of the CDO marketplace is limited only by the imagination of money managers, banks, and investment bankers to bundle new assets into trust structures. The limiting factor is getting the rating agencies to review and issue an investment-grade credit rating for the tranches of the CDO trust securities. To that end, the rating agencies must be able to develop a coherent method for analyzing the underlying collateral. Without investment-grade credit ratings, CDOs will not be able to sell their securities.

31

Risks and New Developments in CDOs

We finish our section on CDOs by discussing the many new products that this credit derivative structure has brought to the market. While the CDO structure was initially developed for collateralized loan obligations (CLOs) and collateralized debt obligations (CDOs), the creativity of the financial markets has taken this structure to new levels of complexity and ingenuity. We also finish our discussion of CDOs with a discussion of the risks. The credit crisis of 2007 to 2009 has demonstrated how fragile the CDO market and infrastructure really was. But first, we begin with new developments in CDOs.

NEW DEVELOPMENTS IN CDOs

There have been many new developments in the CDO marketplace such as extending the CDO structure to distressed debt, hedge funds, commodity exposure, private equity CDOs, single-tranche CDOs, unfunded CDO tranches, and even CDOs on top of CDOs. We take a brief look at all of these newfangled CDO ideas. In our discussion of distressed debt investing in Chapter 26, we noted how default rates have increased in the United States during the time period 2000–2001 and again in 2008. This increase in default rates has led to an increased interest in distressed debt-backed CDOs.

A second new development has been the extension of CDOs to hedge funds. This comes as a result of the tremendous amount of capital pouring into the hedge fund market. CDOs have also been applied to private equity investments. These three relatively new developments demonstrate how barriers were broken between different segments of the alternative investment market. Indeed, CDOs are now used in commodity swaps.

Distressed Debt CDOs

A recent development in the CDO market is a **distressed debt CDO**. As its name implies, the primary collateral component is distressed debt. Distressed debt includes both securities for which the issuer is in default of the bond payments, and non-defaulted securities that trade in distressed ranges in anticipation of a future default by the issuing entity. Distressed debt securities are generally defined as those loans or subordinated debt that trade at a yield that is at least 10% greater than the U.S. Treasury rate or are in some sort of distress such as default, bankruptcy, or cash flow crisis. In our introductory chapter on credit derivatives, we referred to the group of credit-risky assets as "spread products." Distressed debt may be referred to as "big spread products."

Distressed debt CDOs usually have a combination of defaulted securities, distressed but unimpaired securities, and non-distressed securities. The CDO manager will use historical default rates and estimated recovery amounts, as well as the timing of default and recovery for valuing both distressed assets and non-distressed assets. In addition, for securities already in default, the CDO manager may use simulation models to determine how historical recovery patterns may change in times of additional market stress or lack of liquidity.

The appeal of the CDO structure is the ability to provide a series of tranches of collateralized securities that can have an investment-grade credit rating even though the underlying collateral in the CDO is mostly distressed debt. Investors are then able to sample the distressed debt market more effectively by choosing a distressed debt CDO tranche that matches their level of risk aversion. The CDO securities can receive a higher investment rating than the underlying distressed collateral through one or several of the credit enhancements described in the preceding chapter.

To date, the main suppliers of assets for distressed debt CDOs have been banks. Banks use these CDOs to manage the credit exposure on their balance sheets. Assets for a CDO are purchased at market value. When a bank sells a distressed loan or bond to a distressed debt CDO, it will usually receive a loss because it issued the loan or purchased the bond at par value. It was after the issuance of the loan or bond purchase that the asset became distressed, resulting in a decline in market value.

Still, banks are willing to provide the collateral to distressed debt CDOs for several reasons. First, it stops the deterioration of value on the bank's balance sheet. Any further decline in value of the distressed loan will be at the expense of the CDO and the holders of the CDO's equity tranches. Second, by removing distressed loans from its balance sheet, the bank reduces its nonperforming asset ratio. This allows it to obtain regulatory capital relief from its relevant banking authority, and this regulatory capital can be used for other bank business.[1]

Consider the Patriarch Partners distressed loan CDO. In January 2001, Patriarch purchased a portfolio of $1.35 billion of troubled loans from FleetBoston Financial Corporation representing about 10% of FleetBoston's troubled loan portfolio. The purchase price was $1 billion, a 26% discount from the face value of the loans. The trust collateral consisted of 188 commercial loans from 91 borrowers.[2]

To finance the purchase of the loans, Patriarch Partners sold $925 million in AAA-rated bonds and $75 million of A-rated bonds. To receive an investment-grade credit rating for its CDO bonds, Patriarch had to establish a credit enhancement. It established a large reserve account of about $275 million. Patriarch was able to establish this reserve account because of the $1 billion it paid to FleetBoston; $725 million was in cash and $275 million was in the form of a zero coupon note. Therefore, Patriarch had $275 million from the sale of the trust securities that it could allocate to the reserve account. This CDO structure is presented in Exhibit 31.1.

From Patriarch's perspective, if it could successfully collect on all of the troubled loans, it stood to collect considerable income from the excess spread between the loan collateral and the interest paid on the trust securities. For instance, the AAA-rated CDO tranche was priced at an interest rate of about LIBOR plus 50 basis points, considerably less than that received from the commercial loans.

From FleetBoston's perspective, it could sell the loans without taking a complete write-off. In addition, FleetBoston was able to reduce its loan-loss reserves by $75 million by removing the troubled loans from its balance sheet. FleetBoston could also profit because the value of the $275 million zero coupon bonds was tied to the amount collected from the troubled loans.[3]

Hedge Fund CDOs

In May 2002, the first two collateralized fund obligation (CFO) structures came to the market. One was a $550 million CFO structure offered by Man Group Plc. The second was a $250 offering for the Diversified Strategies CFO. This offering was brought to the market by Investcorp Management Services Ltd. of Bahrain. It contained several tranches of both dollar- and euro-denominated floating

---

[1] The amount of regulatory capital that banks are required to maintain is determined by the Basel Committee on Banking Regulations and Supervisory Practices, which established global regulatory capital standards for industrialized nations. See Mark Anson, *Credit Derivatives* (New Hope, PA: Frank J. Fabozzi Associates, 1999).

[2] See Mark Pittman, "Patriarch Purchase of Fleet Loans a Bet on Collecting on Bad Debts," *Bloomberg News*, January 11, 2001.

[3] See Pittman, "Patriarch Purchase of Fleet Loans."

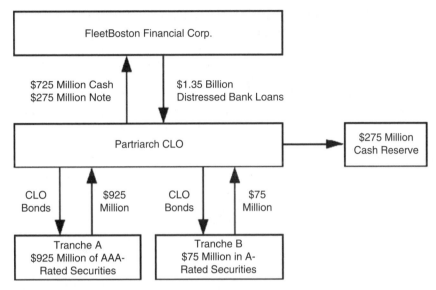

Exhibit 31.1 Patriarch CLO trust of distressed bank loans

rate notes that were rated investment grade by Standard & Poor's. Exhibit 31.2 displays the Diversified Strategies CFO. Five tranches of structured notes were issued, each with five-year bullet maturities. The first four tranches had semiannual interest payments tied to LIBOR.[4]

The equity tranche received a maximum annual coupon of 5% contingent upon the performance of the portfolio of hedge funds.[5] The equity tranche also received any residual appreciated value associated with the DSF II fund of funds. The CFO notes were issued by the Diversified Strategies CFO, a *société anonyme* incorporated in Luxembourg. Diversified Strategies took the cash flow received from the sale of the CFO bonds and invested the proceeds in redeemable shares issued by Diversified Strategies Fund II, a hedge fund of funds (HFOF). In turn, DSF II invested the proceeds received from the sale of its shares in individual hedge funds and separately managed accounts. The redeemable shares in DSF II formed the primary collateral for the Diversified Strategies CFO. JPMorgan Chase served as trustee to the Diversified Strategies CFO, while Investcorp Management Services was the adviser to DSF II.[6]

As trustee, JPMorgan Chase was responsible for notifying Investcorp Management Services when the next coupon payment would be due on the CFO bonds and when the trustee would redeem its shares in DSF II. Investcorp Management Services must then give notices to the individual hedge

---

[4] To protect itself against unusually high floating rates, the Diversified Strategies CFO was required to enter into an interest rate cap agreement to hedge this risk.

[5] The equity tranche received its contingent payment only after the performance of the hedge fund portfolio had appreciated such that the NAV of the portfolio was 150% of the outstanding principal balance of the senior CFO bonds.

[6] Investcorp Management Services also served as the collateral manager to the Diversified Strategies CFO to the extent this SPV held cash or short-term notes in addition to the redeemable shares issued by the DSF II fund. The equity tranche of the CFO structure comprised 26.5% of the capital structure of the SPV. The equity tranche was considered overcollateralized in that this tranche provided subordination to classes A through C-2 of the CFO bonds. Stated more simply, the equity tranche was used as the first-loss tranche. Should the hedge fund of funds decline in net asset value, this tranche would serve as the buffer to protect the senior CFO bond tranches. The rating methodology used by Standard & Poor's took into account the long-term return expectations of the fund of funds as well as the probability of realizing an adequate level of return to meet the debt service requirement of the CFO bonds.

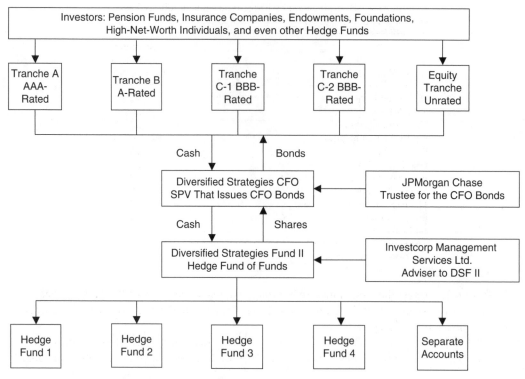

Exhibit 31.2 Structure of the Diversified Strategies CFO

fund managers or the separate accounts so as to have sufficient cash to redeem the shares put to DSF II by the trustee.

Exhibit 31.3 shows the tranche structure for the Diversified Strategies CFO. The weighted average cost of tranches A through C-2 was 105 basis points (bps) over LIBOR. The equity tranche received a contingent coupon and whatever residual return was accrued after the first four tranches received their payments. One reason why the first four tranches were able to obtain an investment-grade rating was because of the large equity contribution.[7]

Exhibit 31.3 Tranche Structure for Diversified Strategies CFO

Tranche	Rating (S&P)	Amount (millions)	Interest Rate
A	AAA	$125	LIBOR + 60 bps
B	A	$32.50	LIBOR + 160 bps
C-1	BBB	€10	LIBOR + 250 bps
C-2	BBB	€16.20	LIBOR + 250 bps
Equity	Unrated	$66.30	5%

Source: Standard & Poor's.

---

[7] See Standard & Poor's, "Resale: Diversified Strategies CFO S.A.," April 4, 2002.

Exhibit 31.4 Diversification by hedge fund strategy followed by
Diversified Strategies CFO

Hedge Fund Strategy	Maximum Allocation by % of NAV
Distressed Debt	12%
Risk Arbitrage	30
Convertible Arbitrage	30
Equity Market Neutral	30
Relative Value	20
U.S. Equity Long/Short	20
International Equity Long/Short	20
Macro Discretionary	15
Macro Systematic	15
Portfolio Insurance	15
Multistrategy	15

Source: Standard & Poor's.

S&P was able to rate the CFO transaction through simulation analysis of the expected net asset value of the hedge fund of funds investments and by using hedge fund indices as proxies for expected returns by hedge fund strategy.[8]

In order to increase the probability of meeting the projected returns needed to redeem the CFO bonds, the hedge fund of funds was subject to a number of diversification requirements, including:[9]

- The number of hedge fund managers in the fund of funds.
- The concentration with any one hedge fund manager.
- The concentration within any one hedge fund strategy.
- A minimum number of hedge fund strategies.
- Liquidation and redemption rules for the hedge fund managers.

Exhibit 31.4 sets the maximum allocation followed by Diversified Strategies CFO by percentage of nest asset value (NAV) and by hedge fund strategy. As this exhibit indicates, the DSF II fund was well diversified across 11 hedge fund strategies. This diversification was an important benefit that we will discuss further. Exhibit 31.5 sets the diversification by investment vehicle. The allocation and diversification requirements were reviewed at the end of each month.

In addition to diversification and allocation requirements, the Diversified Strategies CFO also had to meet certain liquidity requirements. The hedge fund of funds must maintain at least 20% of its total assets in separately managed accounts at all times. Separate accounts are much easier to liquidate than investments in hedge funds because most hedge funds allow liquidations only at appointed times (such as quarterly or semiannually), while a separately managed account can be liquidated at any time. If the 20% liquidity threshold was breached, then Investcorp would be required to immediately liquidate sufficient investments from the separate accounts and convert them to cash or cashlike instruments that would mature before the next coupon payment on the CFO bonds.

Last, to protect the senior tranches of the CFO bonds, an event of default was set at the point where the NAV of the fund of funds portfolio would fall below the total principal amount of the outstanding

---

[8] See Standard & Poor's, "Ratings Assigned to Diversified Strategies CFO's Notes in Structured Hedge Fund of Funds Deal," June 28, 2002.

[9] See Standard & Poor's, "Resale."

Exhibit 31.5 Diversification by investment vehicle followed by Diversified Strategies CFO

Category of Diversification	Limit
Minimum number of investment vehicles	25
Minimum number of managers	20
Single investment vehicle limit	9%
Single manager limit	12%
Maximum number of vehicles with an allocation greater than 6%	8
10 Largest investment vehicles as a % of NAV	50%
Minimum % of assets in managed accounts	20%

senior (rated) CFO bonds. At this point, the first-loss capital associated with the equity tranche would be exhausted. If such an event occurred, the trustee would liquidate the entire collateral (it would put its redeemable shares back to the DSF II fund of funds) and would use the proceeds to pay the principal on the senior notes.

A key benefit of CFOs is that they are constructed of assets that are different from the traditional CDO model. For example, hedge funds, high-yield bonds, and bank loans are the three primary collateral classes that form CFOs, CBOs, and CLOs, respectively. In Exhibit 31.6 we measure the correlation between hedge funds of funds (HFOFs), high-yield bonds, and bank loans over the past 10 years. We can see that HFOFs have a low correlation with bank loans of 0.35 and with high-yield bonds of 0.43. Therefore, CFO structures have the potential to offer diversification with respect to traditional CDO structures.

Collateralized commodity obligations

In early 2005, Barclays Capital launched the first **collateralized commodity obligation (CCO)**. The product was rated by Standard & Poor's and is structured similarly to a synthetic arbitrage CDO. The key difference is that instead of referencing a pool of credit-risky assets via a swap, the underlying assets of the CCO are commodity trigger swaps (CTSs). CTSs are similar to CDSs in that there are trigger events that require a payment by one swap holder to another. These trigger events are based on underlying commodity buckets hitting different price hurdles.

The Barclays CCO references a diversified pool of CTSs, including precious metals, base metals, and energy commodities. The payment of the CCO note principal and coupons is dependent on a short averaging period immediately prior to the five-year maturing of the CCO. In addition, Barclays had to apply certain portfolio construction rules regarding the CTSs and the commodities that they referenced in order to obtain an investment-grade credit rating for its senior tranches of the CCO. These construction rules are presented in Exhibit 31.7.

Exhibit 31.6 Correlation matrix of returns

	HFOF	Lev. Loans	High-Yield
HFOF	1.00		
Lev. Loans	0.35	1.00	
High-Yield	0.43	0.65	1.00

Source: Bloomberg.

Exhibit 31.7   Barclays' collateralized commodity obligation

Portfolio Construction Rules to Earn an Investment-Grade Credit Rating

1. Loss profiles of CTSs are determined by using historical observations.
2. A diversified basket of 16 commodities, including industrial metals, precious metals, and energy commodities. Agriculture and livestock may be added to the CTS at a later date.
3. Commodities cannot be included in the CTS basket if their one-year moving average is greater than 150% of their 5-year moving average. This reduces the likelihood of selling protection against commodity price spikes.
4. Each price trigger must differ by at least 5% from triggers in the same commodity. This reduces the chances of multiple triggers occurring at the same time in one commodity.

The trigger events in the CTSs cut both ways. If commodity prices have increased over the five-year period of the CCO, the CCO note holders will be rewarded and the trigger events will be positive. However, if commodity prices have declined, the CCO note holders will receive less than par value on their notes. Exhibit 31.8 demonstrates the new CCO.

Private equity CDOs

Another intersection in the alternative investment marketplace is that of CDOs and private equity. In July 2001, JP Morgan Partners and Prime Edge sponsored a new CDO trust that raised €150 million (about $128 million at that time) by selling CDO securities that are collateralized by investments in private equity funds.[10] Furthermore, Standard & Poor's issued an investment-grade credit rating for the CDO securities in what was the first stand-alone credit rating for a private equity vehicle.

The €150 million was invested in a diversified pool of 35 preapproved European private equity fund managers. The CDO trust issued three tranches of securities. Tranche A carried an AA rating (with an insurance guarantee from Allianz Risk Transfer), had a term of 12 years, and raised €72 million. Tranche B was rated BBB, also had a term of 12 years, and raised €33 million. The equity or subordinated tranche of €45 million was unrated.

Single-tranche CDOs

Single-tranche CDOs provide a very targeted structure of credit risk exposure. In a **single-tranche CDO**, the sponsor sells only one tranche from the capital structure of a CDO. Consider the Highgate ABS CDO presented in Exhibit 30.13 of the prior chapter. This CDO has six tranches of issued securities.

In a single-tranche CDO, the sponsor could sell just one of these tranches and potentially keep the rest for its balance sheet. A single-tranche CDO uses a CDS just like a normal synthetic CDO. The main difference is that in a single-tranche CDO, only a specific slice of the portfolio risk is transferred to the investors, rather than the entire portfolio risk.

Single-tranche CDOs allow for even more customization for an investor, such as collateral composition, maturity of the single-tranche note, weighted average credit rating, and so on. As a result, single-tranche CDOs are the most finely tuned of any structure. For this reason, single-tranche CDOs are sometimes referred to as "bespoke CDOs" or "CDOs on demand."

---

[10] See Dan Primack, "Prime Edge and JP Morgan Partners Put Private Equity into Debt," *Private Equity Week*, June 11, 2001.

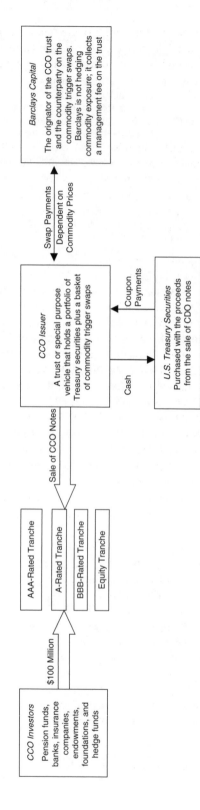

Exhibit 31.8 Barclays' synthetic arbitrage CCO with a commodity trigger swap

There are two main advantages to an investor from a single-tranche CDO. The first has already been alluded to: investors have considerably more control over the terms of a single-tranche CDO than the typical multitranche CDO. Second, there is no waterfall in a single-tranche CDO. All cash flows flow to the investor.

CDO-squareds

Some CDOs invest in the notes and tranches of other CDO structures. CDO structures that invest primarily in the notes and equity tranches from other CDOs are called **CDO-squareds** and are often referred to by the mathematical expression *CDO* to the second power. Similar to traditional CDOs, a CDO-squared can be either cash backed or synthetically constructed. A cash CDO-squared is a CDO backed by a collateral portfolio that consists of tranches of existing cash CDOs. A synthetic CDO-squared consists of a portfolio of credit default swaps that reference specific tranches of other CDOs.

Exhibit 31.9 displays the basic structure of a CDO-squared. A master trust is created that invests in the different tranches of other CDO trusts, called the secondary CDOs. Notice in Exhibit 31.9 that the master CDO can invest across the spectrum of tranches in the secondary CDOs. It may purchase the most creditworthy tranches of a CDO or the equity tranche. Some CDO-squared trusts specialize in purchasing the equity tranches of other CDOs, while some squared transactions concentrate on purchasing only the higher credit rated tranches of CDOs. The master CDO in turn issues its own securities with a similar tranche structure to attract investors.

Notice that at the bottom of Exhibit 31.9 we show that the secondary CDOs can invest in a collective pool of securities in the marketplace. This is important because the secondary CDO portfolios often include some of the same underlying securities. This overlap creates problems of credit concentration for the master CDO.

Exhibit 31.10 shows a hypothetical example of how many overlapping credits can creep into a CDO-squared transaction. We assume that CDOs A through D each invest in 100 underlying credit-risky securities. The greater the overlap of credits, the more fat-tailed the distribution of returns will be for the CDO-squared. This is because overlapping securities will increase the default correlations to the master CDO. In fact, it is the same thing as having two referenced credits with 100% default correlation. This increases the risk of outlier events to the master CDO, fattening up the tails of the return distribution.

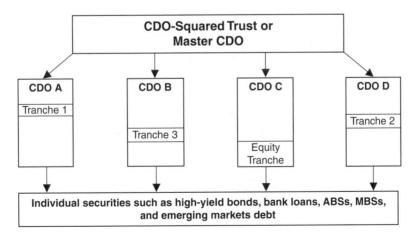

Exhibit 31.9   CDO-squared structure

Exhibit 31.10   Example of overlapping credits

	CDO A	CDO B	CDO C	CDO D
CDO A	100	10	5	0
CDO B	10	100	7	0
CDO C	5	7	100	5
CDO D	0	0	5	100

Hypothetical example.

There are two key rationales for CDO-squared transactions. First, a typical CDO will include 50 to 100 corporate and ABS credits in its portfolio. A typical CDO-squared transaction will invest in the tranches of 4 to 10 secondary CDOs, greatly amplifying the diversification properties of CDO investing. Second, CDO-squared transactions can provide higher spread returns to their investors, particularly if they invest in the lower-rated and equity tranches of the secondary CDOs.

One of the key differences in a master CDO compared to a normal CDO is that where defaults occur is more important than how many defaults occur. Consider the situation that CDOs A, B, C, and D all experience one default each in their underlying portfolios. These defaults will create losses to each of the equity tranches of CDOs A through D. Investors in CDOs A through D will all experience losses because the number of defaults impacts those portfolios. However, for the master CDO, only the default in CDO C (where the master CDO invests in the equity tranche) will create a loss for the CDO-squared investors. Again, the takeaway point is that where losses occur needs to be determined before a conclusion can be made as to whether the loss in a secondary CDO will impact the value of the master CDO. This is a demonstration of the additional diversification that CDO-squared trusts can provide for their investors.

RISKS OF CDOs

There are considerable risks associated with CDO trusts. The meltdown in the subprime mortgage market spilled over into the CDO marketplace with a vengeance. By the end of 2008, large financial institutions such as Citigroup, UBS, Merrill Lynch, and others had written down more than $160 billion of CDOs linked to the mortgage market. All told, a recent article estimates that subprime and CDO bank losses may exceed $285 billion by the time the credit crisis of 2007–2009 runs its course.[11]

In this section we review the major risks associated with CDOs. These are complicated instruments, and the risks are not always apparent. Last, we complete this section with a case study which illustrates what can go wrong.

Default risk of the underlying collateral

Default risk is the single greatest risk associated with an investment in a CDO structure. The lower down the totem pole of tranches the investor acquires, the greater the risk. It is important to note that a CDO structure cannot change the credit risk of the underlying portfolio. The securities acquired by the CDO portfolio do not have their default risks reduced. Instead, the risk of default is shifted between the different tranche holders of the CDO.

---

[11] See Jody Shenn, "S&P Says End in Sight for Writedowns on Subprime Debt," Bloomberg Finance, L.P., March 13, 2008.

One example of the risks associated with CDOs is provided by the American Express Company.[12] As a result of its investments in CDOs, it was forced to take a more than $1 billion pretax charge for losses associated with these investments. The investments were made by the company's money management unit, American Express Financial Advisors (AEFA). In the late 1990s, AEFA decided to increase the high-yield bond portion of its portfolio to 12% of a pool of assets it managed for the parent company, and to include CDO investments in its high-yield bond portfolio. AEFA purchased CDO securities in about 60 different trusts, and in some cases, bought the lower-rated or equity tranches of the CDO.[13]

Unfortunately, with high-yield default rates increasing significantly from prior years, the riskier tranches of CDO structures began to default, resulting in large losses. American Express initially reported a loss from these investments of $182 million in April 2001. In July, the company announced an additional $826 million charge from its investments in CDOs. Of this amount, $403 million was due to problems related to the investment-grade tranches of CDOs it owned, and the remainder was from losses and planned sales of high-yield bonds and lower-grade CDO tranches.[14]

The experience of American Express also illustrates another risk with CDO investing. Investors all too often rely on the reports generated by the CDO manager to determine the value of the collateral in the CDO. To its credit, once the problem came to light, American Express performed its own analysis of the credit risk associated with the CDO collateral. In its analysis, American Express used an estimate that default rates would continue in the 8% to 9% range and stay constant for the next 18 months. This assumption led to the significant charges associated with its CDO portfolio. These estimates were more conservative than the more optimistic estimates generated by the CDO managers. Also, American Express analyzed the credit risk associated with about 8,500 bonds underlying the CDO trusts in which it had invested.[15]

The lesson is that in times of stress, CDO managers may be slower or reluctant to write down or write off the investments contained in the CDO trust. The investor may need to perform its own analysis to determine the extent of the damage.

Another example of CDO default risk is the example of Calpine Corporation. Calpine is the second largest energy producer in California. In December 2005 its credit rating was cut by Moody's to Caa—low-rated junk status. Only a few short weeks later, Calpine declared bankruptcy.

At the time of its bankruptcy, Calpine had $17 billion of debt outstanding. More than half of this debt was contained in CDO trusts. Moody's Investors Service identified 467 CDOs that had Calpine debt in their CDO trusts. The proportion of affected portfolios ranged from 0.2% to a whopping 23%, with a median exposure of 1.4%. Clearly, with more than 400 CDO trusts having exposure to Calpine, its bankruptcy will have a significant impact on the value of CDO notes held by investors. Even with a median exposure of 1.4%, this is a sufficient default risk to have a material impact on the return to the equity tranche of a CDO.

Financial engineering risk

As the American Express example demonstrates, the valuation of CDO tranches can be a very tricky game. Indeed, the $1 billion loss of American Express pales by comparison to the approximately

---

[12] See Paul Beckett, Mitchell Pacelle, and Tom Lauricella, "How American Express Got in Over Its Head with Risky Securities," *Wall Street Journal*, July 27, 2001, A1.

[13] Ibid.

[14] Ibid.

[15] Ibid.

$200 billion in CDO write-downs suffered by major banks as a result of the subprime mortgage crisis. But how did this all go so wrong? Unfortunately, some amount must be attributed to the financial engineering associated with the subprime CDO market. We simply got too smart for ourselves.

Let's start at the beginning. At the heart of the subprime debacle is a mortgage loan to a less than prime grade borrower. Small banks and mortgage lenders made these loans and then sold them in pools to larger financial institutions, primarily Fannie Mae and Freddie Mac. Fannie and Freddie then took these subprime mortgage pools and issued mortgage-backed securities (MBSs), essentially bonds backed by the underlying pool of subprime mortgages. Large investment banks purchased these MBSs and repackaged them yet again into a second pool, a CDO trust. The CDOs then issued a second round of securities backed by the underlying pool of subprime MBSs. Finally, the CDO securities were sliced and diced to offer different risk slices of the subprime MBSs, which were then sold to the clients of the investment banks: hedge funds, high-net-worth individuals, and large institutional investors.

Exhibit 31.11 demonstrates how financial engineering transformed subprime mortgages into reputably suitable investments for hedge funds and other institutional investors. However, you can see that this house of cards quickly got stacked very high based on a weak foundation of shaky subprime mortgages. When the underlying subprime mortgages began to default at much faster rates than previously experienced, the whole financial structured collapsed, bringing down Fannie Mae, Freddie Mac, and the CEOs of most of the Wall Street investment banks.

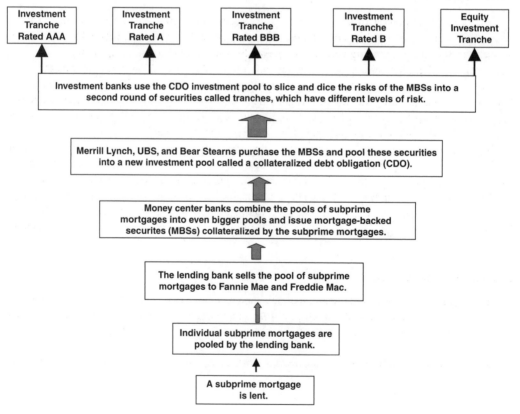

Exhibit 31.11   Transformation of Subprime Mortgages

Downgrade risk

Downgrade risk refers to a reduction in credit rating of the CDO trust securities themselves (and not the underlying collateral). Prior to 2001, no AAA-rated CDO tranche had ever been downgraded. However, with the general slowdown of the U.S. economy and the increase in default rates, downgrades were inevitable. In July 2001, Standard & Poor's (S&P) downgraded six AAA-rated CDO tranches because of losses associated with the underlying trust collateral. While a credit downgrade does not provide an edict of default, it does reduce the value of the CDO tranches. This is most important for market value CDOs. We demonstrated in the prior chapter that in a **market value CDO**, declines in value of the securities in the CDO portfolio can rapidly and dramatically reduce the value of a CDO's tranches.

Now, S&P credit rating transitions for CDOs both up and down are common. For example, in 2005, S&P upgraded the credit rating for 125 CDO tranches while it downgraded 102. Moody's upgraded 49 CDO tranches while downgrading 89. World gross domestic product (GDP) growth was strong in 2005, and consequently the numbers of CDO upgrades and downgrades were fairly well balanced.[16] However, this balance changed dramatically in 2007 and 2008 with the subprime mortgage crisis. For example, in April 2008, Standard & Poor's put 331 classes of 79 CDOs on negative credit watch, affecting adversely the value of over $50 billion of CDO tranches.[17] Even more dramatic, in the first quarter of 2008, rating agencies collectively announced downgrades on the ratings for 4,485 tranches of CDOs.

CDO default rates

The three-year bear market from 2000 to 2002, the recession of 2001 and 2002, and the corporate accounting scandals of 2002 all contributed to rocky times in the credit markets. CDOs did not go unscathed. But this was nothing compared to what 2007 and 2008 brought to the party.

While CDO default rates increased dramatically during 2007 and 2008, nowhere was this more keenly observed than in CDOs backed by subprime mortgages. Standard & Poor's predicted massive losses on CDOs continuing into 2009. Through the first half of 2008, CDO downgrades attributed to subprime securities had reached $351 billion over the prior 12-month period. Over this time period more than 4,000 CDO tranches had been downgraded or entered default.[18]

Furthermore, S&P estimated that recovery rates once a CDO tranche becomes impaired would decline significantly. S&P estimates that impaired CDO tranches rated below A and backed by subprime mortgages will experience a 100% loss of value (i.e. no recovery whatsoever). Further, S&P estimates that even AAA-rated CDO tranches backed by subprime mortgages that become impaired will experience only a 60% recovery value. These lower recovery rates will mean that a larger cushion is needed against potential losses than previously used to establish an investment-grade rating.

Differences in periodicity

It may be that the frequency with which payments are received on the underlying collateral does not coincide with the frequency with which payments must be made on the CDO securities. This risk can be compounded when payments on different assets are received with different frequencies.

---

[16] See Brian McManus, "Year-End Surveillance Review for 2005 and Outlook for 2006," Wachovia Securities, December 19, 2005.

[17] See "Ratings on 331 Classes from 79 US CDOs of ABS Put on Watch Negative; $50.9 Billion in Issuance Affected," Standard & Poor's Ratings Direct, April 16, 2008.

[18] "Standard and Poor's Predicts Massive CDO Losses," Page Perry LLC, April 29, 2008.

For instance, consider a CDO collateralized by both high-yield bonds and commercial loans. High-yield bonds pay interest semiannually while commercial loans typically pay interest quarterly. If the trust's assets (the underlying bond and loan collateral) pay interest more frequently than the trust securities, then the transaction may be subject to negative carry (the trust has to hold the interest payments received from the collateral securities in low-interest-bearing accounts and wait for the payment date on its securities). Alternatively, if the trust assets pay interest less frequently than the securities issued by the trust, the trust may be faced with an interest deficiency (the trust must find some way to fund the interest payments due on its securities).

This problem is often solved through the use of a swap agreement with an outside party, where the trust swaps the payments on the underlying collateral in return for interest payments that are synchronized with those of the trust securities.

Difference in payment dates

A risk due to the difference in payment dates arises from a mismatch between the dates on which payments are received on the underlying trust collateral, and the dates on which the trust securities must be paid. For example, consider a CBO trust whose underlying collateral consists entirely of high-yield bonds that pay semiannual interest each January and July. Unfortunately, the CDO trust securities pay semiannual interest in March and October. Similar to the problem of periodicity, this mismatch can be cured in a swap with an outside counterparty.

Basis risk

Basis risk occurs when the index used for the determination of interest earned on the CDO trust collateral is different from the index used to calculate the interest to be paid on the CDO trust securities. For instance, the interest paid on most bank loans is calculated on LIBOR plus a spread, but other assets may be based on a certificate of deposit rate in the United States. The combination of these assets in a single CDO trust will result in different bases being used to determine the interest payments on the CDO trust securities. One way to counter this problem is to issue one or more tranches with a fixed interest rate. This way the underlying index will not affect the required payments to the CDO securities. However, this may lead to spread compression risk.

Spread compression

Spread compression risk arises when credit spreads decline or compress over time, reducing interest rate receipts from the underlying collateral. Arbitrage CDOs based on high-yield bonds and commercial loans are susceptible to this risk.

For example, suppose a CDO trust is based on a portfolio of leveraged loans earning LIBOR plus 200. The trust issues securities that, in the aggregate, pay an average of LIBOR plus 100 bps. Over the life of the trust, some of the commercial loans mature and must be replaced with new collateral for the CDO trust. However, in the interim, let us also suppose that credit spreads have declined so that the same credit quality loan is now priced at LIBOR plus 100 bps. The CDO trust has now lost its arbitrage, and further, there is no excess spread to cushion any defaults that may occur with the new loans.

Yield curve risk

Any CDO trust portfolios with assets across a spectrum of maturity ranges will be impacted by changes in the yield curve represented by shifts in the curve, its shape, and its steepness.

For example, falling interest rates may result in a reduction of the positive spread between the CDO trust assets and its securities. This will have the same or a similar impact as the spread compression just described if the trust securities have a fixed coupon rate instead of a floating coupon rate. In addition, high-yielding collateral may be called away in the case of high-yield bonds or prepaid in the case of commercial loans and replaced with lower-yielding collateral. This will erode the arbitrage of the CDO trust.

The slope of the yield curve will also impact the profitability of an arbitrage CDO. For example, throughout most of the 1990s, the U.S. yield curve was upward sloping. Consequently, there has been a negative carry between holding cash reserve accounts and the higher interest that must be paid on long-term CDO trust securities.

WARF versus WAS

Every CDO active manager must balance the **weighted average rating factor (WARF)** of the underlying collateral pool with the **weighted average spread (WAS)** over LIBOR. The WARF measures the average credit rating of the underlying collateral contained in the CDO trust. All CDO indentures contain covenants as to the average credit rating of the collateral pool. The flip side is that CDO indentures often have a weighted average spread over LIBOR that they are required to maintain. So there is a trade-off: The CDO active manager can increase the WARF to get more yield, or increase the creditworthiness of the CDO collateral pool (lower the level of WARF), only at the expense of yield.[19]

For example, during 2005 with a reasonably strong U.S. economy, credit spreads remained low and leveraged loan prices experienced price compression as credit spreads were reduced. As a result, many active CDO managers began to look at second lien loans as a way to boost the WAS over LIBOR. Unfortunately, second lien loans are subprime loans and can dramatically reduce the WARF. In fact, most of the second lien loans issued in 2005 were rated B– or lower, low even on the junk debt scale.

Notice that this can lead to competing incentives among the tranche classes of the CDO. For example, for the supersenior and senior classes, their yields are driven strictly by maintaining collateral of good credit quality so that they do not experience any credit losses on their notes. However, for the equity tranche, there might be an incentive to lower the WARF and raise the WAS because any extra or arbitrage income spread accrues to the equity tranche. Bottom line: For higher-rated tranches of a CDO, be wary of the CDO manager lowering the WARF to raise the WAS.

A CASE STUDY OF CDO RISK

One of the hardest hit by the CDO meltdown is the venerable Wall Street banking firm Merrill Lynch. The *Financial Times* of London conducted an analysis of Merrill's CDO losses and concluded that this amounted to 25% of Merrill's total profits earned since it went public in 1971.[20] In its analysis, adjusting for inflation, the *Financial Times* concluded that the $14 billion in after-tax losses recorded by Merrill for the third quarter of 2007 through the second quarter of 2008 equaled 25% of Merrill's inflation-adjusted profits from 1971 through 2006 of $56 billion. One can but wonder: How did all of this happen?

---

[19] Under the convention of the rating agencies, a lower WARF indicates a high credit rating.

[20] See Francesco Guerrera, "Merrill's Recent Losses Calculated at 25% of Profits over 36 Years," *Financial Times*, August 29, 2008, 1.

The story of Merrill's CDO meltdown was documented in a *Fortune* magazine story.[21] The story of its losses stems from a switch in strategy by the bank from conducting a transaction fee business with respect to CDOs to being an investor in CDO tranches. In effect, Merrill was "drinking the Kool-Aid."

Merrill wasn't alone in this change in strategy, but it serves as a good example of what went wrong at many Wall Street, London, and Zurich banks. In the past, Merrill typically did not operate or invest in any CDOs. Instead, it acted as a sort of intermediary to help set up CDOs for its clients, collect a transaction fee, and then exit the party.

In a standard arrangement, a CDO money manager would approach Merrill and ask for financing for a CDO portfolio that would hold, let's say, $1 billion of mortgage-backed securities. Firms such as Pimco, Cohen & Company, and Trust Company of the West could be clients of Merrill for this purpose. Merrill would supply the financing to get the CDO portfolio started; then the CDO issued securities of its own in several tranches and used the proceeds of the CDO securities to pay back the loan from Merrill. For its trouble, Merrill would collect a transaction fee, usually in the range of 1.5% to 2%. On a billion-dollar CDO, this could be $15 million to $20 million of fees paid to Merrill.

Not only would Merrill supply the financing for the CDO, but Merrill's structured finance team also helped to determine how the underlying MBS securities should be repackaged as CDO tranches, while Merrill's sales force helped to sell the different tranches of CDO securities to Merrill customers such as pension funds, hedge funds, and high-net-worth investors.

So far, so good. Conducting this type of business posed little risk to Merrill. Merrill did not hold any of the tranches supported by the MBS collateral, and collected fees for fund-raising, deal structuring, and selling the CDO tranches. Essentially, Merrill treated the CDO market as a client business (provide help, assistance, financing) for a fee, of course, but it did not become an investor in the CDO. Merrill's job was to set up the CDO, sell the risks to someone else, collect a fee, and move on to the next deal.

Merrill became a very large player in helping to construct CDOs. It went from being a small player in mortgage-related CDOs in 2003 to being the leader in underwritings in 2004 to 2006.

By 2006, the U.S. housing market was beginning to slow down. Yet subprime mortgage rates remained low. The reason was that Merrill and other players in the CDO/MBS market needed to buy subprime securities to feed their CDO client business. This kept subprime MBSs at low return rates, when yields should have been rising. With yields on subprime MBSs remaining low well into 2007, the yields on CDO bonds also began to fall. Investors began to reject the investment-grade tranches of CDOs because the yields were too low. They fell to 20 to 50 basis points over LIBOR. This had the potential of wiping out a lucrative market for Merrill.

Merrill faced a tough decision: it could turn off the CDO pump and the fees that went with the business, or it could step in and now purchase the senior tranches of the CDO/MBS products to keep its CDO client business running. Merrill decided on the latter course and began to buy large amounts of the AAA-rated tranches from its CDO clients. By the end of June 2007, Merrill held $41 billion in subprime CDOs and subprime MBSs on its books, more than its $38 billion in outstanding market capitalization.

As the subprime mortgage market melted down in 2007, it became clear that Merrill and other large investment banks had severely underestimated the probability of default in subprime mortgages. Another fault lay in the fact that many CDO issuers/buyers believed that even if subprime loans defaulted, the underlying real estate values would be sufficient to cover the principal obligations on the loans. Unfortunately, the U.S. real estate market fell into one of the most widespread declines in

---

[21] Shawn Tully, "Wall Street's Money Machine Breaks Down," *Fortune*, November 12, 2007.

value since the Great Depression. This amplified the subprime weakness such that many subprime borrowers stopped making payments on their mortgages. The declines in the value of the real estate market meant that many troubled property loans did not have sufficient collateral to ensure loan repayment at liquidation. The loss of value in the subprime market heightened the perception of risk in the mortgage market generally, and this depressed the values of many MBSs and sent investors streaming for the exits. As the value of securities in many CDO portfolios declined sharply, so did the tranches of securities issued by the CDOs, even the investment-grade tranches. In fact, the subprime market became so distressed that remaining cash flows were not sufficient to make interest or principal payments on the highest-rated tranches of the CDOs. This led to massive write-downs and losses by Merrill, Citigroup, UBS, Morgan Stanley, and others.

Merrill learned the lesson not to apply its own proprietary capital unless it was willing to monitor the risks. Furthermore, Merrill hedged its CDO mortgage exposure to only a small extent. Again, if Merrill's goal was to collect fees, and not to speculate on the value of the CDO securities it purchased to keep the CDO machine going, it should have hedged its CDO investments. Ultimately, Merrill exposed its balance sheet to the CDO mess and turned what had been a client business into an investment bet.

Eventually, Merrill was forced to throw in the towel on its CDO assets, selling $30.6 billion of CDO securities for $6.7 billion in July 2008. This amounted to a purchase price of 22 cents on the dollar. The buyer was a distressed debt manager, Lone Star Funds. Furthermore, Merrill financed Lone Star's purchase of the CDOs by lending Lone Star 75% of the $6.7 billion purchase price. Consequently, Lone Star was only required to put up $1.68 billion of its own money. Lone Star effectively purchased a call option on the value of the subprime assets underlying the Merrill CDOs for about 5 cents on the dollar. With this sale of CDOs and from the beginning of 2007, Merrill wrote down in value approximately $27 billion of CDO securities on its balance sheet.

CONCLUSION

The Merrill Lynch case is a stark reminder that all investments contain risk, even if they are AAA-rated CDO tranches. Clearly the assumptions about the rate of default in MBSs, particularly subprime MBSs, and the ability to recover value from a defaulted loan were dramatically underestimated in 2007 and 2008. What we have learned is that CDOs are not a panacea. They cannot eliminate the risk of a market like subprime mortgages. CDOs are repackaging agents. Their goal is to take an underlying fundamental economic risk and slice and dice that risk into different tranches with different risk profiles and return expectations.

However, risk cannot be eliminated. Risk, like energy, has to be conserved. It has to land on someone's balance sheet. What Merrill and other bankers seemed to have forgotten was that the CDO structure did not remove them from subprime mortgage risk. Instead, it provided a reduced likelihood of the risk harming their investments, but not an elimination of the subprime mortgage risk. When the subprime mortgage market melted down, that risk came home to roost with a vengeance.

Appendix A

Basic Principles of Return and Present Value

INTRODUCTION

This appendix presents the basics of return and yield by which all investments are judged. Regardless of whether we invest in a simple U.S. Treasury bond or a newfangled hedge fund, it all comes down to what rate of return we earn on our investment. In the course of this appendix we examine a basic holding period return, compound interest rates, continuous (exponential) compounding, present and future value, internal rate of return (IRR), yield to maturity, yield to call, and current yield. This will form the foundation for thinking about whether we are appropriately rewarded when we invest in alternative assets.

HOLDING PERIOD RETURN, COMPOUNDING, AND EXPECTED RETURN

Consider the purchase of a stock. We pay a current price, $P(0)$, and hold the stock for one year. At the end of one year we receive a dividend, $D(1)$ and we sell the stock for a price of $P(1)$. Our simple holding period return is:

$$1 + R = [P(1) + D(1)]/P(0) \tag{A.1}$$

Let's assume that we purchase one share of stock at a price of $10, so $P(0) = \$10$. We also assume that we hold the stock for one year, and over the course of that year the stock price rises to $P(1) = \$11$. We also receive a dividend, $D(1) = \$1$, at the end of year 1. Our holding period return is then calculated as:

$$1 + R = (\$11 + \$1)/\$10 = 1.20$$

and

$$R = 1.20 - 1 = 0.20 \text{ or } 20\%$$

In this example, our holding period was equal to one year, so conveniently, our annualized return is equal to our holding period return of 20%.

The holding period return of a bond is only slightly more complicated than that of a stock. Bonds pay regular coupons, usually on a semiannual basis, and then face value at maturity. Let's again start with a simple example. We purchase a bond for $980 with a face value of $1,000. The bond matures in one year. At maturity, the bond will pay its holder the face value. Its stated coupon rate is 8%, and it pays its coupons semiannually. This means that there are two coupon payments each year of $40 each. Our one-year holding period return is calculated as:

$$1 + R = (\$1,000 + \$40 + \$40)/\$980 = 1.1020$$

and

$$R = 1.1020 - 1 = 0.1020 \text{ or } 10.20\%$$

Let's now expand our stock example to a two-year holding period. At the end of year 2, the stock price has risen by \$2 so that $P(2) = \$12$, and we receive two dividends of \$1 each at the end of the first and second years; $D(1) = \$1$ and $D(2) = \$1$. Our holding period total return is now:

$$1 + R = (\$12 + \$1 + \$1)/\$10 = 1.40$$

and

$$R = 1.40 - 1 = 0.40 \text{ or } 40\%$$

However, if we wish to annualize this return to determine what our effective annual return was, we must account for the two-year holding period. This introduces the idea of compounding. We need to determine what compound annual rate of return would have produced a total return of 40% over two years. Our formula then would look like:

$$(1 + R) \times (1 + R) = (\$12 + \$1 + \$1)/\$10$$
$$(1 + R)^2 = 1.40$$
$$1 + R = \sqrt{1.40} = 1.1832$$
$$R = 1 - 1.1832 = 18.32\%$$

We can see that with compounding, the effective annual return is less than 20% a year. This simple example demonstrates that compounding (as a result of reinvestment of proceeds) is a powerful tool to increase returns. Simple averaging of 40% over two years would lead one to conclude that the average return is 20% per year, but this ignores the fact that the return on our stock investment needs to be compounded. If we allow for compounding of our returns, then we can earn a smaller return each year of 18.32% and still get to our two-year holding period of 40%. Consider this example another way. If we allow for compounding, then a 20% return compounded over two years will produce a holding period return of 44%:

$$1.20\% \times 1.20\% = 1.44\%$$

Last, we consider the idea of expected return. We saw that a one-year holding period return for our stock returned 20%. But this is an ex post, after the fact, calculation. Going into our purchase of the stock, we need to consider what return we expect to earn over our one-year holding period. Dividends are reasonably predictable, so our expectation over the first year remains at $D(1) = \$1$. However, the future stock price, $P(1)$, is a random variable—it is unknown what its value will be in one year's time. Let's suppose that we expect the stock price to increase by only 50 cents over our one-year holding period. Then our expected return can be calculated as:

$$1 + R = \{E[P(1)] + D(1)\}/P(0) \qquad \text{(A.2)}$$

Notice that in Equation A.2, we use the expectation of the future price, $E[P(1)]$, compared to Equation A.1, where we used the realized price, $P(1)$. Putting in the numbers from our example we get:

$$1 + R = (\$10.50 + \$1)/\$10$$

Solving for R we get 15%. This is our expected return. In fact, our realized holding period return of 20% exceeds our expected return of 15%, giving us a 5% boost.

In practice, expected returns are determined using simple averaging techniques or an asset pricing model such as the capital asset pricing model (CAPM). First, an expectation of a return can be determined by taking an average of a time series of returns for an asset. For example, the average annual return to the S&P 500 since 1980 is 12.6%. This period contains bull and bear markets, booms and busts, tech bubbles and housing bubbles. Given the variety of data and economic cycles over the past 28 years, this is a reasonable estimate of the long-term return to the S&P 500. We can use this average return to form our expectation about future returns.

Another example of a predictive model is the CAPM. The CAPM was invented by William Sharpe in 1964. It is a model to predict the return on an asset over one holding period. It takes the form of:

$$E[R(i)] = R(f) + \beta \times \{E[R(m)] - R(f)\}$$

where

$E[R(i)]$ = the expected return on asset i

$\quad R(f)$ = the risk-free rate—usually a one-year Treasury bill rate

$\quad\quad \beta$ = a measure of systematic, or market risk that is embedded within asset (i). It is determined through a linear regression model.

For example, the beta of IBM is 1.1, the one-year T-bill rate is 2.15%, and the expected return of the market is 12.6%. Using these numbers, the expected one-year return for IBM is:

$$E[R(\text{IBM})] = 2.15\% + 1.1 \times (12.6\% - 2.15\%) = 13.65\%$$

PRESENT VALUE, FUTURE VALUE, INTERNAL RATE OF RETURN, YIELD TO MATURITY, YIELD TO CALL, AND CURRENT YIELD

In the prior section we saw how compounding can be a powerful tool to increase returns. Compounding also highlights two key concepts in return analysis: present value and future value. If we use our previous stock example, its present value is equal to $10, our out-of-pocket costs at the moment we purchase the stock. This is its current market or *present* value. Its future value is the price at which we sell it, or $12. In between we also receive two dividends of $1 each. So the present value of the stock today of $10 is the discounted future value of the stock price we receive in two years' time plus the discounted future value of our two dividend payments.

The basic formula relating present value to future value is:

$$FV(T) = PV \times [1 + (R/N)]^{N \times T} \tag{A.3}$$

where

R = the annual rate of return

N = the number of compounding periods per year

T = the number of years

Assume that we purchase our bond at $900 with the expectation that it will earn 10% a year. We hold the bond for one year. Using Equation A.1, we solve for:

$$PV = \$900$$
$$R = 10\%$$
$$N = 1$$
$$T = 1$$

In this most simple example, we determine future value to be:

$$FV = \$900 \times (1 + 10\%) = \$990$$

Let's expand our example by allowing for different compounding periods of annual, semiannual, quarterly, monthly, daily, and continuous compounding. As we increase the compounding periods, we demonstrate in Exhibit A.1 how the future value grows through the power of compounding.

Exhibit A.1 Growth of the investment for different compounding intervals

Frequency	R/N	Compounding Periods $= T \times N$	Future Value
Annual	10%	1	$900 \times (1 + 10\%) = 990$
Semiannual	5%	2	$900 \times (1 + 5\%)^2 = \$992$
Quarterly	2.5%	4	$900 \times (1 + 2.5\%)^4 = \$993$
Monthly	0.833%	12	$900 \times (1 + 0.833\%)^{12} = \$994$
Daily	0.0274%	365	$900 \times (1 + 0.0274\%)^{365} = \$995$
Continuous			$900 \times e^{0.10} = \$995$

We can see that as the number of compounding periods increases, the future value of the investment increases. The last example of continuous compounding introduces another concept. Continuous compounding essentially means that the number of compounding periods increases to infinity. Since we cannot count to infinity (who can?), we use the exponential component known as e. The number e is a transcendental number (never ending, like my golf score) that allows us to compound continuously. The formula for continuous compounding is:

$$FV = PV \times e^{R \times T} \qquad (A.4)$$

where

$e =$ the exponential operator
$R =$ the annual interest rate
$T =$ the number of compounding periods

So suppose that we invest $900 with continuous compounding at 10% (annually) for three years. Our future value will grow to be:

$$\$900 \times e^{0.10 \times 3} = \$1,214.87$$

Note that if we allow for just annual compounding at 10%, the future value is less than that for continuous compounding:

$$\$900 \times (1 + 10\%) \times (1 + 10\%) \times (1 + 10\%) = \$1,197.90$$

We come to our next step in the process of future value and present value: how to determine the rate of return when there are multiple cash flows across different periods of time. We start with a very simple example. Suppose we purchase a zero coupon bond and hold it until maturity in five years. This is a present value calculation with just a single cash flow, the payment of the bond at maturity. The current price is $800, and the bond pays its face value of $1,000 in five years. Exhibit A.2 demonstrates our problem.

Exhibit A.2 Future value of an investment

$PV \xrightarrow{\qquad 1 \quad 2 \quad 3 \quad 4 \quad 5 \qquad} FV = PV \times (1 + R)^5$

Exhibit A.3 Present values of bond cash flows

1	2	3	4	5	6
$40/(1 + R/2)$					
	$40/(1 + R/2)^2$				
		$40/(1 + R/2)^3$			
			$40/(1 + R/2)^4$		
				$40/(1 + R/2)^5$	
					$1,040/(1 + R/2)^6$
$37.72 +$	$35.58 +$	$33.56 +$	$31.65 +$	$29.85 +$	$731.64 = \$900$

In this case we determine the rate of return as:

$$FV = PV \times (1 + R)^5$$
$$\$1,000 = \$800 \times (1 + R)^5$$
$$\$1,000/800 = (1 + R)^5$$
$$1.25 = (1 + R)^5$$
$$\sqrt[5]{1.25} = 1 + R$$

Solving for R, we get $R = 4.56\%$.

The problem becomes a bit more complicated when we solve for multiple cash flows over a number of years. Then we have to determine the discount rate that will equate the future cash flows to the present value of the investment. This calculation is known as the internal rate of return (IRR).

Consider a bond with three years to maturity. Its face value is $1,000 and its current price is $900. It pays a coupon of 8% semiannually. Our goal is to determine the interest rate that will equate the future face value of $1,000 and the six semiannual coupons of $40 to the present value of $900. Our equation looks like this:

$$\$900 = \$40/(1 + R/2) + \$40/(1 + R/2)^2 + \$40/(1 + R/2)^3$$
$$+ \$40/(1 + R/2)^4 + \$40/(1 + R/2)^5 + \$1,040/(1 + R/2)^6$$

Solving for R, we find that it is equal to 12.06%.[1] The cash flow payment looks like Exhibit A.3.

The rate of return of 12.06% is the discount rate that equates the future coupon payments and face value to the current price of the bond. This is also known as the internal rate of return. The IRR is that rate of interest that, when applied to discount the future cash flows associated with an investment, will equate the discounted future payments to the current price of the investment. In the case of a bond, the IRR calculation has a special name, it is called the yield to maturity.

Another calculation associated with a bond is yield to call. Most corporate bonds have a call feature that allows the issuing company to call the bond back from the bondholder after a certain period of time. Bonds are usually called when interest rates decline and the company wishes to refinance the bonds at a lower coupon rate. Suppose that our bond still has a present value

---

[1] Most financial calculators can do this calculation in a few seconds. If not, then it is a bit of trial and error to find the value of R. If so, an easy starting point is to assume that all of the cash flows, $240 of coupons and face value of $1,000, are all paid at the end of year 3, so that $900 = $1,240/(1 + R/2)^6$. Solving this equation, we come to a value of R of 10.8%. This is our starting point. We know that since the coupon payments are paid earlier than at the end of year 6, we will need a higher discount rate to make the present value equality work.

of $900 but can be called at the end of the second year at its face value. Our calculation then becomes:

$$\$900 = \$40/(1 + R/2) + \$40/(1 + R/2)^2 + \$40/(1 + R/2)^3 + \$1,040/(1 + R/2)^4$$

Again, solving for R, we get a yield to call of 13.9%, which is greater than our yield to maturity. The reason for this is that the most bondholders do not wish to have their bonds called because it typically means that they will have to reinvest their proceeds in a new bond with a lower coupon payment. Therefore, there is more risk associated with a callable bond because the bondholders may end up not getting their coupon payments through the maturity of the bond. To reflect this call risk to bondholders, they must be compensated with a higher internal rate of return in the form of the yield to call. Another way to look at the problem is that the bondholders have sold a call option back to the company and the issuing corporation can exercise this call option to its advantage. In order to compensate them for selling the call option to the company, the bondholders must receive a call premium in the form of a higher internal rate of return.

A last calculation with respect to bonds is the current yield. This is simply the annual coupon amount divided by the current price of the bond:

$$\$80/\$900 = 8.89\%$$

The current yield simply indicates that the bond is trading at a discount and that the yield to maturity will be greater than the 8% coupon rate.

ARITHMETIC MEAN VERSUS GEOMETRIC MEAN

When working with the returns to risky assets, it is sometimes helpful to determine their mean or average return. There are two methods to determine the average return to an asset: the arithmetic mean and geometric mean. The arithmetic mean is simply the sum of the all of the returns divided by the number of periods over which the sum total is calculated. This is also called the average, or average return.

$$\text{Arithmetic Mean} = \frac{1}{N} \sum_{i=1}^{N} \text{S\&P Return}(i) \tag{A.5}$$

where

$\sum_{i=1}^{N}$ = the summation notation that means that we are adding up all of the observations over N periods

S&P Return(i) = the return to the S&P 500 in the ith year

N = the number of periods over which we calculate the average

Consider Exhibit A.4. This is the return to a risky asset X over a 10-year time horizon. We will use this data to demonstrate the difference between the arithmetic and geometric mean.

Using Equation A.5 and the data in Exhibit A.4, the arithmetic mean is calculated as:

$$\begin{aligned} \text{Arithmetic Mean} &= [10\% + 14\% + (-7\%) + (-3\%) + 22\% \\ &\quad + 16\% + 8\% + 13\% + 15\% + 12\%]/10 \\ &= 100\%/10 = 10\% \end{aligned}$$

This is the average annual return produced by risky asset X over the past 10 years.

Equation A.5 is the simplest calculation to determine the average return. The average return on an asset, observed over a long period of time, is often used as the expected return for future years.

Exhibit A.4 The returns to risky asset X

Year	Return
1	10%
2	14
3	-7
4	-3
5	22
6	16
7	8
8	13
9	15
10	12

Although the future return is unknown and cannot be predicted with great accuracy, the historical average return is as good a guess as any of what the return will be in the future.

The geometric mean is a bit more complicated. It uses compounding to determine the mean return. For a set of observations related to an asset return stream, the geometric mean is equal to:

$$1 + R(G) = \sqrt[N]{[1 + R(1)] \times [1 + R(2)] \times \cdots \times [1 + R(N)]} \qquad (A.6)$$

where

$R(G) =$ the return for the geometric mean

$R(1), R(2), R(N) =$ the returns to risky asset X in periods 1, 2, all the way to period N

$N =$ the number of periods over which we calculate the geometric mean

$\sqrt[N]{\ }$ means that we take the Nth root of our compound return stream to determine $R(G)$

Another way to express Equation A.6 is by using a product symbol, $\prod$:

$$1 + R(G) = \left\{ \prod^{N} [1 + R(i)] \right\}^{1/N} \qquad (A.7)$$

where

$\prod =$ the product symbol that means that all of the values of $[1 + R(i)]$ are multiplied against each other rather than added together

$R(i) =$ the return on risky asset X in the ith period

$N =$ the number of periods in our sample

Using the data in Exhibit A.4 and Equation A.6, we calculate the geometric mean as:

$$1 + R(G) = \sqrt[10]{\begin{array}{l}(1 + 10\%)(1 + 14\%)(1 - 7\%)(1 - 3\%)(1 + 22\%)(1 + 16\%)(1 + 8\%) \\ \times (1 + 13\%)(1 + 15\%)(1 + 12\%)\end{array}}$$

$$1 + R(G) = 1.0967$$
$$R(G) = 9.67\%$$

We note that the geometric mean is slightly lower than the arithmetic mean. This is the case when the returns are changing through time. In fact, there is an approximate relationship between the two:

$$R(G) \approx R(A) - \frac{1}{2} Var(R)$$

where $Var(R)$ is the variance of the rate of return on asset X. It can be seen that if the annual rate of return on the asset has no volatility, then geometric and arithmetic means will be equal.

One more observation is appropriate. The geometric mean is also used in the calculation for the cumulative average growth rate (CAGR). CAGR assumes that an asset, cash flow, or some other random variable grows at a constant rate of return compounded over a sample period of time. For example, assume that we purchase a stock of company X at \$50 and hold it for three years until it reaches the value of \$100. What is our CAGR? The calculation is simple: We combine our holding period return calculation with Equation A.5.

First, determine the holding period return as:

$$\$100/\$50 = 2$$

Then our CAGR is equal to:

$$1 + R(G) = \sqrt[3]{2.0} = \sqrt[3]{(1 + \text{CAGR}) \times (1 + \text{CAGR}) \times (1 + \text{CAGR})}$$
$$1 + R(G) = 1.26 = (1 + \text{CAGR})$$
$$R(G) = 26\% = \text{CAGR}$$

CONCLUSION

This appendix is not meant to be an exhaustive dissertation on the subject of present value, expected returns, or compounding. It is meant to arm the reader with the basic tools needed to understand the concepts in the rest of the book with respect to return, risk, average returns, and expected returns. We use these concepts frequently as we explore the world of alternative assets.

Appendix B
Measures of Risk and Risk Management

INTRODUCTION

In Appendix A we provided a discussion of the return earned on an asset. In this appendix we turn to the other side of the coin: risk. In the world of investing, the key issue is whether an investor earns a proper rate of return for the risk underwritten. Risk can be measured by a number of different statistics, such as variance, volatility, skewness, and kurtosis.

In this appendix we introduce the reader to the basic concepts of risk measurement so that she can make informed decisions about the return she has earned on a particular investment, asset class, or product. Risk is also an important topic for alternative assets because alternative investments are often viewed as having different risk characteristics than traditional assets such as stocks and bonds.

RANGE AND LOCATION

Statisticians often make use of what are known as *quantiles* to divide a ranked (on some chosen statistic) data sample into equal fractions. Quantiles are a way to divide a time series of returns into a descriptive pattern. For example, quartiles (a ranked sample divided into four quantiles) are used most frequently when reviewing data (e.g., are a manager's returns in the first quartile of his peer group, in the second quartile, or in the third or fourth?). Dividing the data up into quartiles provides an investor with a quick and convenient way to determine whether a hedge fund manager outperforms his peer group or lags behind. This is another way of determining how a hedge fund manager *ranks* when compared to other hedge fund managers in the same category.

Quantiles divide the data up into fractional units and categorize the return of a risky asset, hedge fund manager, or return stream into one of the fractions below which a portion of the data population lies. Another way to look at the data is that quantiles divide up the *range* of a data sample into groups based on their ranking within the overall sample. Most popular quantiles are quartiles (four fractional units), quintiles (five fractional units) and deciles (10 fractional units). An example might help.

Exhibit B.1 contains the returns for 32 actual equity long/short hedge fund managers for the year 2007. These managers were selected randomly. We note that the worst hedge fund manager had a return of -16% for 2007 whereas the best had a return of 20%. This is the range of the data: from -16% to $+20\%$.

The range is a quick way to measure the dispersion, or risk, of a data sample. Simply, the range is calculated as:

$$\text{Range} = \text{Highest value in a data sample} - \text{Lowest value} \qquad (B.1)$$

In our hedge fund sample, the range is $20\% - (-16\%) = 36\%$.

With 32 hedge fund managers divided up into quartiles, eight hedge fund managers will be in the top quartile of performance, eight in the second quartile, and so forth. Using our quartile rankings, Exhibit B.2 demonstrates how the data can be divided up into a descriptive analysis.

Calculating the average of these hedge fund managers using our methods from Appendix A, the arithmetic average is 6.03%. With the meltdown of the subprime market and the equity markets

Exhibit B.1 Equity long/short hedge fund returns

Hedge Fund	Return
A	−14%
B	7
C	11
D	10
E	8
F	−2
G	−3
H	6
I	12
J	18
K	20
L	13
M	9
N	−12
O	−7
P	9
Q	14
R	3
S	10
T	16
U	−16
V	−2
W	9
X	11
Y	7
Z	2
AA	15
BB	19
CC	8
DD	−4
EE	10
FF	4

with it, equity long/short managers had a tough year. We note that the *median* of this cross section of hedge funds is between 8% and 9%. The median is that value for which one-half of the sample population lies above it and one-half of the sample population lies below it. In a normal, bell-shaped distribution of returns, the mean and the median are equal. The fact that in this case the mean is less than the median indicates that there was significant downside risk associated with equity long/short hedge funds in 2007.

MOMENTS OF THE DISTRIBUTION: THE MEAN, VARIANCE, VOLATILITY, SKEWNESS, AND KURTOSIS

Every asset, whether a stock or a bond or a hedge fund, provides a stream of returns. The business of statistics is to provide descriptive numbers that can paint a picture of what these return patterns look like. A distribution of numbers such as a time series of asset returns is often described by its *moments*. The moments of a distribution are calculations that transcribe the pattern of returns into numbers that paint a picture about the return stream.

Exhibit B.2   Quartile rankings for equity long/short hedge funds

Quartile Ranking	Hedge Funds
Quartile 1	Hedge Fund Manager K = 20% Hedge Fund Manager BB = 19% Hedge Fund Manager J = 18% Hedge Fund Manager T = 16% Hedge Fund Manager AA = 15% Hedge Fund Manager Q = 14% Hedge Fund Manager L = 13% Hedge Fund Manager I = 12%
Quartile 2	Hedge Fund Manager C= 11% Hedge Fund Manager X = 11% Hedge Fund Manager D = 10% Hedge Fund Manager S = 10% Hedge Fund Manager EE = 10% Hedge Fund Manager M = 9% Hedge Fund Manager P = 9% Hedge Fund Manager W = 9%
Quartile 3	Hedge Fund Manager E = 8% Hedge Fund Manager CC = 8% Hedge Fund Manager B = 7% Hedge Fund Manager Y = 7% Hedge Fund Manager H = 6% Hedge Fund Manager FF = 4% Hedge Fund Manager R = 3% Hedge Fund Manager Z = 2%
Quartile 4	Hedge Fund Manager F = −2% Hedge Fund Manager V = −2% Hedge Fund Manager G = −3% Hedge Fund Manager DD = −4% Hedge Fund Manager O = −7% Hedge Fund Manager N = −12% Hedge Fund Manager A = −14% Hedge Fund Manager U = −16%

The first moment of the distribution is one that we discussed thoroughly in the prior appendix; it is the *mean* of the distribution, described as:

$$E[X] = \sum_{i}^{N} X_i / N \tag{B.2}$$

where

$X_i =$ the individual observations in our data population
$N =$ the number of observations in our population
$\sum_{i}^{N} =$ the summation symbol of all of our X observations from i to N

From the cross section of hedge fund returns in Exhibit B.1, we calculate that the value of $E[X] = 6.03\%$. This is the mean of the hedge fund return distribution.

The second moment of the distribution is expressed as:

$$E[X^2] = \sum_i^N X_i^2/N \tag{B.3}$$

Using Exhibit B.1 again, we get a value of 1.208%.

The first two moments are particularly important because they can be used to determine both the mean and variance of a distribution of returns. Specifically, the *variance* of any sample of returns can be determined by the equation:

$$\text{Variance} = E[X^2] - \{E[X]\}^2 \tag{B.4}$$

Inserting the values obtained for $E[X]$ and $E[X^2]$, we find the variance to be:

$$1.208\% - (6.03\%)^2 = 0.008446$$

Taking the square root of the variance gives us the volatility, or standard deviation, of our hedge fund population:

$$\sqrt{.008446} = 9.19\%$$

Another formula to calculate the variance of a data population is given by:

$$\text{Variance} = \sum_i^N (X_i - E[X])^2/N \tag{B.5}$$

Both Equation B.4 and Equation B.5 will lead us to the same calculation of variance of 0.008446. The variance is often represented by the symbol σ^2, and the volatility, or standard deviation, by the square root of σ^2 (which is simply σ).

In many instances of data examination, we can observe only a subset of the overall data population. In such a case both the mean and the variance have to be estimated. Because of this it turns out that the estimated value of variance will be unbiased if the sum of squared differences is divided by $(N - 1)$. Therefore, the formula for the variance is:

$$\sigma^2 = \sum_i^N (X_i - E[X])^2/(N - 1) \tag{B.6}$$

Another risk measure is the *semivariance*. Variance is a symmetrical calculation; it measures the negative and positive dispersion around the mean. However, for risk management purposes, we are more concerned with the downside than the upside. Therefore, another measure, the semivariance, is used to determine the risk of the downside. The semivariance is calculated as:

$$\text{Semivariance} = \sum_i^N (X_i - E[X])^2/N \text{ For all } X_i < E[X] \tag{B.7}$$

In other words, we calculate the dispersion below the mean value of only those values that are less than the mean. This gives us a sense of how much variability exists for those observations that fall below the mean. Using Equation B.7, we calculate the semivariance to equal 0.01435.

Another use of the semivariance is to calculate a *target* semivariance. The difference is that in Equation B.7 we substitute a target rate of return (like 5%) instead of the mean return of 6.03%.

Two other calculations are very important to the analysis of alternative assets: *skewness* and *kurtosis*. For a normal distribution, which is represented by the classic bell-curve pattern of returns, the mean and the variance are all that is needed to describe the pattern of returns associated with an investment. That is because a bell-curve distribution is perfect in its symmetry; each side of the curve, centered at the mean of the return distribution, is a mirror imagine of the other side of the curve. For example, under a normal (bell-curve) distribution, if the mean were 0%, we would expect that losses in the 0% to -1% range would occur with same frequency as gains from 0% to 1%, and so forth. The distribution would be perfectly balanced on each side of the mean. Under these rare circumstances, the mean and the variance can describe perfectly the shape of the return distribution.

Note that there are many other distributions that are perfectly described by only two parameters (e.g., the lognormal distribution is described by only two parameters). However, normal distribution is the only one that is symmetrical and stable, which means the sum of two normal random variables will be normal. In contrast, the sum of two lognormal random variables will not be lognormal.[1]

Unfortunately, most return distributions are not symmetrical. They have unusual shapes and return patterns that cannot be described fully by just the mean and the variance. Gains and losses around the mean are not symmetrical, and therefore we need to have further calculations to fully understand the return pattern. We see these patterns most distinctly when we examine hedge funds, commodities, private equity, and the like.

A distribution that is not symmetrical is *skewed* and its return distribution is described by its *skewness*. A skewed distribution leans either to the right toward more positive gains or to the left toward more negative returns. For example, a positively skewed distribution demonstrates a small number of very large positive gains with small but more frequent losses. Conversely, a negatively skewed distribution has infrequent but very large negative returns combined with frequent but small positive returns. Generally, negatively skewed distributions are to be avoided because they demonstrate the risk of large downside losses. The normal, or bell-curve distribution, has a skew of 0.

Skewed distributions are referred to in terms of *tails* and *mass*. A positively skewed distribution has a long tail to the right, indicating the probability of large upside returns associated with the return pattern. Sometimes this is described as greater mass located in the right-hand (positive) tail of the distribution. This is a good thing because it demonstrates an asset that has the ability to deliver on occasion large positive returns. For a positively skewed distribution, the median is less than the mean.

For a distribution with a negative skew, the mean is less than the median. This demonstrates an asset that has the potential to deliver large negative returns. Negatively skewed return distributions are to be avoided if possible because they demonstrate a risk of large downside returns.

The skew of a distribution is measured by the third moment of the distribution as:

$$\text{Skew} = (1/N) \times \sum_{i}^{N} (X_i - E[X])^3 / \sigma^3 \tag{B.8}$$

Using Equation B.8, we find the skew of our hedge fund distribution to be -0.80.

The last moment of the distribution, called the fourth moment, measures the *kurtosis* of the distribution. Kurtosis is a way to measure the thickness of the tails of the distribution. Often, the return distribution associated with an asset has a significant amount of the return observations that are at the extreme ends of the range of the distribution. These outlier returns add to the mass in the tails of the distribution, increasing the value of kurtosis.

Kurtosis is often measured relative to the normal bell-curve distribution. For a normal, bell-curve distribution, the value of kurtosis is 3. *Leptokurtosis* refers to the condition that more return observations are contained in the tails of the distribution than for a normal distribution. Sometimes this is described as a distribution with fat tails. This simply means that there are more large return deviations from the mean than are associated with a normal distribution. The term *platykurtosis* refers to the condition where the tails of the return distribution are thinner than for a normal,

---

[1] There is a general class of stable symmetrical distributions, of which normal is the most widely used member.

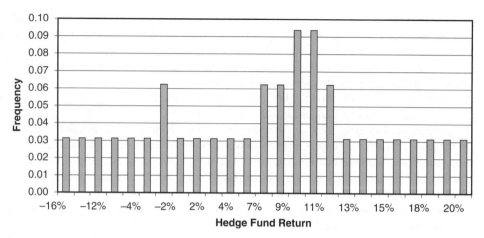

Exhibit B.3   Frequency distribution of hedge fund returns

bell-curve distribution; that is, there are fewer large deviations from the mean than are observed for a normal distribution. In this book, we measure kurtosis relative to a normal distribution. So a positive value of kurtosis indicates fatter tails than a normal distribution (leptokurtosis), and a negative value of kurtosis indicates thinner tails than a normal distribution (platykurtosis).

Kurtosis is measured by:

$$\text{Kurtosis} = 1/N \times \sum_{i}^{N} (X_i - E[X])^4/\sigma^4 - 3 \qquad (B.9)$$

This expression is also referred to as excess kurtosis because it is measured in excess of the kurtosis of a normal distribution. In this book we use the term *kurtosis* to refer to Equation B.9.

We put this all together in Exhibit B.3. This is a frequency distribution for our hedge fund returns. It plots the sample hedge fund returns against the frequency with which those returns occur. This is a probability density graph that provides a picture to demonstrate our hedge fund return pattern. It shows where the greatest mass is located with respect to our hedge fund returns.

We can see that the mass of the distribution is centered around the 7% to 12% range. In fact, we previously observed that the median of the distribution is 8%. Note, however, that the mean of our hedge fund sample is only 6.03%; it is less than the median. This tells us that we have a negatively skewed distribution—a bias toward downside returns. Our calculations prove this; the skew of the distribution is −0.80. We also observe a value of kurtosis that is 0.14. This demonstrates tails of our hedge fund return distribution that are slightly fatter than a normal distribution. This indicates a bias toward outliers that fatten the tails of the distribution.

Taken together, a negative skew and a positive value of kurtosis indicate a return distribution that has a bias to large downside returns. Clearly we would prefer the return scenario of a positive skew and kurtosis, which would indicate a bias toward large positive outliers. Throughout this book, we make great use of the mean, volatility, skew, and kurtosis.

TEST OF HYPOTHESIS

All hypothesis tests are conducted the same way. We state a hypothesis to be tested, design a plan, analyze sample data according to the plan, and accept or reject the null hypothesis based on results of the analysis.

Step 1: State the hypotheses. Every hypothesis test requires the analyst to state a null hypothesis and an alternative hypothesis. The hypotheses are stated in such a way that they are mutually exclusive. That is, if one is true, the other must be false, and vice versa.

Step 2: Design a plan to analyze data. The plan describes how to use sample data to accept or reject the null hypothesis. It should specify the following elements:

- *Significance level.* Often, researchers choose significance levels equal to 0.01, 0.05, or 0.10; but any value between 0 and 1 can be used.

- *Test method.* Typically, the test method involves a test statistic and a sampling distribution. The test statistic is a function of the sample data, and its sampling distribution tells us the distributional properties of the test statistics under some assumptions about the data sample. The test statistic might be the mean, standard deviation, proportion, difference between means, and so on. Given a test statistic and its sampling distribution, a researcher can assess probabilities associated with the test statistic. If the test statistic probability is less than the significance level, the null hypothesis is rejected.

Step 3: Analyze sample data. Using sample data, perform computations called for in the analysis plan. These computations allow you to calculate the test statistic.

- *Test statistic.* When the null hypothesis involves a mean or a proportion, use either of the following equations to compute the test statistic.

$$\text{Test statistic} = (\text{Statistic} - \text{Parameter})/(\text{Standard deviation of statistic})$$
$$\text{Test statistic} = (\text{Statistic} - \text{Parameter})/(\text{Standard error of statistic})$$

where Parameter is the value appearing in the null hypothesis, and Statistic is the point estimate of Parameter. As part of the analysis, you may need to compute the standard error of the statistic.

- *P-value.* The P-value is the probability of observing a sample statistic as extreme as the test statistic, assuming the null hypothesis is true.

Step 4: Interpret the results. If the sample findings are unlikely, given the null hypothesis, the researcher rejects the null hypothesis. Typically, this involves comparing the P-value to the significance level, and rejecting the null hypothesis when the P-value is less than the significance level.

We explain in the following subsections how to conduct a hypothesis test of a mean when the following conditions are met:

- The sampling method is simple random sampling.
- The sample is drawn from a normal or near-normal population.

Generally, the sampling distribution will be approximately normally distributed if any of the following conditions apply.

- The population distribution is normal.
- The sampling distribution is symmetrical, unimodal, and without outliers, and the sample size is 15 or less.
- The sampling distribution is moderately skewed, unimodal, and without outliers, and the sample size is between 16 and 40.
- The sample size is greater than 40, without outliers.

This approach consists of four steps: (1) state the hypotheses, (2) formulate an analysis plan, (3) analyze sample data, and (4) interpret results.

Step 1: State the hypotheses

Every hypothesis test requires the analyst to state a null hypothesis and an alternative hypothesis. The hypotheses are stated in such a way that they are mutually exclusive. That is, if one is true, the other must be false, and vice versa.

Exhibit B.4 shows three sets of hypotheses. Each makes a statement about how the population mean μ is related to a specified value M.

The first set of hypotheses (set 1) is an example of a two-tailed test, since an extreme value on either side of the sampling distribution would cause a researcher to reject the null hypothesis. The other two sets of hypotheses (Sets 2 and 3) are one-tailed tests, since an extreme value on only one side of the sampling distribution would cause a researcher to reject the null hypothesis.

Step 2: Formulate an analysis plan

The analysis plan describes how to use sample data to accept or reject the null hypothesis. It should specify the following elements.

- *Significance level.* Often, researchers choose significance levels equal to 0.01, 0.05, or 0.10; but any value between 0 and 1 can be used.
- *Test method.* Use the one-sample t-test to determine whether the hypothesized mean differs significantly from the observed sample mean.

Step 3: Analyze sample data

Using sample data, conduct a one-sample t-test. This involves finding the standard error, degrees of freedom, test statistic, and the P-value associated with the test statistic.

- *Standard error.* Compute the standard error (SE) of the sampling distribution.

$$SE = s/\sqrt{n}$$

  where s is the standard deviation of the sample and n is the sample size.
- *Degrees of freedom.* The degrees of freedom (DF) is equal to the sample size (n) minus one. Thus, $DF = n - 1$.
- *Test statistic.* The test statistic is a t-score (t) defined by the following equation:

$$t = (x - \mu)/SE$$

  where x is the sample mean, μ is the hypothesized population mean in the null hypothesis, and SE is the standard error.
- *P-value.* The P-value is the probability of observing a sample statistic as extreme as the test statistic. Since the test statistic is a t-score, use the t-distribution.

Exhibit B.4   Null hypothesis and alternative hypothesis

Set	Null Hypothesis	Alternative Hypothesis	Number of Tails
1	$\mu = M$	$\mu \neq M$	2
2	$\mu \geq M$	$\mu < M$	1
3	$\mu \leq M$	$\mu > M$	1

Step 4: Interpret results

If the sample findings are unlikely, given the null hypothesis, the researcher rejects the null hypothesis. Typically, this involves comparing the P-value to the significance level, and rejecting the null hypothesis when the P-value is less than the significance level.

Example: An investor has collected monthly returns in excess of the MSCI World index for an active manager who is benchmarked to that index. The 24 observations are as follows:

	Jan	Feb	Mar	Apr	May	Jun	Jul	Aug	Sep	Oct	Nov	Dec
Year 1	1.79%	0.21%	−0.64%	0.69%	0.37%	−0.16%	−1.93%	−3.70%	1.21%	−0.76%	1.63%	2.09%
Year 2	2.17%	0.03%	3.41%	4.04%	1.63%	0.36%	−0.49%	−1.92%	0.86%	4.23%	−3.18%	4.01%

The null hypothesis is that the manager has no skill and that the mean alpha is less than zero.

$$Null : \mu \leq 0$$
$$Alt : \mu > 0$$

The sample mean is:

$$x = \sum_{t=1}^{24} r_t = 0.66\%$$

The sample standard deviation is:

$$s = \sqrt{\frac{1}{24-1} \sum_{t=1}^{24} (r_t - x)^2} = 2.13\%$$

The standard error of the sample mean is:

$$SE = s/\sqrt{n} = 0.44\%$$

The t-statistic is therefore:

$$t = \frac{0.66\% - 0}{0.44\%} = 1.496$$

This value must be compared to the t-distribution with 23 degrees of freedom. It turns out the Prob($t > 1.496$) = 0.074. This means that if we reject the null hypothesis, there is a 7.4% chance that we rejected the null even if the null is correct. Since this is greater than 5%, we cannot reject the null hypothesis that the manager has no skill under a 5% confidence level. However, if we were satisfied to use a 10% confidence level, then we would reject the null hypothesis because 7.4% is less than 10%.

RISK MANAGEMENT

Value at risk, Monte Carlo simulation, and scenario analysis

The last section of this appendix deals with three basic risk management tools: *value at risk, Monte Carlo simulation*, and *stress testing*. Most asset managers, both traditional and alternative, use some combination of these mathematical concepts in the management of the risk within their investment strategies and portfolios. No one method reigns supreme; they all have their benefits and weaknesses.

Value at risk

Value at risk (VaR) is a measure of probability and loss. It is defined as the maximum amount of money that one could expect to lose with a given level of probability (or confidence) over a specified period of time. VaR is used across derivatives trading desks, bank loan desks, mutual funds, high-net-worth accounts, and the like. It is a widely applied risk management tool, but it is not without risks itself. First, let us define it.

Under the assumption that returns are approximately normally distributed, VaR requires four inputs: (1) an expected change in value, (2) a time horizon over which that value change could occur, (3) a measure of volatility associated with the change in value, and (4) a stated probability of loss.

For example, suppose a mutual fund manager manages a portfolio of $100 million with a portfolio standard deviation of $10 million and an expected increase in the value of the portfolio over one year of $5 million. The manager would like to know: What is the maximum amount he could lose over one year with a 1% confidence (or probability) of greater loss?

Our four inputs are:

1. An expected increase in value of $5 million.
2. A one-year time horizon.
3. A volatility of $10 million.
4. A confidence or probability interval of 1%.

The last input is the one that gives risk managers fits. The trick is how to define the confidence interval with a 1% probability level. Many VaR models use a normal, bell-curve distribution for asset returns, which assumes that asset returns are symmetrically distributed around the mean value. As we have demonstrated for equity long/short hedge funds, this is rarely the case. However, for the moment we will keep this assumption in place. Confidence intervals are determined as the number of standard deviations from the mean. For example, using our VaR test we might be interested to know what is the probability of achieving a portfolio value that is two standard deviations away from our expected return of $5 million.

For a normal distribution, the number of standard deviations from the mean can be looked up under any normal distribution table found at the back of most statistics and financial textbooks. The most common intervals are shown in Exhibit B.5.

Note that these values are for two-tailed tests. This means that VaR is a symmetrical measure. Although we are worried about the downside, the expected change to our portfolio could be a positive $5 million just as it could be a negative $5 million. So our VaR calculation will not only identify for us the amount that could be lost with a 1% probability; it will also calculate the amount that could be gained with a 1% probability. Using a normal distribution, the 1% confidence interval is 2.33 standard deviations, both plus and minus, away from the mean return. This means that, if our returns to the portfolio are normally distributed, we would expect only 1% of the time to see a change in

Exhibit B.5 Probability of observing a value for normal distribution

Confidence Interval	Normal Distribution Value
1%	2.33
2.5%	1.96
5%	1.65

value that is further from the expected return than 2.33 times the standard deviation of the change in the portfolio

Our VaR equation is:

$$VaR(1\%) = E[\text{Change in value}] - 2.33 \times \sigma[\text{Change in Value}] \tag{B.10}$$

Plugging in our numbers we get:

$$VaR(1\%) = \$5 \text{ million} - 2.33 \times \$10 \text{ million}$$
$$VaR(1\%) = -\$18.3 \text{ million}$$

In words, with a 1% probability of occurrence, given that we expect that portfolio to achieve a positive change in value of $5 million, we could have an adverse return worse than −$18.3 million. However, this is an extreme event that we expect to occur only 1% of the time. In other words, we know with 99% confidence that we will not lose more than $18.3 million over the course of the year. Note that the symmetry of VaR means that we could also achieve with a 1% probability an upside return of $28.3 million. If we are less concerned with extreme outcomes and want to assure ourselves of the potential losses that can occur 2.5% and 5% of the time, our calculations would be:

$$VaR(2.5\%) = \$5 \text{ million} - 1.96 \times \$10 \text{ million} = -\$14.6 \text{ million}$$
$$VaR(5\%) \ = \$5 \text{ million} - 1.65 \times \$10 \text{ million} = -\$11.5 \text{ million}$$

Exhibit B.6 demonstrates this range of outcomes. Again, notice that VaR is a symmetrical calculation. Even though we are most concerned about our downside loss, VaR calculates the expected change in the portfolio both up and down.

The major weakness of VaR is that it requires us to make some assumptions about the distribution of returns associated with an asset. As indicated before, the normal distribution is most often used when making VaR calculations. However, as we demonstrated with our equity long/short hedge fund examples, it is very likely that the distribution of returns associated with alternative assets will not follow a normal, bell-curve distribution. Another way to say this is that the VaR calculations we performed do not take into account the skew or kurtosis of the distribution of returns. This can lead to inaccurate predictions.

In practice, VaR calculations are enhanced with either Monte Carlo simulation or stress testing, discussed next.

Monte Carlo simulation

Although the normal distribution is most often used to determine VaR, any distribution can be substituted into Equation B.10. Another method used to determine VaR is *Monte Carlo simulation*.

Monte Carlo simulation is a method to use random numbers and probability to solve problems. It is a sampling method that uses randomly selected inputs to determine how lack of knowledge, changes to variance, sensitivity to certain factors, and so on will affect the value of the system being modeled. Monte Carlo simulation is often use in option pricing models and other financial calculations to project the trajectory of an underlying asset price so that an option or swap value can be calculated from the expected future value of the asset.

2.33 SD	1.96 SD	1.65 SD	E[Change]	1.65 SD	1.96 SD	2.33 SD
−$18,300,000	−$14,600,000	−$11,500,000	$5,000,000	$21,500,000	$24,600,000	$28,300,000

Exhibit B.6 Range of extreme returns

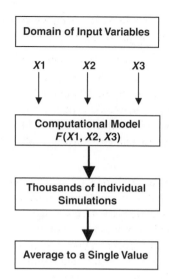

Exhibit B.7   Monte Carlo simulation

Monte Carlo simulation was invented in the 1940s by the scientists working on developing the atomic bomb at the Los Alamos nuclear research facility in New Mexico. The scientists working on the Manhattan Project had to determine the probability that one neutron exploding from one fissioning uranium atom would bombard another uranium atom and cause it to fission, setting off a chain reaction that would result in a nuclear explosion. To calculate the right amount of uranium they would need to explode an atomic bomb, they had to determine the trajectory of neutrons and calculate the probability that a neutron would either be absorbed by another uranium atom, escape the bomb, or contribute to the fission chain reaction. This required hundreds of calculations that the scientists were able to reduce through the use of Monte Carlo simulation.

There is no single method of Monte Carlo simulation. The four steps in the simulation, however, are consistent:

1. Define a domain of possible inputs that affect the underlying value being studied (e.g., the impact of inflation on the price of a bank stock over the next year).
2. Generate a system of randomly selected inputs from the domain of variables and perform a computation on the value of the stock price. This process is often accomplished using a random number selector that is incorporated in most software packages, including Microsoft Excel.
3. Perform this computation again and again—most Monte Carlo simulations run 10,000 or more simulations.
4. Aggregate the results of the individual simulations into a final result. This is typically done by taking the simple average of all of the individual simulations.

Exhibit B.7 shows the basic design of a Monte Carlo system.

Let's take a birthday example. What is the probability that in a classroom of 30 students two students will have the same birthday?[2] Ignoring leap years, there are 365 days each year, and we

---

[2] We have adapted this simulation from Greg Kochanski, "Monte Carlo Simulation," at http://kochanski.org/gbk (2005).

need to find out within that range the probability that two people in a room of 30 will have overlapping birthdays. Our four-step Monte Carlo simulation is as follows:

1. Pick 30 random numbers in the range of 1 to 365. Each randomly selected number represents one day of the year.
2. Check to see if there is any match among the 30 randomly selected numbers.
3. Repeat step 1 multiple times—typically 10,000 simulations will do.
4. Add up the total number of simulations from step 3 that resulted in matching birthdays. Divide this value by 10,000—this is the probability that two people will have overlapping birthdays in a group of 30.

If we do our simulation correctly, we will come up with the surprising probability that 71% of the time in a room of 30 people there will be two people with matching birthdays. Amazing.

The downside of Monte Carlo simulation is that it takes many, many simulations to get a sufficiently large population of results from which to draw accurate conclusions. This is less of an issue now, but can you imagine how many slide rules were working overtime on the Manhattan Project without the benefit of computers? Second, you need to make certain that you have the right functional formula as specified in Exhibit B.7. Monte Carlo simulation is only as good as the robustness of the computational model used to calculate the simulated values.

Stress testing and scenario analysis

Our last bit of work in this appendix is to discuss *scenario analysis* and *stress testing*. These terms are used interchangeably and boil down to the same thing. We use this technique when we wish to consider alternative return patterns, shocks to the financial system, or other out-of-the-ordinary events that could affect the value of an underlying financial analysis. If this sounds a bit like Monte Carlo simulation, that is intended, as the two are closely related.

Another way to consider stress testing/scenario analysis is that it is a form of testing that is used to determine the stability of a given system when it operates beyond normal capacity or limits. For example, stress testing can be used by banks to determine the adequacy of their capital reserves to cover potential losses incurred during extreme events. These extreme events are considered rare, but possible. Another good example is to stress test the diversification of an investment portfolio. Most diversified portfolios contain a blend of stocks, bonds, hedge funds, private equity, commodities, and real estate. Over long periods of time, these asset classes are less than perfectly correlated and provide good long-term diversification to an investor. However, during times of stress, the correlations associated with these asset classes can converge, resulting in less diversification than expected by the investor. Hence the term *stress* testing.

Like Monte Carlo simulation, there is no uniform method of stress testing. The test will depend on the construction of the investment portfolio by the investor and the type of event she wishes to test. Exhibit B.8 demonstrates how stress testing works.

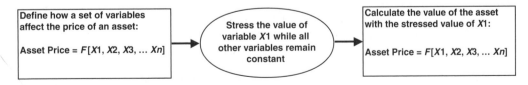

Exhibit B.8   Stress testing

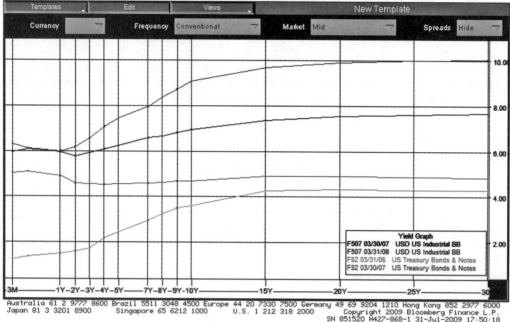

Exhibit B.9   The spread for high-yield bonds

Source: Bloomberg Finance, L.P.

As an example, in the summer of 2007 a meltdown in the subprime mortgage market led to a credit and liquidity crisis around the globe. Spreads on BB-rated industrial bonds in the United States (junk or high-yield bonds) compared to U.S. Treasury bonds doubled from 300 basis points over U.S. Treasuries to 600 basis points over U.S. Treasuries. There was a twin effect at work during this time. First, there was a flight to safety so that the yields on U.S. Treasury bonds declined by 100 basis points. At the same time, riskier bonds like high-yield bonds sold off in the market so that their yields increased by 200 basis points. The net effect was a spread widening of 300 basis points.

Exhibit B.9 shows what happened to in the high-yield and U.S. Treasury bond market. The lowest line in Exhibit B.9 was the U.S. Treasury yield curve in May 2008. This shows an upward-sloping yield curve topping off at around 4%. The next line up was the yield curve in May 2007, which shows a relatively flat yield curve at 5%. The next line above that was the high-yield curve for May 2007, with high-yield bonds peaking at just under 8%, indicating a high-yield spread over U.S. Treasury bonds in May 2007 of about 3%. The last line at the top of the chart shows the high-yield curve as of May 2008 with high-yield bonds maxing out at 10%.

From this we could devise a simple stress test as follows:

1. Purchase $10,000,000 of high-yield bonds in May 2007.
2. Determine the current yield of these bonds compared to U.S. Treasury bonds. This spread amount represents the current perceived riskiness of high-yield bonds compared to U.S. Treasury bonds—it was 3% at that time.

3. Assume that a shock to the financial system causes the spread for high-yield bonds to increase by 300 basis points while the yield for U.S. Treasury bonds remains constant.
4. Calculate a new discount rate for high-yield bonds by adding 300 basis points to the prior high-yield spread over the U.S. Treasuries—effectively raising the high-yield spread to 6% and increasing the discount rate by 3%.
5. Using the new discount rate for high-yield bonds from step 4, calculate the new value of the high-yield bonds.

Clearly, if the spreads for high-yield bonds increase dramatically, their value will go down equally drastically. Such was the case in 2007 when in a matter of a few months the spread for BB-rated industrial bonds increased from 300 basis points over U.S. Treasuries to 600 basis points over U.S. Treasuries, a nasty scenario indeed.

CONCLUSION

This appendix was meant as introduction to basic statistics that are used throughout this text. It was not meant to turn the reader into a mathematician or a statistician, but rather to provide some intuition into the use of numbers to help us better understand the alternative asset world. It is best to be armed and ready when we venture forth into the brave new world of alternatives.

Appendix C
Correlation and Regression Analysis

INTRODUCTION

One of the key methods of any data analysis is correlation and regression analysis. Simply, this part of statistics determines how two variables move together. Are they closely related, somewhat related, or third cousins, twice removed? More seriously, one of the claimed advantages of alternative assets is that they are good diversifiers of traditional assets such as stocks and bonds. Therefore, it is necessary to determine how correlated their movements are to better understand the relationship between alternative assets and traditional financial assets.

We begin this chapter with a simple scatter plot. We then move on to correlation analysis as this is a key part of our analysis of alternative assets. Last, we use regression analysis to provide a more formal background for analyzing alternative assets.

SCATTER PLOTS AND CORRELATION ANALYSIS

A *scatter plot* is a graphical demonstration of the relationship between two variables, X and Y. We simply plot the intersection of the data points for X and Y on a chart to see if there is any discernible pattern. For example, suppose we wish to get a picture of the relationship between the S&P 500 and the net asset value (NAV) of a stock mutual fund. We define the S&P 500 to be the X variable and the NAV of the mutual fund to be the Y variable. In a scatter plot, the X variable is always along the horizontal axis and the Y variable is plotted along the vertical axis.

Exhibit C.1 shows our scatter plot. For each point, the X axis value is the S&P 500 while the Y axis value is the NAV of the stock mutual fund. We synchronize the data so that the data points we plot for the mutual fund and the S&P 500 are from the same month. We can see that there is an upward-sloping relationship between the NAV of the mutual fund and the S&P 500. This is not surprising given that the mutual fund defines its benchmark as the S&P 500 and makes its active stock selections from this universe. The fact that the mutual fund does not precisely track the S&P 500 reflects the active management of the portfolio manager.

Nonetheless, we can see a very close relationship between the NAV of the mutual fund and the S&P 500. To measure the relationship between the mutual fund and the S&P 500 index it is not appropriate to work with values. Because the current value represents the sum previous returns, using a series of values to measure the relationship will give us biased estimates. It is generally more appropriate to use returns or changes in values to measure the relationship between two investments.

The scatter plot changes when we switch from net asset values and the level of the S&P 500 to a scatter plot of the monthly returns to the equity mutual fund versus the returns to the S&P 500. Exhibit C.2 presents this scatter plot. First, we notice more variation in the scattering of the dots. True, there still appears to be an upward-sloping relationship, but the scatter dots are not as tightly grouped. This is because there is more variation on a monthly basis among returns than there is variation on a monthly return for the NAV of the equity fund. This is borne out by our second observation, which is that the monthly returns can be both positive and negative, while the monthly NAV for the equity fund is always positive. Simply, there is much more variation with respect to monthly returns than there is to monthly changes in NAV.

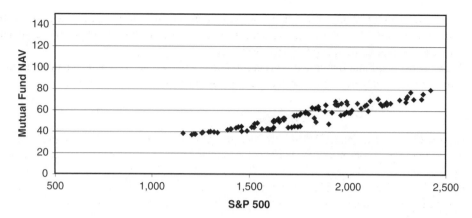

Exhibit C.1   Scatter plot of stock mutual fund NAV versus the S&P 500

The next step in our analysis is to determine the strength of the relationship between the returns for the mutual fund and the returns for the S&P 500. *Correlation* analysis performs the same function as our scatter plot but distills the relationship of the two data series down to a single number called the *correlation coefficient*. More specifically, the correlation coefficient measures the direction and extent of the linear association between two variables.

The correlation coefficient can have a maximum value of +1 and a minimum value of −1. If two variables have a correlation coefficient of +1, they are perfectly correlated and move in lockstep with one another. If the variables have a correlation coefficient of −1, they move in exactly the opposite direction. A correlation coefficient of 0 means that the two variables bear no relationship to one another. Mathematicians sometimes refer to this as an orthogonal relationship. For portfolio diversification purposes, we want to find asset classes or investment products that, when blended together, have a correlation coefficient less than 1. This would demonstrate diversification potential. The smaller the correlation coefficient, the greater the diversification. In fact, we strive to find investment products and asset classes that have a negative correlation coefficient with stocks and bonds; this would be the ideal alternative asset.

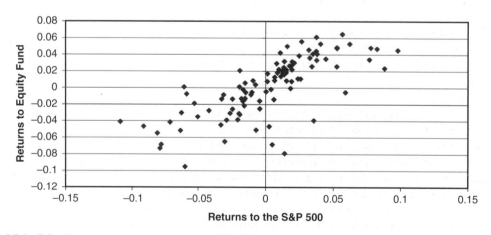

Exhibit C.2   Scatter plot of returns versus the S&P 500

Returning to Exhibit C.2, the correlation coefficient between the returns to the stock mutual fund and those for the S&P 500 is 0.74. This represents a high degree of linear and positive association between the stock mutual fund and the S&P 500.

To better understand and define the correlation coefficient, we need to define another term, the *covariance* of two variables. The covariance of two variables, X and Y, is defined as:

$$\text{Cov}(X, Y) = \sum_{i}^{N} (X_i - E[X]) \times (Y_i - E[Y])/(N - 1) \tag{C.1}$$

We divide by $N - 1$ to reflect that we are measuring the covariance of a data sample rather than the whole population of observations. If indeed we had the values for every data point in the whole population, then we would divide Equation C.1 by N. In words, covariance is a measure of the deviations of two random variables around their respective mean values. A higher covariance will lead to a higher correlation coefficient. The formula for the correlation coefficient is then:

$$r = \text{Cov}(X, Y)/\sigma_X \sigma_Y \tag{C.2}$$

The correlation coefficient is often represented by the letter r and it is the covariance of the two random variables, X and Y, divided by the product of the standard deviations of X and Y. One of the neat things about Equation C.2 is that it cancels out all units associated with X and Y. It does not matter whether X and Y are measured in dollar terms, percentages, bushels of corn, or any other form of denominator. The correlation coefficient is constructed so that these unit forms cancel each other out, and all that is left is a simple number between -1 and $+1$.

Using Equations C.1 and C.2, we find the values for our calculation to be:

$$r = 0.001049/(0.039972 \times 0.035541) = 0.74$$

While the correlation coefficient is a neat statistic to describe the relationship of two random variables, it does have its limitations. First, it is subject to distortion from outlier returns. Outliers are a small number of extreme observations that exist in the tail ends of our data samples. Sometimes statisticians refer to these data points as noise in the data, outliers that have no bearing on the relationship between two variables and seem to exist for no good reason. Often, these outliers are scrubbed out of the data because they are too extreme to be considered reasonable data points. This is where judgment and science meet. Tossing out a few outliers can greatly improve the predictive power of the correlation coefficient. We must use our good judgment to determine whether outlier events contain legitimate information that should be part of the correlation coefficient or are simply the noise in the data.

A second shortcoming is that the correlation coefficient is a *linear* measure of the relationship of two variables. It could be that two variables have a curved relationship that cannot be captured by a linear measure. Consider the following relationship between the two variables X and Y:

$$Y = X^2 \tag{C.3}$$

Clearly, this is a well-defined relationship between X and Y. Exhibit C.3 lists some of the values for this relationship. We can see that while X can take on a negative value, the values for Y will always be positive because of the squared relationship between X and Y. Exhibit C.4 provides the scatter plot for X and Y based on Equation C.3. We can see that X and Y are related to each other in a well-defined manner, but not in a linear fashion. In fact, there is an *exact* relationship between X and Y as spelled out in Equation C.3. However, using our correlation coefficient calculation, we find that the value of r is close to zero. How can this be given that we know that there is a clear relationship between X and Y based on Equation C.3? The answer lies in Exhibit C.4. We can see that there is a symmetrical plotting of the dots around zero. In fact, the plotted dots to the

Exhibit C.3 $Y = X$ squared

X	Y
−10	100
−9	81
−8	64
−7	49
−6	36
−5	25
−4	16
3	9
−2	4
−1	1
0	0
1	1
2	4
3	9
4	16
5	25
6	36
7	49
8	64
9	81
10	100
Correlation = −0.04	−0.03999

right of zero are exactly equal and opposite to the dots plotted to the left of zero. If we divide the graph in Exhibit C.4 in half, centered around zero, we can see that the two halves of the chart are mirror imagines of one another. Each side of Exhibit C.4 effectively cancels out the other so that the correlation coefficient calculates as zero, no net effect. Therefore, we must be cautious when we use the correlation coefficient. In the example of a nonlinear relationship, the correlation coefficient will provide misleading conclusions.

As a last note, we can test the *significance* of the correlation coefficient. Significance tests allow us to assess whether the relationship between two random variables as identified by the correlation coefficient is the result of chance or a legitimate relationship. The hypothesis that we test is that there is no relationship between two variables, or that $r = 0$. This is called the *null hypothesis*.

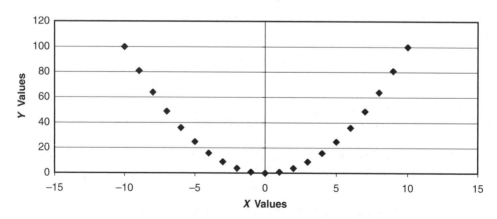

Exhibit C.4 $Y + X$ squared

Alternatively, we can test a second hypothesis that the value of r is not equal to zero: $r \neq 0$. If we accept the null hypothesis in our significance test, it means that there is no basis in our data for accepting that there is a legitimate relationship between two random variables. Alternatively, if we reject the null hypothesis it means that the value of r is significantly different from zero and there is a legitimate relationship between two economic variables. Our significance test statistic is defined as:

$$t = r \times \frac{\sqrt{N - 2}}{\sqrt{(1 - r)^2}} \tag{C.4}$$

Equation C.4 calculates a *Student's t-statistic*. If we assume that the two underlying variables approximate a normal distribution, we can use Equation C.4 to determine whether there is a legitimate relationship. In Exhibit C.1, we used 100 months of NAV and S&P 500 observations, so $N = 100$. Plugging our values into Equation C.4, we get:

$$t = 0.74 \times \frac{\sqrt{98}}{\sqrt{(1 - 0.74^2)}} = 16.19$$

We can look up the statistical significance of this *t*-statistic in any financial or statistical textbook. Generally, a *t*-statistic equal to 1.96 is significant at the 2.5% level of confidence for a two-tailed test, and a *t*-statistic of 2.33 is significant at a 0.5% level for a two-tailed test. Equation C.4 is a two-tailed test because we are trying to determine whether the correlation coefficient is significantly different from 0, either positive or negative. With a *t*-statistic of 16.19, our conclusion is that the correlation coefficient between the stock mutual fund and the S&P 500 demonstrates a legitimate economic relationship at an extremely high level of confidence.

REGRESSION ANALYSIS

Another way to study the relationship of two variables is through *regression analysis*. Linear regression allows us to study the past relationship of two variables and make predictions about their future relationship. Regression analysis starts with a dependent variable, typically denoted by the notation Y, whose properties we are trying to explain or predict. Variable Y is analyzed using independent variable X to determine how changes in the value of X will impact changes in the value of Y.

Simple regression

Linear regression analysis assumes a linear relationship between the two variables and assumes the following form:

$$Y = b_0 + b_1 X + \varepsilon \tag{C.5}$$

where

$Y =$ the dependent variable.

$b_0 =$ a constant amount often called the intercept. It represents the value of Y when the value of $X = 0$.

$b_1 =$ the slope of the linear line. It is a measure of how sensitive the dependent variable Y is to movements in the independent variable X.

$\varepsilon =$ a random error term representing the noise in the data.

Equation C.5 is called linear regression because this equation attempts to draw the best straight line through the data points presented by X and Y. Equation C.5 is also called *least squares regression* because in plotting a straight line that best fits the observations, it is designed to minimize the squared deviations around the estimated line. Mathematically, this condition is stated as:

$$\text{Minimize} \left[\sum_i^N (Y_i - b_0 - b_1 X_i)^2 \right] \tag{C.6}$$

Linear regression works by selecting the best values of b_0 and b_1 so as to minimize the squared deviations around the linear regression line. It is a method of finding the best fit within the data to ensure that there is the least amount of variation in describing the relationship between X and Y.

Regression analysis can be used for time series data, cross-sectional data, or a combination of the two. Let's continue with our example of the returns to the stock mutual fund contained in Exhibit C.2. This is a time series analysis; we have collected the monthly returns for the S&P 500 and for our mutual fund from January 2000 through April 2008. The slope of this line, or the beta, is calculated as:

$$\begin{aligned} \text{Slope} &= \text{Cov}(X, Y)/\text{Var}(X) \\ &= 0.001049/0.001598 = 0.66 \end{aligned} \tag{C.7}$$

Using our regression analysis, we also get a value of the intercept of 0.0007. Going back to Equation C.5, we can describe the relationship between the value of Y and the value of X as:

$$Y = 0.0007 + 0.66 \times X + \varepsilon \tag{C.8}$$

Exhibit C.5 shows the same scatter plot as Exhibit C.2 but now with the linear regression line of Equation C.8 fitted to the data. We can see that this line crosses the Y axis at above zero, indicating a positive amount of extra return to the Y variable (stock mutual fund return) in addition to the return derived from the movement of the stock market—the beta of 0.66 applied to our independent variable, the S&P 500.

A vital statistic to determine the goodness of fit of the regression line is the *coefficient of determination*, usually denoted by the term R^2. This number tells us how well the independent variable X explains the variation in the dependent variable Y. The coefficient of determination ranges from 0.0 to 1.0. At 1.0, there is a perfect fit between the dependent variable Y and the independent variable X. At a value of 0, there is no linear relationship between X and Y. Specifically, the coefficient of

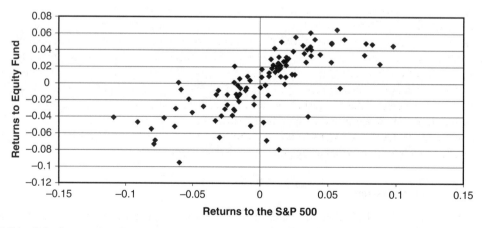

Exhibit C.5   Scatter plot of returns

determination tells us what percentage of the total variation in Y is explained by the variation in X. The calculation is as follows:

$$R^2 = \frac{\text{Total variation in } Y - \text{Unexplained variation in } Y}{\text{Total variation in } Y} \qquad (C.9)$$

A much simpler way to calculate R^2 is to take the correlation coefficient between X and Y and square it. This may seem like a cheater's way to calculate R^2, but it gets us to the same value.

$$R^2 = (\text{Correlation coefficient})^2$$
$$= 0.74 \times 0.74 = 0.5476 \qquad (C.10)$$

This is a large value for the coefficient of determination, demonstrating a strong relationship between the variables X and Y.

Another key statistic is the Student's t-statistic, calculated earlier in Equation C.4. This tests the significance of the intercept term (b_0) and the slope coefficient for X, b_1. The t-test is used to determine if the value of the intercept or the slope coefficient are significantly different from zero. If so, then we can conclude that our regression Equation C.5 has significant explanatory power for the movement of our dependent variable, Y.

To test the hypothesis that b_0 and b_1 are significantly different from zero, we use the following t-tests:

$$\text{Student's } t\text{-statistic for the slope coefficient} = b_1/s_{b1} \qquad (C.11)$$

$$\text{Student's } t\text{-statistic for the intercept} = b_0/s_{b0} \qquad (C.12)$$

where t is the Student's t-distribution distributed with $n - 2$ degrees of freedom because we are estimating two values, b_0 and b_1. For each variable that we have to estimate, we lose one degree of freedom. The terms s_{b0} and s_{b1} are the standard errors of the intercept and the slope coefficient.

The standard error is a measure of the standard deviation of the slope coefficient and the intercept, adjusted for $n - 1$ degrees of freedom. We showed in Appendix B how to calculate the variance and standard deviation using $n - 1$ degrees of freedom. The standard errors for the intercept and the slope coefficient as 0.00052 and 0.18. Using Equations C.11 and C.12, we get t-statistics of:

$$t\text{-statistic for the slope coefficient} = 0.66/0.18 = 3.67$$
$$t\text{-statistic for the intercept} = 0.0007/0.00052 = 1.35$$

Generally, a t-statistic of 1.67 indicates that we can say with 90% confidence that a regression value is significantly different than 0, a t-statistic of 1.96 indicates a 95% level of confidence, and a t-statistic of 2.33 indicates a 99% level of confidence. Looking at our t values, we conclude that the t-statistic for the slope intercept, b_1, is very large and therefore statistically significant beyond the 99% level of confidence. This indicates that the value of b_1 is not due to random chance but has a very high degree of probability of providing significant explanatory power for our dependent variable, Y. Conversely, the t-statistic for the intercept value, b_0, is smaller, indicating that we have much less confidence in its impact on the value of Y. Generally, t-tests are conducted at the 10%, 5%, and 1% levels. A t-statistic that falls below the 90% confidence level is not considered significant enough to have explanatory power on the dependent Y value.

Multiple linear regression

Unfortunately, the world of economics and finance is not so clean and neat that one independent variable is all that is sufficient to describe the behavior of one dependent variable. When this is the case, we need to expand Equation C.5 to include multiple independent variables and their impact on our dependent variable:

$$Y = b_0 + b_1X_1 + b_2X_2 + \cdots b_nX_n + \varepsilon \qquad (C.13)$$

where

Y = our dependent variable

b_0 = our intercept term

b_1 = measures how sensitive the dependent variable Y is to movements in our first independent variable, X_1

b_2 = measures how sensitive the dependent variable Y is to movements in our second independent variable, X_2

b_n = measures the sensitivity of Y to the nth independent variable, X_n

ε = our error term, essential accounting for random noise in Equation C.13

The slope values, $b_1, b_2, \ldots b_n$ are referred to as the *regression coefficients*, and collectively they explain the sensitivity of the Y variable to the multiple X variables.

We go back to Appendix B and use the return data from our initial sample of 32 hedge funds. In Exhibit C.6 we list the returns to these hedge funds in addition to two other variables: the age of the hedge fund and the size of assets under management. We plan to regress the returns to the hedge fund managers (our Y variable) against the independent variables of age and size, and single fund.

This regression is a cross sectional regression. This means that we are defining the independent variable across a class of hedge funds. This is different from the simple linear regression equation that we used earlier to regress a time series of mutual fund returns against the returns to the S&P 500. This demonstrates why regression analysis is so widely used in economics and finance: It can identify and quantify relationships across an asset class as well as across time.

We postulate three hypotheses to test. First, we believe that younger hedge funds earn better returns. There is some empirical support for this. Generally, hedge funds in their first one to three years find new ways to exploit profit opportunities in the financial markets. This works fine until competitors begin to mimic them or follow in their footsteps to gain the same alpha that the original hedge fund had discovered. Unfortunately, as more competitors enter the hedge fund's space, its returns erode to reflect a more crowded space for alpha generation.

Our second hypothesis is that smaller hedge funds earn better returns. This hypothesis can really go either way. Some argue that larger, more established hedge fund managers can exploit profit opportunities more efficiently, and further, they have a larger staff to find pockets of market inefficiency. Conversely, smaller hedge fund managers can move faster and be more flexible to exploit an opportunity when they find it. It has also been argued that larger hedge funds may become more conservative in their risk profiles and more concerned with preserving wealth than in creating wealth, whereas newer hedge funds tend to be more aggressive. Our regression equation looks like:

$$\text{Hedge fund returns} = b_0 + b_1(\text{Age}) + b_2(\text{Size}) + b_3(\text{Single fund}) + \varepsilon \qquad (C.14)$$

Our third hypothesis is that hedge fund managers that manage only one fund produce better returns than hedge fund managers that have multiple products. The hypothesis is that if a hedge fund manager has only one fund to manage, that fund will get all of her best ideas and attention. We test this hypothesis using a *dummy variable*. A dummy variable takes the value of 1 if the condition we are testing is true, and the value of 0 otherwise. Dummy variables are often called *binary variables* because they divide up the world into two states (night/day, on/off, Democrat/Republican, recession/no recession). In our regression, if the hedge fund manager manages only one hedge fund, then the value of $X_3 = 1$. Otherwise, the value is 0 if the hedge fund manager manages multiple hedge funds.

Exhibit C.6 Cross-sectional multiple linear regression of hedge fund returns

Hedge Fund	Return	Age	Size	Single Fund
K	20%	2	600	1
BB	19	1	500	1
J	18	3	800	1
T	16	2	100	1
AA	15	4	200	1
Q	14	3	300	1
L	13	3	400	0
I	12	4	300	1
C	11	2	200	1
X	11	1	300	1
D	10	3	150	1
S	10	4	250	0
EE	10	2	225	1
M	9	6	400	1
P	9	3	225	0
W	9	4	600	1
EE	8	3	200	1
CC	8	2	400	1
BB	7	5	500	0
Y	7	2	450	1
H	6	3	500	1
FF	4	5	550	1
R	3	6	600	0
Z	2	3	500	0
FF	−2	4	200	1
V	−2	5	500	0
G	−3	6	850	0
DD	−4	4	700	0
O	−7	8	1,100	0
N	−12	7	750	0
AA	−14	5	500	0
U	−16	5	600	0

Exhibit C.7 presents our results. First we note that the intercept term, b_0, is equal to 0.1175 with a t-statistic of 2.43. This indicates that the intercept term is both economically and statistically significant; the t-test is significant with a 97.8% level of confidence.

We next look at our first independent variable, Age. We had hypothesized that the younger the hedge fund, the better its performance. This means that there would be an inverse relationship between Age and hedge fund returns, and that we would expect to see a negative regression coefficient to demonstrate the fact that Age and returns might move in opposite directions. Indeed, Exhibit C.7

Exhibit C.7 Hedge fund regression results

Variable	Regression Coefficient	t-Statistic	Confidence Level	R-Squared	F-Statistic	F Confidence Level
Intercept	0.1175	2.43	97.80%	55%	11.35	99.90%
Age	−0.0246	−2.58	98.50%			
Size	−0.00013	−0.195	15% → weak			
Single fund	0.0674	2.29	97%			

demonstrates that this is true. The regression coefficient for age, b_1, is a negative -0.0246 and has a t-statistic of -2.58. This regression coefficient is significant at the 98.5% confidence level. Our sample of hedge fund managers demonstrates that younger hedge funds do indeed perform better than older hedge funds.

For the independent variable, size, we find a regression coefficient that is close to zero. The value of b_2 is -0.00013, which demonstrates that this independent variable has almost no impact on hedge fund returns. This is confirmed with a very weak t-statistic of -0.195, which is significant at only a 15% level of confidence. Size doesn't matter in our hedge fund sample.

Last, we examine the dummy variable, single fund. Again, if the hedge fund manager manages only one hedge fund, then the value of this variable is set equal to 1. If the hedge fund manager manages more than one hedge fund, then the value of single fund is set to 0. The value of b_3 is 0.0674 with a t-statistic of 2.29. The t-statistic is significant at the 97% level. This indicates that there is an economically and statistically significant impact of managing multiple hedge funds on hedge fund performance. Given the way we constructed our dummy variable, a positive regression coefficient for the variable single fund demonstrates that those hedge fund managers that manage only one hedge fund perform significantly better than those managers that manage more than one hedge fund.

Briefly, we consider two more statistics in Exhibit C.7. First, the R-squared measure is very high at 55%. This means that 55% of the variation in the dependent variable, hedge fund returns, is explained by our three independent variables. This is a considerable amount of variance explained by our variable regression model. Further, the strength of these relationships is confirmed by the F-statistic.

The F-test is used to determine the overall significance of the regression equation in explaining the variability of the dependent variable Y. More specifically, the F-statistic provides a test as to whether all of the regression coefficients in Equation C.12 are zero. The larger the value of the F-statistic, the greater the explanatory power of the independent variables. If there is no explanatory power of any of the X variables on Y, then the regression coefficients will be close to zero and the F-statistic will also be close to zero. With an F-statistic of 11.35 and a confidence level of 99.9%, we can conclude easily that there is significant explanatory power between the independent X variables and our cross section of hedge fund returns.

Problems with linear regression

Generally, there are three problems with using linear regression. They are autocorrelation, multicollinearity, and heteroskedasticity. Each of these problems can erode the confidence and robustness that we have in the regression coefficients from Equation C.14. Starting with autocorrelation (sometimes called serial correlation), one of the assumptions of linear regression is that the observations of the Ys and the Xs are not correlated with prior observations of Y or X. Mathematically, the assumption is:

$$\text{Correlation Coefficient } (Y_t, Y_{t-1}) = 0 \tag{C.15}$$

and

$$\text{Correlation Coefficient } (X_t, X_{t-1}) = 0 \tag{C.16}$$

and

$$\text{Correlation Coefficient } (\varepsilon_t, \varepsilon_{t-1}) = 0 \tag{C.17}$$

Equations C.15, C.16, and C.17 simply mean that each observation of Y and X is independent of every other observation of Y and X, and, in addition, it is assumed that the regression residual terms associated with every observation from Equation C.14 are uncorrelated. The main problem with autocorrelation is that the standard errors estimated for the regression coefficients may be underestimated, which can lead to inflated t-statistics and incorrect conclusions regarding the significance of the regression coefficients. Typically, this is a problem for time series analysis where the returns in one period might influence the returns in the next period. In our cross-sectional regression analysis, this would not be a problem because all of the returns come from the same period, 2007.

Two methods are used to correct for serial correlation. The first is to use statistical techniques to adjust upward the standard errors of the regression coefficients. This leads to smaller but more robust t-statistics for the regression coefficients. Second, the regression equation itself can be corrected by eliminating a variable from the equation that causes the serial correlation. The culprit is often an independent variable, X, that in reality is nothing more than a lagged observation of Y.

Multicollinearity exists when two of the independent variables in a regression equation are related. In our regression equation, it is assumed that the independent variables are just that: *independent* of one another. However, if they are correlated in some fashion, then our estimates of the standard errors of the regression coefficients will be *higher* than reality, leading to *lower* t-statistics (the exact opposite effect of serial correlation). For example, we might suspect that age and size are related; that is, the longer a hedge fund is in existence, the larger it will be in size. The easiest way to detect multicollinearity is to witness a high R^2 and F-statistic from the regression analysis while none of the individual regression coefficients are statistically significant. In practice, some amount of multicollinearity exists in all regression equations. Given the significance of our regression coefficients from Equation C.14 and the high R^2, we can conclude that this is not a significant problem in our analysis.

Heteroskedasticity is a condition commonly associated with cross-sectional data. This is the condition whereby the residual error term in Equation C.13 is not constant across all observations. It is often the case that the error term increases as the size of the independent variables increase in size. If there is evidence of heteroskedasticity in the regression equation, then the t-tests of the regression coefficients and the F-test are unreliable because the standard errors will underestimate the true variance of the regression coefficients and the t-statistics can be inflated. A simple test to determine if there is heteroskedasticity in the regression equation is to regress the squared residuals from the estimated regression equation on the independent variables. If there is no statistical relationship between the independent variables and the residual term, one can reasonably conclude that there is no heteroskedasticity.

There are two methods for correcting for heteroskedasticity. The first is known as generalized least squares. This is a method whereby the regression equation is modified to try to eliminate heteroskedasticity from the original regression equation. The way this is most often done is to weight each of the independent variables by their standard deviations. Typically, this means taking the X variables and dividing them by their standard deviations, and using this value as the new value of X in the regression equation.

The second method for correcting for heteroskedasticity is called robust standard errors, and it corrects the standard errors of the regression coefficients. Essentially, this method adjusts upward the standard errors of the regression coefficients so that t-statistics calculated for the regression coefficients are more robust and less inflated.

CONCLUSION

This appendix is not meant to provide an exhaustive review of regression analysis. There are many other statistical and econometric textbooks for that purpose. The key here is to gain an understanding of simple and multiple linear regression, the statistics created by this type of analysis, and some of the pitfalls associated with regression analysis. Thus armed, we can tackle alternative assets much more robustly.

Appendix D

The Quantitative Analysis
of 130/30 Products

To demonstrate the impact that 130/30 products can have over traditional actively management products, we start with a standard mean-variance optimization problem.[1] If we consider an active equity portfolio to be constructed from selecting stocks from the Russell 1000, we have a $1,000 \times 1$ vector of portfolio weights, $X = [x_1, x_2, \ldots x_{1,000}]$. Further, for each stock in the Russell 1000, there is a corresponding $1,000 \times 1$ vector of expected returns associated with each stock in the index: $R = [r_1, r_2, \ldots r_{1,000}]$. The goal for the portfolio manager is to maximize the return of the actively managed portfolio:

$$E[R_p] = \sum_{i=1}^{1000} x_i \times r_i = X^T R \tag{D.1}$$

where X^T means matrix transpose.

However, the portfolio manager must consider the overall risk of her portfolio. Higher returns comes only with a higher level of risk. Therefore, her optimization problem is a constrained one in that clients like to achieve higher portfolio returns but generally do not like higher levels of risk. If we express the covariance between security j and security k as σ_{jk}, then we can construct a variance-covariance matrix identified by V, where the terms along the diagonal, $\sigma_{jj}, \sigma_{kk}, \ldots \sigma_{nn}$ are the variances associated with the returns to securities $j, k \ldots n$. We can then express the risk of the active portfolio as:

$$V_R = \text{Cov}[R, R^T] \tag{D.2}$$

$$\sigma_P^2 = X^T V_R X \tag{D.3}$$

The portfolio manager's task is then to maximize the expected utility of the client, generally expressed in the format:

$$E[U_i] = X^T R - 1/(2A) \times X^T V_R X \tag{D.4}$$

where $E[U_i]$ is the utility function for client i and A is a measure of the client's risk tolerance. As A decreases, the higher the weight that is given to reducing the variance.

To start with, we maximize the utility function for client i without regard to the long-only constraint.

Taking first order derivative of expected utility with respect to security weights, we get:

$$\partial E[U_i]/\partial X = R - (1/A) \times X^T \times V_R = 0 \tag{D.5}$$

---

[1] We discuss in Appendix B the problems associated with using the first two moments of a return distribution (the mean and the variance) to maximize the utility of an investment portfolio.

If we set Equation D.5 equal to zero, we can solve for the optimal portfolio for client i:

$$X = A \times R \times V_R^{-1} \tag{D.6}$$

where X is an $N \times 1$ vector of weights for the stocks in the Russell 1000.[2]

The stock portfolio represented by $X = A \times R \times V_R^{-1}$ is the minimally constrained portfolio. This portfolio permits short positions because there was no restriction that the portfolio weights $X = [x_1, x_2, \ldots x_n]$ be positive. Also, this is a demonstration of integrated portfolio management because the long and short positions were determined concomitantly. As a result, there is only one alpha for the total portfolio instead of a separate alpha for the long portfolio and for the short portfolio.

Two other observations are apparent. First, this long/short portfolio is unlikely to be market neutral. Market neutrality typically means that the portfolio has no dollar exposure to the systematic risk of a broad stock market index. To show this, market neutrality requires that the sum of the portfolio weights $[x_1 + x_2 + x_n] = 0$. This means that:

$$\sum_{n} x_j = 0 = 1^T X = 0$$

where 1^T is a $1 \times N$ vector of ones that when multiplied by the optimal $N \times 1$ vector or portfolio weights X provides a summation of all of the weights in the portfolio. From Equation D.6 we know that the optimal portfolio is defined as:

$$X = A \times R \times V_R^{-1}$$

This means that the condition of dollar neutrality requires that:

$$1^T X = 0 \rightarrow 1^T \times X = A \times 1^T \times R \times V_R^{-1} = 0 \tag{D.7}$$

One way to satisfy Equation D.7 is to have $1^T R = 0$, a possible but most unlikely condition. The goal of every active manager is to produce a positive return on the portfolio, and even though many active managers produce a negative return, it is very rare for an active manager to produce *no* return.

Turning back to our constraints, for traditional long-only active portfolios, Equation D.4 is solved subject to two constraints:

$$\sum_{n} x_j = 1 \tag{D.8}$$

$$x_j \geq 0 \text{ for all } j \tag{D.9}$$

Equation D.8 requires the portfolio manager to fully invest the investment capital allocated by the client, while Equation D.9 requires only positive (long-only) security weights in the active portfolio.

Generally, the constraint in Equation D.8 also applies to 130/30 portfolios. Most of these products are constrained to have 100% exposure to the stock market index that acts as its benchmark. This has led the industry to occasionally label 130/30 products "beta one" products because even though the portfolio manager can go long and short the market, the portfolio is constrained to have a beta that matches that of its benchmark. The reason for beta one portfolios is that asset owners want active

---

[2] We note that it is not possible for an active manager to include every stock in the Russell 1000 into her optimal portfolio. The value of N will be some number less than 1,000.

management for tactical portfolio reasons, but don't want their active managers to stray too far from their equity benchmark for purposes of strategic asset allocation.[3]

The advantage that 130/30 managers have is that Equation D.9 is eliminated as a constraint in their portfolio. As discussed previously, Equation D.9 is the most restrictive constraint placed on portfolio managers and can lead to significant erosion of the transfer coefficient identified in Equation 5.13. 130/30 managers remove Equation D.9 and replace it with two other constraints that, while potentially reducing the transfer coefficient, do not erode it to the same extent as Equation D.8. The two constraints are:

$$\sum_{}^{n} x_k \geq -0.30 \text{ for all } x_k \leq 0 \tag{D.10}$$

$$\sum_{}^{n} x_j \leq 1.30 \text{ for all } x_j \geq 0 \tag{D.11}$$

Equation D.10 limits the short positions in the portfolio to no more than 30% of the portfolio exposure, while Equation D.11 allows the long portfolio to be leveraged no more than 130%.

---

[3] See Mark Anson, "The Beta Continuum," *Journal of Portfolio Management* (Winter 2008), and "Strategic vs. Tactical Asset Allocation: Beta Drivers vs. Alpha Drivers," *Journal of Portfolio Management* (2004).

Index

Notes